The American Freshman

Forty Year Trends, 1966–2006

By

John H. Pryor
Sylvia Hurtado
Victor B. Saenz
José Luis Santos
William S. Korn

Higher Education Research Institute
Graduate School of Education & Information Studies
University of California, Los Angeles

April, 2007

Higher Education Research Institute
University of California, Los Angeles
Sylvia Hurtado, Professor and Director

HERI Affiliated Scholars

Walter R. Allen, Allan Murray Cartter Professor of Higher Education
Alexander W. Astin, Founding Director and Senior Scholar
Helen S. Astin, Senior Scholar
Mitchell J. Chang, Associate Professor
Patricia M. McDonough, Professor
José Luis Santos, Assistant Professor
Linda J. Sax, Associate Professor in Residence
Rick Wagoner, Assistant Professor

The Higher Education Research Institute (HERI) is based in the Graduate School of Education & Information Studies at the University of California, Los Angeles. The Institute serves as an interdisciplinary center for research, evaluation, information, policy studies, and research training in postsecondary education.

CIRP Advisory Committee

Anthony L. Antonio
Associate Professor
Stanford University

Betsy O. Barefoot
Co-Director and Senior Scholar
Policy Center on the First Year of College

Victor M. H. Borden
Associate Vice Chancellor and
Associate Professor
Indiana University Purdue University Indianapolis

C. Anthony Broh
Director of Research
Consortium on Financing Higher Education

Patrick M. Callan
President
National Center for Public Policy and
Higher Education

Mark L. Gunty
Assistant Director of Institutional Research
University of Notre Dame

Kurt J. Keppler
Vice President for Student Affairs
Valdosta State University

Berta Vigil Laden
Associate Professor
University of Toronto

Alexander C. McCormick
Senior Scholar
The Carnegie Foundation for the
Advancement of Teaching

Sylvia Hurtado
Professor and Director, HERI
(ex-officio)

John H. Pryor
Director, CIRP
(ex-officio)

Published by the Higher Education Research Institute. Suggested citation:

Pryor, J.H., Hurtado, S., Saenz, V.B., Santos, J.L., Korn, W.S. (2007). *The American Freshman: Forty Year Trends.* Los Angeles: Higher Education Research Institute, UCLA.

Additional copies of this report may be purchased from the Higher Education Research Institute, UCLA Graduate School of Education & Information Studies, 3005 Moore Hall/Mailbox 951521, Los Angeles, CA 90095-1521.

Please remit $25.00 plus $5.00 for shipping. Website: www.gseis.ucla.edu/heri/heri.html; Telephone: 310/825-1925.

The American Freshman

Forty Year Trends

CONTENTS

TABLES

FIGURES

PREFACE

In celebration of 40 years of data collection on American freshmen, the Higher Education Research Institute (HERI) is pleased to present this report as well as a series of new reports on specific student populations. These trends data now constitute a national treasure, documenting the changing nature of students' characteristics, aspirations, values, attitudes, expectations, and behaviors. As college participation and high school graduation rates increase, these data become ever more important in documenting the changing nature of students seeking access to higher education. The CIRP Freshman Survey trends are a result of the joint effort between participating colleges and universities who use and administer the surveys on campus, higher education associations that foresaw the need to assess higher education impact, numerous foundations and three federal agencies that have offered financial support over the years, and the involvement of key researchers and advisors who have guided the development of the CIRP as the longest continuing study of higher education. Special thanks are due to each and every individual and organization that has contributed over the last 40 years. Without continuing interest and commitment to the CIRP, we would not have been able to generate the data that serves as the basis of this report and many others to be released in the future (visit http://www.gseis.ucla.edu/heri/publications.html for reports).

The most significant contribution to the CIRP over the years has been the insight and energy of Alexander W. Astin. He conceptualized and implemented the survey in 1965, transferred operations from the American Council on Education to UCLA in 1973, and successfully directed the project during its first 25 years. He has single-handedly influenced institutional research efforts and shaped our knowledge about higher education and its practice using the CIRP as empirical evidence on students. His national research projects, 21 books, and hundreds of research articles make use of CIRP data to tell the story of students and institutions in American higher education. As a result of his research design, we have maintained nationally normative data on students at four-year colleges and universities. A core group of institutional participants also have 40 years of data to use on their own campuses. At each five-year anniversary, we provide all institutions with their own trends report, and in any single year, they are able to compare themselves with similar types of institutions.

The influence of Helen S. Astin is also evident in these data in that we have produced reports separately for men and women over the 40 years. These data have served to document significant gender shifts in higher education as well as the impact of college on women's development. Together, through their research using CIRP data, the Astins have contributed to our understanding of many areas of student development, questioned our assumptions about higher education, and promoted institutional change and transformation. Many others have now followed in their footsteps in analyzing the data and addressing significant problems in higher education. We thank them for their contributions and seek to encourage other researchers to use the data to study emerging issues that may help improve institutional practice as we move further into the 21st century.

CIRP data have served several important purposes over the years. First, the data have served as an alert to the public and helped shape public opinion about key issues associated with the concerns of college youth. This has been accomplished through release of the data at national conferences, in national, local and student newspapers, as well as through television and radio interviews about the findings. This general public interest is often linked with key policy considerations in education, making CIRP data relevant to these decisions. Most importantly, however, is that these freshmen data document student predispositions, which help colleges to determine their impact on student recruitment, student development, and student retention and career preparation. The trends data in this report, and reports provided to institutions, help campuses determine how much their student body has changed over the years as a result of institutional policy and how they might design more effective ways of reaching students new to higher education. CIRP data have also served as the basis for numerous national studies that have expanded the scholarly literature in higher education in such important areas as college access, retention, college impact on a wide range of cognitive and affective outcomes, student transition to college, and diversity in higher education (for example, see Astin, 1977; Astin, 1993; McDonough, Antonio, Walpole, & Perez, 1998; Sax, 2001; Astin & Oseguera, 2002; Gurin, Dey, Hurtado, & Gurin, 2002; Keup & Stolzenberg, 2004; Allen, Jayakumar, Griffin, Korn, & Hurtado, 2005; Chang, Denson, Saenz, & Misa, 2006; Sax, forthcoming). Over the years, many institutions have been asked to take part in specific national studies that have been vital to our understanding of the long-term impact on students and the particular institutions they attend. Finally, CIRP data have been an important focus for training in evaluation and assessment. Since 1973, CIRP data have been used to train hundreds of students preparing for careers in higher education. Many of them have become institutional researchers, research-informed practitioners, and/or noted scholars of higher education. Since 1995, the Higher Education Research Institute has offered a summer workshop to institutional researchers to make the best use of CIRP data for institutional assessment and reporting.

One can easily see that CIRP data have become a national resource in more ways than one. I want to offer special thanks to all the staff and graduate students at HERI that have helped make our surveys successful and worked with campuses to make their institutional efforts successful over the years. We are committed to generating studies and data that will improve higher education's ability to develop the talent of its students and the next generation of leaders. We offer this report with this goal in mind. Special thanks for preparation of this report are due to John Pryor who manages the surveys and manages to do just about everything, William S. Korn whose wizardry prevents us from becoming hopelessly mired in the decades of data, Victor Saenz who manages research with optimism and keeps us connected to policy, Jose Luis Santos who has offered his economist's lens to our work, Jessica Korn who assisted with publication, and graduate students Hoi Ning Ngai and Hanna Song for helping us to prepare the report.

Sylvia Hurtado
Director, Higher Education Research Institute

THE AMERICAN FRESHMAN: FORTY-YEAR TRENDS, 1966–2006

Many changes have occurred in American higher education in the last 40 years. Most significant has been the unprecedented growth in enrollments accompanied by changes in the proportions who are female, who are students of color, who attend full time, and who attend four-year institutions (NCES, 2006). The opening of pathways to the baccalaureate for women, racial/ethnic minority students, first-generation college students, and low-income students who had limited opportunity before the 1960s occurred as a result of the civil rights and women's movements and a series of policy initiatives to increase access to higher education. The baccalaureate degree has become a minimum and essential credential for employers in a wide array of occupations, as higher education and training beyond high school is no longer optional for those who aspire towards upward social and economic mobility in American life (NCPPHE, 2002). As a result, we could not have predicted the number of high school graduates who would take advantage of expanded opportunity to higher education. Moreover, higher education enrollments are projected to continue increasing from 2006 through 2015: Full-time undergraduate enrollment is expected to continue growing more rapidly than part-time enrollment, and the growth in enrollment at four-year institutions is expected to be greater than at two-year institutions during this period (NCES, 2006).

From 1972 to 2004, college participation rates increased, with high school graduates enrolled in college immediately after high school increasing from 49 to 67 percent (NCES, 2006). Additionally, for the past 35 years, undergraduate enrollment has been larger in four-year institutions than in two-year institutions, and aside from a slowdown in the early 1990s, enrollment has grown fairly steadily at four-year institutions since 1970 (NCES, 2006). These changes were greatly facilitated by the introduction of policy initiatives (e.g., Higher Education Act of 1965 and subsequent reauthorizations; Middle-Income Student Assistance Act of 1978) and financial aid grant and loan programs (e.g., Pell Grants, Perkins Loans, Stafford Loans) that provided aid directly to students to allow them mobility and choice regardless of income.

The contributions of the women's and civil rights movement were equally felt in American higher education, as well as a new set of institutionally-based policies and programs to help reduce educational and societal inequalities and enhance the racial/ethnic diversity of institutions. However, substantial gaps remain between racial/ethnic groups, schools, and states in raising levels of educational attainment. More recently, new initiatives, such as the federally-sponsored GEAR UP program, have been developed to support educational alliances between schools and colleges, with the goal of improving college access (see Pathways to College Network at: www.pathwaystocollege.net/aboutus).

At the same time that access has reached unprecedented levels, additional issues have emerged that raise serious questions about whether four-year colleges and universities are doing their fair share of achieving educational equity, meeting students' needs and aspirations, and developing students' values, skills, and knowledge that equip them for an increasingly complex and global society. Institutions do not operate entirely autonomously from larger social and political pressures in society. Some contend our higher education system has become more stratified in terms of students and institutions (Bastedo & Gumport, 2003; Astin & Oseguera, 2004), preserving education of the elite in an era of increased access. Our system is strongly driven by economic and market forces that increase competition for resources and talented students, promote the view of students as self-interested consumers who know how to best meet their educational needs, result in declining funds for public higher education, and increase privatization of many previously public services. With such driving forces, how are students today to develop a commitment to the public good, a life of service, and ethical decision-making skills that may involve a departure from goals of self-interest? While the documentation of all these forces that shape higher education and student development in college is beyond the scope of this report, we are fortunate to have national data at our disposal to observe changes in students' aspirations, values, attitudes, and behaviors to understand both the continuing advances and new challenges that have emerged in educating the American college student.

The Cooperative Institutional Research Program

The Cooperative Institutional Research Program (CIRP) Freshman Survey is coordinated by the staff of the Higher Education Research Institute (HERI), located in the Graduate School of Education and Information Studies at the University of California at Los Angeles (UCLA). While the CIRP Freshman Survey is designed to be the initial instrument in a program of assessment that includes two follow-up surveys, the Your First College Year (YFCY) and College Senior Survey (CSS), it also provides a unique snapshot of the changes in cohorts of American college freshmen over the past four decades.

The fall of 2006 marked the 40th anniversary of the CIRP Freshman Survey. Since 1966, the first year of the survey, 8,309,318 incoming first-year students at 1,201 colleges and universities across the United States have completed the instrument and been included in the national normative reports published by HERI. The CIRP Freshman Survey is the largest and longest-running survey of American college students. Hundreds of journal articles, monographs, and books have been written in the past 40 years using CIRP data, adding to what we know about the college experience and the characteristics of college students.

The 40th anniversary of the CIRP has been the occasion for a series of publications addressing issues of equity and progress for different groups. In 2005, HERI published *Black Undergraduates from* Bakke *to* Grutter*: Freshmen Status, Trends, and Prospects, 1971–2004* (Allen, Jayakumar, Griffin, Korn, & Hurtado, 2005). We have a report in press, *First In My Family: A Profile of First-Generation College Students at Four-Year Institutions Since 1971*, that examines first-generation college students (Saenz,

Hurtado, Barrera, Wolf, & Yeung, 2007). Manuscripts in preparation, to be released later this year, will illustrate trends for Latinos and Asian Americans. Finally, the former director of the CIRP, Linda Sax, will release a book later this year entitled *The Gender Gap in College: Differential Patterns of Change and Development for Women and Men.*

Changing Demographic Trends

One of the most dramatic changes in higher education over the last 40 years has been the composition of entering students that has accompanied increased enrollments at baccalaureate-granting institutions. Four decades of CIRP Freshman Survey data reveal several interesting trends with regard to the increased diversification of baccalaureate-granting colleges and universities.

Racial/Ethnic Diversity Reflects Distinct Group Dynamics

White students represented 90.9 percent of the first-time, full-time freshmen in 1971 and their proportion declined to 76.5 percent in 2006, indicating proportional increases in the representation of other racial/ethnic groups and demographic shifts in the U.S. population (Table 1). Most notably, Asian/Asian American students' representation has nearly doubled *each decade*, constituting 0.6 percent of freshmen in 1971 and now representing 8.6 percent of first-time, full-time freshmen. Similarly, although they are more likely than other groups to begin at community colleges, the percentage of Latinos entering baccalaureate-granting institutions has also steadily increased, due primarily to sheer demographic growth. Their representation among first-time, full-time freshmen increased from .06 percent in 1971 to 7.3 percent in 2006, with trends indicating their representation doubled from 1971 to 1980 and then tripled from 1990 to 2000. In contrast, the representation of African American/Black students has increased, stalled, and slightly declined over time. While African American/Black students represented 7.5 percent of freshmen in 1971 and increased to 12.5 percent

Table 1. Racial/Ethnic Representation of First-Time, Full-Time Freshmen (CIRP Survey)

Racial/Ethnic Group	Percent in				
	1971	1980	1990	2000	2006
White/Caucasian	90.9	84.1	80.7	76.1	76.5
African American/Black	7.5	12.5	12.1	10.4	10.5
American Indian	0.9	0.8	1.3	1.9	2.2
Asian/Asian American/Pacific Islander	0.6	1.4	3.8	7.1	8.6
Latina/o	0.6	1.4	2.2	6.7	7.3
Other Race	1.0	1.7	1.8	3.6	3.6
Multiracial (two or more groups)	1.3	1.2	1.7	4.8	7.2

Note: Percentages may total more than 100.0 since respondents were allowed to mark more than one category. The "Asian/Asian American" category includes students who reported being a "Native Hawaiian/Pacific Islander," which was first included in the 2002 survey. The "Multiracial" category includes students that reported two or more groups, and are counted in the previous cells as well.

of all students in 1980, this group subsequently declined to represent 10.5 percent in 2006 across all baccalaureate-granting institutions (inclusive of historically Black colleges and universities or HBCUs). (See Allen, Jayakumar, Griffin, Korn, & Hurtado, 2005 for a full report on the status and trends.) Overall, these differences across groups reflect U.S. population shifts, changes in college admissions criteria (from race-conscious to race-neutral), and variability in access and opportunity within and between schools for various groups.

These numbers do not exactly map onto IPEDS figures for different racial/ethnic groups entering baccalaureate-granting institutions primarily because CIRP surveys give students the opportunity to indicate more than one racial/ethnic category, and also because IPEDS does not capture the racial/ethnic make-up of students who indicate they are not U.S. citizens. However, the survey has allowed us to identify another important national trend: an increasing proportion of multi-racial/ethnic students or students who identify themselves as belonging to more than one racial/ethnic group. In 1971, relatively few students (1.3 percent) categorized themselves in more than one group, but by 2006 this figure had increased to 7.4 percent of all entering college students.

Other Key Demographic Trends

First-time, Full-time Women Become a Stable Majority. In previous decade reports, we have noted the significant shift in gender composition of college freshmen (Astin, Green & Korn, 1987; Astin, Parrott, Korn, & Sax, 1997). During the first five years of the Freshman Survey (1966–70), most entering college students were men (53–55 percent). From 1971 on, however, the percentage of women steadily increased, overtaking the percentage of men in 1976 and increasing until 2001, when women constituted about 55 percent of entering students. In the last five years, this proportion has remained relatively stable. This trend is beginning to manifest itself in graduate/professional schools, as women do better than men with regard to retention and grades in college.

Religious Preferences Decline. Increasing numbers of students report having no religious affiliation, from 13.6 percent in 1966 to 19.1 percent in 2006. A decline was reported in categories aggregated as Protestant (Christian), moving from more than half (54.5 percent) to 48.0 percent; Catholic members remained fairly stable and are currently at 27.7 percent; and a decline was noted for students who identified as Jewish, dropping by almost half (moving from 4.9 percent of freshmen to 2.6 percent). A similar pattern of decline in religious affiliation among mothers and fathers was evident. While more than three-quarters of students (76.9) reported in 2006 that they attended a religious service in the last year of high school, this proportion has steadily declined since 1968 (91.1 percent).

Older Students Entering College for the First Time. Although up to 67 percent of high school graduates enter college immediately after high school today, we have noted a shift in students that enter college at a later age. In 1967, 80.5 percent of entering first-year students were

18 years old, while only 13.7 percent was 19 and older. By 2006, 68.5 percent of entering students was 18, while the percentage of students 19 and older more than doubled to 29.6 percent. This shift was more substantial in the last 20 years than in the first 20 years of the survey, perhaps indicating some students may take longer to meet new standards and/or pursue postgraduate work at private high schools to increase their chances of getting into the colleges of their choice.

Increase in Learning-Disabled Students. The percentage of incoming students reporting a learning disability was 2.8 percent in 2004 (the most recent year we asked about disabilities)— more than five times the 0.5 percent reported in 1983. This increase in the proportion of learning-disabled students entering college is mirrored in similar trends in elementary and secondary school populations (NCES, 2006).

Fewer Students Report Parents are Married or Living Together. In 1972, we started to ask regularly about the marital status of students' parents. At that time, 84.8 percent of students' parents lived with each other, 7.9 percent had parents that lived apart, and 7.3 percent had one or both parents deceased. By 2006, the percentage of students with two parents that lived together had dropped to 71.2 percent, those with parents who lived apart increased to one out of four students (25.2 percent), and those with one or more deceased parents dropped to 3.7 percent.

Parental Income Steadily Increases Among Entering Freshmen. Parental income for the entering college freshmen is rising faster than national median income, a pattern that acceler-ated during the mid 1980s. Freshmen are coming from more economically advantaged homes than their predecessors. This shift has occurred at both public and private institutions, but parental incomes are rising faster among students attending public institutions, indicating more advantaged families may be choosing public institutions because the costs are lower. (See details in section on Parental Income, Affordability, and Financial Concerns.)

Decline in Proportion of First-Generation Freshmen. Since 1971, CIRP Freshman Survey data has monitored the educational background of parents. (See mother's and father's education levels in Weighted National Norms in the statistical tables section of this report.) However, aggregating data for those students whose parents have had no college or post-secondary experiences—first-generation college students—has allowed us to determine how these students fare in access and success. The trends show that the proportion of first-generation college students at baccalaureate-granting institutions has steadily declined. In 1971, first-generation students represented 39.3 percent of all first-time, full-time college freshmen, a figure that drops in half by 1992. By 2005, the proportion of first-generation college students declined to 16.5 percent of all entering freshmen. A closer look at the demographic data reveals some slight differences by gender since the late 1980s, with women somewhat more likely than men to be first-generation students. However, differences across racial/ethnic groups remain evident: The proportion of first-generation students was much higher for Hispanics (57.7 percent) in 1975 and remains the highest (38.2 percent) of all groups in 2005; African Americans show the fastest rate of decline of first-generation students compared to other groups (from 51.5 percent to 20.4 percent). (For a complete report, see Saenz, Hurtado, Barrera, Wolf, & Yeung, 2007).

Preparation for a Diverse Society: Attitudes and Interactions

The past 40 years of CIRP Freshman Survey data show that the incoming first-year class at baccalaureate-granting institutions has become increasingly more diverse and somewhat more socioeconomically homogeneous (based on parental income and education). However, the question remains whether racial/ethnic experiences and racial tolerance are salient for freshmen who must eventually be prepared to enter an increasingly diverse workforce and society. We examined several items that tap into students' experiences with diverse racial groups, cross-racial interactions in high school, expectations for college, and students' goals and beliefs.

In 1983, we began monitoring the racial composition of the neighborhood and high schools of entering college freshmen (Table 2). At that time, 78.5 percent of freshmen came from mostly or completely White high schools and 85.1 percent grew up in mostly or completely White neighborhoods. By 2006, 64.1 percent came from mostly or completely White high schools and 73.7 percent grew up in mostly or completely White neighborhoods. While this may indicate some desegregation of high schools in particular, a breakdown by racial group over this time period

Table 2. Racial Composition of Neighborhood and High School by Race/Ethnicity

		Percent in			Percent Change
	Race/Ethnic Group	1983	1990	2006	1983–2006
Completely/mostly White: Neighborhood where you grew up	All Students	85.1	81.6	73.7	–13.4
	White	94.6	93.2	87.3	–7.7
	African American	17.6	19.1	23.1	31.7
	American Indian	54.9	63.3	49.9	–9.2
	Asian/Pacific Islander	69.4	65.1	42.1	–39.3
	Hispanic	46.7	42.0	33.3	–28.7
	Other Race	58.2	56.0	51.5	–11.5
	Multiracial	75.8	70.8	61.7	–18.6
Completely/mostly White: High School you last attended	All Students	78.5	73.9	64.1	–18.4
	White	84.9	82.2	74.8	–11.9
	African American	35.3	33.2	29.0	–17.8
	American Indian	52.4	58.6	44.8	–14.6
	Asian/Pacific Islander	64.5	57.2	37.5	–41.9
	Hispanic	46.3	37.5	31.7	–31.5
	Other Race	57.2	52.1	44.0	–23.1
	Multiracial	73.5	63.2	52.8	–28.2

Note: The racial composition scale ranged from Completely White, Mostly White, Half White/Half non-White, Mostly non-White, and Completely non-White.

reveals distinct differences across groups in the racial composition of pre-college contexts. African Americans continue to be most highly represented in predominantly non-White pre-college contexts and it is the group least likely to be represented in predominantly White schools or neighborhoods (see also Pryor, Hurtado, Saenz, Korn, Santos, & Korn, 2006). In contrast, White students are more likely to be socialized in predominantly White environments. Specifically, Table 2 shows that about three-quarters of White students attended a predominantly White high school (74.9 percent) and 87.3 percent grew up in predominantly White neighborhoods in 2006—it is the group least likely to have changed over time. Asian and Latino students are less likely to come from predominantly White contexts compared to

20 years ago, indicating they are more likely to be in mixed-race schools and neighborhoods.

We further investigated the extent to which students were socially integrated and interacted across race/ethnicity (Figure 1). In 2006, more than two-thirds (66.9 percent) of students stated that they socialized with someone of another racial/ethnic group in high school—a proportion that has varied between 65 and 70 percent over the last ten years, up from 58.4 percent in 1992 (when we first asked this question). Moreover, an almost equal percentage (64.8 percent) of students in 2006 expected to socialize with someone from another racial/ethnic group in college, a slight decrease from 65.6 percent in 2000.

While there are obvious differences in cross-racial contact across groups, students' personal

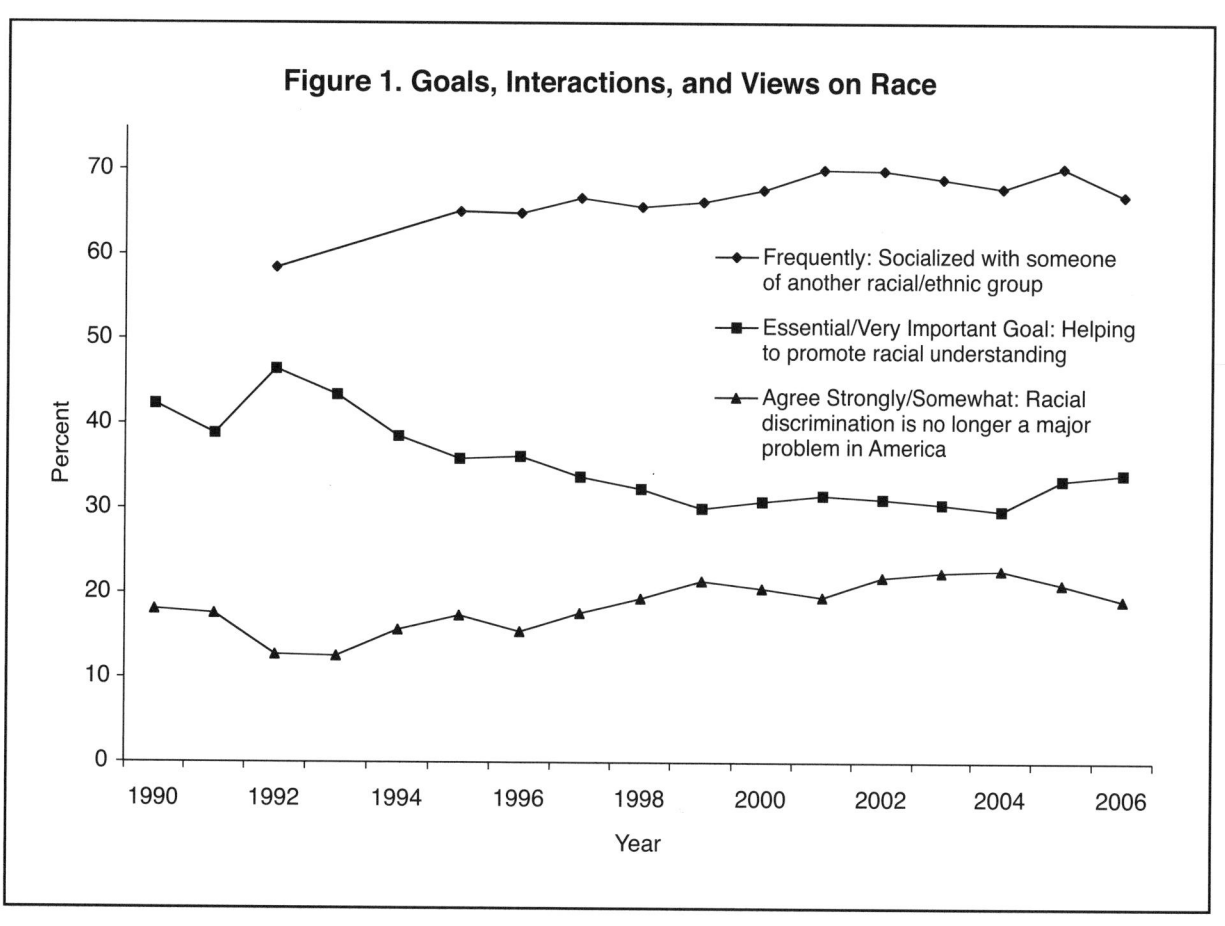

Figure 1. Goals, Interactions, and Views on Race

- Frequently: Socialized with someone of another racial/ethnic group
- Essential/Very Important Goal: Helping to promote racial understanding
- Agree Strongly/Somewhat: Racial discrimination is no longer a major problem in America

goals and beliefs at college entry may be cause for concern. Only slightly more than a third of students (34.0 percent) rated the objective of helping to promote racial understanding as "essential" or "very important," a goal that has declined since it peaked in 1992 (46.4 percent), when the Rodney King decision and riots in Los Angeles provoked national discussions about race.

Over the same time period, the proportion of students who agreed "strongly" or "somewhat" with the statement that "racial discrimination is no longer a major problem in America" reached a low in 1992, but steadily increased to 22.7 percent in 2004 and is now at 19.1 percent. This suggests that students may be less likely to see problems associated with race compared with previous cohorts 14 or 15 years ago, and it is interesting to note that these shifts also coincided with presidential election years. In order to encourage students to address diversity and racial inequalities after college, institutions should seek to capitalize on students' expectations by providing opportunities for meaningful contact experiences, broad knowledge about different racial/ethnic groups, and tools that allow students to confidently assume social responsibility for addressing difficult social problems associated with diversity and inequality. One positive note is that, since 9/11, all students have steadily increased in their personal goal of improving their understanding of other countries or cultures (from 43.2 percent in 2002 to 49.1 percent in 2006). This suggests students enter college willing to develop greater awareness of important issues associated with diversity.

Academic Preparation for College-Level Work

Within the last few years, the release of several national reports has placed renewed emphasis on the academic preparation of all students who aspire to a college education (U.S. DOE, 2006; AACU, 2007). Since the National Commission on Excellence in Education released its report, *A Nation at Risk* (NCEE, 1982), we have monitored basic levels of high school preparation in various subject areas to document whether college freshmen meet or exceed recommendations for the minimum number of years of study. After the call for reform in high school curriculum to establish baseline levels for college preparation, several states instituted their own recommended years of study beyond the initial national imperative to ensure that students are sufficiently prepared for college level work. Figure 2 shows the percentage of freshmen cohorts by subject area that meet or exceed requirements for years of study. The good news is that the percentage of entering freshmen taking the recommended number of courses in all key subject areas has increased, with the exception of history or American government, which was already at its highest point (99 percent) in 1984. The largest increases between 1984 and 2006 occurred in foreign language study (20 percentage point increase), arts and music (19 percentage point increase), biological science (11 percentage point increase), and mathematics (9 percentage point increase). Comparing cohorts in 1984, 1994, and 2006, however, it appears that most of the improvement in students' course-taking patterns occurred within the

Figure 2. Percentage of Freshman Cohorts Meeting or Exceeding Recommended Years of High School Study in Key Subject Areas

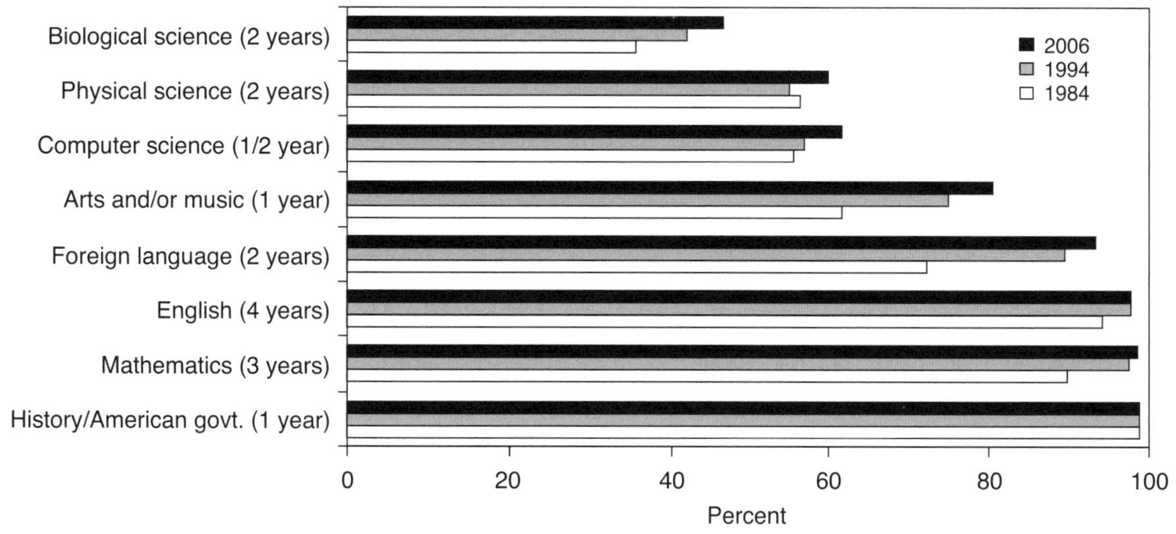

Biological science (2 years)
Physical science (2 years)
Computer science (1/2 year)
Arts and/or music (1 year)
Foreign language (2 years)
English (4 years)
Mathematics (3 years)
History/American govt. (1 year)
2006
1994
1984
0
20
40
60
80
100
Percent

Note: Trends data from 1984 are used because these survey items were first asked in that year. Years of study for each discipline are based on the high school curriculum recommendations of the National Commission on Excellence in Education.

first ten years of the call for reform. In the last ten years, very modest but important increases have occurred in the percentage of students taking at least two years of physical science and a half-year of computer science. This may reflect some state initiatives to ensure high school preparation for careers that will attract higher wages and jobs to their state. However, the percentage of students in 2006 taking the recommended years of study in biology (46.8 percent), physical science (59.9 percent), and computer science (61.6 percent) is well below that of other subject areas, indicating there is substantial room for improvement. It could be an indication that high schools are having difficulty providing a second year of physical science and biology, and a half-year of computer science, to large numbers of high school students, many of them bound for studies at four-year colleges.

Even after 20 years of progress in which all students increased their minimum levels of preparation, gender differences persist in the science-related disciplines in two important areas: Women are less likely to have taken two years of physical science (56.7 percent) and a half year of computer science (56.9 percent) than men (63.7 percent and 67.2 percent, respectively) (Table 3). However, the gender gap has closed in terms of the minimum standards for mathematics preparation. In 1984, about 87.8 percent of female students and 91.9 percent of male students reported three or more years of mathematics study in high school, figures that have increased to 98.6 percent for women and 98.5 percent for men in the last 22 years. Both male and female students showed significant increases in terms of the proportions reporting two or more years of

Table 3. Years of High School Study in Subject Areas by Gender

	Women			Men		
	1984	2006	Percent change	1984	2006	Percent change
Mathematics (3 years)	87.8	98.6	12.3	91.9	98.5	7.2
Physical science (2 years)	50.5	56.7	12.3	62.4	63.7	2.1
Biological science (2 years)	37.9	48.5	28.0	33.3	44.8	34.5
Computer science (1/2 year)	50.1	56.9	13.6	61.4	67.2	9.4

Note: Trends data from 1984 are used because these items were first asked in that year. Years of study for each discipline are based on the curriculum recommendations of the National Commission on Excellence in Education. Percent change refers to proportion or relative percent change between 1984 and 2006.

biological science study, increasing by 34.5 percent for male students and 28.0 percent for female students since 1984. It is important to note that women were always somewhat more likely than men to have taken two years of biology prior to college entry, an advantage that now appears to have multiplied with the increased representation of women in baccalaureate-granting institutions, likely contributing to higher percentages of women applying to medical schools (www.aamc.org/data/facts/2006/2006summary.htm). (For additional trends in gender differences using CIRP data, see Sax, forthcoming; trends by racial/ethnic group are also available in forthcoming reports from the Higher Education Research Institute.)

Trends for Remedial Education

In the last ten years, no less than 41 state legislatures, governing boards, and higher education systems have considered or enacted policy initiatives directed at limiting or reforming remedial education in two- and four-year institutions (Mazzeo, 2002). In 2000, an NCES survey of all Title IV degree-granting, 2-year and 4-year institutions found that 76 percent offered at least one

remedial reading, writing, or mathematics course (NCES, 2003). Over 98 percent of public 2-year institutions offered remedial courses, while 80 percent of public four-year institutions and 59 percent of private four-year institutions offered such courses. Over time, more four-year institutions have moved away from offering remedial or developmental courses (NCES, 2003). However, many policy and empirical questions remain as to whether remediation should continue to be offered by all sectors of higher education or whether it should be relegated to the two-year sector and/or the K-12 public education system. Perhaps the most central policy concern is the challenge of the under-prepared student and the attendant effects of remedial programs on student achievement and matriculation through the higher education pipeline.

CIRP Freshman Survey trends data offer an additional dimension to these institutional trends on remediation, as they indicate that the need to help students meet college-level expectations persists and requires creative, new initiatives that bridge the gap between high school curricula and basic college preparation. While many more students are meeting the minimum standards for coursework in high school, these data do not delve into the quality of these courses. We do not know, for example, whether three years of mathematics coursework actually prepares students for college-level work. For this reason, we ask students to indicate whether they had special tutoring or remedial work in high school in each of these key subject areas (Table 4).

While there have been some increases since 1979 in the percentage of students reporting they had special tutoring or remedial work in high school, the largest increases have occurred in mathematics, with 12.7 percent of students in 2005 compared with 7.5 percent in 1979. However, there have been remarkably small changes in the last ten years. In general, the percentage of students reporting they feel they need remediation upon college entry has declined since 1971, particularly in foreign language, science, and mathematics.

More significantly, there has been virtually no change over the last ten years in the percentage of students who feel they need tutoring or remedial work in college. Almost a quarter of students entering college (24.1 percent) still feel they need special tutoring or remedial work in mathematics. This is occurring at the same time that many public four-year colleges have begun to move away from offering remedial or developmental coursework and relegated such offerings to community colleges and high schools (Ignash, 1997). As such, state legislators are concerned for those students who have done well in high school but find that they are unable to meet college-level standards for academic performance (Mazzeo, 2002).

Perhaps even more compelling are the trends for remedial education across racial/ethnic groups. Figures 3 and 4 reveal important differences across race/ethnicity that serve to reaffirm the

Table 4. Percentage of Students Reporting Special Tutoring or Remedial Work

	Percent in			
	1971*	1979*	1995	2005
Had tutoring or remedial work in high school				
English	NA	5.8	4.9	6.0
Reading	NA	5.9	4.4	5.0
Mathematics	NA	7.5	11.2	12.7
Social studies	NA	4.9	3.2	3.6
Science	NA	4.6	4.3	4.9
Foreign language	NA	3.8	4.4	5.0
Will need special tutoring or remedial work in college				
English	14.7	10.9	9.9	9.4
Reading	10.0	4.9	4.4	4.4
Mathematics	34.6	21.5	24.6	24.1
Social studies	3.4	2.5	3.3	3.3
Science	22.3	9.7	11.1	10.9
Foreign language	23.0	9.5	11.3	11.1

Note: * Indicates first year survey item was introduced on the survey.

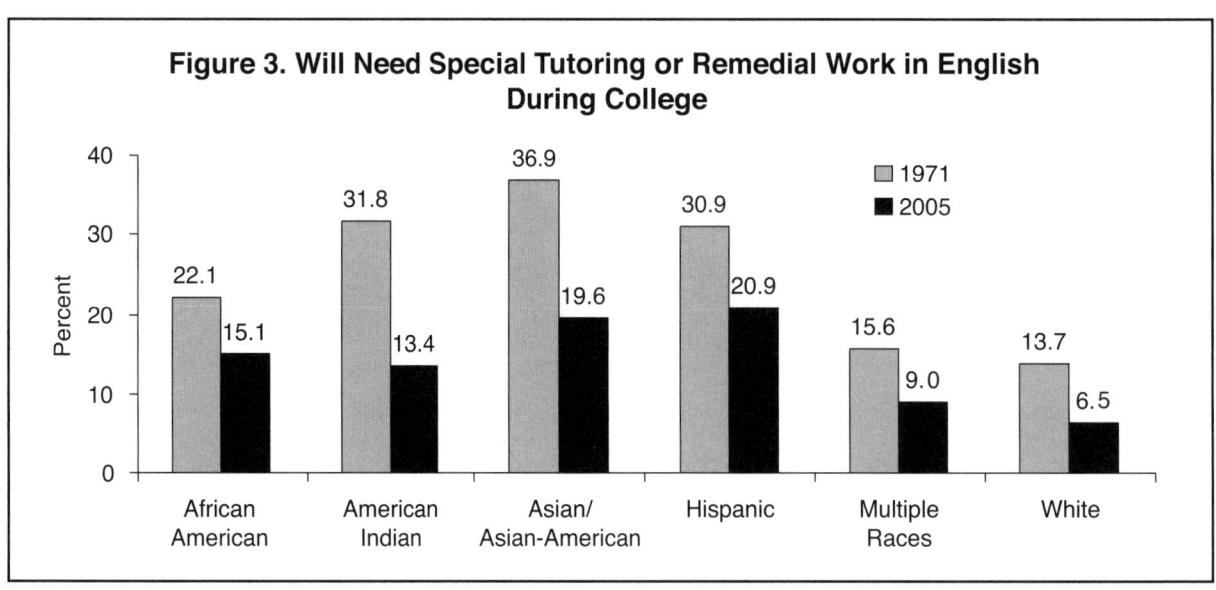

Figure 3. Will Need Special Tutoring or Remedial Work in English During College

academic preparation gap that exists at college entry. Over the last 35 years, student expectations for needing college remedial work in English and mathematics have decreased for all groups, although persistent gaps remain.

For example, in 1971, White students reported the lowest expectation for needing remedial work in English (13.7 percent), a figure that was about half that for African-American students (22.1 percent) and almost two-thirds less than for Asian students (36.9 percent). By 2005, the percentage point differences between these comparison groups had dropped significantly. Asians and Hispanics (most likely second language users) reported considerable drops, yet these are the groups still most likely to report some tutoring or coursework needed in English preparation at college entry.

Mathematics preparation at the K-12 level is acknowledged as the critical gatekeeper for entry into many science, technology, and engineering disciplines and career paths for students. Student trends data suggest that critical differences persist across groups, with racial/ethnic minority students still lagging behind their Asian and White peers with respect to academic preparedness in mathematics upon college entry. In 1971, over half of all entering students from African American, American Indian, and Hispanic racial/ethnic backgrounds expected to need college remedial work in mathematics, figures that have steadily dropped to the 2005 levels observed in Figure 4. Yet, while drops are apparent for all groups, the between-group differences have been preserved over time, and they remain a cause for continuing concern as well as a driver of policy and programmatic intervention. American Indians reported the greatest decline in need for remedial work, while African Americans (43.4 percent) and Hispanics (38.5 percent) are more likely to report they will need some type of special tutoring or coursework in mathematics. In addition, one in five White students enters college reporting a need for remedial work or special tutoring in mathematics. Placement tests administered during orientation, about the same time that

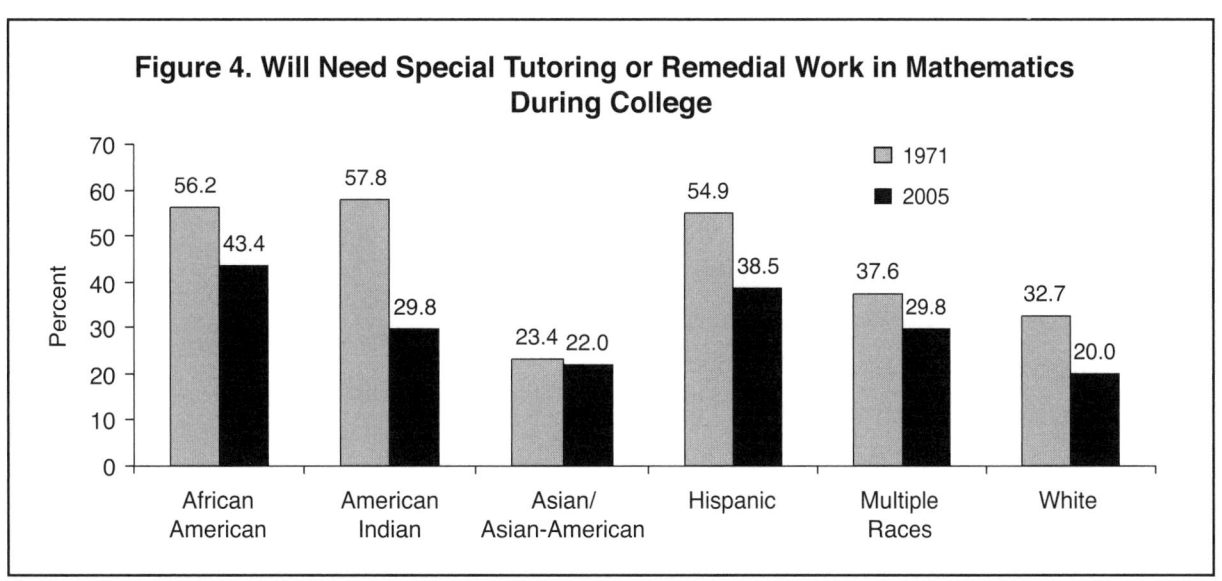

Figure 4. Will Need Special Tutoring or Remedial Work in Mathematics During College

	1971	2005
African American	56.2	43.4
American Indian	57.8	29.8
Asian/Asian-American	23.4	22.0
Hispanic	54.9	38.5
Multiple Races	37.6	29.8
White	32.7	20.0

students take the Freshman Survey, may have influenced their expressed need to meet the demands of college level work.

While the data indicate that today's freshmen, compared with cohorts 35 years ago, report less of a need for remedial English and math preparation, it is important to note that many of these figures have changed very little in the last ten years despite the "No Child Left Behind" initiative and state interest in removing remedial education in many four-year college and university systems. It may be premature to abandon special coursework to help students meet the demands of college-level work, particularly in mathematics

and English. Recent research on the impact of remediation at the college level reveals that students required to take remedial coursework in English or mathematics in college were more likely to persist, transfer to a higher-level college, and complete a baccalaureate degree; thereby increasing degree attainment in states that need it most to improve their economies (Bettinger & Long, 2005).

Perceived Abilities

At the same time that students have indicated a continuing need for better high school preparation, we have witnessed changes in students'

Table 5. Student Self-Ratings: Above Average or Highest 10% Compared to Average Peer

	Percent in		
	1966	1991	2006
Academic ability	64.3	64.2	68.6
Creativity	NA	NA	56.6
Drive to achieve	60.2	72.0	72.6
Mathematical ability	39.2	43.1	43.7
Self confidence (intellectual)	NA	58.5	59.7
Writing ability	30.0	45.9	47.7

self-ratings of academic ability. Table 5 shows the trend for increases in key academic self-ratings. Most significantly, from 1966 to 2006, the highest increases have occurred in intellectual self-confidence (20.7 percentage point increase from 39.0 percent to 59.7 percent), writing ability (17.7 percentage point increase from 30.0 percent to 47.7 percent) and drive to achieve (12.4 percentage point increase from 60.2 percent to 72.6 percent). In fact, students' self-ratings indicating their drive to achieve are at an all-time high in 2006.

However, as the trend lines indicate, it should be noted that most of the dramatic increases occurred during the first 20 years of the survey. That is, a heightened sense of academic ability is not characteristic only of the millennial cohorts. Much smaller increases were reported in areas of mathematics ability and academic self-confidence, while self-ratings of creativity posted the largest increase in the last ten years.

Other Key Academic Trends

Higher Proportions Report Coming Late to Class, Signs of Abatement. The proportion of students who report coming late to class in the last year of high school increased from 48.2 percent in 1966 to 60.6 percent in 2006. This may well be a sign of "senioritis," although it is important to note that this is an improvement from its all-time high five years ago (65.1 percent in 2001). That is, in the last five years, there has been a slight reversal of this trend. It could be that students are aware that more college admissions officers are evaluating academic rigor and involvement through the senior year of high school.

Recent national reports call for greater attention to better preparing students in the last year of high school for college (AACU, 2007).

Declining Proportion of Students Report Studying/Doing Homework. Fewer students in 2006 (32.8 percent) report spending six or more hours per week studying or doing homework as seniors in high school than in 1987 (47.0 percent), when we first introduced a time diary to record student involvement. The proportion of students who spent at least six hours represents an all-time low in the last two years. A little over half (52.9 percent) spent between 1 and 5 hours a week studying in high school.

Declining Interaction With High School Teachers. The percentage of students who report having been a guest in a teacher's home at least occasionally has dropped from 39.7 percent in 1967 to almost half that level, 22.9 percent in 2006. Those who reported frequently asking teachers for advice after class dropped slightly, from 28.2 percent in 1967 to 26.0 percent in 2006. The students' time diary gives a more exact account of how frequently they interact with teachers: About 10 percent of students report that they do not talk to teachers outside of class at all on a weekly basis (an increase from 6 percent in 1987), and about 43 percent indicate they spend less than an hour. Fewer students spend an hour (or more) per week compared to cohorts 20 years ago. These statistics are concerning given that faculty interaction in college is associated with a host of educational outcomes (Astin, 1993; Pascarella & Terenzini, 2005). Moreover, interaction with instructors may be critical to students

Table 6. AP Course/Exam Patterns by High School Grade Point Average (2006 only)

		Percent in 2006		
		C+ or less	B– to B+	A– or higher
AP COURSES taken	None offered at my high school	5.6	44.5	49.8
	No AP Courses	9.2	66.9	23.9
	1 to 4	2.4	45.7	51.9
	5 to 9	0.6	23.3	76.2
	10 or more	1.3	19.1	79.5
	Total	4.5	49.0	46.5
AP EXAMS taken	None offered at my high school	5.6	45.2	49.1
	No AP Exams	7.9	63.9	28.2
	1 to 4	1.9	41.8	56.3
	5 to 9	0.5	21.2	78.3
	10 or more	1.2	16.7	82.1
	Total	4.5	49.0	46.5

understanding course content, acquiring academic skills, and feeling academically integrated.

Low Grades a Thing of the Past? Only 1.3 percent of entering freshmen in 2006 report making a C average in high school compared with 8.6 percent of students in 1966. This trend of high grades, referred to as "grade inflation," has continued unabated since we first reported it in 1987 (Astin, Green, & Korn, 1987), with the most dramatic increases in the last 20 years. In the last ten years, increases have continued to occur in the proportion of students reporting an A– average, reaching a high point in 2006 (24.1 percent). The highest proportion of students who reported an A or A+ high school grade point average was reached in 2004 (23.7 percent). A deeper examination of the trends data confirms that, as students take a higher proportion of honors and AP courses, they are more likely to report a higher high school grade point average at college entry (Table 6). Moreover, upon college entry, 60.6 percent of freshmen in 2006 state that they expect to earn at least a B average in college compared to only 26.7 percent in 1967.

Trends in Technology Use Among Entering College Students

In more recent years, entering college students have likely grown up in a world that is fully wired, integrated, and web-enabled, resulting in some interesting trends related to their use of computer and internet technologies. In its 2004 report, *A Nation Online,* the National Telecommunications and Information Administration reported that 86.7 percent of the "in-school population between the ages of 18–24 had some form of internet access (e.g., at home, at school, local library)" (NTIA, 2004). This represented the highest rate among any age subgroup in the entire survey, including adults in the age range of 25 to 49 that were in the labor force (71.7 percent).

This same age cohort for young adults (18–24) closely resembles the entering college student population within our CIRP Freshman Survey

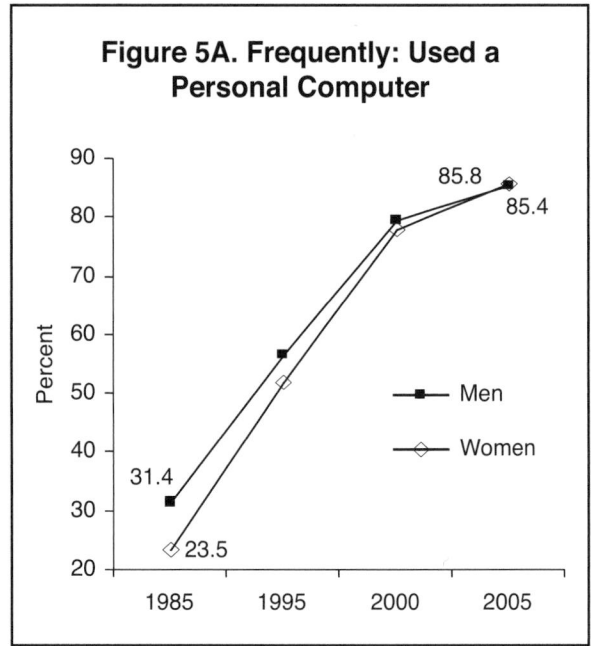

Figure 5A. Frequently: Used a Personal Computer

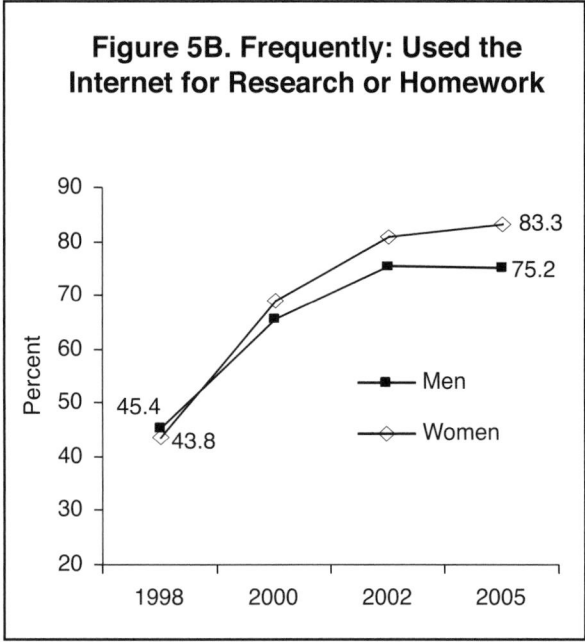

Figure 5B. Frequently: Used the Internet for Research or Homework

trends data. Figures 5A and 5B display students' frequency of use of personal computers in general as well as their use of the internet for research and homework. Not surprisingly, given the broader trends noted by NTIA, entering college students have reported more frequent use of computers and the internet over the last decade. In fact, frequent use of a personal computer among entering female students has more than tripled in the last 20 years, from 23.5 percent in 1985 to 85.8 percent in 2005. Frequent computer usage rates for male students have also increased dramatically in this time span (85.4 percent in 2005).

Female incoming students have surpassed their male counterparts in their utilization of the internet for research or homework, as their rates of frequent use have almost doubled from 43.8 percent in 1998 to 83.3 percent in 2005. Entering college male students have also shown an increased utilization of the internet for educational purposes, increasing from 45.4 percent in 1998 to 75.2 percent in 2005. Growth in frequent use of

the internet for both groups is clearly evident, and it is a sign of the increased utility of the internet as a medium for educational intervention and instructional practice. However, there does appear to be an increasing gap between male and female students in their use of the internet for educational purposes, which may be emblematic of their varied interests and motivations for using the internet. This growing dichotomy in the use of the internet should be closely watched by institutions that are increasingly moving towards more web-based and interactive methods of instruction. A recent set of questions on the CIRP Freshman Survey indicates that incoming women are more likely to frequent blogs, while men are more likely to access internet news sites.

Other prominent gaps in computer and internet use are also evident when examining trends data along racial/ethnic and socioeconomic lines (Table 7). Within the broader U.S. population, NTIA (2004) reported that 65.1 percent of the White (only) population and 63.0 percent of the

Table 7. Internet Use by Racial/Ethnic Group and Family Income

Category	Internet Users, U.S. Pop. (2004)	"Frequent" Use of the Internet for Research or Homework	
		Entering College Freshmen (1998)	Entering College Freshmen (2005)
Racial/Ethnic Group	%	%	%
White (only)	65.1	40.5	80.0
Black (only)	45.2	32.1	75.9
Asian Amer. and Pac. Isl. (only)	63.0	51.0	82.2
Hispanic (of any race)	37.2	34.2	77.8
Family Income			
Less than $15,000	31.2	30.6	72.9
$50,000–$74,999	71.8	42.5	79.3
$75,000–$99,999	79.8	45.9	80.7
$150,000 and above	86.1	52.1	83.5

Note: The word "only" in parentheses indicates that students in this group include only those students that reported belonging to this racial/ethnic group at the exclusion of all others. Hispanics can be of any race.
Sources: U.S. population data is from NTIA, 2004; CIRP Freshman Survey Trends Data is from 1998 and 2005.

Asian American/Pacific Islander population were internet users, while these rates were significantly lower for the Black (45.2 percent) and Hispanic (37.2 percent) populations. Comparing these data with our CIRP trends data reveals similar differences across racial/ethnic groups for entering college students. In 1998, 40.5 percent of White (only) and 51.0 percent of Asian American/ Pacific Islanders reported frequent use of the internet for research or homework, a significant difference when compared against Black (only) and Hispanic students (at 32.1 percent and 34.2 percent, respectively). By 2005, all racial/ethnic groups showed dramatic increases in the frequent use of the internet for research or homework. More importantly, while the racial/ethnic group differences in this kind of internet use have diminished somewhat, these differences remain salient for institutions as they contend with pervasive gaps in other benchmarks, such as academic achievement, success, and retention for underrepresented groups.

Even greater gaps in internet use were noted across household income categories, as only 30.6 percent of entering college students in 1998 from the lowest income range reported using the internet for research or homework compared to 52.1 percent of those in the highest income range. Seven years later, the gap in internet use (i.e., for research or homework) between the lowest and highest income range students had diminished considerably, from a difference of 21.5 percentage points in 1998 to 11.0 percentage points in 2005. In short, persistent gaps between student groups in the use of the internet as a tool in the educational experience remain, but much progress has been made in recent years in closing these gaps across race and family income levels.

Interest in Biological and Health Science is on the Rise, Women Take the Lead

In recent years, policy imperatives have been continually raised with regards to science and math preparation as well as the attendant shortages in those professions that require strong science and math orientations. The Spellings Commission report (U.S. DOE, 2006) highlighted these shortages as a key area of concern for the future of higher education. CIRP Freshman Survey trends data reveal some promising developments with regards to growing interest in the sciences and health professions as fields of study.

Figures 6A–C track probable majors in the biological sciences, health professions, and nursing. Trend data on these probable majors reveal a mixed portrait of changing interests for both male and female students at college entry. In the biological sciences, a key finding is that interest in this field has been on an upswing since the early

1980s. Even more interesting is the fact that female students have eclipsed male students since the mid 1990s in reporting a strong interest in majoring in this field. Most importantly, the proportions of female (9.2 percent) and male (7.3 percent) students who reported a probable major in the biological sciences are at their highest levels since 1976. The challenge for institutions is to sustain and nurture interest in these critical science fields through the college years.

Similarly, interest in the health professions has been stronger among female students than their male counterparts since the mid 1970s, as women have surpassed men in reporting interest in the fields within this category. The cyclical

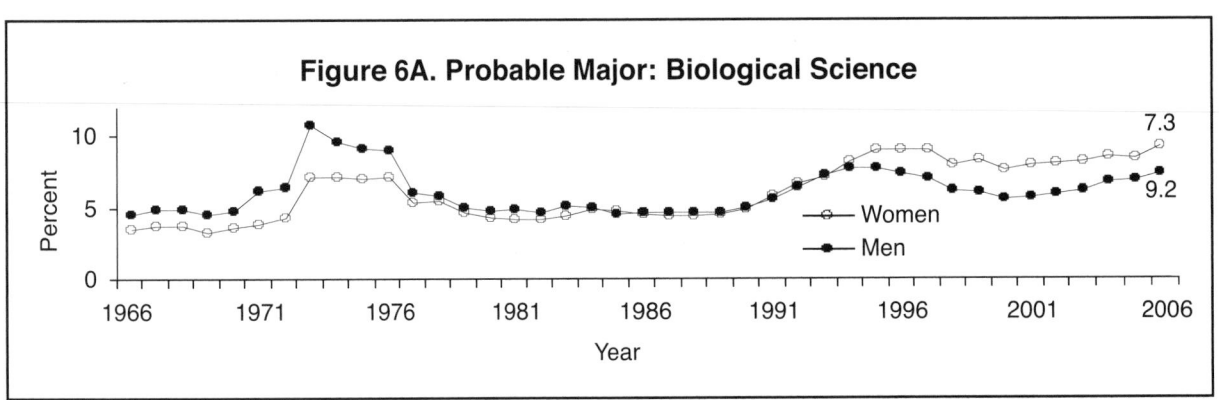

Figure 6A. Probable Major: Biological Science

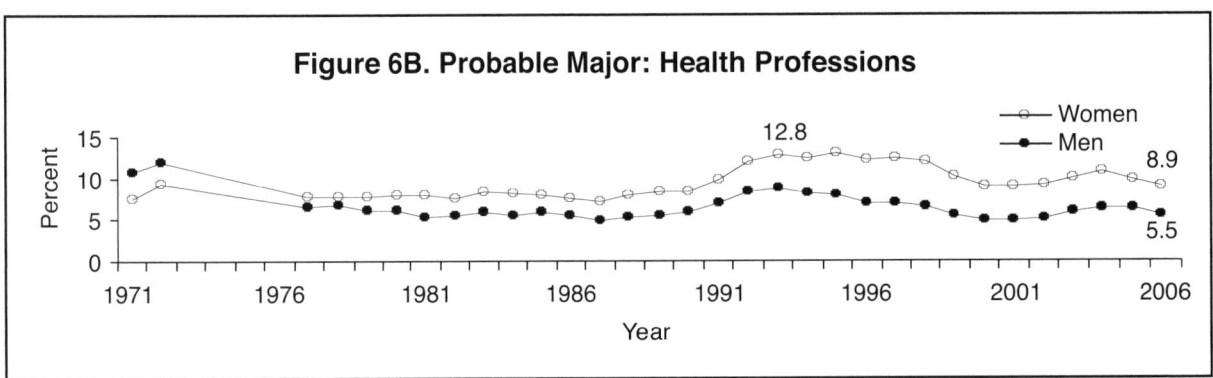

Figure 6B. Probable Major: Health Professions

Note: The health professional major includes Medical, Dental, Veterinary, Pharmacy, and Therapy (occupational, physical, speech). For purposes of this trend, it excludes nursing, which is illustrated in the following figure dashed lines indicate that data for these major categories were not available for the corresponding years.

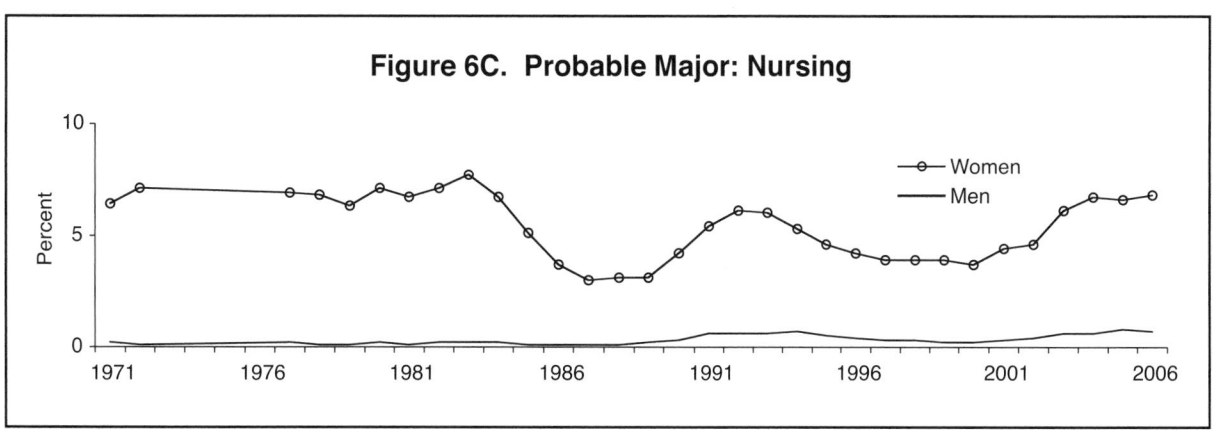

Figure 6C. Probable Major: Nursing

popularity of these major fields over the last 15 years is evident in the various periods of up and down trends for each group. Interest in these majors for female students reached a high point in 1993 with 12.8 percent reporting an interest in the health professions, and this trend has steadily declined since then to its current level of 8.9 percent for 2006. Meanwhile, the trend for male students majoring in these fields has also declined since the mid 1990s.

A more striking gender gap has persisted in students' interest in the nursing major over the last 40 years (Figure 6C). In fact, male student interest in nursing (or lack thereof) has continued to be a dilemma for both higher education institutions and for this health profession sector, which is intent on diversifying and growing its labor force, which is in dire need of more skilled workers. On a positive note, in 2006, women reported their highest level of interest since 1983 for this probable major. Women have remained significantly more interested than men in the nursing major at college entry, and this persistent difference is also manifested in students' career aspirations and their general over-representation in

the nursing field (Astin, Oseguera, Sax & Korn, 2002).

Given the increasing workforce demands for skilled professionals in these critical health profession fields, institutions should pay close attention to the changing interests of their entering student populations, with an eye towards supporting and sustaining student interest in the science and health profession majors and career tracks. Students' commitment to science and innovation remain most apparent in their strong desire to make a theoretical contribution to their chosen science fields. Student commitment has grown in recent years, and is strongest for male students (22.3 percent), who report this goal as essential or very important at college entry in 2006. Women, as well, have reported an increased commitment to this goal in recent years. Such a trend among incoming student populations should serve as notice that interest and commitment to science should to be nourished with appropriate new pedagogies, curricula, and technologies to improve learning in these fields, a priority articulated by both policy imperatives (U.S. DOE, 2006) and workforce needs and realities (NSB, 2002).

College Access and Choice

In recent years, higher education researchers and administrators have paid greater attention to the college choice process for students and their parents. In truth, an entire for-profit cottage industry has arisen that offers students a variety of services, resources, how-to books, and multi-college tours, all designed to influence the college choice process. Colleges and universities too have succumbed to market pressures, as they have grown increasingly proactive in their marketing and outreach campaigns, intended to attract the best and brightest to their campuses. Jostling for students, resources, top-notch campus facilities, and high rankings is emblematic of the re-defined cultural norms of the college choice process in the four-year sector. Institutions have had to become smarter about their packaging and marketing, and students and families in turn are becoming savvier about "shopping" for the best educational value in making their final college choice.

Students Increasingly Apply to More Colleges

In tracking the various factors involved in affecting a student's decision to attend a particular college, the CIRP Freshman Survey trends data highlight many important changes that reflect the evolving nature of the college choice process. One very important contextual fact to establish about the choice process is that students are more likely than ever to apply to a higher number of institutions (Figure 7). In 1967, less than one in five entering college students (19.9 percent) reported applying to four or more colleges, a figure that has nearly tripled to 56.5 percent in 2006. In contrast, the number of students who reported submitting only one college application has declined by more than half during this same time span (from 43.1 percent to 17.7 percent). A closer look at the actual number of college applications submitted by students indicates that this figure has doubled over the last 40 years, a trend that shows little sign of slowing down as the application process becomes increasingly streamlined and web-enabled.

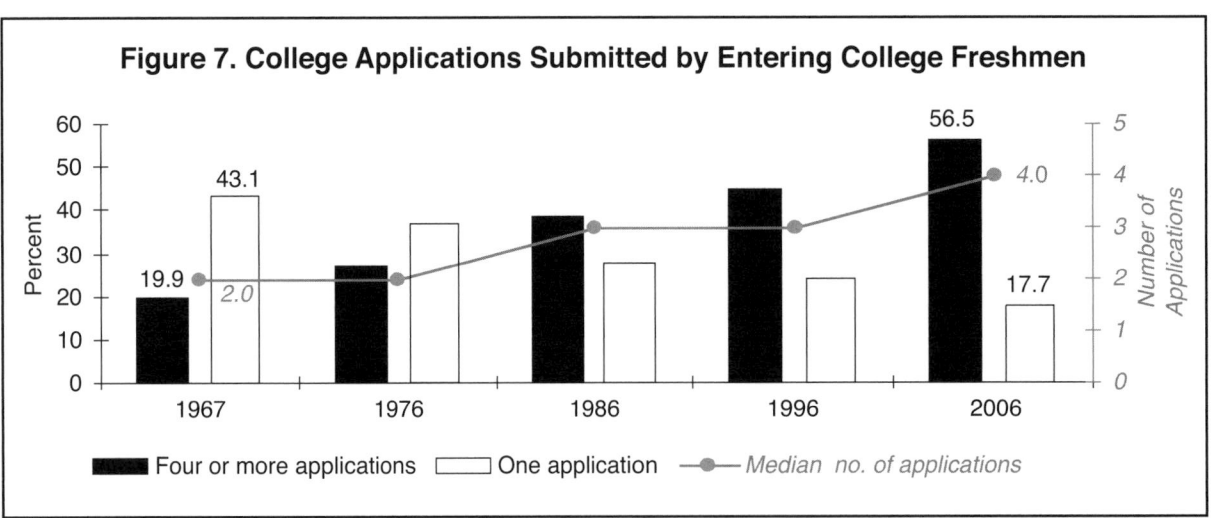

Note: The scale for median number of applications is reflected on the right-hand side of this figure.

Every spring, when admissions decisions are communicated, one hears stories about the student who applied to 20 or more colleges. In fact, only 2.2 percent of students in 2006 had applied to twelve or more schools, a figure that has increased from 1.3 percent in 2000, but still represents a very low proportion of all students submitting applications.

Perceived Importance of a College Education Increases

It is interesting to note that almost all listed reasons for attending college have increased in importance over time. This suggests that, over the last 40 years, the college experience is increasingly seen as more multi-faceted by today's incoming students, leading one to infer that the expectations of these students might be even higher than students in the past. This also suggests that students increasingly view a college education as a necessary component to achieving their goals in life.

Many of the same reasons for attending college in 1976 (when this question was first regularly asked on the CIRP Freshman Survey) remain important to students making those same decisions today. The top two important reasons in 1976 ("to learn about things that interest me" and "to get a better job") are the top two important reasons 30 years later in 2006. One change has been seen in the importance of seeing the college degree as a way "to be able to make more money." This was a very important reason to go to college for only half (49.9 percent) of incoming students in 1976, but moved up dramatically over the following seven years to 64.9 percent before staying relatively stable in the late 1980s and reaching 69.0 percent in 2006. Another change has been in the proportion of students who reported that preparation for graduate or professional school was a "very important" reason for attending college: from 34.9 percent in 1971 to 57.7 percent in 2006, an increase of about one-third.

Greater Influence of Parents

Trends data in Figure 8 show that entering college students are placing more importance on

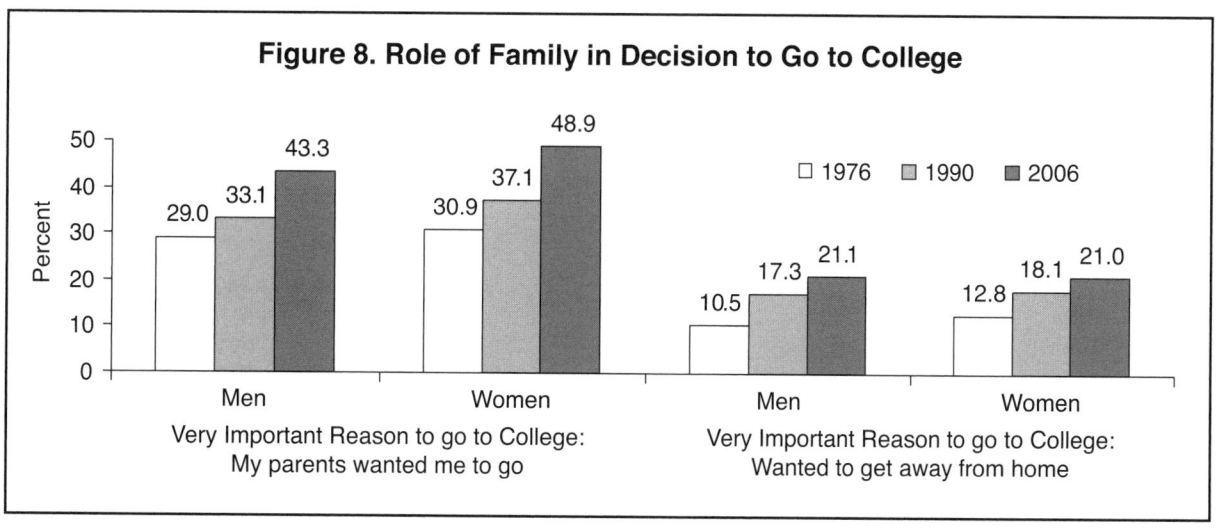

Figure 8. Role of Family in Decision to Go to College

parental encouragement in deciding to attend college. In 1976, 29.0 percent of male students and 30.9 percent of female students reported parental encouragement as a very important reason for going to college. This figure has increased steadily for both groups through 2006, with female students slightly outpacing their male counterparts. On the other hand, students are also increasingly reporting that getting away from home is a "very important" reason for going to college, nearly doubling in the last 30 years.

The trends for each group in Figure 8 show the relative similarity with which parents of female students encourage them to pursue higher education compared to the parents of male students. The awareness and the value placed on higher education align with larger societal shifts from the industrial employment sector to more technological fields, shifts that are emblematic of how more education is essential in the new global economy. These results further suggest that par-

ents may have increasingly central roles in shaping student's orientation for higher education. Recognizing the perceived increased influence of parents in the college experience, we introduced a new set of items to the 2007 CIRP Freshman Survey that will examine this phenomenon more closely.

Choosing Your College:
Relative Importance of Rankings

Entering freshmen are apt to consider a college's academic reputation, the likelihood of gaining entry into a top graduate/professional program, and an institution's national ranking as very important reasons for choosing their respective colleges, and these reasons have not changed much in importance to students in the last 20 years (Figure 9). In 2006, more than half (57.4 percent) of all entering college students indicated that the school's good academic reputation was a "very important" reason for selecting their particular

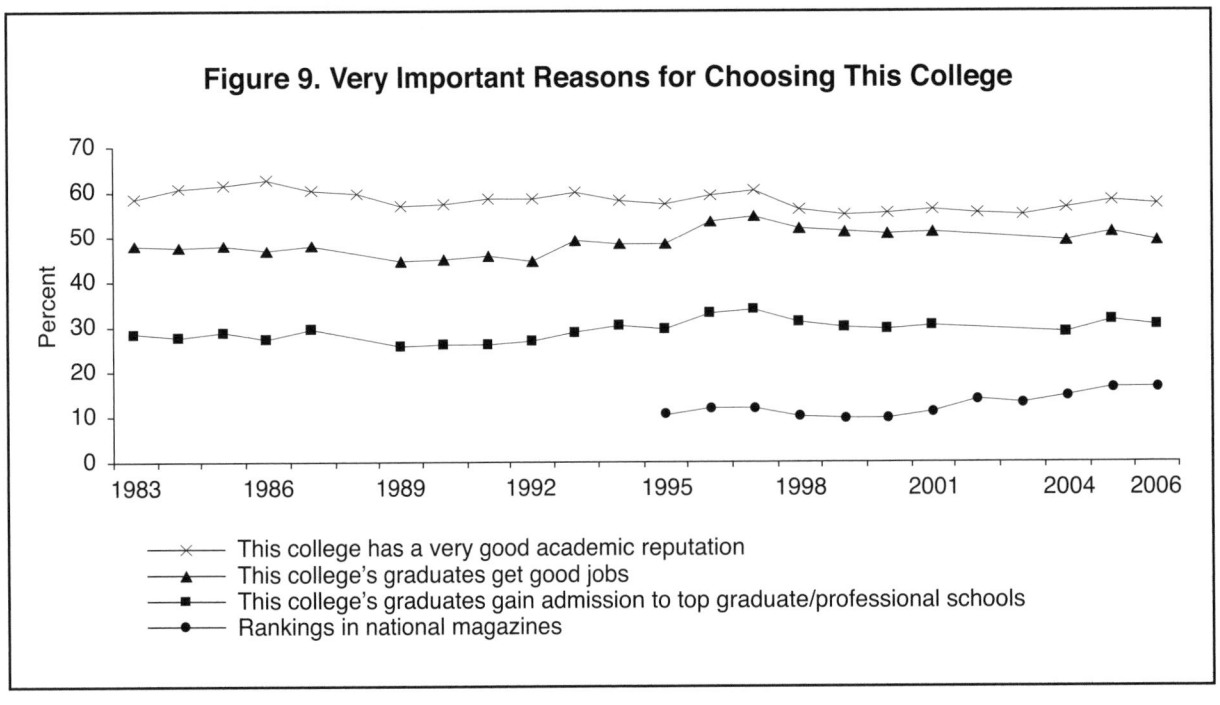

Figure 9. Very Important Reasons for Choosing This College

- —×— This college has a very good academic reputation
- —▲— This college's graduates get good jobs
- —■— This college's graduates gain admission to top graduate/professional schools
- —●— Rankings in national magazines

college, almost equivalent to the proportion in 1983 (58.4 percent). Two other characteristics that have held steady as very important reasons for colleges being selected by students are institutional track records of placing graduates in good jobs and in graduate school.

In the last decade, more students relied on rankings to choose a particular college. It should be noted, however, that despite all the hype, only 16.4 percent of incoming students in 2006 reported that rankings were very important in their decision to attend their particular college. Finally, the proportion of students who report that information from a website helped them to choose a particular college has more than doubled in the last five years, from 6.8 percent in 2000 to 17.0 percent in 2006.

During the spring college decision season, the advent of college rankings has reinforced the competitive dynamic within the higher education marketplace. In some ways, the increasing popularity and use of rankings that purport to categorize the "best colleges" (e.g., U.S. News & World Report) or the "best college buys" (e.g., Money Magazine) or the "best sports schools" (e.g., Sports Illustrated) has re-normalized the entire college decision process to give additional advantage to more affluent students and families. McDonough et al. (1998) contend that, while some may characterize college rankings as the further democratization of college knowledge for the benefit of all, their findings suggested quite the contrary. Namely, they found that more affluent families were much more likely to value college rankings and use them in informing their college choice. The patterns of use of college

rankings point to the further reinforcement of advantages that more affluent students already possess with respect to the college choice process, which can lead to greater challenges for lower socioeconomic groups wanting to gain access to the most selective institutions.

Fewer Students Attending Their First Choice Institutions

Fewer students today are attending their first choice institution compared with students in the 1970s. In 1975, 79.7 percent of freshmen reported they were attending their first choice institution. This has reached a new low in 2006, with only 67.3 percent enrolled in their first choice. Further, the percentage of students who report they chose a particular college because they received financial assistance rose from 19.5 percent in 1972 to over one third in 2006 (34.3 percent)—a percentage that has hovered in that range since 1995. In fact, our analysis of college choice and financial concerns indicate that significant numbers of students who had been admitted to their first-choice college are deciding to attend second, third, or fourth (or more) choice institutions based upon economic factors (Pryor et al., 2006).

Parental Income, Affordability, and Financial Concerns

Entering College Freshmen Increasingly Coming from Wealthier Households

Overall, parental income for entering freshmen has markedly increased as measured by students' reported parents' median household income and the U.S. median household income (inflation-adjusted). In addition, parental income for entering college freshmen is rising faster than national income for students attending both private and public institutions, having accelerated during the mid 1980s. In short, today's entering freshmen are more financially advantaged than their predecessors 35 or so years earlier, as they come from households whose incomes are much higher—and the gap is widening. Meanwhile, the percentage of incoming students who report having major concerns about financing their education was at 11.6 percent in 2006, the lowest since 1971 (also 11.6 percent) and down from a high of 19.1 percent in 1995.

CIRP Median Household Income vs. National Median Household Income (Current $)

One way to look at the shift in students' parental income is by comparing students' reported median household income and the official national median household income. In 1971, students' median household income was $13,200 while the U.S. median household income stood at $9,028. In 2005, students' median household income was $74,000 while the national median household income in the same year stands at $46,326. As a result, in 1971, entering freshmen came from households where the parental median income was 46 percent above the national median income, and in 2005, that figure increased to 60 percent above the national median income, representing an increase of 14 percentage points. Today's entering freshmen are increasingly coming from wealthier households.

CIRP Median Household Income vs. National Median Household Income (2006 Constant $)

Perhaps the best way to ascertain the relative changes in college students' parental wealth is to compare their median household income with the national median household income while adjusting for inflation. Figure 10A illustrates the general tendencies of college students' parental wealth. Students' parental income rose from $13,200 to $74,000 in current dollars over the 35-year period, representing a 461 percent increase—over five and a half times higher in 2005 than in 1971. National income rose from $9,028 to $46,326 in current dollars from 1971 to 2005, representing a 413 percent increase—five times higher in 2005. Both trends overlaid, and measured in 2006 constant dollars, paint a clearer picture of the sharp increase in college students' parental income relative to national income.

In the last 35 years, college student parental income rose from $65,700 to $76,400 (inflation-adjusted), representing a 16 percent increase, while national income rose from $44,900 to $47,800 (inflation-adjusted), representing a 6.5 percent increase. That is, parental income for the entering college freshmen is outpacing the national income by more than a two-to-one margin. Of particular note is that the mid-1980s ushered in an era where differences between college students' family income and national income were the most pronounced. Between 1983 and 1987, student family income increased from $62,900 to $76,100, representing a 21 percent

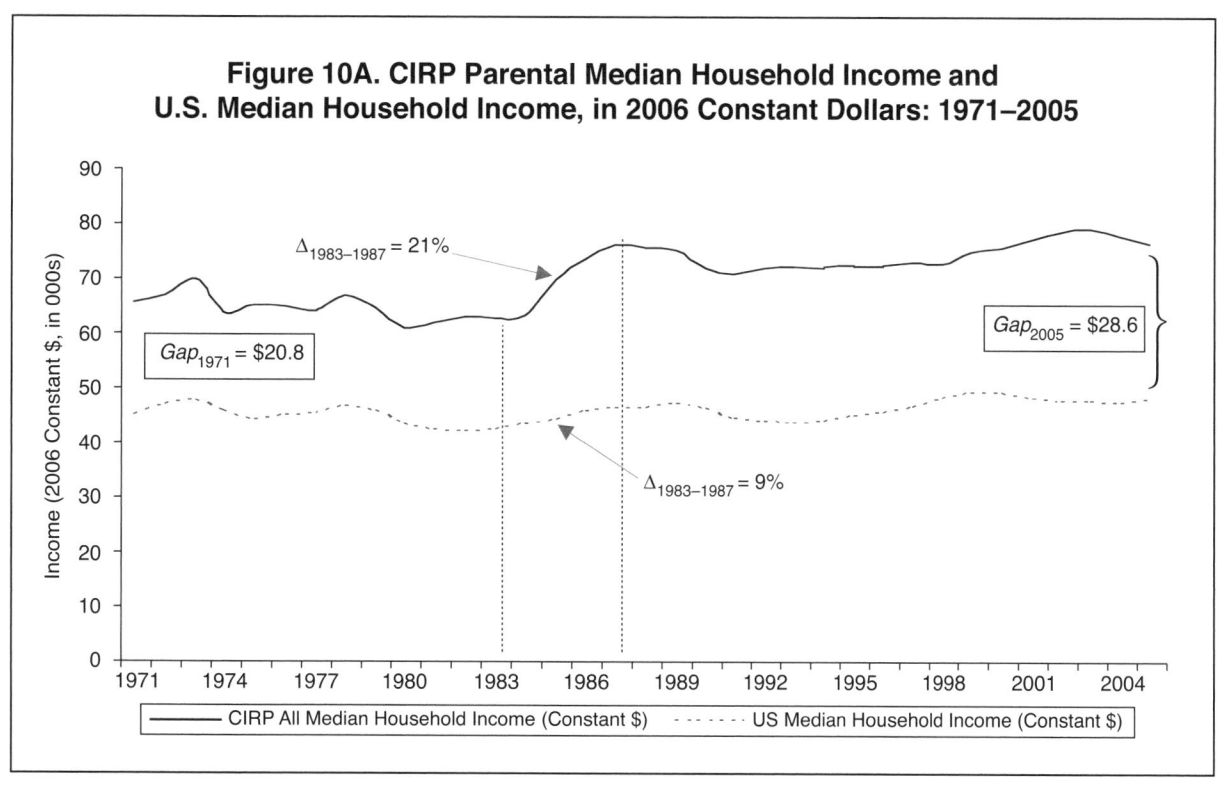

Figure 10A. CIRP Parental Median Household Income and U.S. Median Household Income, in 2006 Constant Dollars: 1971–2005

Note: US Census Official Median Household Income is reported from 1967 to 2005.
Source: Bureau of Labor Statistics, CPI-U Annual Average; US Census Table H-5. Race and Hispanic Origin of Householder—Households by Median and Mean Income: 1967 to 2005; Author's Calculations.

relative increase, while national income only rose from $42,300 to $46,200, a nine percent relative increase. Thus the 1980s signaled the beginning of an enduring and widening gap: In 1971, students' parental income was $65,700 while national income was $44,900, representing a $20,800 gap (inflation-adjusted), and in 2005, parental income was $76,400 while national income was $47,800, representing a much larger $28,600 gap.

CIRP Median Household Income by Institutional Control (Public/Private) vs. National Median Household Income (2006 Constant $)

Figure 10A illustrates the tendencies of entering college freshmen's parental income compared to national median household income

across a 35-year period. But what differences exist between entering college students' parental income at public and private institutions relative to national household median income for the same period, 1971–2005, when adjusted for inflation? Moreover, what differences exist between entering college students' parental income at private institutions relative to entering college students' parental income at public institutions? By disaggregating CIRP median household income by public and private institutions and comparing each set of reporting students, we are able to tease out the differences in parental income over time relative to each other and relative to the national median household income (Figure 10B).

Private and Public Differences

For entering students at private colleges, parental income rose from $14,500 to $80,900 in current dollars between 1971 and 2005, representing a 458 percent increase. Measured in 2006 constant dollars during the same time period, parental income for students at privates rose from $72,200 to $83,500 (inflation-adjusted), representing a 15.7 percent increase. Relative to national income, in 1971 the gap (inflation-adjusted) was $27,300, while in 2005 the gap widened to $35,700.

For entering students at public colleges, parental income rose from $12,600 to $71,100 in current dollars between 1971 and 2005, representing a 464 percent increase. Measured in 2006 constant dollars during the same time period, parental income for students at publics rose from $62,700 to $73,400 (inflation-adjusted), representing a 17.1 percent increase. Relative to national income, in 1971, the gap (inflation-adjusted) was $17,800, while in 2005 the gap widened to $25,600.

Thus the rate of increase in students' parental income at publics is faster than for students' parental income at privates, thereby reflecting a closing of the income gap for students' parental income between the two sectors.

A Widening Economic Gap: Explanations and Implications

Parental income for all entering college freshmen is rising faster than national income and contributing to the widening gap as illustrated by Figure 10A. This trend supports the increased social inequality in the U.S. In fact, the gaps between rich and poor in terms of four-year college matriculation widened from about 1979 to the beginning of the new century and has led to increased economic inequality (Neckerman, 2004).

From Figure 10B, two stories emerge. First, the gap between parental income for those students attending publics compared to national income has widened from 40 to 54 percent. Second, parental income in real terms for those students attending publics rose at a faster rate than for those students attending privates, at 15.7 and 17.1 percent, respectively.

Some possible explanations for the widening gaps between parental income for incoming freshmen and national income and the decreasing gap between parental income for those students attending publics versus privates, center around finance policy over the last 30 years or so. According to the College Board (2006), between academic years 1981–82 and 1986–87, the five-year percent change for tuition and fees in 2006 constant dollars increased by 31 percent at public four-year colleges and universities. During the same time period, tuition and fees rose 36 percent at private four-year colleges and universities. It is likely that this large percent change (inflation-adjusted) adversely affected low-income students as these students are most responsive to changes in posted tuition and fee increases, thereby changing the composition of students entering college as measured by median income for the years 1983 through 1987. Between academic years 2001–02 and 2006–07, the five-year percent change for tuition and fees in 2006 constant dollars increased by 35 percent at public four-years and only 11 percent at private

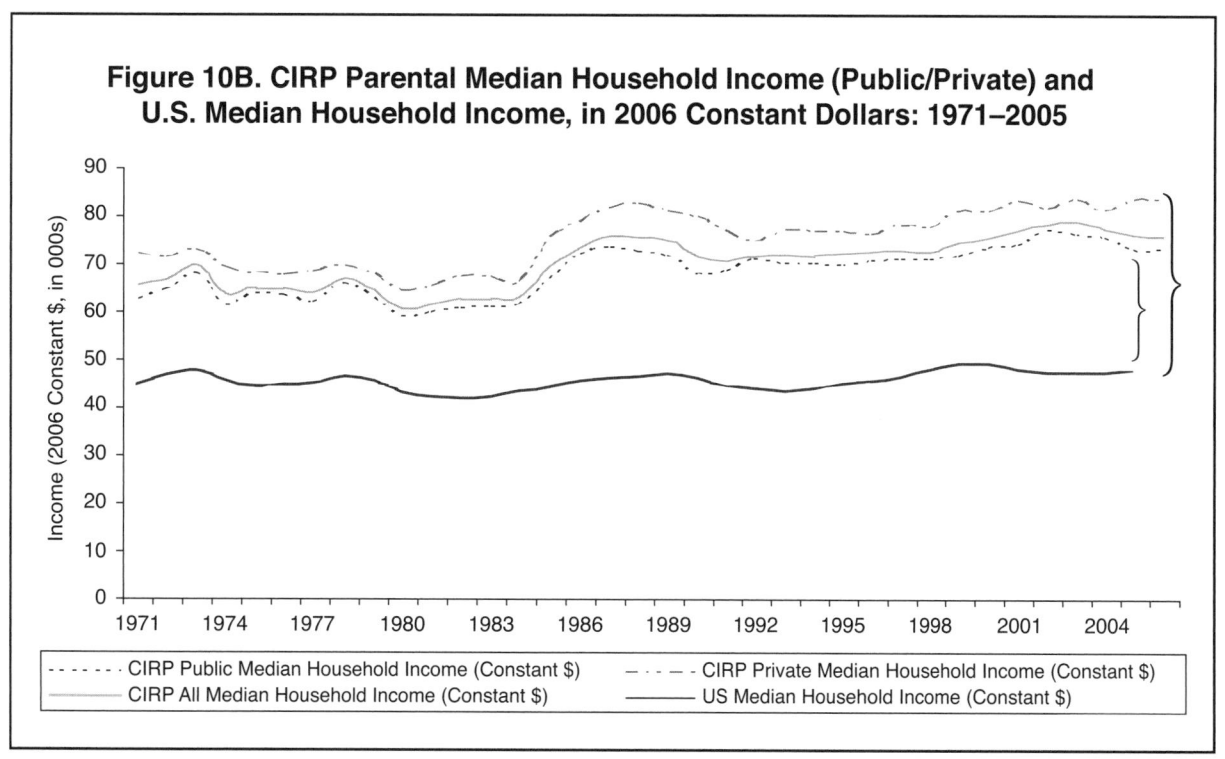

Figure 10B. CIRP Parental Median Household Income (Public/Private) and U.S. Median Household Income, in 2006 Constant Dollars: 1971–2005

- - - - - - CIRP Public Median Household Income (Constant $)　　- · - · - CIRP Private Median Household Income (Constant $)
———— CIRP All Median Household Income (Constant $)　　———— US Median Household Income (Constant $)

four-years. As tuition and fees continue to rise faster (inflation-adjusted) at public-four years than at private four-years, students from lower income families are most affected.

From 2000 through 2005, colleges and universities increased tuition prices at twice the rate of inflation during each year. Moreover, government subsidies have decreased dramatically during the same time period as the federal government has shifted its financial aid policies from grants to loans. State policy has also shifted in some states, favoring merit aid versus need-based aid.

Since the mid to late 1980s, public universities have experienced decreasing state funds in terms of market share in their revenue sources (Mumper, 1996; Hovey, 1999; Boyd, 2002; Santos, 2007) as a share of their revenue sources. This reality has led universities to increase tuition

and fees in an effort to offset state appropriation shortfalls—leading to large percent increases from time to time.

Taken together, major shifts in finance policy have contributed to these results. Moving forward, if finance policy from the federal, state, and institutions continues in this way, we can project that students coming from poorer households will be priced out of the college-going market.

Political Affiliation and Views Become More Polarized in Some Areas

Fewer of today's students self-report their political ideology as middle-of-the-road, and increasing percentages are identifying as liberal or conservative, with both liberal and conservative numbers moving up to higher levels (Figure 11). In 1970 (the first year in which this question was asked), 35.7 percent of students identified

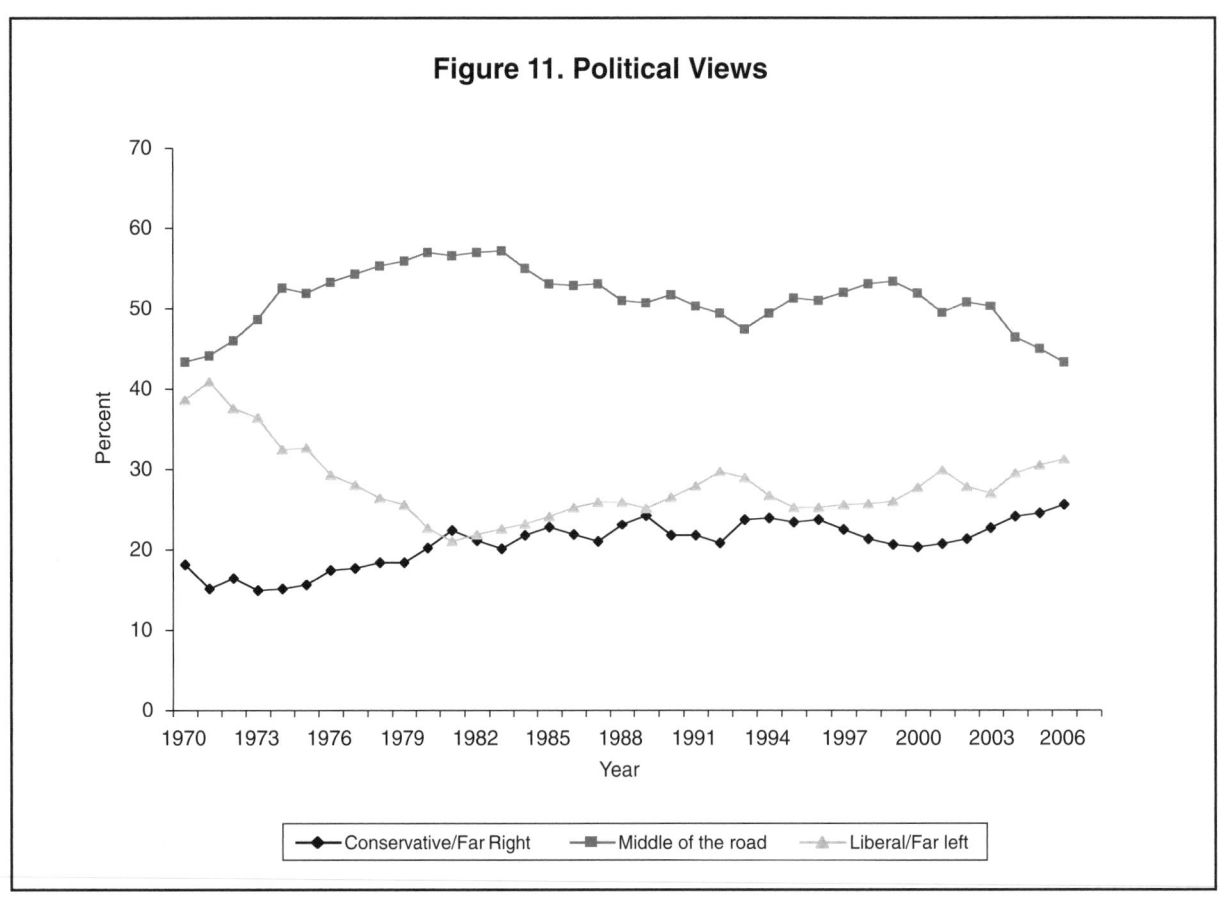

Figure 11. Political Views

Conservative/Far Right — Middle of the road — Liberal/Far left

as liberal, but the percentage quickly declined to under 30 percent in 1976. The 2006 level of 28.4 percent is the highest since the mid 1970s. Students identifying as conservative are at an all-time high in 2006 (23.9 percent). Although the trend has been cyclic over time, there has been a movement away from having a moderate political stance and towards identifying as liberal or conservative since 1999. Accompanying this change has been the increased tendency of students to have discussed politics frequently in high-school, now at an all-time high in 2006 at 33.8 percent.

The social and political views examined in the CIRP Freshman Survey can be analyzed by self-reported political affiliation as liberal or conservative, and doing so can illustrate how the views of such students have changed relative to each other over time. In examining the following trends, we have combined data from conservative and far right students as well as the data from liberal and far left students.

One of the more dramatic changes in the views of incoming students has been towards the legalization of abortion, as relative support has fluctuated over the decades (Figure 12). The percentage of incoming students who agreed that "abortion should be legal" was first measured in 1969 at 78.8 percent, and then rose to what would be the all-time high at 85.7 percent in 1970. When next measured in 1977, support for legalization had dropped to 55.6 percent, a drop of 30.1 percentage points. The next period of growth in support was in the mid to late 1980s and early 1990s, reaching 67.2 percent in 1992 but then dropping

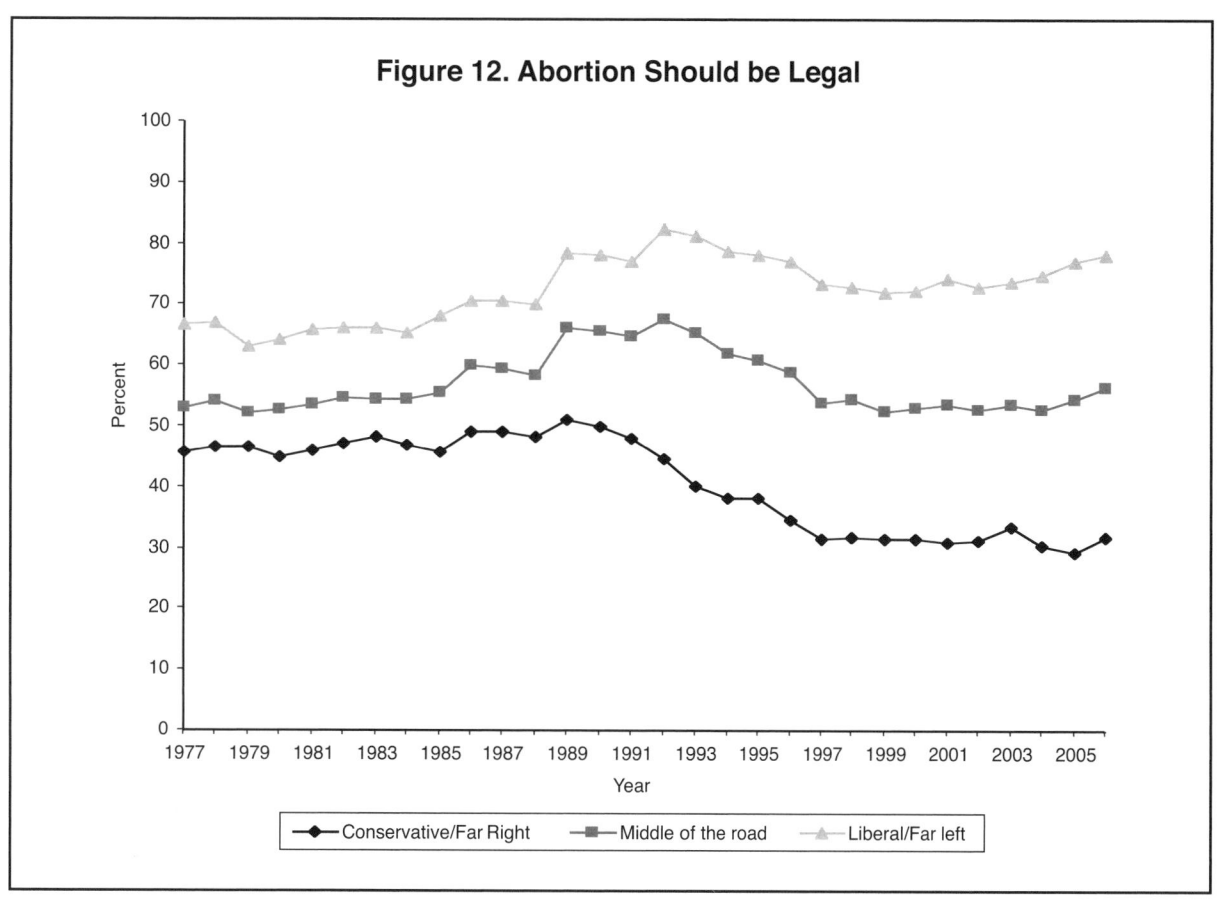

Figure 12. Abortion Should be Legal

to an all-time low in 1999 of 53.2 percent. Since then, support for the legalization of abortion has risen slightly to the 2006 level of 56.8 percent. Thus, overall, there is a cyclical pattern of support. We currently seem to be in a moderate phase that is moving in a more liberal direction.

The pattern of change is even more interesting when we break out support by political ideology. In 1977, there was a 21.1 percentage point spread between liberal/far left students and conservative/far right students on this issue, with 45.7 percent of conservatives/far right agreeing that abortion should be legal compared with 66.8 percent of liberals/far left. Middle-of-the-road students agreed with the statement at 53.2 percent, and while slightly more aligned with conservatives, ultimately situated themselves, as their label indi-

cates, in the middle of the road. There were slight changes up and down a few points for the next few years until the early 1990s, when the liberal/far left students and conservative/far right students broke away in opposite directions: Liberals more likely to support legalized abortion, and conservatives less likely to do so. Since that time, the spread has become even greater, such that in 2006, liberal/far left students supported the legalization of abortion at a much higher 78.3 percent compared to 56.3 percent for middle-of-the-road students, and a much lower 31.8 percent for conservative/far right students. The 21.1 percentage point difference between these two groups in 1977 had grown to 46.5 percentage points in 2006, reflecting a huge difference in opinion.

Another large change in socio-political views among incoming first-year students is reflected in the decline of support for laws against "homosexual relationships." The prevalence of the belief that such laws are important fell since first asked in 1976, from 43.6 percent to 25.6 percent in 2006, a drop of 18.0 percentage points. Over a shorter period of time, we saw an increase in those who believe that same-sex couples have a right to legal marital status, from 50.9 percent in 1997 to 61.2 percent in 2006, a move of 10.3 percentage points.

This is another area in which we see a widening gap between conservative/far right and liberal/far left students. In 1976, 32.0 percent of liberal/far left students believed that it was important to have laws that prohibit homosexual relationships,

compared to 54.7 percent of conservative/far right students. While the support for such a position has dropped in both cases, the drop is far more pronounced with the liberal/far left students, such that only 11.0 percent support having laws to prohibit homosexual relationships compared to 48.5 percent of conservative/far right students. The spread has moved from 22.7 percentage points to 37.5 percentage points, and while only a small minority of liberal/far left students supports such laws, almost half of the conservative/far right students do so.

A different pattern can be seen in two other sociopolitical views: the legalization of marijuana (Figure 13) and the use of affirmative action in college admissions. In 1971, only 17.2 percent of conservatives supported the legalization of

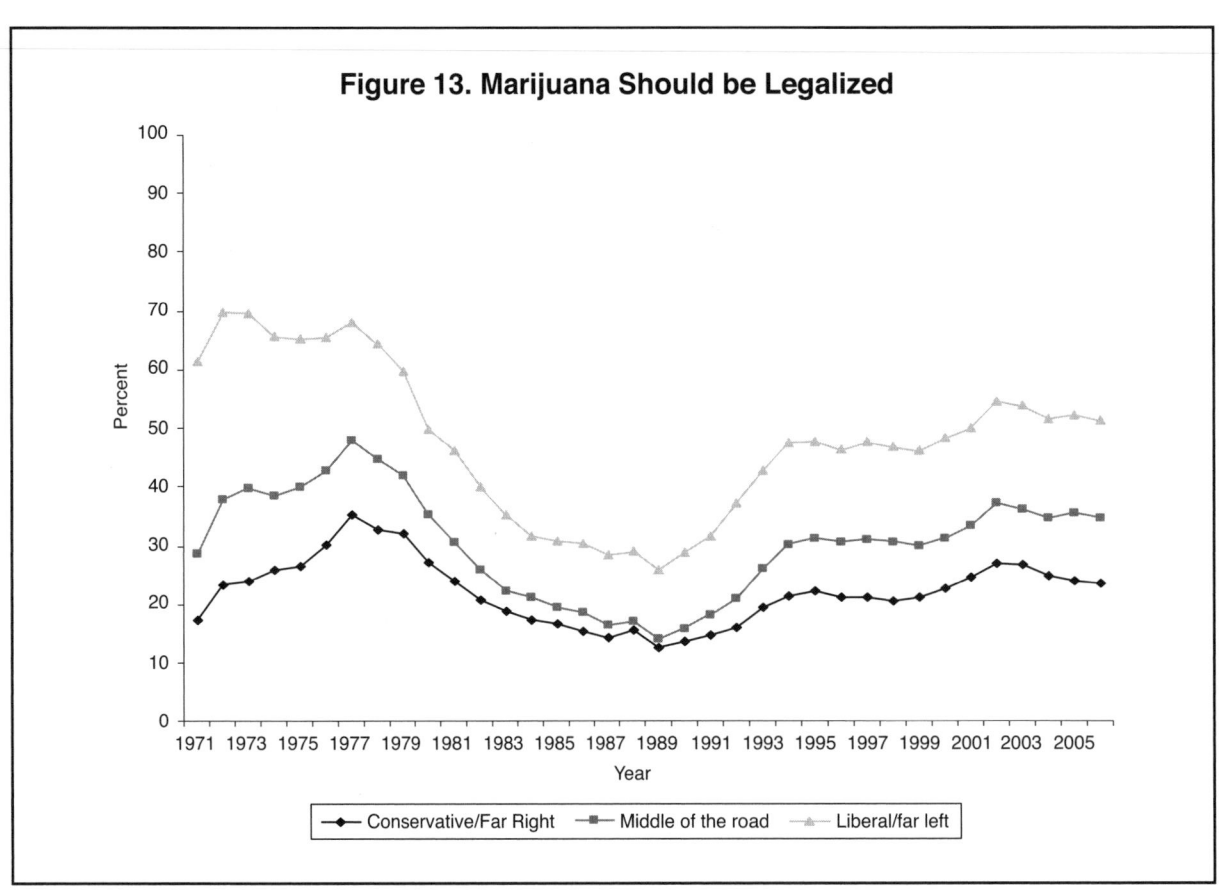

Figure 13. Marijuana Should be Legalized

marijuana, compared to 28.6 percent of middle-of-the-road students and a much higher 61.4 percent of liberals. For the most part, these percentages rose until 1978, when they started a massive plunge to the point (in 1989) where only 25.9 percent of liberal/far left students, 14.0 percent of middle-of-the-road, and 12.4 percent of conservative/far right students supported legalization of marijuana. After 1989, these figures were again on the move, but in the opposite direction. Support for legalizing marijuana jumped, but this time at a fast rate for liberal/far left students and middle-of-the-roaders such that the gap between liberal/far left (at 51.5 percent) and conservative/far right (at 23.5 percent) had diminished from 44.2 percentage points in 1971 to 13.5 percentage points in 1989 and widened again to 28.0 percentage points in 2006. Another way of looking at these trends is that students of all political orientations have changed their opinions about marijuana over time, but the conservatives tend to change less while the liberals tend to change more.

The trend with regard to affirmative action shows yet another pattern. Since 1995, we asked students if they agreed with the statement that "affirmative action in college admissions should be abolished." What we see over the subsequent nine years is that liberal/far left students and middle-of-the-roaders track very closely, and remain fairly stable over time at about 45 percent. During the same time period, the conservative/far right students have moved toward the liberal and middle-of-the-road views, dropping from 63.7 percent agreement with the statement to 52.7 percent agreement, a drop of 11.0 percentage points

compared to the drop of 1.3 percentage points for liberal/far left students.

Thus, we see in these data that some student views have shifted dramatically over time. Conservative/far right and liberal/far left students are more polarized on abortion and gay rights, and less polarized on issues to do with the use of affirmative action in college admissions and the legalization of marijuana. With both percentages of students identifying as liberal and as conservative increasing on American college campuses, and the significant increase in 2006 of the percentages of students who report discussing politics, we should expect to see increasing debate on these more polarizing issues.

Not only are liberal and conservative students even more likely to disagree on some of these sociopolitical views, but they also disagree on whether or not colleges have the right to ban extreme speakers on campus. Over half (55.1 percent) of conservative (and far right) students believe that colleges have the right to ban extreme speakers compared to only 28.5 percent of liberal (and far left) students. Thus, not only may some polarizing issues divide students, but the method by which they engage each other in dialogue concerning these issues may also be a point of disagreement. Facilitating dialogue and promoting civil discourse will be a challenge for student affairs professionals and faculty alike.

Trends in Students' Values: A Better Quality of Life and Altruism

Are current students more materialistic now than in the past? Are they more apathetic? Popular media might lead one to believe that materialism reigns alongside civic disengagement, but CIRP Freshman Survey data indicates the issue is more complex. By far, students' top personal objective that they consider to be "essential" or "very important" is "raising a family." Over the years, this has been consistently high compared with other objectives, showing some growth over the years so that now over three-quarters of both men and women view this as a top objective, compared with earlier cohorts where differences between men and women were greater. Figure 14 shows that this goal or value has risen and closely follows students' objective of "being very well off financially." When viewed together, these data speak to students' interest in quality of life as well as an interest in social mobility.

Materialism might be involved in the desire to be financially well off, but it is not the only explanation for its rise, nor is it only characteristic of the millennial generation. Figure 14 shows that much of the growth in the percentage of students who rate highly the importance of being well off financially occurred from 1966 to 1987 (from 42.2 percent to 74.1 percent) and has remained fairly stable since then (73.4 percent in 2006). Several forces may be at work to drive and sustain interest in being well off financially. First, both economists and sociologists are concluding

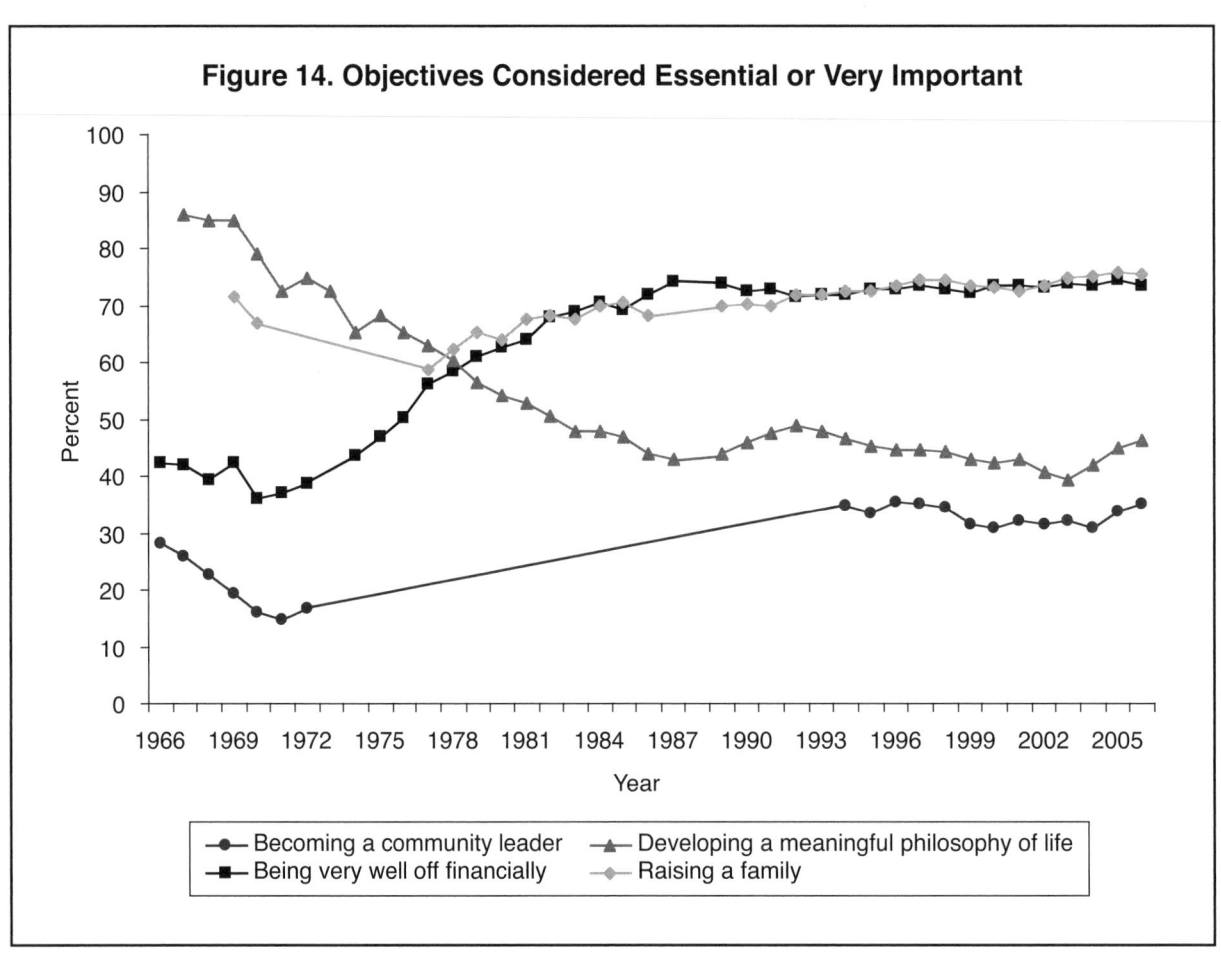

Figure 14. Objectives Considered Essential or Very Important

that individuals born in the 1960s and 1970s were among the first generations where upward mobility (doing better than their parents) was less likely, downward mobility is almost as prevalent as upward mobility, and immobility rose to one-third. (See the futureofchildren.org for a summary of this work). Additionally, the desire for social mobility is high when income inequality is on the rise, with downward mobility likely to come at a higher cost. Given the rise in parental income and changes noted in parents' occupations in previous reports (Astin, Oseguera, Sax & Korn, 2002), it is much harder for students to do better than their parents, one is first-generation, African American, and/or low-income—all of whom tend to rate the goal of being well off financially higher than their peers in their desire for social mobility (Saenz et al., forthcoming, Allen et al., 2005). Second, high corporate salaries, young entrepreneurs riding the wave of technology, and stories of common people becoming millionaires (in state lotteries instituted as a result of efforts to create additional revenues for education) convey the notion that being financially well off is not only desirable but also within their reach. These influences work to increase students' interest in social mobility and sustain it.

While there has been stability in the goal of being well off financially, another trend we have observed over the decades that had shown the largest declines among incoming college students now shows signs of reversal. The percentage who report that "developing a meaningful philosophy of life" is a "very important" or "essential" personal goal declined steadily from 1967 at 85.8 percent to the all-time low of 39.3 percent in

2003. Since that time, however, there has been a slight reversal of this trend and the percentage has moved upward to 46.3 percent in 2006. This indicates that students as of late are seeking ways to bring meaning into their lives at the same time they encounter strong pressures for economic success.

Students show a resurgent interest in altruistic values. The importance of "helping others in difficulty" is at 66.7 percent, the highest it has been in 20 years (compared with 1986), and in 2006, it was the third highest common value held by incoming students. Becoming a community leader is more important now than ever, with 35.2 percent of students rating it "very important" or "essential." One trend that has increased over time has been participation in community service or volunteer work. When this item was introduced in 1990, 16.9 percent of incoming students reported that there was a very good chance they would participate in such activities in college, a percentage that steadily increased to 26.8 percent in 2006. Also steady has been the relative participation of men versus women, with women outperforming men in expectations for service in college by about 2-to-1 throughout this period.

We have previously reported on the increase of civic engagement both on campus and on the national and international scale (Pryor et al., 2006). One piece of good news is that more students are engaged in volunteer work in high school, 72.5% in 1984 moving up to 82.1% in 2006. Moving in the opposite direction, however, has been the percentage of incoming college students who frequently voted in student elections when in high school, a drop from 72.9 percent in

1966 to a low 21.5 percent in 2006. In recent years we asked about students' intention to be involved in student government in college, and the resulting percentage has been very low, at 7.5 percent in 2006 (with almost no change since 2000 when it was first monitored). It appears that students are distinguishing between political engagement and service to communities, an aspect we intend to continue to monitor in understanding students' civic engagement.

Community service and civic engagement have been of particular interest to HERI over the last 15 years. (Readers interested in more detail should view the HERI website at: www.gseis. ucla.edu/heri.) Many institutions are meeting students' expectations by increasing the opportunities for curricular and co-curricular service learning opportunities, pairing up with local volunteering efforts, and in response to recent events in the Gulf coast, even facilitating opportunities to serve abroad. CIRP data on students' interest in and expectations of community service opportunities indicate that, not only will the demand for such opportunities increase, but they can also affect students' assessment of their own abilities and skills (Astin, Vogelgesang, Ikeda, & Yee, 2000).

Conclusion and Implications for Higher Education

In many ways, the trends we have observed over the 40 years say as much about American society as it does about the students whom we educate and to whom we entrust the future. Different generations of students have been influenced by economic and social forces as well as immediate socialization contexts that are under direct parental influence. One thing is clear across the broad patterns we observed: Though some progress is evident, educational equity continues to be an elusive goal and key challenges remain in addressing diversity, improving teaching and learning, and helping students to acquire the values, skills and knowledge to advance American society. With projected enrollments expected to continue to increase in the future, it is imperative to continue monitoring a variety of trends we identified here among entering freshmen.

At the same time that campuses have become more diverse in many ways, they have also grown more homogeneous in terms of rising levels of parental income and declining proportions of first-generation students relative to changes in education and income in the national population. Though two-thirds of students claim to have racial/ethnic contact in high school, many of them live in neighborhoods and attend schools that reveal less meaningful contact is probable prior to college entry. Moreover, controversial issues that split students along lines of political ideology suggest that contact across differences can lead to conflict. Educating students about diversity, promoting opportunities for practicing modes of civil discourse, and handling conflict more constructively will be an important skill for student affairs professionals and faculty in classrooms.

Of key national interest is the extent to which students come prepared with the habits of mind, skills, and content knowledge to successfully navigate college-level expectations for academic work. While more students are taking the recommended courses specified in the call for reform in most subject areas, there has been less change among these trends in the last ten years. More improvement is needed in key areas of biology, physical sciences, and computer science to meet minimum benchmarks set 20 years ago as well as more recent national imperatives for science education.

While more students are getting help in mathematics in high school, and students entering college are less likely to report needing tutoring or remedial education than students in the 1970s, it is important to note that progress has stagnated. In the last decade, we have witnessed the educational reform initiatives of "No Child Left Behind," the institutionalization of high school exit exams, and the continuing move by state legislatures to curtail remedial education at four-year colleges. Nonetheless, a steady proportion of students continue to report that they will need remedial work in critical content areas once in college. Rather than dismissing the challenge of remedial/developmental education or relegating it to another educational sector, four-year colleges and universities should reconsider the important stake and responsibility they have in facilitating greater access for all students. New initiatives are needed that link colleges and universities with schools in order to convey expectations for college-level work. In one initiative in California, for example, the state system is providing college placement examinations to juniors in high school so that they are able to use the senior year to prepare for college. Making better use of the senior year in high school to reinforce the behaviors and skills needed to be successful in college is key, and some colleges already offer coursework for

seniors. On campus, many colleges are introducing living-learning programs that offer supplemental education for gateway courses to address students' needs.

One area where we have observed some progress over the last ten years is in the use of technology. Greater use of the computer and internet for academic work is evident among all freshmen entering college. In the information age, more students seek sources of information on the internet for a variety of topics, and while it might make work in college classrooms easier, it also presents new challenges. Students today will need a solid general education that helps them to evaluate sources of information, understand the scientific method, and weigh perspectives they encounter from a wide range of sources now online. Libraries with online resources have to make sure that their students have access to appropriate journals and classic works including online books and workshops to ensure that students include the best set of references in papers and arguments. Constructing teaching aids and course websites, and generating discussions online, require that faculty have access to skills and resources, and time, to construct new e-learning environments. Technology will not result in the improvement of teaching and learning without identifying and addressing these new challenges.

As of late, the millennial generation has taken much criticism for being too narcissistic and materialistic relative to prior generations of young people. However, 40 years of data indicate that most of the upward growth in trends occurred during the mid 1980s, as evidenced in increases to academic self-concept and student desires to be well off financially. Both patterns have been relatively stable—though admittedly high—since that time period. We posit the theory that students' values are largely influenced by economic and social forces, not the least of which has been a concern regarding social mobility in a society where doing well economically constitutes a better quality of life. At the same time, we identify increasing altruistic tendencies in community service and the desire to help others in difficulty. Colleges have a great opportunity to expand students' thinking, help them reflect on their values, and encourage the development of responsible citizenship. Educating citizens has historically been a mission of higher education, and this central goal experienced renewal in the many service learning initiatives, units devoted to community partnership, and associations of institutions such as NASULGC and AAC&U that have adopted a stance on education for the public good (Kellogg, 2000; AAC&U, 2007).

Meanwhile, market forces continue to shape college access and affordability patterns, leading to increased stratification, more competition for the best students, and the commodification of students and their families. Students are applying to many more colleges (with 56.5 percent applying to four or more colleges, a figure that has nearly tripled since 1967) and higher education has facilitated this through aggressive recruitment and admissions processes that have made it easier for students to apply (e.g., web-enabled application, multiple-application procedures). Getting into the college of one's choice is important, but a student's top choice may not be as affordable as other choice options—manifested in the fact that fewer freshmen report they are enrolling in their first-choice institution and more students are stating they selected a particular college because they were offered financial aid.

Moreover, the rising family income of entering college students—outpacing inflation and the national income levels—suggests that low- and middle-income students may be making other choices (e.g., two-year colleges, for-profit higher education, distance learning). From a market perspective, given the increasing demand for higher education, colleges charge what parents will pay and they can charge significantly more than they do now if demand continues to exceed the supply. Higher income families can absorb college price and cost fluctuation while other families think harder before doing so, a factor that is clearly affecting the make-up of entering college students. Declining state appropriations for public higher education—which often constitute a major revenue stream—has resulted in public institutions seeking more resources and increasing tuition and fees. Nonetheless, the costs are still low enough that middle- and high-income families are turning to these as a good "bargain." Enabling more low-income students to have good choices, minimizing the competition between institutions, and admitting students using a broad definition of talent are steps that some colleges are taking. More changes are needed, however, to bring the market perspective in line with the broader goals of higher education in advancing social progress.

We are indeed fortunate, through the foresight of Alexander Astin (founding director) and the hard work of those who have facilitated and extended the CIRP over a 40-year time period, to have this extensive database on the American Freshman. As we embark on this fifth decade of data collection, we are also pleased to broaden access to this database to a wider field of scholars. The changing scene of education has aspects that can only be uncovered by research using this rich collection of information.

REFERENCES

Allen, W.R., Jayakumar, U.M., Griffin, K.A., Korn, W.S., & Hurtado, S. (2005). Black Undergraduates from *Bakke* to *Grutter*: Freshmen Status, Trends, and Prospects, 1971–2004. Los Angeles: Higher Education Research Institute, UCLA.

Association of American Colleges and Universities (AAC&U). (2007). College Learning for the New Global Century: A Report From the National Leadership Council for Liberal Education & America's Promise. Washington, DC.

Astin, A. W. (1977). Four Critical Years. San Francisco: Jossey-Bass, Inc.

Astin, A. W. (1993). What Matters in College: Four Critical Years Revisited. San Francisco: Jossey-Bass, Inc.

Astin, A.W., Ikeda, E.K., Vogelgesang, L.J., & Yee, J.A. (2000). How Service Learning Affects Students. Los Angeles: Higher Education Research Institute, UCLA.

Astin, A.W., Green, K.C., & Korn, W.S. (1987). The American Freshman: Twenty Year Trends. Los Angeles: Higher Education Research Institute, UCLA.

Astin, A.W. & Oseguera, L. (2002). Degree Attainment Rates at American Colleges and Universities. Los Angeles: Higher Education Research Institute, UCLA.

Astin, A.W., & Oseguera, L. (2004). The declining "equity" of American higher education. The Review of Higher Education, 27, 3: 321–341.

Astin, A.W., Oseguera, L., Sax L.J., & Korn, W.S. (2002). The American Freshman: Thirty-Five Year Trends. Los Angeles: Higher Education Research Institute, UCLA.

Astin, A.W., Parrott, S.A., Korn, W.S., & Sax L.J. (1997). The American Freshman: Thirty Year Trends. Los Angeles: Higher Education Research Institute, UCLA.

Bastedo, M., & Gumport, P. (2003) Access to what? Mission differentiation and academic stratification in U.S. public higher education. Higher Education, 46, 3: 341–359.

Bettinger, E.P. & Long, B.T. (2005). Addressing the Needs of Under-Prepared Students in Higher Education: Does College Remediation Work? National Bureau of Economic Research, Working Paper W11325. Cambridge, MA: Harvard University.

Boyd, D. (2002). State Spending for Higher Education in the Coming Decade. Report prepared for the National Center for Higher Education Management Systems.

Chang, M.J., Denson, N., Saenz, V., & Misa, K. (2005). The educational benefits of sustaining cross-racial interaction among undergraduates. The Journal of Higher Education, 77, 3: 430–455.

College Board (2006). Trends in College Pricing and Financial Aid 2006. Report retrieved from: http://www.collegeboard.com/press/releases/150634.html.

Gurin, P., Dey, E.L., Hurtado, S., & Gurin, G. (2002). Diversity and higher education: Theory and impact on educational outcomes. Harvard Educational Review, 72, 3: 330–336.

Hovey, H.A. (1999). State Spending for Higher Education in the Next Decade: The Battle to Sustain Current Support. Report prepared by State Policy Research, Inc. for the National Center for Public Policy and Higher Education.

Ignash, J.M. (1997). Who should provide postsecondary remedial/developmental education? In J. Ignash (Ed.), New Directions for Community College, No. 100 (pp. 5–20). San Francisco: Jossey-Bass.

Kellogg (2000). Renewing the Covenant Learning, Discovery, and Engagement in a New Age and Different World. http://www.nasulgc.org/publications/Kellogg/Kellogg2000_covenant.pdf

Keup, J.R. & Stolzenberg, E.B. (2004). Your First College Year Survey: Exploring the Academic and Personal Experiences of First-Year Students. Columbia, SC: University of South Carolina, National Resource Center for the First Year Experience and Students in Transition.

Mazzeo, C. (2002). Stakes for students: Agenda-setting and remedial education. The Review of Higher Education, 26, 1:19–39.

McDonough, P.M., Antonio, A.L., Walpole, A.M., & Perez, L.X. (1998). College rankings: Democratized college knowledge for whom? Research in Higher Education, 39, 5: 513–537.

Mumper, M. (1996). Removing College Price Barriers: What Government Has Done and Why It Hasn't Worked. Albany: State University of New York Press.

National Center for Education Statistics (NCES). (2003). Remedial Education at Degree-Granting Postsecondary Institutions in Fall 2000, NCES 2004-010, by Basmat Parsad and Laurie Lewis. Project Officer: Bernard Greene. Washington, DC: U.S. Government Printing Office.

National Center for Education Statistics (NCES). (2006). The Condition of Education, 2006. U.S. Department of Education. Washington, DC: U.S. Government Printing Office. Retrieved from: http://nces.ed.gov/programs/coe/index.asp.

National Center for Public Policy and Higher Education (NCPPHE). (2002). Losing Ground: A National Status Report on the Affordability of American Higher Education. San Jose, CA. Retrieved from: http://www.highereducation.org/reports/losing_ground/ar.shtml.

National Commission on Excellence in Education (NCEE). (1982). A Nation at Risk. Washington, DC.

National Science Board (2002), *Science and Engineering Indicators. Arlington, VA: National Science Foundation, 2002 (NSB-02-1).*

National Telecommunications and Information Administration (NTIA). (2004). A Nation Online: How Americans Are Expanding Their Use of the Internet. Washington, DC.

Neckerman, K. (Ed.) (2004). Social Inequality. New York: Russell Sage Foundation.

Pascarella, E.T. & Terenzini, P.T. (2005). How College Affects Students: A Third Decade of Research. San Francisco: Jossey-Bass.

Pryor, J.H., Hurtado, S., Saenz, V.B., Korn, J.S., Santos, J.L., & Korn, W.S. (2006). The American Freshman: National Norms for Fall 2006. Los Angeles: Higher Education Research Institute, UCLA.

Saenz, V., Hurtado, S., Barrera, D., Wolf, D., & Yeung, F. (2007). First in My Family: A Profile of First-Generation College Students at Four-Year Institutions Since 1971. Los Angeles: Higher Education Research Institute, UCLA.

Santos, J.L. (2007). Resource allocation within public research universities. The Review of Higher Education, 30, 2: 125–144.

Sax, L.J. (2001). Undergraduate science majors: Gender differences in who goes to graduate school. The Review of Higher Education, 24, 2: 153–172.

Sax, L.J. (Forthcoming). The Gender Gap in College: Differential Patterns of Change and Development for Women and Men. San Francisco: Jossey-Bass.

U.S. Census (2007). U.S. Census Table H-5. Race and Hispanic Origin of Householder—Households by Median and Mean Income: 1967 to 2005. Table retrieved from: http://www.census.gov/hhes/www/income/histinc/h05.html.

U.S. Department of Education (DOE). (2006). A Test of Leadership: Charting the Future of U.S. Higher Education. Washington, DC.

Forty Year Trends
for All Freshmen

NOTES

These notes refer to report items that are followed by numbers or asterisks in [brackets].

[*]   Changes in the question text and/or the text of the response options have occurred over the years. The text used in this report reflects the most recent year the question was asked. The text changes were deemed by HERI to have had no significant effect on the results for this item.

[1]   Percentages will total more than 100.0 if any respondents marked more than one response.

[2]   Disaggregated responses for this item can be found at the end of this report.

[3]   See Appendix D for special circumstances affecting this item.

[4]   Based on curriculum recommendations of the National Commission on Excellence in Education.

[5]   Percentage responding "frequently" only. Results for other items in this group represent the percentage responding "frequently" or "occasionally."

DEMOGRAPHICS
ALL FRESHMEN

ITEM	1966	1967	1968	1969	1970	1971	1972	1973	1974	1975	1976	1977	1978	1979	1980	1981	1982	1983	1984	1985
Your sex																				
Male	53.0	54.0	54.7	54.0	54.7	52.1	52.8	51.1	51.5	51.3	50.6	50.7	49.2	48.9	48.8	48.5	49.1	48.7	48.5	48.9
Female	47.0	46.0	45.3	46.0	45.3	47.9	47.2	48.9	48.5	48.7	49.4	49.3	50.8	51.1	51.2	51.5	50.9	51.3	51.5	51.1
How old will you be on December 31 of this year?																				
16 or younger	—	0.3	0.1	0.2	0.1	0.1	0.1	0.1	0.1	0.1	0.1	0.2	0.1	0.1	0.1	0.1	0.1	0.1	0.1	0.1
17	—	5.6	5.4	4.6	4.5	4.2	4.6	5.0	4.2	4.0	3.9	3.4	3.3	2.9	2.8	2.6	2.6	2.6	2.7	2.8
18	—	80.5	79.7	79.7	80.4	79.0	78.5	79.0	77.7	77.8	77.9	76.7	77.7	75.9	75.4	75.9	76.4	75.7	76.2	75.5
19	—	11.2	11.4	12.1	11.9	13.5	13.9	13.8	15.0	15.4	15.2	16.5	16.3	17.9	18.5	18.6	18.5	19.1	18.5	19.2
20	—	1.0	1.3	1.2	1.0	1.1	1.4	1.0	1.4	1.2	1.3	1.5	1.2	1.5	1.5	1.4	1.2	1.2	1.3	1.2
21 or older	—	1.5	2.2	2.5	2.0	2.1	1.6	1.1	1.6	1.4	1.5	1.8	1.3	1.7	1.7	1.4	1.3	1.3	1.1	1.1
Are you: (mark all that apply) [1,3]																				
White/Caucasian	—	—	—	—	—	90.9	88.4	89.9	88.7	87.4	86.3	85.1	86.5	84.6	84.1	85.8	85.1	85.3	85.0	85.0
African American/Black	—	—	—	—	—	7.5	9.3	7.9	8.5	9.8	10.5	11.0	10.0	11.2	12.5	11.0	11.1	11.0	11.3	10.5
American Indian	—	—	—	—	—	0.9	1.0	0.9	0.8	0.7	1.0	0.7	0.7	0.9	1.1	1.1	1.1	1.2	1.1	1.1
Asian American/Asian	—	—	—	—	—	0.6	0.9	0.8	1.0	1.2	1.2	1.3	1.3	1.4	1.4	1.4	1.7	1.9	1.8	2.7
Mexican American/Chicano	—	—	—	—	—	0.3	0.4	0.5	0.6	0.7	0.7	0.8	0.9	0.9	0.5	0.7	0.9	0.7	0.7	0.8
Puerto Rican American	—	—	—	—	—	0.3	0.7	0.3	0.5	0.6	0.5	1.1	0.8	1.1	1.0	0.6	1.1	0.5	0.6	0.5
Other Latino	—	—	—	—	—	—	—	—	—	—	—	—	—	—	—	—	—	—	—	—
Other	—	—	—	—	—	1.0	1.4	1.1	1.4	1.4	1.4	1.6	1.6	1.9	1.7	1.5	1.6	1.3	1.3	1.3
Is English your native language?																				
Yes	—	—	—	—	—	—	—	—	—	—	—	—	—	—	—	—	—	—	—	—
No	—	—	—	—	—	—	—	—	—	—	—	—	—	—	—	—	—	—	—	—
Are you presently married? [*]																				
No	—	—	—	—	—	98.4	99.1	99.3	99.1	99.2	99.2	99.1	99.3	99.3	99.3	99.3	99.4	99.4	99.5	99.4
Yes	—	—	—	—	—	1.6	0.9	0.7	0.9	0.8	0.8	0.9	0.7	0.7	0.7	0.7	0.6	0.6	0.5	0.6
Citizenship status																				
Yes	—	—	—	98.7	98.7	—	98.5	98.8	—	—	—	—	—	—	—	—	97.3	97.9	97.7	97.8
No	—	—	—	1.3	1.3	—	1.5	1.2	—	—	—	—	—	—	—	—	2.7	2.1	2.3	2.2
U.S. Citizen	—	—	—	—	—	—	—	—	—	—	—	—	—	—	—	—	—	—	—	—
Permanent resident (green card)	—	—	—	—	—	—	—	—	—	—	—	—	—	—	—	—	—	—	—	—
Neither	—	—	—	—	—	—	—	—	—	—	—	—	—	—	—	—	—	—	—	—
Do you have a disability? [3]																				
Hearing	—	—	—	—	—	—	—	—	—	—	—	—	—	—	—	—	—	0.7	0.8	0.8
Speech	—	—	—	—	—	—	—	—	—	—	—	—	—	—	—	—	—	0.2	0.2	0.2
Orthopedic	—	—	—	—	—	—	—	—	—	—	—	—	—	—	—	—	—	0.8	0.9	0.8
Learning disability	—	—	—	—	—	—	—	—	—	—	—	—	—	—	—	—	—	0.5	0.7	0.7
Health related	—	—	—	—	—	—	—	—	—	—	—	—	—	—	—	—	—	0.8	1.0	1.1
Partially sighted or blind	—	—	—	—	—	—	—	—	—	—	—	—	—	—	—	—	—	2.3	2.0	2.2
Other	—	—	—	—	—	—	—	—	—	—	—	—	—	—	—	—	—	1.1	1.2	1.0
Which of the following statements applies to you?																				
I was born in the United States	—	—	—	—	—	—	—	—	—	—	—	—	—	—	—	—	—	—	—	—
I came to the U.S. before age 6	—	—	—	—	—	—	—	—	—	—	—	—	—	—	—	—	—	—	—	—
I came to the U.S. between ages 6–12	—	—	—	—	—	—	—	—	—	—	—	—	—	—	—	—	—	—	—	—
I came to the U.S. after age 12	—	—	—	—	—	—	—	—	—	—	—	—	—	—	—	—	—	—	—	—

DEMOGRAPHICS
ALL FRESHMEN

ITEM	1986	1987	1988	1989	1990	1991	1992	1993	1994	1995	1996	1997	1998	1999	2000	2001	2002	2003	2004	2005	2006
Your sex																					
Male	48.1	47.9	47.2	47.1	47.0	47.3	47.4	46.2	45.8	45.6	45.7	45.5	45.5	45.3	45.2	44.9	45.0	45.1	44.9	45.0	45.1
Female	51.9	52.1	52.8	52.9	53.0	52.7	52.6	53.8	54.2	54.4	54.3	54.5	54.5	54.7	54.8	55.1	55.0	54.9	55.1	55.0	54.9
How old will you be on December 31 of this year?																					
16 or younger	0.1	0.1	0.1	0.1	0.1	0.1	0.1	0.1	0.1	0.1	0.1	0.0	0.0	0.0	0.1	0.0	0.1	0.1	0.1	0.0	0.0
17	2.8	2.7	2.5	2.3	2.3	2.4	2.3	2.3	2.3	2.1	2.1	2.0	1.9	1.8	1.9	1.8	1.8	1.7	1.6	1.7	1.8
18	75.9	76.2	76.5	74.5	72.9	72.3	72.9	72.1	71.6	71.1	70.6	70.2	70.4	68.6	68.9	67.8	67.4	68.2	66.7	69.1	68.5
19	18.8	19.2	18.9	20.9	22.2	22.2	22.2	23.4	23.9	24.6	25.4	25.8	25.8	27.7	27.4	28.7	29.1	28.7	29.9	27.8	28.2
20	1.2	1.0	1.1	1.2	1.5	1.6	1.3	1.1	1.2	1.2	1.2	1.2	1.1	1.1	1.0	1.0	1.0	0.9	1.0	0.9	0.9
21 or older	1.2	0.8	0.8	1.0	1.1	1.5	1.3	0.9	1.0	0.8	0.7	0.7	0.7	0.7	0.7	0.7	0.7	0.5	0.6	0.5	0.5
Are you: (mark all that apply) [1,3]																					
White/Caucasian	85.1	85.4	81.8	83.2	80.7	79.5	81.3	81.3	79.4	79.3	78.7	79.5	78.9	78.3	76.1	73.9	75.8	75.7	76.5	74.4	76.5
African American/Black	9.6	9.5	12.0	10.8	12.1	12.2	10.3	10.3	10.8	10.7	10.9	10.6	11.0	9.9	10.4	10.6	10.1	9.6	9.7	11.3	10.5
American Indian	0.9	0.9	0.9	0.9	1.3	1.7	1.8	1.9	2.2	2.2	2.4	3.1	2.1	2.3	1.9	1.2	1.3	1.3	1.9	1.7	2.2
Asian American/Asian	3.0	2.9	3.3	3.3	3.8	4.3	4.2	4.4	5.7	5.5	5.6	6.0	5.6	6.5	7.1	7.6	7.8	8.5	7.9	8.9	8.6
Mexican American/Chicano	1.2	1.0	1.6	1.4	1.7	2.1	2.3	2.0	2.1	2.2	2.4	2.0	2.6	3.1	3.8	4.3	3.4	3.7	3.5	3.8	3.4
Puerto Rican American	0.6	0.6	0.6	0.6	0.6	0.7	0.6	0.7	0.7	0.7	0.8	0.8	1.0	0.9	1.0	0.9	0.9	0.9	1.1	1.2	1.4
Other Latino	—	—	—	—	—	—	1.1	1.1	1.4	1.5	1.6	1.8	1.7	1.8	2.2	2.2	2.1	2.2	2.4	3.0	3.4
Other	1.6	1.6	1.7	1.6	1.8	2.2	1.8	1.8	2.1	2.2	2.7	3.0	2.7	3.3	3.6	3.3	3.1	3.0	4.0	2.8	3.6
Is English your native language?																					
Yes	—	—	95.6	95.7	95.0	94.5	94.8	94.6	93.5	93.2	93.1	93.7	94.1	93.6	92.1	91.9	92.7	92.3	92.5	92.0	92.5
No	—	—	4.4	4.3	5.0	5.5	5.2	5.4	6.5	6.8	6.9	6.3	5.9	6.4	7.9	8.1	7.3	7.7	7.5	8.0	7.5
Are you presently married? [*]																					
No	99.4	—	—	—	—	—	—	99.3	—	—	—	—	—	—	99.7	99.6	—	—	—	—	—
Yes	0.6	—	—	—	—	—	—	0.7	—	—	—	—	—	—	0.3	0.4	—	—	—	—	—
Citizenship status																					
	97.6	98.4	98.4	97.7	—	—	—	—	—	—	—	—	—	—	—	—	—	—	—	—	—
	2.4	1.6	1.6	2.3	—	—	—	—	—	—	—	—	—	—	—	—	—	—	—	—	—
U.S. Citizen	—	—	—	—	97.3	96.8	97.1	97.1	96.4	96.1	96.0	96.5	96.4	96.2	95.7	95.9	96.4	96.6	96.4	96.5	96.6
Permanent resident (green card)	—	—	—	—	2.0	2.2	2.1	2.1	2.7	2.9	3.0	2.6	2.6	2.7	3.1	2.9	2.4	2.3	2.3	2.3	2.1
Neither	—	—	—	—	0.8	1.0	0.8	0.9	0.9	1.0	1.0	0.9	1.0	1.1	1.2	1.2	1.1	1.1	1.2	1.3	1.3
Do you have a disability? [3]																					
Hearing	0.5	0.6	0.8	—	—	0.8	0.8	—	0.8	—	0.7	—	—	—	0.5	—	0.5	—	0.6	—	—
Speech	0.1	0.2	0.2	—	—	0.3	0.3	—	0.3	—	0.3	—	0.4	—	0.2	—	0.2	—	0.2	—	—
Orthopedic	0.6	0.7	0.9	—	—	1.0	0.9	—	0.8	—	0.7	—	0.7	—	0.4	—	0.5	—	0.5	—	—
Learning disability	0.6	1.0	1.0	—	—	1.4	1.8	—	2.0	—	2.3	—	2.6	—	2.4	—	2.5	—	2.8	—	—
Health related	0.7	0.8	1.0	—	—	1.2	1.3	—	1.5	—	1.4	—	1.5	—	0.9	—	1.0	—	1.1	—	—
Partially sighted or blind	1.8	2.0	2.0	—	—	2.5	2.3	—	2.3	—	1.9	—	1.1	—	1.0	—	1.0	—	1.1	—	—
Other	0.7	0.9	1.2	—	—	1.5	1.4	—	1.5	—	1.5	—	—	—	1.0	—	1.1	—	1.2	—	—
Which of the following statements applies to you?																					
I was born in the United States	—	—	—	—	—	—	—	—	94.0	—	—	—	—	—	—	—	—	93.2	—	93.0	—
I came to the U.S. before age 6	—	—	—	—	—	—	—	—	2.8	—	—	—	—	—	—	—	—	3.0	—	3.2	—
I came to the U.S. between ages 6–12	—	—	—	—	—	—	—	—	1.5	—	—	—	—	—	—	—	—	1.9	—	1.9	—
I came to the U.S. after age 12	—	—	—	—	—	—	—	—	1.7	—	—	—	—	—	—	—	—	1.9	—	1.9	—

45

DEMOGRAPHICS
ALL FRESHMEN

ITEM	1966	1967	1968	1969	1970	1971	1972	1973	1974	1975	1976	1977	1978	1979	1980	1981	1982	1983	1984	1985
Your religious preference [2,3]																				
Protestant (Christian)	54.8	50.4	46.4	49.3	52.3	42.5	41.2	50.2	50.4	50.8	48.5	49.5	49.8	37.0	36.9	36.5	35.2	33.5	45.4	46.8
Roman Catholic	28.3	29.4	30.0	27.4	28.2	27.7	27.4	30.3	30.8	29.6	31.6	32.9	33.4	34.2	33.9	34.6	35.8	36.3	36.5	34.5
Jewish	4.9	6.3	5.5	4.6	5.4	3.6	4.4	5.2	4.1	4.4	4.7	4.0	4.4	4.1	3.8	3.7	3.8	3.7	3.4	3.6
Other	5.4	5.7	8.0	3.3	3.0	10.8	12.0	3.5	3.8	4.3	4.9	4.4	4.1	16.3	17.2	17.5	17.5	18.2	5.9	5.7
None	6.6	8.0	10.1	13.6	10.7	15.4	15.0	10.8	10.9	10.9	10.2	9.1	8.3	8.3	8.2	7.6	7.6	8.3	8.8	9.4
Do you consider yourself a born-again Christian?																				
No	—	—	—	—	—	—	—	—	—	—	—	—	—	—	—	—	—	—	—	75.4
Yes	—	—	—	—	—	—	—	—	—	—	—	—	—	—	—	—	—	—	—	24.6
Which of your parents were born in the U.S.?																				
Both	—	—	—	—	—	—	—	—	—	—	—	—	—	—	—	—	—	—	—	—
Father only	—	—	—	—	—	—	—	—	—	—	—	—	—	—	—	—	—	—	—	—
Mother only	—	—	—	—	—	—	—	—	—	—	—	—	—	—	—	—	—	—	—	—
Neither	—	—	—	—	—	—	—	—	—	—	—	—	—	—	—	—	—	—	—	—
What is the best estimate of your parents' total income last year? Consider income from all sources before taxes. [3]																				
Less than $6,000	18.4	—	14.8	12.3	10.1	10.3	11.3	8.7	9.1	8.8	9.0	8.9	7.0	6.8	6.6	5.4	4.7	4.7	4.9	4.0
$6,000 to $9,999	33.3	—	30.1	27.4	21.5	19.8	16.6	12.7	12.1	9.9	9.3	8.8	7.3	7.0	6.3	5.3	4.8	4.4	4.3	3.6
Less than $10,000	—	—	—	—	—	—	—	—	—	—	—	—	—	—	—	—	—	—	—	—
$10,000 to $14,999	25.4	—	27.9	29.3	31.8	31.9	29.1	27.6	26.9	23.1	20.8	18.7	15.8	13.3	12.1	10.4	9.1	9.3	8.5	6.1
$15,000 to $19,999	9.8	—	12.2	13.8	14.7	15.4	16.0	17.6	17.1	17.6	17.0	16.4	14.8	12.6	11.1	9.4	8.1	7.8	7.1	6.1
$20,000 to $24,999	5.0	—	6.1	7.1	8.8	9.3	10.3	12.5	13.0	13.8	14.3	15.0	16.0	16.1	15.3	14.0	12.2	11.3	10.3	7.5
$25,000 to $29,999	2.7	—	3.0	3.4	4.2	4.6	5.3	6.4	6.8	8.0	8.3	9.2	10.4	10.9	10.9	11.1	10.6	10.0	9.4	7.7
$30,000 or more	5.4	—	5.9	6.5	—	—	—	—	—	—	—	—	—	—	—	—	—	—	—	—
$30,000 to $39,999	—	—	—	—	—	—	—	—	—	—	—	—	—	—	—	—	—	—	—	—
$30,000 to $34,999	—	—	—	—	2.9	2.9	3.6	4.6	4.7	5.7	6.5	7.0	8.9	9.2	10.0	10.7	11.6	11.3	10.7	10.5
$35,000 to $39,999	—	—	—	—	1.6	1.6	2.2	2.7	2.9	3.6	4.1	4.4	5.3	6.3	7.0	8.3	8.7	9.0	9.2	9.6
$40,000 or more	—	—	—	—	4.3	4.3	—	—	—	—	—	—	—	—	—	—	—	—	—	—
$40,000 to $49,999	—	—	—	—	—	—	2.1	2.6	2.7	3.5	4.0	4.2	5.3	7.2	8.5	10.3	11.6	12.5	13.3	12.3
$50,000 or more	—	—	—	—	—	—	3.5	4.6	4.8	6.1	6.7	7.3	9.2	—	—	—	—	—	—	—
$50,000 to $59,999	—	—	—	—	—	—	—	—	—	—	—	—	—	—	—	—	—	—	—	10.8
$50,000 to $99,999	—	—	—	—	—	—	—	—	—	—	—	—	—	7.9	9.2	11.4	13.9	15.1	16.8	—
$60,000 to $74,999	—	—	—	—	—	—	—	—	—	—	—	—	—	—	—	—	—	—	—	8.5
$75,000 to $99,999	—	—	—	—	—	—	—	—	—	—	—	—	—	—	—	—	—	—	—	5.4
$100,000 or more	—	—	—	—	—	—	—	—	—	—	—	—	—	2.6	3.0	3.7	4.5	4.6	5.4	—
$100,000 to $149,999	—	—	—	—	—	—	—	—	—	—	—	—	—	—	—	—	—	—	—	4.0
$150,000 or more	—	—	—	—	—	—	—	—	—	—	—	—	—	—	—	—	—	—	—	3.9
$150,000 to $199,999	—	—	—	—	—	—	—	—	—	—	—	—	—	—	—	—	—	—	—	—
$200,000 or more	—	—	—	—	—	—	—	—	—	—	—	—	—	—	—	—	—	—	—	—
$200,000 to $249,999	—	—	—	—	—	—	—	—	—	—	—	—	—	—	—	—	—	—	—	—
$250,000 or more	—	—	—	—	—	—	—	—	—	—	—	—	—	—	—	—	—	—	—	—
MEDIAN INCOME (in thousands of dollars)	9.8	—	10.9	11.8	12.9	13.1	13.8	15.3	15.6	17.3	18.2	19.1	21.6	23.2	24.5	27.5	30.2	31.1	32.6	37.3
Are your parents:																				
Both alive and living with each other?	—	—	—	—	—	—	84.8	—	—	—	—	—	—	—	—	—	—	—	—	—
Both alive, divorced or living apart?	—	—	—	—	—	—	7.9	—	—	—	—	—	—	—	—	—	—	—	—	—
One or both deceased?	—	—	—	—	—	—	7.3	—	—	—	—	—	—	—	—	—	—	—	—	—

DEMOGRAPHICS
ALL FRESHMEN

ITEM	1986	1987	1988	1989	1990	1991	1992	1993	1994	1995	1996	1997	1998	1999	2000	2001	2002	2003	2004	2005	2006
Your religious preference [2,3]																					
Protestant (Christian)	31.3	46.4	45.3	47.7	46.5	47.1	47.3	44.9	49.2	47.5	48.7	49.0	49.1	49.8	46.4	45.6	44.7	44.9	46.9	46.5	45.0
Roman Catholic	33.7	33.5	32.2	31.1	32.1	31.7	30.4	32.4	30.2	31.0	29.8	30.3	29.0	28.5	30.5	30.3	30.1	29.7	27.7	28.0	27.7
Jewish	3.6	3.4	3.4	3.0	2.8	2.2	2.4	2.5	2.4	2.5	2.4	2.2	2.2	2.1	2.8	2.6	2.4	2.4	2.5	2.6	2.6
Other	20.9	5.6	6.1	5.8	6.3	6.3	6.4	6.7	4.8	5.0	5.2	5.2	5.2	5.2	5.5	5.8	5.7	5.4	5.3	5.5	5.6
None	10.5	11.0	13.0	12.3	12.3	12.8	13.4	13.5	13.4	14.0	14.0	13.2	14.6	14.3	14.9	15.8	17.2	17.6	17.5	17.4	19.1
Do you consider yourself a born-again Christian?																					
No	—	—	76.6	72.2	72.4	71.3	71.0	73.4	72.3	74.2	71.4	71.5	—	—	—	74.9	—	—	76.0	—	—
Yes	—	—	23.4	27.8	27.6	28.7	29.0	26.6	27.7	25.8	28.6	28.5	—	—	—	25.1	—	—	24.0	—	—
Which of your parents were born in the U.S.?																					
Both	—	—	—	—	—	—	—	—	85.5	—	—	—	—	—	—	—	—	80.4	—	—	—
Father only	—	—	—	—	—	—	—	—	2.7	—	—	—	—	—	—	—	—	3.0	—	—	—
Mother only	—	—	—	—	—	—	—	—	2.4	—	—	—	—	—	—	—	—	3.2	—	—	—
Neither	—	—	—	—	—	—	—	—	9.4	—	—	—	—	—	—	—	—	13.4	—	—	—
What is the best estimate of your parents' total income last year? Consider income from all sources before taxes. [3]																					
Less than $6,000	3.0	2.8	2.8	2.4	2.6	2.9	2.5	2.5	2.5	2.2	2.2	1.9	2.0	1.9	1.9	1.9	—	—	—	—	—
$6,000 to $9,999	2.9	2.5	2.5	2.3	2.3	2.5	2.3	2.3	2.2	2.1	1.9	1.8	1.7	1.7	1.8	1.5	—	—	—	—	—
Less than $10,000	—	—	—	—	—	—	—	—	—	—	—	—	—	—	—	—	3.0	3.1	3.2	3.4	3.2
$10,000 to $14,999	5.3	4.5	4.3	4.2	4.1	4.4	3.9	3.9	3.8	3.4	3.4	3.1	3.1	2.9	2.8	2.7	2.7	2.8	2.7	2.9	2.6
$15,000 to $19,999	5.3	5.1	5.0	4.5	4.6	4.5	4.2	3.9	3.8	3.5	3.5	3.2	3.1	3.0	2.8	2.7	2.6	2.7	2.5	2.6	2.4
$20,000 to $24,999	7.0	6.7	6.4	6.1	6.0	5.9	5.5	5.2	5.1	4.9	4.7	4.5	4.5	4.3	4.0	3.9	3.7	3.7	3.7	3.6	3.3
$25,000 to $29,999	7.1	6.6	6.4	6.2	6.2	6.4	6.0	5.8	5.7	5.4	5.0	4.9	4.8	4.5	4.1	4.0	3.8	3.5	3.6	3.4	3.3
$30,000 or more	—	—	—	—	—	—	—	—	—	—	—	—	—	—	—	—	—	—	—	—	—
$30,000 to $39,999	—	—	—	—	—	13.0	12.4	11.7	11.1	10.9	10.4	10.1	9.7	8.9	8.5	8.0	7.2	6.7	6.6	6.8	6.2
$30,000 to $34,999	9.8	8.9	8.4	8.2	8.0	—	—	—	—	—	—	—	—	—	—	—	—	—	—	—	—
$35,000 to $39,999	9.6	9.2	8.7	8.4	8.1	—	—	—	—	—	—	—	—	—	—	—	—	—	—	—	—
$40,000 or more	—	—	—	—	—	—	—	—	—	—	—	—	—	—	—	—	—	—	—	—	—
$40,000 to $49,999	12.7	12.7	12.4	12.5	12.3	13.1	13.1	12.5	12.1	11.8	11.0	10.6	10.6	10.2	9.4	8.8	8.6	8.1	8.2	7.8	7.4
$50,000 or more	—	—	—	—	—	—	—	—	—	—	—	—	—	—	—	—	—	—	—	—	—
$50,000 to $59,999	11.3	11.7	12.0	12.3	12.1	12.1	12.4	12.3	12.1	12.2	12.1	11.9	11.8	11.1	10.6	10.0	10.1	9.8	9.6	9.0	8.9
$50,000 to $99,999	—	—	—	—	—	—	—	—	—	—	—	—	—	—	—	—	—	—	—	—	—
$60,000 to $74,999	10.1	11.3	12.0	12.2	12.6	12.8	13.5	13.7	13.9	14.0	14.3	14.3	14.2	14.2	13.9	13.4	13.1	12.7	12.5	12.0	12.0
$75,000 to $99,999	6.6	7.6	8.0	8.8	9.0	9.6	10.3	11.0	11.5	12.1	12.8	13.4	13.9	14.6	14.6	15.4	15.6	15.7	15.3	15.0	14.9
$100,000 or more	—	—	—	—	—	—	—	—	—	—	—	—	—	—	—	—	—	—	—	—	—
$100,000 to $149,999	4.7	5.3	5.7	6.0	6.2	6.6	7.2	8.0	8.7	9.3	10.3	11.0	11.7	12.5	14.2	15.3	15.8	16.4	16.6	16.9	17.3
$150,000 or more	4.7	5.2	5.4	5.8	5.8	—	—	—	—	—	—	—	—	—	—	—	—	—	—	—	—
$150,000 to $199,999	—	—	—	—	—	2.6	2.8	3.0	3.2	3.5	3.7	4.1	4.0	4.6	5.2	5.6	6.0	6.3	6.5	7.0	7.4
$200,000 or more	—	—	—	—	—	3.7	3.9	4.2	4.3	4.5	4.7	5.2	4.9	5.6	6.3	6.8	—	—	—	—	—
$200,000 to $249,999	—	—	—	—	—	—	—	—	—	—	—	—	—	—	—	—	2.7	3.0	3.1	3.4	3.8
$250,000 or more	—	—	—	—	—	—	—	—	—	—	—	—	—	—	—	—	5.1	5.5	6.0	6.5	7.1
MEDIAN INCOME (in thousands of dollars)	**40.0**	**42.9**	**44.4**	**46.2**	**46.6**	**47.9**	**50.1**	**51.8**	**53.1**	**54.8**	**56.5**	**58.3**	**58.9**	**61.7**	**64.7**	**67.8**	**70.1**	**72.1**	**72.7**	**74.0**	**76.2**
Are your parents:																					
Both alive and living with each other?	76.0	75.5	73.4	73.1	72.7	72.3	72.5	73.1	72.8	72.7	72.5	73.3	72.4	73.0	72.9	72.3	72.3	72.7	72.0	71.4	71.2
Both alive, divorced or living apart?	19.2	19.8	21.9	22.4	22.7	23.2	23.2	22.8	23.2	23.3	23.5	23.0	23.7	23.3	23.3	24.1	24.1	23.8	24.3	24.9	25.2
One or both deceased?	4.8	4.7	4.7	4.5	4.6	4.6	4.3	4.1	4.0	3.9	3.9	3.8	3.8	3.7	3.8	3.7	3.6	3.5	3.7	3.7	3.7

DEMOGRAPHICS
ALL FRESHMEN

ITEM	1966	1967	1968	1969	1970	1971	1972	1973	1974	1975	1976	1977	1978	1979	1980	1981	1982	1983	1984	1985
WHAT IS THE HIGHEST LEVEL OF FORMAL EDUCATION OBTAINED BY:																				
Your father?																				
Grammar school or less	8.5	8.2	8.6	8.2	7.3	7.3	7.0	5.6	6.2	5.7	5.9	6.0	5.0	5.4	5.2	4.7	4.3	4.2	4.0	3.5
Some high school	13.9	13.0	14.6	13.6	13.1	13.4	12.2	10.6	10.6	10.6	10.4	10.4	9.2	9.8	9.6	8.9	8.2	8.2	7.7	7.2
High school graduate	28.3	27.5	28.8	28.3	28.1	28.3	27.7	24.2	25.6	25.2	25.1	26.0	24.3	25.1	25.2	25.1	25.0	24.9	25.0	23.3
Postsecondary school other than college	—	—	—	—	—	—	4.7	4.6	4.2	4.0	4.2	4.2	4.2	4.1	4.1	4.2	4.6	5.0	4.6	
Some college	19.2	18.9	18.7	18.8	18.0	17.5	16.9	15.3	14.4	14.2	13.6	13.8	14.2	13.7	13.7	13.9	14.0	14.2	14.2	14.1
College degree	18.4	19.3	18.5	19.7	21.1	21.3	19.2	20.6	20.3	21.0	21.5	20.8	22.1	21.4	21.3	21.9	22.2	21.8	22.1	22.1
Some graduate school	—	—	—	—	—	—	3.1	3.1	2.9	2.9	3.0	2.8	3.1	3.0	2.9	3.0	2.9	3.0	3.0	3.4
Graduate degree	11.5	12.6	10.8	11.6	12.3	12.2	13.9	16.1	15.4	16.3	16.4	16.0	17.9	17.6	17.9	18.4	19.2	19.2	19.0	21.8
Your mother?																				
Grammar school or less	5.2	4.9	5.3	4.8	4.5	4.3	4.3	3.2	3.7	3.4	3.5	3.9	3.2	3.6	3.3	2.8	2.8	2.7	2.6	2.3
Some high school	11.8	10.9	12.5	11.6	11.2	11.4	10.4	8.9	9.2	9.1	9.0	9.2	7.9	8.6	8.0	7.6	6.8	6.6	6.2	6.0
High school graduate	41.8	41.4	42.6	42.4	42.4	42.8	41.8	38.4	38.6	38.8	38.3	39.1	37.9	37.6	37.5	37.2	36.3	35.8	35.3	32.9
Postsecondary school other than college	—	—	—	—	—	—	—	7.8	7.9	7.3	7.5	7.2	7.3	7.0	7.0	6.9	7.3	7.7	7.9	7.6
Some college	21.0	21.3	20.6	20.8	20.4	19.8	19.6	16.8	15.9	15.8	15.4	15.3	16.0	15.7	16.2	16.3	16.5	16.5	16.7	17.3
College degree	17.1	17.7	16.0	16.9	17.6	17.8	16.3	16.8	16.9	17.2	17.8	16.8	18.1	17.8	18.2	19.1	19.6	19.2	19.8	20.4
Some graduate school	—	—	—	—	—	—	2.8	2.7	2.6	2.6	2.5	2.5	2.7	2.7	2.7	2.6	2.7	2.8	2.9	3.4
Graduate degree	3.2	3.6	3.1	3.6	3.8	3.9	4.8	5.3	5.2	5.9	5.9	6.0	6.9	7.0	7.2	7.5	8.1	8.6	8.7	10.0
Your father's occupation [2,3]																				
Artist	—	0.9	0.8	0.9	1.0	0.8	0.9	—	—	—	1.0	1.0	0.9	0.9	0.9	0.9	1.0	1.0	1.0	0.9
Business	—	34.4	32.3	32.1	33.2	31.7	32.7	—	—	—	31.7	30.9	31.8	31.3	31.3	31.3	32.0	31.5	31.5	31.6
Clerical	—	—	—	—	—	1.3	1.4	—	—	—	0.9	0.9	0.9	0.9	0.9	0.8	0.8	0.7	0.8	0.7
Clergy	—	1.3	1.0	1.1	1.2	1.0	1.1	—	—	—	1.4	1.3	1.4	1.3	1.3	1.2	1.2	1.2	1.1	1.2
College teacher	—	0.9	0.9	0.9	1.1	1.0	1.1	—	—	—	1.2	1.1	1.2	1.2	1.2	1.2	1.2	1.2	1.2	1.4
Doctor (MD or DDS)	—	3.2	2.6	2.6	2.7	2.5	2.7	—	—	—	3.2	2.9	3.1	3.0	3.1	3.1	3.2	3.2	2.9	3.2
Education (secondary)	—	2.3	2.2	2.4	2.5	2.5	2.8	—	—	—	3.4	3.2	3.5	3.6	3.5	3.8	3.8	3.8	3.7	4.0
Education (elementary)	—	0.3	0.3	0.3	0.3	0.4	0.4	—	—	—	0.6	0.6	0.6	0.6	0.6	0.6	0.7	0.7	0.7	0.8
Engineer	—	7.3	7.6	7.7	8.1	8.2	8.4	—	—	—	9.0	8.7	9.4	8.7	8.6	8.7	8.7	8.6	8.8	9.1
Farmer or forester	—	6.1	6.0	5.3	4.9	5.4	4.9	—	—	—	4.1	3.5	3.1	3.2	3.6	4.0	3.6	3.2	3.2	3.7
Health professional	—	1.1	1.2	1.2	1.3	1.3	1.2	—	—	—	1.4	1.4	1.4	1.4	1.3	1.4	1.3	1.3	1.3	1.3
Homemaker	—	—	—	—	—	0.2	0.0	—	—	—	0.1	0.1	0.1	0.1	0.1	0.1	0.1	0.1	0.1	0.1
Lawyer	—	1.8	1.5	1.6	1.7	1.6	1.8	—	—	—	1.9	1.9	1.9	2.0	2.0	2.1	2.2	2.0	2.0	2.2
Military	—	1.6	1.8	1.7	2.0	2.2	2.0	—	—	—	2.2	2.3	2.2	2.0	2.0	2.1	2.0	2.1	1.9	1.7
Nurse	—	—	—	—	—	0.1	0.1	—	—	—	0.1	0.1	0.1	0.1	0.1	0.1	0.1	0.1	0.1	0.1
Research scientist	—	0.6	0.7	0.7	0.8	0.8	0.8	—	—	—	0.8	0.7	0.8	0.7	0.8	0.7	0.7	0.8	0.7	0.8
Social worker	—	—	—	—	—	0.3	0.3	—	—	—	0.4	0.4	0.4	0.4	0.4	0.4	0.4	0.4	0.5	0.4
Skilled worker	—	11.0	11.7	12.1	11.2	11.0	10.8	—	—	—	9.4	9.9	9.3	9.5	9.5	9.4	9.3	9.1	9.3	8.2
Semi skilled worker	—	6.7	7.7	7.0	6.6	6.6	5.8	—	—	—	4.9	5.3	4.4	4.7	4.6	4.2	4.1	4.4	4.1	4.1
Laborer	—	3.0	3.6	3.4	3.2	3.5	3.5	—	—	—	3.3	3.3	2.9	3.1	3.2	2.9	2.8	2.7	2.8	2.7
Unemployed	—	0.8	1.0	1.1	1.2	1.2	1.8	—	—	—	2.0	2.2	2.1	2.2	2.4	1.9	2.0	2.7	2.4	2.3
Other occupation	—	16.4	17.2	17.5	17.1	16.6	15.4	—	—	—	17.1	18.4	18.3	19.2	18.5	19.3	19.0	19.2	20.1	19.4

DEMOGRAPHICS ALL FRESHMEN

ITEM	1986	1987	1988	1989	1990	1991	1992	1993	1994	1995	1996	1997	1998	1999	2000	2001	2002	2003	2004	2005	2006
WHAT IS THE HIGHEST LEVEL OF FORMAL EDUCATION OBTAINED BY:																					
Your father?																					
Grammar school or less	3.0	2.7	3.0	2.6	3.2	2.9	2.5	2.3	2.6	3.2	3.1	2.7	2.1	2.7	2.9	2.8	2.3	2.5	2.7	2.8	3.4
Some high school	6.1	5.7	5.7	5.4	5.6	5.6	4.8	4.7	4.4	4.3	4.3	4.0	4.3	4.1	4.3	4.5	4.3	4.1	4.2	4.6	4.4
High school graduate	22.4	22.2	22.8	22.8	23.6	23.1	21.0	22.6	22.0	21.9	21.1	21.2	21.8	21.1	20.8	20.7	20.8	20.7	21.0	21.3	20.8
Postsecondary school other than college	4.6	5.0	4.8	5.0	5.1	5.0	5.1	5.0	4.6	4.8	4.3	4.5	4.3	4.1	3.9	3.9	3.9	4.0	4.0	3.6	3.8
Some college	14.5	14.3	14.8	15.0	15.4	15.7	16.4	15.4	15.6	15.6	15.7	15.5	16.0	15.7	15.7	15.7	15.7	15.2	14.8	14.8	14.7
College degree	23.1	23.5	22.8	23.7	22.9	23.3	25.0	24.7	25.9	26.4	26.9	27.5	27.5	27.3	27.3	27.3	27.9	28.2	28.1	27.9	27.9
Some graduate school	3.4	3.5	3.4	3.1	3.0	3.1	3.2	2.9	2.9	2.7	2.7	2.6	2.5	2.4	2.2	2.2	2.2	2.3	2.2	2.1	2.2
Graduate degree	22.8	23.2	22.7	22.3	21.3	21.4	21.9	22.4	21.9	21.1	21.9	22.0	21.7	22.5	22.8	23.0	23.0	23.0	23.0	22.9	22.8
Your mother?																					
Grammar school or less	2.1	2.0	2.2	2.0	2.5	2.3	2.0	1.8	2.2	2.8	2.8	2.4	1.8	2.5	2.8	2.5	2.1	2.3	2.4	2.4	2.9
Some high school	4.9	4.2	4.4	4.2	4.5	4.6	3.9	3.6	3.5	3.4	3.3	3.0	3.1	3.1	3.3	3.4	3.1	3.1	3.2	3.4	3.2
High school graduate	30.9	30.5	30.1	29.7	29.9	28.9	27.0	28.1	26.5	26.0	25.1	24.3	24.5	23.4	22.9	22.0	21.5	21.0	20.9	20.7	20.2
Postsecondary school other than college	7.9	8.2	7.8	8.0	7.9	7.6	7.6	7.3	6.9	6.5	5.9	5.9	5.5	5.2	5.2	4.8	4.6	4.8	4.7	4.1	4.2
Some college	18.4	17.6	18.3	18.1	18.0	18.4	19.0	17.8	18.2	17.5	17.8	17.9	18.1	17.9	17.7	18.1	18.2	17.6	17.4	17.1	16.7
College degree	21.5	22.2	21.9	22.4	22.0	22.5	24.1	24.3	25.5	26.4	27.1	28.2	28.6	29.0	28.7	29.4	30.8	31.2	31.4	31.8	32.0
Some graduate school	3.7	3.7	3.6	3.5	3.7	3.6	3.7	3.5	3.5	3.3	3.3	3.2	3.3	3.0	2.9	2.9	2.8	2.9	2.7	2.7	2.9
Graduate degree	10.7	11.4	11.7	11.8	11.8	12.1	12.7	13.6	13.7	14.0	14.7	15.0	15.0	16.0	16.6	16.8	16.9	17.1	17.4	17.7	17.9
Your father's occupation [2,3]																					
Artist	1.0	1.0	1.0	0.9	0.8	0.8	0.8	0.8	0.8	0.8	0.9	0.8	0.9	0.9	1.0	1.0	1.0	1.0	1.0	1.0	1.1
Business	33.1	33.4	31.5	31.6	29.9	29.1	29.4	29.0	28.7	28.5	28.2	28.7	28.9	29.1	29.3	29.1	28.9	29.3	29.0	28.7	28.8
Clerical	0.7	0.8	0.7	0.7	0.7	0.7	0.7	0.7	0.8	0.8	0.7	0.8	0.9	0.9	1.0	1.1	1.1	1.1	1.1	1.1	1.2
Clergy	1.2	1.1	1.0	1.2	1.2	1.2	1.2	1.1	1.2	1.1	1.3	1.2	1.2	1.2	1.1	1.0	1.0	1.0	1.0	1.0	0.9
College teacher	1.3	1.3	1.2	1.1	1.0	1.0	1.0	0.9	0.9	0.8	0.8	0.8	0.8	0.8	1.0	0.8	0.8	0.8	0.8	0.7	0.8
Doctor (MD or DDS)	3.2	3.3	3.2	3.1	2.9	2.7	2.8	2.8	2.9	2.8	2.7	3.0	2.8	2.9	3.0	3.1	3.0	3.0	3.0	2.9	2.9
Education (secondary)	4.2	4.2	4.3	4.3	4.1	4.1	4.2	4.2	4.0	3.9	3.9	3.7	3.4	3.3	3.1	2.9	2.8	2.7	2.6	2.5	2.4
Education (elementary)	0.8	0.9	0.9	1.0	1.0	1.0	1.1	1.1	1.1	1.1	1.2	1.1	1.1	1.0	0.9	0.9	0.9	0.9	0.8	0.8	0.7
Engineer	8.8	8.6	8.3	8.2	8.0	8.0	8.1	8.1	7.9	7.9	8.0	7.9	8.1	8.2	8.1	8.4	8.3	8.6	8.7	8.5	8.5
Farmer or forester	2.7	2.7	2.5	2.8	2.9	3.0	2.6	2.9	3.2	3.2	2.7	3.0	2.6	2.7	2.4	2.1	2.0	1.7	1.9	1.5	1.5
Health professional	1.4	1.4	1.4	1.4	1.3	1.3	1.4	1.3	1.4	1.3	1.4	1.5	1.4	1.4	1.5	1.4	1.5	1.5	1.5	1.5	1.5
Homemaker	0.1	0.1	0.1	0.1	0.2	0.2	0.2	0.2	0.1	0.2	0.1	0.2	0.2	0.2	0.2	0.2	0.2	0.2	0.2	0.2	0.2
Lawyer	2.3	2.4	2.4	2.2	2.1	2.0	2.1	2.2	2.2	2.2	2.2	2.4	2.2	2.3	2.3	2.3	2.4	2.3	2.3	2.4	2.5
Military	2.0	1.9	2.0	2.1	2.0	2.3	2.2	1.8	1.8	1.7	1.7	1.5	1.6	1.6	1.5	1.7	1.6	1.5	1.5	1.5	1.5
Nurse	0.1	0.1	0.1	0.2	0.2	0.2	0.2	0.3	0.3	0.3	0.3	0.4	0.4	0.4	0.4	0.4	0.5	0.5	0.5	0.5	0.5
Research scientist	0.8	0.7	0.7	0.6	0.6	0.7	0.6	0.6	0.6	0.6	0.6	0.6	0.6	0.6	0.7	0.7	0.7	0.7	0.7	0.7	0.7
Social worker	0.4	0.5	0.5	0.5	0.5	0.6	0.5	0.6	0.6	0.6	0.6	0.6	0.6	0.6	0.6	0.6	0.6	0.6	0.5	0.6	0.6
Skilled worker	8.4	8.3	8.8	8.8	9.0	9.0	8.4	9.2	8.6	8.5	8.4	8.4	8.4	7.9	7.7	8.3	8.2	7.9	8.0	7.6	7.6
Semi skilled worker	3.4	3.2	3.6	3.6	3.8	4.0	3.6	3.5	3.6	3.6	3.4	3.4	3.3	3.1	3.0	3.2	3.1	3.0	3.0	3.0	2.8
Laborer	2.3	2.1	2.5	2.4	2.8	2.9	2.6	2.9	2.7	2.6	2.7	2.5	2.7	2.5	2.6	3.1	3.1	3.1	3.1	3.3	3.0
Unemployed	2.2	1.9	2.0	2.0	2.2	2.8	2.9	2.9	2.9	2.7	2.9	2.5	2.4	2.2	2.4	2.0	2.4	2.6	2.5	2.6	2.5
Other occupation	19.5	20.1	21.1	21.3	22.9	22.5	23.2	22.8	23.7	24.7	25.3	25.3	25.7	26.1	26.4	25.7	25.7	26.1	26.2	27.3	27.7

DEMOGRAPHICS
ALL FRESHMEN

ITEM	1966	1967	1968	1969	1970	1971	1972	1973	1974	1975	1976	1977	1978	1979	1980	1981	1982	1983	1984	1985
Your mother's occupation [2,3]																				
Artist	—	—	—	—	—	1.0	1.0	—	—	—	1.4	1.4	1.4	1.4	1.4	1.6	1.7	1.7	1.6	1.8
Business	—	—	—	—	—	4.8	5.7	—	—	—	6.4	6.9	7.7	8.1	8.9	9.8	10.3	10.8	11.4	12.9
Clerical	—	—	—	—	—	8.7	10.7	—	—	—	9.7	9.7	10.0	10.4	10.9	11.0	11.1	10.8	11.3	10.5
Clergy	—	—	—	—	—	0.1	0.1	—	—	—	0.1	0.1	0.1	0.1	0.1	0.1	0.1	0.1	0.1	0.2
College teacher	—	—	—	—	—	0.3	0.4	—	—	—	0.4	0.4	0.4	0.4	0.4	0.3	0.4	0.3	0.4	0.5
Doctor (MD or DDS)	—	—	—	—	—	0.1	0.1	—	—	—	0.2	0.2	0.2	0.2	0.3	0.3	0.3	0.3	0.4	0.5
Education (secondary)	—	—	—	—	—	2.6	3.0	—	—	—	3.1	3.0	3.2	3.2	3.3	3.8	3.9	3.6	3.8	4.2
Education (elementary)	—	—	—	—	—	4.8	5.4	—	—	—	6.3	6.2	6.5	6.4	6.3	6.7	6.9	6.3	6.3	6.8
Engineer	—	—	—	—	—	0.1	0.0	—	—	—	0.1	0.1	0.1	0.1	0.1	0.1	0.1	0.1	0.2	0.2
Farmer or forester	—	—	—	—	—	0.1	0.2	—	—	—	0.2	0.2	0.2	0.2	0.2	0.2	0.3	0.2	0.3	0.3
Health professional	—	—	—	—	—	1.1	1.2	—	—	—	1.6	1.6	1.5	1.6	1.7	1.8	1.9	1.9	2.0	2.0
Homemaker	—	—	—	—	—	52.4	35.6	—	—	—	35.1	32.6	31.9	29.4	27.9	23.6	22.7	24.9	23.6	21.9
Lawyer	—	—	—	—	—	0.1	0.1	—	—	—	0.1	0.1	0.1	0.1	0.2	0.2	0.2	0.2	0.2	0.3
Military	—	—	—	—	—	0.0	0.0	—	—	—	0.0	0.0	0.0	0.0	0.0	0.0	0.0	0.0	0.1	0.0
Nurse	—	—	—	—	—	4.6	4.9	—	—	—	6.3	6.5	6.5	6.7	6.8	7.4	7.5	7.4	7.5	7.4
Research scientist	—	—	—	—	—	0.1	0.1	—	—	—	0.1	0.1	0.1	0.1	0.1	0.1	0.1	0.2	0.1	0.2
Social worker	—	—	—	—	—	0.7	0.9	—	—	—	1.2	1.2	1.1	1.3	1.2	1.3	1.3	1.3	1.4	1.3
Skilled worker	—	—	—	—	—	1.3	1.8	—	—	—	1.5	1.6	1.7	1.7	1.7	1.8	1.9	1.8	1.9	1.8
Semi skilled worker	—	—	—	—	—	2.6	3.0	—	—	—	2.9	3.1	2.7	2.9	3.0	3.0	2.9	2.9	2.7	2.6
Laborer	—	—	—	—	—	1.5	1.9	—	—	—	1.9	2.0	1.8	2.0	2.1	2.0	1.9	1.8	1.8	1.8
Unemployed	—	—	—	—	—	3.1	11.2	—	—	—	8.4	8.7	8.1	8.3	8.1	8.1	7.5	6.7	6.1	6.3
Other occupation	—	—	—	—	—	10.0	12.7	—	—	—	13.1	14.3	14.6	15.2	15.3	16.9	17.0	16.3	16.8	16.5
Your father's religious preference [2,3]																				
Protestant (Christian)	—	—	—	—	—	—	—	54.4	54.2	54.2	51.5	52.0	52.0	39.1	39.0	38.4	36.9	35.5	46.8	47.9
Roman Catholic	—	—	—	—	—	—	—	30.9	31.2	29.6	31.7	33.0	32.9	33.7	33.3	33.7	34.8	35.3	35.9	34.0
Jewish	—	—	—	—	—	—	—	6.2	4.9	5.1	5.4	4.6	5.0	4.7	4.3	4.2	4.4	4.2	4.0	4.2
Other	—	—	—	—	—	—	—	2.1	2.4	3.0	3.6	3.3	3.2	15.6	16.2	16.7	17.0	17.5	5.2	5.1
None	—	—	—	—	—	—	—	6.4	7.4	8.0	7.8	7.1	6.9	6.9	7.1	7.0	6.9	7.6	8.1	8.9
Your mother's religious preference [2,3]																				
Protestant (Christian)	—	—	—	—	58.0	—	—	56.4	56.5	56.9	53.9	54.4	54.2	40.2	39.8	39.2	37.9	36.2	48.8	50.1
Roman Catholic	—	—	—	—	29.7	—	—	32.3	32.7	31.1	33.4	34.3	34.3	35.2	34.9	35.3	36.4	37.0	37.2	35.4
Jewish	—	—	—	—	6.5	—	—	6.0	4.7	4.9	5.2	4.4	4.8	4.5	4.2	4.1	4.2	4.0	3.8	4.0
Other	—	—	—	—	3.0	—	—	2.2	2.6	3.2	3.9	3.5	3.5	16.4	17.3	17.6	17.8	18.5	5.8	5.6
None	—	—	—	—	3.1	—	—	3.1	3.5	3.8	3.7	3.4	3.3	3.7	3.8	3.9	3.7	4.2	4.5	4.9
How many persons are currently dependent on your parents?																				
One	—	—	—	—	—	—	—	—	—	—	—	—	4.4	5.2	4.9	4.7	5.1	5.5	5.7	6.2
Two	—	—	—	—	—	—	—	—	—	—	—	—	7.9	9.2	9.1	9.7	10.5	11.5	12.2	12.9
Three	—	—	—	—	—	—	—	—	—	—	—	—	18.9	19.4	19.8	20.0	20.6	23.2	23.1	21.0
Four	—	—	—	—	—	—	—	—	—	—	—	—	26.3	25.7	26.8	27.3	27.8	29.7	30.1	29.3
Five	—	—	—	—	—	—	—	—	—	—	—	—	23.1	22.0	22.3	22.1	21.1	18.9	18.8	18.8
Six or more	—	—	—	—	—	—	—	—	—	—	—	—	19.4	18.4	17.0	16.2	14.9	11.2	10.2	11.8

DEMOGRAPHICS
ALL FRESHMEN

ITEM	1986	1987	1988	1989	1990	1991	1992	1993	1994	1995	1996	1997	1998	1999	2000	2001	2002	2003	2004	2005	2006
Your mother's occupation [2,3]																					
Artist	1.9	1.9	1.9	1.7	1.6	1.6	1.6	1.5	1.6	1.6	1.5	1.6	1.6	1.6	1.7	1.7	1.7	1.8	1.8	1.8	1.8
Business	13.9	14.7	14.4	14.7	14.1	13.9	13.8	13.5	13.6	13.6	13.3	14.0	14.4	15.0	14.9	15.8	15.9	16.1	16.5	16.6	16.7
Clerical	11.1	11.2	10.6	10.6	10.1	9.6	9.2	8.8	8.4	8.1	7.7	7.5	7.7	7.2	7.0	6.8	6.2	5.9	5.3	5.0	5.0
Clergy	0.2	0.2	0.2	0.5	0.5	0.2	0.6	0.2	0.2	0.2	0.2	0.5	0.3	0.2	0.3	0.2	0.3	0.3	0.3	0.3	0.3
College teacher	0.5	0.5	0.5	0.5	0.5	0.6	0.6	0.6	0.6	0.6	0.5	0.5	0.6	0.6	0.6	0.6	0.6	0.5	0.6	0.5	0.5
Doctor (MD or DDS)	0.4	0.5	0.5	0.5	0.5	0.5	0.6	0.6	0.7	0.7	0.7	0.8	0.9	1.0	1.0	1.1	1.1	1.2	1.3	1.3	1.4
Education (secondary)	4.4	4.6	4.8	4.7	4.7	5.0	5.3	5.4	5.7	5.7	5.8	5.7	5.6	5.6	5.4	5.3	5.3	5.0	5.0	4.9	4.9
Education (elementary)	7.1	7.5	7.7	7.9	8.0	8.7	9.3	9.7	10.1	10.2	10.8	11.0	10.8	10.7	10.3	10.1	9.9	9.5	8.9	8.8	8.5
Engineer	0.2	0.2	0.2	0.2	0.2	0.2	0.3	0.3	0.3	0.3	0.4	0.3	0.4	0.4	0.4	0.5	0.6	0.6	0.7	0.7	0.8
Farmer or forester	0.3	0.3	0.3	0.3	0.4	0.4	0.3	0.3	0.4	0.4	0.4	0.4	0.3	0.4	0.3	0.3	0.3	0.3	0.3	0.2	0.2
Health professional	2.0	2.0	2.0	2.1	2.2	2.2	2.2	2.3	2.3	2.4	2.4	2.6	2.7	2.8	2.9	3.0	3.0	3.1	3.3	3.1	3.2
Homemaker	20.1	17.9	16.9	16.0	14.9	14.7	14.0	13.5	12.9	11.9	11.7	11.1	11.1	11.0	11.1	10.9	10.5	10.4	10.2	9.5	8.9
Lawyer	0.3	0.3	0.3	0.3	0.3	0.3	0.3	0.3	0.4	0.4	0.4	0.4	0.4	0.5	0.6	0.6	0.7	0.7	0.8	0.9	1.0
Military	0.0	0.0	0.1	0.1	0.1	0.1	0.1	0.1	0.1	0.1	0.1	0.1	0.1	0.1	0.1	0.2	0.2	0.2	0.2	0.2	0.2
Nurse	7.4	7.5	7.6	7.8	7.8	7.9	8.0	8.2	8.2	8.6	8.5	8.8	8.7	8.7	8.6	8.6	8.8	8.8	8.9	8.8	8.8
Research scientist	0.2	0.2	0.2	0.2	0.2	0.2	0.2	0.2	0.2	0.2	0.2	0.2	0.2	0.2	0.2	0.3	0.3	0.3	0.3	0.4	0.4
Social worker	1.4	1.5	1.6	1.5	1.5	1.7	1.6	1.7	1.7	1.8	1.8	1.8	1.9	1.8	1.9	1.9	1.8	1.8	1.7	1.9	1.9
Skilled worker	1.9	2.0	1.9	2.0	2.1	2.1	1.9	2.1	1.9	1.9	1.8	1.7	1.7	1.7	1.6	1.8	1.7	1.6	1.6	1.5	1.5
Semi skilled worker	2.4	2.3	2.3	2.5	2.6	2.6	2.4	2.4	2.4	2.4	2.3	2.2	2.1	2.0	1.9	2.2	2.1	2.0	2.0	2.0	1.8
Laborer	1.5	1.4	1.6	1.6	1.8	1.8	1.7	2.1	1.7	1.6	1.6	1.5	1.5	1.5	1.5	1.8	1.8	1.7	1.7	1.8	1.7
Unemployed	5.8	5.7	5.5	5.2	5.2	5.6	5.4	5.2	5.3	5.1	5.5	5.0	4.8	4.6	4.9	4.3	4.5	4.9	5.0	5.4	5.4
Other occupation	17.0	17.6	18.9	19.3	21.0	20.3	21.1	21.0	21.4	22.2	22.5	22.6	22.4	22.5	22.7	22.1	22.7	23.3	23.7	24.6	25.1
Your father's religious preference [2,3]																					
Protestant (Christian)	33.3	48.4	47.2	49.6	47.9	48.6	49.1	46.7	50.0	49.0	49.1	49.5	49.4	50.0	46.5	46.1	45.2	45.1	47.0	46.7	45.8
Roman Catholic	33.4	33.4	32.2	32.3	33.2	33.0	31.7	34.2	31.5	33.0	32.0	32.0	30.7	30.1	32.5	32.4	32.6	32.2	30.0	30.4	30.4
Jewish	4.1	4.1	4.1	3.7	3.5	2.8	3.0	3.2	3.1	3.2	3.1	2.9	2.8	2.7	3.5	3.3	3.1	3.1	3.3	3.3	3.4
Other	20.4	4.9	5.5	5.0	5.6	5.7	5.7	6.0	4.8	4.9	5.2	5.1	5.1	5.3	5.7	5.8	5.6	5.7	5.5	5.7	5.5
None	8.8	9.2	10.9	9.3	9.9	10.0	10.5	10.0	10.6	10.0	10.6	10.5	11.9	11.9	11.9	12.4	13.5	13.9	14.2	13.9	14.9
Your mother's religious preference [2,3]																					
Protestant (Christian)	34.4	50.8	49.8	52.0	50.3	50.8	51.6	49.0	52.9	51.6	52.1	52.4	52.9	53.2	49.5	49.4	48.6	48.5	50.7	50.3	49.5
Roman Catholic	34.9	34.8	34.0	33.5	34.4	34.3	33.0	35.6	33.0	34.4	33.3	33.5	32.1	31.7	34.0	34.0	34.2	33.9	31.7	32.0	32.0
Jewish	4.0	3.9	3.9	3.5	3.3	2.6	2.8	2.9	2.8	2.9	2.8	2.6	2.6	2.5	3.3	3.1	2.9	2.9	3.0	3.0	3.2
Other	21.3	5.4	6.0	5.5	6.1	6.1	6.1	6.4	4.9	4.9	5.2	5.0	5.0	5.3	5.5	5.7	5.6	5.6	5.4	5.6	5.5
None	5.4	5.1	6.3	5.6	6.0	6.2	6.6	6.1	6.4	6.2	6.5	6.4	7.3	7.3	7.4	7.8	8.7	9.1	9.2	9.1	9.8
How many persons are currently dependent on your parents?																					
One	6.5	7.9	—	—	—	—	—	—	—	—	8.7	8.8	—	—	—	—	—	—	—	—	8.9
Two	14.3	17.3	—	—	—	—	—	—	—	—	17.7	17.4	—	—	—	—	—	—	—	—	17.7
Three	21.9	22.2	—	—	—	—	—	—	—	—	21.3	21.7	—	—	—	—	—	—	—	—	22.4
Four	29.3	28.1	—	—	—	—	—	—	—	—	28.1	28.7	—	—	—	—	—	—	—	—	29.3
Five	17.6	16.0	—	—	—	—	—	—	—	—	15.7	15.5	—	—	—	—	—	—	—	—	14.6
Six or more	10.4	8.5	—	—	—	—	—	—	—	—	8.5	8.0	—	—	—	—	—	—	—	—	7.1

HIGH SCHOOL EXPERIENCES
ALL FRESHMEN

ITEM	1966	1967	1968	1969	1970	1971	1972	1973	1974	1975	1976	1977	1978	1979	1980	1981	1982	1983	1984	1985
From what kind of secondary school did you graduate? [*]																				
Public	81.5	—	—	81.8	81.6	—	82.7	—	—	—	—	—	—	83.0	83.1	—	—	81.8	81.3	—
Private, denominational	14.0	—	—	13.9	15.1	—	12.6	—	—	—	—	—	—	12.8	12.6	—	—	13.0	13.5	—
Private, nondenominational	4.5	—	—	4.3	3.3	—	4.8	—	—	—	—	—	—	4.2	4.4	—	—	5.2	5.2	—
In what year did you graduate from high school?																				
This year	—	—	—	—	—	—	—	96.6	95.4	95.7	95.9	95.3	96.1	95.2	95.4	96.1	96.5	96.3	96.4	96.5
One year ago	—	—	—	—	—	—	—	1.8	2.5	2.4	2.1	2.3	2.1	2.6	2.4	1.9	1.8	2.0	2.0	1.9
Two years ago	—	—	—	—	—	—	—	0.4	0.6	0.5	0.5	0.6	0.5	0.6	0.6	0.5	0.5	0.4	0.5	0.5
Three or more years ago	—	—	—	—	—	—	—	0.7	1.0	0.9	0.9	1.1	0.7	0.9	1.0	0.9	0.8	0.9	0.8	0.7
Did not graduate but passed G.E.D. test	—	—	—	—	—	—	—	0.2	0.3	0.3	0.3	0.5	0.3	0.5	0.5	0.4	0.4	0.3	0.3	0.3
Never completed high school	—	—	—	—	—	—	—	0.2	0.2	0.2	0.2	0.3	0.2	0.2	0.2	0.2	0.1	0.1	0.1	0.1
HOW WOULD YOU DESCRIBE THE RACIAL COMPOSITION OF THE:																				
High school you last attended																				
Completely non-White	—	—	—	—	—	—	—	—	—	—	—	—	—	—	—	—	—	1.2	—	—
Mostly non-White	—	—	—	—	—	—	—	—	—	—	—	—	—	—	—	—	—	4.7	—	—
Roughly half non-White	—	—	—	—	—	—	—	—	—	—	—	—	—	—	—	—	—	15.7	—	—
Mostly White	—	—	—	—	—	—	—	—	—	—	—	—	—	—	—	—	—	60.5	—	—
Completely White	—	—	—	—	—	—	—	—	—	—	—	—	—	—	—	—	—	18.0	—	—
Neighborhood where you grew up																				
Completely non-White	—	—	—	—	—	—	—	—	—	—	—	—	—	—	—	—	—	3.9	—	—
Mostly non-White	—	—	—	—	—	—	—	—	—	—	—	—	—	—	—	—	—	5.8	—	—
Roughly half non-White	—	—	—	—	—	—	—	—	—	—	—	—	—	—	—	—	—	5.3	—	—
Mostly White	—	—	—	—	—	—	—	—	—	—	—	—	—	—	—	—	—	39.3	—	—
Completely White	—	—	—	—	—	—	—	—	—	—	—	—	—	—	—	—	—	45.8	—	—
Did your high school require community service for graduation?																				
No	—	—	—	—	—	—	—	—	—	—	—	—	—	—	—	—	—	—	—	—
Yes	—	—	—	—	—	—	—	—	—	—	—	—	—	—	—	—	—	—	—	—
Did you meet or exceed recommended years of high school (grades 9–12) study in the following subjects [4]																				
English (4 years)	—	—	—	—	—	—	—	—	—	—	—	—	—	—	—	—	—	—	94.2	94.4
Mathematics (3 years)	—	—	—	—	—	—	—	—	—	—	—	—	—	—	—	—	—	—	89.8	90.4
Foreign language (2 years)	—	—	—	—	—	—	—	—	—	—	—	—	—	—	—	—	—	—	72.3	73.0
Physical science (2 years)	—	—	—	—	—	—	—	—	—	—	—	—	—	—	—	—	—	—	56.2	59.1
Biological science (2 years)	—	—	—	—	—	—	—	—	—	—	—	—	—	—	—	—	—	—	35.7	37.4
History/American govt. (1 year)	—	—	—	—	—	—	—	—	—	—	—	—	—	—	—	—	—	—	99.0	99.3
Computer science (1/2 year)	—	—	—	—	—	—	—	—	—	—	—	—	—	—	—	—	—	—	55.5	61.6
Arts and/or music (1 year)	—	—	—	—	—	—	—	—	—	—	—	—	—	—	—	—	—	—	61.6	61.9
Have you had any special tutoring or remedial work in:																				
English	—	—	—	—	—	—	—	—	—	—	—	—	—	5.8	5.9	4.8	4.9	—	5.0	—
Reading	—	—	—	—	—	—	—	—	—	—	—	—	—	5.9	6.1	4.6	4.9	—	4.7	—
Mathematics	—	—	—	—	—	—	—	—	—	—	—	—	—	7.5	7.8	6.7	7.5	—	8.7	—
Social studies	—	—	—	—	—	—	—	—	—	—	—	—	—	4.9	5.8	3.6	3.8	—	3.6	—
Science	—	—	—	—	—	—	—	—	—	—	—	—	—	4.6	5.2	3.6	3.9	—	4.0	—
Foreign language	—	—	—	—	—	—	—	—	—	—	—	—	—	3.8	3.8	3.1	3.5	—	3.7	—

HIGH SCHOOL EXPERIENCES
ALL FRESHMEN

ITEM	1986	1987	1988	1989	1990	1991	1992	1993	1994	1995	1996	1997	1998	1999	2000	2001	2002	2003	2004	2005	2006
From what kind of secondary school did you graduate? [*]																					
Public	—	—	—	—	—	82.9	—	83.1	—	—	—	—	83.0	—	—	82.6	—	—	—	—	—
Private, denominational	—	—	—	—	—	12.2	—	12.1	—	—	—	—	13.1	—	—	13.2	—	—	—	—	—
Private, nondenominational	—	—	—	—	—	4.9	—	4.9	—	—	—	—	3.9	—	—	4.3	—	—	—	—	—
In what year did you graduate from high school?																					
this year	96.5	97.3	97.2	96.8	96.6	96.3	97.0	97.3	97.4	97.4	97.8	97.8	97.8	97.7	98.0	97.9	98.0	98.3	97.9	98.3	98.1
one year ago	1.8	1.6	1.6	1.8	1.9	1.7	1.5	1.5	1.3	1.4	1.3	1.3	1.2	1.3	1.1	1.2	1.1	1.0	1.2	1.0	1.2
two years ago	0.5	0.4	0.4	0.4	0.4	0.5	0.3	0.3	0.3	0.3	0.3	0.3	0.2	0.2	0.2	0.3	0.3	0.3	0.3	0.2	0.3
three or more years ago	0.8	0.5	0.6	0.7	0.7	1.0	0.9	0.6	0.7	0.6	0.4	0.5	0.5	0.5	0.4	0.4	0.4	0.3	0.4	0.3	0.3
did not graduate but passed G.E.D. test	0.3	0.2	0.2	0.2	0.3	0.4	0.3	0.2	0.2	0.2	0.2	0.2	0.2	0.2	0.2	0.2	0.2	0.1	0.2	0.2	0.1
never completed high school	0.1	0.1	0.0	0.0	0.1	0.1	0.1	0.1	0.1	0.1	0.1	0.1	0.0	0.0	0.0	0.0	0.0	0.1	0.0	0.0	0.0
HOW WOULD YOU DESCRIBE THE RACIAL COMPOSITION OF THE:																					
High school you last attended																					
Completely non-White	—	—	1.7	—	1.9	—	—	—	—	—	—	—	—	—	—	—	—	—	—	—	2.5
Mostly non-White	—	—	6.0	—	6.7	—	—	—	—	—	—	—	—	—	—	—	—	—	—	—	10.6
Roughly half non-White	—	—	17.1	—	17.5	—	—	—	—	—	—	—	—	—	—	—	—	—	—	—	22.9
Mostly White	—	—	59.3	—	59.9	—	—	—	—	—	—	—	—	—	—	—	—	—	—	—	54.5
Completely White	—	—	15.8	—	14.0	—	—	—	—	—	—	—	—	—	—	—	—	—	—	—	9.5
Neighborhood where you grew up																					
Completely non-White	—	—	4.2	—	4.8	—	—	—	—	—	—	—	—	—	—	—	—	—	—	—	4.8
Mostly non-White	—	—	6.7	—	6.8	—	—	—	—	—	—	—	—	—	—	—	—	—	—	—	9.4
Roughly half non-White	—	—	6.6	—	6.9	—	—	—	—	—	—	—	—	—	—	—	—	—	—	—	12.2
Mostly White	—	—	43.2	—	44.1	—	—	—	—	—	—	—	—	—	—	—	—	—	—	—	50.3
Completely White	—	—	39.4	—	37.4	—	—	—	—	—	—	—	—	—	—	—	—	—	—	—	23.2
Did your high school require community service for graduation?																					
No	—	—	—	—	—	—	—	—	—	—	—	—	77.5	75.9	72.7	71.8	70.7	68.7	69.7	68.2	—
Yes	—	—	—	—	—	—	—	—	—	—	—	—	22.5	24.1	27.3	28.2	29.3	31.3	30.3	31.8	—
Did you meet or exceed recommended years of high school (grades 9–12) study in the following subjects [4]																					
English (4 years)	95.7	96.6	96.2	—	97.1	—	97.7	—	97.7	—	97.8	—	98.0	—	—	—	—	—	97.7	—	97.8
Mathematics (3 years)	92.7	93.8	94.2	—	95.3	—	96.9	—	97.5	—	97.9	—	98.1	—	—	—	—	—	98.1	—	98.5
Foreign language (2 years)	77.8	81.9	82.2	—	84.3	—	88.4	—	89.6	—	90.7	—	92.2	—	—	—	—	—	92.2	—	93.5
Physical science (2 years)	57.0	53.3	52.7	—	52.6	—	53.5	—	54.9	—	55.9	—	53.7	—	—	—	—	—	58.6	—	59.9
Biological science (2 years)	37.4	35.2	36.6	—	36.8	—	39.7	—	41.9	—	43.4	—	42.9	—	—	—	—	—	44.0	—	46.8
History/American govt. (1 year)	99.3	99.4	99.3	—	99.1	—	99.1	—	99.0	—	98.9	—	98.9	—	—	—	—	—	98.8	—	98.8
Computer science (1/2 year)	62.6	60.1	59.5	—	55.6	—	55.4	—	56.9	—	58.7	—	59.9	—	—	—	—	—	62.5	—	61.6
Arts and/or music (1 year)	62.8	64.3	66.1	—	72.3	—	73.3	—	75.1	—	75.3	—	76.9	—	—	—	—	—	80.1	—	80.6
Have you had any special tutoring or remedial work in:																					
English	—	—	—	5.0	—	5.3	—	4.3	—	4.9	—	4.7	—	5.6	5.7	5.7	5.4	5.1	—	6.0	—
Reading	—	—	—	4.5	—	4.9	—	4.0	—	4.4	—	4.1	—	4.8	5.0	5.0	4.7	4.3	—	5.0	—
Mathematics	—	—	—	10.1	—	11.1	—	10.7	—	11.2	—	11.3	—	12.2	12.7	12.7	12.8	11.6	—	12.7	—
Social studies	—	—	—	3.6	—	4.0	—	2.9	—	3.2	—	3.0	—	3.5	3.7	3.7	3.4	3.1	—	3.6	—
Science	—	—	—	4.3	—	4.7	—	3.9	—	4.3	—	4.3	—	4.8	5.0	4.9	4.7	4.4	—	4.9	—
Foreign language	—	—	—	4.4	—	4.8	—	4.1	—	4.4	—	4.5	—	5.1	5.2	5.2	5.0	4.5	—	5.0	—

HIGH SCHOOL EXPERIENCES
ALL FRESHMEN

ITEM	1966	1967	1968	1969	1970	1971	1972	1973	1974	1975	1976	1977	1978	1979	1980	1981	1982	1983	1984	1985
Do you feel you will need any special tutoring or remedial work in:																				
English	—	—	—	—	—	14.7	—	—	—	—	—	12.3	13.0	10.9	10.6	10.0	9.8	—	9.9	—
Reading	—	—	—	—	—	10.0	—	—	—	—	—	7.1	7.5	4.9	4.8	3.9	3.8	—	3.6	—
Mathematics	—	—	—	—	—	34.6	—	—	—	—	—	24.7	23.5	21.5	21.2	20.2	21.1	—	22.3	—
Social studies	—	—	—	—	—	3.4	—	—	—	—	—	2.4	3.8	2.5	2.6	2.3	2.4	—	2.5	—
Science	—	—	—	—	—	22.3	—	—	—	—	—	10.7	13.0	9.7	9.6	8.7	9.3	—	10.2	—
Foreign language	—	—	—	—	—	23.0	—	—	—	—	—	12.7	14.7	9.5	10.1	8.5	8.6	—	9.4	—
What was your average grade in high school? [3]																				
A or A+	7.3	7.1	6.2	6.2	7.3	8.0	9.4	10.8	10.7	11.2	12.0	11.5	13.9	12.3	12.1	12.2	12.8	12.8	12.4	13.4
A-	12.1	12.0	11.4	11.5	12.2	12.4	14.1	13.6	14.9	14.4	15.4	14.2	16.3	14.4	14.5	14.3	14.1	13.7	13.5	15.3
B+	20.3	20.4	19.5	20.3	21.3	21.4	22.8	24.7	22.4	22.9	23.9	22.6	22.1	20.8	20.8	20.9	21.2	20.7	20.5	21.4
B	24.2	24.4	24.8	26.1	25.9	25.6	25.9	25.5	25.8	25.1	25.0	25.7	24.4	25.0	25.5	24.9	24.8	24.4	24.5	23.9
B-	14.2	14.5	15.2	15.1	15.3	14.9	12.7	12.8	11.6	12.5	11.0	11.9	10.9	12.1	11.9	12.6	12.3	12.5	12.7	11.8
C+	12.9	12.5	13.4	12.3	11.6	11.2	9.8	7.4	9.2	8.4	8.1	8.9	8.0	9.8	9.3	9.6	9.6	10.1	10.2	8.8
C	8.6	8.4	9.2	7.9	6.1	6.2	5.1	5.0	5.2	5.3	4.5	5.0	4.4	5.4	5.6	5.2	4.9	5.6	5.9	5.2
D	0.4	0.4	0.5	0.5	0.3	0.3	0.2	0.2	0.2	0.2	0.2	0.3	0.2	0.2	0.2	0.3	0.2	0.2	0.3	0.2
Indicate which activities you did during the past year																				
Asked teacher for advice after class [5]	—	28.2	22.9	26.4	24.2	24.1	—	—	—	—	—	—	—	—	—	—	25.7	—	28.2	27.1
Attended a public recital or concert	68.2	—	—	—	—	—	—	—	—	—	—	—	84.3	82.3	—	81.4	80.2	78.7	77.0	80.0
Attended a religious service	66.1	—	91.7	91.0	89.0	87.4	—	—	—	—	—	—	87.5	87.2	—	87.9	87.8	87.3	87.3	86.5
Came late to class	48.2	56.9	53.3	58.7	59.5	53.8	—	—	—	—	—	—	—	—	—	—	—	—	—	—
Checked out a book or journal from the school library [5]	55.1	57.0	51.9	51.9	47.2	45.2	—	—	—	—	—	—	—	—	—	—	—	—	—	—
Communicated via e-mail [5]	—	—	—	—	—	—	—	—	—	—	—	—	—	—	—	—	—	—	—	—
Discussed politics [5]	—	27.4	33.6	30.5	31.3	24.4	—	—	—	—	—	—	—	—	—	—	—	—	—	—
Discussed religion [5]	—	36.8	32.1	31.8	29.8	29.2	—	—	—	—	—	—	—	—	—	—	—	—	—	—
Drank beer	53.8	54.3	51.0	54.1	56.0	58.1	—	—	—	—	—	—	71.6	72.3	—	73.5	73.7	71.7	68.8	66.3
Drank wine or liquor	—	—	—	—	—	—	—	—	—	—	—	—	—	—	—	—	—	—	—	—
Felt depressed [5]	—	—	—	—	—	—	—	—	—	—	—	—	—	—	—	—	—	—	—	8.6
Felt overwhelmed by all I had to do [5]	—	—	—	—	—	—	—	—	—	—	—	—	—	—	—	—	—	—	—	18.1
Overslept and missed a class or appointment	19.6	20.4	17.8	22.6	22.1	20.2	—	—	—	—	—	—	16.6	18.4	—	20.1	21.8	25.7	28.2	28.8
Participated in organized demonstrations	15.8	16.5	—	—	—	—	—	—	—	—	—	—	—	—	—	—	—	21.3	—	—
Performed community service as part of a class	—	—	—	—	—	—	—	—	—	—	—	—	—	—	—	—	—	—	—	—
Performed volunteer work	—	—	—	—	—	—	—	—	—	—	—	—	—	—	—	—	—	—	72.5	73.3
Played a musical instrument [5]	53.8	48.0	42.4	42.7	41.6	40.8	—	—	—	—	—	—	47.3	45.5	—	44.9	48.5	46.3	45.7	45.7
Smoked cigarettes [5]	15.0	15.2	13.4	12.6	12.2	12.4	—	—	—	—	—	—	10.9	11.0	—	9.4	9.0	8.3	7.3	6.5
Socialized with someone of another racial/ethnic group [5]	—	—	—	—	—	—	—	—	—	—	—	—	—	—	—	—	—	—	—	—
Studied with other students	—	91.1	—	—	—	—	—	—	—	—	—	—	—	—	—	—	—	—	—	90.9
Tutored another student	—	52.1	51.5	50.1	50.9	49.1	—	—	—	—	—	—	—	—	—	—	—	—	—	49.5
Used a personal computer [5]	—	—	—	—	—	—	—	—	—	—	—	—	—	—	—	—	—	—	—	—
Used the Internet for research or homework [5]	—	—	—	—	—	—	—	—	—	—	—	—	—	—	—	—	—	—	—	—
Visited an art gallery or museum	—	74.3	72.6	73.6	71.0	69.2	—	—	—	—	—	—	—	—	—	—	—	—	—	27.3

HIGH SCHOOL EXPERIENCES
ALL FRESHMEN

ITEM	1986	1987	1988	1989	1990	1991	1992	1993	1994	1995	1996	1997	1998	1999	2000	2001	2002	2003	2004	2005	2006
Do you feel you will need any special tutoring or remedial work in:																					
English	—	—	—	9.6	—	11.2	—	10.0	—	9.9	—	9.3	—	9.7	8.9	9.3	8.8	10.1	—	9.4	—
Reading	—	—	—	3.6	—	4.8	—	4.0	—	4.4	—	4.0	—	4.1	4.2	4.5	4.1	4.5	—	4.4	—
Mathematics	—	—	—	24.0	—	27.4	—	26.3	—	24.6	—	24.1	—	24.2	24.3	24.4	23.2	24.4	—	24.1	—
Social studies	—	—	—	2.9	—	3.5	—	3.1	—	3.3	—	2.8	—	3.1	3.3	3.3	3.0	3.3	—	3.3	—
Science	—	—	—	10.1	—	12.1	—	12.0	—	11.1	—	10.7	—	10.9	10.5	10.3	10.3	11.1	—	10.9	—
Foreign language	—	—	—	10.6	—	11.9	—	11.5	—	11.3	—	11.3	—	11.8	11.1	11.0	11.2	11.3	—	11.1	—
What was your average grade in high school? [3]																					
A or A+	14.2	14.0	14.2	14.3	13.7	14.7	15.6	16.5	17.6	17.7	19.5	20.7	19.6	21.1	21.2	21.7	22.9	23.2	23.7	22.9	21.9
A-	14.9	14.0	15.2	16.3	15.7	16.1	16.9	17.8	18.7	18.4	19.7	20.5	20.2	21.6	21.7	22.4	22.8	23.4	23.8	23.7	24.1
B+	20.2	21.2	19.5	20.7	20.3	20.4	20.9	20.9	20.8	20.4	20.8	20.7	20.9	21.0	20.8	20.9	21.0	20.8	20.4	21.1	21.6
B	23.5	21.6	23.4	24.6	24.3	23.9	23.6	23.3	23.1	23.3	22.0	21.6	22.4	21.4	21.5	20.8	20.7	20.4	20.2	20.1	20.7
B-	12.5	14.9	12.6	12.0	12.4	11.9	11.4	10.9	10.2	10.5	9.4	8.9	9.0	8.3	8.2	7.8	7.3	7.1	7.0	6.8	7.1
C+	9.4	7.9	9.4	8.2	8.9	8.7	7.8	7.2	6.6	6.6	5.8	5.2	5.3	4.6	4.5	4.3	3.5	3.4	3.2	3.8	3.3
C	5.0	6.2	5.4	3.9	4.5	4.1	3.6	3.2	3.0	3.0	2.7	2.4	2.4	1.9	2.0	1.9	1.7	1.6	1.8	1.6	1.3
D	0.2	0.2	0.2	0.2	0.2	0.2	0.2	0.1	0.1	0.1	0.1	0.1	0.1	0.1	0.1	0.1	0.1	0.1	0.1	0.1	0.1
Indicate which activities you did during the past year																					
Asked teacher for advice after class [5]	80.1	—	—	—	31.2	21.0	21.5	20.9	21.7	21.8	24.6	24.4	24.9	25.1	23.9	24.7	24.4	24.1	24.9	24.9	26.0
Attended a public recital or concert	—	82.1	—	—	—	—	81.4	—	—	—	—	—	78.8	78.8	79.5	79.8	79.9	—	—	—	—
Attended a religious service	85.5	85.1	82.6	84.1	85.0	85.5	85.3	85.1	85.3	84.5	84.8	85.4	84.5	84.1	82.8	83.1	81.9	80.4	80.4	79.6	76.8
Came late to class	—	—	—	—	60.2	58.1	57.7	57.5	57.2	—	—	—	64.1	64.5	64.5	65.1	63.2	62.6	63.2	62.3	60.6
Checked out a book or journal from the school library [5]	—	—	—	—	29.2	—	—	—	—	—	—	—	21.4	20.1	—	—	—	—	—	—	—
Communicated via e-mail [5]	—	—	—	—	—	—	—	—	—	—	—	—	42.1	56.6	65.3	69.3	67.4	64.1	—	—	—
Discussed politics [5]	—	—	21.5	—	—	24.9	29.7	22.7	19.2	17.9	18.7	16.5	16.5	16.9	16.4	20.9	19.4	22.5	25.5	35.0	33.8
Discussed religion [5]	—	—	23.2	—	—	—	—	—	24.2	—	—	—	29.6	30.7	29.8	30.5	30.5	29.6	—	35.0	31.3
Drank beer	66.1	65.4	64.7	59.7	56.7	55.2	53.7	53.5	51.7	52.4	51.5	50.7	50.0	48.6	47.1	47.1	46.5	44.8	45.5	43.4	42.3
Drank wine or liquor	—	67.8	67.2	61.6	57.7	56.2	54.5	54.8	52.5	54.0	54.7	54.9	54.8	53.2	53.9	53.7	52.5	50.7	51.9	50.5	48.6
Felt depressed [5]	8.7	9.0	10.6	8.9	8.6	8.8	8.8	8.8	9.3	9.0	9.1	8.6	8.6	8.4	8.1	7.8	7.5	7.4	7.7	7.0	7.3
Felt overwhelmed by all I had to do [5]	19.6	18.6	23.7	21.0	21.4	22.1	23.8	24.6	26.1	26.5	29.5	29.5	29.9	30.7	28.1	28.0	26.8	26.5	27.4	26.8	28.7
Overslept and missed a class or appointment	31.2	30.9	—	—	—	—	—	30.4	29.7	33.6	34.0	32.9	34.8	34.9	35.3	35.6	33.9	32.4	—	—	—
Participated in organized demonstrations	—	—	35.4	37.3	39.6	39.3	41.1	38.5	40.5	41.1	42.0	42.4	45.9	46.4	45.4	47.5	46.7	46.5	49.2	49.7	50.2
Performed community service as part of a class	—	—	—	—	—	—	—	—	—	—	—	—	—	55.1	55.8	57.1	52.7	52.3	53.0	54.6	53.7
Performed volunteer work	72.3	—	—	66.0	66.4	68.8	70.2	72.6	74.3	74.9	76.9	78.9	79.6	81.1	81.0	82.6	82.6	83.1	82.1	83.2	82.1
Played a musical instrument	45.4	45.1	—	—	41.1	40.6	39.8	40.7	40.7	41.2	41.0	41.3	40.7	40.9	41.5	42.3	42.8	42.6	43.2	43.7	41.9
Smoked cigarettes [5]	6.9	7.2	8.0	7.7	7.6	8.2	8.8	9.2	9.7	11.3	11.6	11.8	12.7	10.7	10.0	8.6	7.4	6.3	6.4	5.7	5.3
Socialized with someone of another racial/ethnic group [5]	—	—	—	—	—	—	58.4	—	—	64.9	64.8	66.6	65.6	66.2	67.6	70.0	69.9	68.9	67.8	70.2	66.9
Studied with other students	90.7	89.5	—	87.9	87.7	87.6	88.3	88.6	88.4	88.1	88.8	88.6	87.3	87.4	87.4	87.2	87.1	86.8	86.6	86.5	85.5
Tutored another student	48.2	49.4	49.6	51.0	51.7	52.2	55.2	55.5	56.6	55.1	55.8	55.3	54.5	54.3	53.8	56.2	55.3	54.4	55.3	54.2	52.5
Used a personal computer [5]	26.7	27.2	29.6	32.6	—	41.2	55.2	42.0	—	54.0	—	63.4	—	68.4	78.5	82.0	83.9	84.5	85.7	85.6	—
Used the Internet for research or homework [5]	—	—	—	—	—	—	—	—	—	—	—	—	44.5	58.2	67.4	74.5	78.4	81.7	77.7	79.7	—
Visited an art gallery or museum	—	58.6	—	58.6	57.3	—	—	—	62.7	—	—	—	58.5	57.9	59.4	60.1	58.1	57.1	—	—	—

HIGH SCHOOL EXPERIENCES
ALL FRESHMEN

ITEM	1966	1967	1968	1969	1970	1971	1972	1973	1974	1975	1976	1977	1978	1979	1980	1981	1982	1983	1984	1985
Indicate which activities you did during the past year																				
Voted in a student election [5]	72.9	75.2	78.7	71.4	70.9	66.8	—	—	—	—	—	—	—	—	—	—	—	—	—	—
Was bored in class [5]	—	—	—	—	—	—	—	—	—	—	—	—	—	—	—	—	—	—	29.8	29.3
Was a guest in a teacher's home	—	39.7	—	—	—	—	—	—	—	—	—	—	—	—	—	—	—	—	—	35.8
Worked in a local, state or national political campaign	—	—	—	—	—	15.4	—	—	—	—	—	—	10.6	10.0	—	10.2	9.5	9.2	10.4	—
DURING YOUR LAST YEAR IN HIGH SCHOOL, HOW MUCH TIME DID YOU SPEND IN A TYPICAL WEEK DOING THE FOLLOWING ACTIVITIES?																				
Studying/homework																				
None	—	—	—	—	—	—	—	—	—	—	—	—	—	—	—	—	—	—	—	—
Less than one hour	—	—	—	—	—	—	—	—	—	—	—	—	—	—	—	—	—	—	—	—
1 to 2 hours	—	—	—	—	—	—	—	—	—	—	—	—	—	—	—	—	—	—	—	—
3 to 5 hours	—	—	—	—	—	—	—	—	—	—	—	—	—	—	—	—	—	—	—	—
6 to 10 hours	—	—	—	—	—	—	—	—	—	—	—	—	—	—	—	—	—	—	—	—
11 to 15 hours	—	—	—	—	—	—	—	—	—	—	—	—	—	—	—	—	—	—	—	—
16 to 20 hours	—	—	—	—	—	—	—	—	—	—	—	—	—	—	—	—	—	—	—	—
Over 20 hours	—	—	—	—	—	—	—	—	—	—	—	—	—	—	—	—	—	—	—	—
Socializing with friends																				
None	—	—	—	—	—	—	—	—	—	—	—	—	—	—	—	—	—	—	—	—
Less than one hour	—	—	—	—	—	—	—	—	—	—	—	—	—	—	—	—	—	—	—	—
1 to 2 hours	—	—	—	—	—	—	—	—	—	—	—	—	—	—	—	—	—	—	—	—
3 to 5 hours	—	—	—	—	—	—	—	—	—	—	—	—	—	—	—	—	—	—	—	—
6 to 10 hours	—	—	—	—	—	—	—	—	—	—	—	—	—	—	—	—	—	—	—	—
11 to 15 hours	—	—	—	—	—	—	—	—	—	—	—	—	—	—	—	—	—	—	—	—
16 to 20 hours	—	—	—	—	—	—	—	—	—	—	—	—	—	—	—	—	—	—	—	—
Over 20 hours	—	—	—	—	—	—	—	—	—	—	—	—	—	—	—	—	—	—	—	—
Talking with teachers outside of class																				
None	—	—	—	—	—	—	—	—	—	—	—	—	—	—	—	—	—	—	—	—
Less than one hour	—	—	—	—	—	—	—	—	—	—	—	—	—	—	—	—	—	—	—	—
1 to 2 hours	—	—	—	—	—	—	—	—	—	—	—	—	—	—	—	—	—	—	—	—
3 to 5 hours	—	—	—	—	—	—	—	—	—	—	—	—	—	—	—	—	—	—	—	—
6 to 10 hours	—	—	—	—	—	—	—	—	—	—	—	—	—	—	—	—	—	—	—	—
11 to 15 hours	—	—	—	—	—	—	—	—	—	—	—	—	—	—	—	—	—	—	—	—
16 to 20 hours	—	—	—	—	—	—	—	—	—	—	—	—	—	—	—	—	—	—	—	—
Over 20 hours	—	—	—	—	—	—	—	—	—	—	—	—	—	—	—	—	—	—	—	—
Exercising or sports																				
None	—	—	—	—	—	—	—	—	—	—	—	—	—	—	—	—	—	—	—	—
Less than one hour	—	—	—	—	—	—	—	—	—	—	—	—	—	—	—	—	—	—	—	—
1 to 2 hours	—	—	—	—	—	—	—	—	—	—	—	—	—	—	—	—	—	—	—	—
3 to 5 hours	—	—	—	—	—	—	—	—	—	—	—	—	—	—	—	—	—	—	—	—
6 to 10 hours	—	—	—	—	—	—	—	—	—	—	—	—	—	—	—	—	—	—	—	—
11 to 15 hours	—	—	—	—	—	—	—	—	—	—	—	—	—	—	—	—	—	—	—	—
16 to 20 hours	—	—	—	—	—	—	—	—	—	—	—	—	—	—	—	—	—	—	—	—
Over 20 hours	—	—	—	—	—	—	—	—	—	—	—	—	—	—	—	—	—	—	—	—

HIGH SCHOOL EXPERIENCES
ALL FRESHMEN

ITEM	1986	1987	1988	1989	1990	1991	1992	1993	1994	1995	1996	1997	1998	1999	2000	2001	2002	2003	2004	2005	2006
Indicate which activities you did during the past year																					
Voted in a student election [5]	32.5	33.0	35.9	36.1	—	35.0	34.4	—	—	26.2	26.9	24.9	24.6	23.9	22.8	24.5	22.3	21.5	21.6	23.3	21.5
Was bored in class [5]	36.0	—	—	—	31.4	33.4	33.2	35.3	36.7	36.4	37.6	38.4	39.0	40.6	39.7	41.1	40.3	40.1	42.8	40.5	40.9
Was a guest in a teacher's home	—	—	32.1	31.6	31.6	30.6	29.5	29.9	29.5	28.6	29.8	30.7	29.1	29.8	27.7	28.1	27.3	24.6	24.0	23.9	22.9
Worked in a local, state or national political campaign	—	—	10.1	—	—	—	9.0	—	—	9.3	7.7	9.5	—	—	—	—	—	—	8.9	12.0	—
DURING YOUR LAST YEAR IN HIGH SCHOOL, HOW MUCH TIME DID YOU SPEND IN A TYPICAL WEEK DOING THE FOLLOWING ACTIVITIES?																					
Studying/homework																					
None	—	1.2	1.2	1.0	1.2	1.2	1.3	1.6	1.7	1.9	1.9	2.0	2.1	2.3	2.3	2.3	2.7	2.7	2.4	2.9	2.6
Less than one hour	—	7.3	7.3	7.1	7.4	8.3	8.3	10.5	9.2	10.4	9.8	10.4	10.6	11.8	11.8	11.8	13.2	13.4	12.1	14.1	12.6
1 to 2 hours	—	15.2	16.9	16.7	17.2	17.9	18.0	20.6	18.6	19.5	19.1	19.6	19.9	20.7	21.1	21.6	22.0	21.6	22.0	23.3	23.0
3 to 5 hours	—	29.2	29.5	29.2	29.4	29.6	30.0	28.8	28.9	28.4	29.3	28.8	29.3	28.4	28.7	29.3	28.6	28.4	29.1	27.8	29.0
6 to 10 hours	—	26.2	25.1	25.4	25.0	24.0	24.0	21.8	23.0	21.9	22.2	21.5	21.1	20.2	20.0	19.7	18.7	18.7	19.0	17.7	18.5
11 to 15 hours	—	12.2	11.5	11.5	11.5	10.9	10.9	9.8	10.7	10.1	10.1	10.0	9.6	9.2	8.8	8.5	8.1	8.4	8.4	7.7	7.9
16 to 20 hours	—	5.3	5.2	5.4	5.1	5.0	4.6	4.3	4.8	4.6	4.5	4.5	4.4	4.3	4.2	4.0	3.9	4.1	4.1	3.8	3.7
Over 20 hours	—	3.3	3.1	3.3	3.2	3.2	2.9	2.8	3.2	3.1	3.1	3.1	3.0	3.1	3.0	2.7	2.7	2.8	2.8	2.7	2.7
Socializing with friends																					
None	—	0.2	0.2	0.2	0.2	0.2	0.2	0.2	0.3	0.3	0.2	0.3	0.2	0.2	0.3	0.3	0.3	0.3	0.3	0.3	0.3
Less than one hour	—	1.0	1.2	1.3	1.1	1.1	0.9	1.1	1.2	1.2	1.1	1.1	1.0	1.1	1.2	1.2	1.3	1.3	1.3	1.4	1.4
1 to 2 hours	—	3.7	4.8	5.0	4.6	4.7	4.3	4.8	4.6	4.9	4.6	4.9	4.6	4.8	4.8	5.2	5.5	5.5	5.4	5.9	6.0
3 to 5 hours	—	13.2	14.5	14.2	14.4	14.8	14.6	15.2	15.4	14.9	15.1	15.2	15.0	15.3	15.3	16.6	17.2	17.1	17.1	18.3	18.5
6 to 10 hours	—	23.6	23.4	22.2	23.7	23.9	24.2	24.6	24.5	23.4	24.3	24.6	24.0	24.0	24.0	25.3	25.2	25.2	25.3	25.7	26.4
11 to 15 hours	—	20.5	19.8	19.5	20.2	19.6	20.3	20.8	20.3	19.7	20.2	19.9	20.0	19.3	19.4	19.2	18.8	18.9	19.4	18.5	18.9
16 to 20 hours	—	14.6	14.5	14.5	14.6	14.1	14.4	13.7	13.6	13.8	13.8	13.4	14.0	13.5	13.6	12.8	12.5	12.6	12.8	11.7	11.6
Over 20 hours	—	23.3	21.7	23.0	21.2	21.5	21.0	19.5	20.1	21.8	20.7	20.5	21.1	21.8	21.6	19.4	19.3	19.2	18.4	18.1	17.0
Talking with teachers outside of class																					
None	—	6.0	6.7	5.6	6.9	7.1	7.4	7.8	8.6	9.1	8.6	9.2	9.0	9.0	9.2	8.8	9.4	9.7	9.7	10.5	10.3
Less than one hour	—	37.6	34.6	31.4	40.7	41.2	40.4	42.2	42.4	42.6	42.2	43.7	42.3	42.2	41.9	41.9	43.3	43.4	43.3	44.1	42.0
1 to 2 hours	—	33.1	33.7	30.5	33.7	32.9	33.7	31.8	31.8	31.1	31.9	30.9	31.6	31.7	31.7	32.2	31.1	30.7	30.8	29.9	31.4
3 to 5 hours	—	16.6	16.2	17.0	13.5	13.3	13.4	12.7	12.4	12.2	12.5	11.7	12.3	12.0	12.2	12.3	11.6	11.5	11.5	10.9	11.7
6 to 10 hours	—	4.5	5.3	7.6	3.5	3.5	3.5	3.6	3.2	3.4	3.1	3.0	3.2	3.2	3.2	3.2	3.0	3.0	3.0	2.9	3.1
11 to 15 hours	—	1.3	1.9	3.7	1.0	1.1	1.0	1.1	0.9	1.0	1.0	0.9	0.9	1.0	1.1	1.0	0.9	0.9	0.9	1.0	0.9
16 to 20 hours	—	0.5	0.9	2.0	0.4	0.4	0.4	0.4	0.3	0.4	0.4	0.4	0.4	0.4	0.4	0.4	0.4	0.4	0.3	0.4	0.3
Over 20 hours	—	0.5	0.9	2.2	0.3	0.4	0.4	0.3	0.3	0.4	0.4	0.3	0.3	0.4	0.4	0.3	0.4	0.4	0.4	0.4	0.4
Exercising or sports																					
None	—	3.6	3.6	3.4	4.1	3.9	3.5	3.3	4.1	4.3	4.1	4.4	4.2	4.5	4.7	4.7	5.4	5.3	4.7	4.9	4.6
Less than one hour	—	9.3	9.0	8.6	9.4	9.1	8.6	8.9	9.2	8.7	8.5	9.1	9.0	9.3	9.3	9.8	10.1	9.8	9.3	9.8	9.2
1 to 2 hours	—	15.4	16.5	16.0	16.1	15.8	15.7	15.5	15.7	15.0	15.2	15.1	15.6	15.3	15.7	16.0	15.5	15.2	15.2	15.7	15.7
3 to 5 hours	—	21.0	21.5	21.5	20.3	20.1	20.0	19.3	20.2	19.6	19.6	19.3	19.6	19.1	19.1	19.3	19.1	18.9	19.2	19.3	19.8
6 to 10 hours	—	19.1	19.0	19.4	18.6	18.3	19.2	18.3	18.4	18.3	18.5	18.5	18.2	18.0	17.7	18.1	18.2	18.1	18.4	18.4	18.6
11 to 15 hours	—	14.1	13.7	14.3	14.1	14.3	14.5	14.7	14.5	14.7	14.9	14.6	14.4	14.5	13.9	14.0	13.8	13.9	14.3	13.7	14.0
16 to 20 hours	—	7.6	7.6	7.8	8.0	8.1	8.4	8.5	7.9	8.3	8.6	8.5	8.5	8.4	8.3	8.1	7.9	8.3	8.5	8.0	8.1
Over 20 hours	—	10.0	9.2	9.0	9.4	10.4	9.9	11.3	9.7	11.1	10.6	10.7	10.5	11.0	11.3	10.0	10.0	10.5	10.5	10.3	10.1

HIGH SCHOOL EXPERIENCES
ALL FRESHMEN

ITEM	1966	1967	1968	1969	1970	1971	1972	1973	1974	1975	1976	1977	1978	1979	1980	1981	1982	1983	1984	1985
DURING YOUR LAST YEAR IN HIGH SCHOOL, HOW MUCH TIME DID YOU SPEND IN A TYPICAL WEEK DOING THE FOLLOWING ACTIVITIES?																				
Partying																				
None																				
Less than one hour																				
1 to 2 hours																				
3 to 5 hours																				
6 to 10 hours																				
11 to 15 hours																				
16 to 20 hours																				
Over 20 hours																				
Working (for pay)																				
None																				
Less than one hour																				
1 to 2 hours																				
3 to 5 hours																				
6 to 10 hours																				
11 to 15 hours																				
16 to 20 hours																				
Over 20 hours																				
Volunteer work																				
None																				
Less than one hour																				
1 to 2 hours																				
3 to 5 hours																				
6 to 10 hours																				
11 to 15 hours																				
16 to 20 hours																				
Over 20 hours																				
Student clubs/groups																				
None																				
Less than one hour																				
1 to 2 hours																				
3 to 5 hours																				
6 to 10 hours																				
11 to 15 hours																				
16 to 20 hours																				
Over 20 hours																				
Watching TV																				
None																				
Less than one hour																				
1 to 2 hours																				
3 to 5 hours																				
6 to 10 hours																				
11 to 15 hours																				
16 to 20 hours																				
Over 20 hours																				

HIGH SCHOOL EXPERIENCES
ALL FRESHMEN

ITEM	1986	1987	1988	1989	1990	1991	1992	1993	1994	1995	1996	1997	1998	1999	2000	2001	2002	2003	2004	2005	2006
DURING YOUR LAST YEAR IN HIGH SCHOOL, HOW MUCH TIME DID YOU SPEND IN A TYPICAL WEEK DOING THE FOLLOWING ACTIVITIES?																					
Partying																					
None	—	11.6	12.2	13.2	14.5	15.0	16.1	15.1	17.4	17.5	18.2	18.2	17.8	18.8	18.0	18.9	21.0	22.8	23.8	25.1	25.5
Less than one hour	—	11.5	11.6	12.6	12.8	13.0	13.8	14.6	13.8	13.7	13.8	13.6	13.2	13.3	13.2	14.0	14.8	14.9	15.2	15.4	14.7
1 to 2 hours	—	15.8	16.9	17.3	17.4	17.4	17.8	17.9	17.5	17.3	17.7	17.7	17.9	17.7	17.8	18.6	18.1	17.9	17.9	17.8	17.9
3 to 5 hours	—	24.4	24.5	24.5	23.5	23.0	22.7	22.2	22.2	21.6	21.9	21.9	21.9	21.8	22.0	21.7	21.0	20.3	19.8	19.6	19.9
6 to 10 hours	—	19.1	18.6	17.9	17.2	16.8	15.9	16.0	15.3	15.3	14.9	15.0	15.2	15.0	15.1	14.3	13.3	13.0	12.7	11.9	12.2
11 to 15 hours	—	8.8	8.2	7.4	7.6	7.3	7.0	7.3	7.0	7.1	6.7	6.8	6.9	6.7	6.9	6.4	6.0	5.6	5.5	5.2	5.0
16 to 20 hours	—	4.0	3.8	3.4	3.5	3.5	3.3	3.4	3.2	3.5	3.2	3.1	3.4	3.2	3.4	3.0	2.7	2.7	2.6	2.4	2.3
Over 20 hours	—	4.9	4.2	3.7	3.6	4.0	3.4	3.6	3.7	4.1	3.6	3.7	3.6	3.5	3.7	3.1	3.1	2.8	2.5	2.6	2.4
Working (for pay)																					
None	—	26.1	26.4	26.8	27.4	29.7	30.7	27.6	29.0	27.0	28.1	28.0	26.9	27.3	26.9	27.5	29.1	30.5	30.1	30.7	30.2
Less than one hour	—	2.4	2.4	2.3	2.2	2.6	2.5	2.9	2.4	2.3	2.1	2.2	2.0	2.2	2.1	2.2	2.5	2.6	2.7	2.9	2.7
1 to 2 hours	—	3.4	3.4	3.4	3.2	3.5	3.7	3.7	3.4	3.3	3.3	3.2	3.2	3.2	3.2	3.2	3.4	3.7	3.8	4.0	4.1
3 to 5 hours	—	6.1	6.4	6.0	6.0	6.5	6.5	6.6	6.3	6.2	6.1	6.2	6.1	6.3	6.3	6.4	6.6	7.0	7.2	7.2	7.4
6 to 10 hours	—	10.4	10.7	10.9	11.2	11.2	11.4	11.2	11.3	11.3	11.4	11.5	11.5	11.5	11.6	12.0	12.1	12.1	12.1	12.1	12.2
11 to 15 hours	—	12.8	12.7	13.2	13.4	13.0	13.5	13.7	13.5	13.5	13.8	13.8	13.8	13.6	13.8	14.3	13.8	13.8	13.6	13.0	13.4
16 to 20 hours	—	17.0	16.9	16.9	17.1	15.4	15.2	15.6	16.0	16.6	16.4	16.4	16.7	16.4	16.5	16.4	15.6	14.5	14.6	13.8	14.2
Over 20 hours	—	21.9	21.0	20.5	19.4	18.0	16.4	18.7	18.1	19.8	18.9	18.7	19.8	19.6	19.6	18.0	16.8	15.8	16.0	16.2	15.8
Volunteer work																					
None	—	56.3	55.3	46.3	46.2	43.5	42.4	37.3	38.4	37.8	36.5	33.8	31.7	30.8	31.0	29.6	29.9	29.4	27.4	29.4	29.3
Less than one hour	—	15.5	16.1	20.1	20.2	20.6	20.3	22.6	21.6	21.6	21.9	22.7	22.3	22.4	22.2	23.1	23.1	23.0	23.8	23.3	22.7
1 to 2 hours	—	14.6	15.4	18.7	18.4	19.2	19.9	21.0	21.0	20.9	21.8	22.4	23.5	23.7	23.5	24.2	23.4	23.6	25.2	23.6	24.4
3 to 5 hours	—	8.2	8.2	9.3	9.3	10.2	10.5	11.6	11.6	11.5	11.8	12.7	13.3	13.5	13.5	13.8	13.6	13.9	14.3	13.6	13.8
6 to 10 hours	—	3.0	3.0	3.2	3.4	3.7	4.0	4.3	4.2	4.5	4.5	4.7	5.0	5.3	5.4	5.3	5.4	5.5	5.3	5.3	5.3
11 to 15 hours	—	1.0	0.9	1.0	1.1	1.2	1.3	1.5	1.5	1.6	1.6	1.7	1.8	1.9	1.9	1.8	1.9	2.0	1.9	2.0	2.0
16 to 20 hours	—	0.5	0.5	0.5	0.6	0.6	0.6	0.7	0.7	0.8	0.7	0.8	0.9	1.0	1.0	0.9	1.0	1.0	0.9	1.0	1.0
Over 20 hours	—	0.9	0.8	0.8	0.9	1.0	1.0	1.1	1.1	1.2	1.2	1.3	1.4	1.5	1.5	1.4	1.7	1.7	1.3	1.7	1.6
Student clubs/groups																					
None	—	25.8	26.2	22.9	24.1	23.0	23.9	23.6	24.6	26.8	26.9	26.1	25.9	25.4	27.2	26.9	27.4	27.5	28.4	27.3	27.9
Less than one hour	—	12.4	12.6	13.2	13.1	13.3	13.6	15.0	14.1	14.4	14.0	14.8	14.6	14.8	14.4	14.8	15.6	15.5	15.0	15.7	14.8
1 to 2 hours	—	24.6	25.3	26.1	25.8	25.8	26.3	25.3	26.2	25.2	26.2	25.7	26.3	25.9	25.1	25.9	25.4	25.2	25.5	25.4	25.2
3 to 5 hours	—	20.4	19.6	20.7	20.4	20.2	19.6	19.1	19.2	18.3	18.3	18.6	18.5	18.5	17.9	18.0	17.6	17.8	17.4	17.4	17.7
6 to 10 hours	—	9.5	9.2	9.6	9.2	9.5	9.1	9.1	8.8	8.3	8.1	8.1	8.1	8.3	8.2	7.9	7.5	7.5	7.5	7.6	7.7
11 to 15 hours	—	3.7	3.5	3.6	3.6	3.8	3.6	3.8	3.6	3.4	3.2	3.3	3.3	3.4	3.4	3.1	3.1	3.1	3.0	3.1	3.1
16 to 20 hours	—	1.6	1.7	1.7	1.7	1.8	1.7	1.7	1.6	1.6	1.4	1.5	1.5	1.6	1.6	1.5	1.4	1.5	1.5	1.5	1.5
Over 20 hours	—	2.0	2.0	2.2	2.0	2.5	2.1	2.3	2.0	2.0	1.9	1.9	1.9	2.1	2.2	1.9	2.0	1.9	1.8	2.0	2.0
Watching TV																					
None	—	5.3	5.5	5.3	4.5	4.5	4.4	5.0	5.4	5.7	5.3	5.8	5.5	5.8	5.7	5.8	6.1	5.7	5.3	5.7	6.3
Less than one hour	—	12.5	13.0	13.5	12.8	12.9	13.0	15.0	14.5	15.2	14.5	15.8	14.6	15.2	15.1	15.7	16.5	15.4	14.6	14.9	14.7
1 to 2 hours	—	21.5	21.7	21.8	21.5	21.4	22.2	23.3	22.9	23.2	23.5	23.6	23.7	24.2	24.0	24.3	24.8	23.9	24.2	24.0	24.8
3 to 5 hours	—	28.3	27.7	27.6	27.6	27.1	27.6	26.6	26.6	26.3	27.1	26.4	27.2	26.6	26.8	27.1	26.6	27.2	28.0	27.4	27.9
6 to 10 hours	—	18.5	18.0	17.8	18.2	18.1	17.9	16.6	16.6	16.4	16.6	15.9	16.2	15.6	15.8	15.3	14.7	15.7	15.9	15.7	15.4
11 to 15 hours	—	7.1	7.1	7.0	7.3	7.6	7.3	6.8	6.6	6.4	6.4	6.3	6.3	6.3	6.1	5.9	5.5	6.0	6.1	6.0	5.6
16 to 20 hours	—	3.0	3.2	3.1	3.7	3.5	3.3	2.9	2.9	2.8	2.8	2.7	2.8	2.7	2.7	2.5	2.4	2.6	2.6	2.6	2.3
Over 20 hours	—	3.7	3.8	3.8	4.4	4.9	4.3	3.8	3.8	3.9	3.7	3.5	3.8	3.6	3.7	3.4	3.4	3.4	3.2	3.6	3.0

ITEM	1966	1967	1968	1969	1970	1971	1972	1973	1974	1975	1976	1977	1978	1979	1980	1981	1982	1983	1984	1985
DURING YOUR LAST YEAR IN HIGH SCHOOL, HOW MUCH TIME DID YOU SPEND IN A TYPICAL WEEK DOING THE FOLLOWING ACTIVITIES?																				
Housework/childcare																				
None	—	—	—	—	—	—	—	—	—	—	—	—	—	—	—	—	—	—	—	—
Less than one hour	—	—	—	—	—	—	—	—	—	—	—	—	—	—	—	—	—	—	—	—
1 to 2 hours	—	—	—	—	—	—	—	—	—	—	—	—	—	—	—	—	—	—	—	—
3 to 5 hours	—	—	—	—	—	—	—	—	—	—	—	—	—	—	—	—	—	—	—	—
6 to 10 hours	—	—	—	—	—	—	—	—	—	—	—	—	—	—	—	—	—	—	—	—
11 to 15 hours	—	—	—	—	—	—	—	—	—	—	—	—	—	—	—	—	—	—	—	—
16 to 20 hours	—	—	—	—	—	—	—	—	—	—	—	—	—	—	—	—	—	—	—	—
Over 20 hours	—	—	—	—	—	—	—	—	—	—	—	—	—	—	—	—	—	—	—	—
Prayer/meditation																				
None	—	—	—	—	—	—	—	—	—	—	—	—	—	—	—	—	—	—	—	—
Less than one hour	—	—	—	—	—	—	—	—	—	—	—	—	—	—	—	—	—	—	—	—
1 to 2 hours	—	—	—	—	—	—	—	—	—	—	—	—	—	—	—	—	—	—	—	—
3 to 5 hours	—	—	—	—	—	—	—	—	—	—	—	—	—	—	—	—	—	—	—	—
6 to 10 hours	—	—	—	—	—	—	—	—	—	—	—	—	—	—	—	—	—	—	—	—
11 to 15 hours	—	—	—	—	—	—	—	—	—	—	—	—	—	—	—	—	—	—	—	—
16 to 20 hours	—	—	—	—	—	—	—	—	—	—	—	—	—	—	—	—	—	—	—	—
Over 20 hours	—	—	—	—	—	—	—	—	—	—	—	—	—	—	—	—	—	—	—	—
Reading for pleasure																				
None	—	—	—	—	—	—	—	—	—	—	—	—	—	—	—	—	—	—	—	—
Less than one hour	—	—	—	—	—	—	—	—	—	—	—	—	—	—	—	—	—	—	—	—
1 to 2 hours	—	—	—	—	—	—	—	—	—	—	—	—	—	—	—	—	—	—	—	—
3 to 5 hours	—	—	—	—	—	—	—	—	—	—	—	—	—	—	—	—	—	—	—	—
6 to 10 hours	—	—	—	—	—	—	—	—	—	—	—	—	—	—	—	—	—	—	—	—
11 to 15 hours	—	—	—	—	—	—	—	—	—	—	—	—	—	—	—	—	—	—	—	—
16 to 20 hours	—	—	—	—	—	—	—	—	—	—	—	—	—	—	—	—	—	—	—	—
Over 20 hours	—	—	—	—	—	—	—	—	—	—	—	—	—	—	—	—	—	—	—	—
Playing video games																				
None	—	—	—	—	—	—	—	—	—	—	—	—	—	—	—	—	—	—	—	—
Less than one hour	—	—	—	—	—	—	—	—	—	—	—	—	—	—	—	—	—	—	—	—
1 to 2 hours	—	—	—	—	—	—	—	—	—	—	—	—	—	—	—	—	—	—	—	—
3 to 5 hours	—	—	—	—	—	—	—	—	—	—	—	—	—	—	—	—	—	—	—	—
6 to 10 hours	—	—	—	—	—	—	—	—	—	—	—	—	—	—	—	—	—	—	—	—
11 to 15 hours	—	—	—	—	—	—	—	—	—	—	—	—	—	—	—	—	—	—	—	—
16 to 20 hours	—	—	—	—	—	—	—	—	—	—	—	—	—	—	—	—	—	—	—	—
Over 20 hours	—	—	—	—	—	—	—	—	—	—	—	—	—	—	—	—	—	—	—	—
Playing video/computer games																				
None	—	—	—	—	—	—	—	—	—	—	—	—	—	—	—	—	—	—	—	—
Less than one hour	—	—	—	—	—	—	—	—	—	—	—	—	—	—	—	—	—	—	—	—
1 to 2 hours	—	—	—	—	—	—	—	—	—	—	—	—	—	—	—	—	—	—	—	—
3 to 5 hours	—	—	—	—	—	—	—	—	—	—	—	—	—	—	—	—	—	—	—	—
6 to 10 hours	—	—	—	—	—	—	—	—	—	—	—	—	—	—	—	—	—	—	—	—
11 to 15 hours	—	—	—	—	—	—	—	—	—	—	—	—	—	—	—	—	—	—	—	—
16 to 20 hours	—	—	—	—	—	—	—	—	—	—	—	—	—	—	—	—	—	—	—	—
Over 20 hours	—	—	—	—	—	—	—	—	—	—	—	—	—	—	—	—	—	—	—	—

HIGH SCHOOL EXPERIENCES
ALL FRESHMEN

ITEM	1986	1987	1988	1989	1990	1991	1992	1993	1994	1995	1996	1997	1998	1999	2000	2001	2002	2003	2004	2005	2006
DURING YOUR LAST YEAR IN HIGH SCHOOL, HOW MUCH TIME DID YOU SPEND IN A TYPICAL WEEK DOING THE FOLLOWING ACTIVITIES?																					
Housework/childcare																					
None	—	—	—	—	—	—	—	14.7	19.7	19.4	20.2	20.8	20.0	21.0	22.1	20.7	21.7	21.2	20.4	20.3	20.3
Less than one hour	—	—	—	—	—	—	—	19.1	19.1	23.0	22.4	24.0	22.2	23.3	20.9	21.2	22.7	22.3	20.6	22.0	20.4
1 to 2 hours	—	—	—	—	—	—	—	30.3	30.0	29.8	30.4	29.7	30.6	29.9	29.9	30.8	29.9	29.9	30.4	30.0	30.7
3 to 5 hours	—	—	—	—	—	—	—	22.1	19.9	17.6	17.3	16.4	17.5	16.7	17.5	18.1	16.9	17.4	18.5	17.7	18.5
6 to 10 hours	—	—	—	—	—	—	—	8.1	6.6	6.0	5.7	5.3	5.6	5.5	5.7	5.5	5.2	5.4	6.0	5.8	6.0
11 to 15 hours	—	—	—	—	—	—	—	2.7	2.2	2.0	1.9	1.8	2.0	1.8	1.9	1.8	1.7	1.8	2.0	1.9	2.0
16 to 20 hours	—	—	—	—	—	—	—	1.2	0.9	0.8	0.8	0.8	0.8	0.8	0.8	0.7	0.7	0.7	0.8	0.8	0.8
Over 20 hours	—	—	—	—	—	—	—	1.9	1.6	1.4	1.3	1.2	1.3	1.2	1.4	1.3	1.2	1.2	1.3	1.4	1.3
Prayer/meditation																					
None	—	—	—	—	—	—	—	—	—	—	33.1	31.4	32.1	31.5	32.3	34.3	34.8	36.2	37.5	37.4	—
Less than one hour	—	—	—	—	—	—	—	—	—	—	34.4	35.7	34.3	34.3	34.6	34.2	34.7	33.8	33.2	34.1	—
1 to 2 hours	—	—	—	—	—	—	—	—	—	—	21.3	21.5	21.5	21.7	21.2	20.2	19.4	19.1	18.8	18.2	—
3 to 5 hours	—	—	—	—	—	—	—	—	—	—	7.1	7.2	7.6	7.8	7.4	7.1	6.9	6.9	6.7	6.3	—
6 to 10 hours	—	—	—	—	—	—	—	—	—	—	2.3	2.3	2.5	2.6	2.4	2.4	2.3	2.2	2.2	2.1	—
11 to 15 hours	—	—	—	—	—	—	—	—	—	—	0.7	0.7	0.8	0.8	0.8	0.7	0.8	0.7	0.7	0.7	—
16 to 20 hours	—	—	—	—	—	—	—	—	—	—	0.3	0.4	0.4	0.4	0.4	0.3	0.3	0.4	0.3	0.4	—
Over 20 hours	—	—	—	—	—	—	—	—	—	—	0.8	0.8	0.9	0.9	0.8	0.7	0.7	0.8	0.7	0.8	—
Reading for pleasure																					
None	—	—	—	—	—	—	—	—	19.6	22.7	23.0	24.8	24.9	25.2	24.7	24.8	25.6	25.3	24.6	24.8	24.5
Less than one hour	—	—	—	—	—	—	—	—	25.4	26.0	26.8	27.6	27.0	27.4	27.5	27.4	27.3	26.7	26.1	26.1	25.0
1 to 2 hours	—	—	—	—	—	—	—	—	25.9	24.8	25.4	24.4	25.1	24.8	24.9	25.0	24.0	23.8	24.2	23.8	24.5
3 to 5 hours	—	—	—	—	—	—	—	—	16.9	15.6	14.9	14.2	14.0	13.9	14.1	14.1	14.0	14.6	14.9	15.1	15.5
6 to 10 hours	—	—	—	—	—	—	—	—	7.3	6.5	6.1	5.5	5.5	5.3	5.4	5.4	5.5	5.8	6.1	6.1	6.3
11 to 15 hours	—	—	—	—	—	—	—	—	2.6	2.4	2.1	2.0	1.8	1.9	1.9	1.8	2.0	2.1	2.2	2.1	2.2
16 to 20 hours	—	—	—	—	—	—	—	—	1.0	0.9	0.8	0.8	0.7	0.7	0.7	0.7	0.7	0.8	0.9	0.9	0.9
Over 20 hours	—	—	—	—	—	—	—	—	1.2	1.0	0.9	0.8	0.9	0.8	0.8	0.8	0.9	0.9	0.9	1.0	1.0
Playing video games																					
None	—	—	—	—	—	—	—	—	—	61.3	63.6	61.4	53.5	52.6	—	—	—	—	—	—	—
Less than one hour	—	—	—	—	—	—	—	—	—	18.8	17.3	18.2	20.0	19.8	—	—	—	—	—	—	—
1 to 2 hours	—	—	—	—	—	—	—	—	—	10.2	9.9	10.4	12.7	13.0	—	—	—	—	—	—	—
3 to 5 hours	—	—	—	—	—	—	—	—	—	5.6	5.4	5.8	7.8	8.1	—	—	—	—	—	—	—
6 to 10 hours	—	—	—	—	—	—	—	—	—	2.3	2.2	2.4	3.4	3.6	—	—	—	—	—	—	—
11 to 15 hours	—	—	—	—	—	—	—	—	—	0.9	0.8	0.9	1.3	1.4	—	—	—	—	—	—	—
16 to 20 hours	—	—	—	—	—	—	—	—	—	0.4	0.3	0.4	0.6	0.6	—	—	—	—	—	—	—
Over 20 hours	—	—	—	—	—	—	—	—	—	0.6	0.5	0.5	0.8	0.9	—	—	—	—	—	—	—
Playing video/computer games																					
None	—	—	—	—	—	—	—	—	—	—	—	—	—	—	36.9	35.9	39.1	38.7	39.9	40.9	40.6
Less than one hour	—	—	—	—	—	—	—	—	—	—	—	—	—	—	24.4	24.2	23.6	22.2	21.0	20.7	20.1
1 to 2 hours	—	—	—	—	—	—	—	—	—	—	—	—	—	—	17.6	17.9	16.2	16.4	15.9	15.1	15.6
3 to 5 hours	—	—	—	—	—	—	—	—	—	—	—	—	—	—	11.4	11.8	11.1	11.6	11.7	11.5	11.7
6 to 10 hours	—	—	—	—	—	—	—	—	—	—	—	—	—	—	5.2	5.5	5.3	5.7	6.0	6.0	6.1
11 to 15 hours	—	—	—	—	—	—	—	—	—	—	—	—	—	—	2.1	2.2	2.3	2.5	2.6	2.7	2.6
16 to 20 hours	—	—	—	—	—	—	—	—	—	—	—	—	—	—	1.0	1.0	1.0	1.1	1.2	1.2	1.2
Over 20 hours	—	—	—	—	—	—	—	—	—	—	—	—	—	—	1.4	1.5	1.5	1.7	1.7	2.0	2.0

HIGH SCHOOL EXPERIENCES
ALL FRESHMEN

ITEM	1966	1967	1968	1969	1970	1971	1972	1973	1974	1975	1976	1977	1978	1979	1980	1981	1982	1983	1984	1985
Student rated self above average or highest 10% as compared with the average person of his/her age in:																				
Academic ability	64.3	—	—	—	—	62.5	—	—	63.8	—	62.5	—	—	—	61.0	—	—	—	—	67.3
Artistic ability	18.8	—	—	—	—	18.8	—	—	20.7	—	22.7	—	—	—	23.3	—	—	—	—	24.9
Athletic ability	35.3	—	—	—	—	36.8	—	—	39.8	—	41.2	—	—	—	43.1	—	—	—	—	—
Competitiveness	—	—	—	—	—	—	—	—	—	—	—	—	—	—	—	—	—	—	—	—
Computer skills	—	—	—	—	—	—	—	—	—	—	—	—	—	—	—	—	—	—	—	—
Cooperativeness	—	—	—	—	—	—	—	—	—	—	—	—	—	—	—	—	—	—	—	—
Creativity	—	—	—	—	—	—	—	—	—	—	—	—	—	—	—	—	—	—	—	—
Drive to achieve	60.2	—	—	—	—	57.8	—	—	65.3	—	67.7	—	—	—	69.8	—	—	—	—	68.4
Emotional health	—	—	—	—	—	—	—	—	—	—	—	—	—	—	—	—	—	—	—	63.6
Leadership ability	41.1	—	—	—	—	39.7	—	—	46.7	—	50.1	—	—	—	53.3	—	—	—	—	56.6
Mathematical ability	39.2	—	—	—	—	38.4	—	—	39.8	—	40.0	—	—	—	40.5	—	—	—	—	46.1
Physical health	—	—	—	—	—	—	—	—	—	—	—	—	—	—	—	—	—	—	—	63.9
Popularity	33.5	—	—	—	—	31.8	—	—	33.9	—	35.4	—	—	—	38.3	—	—	—	—	46.6
Public speaking ability	24.5	—	—	—	—	22.9	—	—	24.7	—	26.9	—	—	—	28.6	—	—	—	—	—
Self confidence (intellectual)	39.0	—	—	—	—	41.4	—	—	47.1	—	49.6	—	—	—	52.9	—	—	—	—	61.0
Self confidence (social)	30.0	—	—	—	—	29.5	—	—	36.7	—	40.0	—	—	—	44.5	—	—	—	—	49.9
Self understanding	—	—	—	—	—	—	—	—	—	—	—	—	—	—	—	—	—	—	—	—
Spirituality	—	—	—	—	—	—	—	—	—	—	—	—	—	—	—	—	—	—	—	—
Understanding of others	61.4	—	—	—	—	65.1	—	—	68.2	—	69.7	—	—	—	73.3	—	—	—	—	—
Writing ability	30.0	—	—	—	—	32.6	—	—	35.6	—	38.3	—	—	—	38.7	—	—	—	—	44.4

COLLEGE CHOICE
ALL FRESHMEN

ITEM	1966	1967	1968	1969	1970	1971	1972	1973	1974	1975	1976	1977	1978	1979	1980	1981	1982	1983	1984	1985
Reasons noted as very important in deciding to go to college																				
A mentor/role model encouraged me to go	—	—	—	—	—	—	—	—	—	—	—	—	—	—	—	—	—	—	—	—
I could not find a job	—	—	—	—	—	—	—	—	—	—	4.2	4.9	3.5	4.3	4.8	4.9	5.9	4.8	4.1	—
My parents wanted me to go	—	—	—	—	—	23.0	—	—	—	—	29.9	30.0	29.2	31.0	33.1	33.6	34.6	32.7	31.5	—
There was nothing better to do	—	—	—	—	—	2.2	—	—	—	—	2.7	2.5	1.8	2.0	2.1	2.3	2.2	2.2	2.0	2.4
To be able to get a better job	—	—	—	—	—	70.1	—	—	—	—	67.9	74.5	73.1	76.4	74.9	74.0	75.3	73.3	73.0	—
To be able to make more money	—	—	—	—	—	44.6	—	—	—	—	49.9	59.1	57.9	62.2	61.4	64.4	67.5	64.9	65.8	66.7
To get training for a specific career	—	—	—	—	—	—	—	—	—	—	—	—	—	—	—	—	—	—	—	—
To gain a general education and appreciation of ideas	—	—	—	—	—	62.7	—	—	—	—	67.5	73.9	71.5	71.0	69.5	70.5	69.6	66.6	67.4	63.7
To improve my reading and study skills	—	—	—	—	—	20.9	—	—	—	—	35.2	43.5	38.6	39.3	40.6	40.9	41.1	42.4	41.6	39.7
To learn more about things that interest me	—	—	—	—	—	70.4	—	—	—	—	74.8	80.9	75.6	75.1	75.8	75.1	74.6	73.1	73.4	74.3
To make me a more cultured person	—	—	—	—	—	29.8	—	—	—	—	35.6	41.8	36.5	36.5	37.8	37.1	37.8	35.2	36.7	35.4
To prepare for graduate or professional school	—	—	—	—	—	34.9	—	—	—	—	45.3	48.5	47.5	46.9	48.7	47.8	48.3	49.7	49.9	47.8
Wanted to get away from home	—	—	—	—	—	—	—	—	—	—	11.6	10.9	8.7	9.3	10.1	10.4	11.6	12.0	12.9	—

HIGH SCHOOL EXPERIENCES
ALL FRESHMEN

ITEM	1986	1987	1988	1989	1990	1991	1992	1993	1994	1995	1996	1997	1998	1999	2000	2001	2002	2003	2004	2005	2006
Student rated self above average or highest 10% as compared with the average person of his/her age in:																					
Academic ability	66.0	64.8	65.4	67.1	64.8	64.2	65.2	65.3	65.8	66.0	67.1	68.1	66.8	67.9	67.4	67.9	69.5	69.7	—	69.4	68.6
Artistic ability	25.3	27.0	26.2	26.1	26.4	26.0	27.1	25.8	27.0	26.9	27.5	27.7	29.1	28.3	29.4	30.6	29.7	29.8	—	29.7	29.2
Athletic ability	—	—	—	—	—	—	—	—	—	—	—	—	42.6	—	—	—	—	—	—	—	—
Competitiveness	—	—	58.4	58.8	58.5	58.5	58.8	59.0	58.4	58.6	57.6	57.9	57.0	57.4	56.2	55.9	—	—	—	—	—
Computer skills	—	—	—	—	—	—	—	—	—	—	—	—	—	31.7	33.6	34.2	37.6	38.8	—	38.7	37.9
Cooperativeness	—	—	—	—	73.1	73.2	72.2	72.8	72.3	73.4	72.2	73.3	72.1	73.2	72.6	72.2	72.2	72.9	—	72.9	73.3
Creativity	—	—	—	—	—	—	—	51.8	51.2	52.9	52.5	53.7	55.3	56.3	56.9	56.7	57.5	57.7	—	57.4	56.6
Drive to achieve	67.4	65.2	68.8	70.5	71.2	72.0	72.3	70.1	70.1	70.7	70.4	71.2	70.8	71.8	70.6	70.9	70.5	71.6	—	72.3	72.6
Emotional health	62.7	60.1	59.6	60.3	60.3	59.7	59.2	57.9	57.1	57.1	56.4	57.7	56.7	56.3	53.8	53.4	53.9	54.5	—	54.3	54.6
Leadership ability	57.8	56.0	56.3	56.7	55.7	55.0	55.4	56.6	56.9	59.0	58.0	59.7	59.9	61.2	60.8	59.9	60.2	60.6	—	61.3	61.0
Mathematical ability	46.3	46.1	45.9	46.0	43.7	43.1	43.8	43.2	44.5	44.7	44.7	45.0	44.6	44.5	44.3	44.2	45.2	45.0	—	44.3	43.7
Physical health	64.3	62.1	61.2	61.5	61.1	60.0	60.1	59.8	56.2	56.0	58.3	58.7	58.9	57.7	56.4	55.2	56.4	56.6	—	55.8	55.7
Popularity	48.6	47.3	46.8	46.5	45.8	44.2	42.7	42.9	39.3	39.7	41.0	42.7	41.1	40.9	40.7	39.0	38.8	38.1	—	—	—
Public speaking ability	—	33.8	33.5	34.2	32.8	33.7	33.0	33.9	33.8	34.1	34.2	35.5	35.9	37.5	37.4	36.5	36.7	36.3	—	36.6	37.0
Self confidence (intellectual)	61.1	54.8	55.5	57.2	55.0	58.5	58.2	59.3	58.1	58.1	59.1	60.3	60.3	61.2	60.3	58.9	60.1	60.1	—	60.1	59.7
Self confidence (social)	51.7	47.0	47.0	47.4	46.9	49.3	49.1	50.0	48.0	49.4	50.4	51.6	52.3	52.8	52.1	50.7	50.3	49.9	—	52.6	52.8
Self understanding	—	—	—	—	—	—	—	—	—	—	58.4	59.0	58.8	58.3	57.1	55.5	55.8	55.6	—	55.7	57.3
Spirituality	—	—	—	—	—	—	—	—	—	—	44.0	45.1	46.2	46.4	44.9	39.3	39.1	38.3	—	37.6	36.7
Understanding of others	—	—	—	—	70.5	69.8	70.0	70.0	71.7	71.9	66.3	66.4	65.9	66.4	65.6	65.6	65.8	65.7	—	66.5	66.8
Writing ability	46.1	44.5	45.1	45.9	44.8	45.9	45.5	45.9	44.2	44.7	46.3	46.7	46.0	46.9	45.9	45.9	46.4	46.6	—	47.3	47.7

COLLEGE CHOICE
ALL FRESHMEN

ITEM	1986	1987	1988	1989	1990	1991	1992	1993	1994	1995	1996	1997	1998	1999	2000	2001	2002	2003	2004	2005	2006
Reasons noted as very important in deciding to go to college																					
A mentor/role model encouraged me to go	—	—	—	—	—	—	13.7	14.1	13.5	14.4	14.2	13.9	15.4	12.8	13.3	13.2	13.9	13.5	—	15.8	17.2
I could not find a job	—	—	—	5.8	5.7	5.5	5.9	7.2	6.0	5.8	5.8	5.2	6.0	4.1	4.9	4.9	5.4	5.7	6.0	6.5	5.6
My parents wanted me to go	—	—	—	33.7	35.2	33.6	33.4	32.9	34.4	33.3	37.4	34.5	38.9	33.3	35.7	33.5	35.4	35.1	41.8	43.7	46.4
There was nothing better to do	—	2.4	2.5	2.5	2.5	2.9	2.7	2.9	3.4	3.4	3.3	3.1	—	3.2	3.4	3.5	4.0	3.9	4.0	4.0	4.1
To be able to get a better job	67.5	68.3	70.3	74.0	75.6	75.6	76.0	80.3	75.6	75.5	75.5	72.6	75.3	71.6	71.6	70.3	71.6	70.1	71.8	72.2	70.4
To be able to make more money	—	—	—	70.3	71.0	71.4	70.3	72.0	70.3	70.5	71.0	69.9	72.1	69.3	70.0	69.8	70.5	69.4	70.1	71.0	69.0
To get training for a specific career	—	—	—	—	—	—	—	—	—	—	—	—	—	71.6	71.8	71.3	71.1	70.0	74.6	69.4	69.2
To gain a general education and appreciation of ideas	63.6	62.5	61.1	64.4	65.1	63.0	64.8	66.8	61.9	65.4	64.6	62.6	64.6	62.8	64.5	65.8	66.0	65.4	64.6	65.4	64.3
To improve my reading and study skills	39.8	39.1	38.4	40.1	43.3	39.0	41.1	41.2	41.4	43.4	43.1	40.4	42.4	39.4	41.1	41.7	41.1	40.6	—	—	—
To learn more about things that interest me	75.1	73.4	74.4	73.5	74.2	74.3	74.7	76.5	75.1	76.0	76.6	76.3	—	74.8	76.6	77.8	77.5	76.9	76.8	77.7	76.8
To make me a more cultured person	35.6	36.6	37.6	38.8	43.5	42.0	42.5	46.0	40.9	43.6	41.2	40.0	—	39.5	40.5	42.0	42.1	40.7	40.5	42.5	41.7
To prepare for graduate or professional school	48.4	48.7	51.3	53.3	55.3	56.8	56.2	61.3	58.0	—	—	—	—	56.2	56.9	57.4	57.8	57.4	56.7	58.1	57.7
Wanted to get away from home	—	—	—	17.4	17.7	18.2	19.1	20.3	20.9	20.6	20.1	20.3	20.3	20.1	21.4	20.9	22.3	21.6	21.5	21.7	21.1

63

COLLEGE CHOICE
ALL FRESHMEN

ITEM	1966	1967	1968	1969	1970	1971	1972	1973	1974	1975	1976	1977	1978	1979	1980	1981	1982	1983	1984	1985
Reasons noted as very important in influencing student's decision to attend this particular college																				
A college rep. recruited me	—	—	—	—	—	—	—	—	—	4.8	4.7	5.4	5.1	5.2	5.8	5.5	5.4	3.4	3.6	4.1
A friend suggested attending	—	—	—	—	—	—	—	—	—	7.2	7.3	8.2	6.6	6.8	6.9	7.1	7.2	6.7	6.7	7.0
I wanted to go to a school about the size of this college	—	—	—	—	—	—	—	—	—	—	—	—	—	—	—	—	—	—	—	—
I wanted to live at home	—	—	—	—	—	8.1	7.2	7.7	7.2	8.1	6.9	8.3	7.2	7.0	7.2	7.1	7.0	—	—	—
I wanted to live near home	—	—	—	—	—	—	—	—	—	—	—	—	—	—	—	—	—	16.6	16.0	14.8
I was admitted through an Early Action or Early Decision program	—	—	—	—	—	—	—	—	—	—	—	—	—	—	—	—	—	—	—	—
I was attracted by the religious affiliation/orientation of the college	—	—	—	—	—	—	—	—	—	—	—	—	—	—	—	—	—	—	—	—
I was offered financial assistance	—	—	—	—	—	—	19.5	18.9	20.5	19.7	16.6	17.9	16.6	17.8	18.4	17.2	19.2	23.7	22.4	23.2
Information from a website	—	—	—	—	—	—	—	—	—	—	—	—	—	—	—	—	—	—	—	—
My guidance counselor advised me	—	—	—	—	—	5.6	5.8	8.1	8.3	7.4	6.5	7.4	6.6	6.8	6.8	6.5	6.6	7.0	6.7	6.4
High school guidance counselor advised me	—	—	—	—	—	—	—	—	—	—	—	—	—	—	—	—	—	—	—	—
Private college counselor advised me	—	—	—	—	—	—	—	—	—	—	—	—	—	—	—	—	—	—	—	—
My relatives wanted me to come here	—	—	—	—	—	7.5	—	—	6.5	—	6.9	6.6	5.8	6.0	6.5	6.5	6.5	6.4	6.4	6.2
My teacher advised me	—	—	—	—	—	—	—	5.1	5.3	4.8	4.1	4.3	3.9	4.0	4.2	3.9	3.9	3.9	3.9	4.0
Not accepted anywhere else	—	—	—	—	—	2.5	2.7	—	—	—	—	2.5	2.1	2.3	2.4	2.4	2.3	—	—	—
Rankings in national magazines	—	—	—	—	—	—	—	—	—	—	—	—	—	—	—	—	—	—	4.4	4.7
The athletic dept. recruited me	—	—	—	—	—	—	—	—	—	—	—	—	—	—	—	—	—	4.9	4.8	5.1
This college's graduates gain admission to top graduate/professional schools	—	—	—	—	—	—	—	—	—	—	—	—	—	—	—	—	—	28.3	27.8	28.8
This college's graduates get good jobs	—	—	—	—	—	—	—	—	—	—	—	—	—	—	—	—	—	48.0	47.8	48.1
This college has a good reputation for its social activities	—	—	—	—	—	—	—	—	—	—	—	—	—	—	—	—	—	23.6	25.1	25.1
This college has low tuition	—	—	—	—	—	15.1	15.5	19.8	21.3	18.6	12.5	15.9	14.3	13.6	13.6	14.5	16.6	18.6	19.0	18.7
The cost of attending this college	—	—	—	—	—	—	—	—	—	—	—	—	—	—	—	—	—	—	—	—
This college has a very good academic reputation	—	—	—	—	—	—	57.7	59.2	59.7	56.4	52.4	55.0	57.8	56.0	57.0	57.6	58.7	58.4	60.6	61.7
This college offers special educational programs	—	—	—	—	—	32.2	27.3	29.6	30.7	28.5	26.2	30.0	26.8	28.0	28.3	27.3	26.2	22.4	22.0	21.7
Is this college your:																				
First choice?	—	—	—	—	—	—	—	—	77.2	79.7	77.3	75.6	76.4	75.3	75.3	74.4	73.5	73.7	72.7	72.4
Second choice?	—	—	—	—	—	—	—	—	18.1	16.5	17.5	18.6	18.5	19.0	19.0	19.7	20.3	20.2	21.0	20.9
Less than second choice?	—	—	—	—	—	—	—	—	4.7	3.8	5.2	5.7	5.2	5.7	5.7	5.9	6.2	—	—	—
Third choice?	—	—	—	—	—	—	—	—	—	—	—	—	—	—	—	—	—	4.3	4.4	4.5
Less than third choice?	—	—	—	—	—	—	—	—	—	—	—	—	—	—	—	—	—	1.8	1.8	2.2
How many miles is this college from your permanent home? [*]																				
10 or less	—	—	—	15.1	15.3	16.3	14.9	14.4	—	14.9	15.8	17.5	16.0	15.5	15.9	14.7	14.6	14.7	14.1	12.7
11 to 50	—	—	—	20.8	20.4	21.5	19.4	19.3	—	20.5	22.0	22.0	22.0	20.2	21.7	20.0	20.5	23.7	24.5	22.6
51 to 100	—	—	—	15.8	16.1	15.7	17.1	16.8	—	16.1	16.5	17.0	16.5	17.8	17.4	18.3	18.5	18.4	17.3	18.8
101 to 500	—	—	—	34.9	36.3	35.5	36.6	37.5	—	36.4	34.0	32.8	33.6	35.1	33.2	35.5	34.6	31.4	32.2	33.4
More than 500	—	—	—	13.2	11.9	10.9	12.0	11.9	—	12.2	11.6	10.6	11.9	11.4	11.8	11.4	11.8	11.7	11.9	12.5

COLLEGE CHOICE
ALL FRESHMEN

ITEM	1986	1987	1988	1989	1990	1991	1992	1993	1994	1995	1996	1997	1998	1999	2000	2001	2002	2003	2004	2005	2006
Reasons noted as very important in influencing student's decision to attend this particular college																					
A college rep. recruited me	4.2	4.0	4.0	4.0	4.3	4.7	4.7	4.8	4.7	4.7	4.8	4.7	—	—	—	—	—	—	—	—	—
A friend suggested attending	8.2	7.9	8.0	7.8	8.5	8.7	8.2	9.2	8.9	8.3	8.7	8.8	—	—	—	—	—	—	—	—	—
I wanted to go to a school about the size of this college	—	—	—	35.3	37.5	39.2	40.0	42.8	39.8	37.8	38.5	39.0	36.5	36.3	35.0	35.2	33.7	32.9	35.8	38.6	38.9
I wanted to live at home	15.8	14.5	15.6	16.0	16.5	16.6	16.5	16.0	16.7	16.7	17.4	17.2	16.7	16.0	16.9	16.9	17.6	16.8	17.0	18.7	18.3
I wanted to live near home	—	—	—	—	—	—	—	—	—	—	—	—	—	6.9	7.1	7.7	8.5	8.8	8.6	10.1	10.9
I was admitted through an Early Action or Early Decision program	—	—	—	—	—	—	—	—	—	—	—	—	—	—	—	—	—	—	—	—	—
I was attracted by the religious affiliation/orientation of the college	—	—	—	5.3	6.0	6.0	6.3	6.4	6.6	6.2	7.4	7.3	7.6	7.2	7.3	6.4	5.9	5.6	6.7	6.9	7.3
I was offered financial assistance	23.6	22.6	23.5	25.1	26.4	30.2	31.0	33.4	31.7	33.5	35.9	35.9	34.4	33.1	32.0	33.2	34.1	33.6	33.7	35.4	34.3
Information from a website	—	—	—	—	—	—	—	—	—	—	—	—	—	—	6.8	8.5	11.1	12.0	13.5	15.9	17.0
My guidance counselor advised me	7.3	6.2	7.0	6.0	6.6	6.9	6.4	6.6	6.6	6.4	6.3	6.6	5.9	5.6	6.1	6.4	6.5	6.4	—	—	—
High school guidance counselor advised me	—	—	—	—	—	—	—	—	—	—	—	—	—	—	—	—	—	—	7.4	8.0	8.6
Private college counselor advised me	—	—	—	—	—	—	—	1.7	2.2	2.1	2.1	1.7	1.9	2.0	2.1	2.1	2.1	2.2	2.4	2.7	2.9
My relatives wanted me to come here	8.0	7.2	6.7	8.2	8.5	8.2	8.0	8.5	8.5	8.1	8.6	8.0	7.7	7.3	7.8	7.5	9.0	8.8	9.4	10.6	11.6
My teacher advised me	4.2	3.7	3.9	3.3	3.8	3.8	3.8	4.0	3.8	3.7	3.8	3.4	3.4	3.4	3.6	3.9	4.4	4.3	4.8	5.4	6.0
Not accepted anywhere else	—	—	—	—	—	1.8	2.2	1.9	2.0	2.1	2.3	2.2	2.7	2.7	3.2	3.3	—	—	—	—	—
Not offered aid by first choice	5.1	4.7	5.0	5.6	5.4	—	—	—	—	—	—	—	—	—	—	—	—	5.9	6.1	6.6	6.5
Rankings in national magazines	—	—	—	—	—	—	—	—	—	10.5	11.4	11.8	9.9	9.7	9.8	11.1	13.3	13.0	14.7	16.6	16.4
The athletic dept. recruited me	5.4	5.3	5.2	5.3	5.4	6.1	6.4	6.3	6.4	6.8	6.8	6.9	—	—	—	—	6.7	—	—	—	8.0
This college's graduates gain admission to top graduate/professional schools	27.5	29.6	—	25.6	26.2	26.3	27.1	28.8	30.3	29.7	33.1	33.7	31.0	29.9	29.7	30.3	—	—	28.9	31.5	30.2
This college's graduates get good jobs	47.0	48.2	33.5	44.8	45.0	45.8	44.8	49.2	48.5	48.6	53.3	54.7	51.8	51.0	50.9	51.0	—	—	49.1	51.2	49.3
This college has a good reputation for its social activities	30.4	29.4	24.5	24.6	24.7	25.5	27.0	29.3	25.8	26.0	27.3	29.0	27.6	26.9	27.9	27.9	28.7	27.8	28.3	31.2	32.2
This college has low tuition	20.3	18.2	18.9	20.6	22.5	24.2	24.4	26.7	24.7	24.1	25.1	25.7	22.7	21.2	20.3	20.8	21.7	20.6	—	—	—
The cost of attending this college	—	—	—	—	—	—	—	—	—	—	—	—	—	—	—	—	—	—	31.0	32.4	32.2
This college has a very good academic reputation	62.8	60.4	59.6	57.1	57.3	58.5	58.5	60.0	58.0	57.2	59.2	60.2	56.2	55.1	55.2	56.2	55.4	55.1	56.7	57.9	57.4
This college offers special educational programs	22.7	21.8	22.4	20.2	22.0	22.1	23.0	24.0	22.5	21.6	22.9	22.0	20.6	21.0	21.2	21.6	21.1	21.2	—	—	—
Is this college your:																					
First choice?	70.7	68.8	66.7	69.2	71.3	72.2	72.1	72.1	73.4	72.1	71.5	71.0	71.5	72.0	70.6	69.7	69.2	68.7	69.5	69.8	67.3
Second choice?	22.0	23.2	24.2	23.0	21.8	21.1	21.2	20.9	19.9	20.4	20.8	20.8	20.5	20.0	20.8	21.6	21.4	21.9	21.4	21.2	22.8
Less than second choice?	—	—	—	—	—	—	—	—	—	—	—	—	—	—	—	—	—	—	—	—	—
Third choice?	5.0	5.5	6.2	5.3	4.8	4.5	4.6	4.9	4.5	5.0	5.0	5.3	5.2	5.2	5.5	5.6	5.9	5.9	5.8	5.8	6.2
Less than third choice	2.3	2.6	2.9	2.5	2.1	2.2	2.0	2.2	2.2	2.5	2.7	2.8	2.7	2.8	3.1	3.1	3.5	3.5	3.3	3.3	3.7
How many miles is this college from your permanent home? [*]																					
10 or less	11.6	10.3	10.2	10.8	10.1	10.6	9.9	10.1	10.2	10.8	10.4	10.3	10.3	10.3	11.4	11.4	11.6	11.0	10.6	10.9	10.7
11 to 50	22.6	21.6	21.8	21.2	23.0	22.1	21.0	20.7	21.6	21.9	21.6	22.3	22.8	22.5	24.1	25.3	23.8	25.6	24.4	26.9	24.6
51 to 100	17.9	19.7	17.0	16.9	18.5	17.0	16.7	17.4	17.3	16.7	17.1	17.4	18.3	17.3	16.9	16.8	17.3	16.9	17.6	18.1	18.8
101 to 500	33.5	34.7	36.0	36.9	35.0	36.8	38.9	38.4	37.4	37.5	37.5	36.2	36.9	37.3	35.0	34.1	34.8	34.1	34.9	31.5	32.5
More than 500	14.4	13.8	15.0	14.2	13.4	13.4	13.4	13.3	13.5	13.1	13.3	13.9	11.7	12.5	12.6	12.4	12.4	12.4	12.6	12.6	13.5

COLLEGE CHOICE
ALL FRESHMEN

ITEM	1966	1967	1968	1969	1970	1971	1972	1973	1974	1975	1976	1977	1978	1979	1980	1981	1982	1983	1984	1985
To how many colleges other than this one did you apply for admission this year?																				
None	—	43.1	45.1	43.7	—	—	38.2	39.6	—	40.5	36.9	35.2	33.9	33.2	33.6	32.2	31.3	30.0	28.9	27.7
One	—	20.8	21.1	21.7	—	—	20.0	20.4	—	21.7	19.5	18.9	18.1	17.7	17.1	18.1	17.1	17.9	17.1	19.4
Two	—	16.3	15.6	16.1	—	—	17.3	16.7	—	15.5	16.5	17.9	18.2	18.0	17.8	18.4	18.0	18.7	18.6	17.5
Three	—	10.3	9.7	9.5	—	—	11.2	10.6	—	10.3	12.7	13.3	14.1	14.7	14.6	14.5	15.0	15.2	15.8	15.1
Four	—	5.1	4.6	4.8	—	—	6.2	6.1	—	5.7	6.6	6.7	7.2	7.3	7.6	7.6	8.2	8.2	8.7	8.5
Five	—	2.6	2.3	2.4	—	—	3.7	3.4	—	3.1	3.8	4.0	4.3	4.5	4.7	4.3	4.9	4.8	5.1	5.4
Six or more	—	1.8	1.7	1.8	—	—	3.4	3.1	—	3.2	4.0	4.0	4.3	4.5	4.6	4.8	5.5	5.3	5.7	6.4
Six	—	—	—	—	—	—	—	—	—	—	—	—	—	—	—	—	—	—	—	—
Seven to ten	—	—	—	—	—	—	—	—	—	—	—	—	—	—	—	—	—	—	—	—
Eleven or more	—	—	—	—	—	—	—	—	—	—	—	—	—	—	—	—	—	—	—	—
How many other acceptances did you receive this year?																				
None	—	37.0	38.5	—	—	—	—	—	—	20.3	19.0	18.4	15.9	16.1	15.4	15.0	—	12.3	11.8	11.8
One	—	29.8	29.9	—	—	—	—	—	—	34.4	31.3	31.5	30.7	30.1	29.5	30.3	—	29.4	28.7	28.0
Two	—	20.0	19.1	—	—	—	—	—	—	23.0	23.3	24.6	24.8	24.9	25.1	25.6	—	25.8	25.6	25.4
Three	—	8.8	8.3	—	—	—	—	—	—	12.3	14.9	14.6	16.1	16.4	16.8	16.2	—	17.7	18.4	18.4
Four	—	2.9	2.6	—	—	—	—	—	—	5.7	6.3	6.1	7.0	6.9	7.4	7.2	—	8.1	8.4	8.8
Five	—	1.0	0.9	—	—	—	—	—	—	2.2	2.7	2.5	3.1	3.0	3.0	2.9	—	3.4	3.8	4.0
Six or more	—	0.6	0.6	—	—	—	—	—	—	2.1	2.5	2.2	2.6	2.6	2.7	2.7	—	3.3	3.4	3.6
Six	—	—	—	—	—	—	—	—	—	—	—	—	—	—	—	—	—	—	—	—
Seven to ten	—	—	—	—	—	—	—	—	—	—	—	—	—	—	—	—	—	—	—	—
Eleven or more	—	—	—	—	—	—	—	—	—	—	—	—	—	—	—	—	—	—	—	—
Prior to this term, have you ever taken courses for credit at this institution?																				
No	—	—	—	—	—	—	97.5	98.0	98.0	97.0	97.3	97.4	97.4	97.4	97.2	97.6	97.4	97.4	97.4	97.3
Yes	—	—	—	—	—	—	2.5	2.0	2.0	2.5	2.7	2.6	2.6	2.6	2.8	2.4	2.6	2.6	2.6	2.7

PLANS, GOALS, AND EXPECTATIONS
ALL FRESHMEN

ITEM	1966	1967	1968	1969	1970	1971	1972	1973	1974	1975	1976	1977	1978	1979	1980	1981	1982	1983	1984	1985
What is the highest academic degree you intend to obtain anywhere?																				
None	3.8	2.2	2.5	0.7	0.8	—	1.5	—	2.1	2.1	1.9	1.6	1.4	1.2	1.5	1.6	1.4	1.5	1.2	1.5
Vocational certificate	—	—	—	—	—	—	—	—	—	—	—	—	—	—	—	—	—	—	0.4	0.4
Associate (A.A.) or equivalent	1.7	1.3	1.7	1.3	1.6	—	1.5	—	1.7	1.5	1.5	2.0	1.6	2.2	1.7	1.7	1.7	1.1	1.2	0.8
Bachelor's (B.A., B.S., etc.)	39.0	37.1	37.7	38.0	38.6	—	38.1	—	37.2	34.7	34.2	33.9	35.1	34.1	35.3	36.0	35.6	33.8	34.5	34.0
Master's degree (M.A., M.S., etc.)	35.0	37.3	36.5	38.1	35.3	—	31.3	—	30.4	31.7	32.3	33.5	33.7	35.3	33.9	35.2	34.8	35.1	35.4	35.6
Ph.D. or Ed.D.	11.4	13.0	13.1	13.3	12.2	—	11.2	—	11.1	11.4	11.4	11.7	11.4	10.8	10.3	10.2	10.5	11.1	11.7	12.3
M.D., D.D.S., D.V.M. or D.O.	5.7	5.8	5.1	5.3	5.6	—	8.9	—	9.6	9.3	9.4	8.1	8.5	8.1	8.4	7.7	8.0	8.4	8.0	8.6
LL.B. or J.D. (law)	1.8	1.8	1.7	2.0	4.4	—	5.7	—	5.6	6.2	6.4	6.2	6.0	5.8	5.8	5.3	5.8	5.4	5.2	4.9
B.D. or M.Div. (divinity)	0.2	0.3	0.2	0.3	0.4	—	0.4	—	0.4	0.6	0.6	0.6	0.4	0.6	0.6	0.5	0.5	0.6	0.5	0.4
Other	1.4	1.1	1.3	1.1	1.0	—	1.5	—	1.8	2.3	2.3	2.3	1.8	1.9	2.4	1.8	1.7	2.4	1.8	1.4

COLLEGE CHOICE
ALL FRESHMEN

ITEM	1986	1987	1988	1989	1990	1991	1992	1993	1994	1995	1996	1997	1998	1999	2000	2001	2002	2003	2004	2005	2006
To how many colleges other than this one did you apply for admission this year?																					
None	27.7	26.4	24.5	24.7	23.7	25.4	22.8	21.4	23.6	24.3	23.8	24.4	22.8	22.1	20.4	19.9	20.2	18.3	19.3	17.5	17.7
One	16.7	15.7	14.7	14.7	15.4	15.0	15.0	15.3	14.6	14.4	14.2	15.0	14.2	13.8	13.0	12.8	13.0	12.2	12.6	12.0	10.9
Two	17.2	17.1	17.4	17.2	17.9	17.7	17.9	18.0	17.6	16.9	16.9	16.4	16.6	16.4	16.1	16.1	15.9	15.4	15.4	15.1	14.8
Three	15.9	16.3	16.8	16.4	16.6	16.6	17.4	17.3	16.6	16.0	16.0	16.0	16.9	16.9	17.4	17.1	16.8	16.7	16.5	16.8	16.8
Four	9.4	10.2	10.6	10.5	10.5	10.3	10.9	11.2	11.0	10.7	11.0	10.4	11.3	11.6	12.1	12.3	12.2	12.7	12.0	12.5	12.7
Five	6.1	6.4	7.0	7.2	7.0	6.8	7.1	7.5	7.1	7.3	7.5	6.9	7.1	7.6	7.9	8.3	8.1	8.8	8.2	8.7	9.2
Six or more	7.0	7.9	9.0	9.2	8.8	8.3	8.9	9.3	9.6	10.4	10.6	—	—	—	—	—	—	—	—	—	—
Six	—	—	—	—	—	—	—	—	—	—	—	4.5	4.5	4.7	5.3	5.3	5.4	6.0	5.8	6.2	6.3
Seven to ten	—	—	—	—	—	—	—	—	—	—	—	5.3	5.5	5.9	6.5	6.9	6.9	8.1	8.4	9.1	9.3
Eleven or more	—	—	—	—	—	—	—	—	—	—	—	1.0	1.0	1.0	1.3	1.4	1.4	1.8	1.9	2.1	2.2
How many other acceptances did you receive this year?																					
None	12.7	11.8	10.5	9.8	—	—	—	—	—	7.6	7.4	8.4	8.3	—	—	—	—	—	—	—	—
One	27.0	27.0	26.3	25.4	—	—	—	—	—	23.1	22.7	23.8	22.9	—	—	—	—	—	—	—	—
Two	24.9	24.7	25.3	24.9	—	—	—	—	—	23.8	24.0	23.2	23.3	—	—	—	—	—	—	—	—
Three	18.2	18.9	19.1	19.2	—	—	—	—	—	19.6	19.9	19.4	20.0	—	—	—	—	—	—	—	—
Four	9.2	9.4	9.9	10.5	—	—	—	—	—	11.9	12.0	11.4	11.9	—	—	—	—	—	—	—	—
Five	4.2	4.2	4.5	5.1	—	—	—	—	—	6.4	6.6	6.6	6.3	—	—	—	—	—	—	—	—
Six or more	3.9	3.9	4.3	5.1	—	—	—	—	—	7.5	7.3	—	—	—	—	—	—	—	—	—	—
Six	—	—	—	—	—	—	—	—	—	—	—	3.2	3.2	—	—	—	—	—	—	—	—
Seven to ten	—	—	—	—	—	—	—	—	—	—	—	3.6	3.5	—	—	—	—	—	—	—	—
Eleven or more	—	—	—	—	—	—	—	—	—	—	—	0.6	0.6	—	—	—	—	—	—	—	—
Prior to this term, have you ever taken courses for credit at this institution?																					
No	97.2	96.8	96.9	96.7	96.9	96.7	96.9	96.8	96.5	96.6	96.1	96.4	95.6	96.0	96.0	95.9	96.1	96.6	96.3	96.7	96.5
Yes	2.8	3.2	3.1	3.3	3.1	3.3	3.1	3.2	3.5	3.4	3.9	3.6	4.4	4.0	4.0	4.1	3.9	3.4	3.7	3.3	3.5

PLANS, GOALS, AND EXPECTATIONS
ALL FRESHMEN

ITEM	1986	1987	1988	1989	1990	1991	1992	1993	1994	1995	1996	1997	1998	1999	2000	2001	2002	2003	2004	2005	2006
What is the highest academic degree you intend to obtain anywhere?																					
None	1.5	1.3	1.3	0.7	1.1	0.9	2.1	0.5	0.6	0.6	0.6	0.5	0.6	0.5	—	0.6	0.8	0.8	1.1	0.8	0.9
Vocational certificate	0.2	0.2	0.2	0.1	0.2	0.2	0.2	0.1	0.1	0.1	0.2	0.1	0.2	0.1	—	0.1	0.1	0.1	0.1	0.1	0.1
Associate (A.A.) or equivalent	0.8	0.7	1.0	0.7	0.7	0.8	0.6	0.5	0.5	0.5	0.6	0.5	0.6	0.5	—	0.4	0.5	0.4	0.6	0.5	0.5
Bachelor's (B.A., B.S., etc.)	33.2	31.8	28.2	27.8	27.0	25.4	29.0	24.2	23.9	24.5	23.1	22.9	24.3	24.0	—	23.3	23.5	24.2	23.7	23.7	23.5
Master's degree (M.A., M.S., etc.)	38.0	39.1	39.8	40.8	40.2	39.9	39.9	40.4	39.8	40.1	40.8	41.4	42.7	42.3	—	43.1	42.4	41.3	41.0	41.7	42.0
Ph.D. or Ed.D.	12.5	13.1	14.5	14.7	15.0	16.5	13.5	17.1	17.5	17.1	17.8	18.2	16.8	16.8	—	17.3	17.4	17.5	17.4	17.0	16.9
M.D., D.D.S., D.V.M. or D.O.	7.3	6.9	7.1	7.2	7.8	8.9	8.7	10.5	10.8	11.0	10.7	10.5	9.2	9.2	—	8.8	8.8	9.0	9.3	9.3	9.2
LL.B. or J.D. (law)	4.7	5.4	6.1	6.2	6.1	5.7	4.5	5.1	5.2	4.4	4.3	4.3	4.0	4.4	—	4.7	4.9	5.0	4.9	5.1	4.7
B.D. or M.Div. (divinity)	0.3	0.3	0.4	0.3	0.4	0.4	0.2	0.3	0.4	0.4	0.4	0.3	0.4	0.5	—	0.3	0.3	0.3	0.3	0.3	0.4
Other	1.4	1.3	1.4	1.4	1.4	1.4	1.2	1.1	1.3	1.3	1.5	1.3	1.4	1.7	—	1.2	1.2	1.4	1.6	1.5	1.7

PLANS, GOALS, AND EXPECTATIONS
ALL FRESHMEN

ITEM	1966	1967	1968	1969	1970	1971	1972	1973	1974	1975	1976	1977	1978	1979	1980	1981	1982	1983	1984	1985
What is the highest academic degree you intend to obtain at this institution?																				
None	—	—	—	—	—	—	4.8	4.2	5.1	5.1	4.9	4.2	3.7	3.2	3.4	3.4	2.9	2.7	2.8	2.5
Vocational certificate	—	—	—	—	—	—	—	—	—	—	—	—	—	—	—	—	—	0.5	0.4	0.4
Associate (A.A.) or equivalent	—	—	—	—	—	—	2.7	2.7	3.8	3.4	3.2	4.1	3.3	4.8	3.8	4.1	3.4	3.0	3.2	2.1
Bachelor's (B.A., B.S., etc.)	—	—	—	—	—	—	73.6	73.1	70.9	70.0	70.9	69.6	71.1	69.6	70.1	70.5	70.3	70.5	71.1	71.6
Master's degree (M.A., M.S., etc.)	—	—	—	—	—	—	12.4	12.9	13.1	13.5	13.3	14.3	14.6	15.1	14.6	15.1	15.8	14.8	15.3	16.3
Ph.D. or Ed.D.	—	—	—	—	—	—	1.9	2.1	2.0	2.1	2.2	2.1	2.1	2.1	2.0	2.0	2.2	2.4	2.3	2.4
M.D., D.D.S., D.V.M. or D.O.	—	—	—	—	—	—	1.9	2.3	2.3	2.2	2.2	2.1	2.2	2.0	2.4	1.9	2.3	2.4	2.0	2.3
LL.B. or J.D. (law)	—	—	—	—	—	—	1.2	1.4	1.2	1.4	1.3	1.5	1.4	1.3	1.4	1.3	1.5	1.4	1.2	1.0
B.D. or M.Div. (divinity)	—	—	—	—	—	—	0.1	0.1	0.2	0.3	0.5	0.4	0.3	0.3	0.4	0.3	0.3	0.6	0.3	0.2
Other	—	—	—	—	—	—	1.3	1.1	1.5	1.9	1.8	1.9	1.4	1.5	1.9	1.4	1.3	1.9	1.3	1.2
Your probable career/occupation [2,3]																				
Artist	6.5	6.2	6.1	6.0	6.4	6.7	6.8	—	—	—	7.8	7.9	7.3	7.9	7.7	7.7	7.5	7.2	6.8	7.2
Business	10.5	9.8	9.5	9.3	9.8	8.7	9.0	—	—	—	14.6	16.6	18.3	18.7	19.0	19.5	19.5	20.1	22.3	23.3
Clerical	—	—	0.7	0.9	—	1.4	1.2	—	—	—	0.9	1.0	0.9	1.1	0.8	0.9	0.8	0.7	0.7	0.8
Clergy	1.0	1.2	1.3	1.3	0.9	0.8	0.8	—	—	—	0.8	0.6	0.5	0.5	0.5	0.5	0.4	0.4	0.3	0.4
College teacher	2.0	1.4	1.3	1.3	1.2	0.9	0.8	—	—	—	0.5	0.4	0.4	0.3	0.3	0.3	0.3	0.3	0.3	0.4
Doctor (MD or DDS)	5.6	5.3	4.6	4.5	5.0	5.9	7.1	—	—	—	7.0	5.9	6.3	6.0	6.2	5.8	6.0	6.5	6.2	6.7
Education (secondary)	15.2	15.9	16.1	15.0	12.9	10.2	7.8	—	—	—	4.7	3.9	3.4	3.4	2.8	2.6	2.2	2.5	2.7	3.1
Education (elementary)	8.1	9.0	9.7	9.9	8.6	7.7	6.5	—	—	—	5.0	4.7	4.1	4.4	4.1	4.0	3.3	3.4	3.4	3.7
Engineer	8.6	8.3	8.5	8.3	8.7	5.3	5.6	—	—	—	7.5	8.3	8.8	8.9	10.1	10.0	11.1	10.3	10.0	10.1
Farmer or forester	1.6	1.3	1.3	1.4	1.4	2.0	2.2	—	—	—	2.2	2.2	1.5	1.7	1.4	1.4	1.1	0.9	0.9	0.8
Health professional	4.7	4.2	4.1	4.1	4.6	6.1	7.3	—	—	—	7.8	7.2	6.5	6.2	5.9	5.6	5.2	5.6	5.6	4.9
Homemaker	—	—	—	—	—	0.5	0.4	—	—	—	0.2	0.2	0.1	0.2	0.1	0.2	0.1	0.1	0.1	0.1
Lawyer	4.4	4.3	4.0	4.7	4.8	5.5	6.1	—	—	—	5.9	6.0	5.9	5.6	5.6	5.2	5.8	5.2	5.2	5.1
Military	—	—	—	—	—	1.9	2.0	—	—	—	1.3	1.4	1.6	1.5	1.4	1.5	1.2	1.6	1.6	1.4
Nurse	2.1	2.0	2.0	2.2	2.7	3.2	3.4	—	—	—	4.2	3.6	3.6	3.4	3.8	3.6	3.7	4.0	3.6	2.7
Research scientist	4.1	3.7	3.6	3.2	3.4	3.3	3.0	—	—	—	3.1	2.8	2.7	2.2	2.0	1.9	1.7	1.8	1.8	1.9
Social worker	—	—	—	—	—	3.4	2.9	—	—	—	2.7	2.5	2.3	2.2	1.9	1.5	1.1	1.2	1.2	1.1
Skilled worker	—	—	—	—	—	—	0.5	—	—	—	0.4	1.0	0.5	0.6	0.7	0.6	0.4	0.3	0.3	0.3
Other career	21.3	16.9	17.1	17.4	17.3	11.8	11.6	—	—	—	12.3	12.9	13.6	14.2	14.6	15.9	17.5	16.5	15.1	14.1
Undecided	4.2	10.5	11.6	12.0	12.2	14.5	15.2	—	—	—	11.1	10.8	11.7	11.2	11.3	11.5	11.0	11.2	11.9	12.0

PLANS, GOALS, AND EXPECTATIONS
ALL FRESHMEN

ITEM	1986	1987	1988	1989	1990	1991	1992	1993	1994	1995	1996	1997	1998	1999	2000	2001	2002	2003	2004	2005	2006
What is the highest academic degree you intend to obtain at this institution?																					
None	2.5	2.2	2.4	2.5	2.4	2.3	—	1.9	1.9	1.8	1.6	1.5	1.5	1.4	—	1.4	1.7	1.4	1.7	1.3	1.5
Vocational certificate	0.3	0.3	0.3	0.3	0.3	0.3	—	0.2	0.2	0.2	0.2	0.2	0.3	0.2	—	0.2	0.2	0.4	0.2	0.2	0.2
Associate (A.A.) or equivalent	2.0	2.0	2.7	2.3	2.2	2.4	—	1.9	1.8	1.8	1.6	1.9	1.8	1.8	—	1.8	1.7	1.5	1.8	1.7	1.6
Bachelor's (B.A., B.S., etc.)	72.9	72.1	69.2	71.3	70.0	69.1	—	69.3	68.3	69.2	68.1	68.5	67.1	71.0	—	69.1	69.6	70.8	69.3	69.7	67.3
Master's degree (M.A., M.S., etc.)	16.2	17.1	18.4	17.1	18.2	18.8	—	19.4	19.9	19.4	20.4	20.1	21.8	19.0	—	20.8	20.2	18.8	19.5	19.8	20.9
Ph.D. or Ed.D.	2.2	2.3	2.5	2.5	2.6	2.7	—	3.0	3.3	3.1	3.4	3.3	3.2	2.4	—	3.2	3.1	3.2	3.5	3.4	3.8
M.D., D.D.S., D.V.M. or D.O.	1.7	1.7	1.8	1.4	1.6	1.8	—	2.2	2.1	2.3	2.4	2.4	2.1	1.6	—	1.7	1.6	1.7	1.7	1.9	2.2
LL.B. or J.D. (law)	0.9	1.1	1.3	1.2	1.1	1.1	—	1.0	1.1	0.8	0.8	0.8	0.7	0.8	—	0.7	0.8	0.8	0.7	0.8	0.9
B.D. or M.Div. (divinity)	0.2	0.2	0.3	0.2	0.3	0.2	—	0.2	0.2	0.2	0.2	0.2	0.2	0.3	—	0.2	0.1	0.2	0.2	0.2	0.2
Other	1.1	1.0	1.2	1.2	1.3	1.2	—	1.0	1.2	1.2	1.3	1.1	1.3	1.5	—	1.0	0.9	1.2	1.4	1.2	1.5
Your probable career/occupation [2,3]																					
Artist	7.9	8.4	7.9	7.3	7.0	6.8	7.3	6.9	7.1	7.5	7.0	7.3	8.1	7.9	8.8	8.4	8.5	8.3	7.8	8.5	8.3
Business	23.9	24.2	23.5	21.8	19.2	16.4	14.6	13.9	14.2	14.6	14.3	14.6	15.0	15.0	15.2	14.4	13.8	13.6	13.9	15.0	15.6
Clerical	0.5	0.5	0.5	0.5	0.6	0.5	0.5	0.5	0.5	0.5	0.5	0.5	0.5	0.6	0.7	0.7	0.6	0.6	0.5	0.6	0.7
Clergy	0.4	0.3	0.3	0.3	0.3	0.4	0.4	0.3	0.4	0.4	0.4	0.5	0.5	0.5	0.5	0.4	0.5	0.4	0.4	0.4	0.4
College teacher	0.4	0.4	0.5	0.5	0.5	0.6	0.6	0.6	0.6	0.6	0.6	0.6	0.6	0.5	0.5	0.5	0.5	0.5	0.5	0.5	0.5
Doctor (MD or DDS)	5.7	5.3	5.5	5.6	5.8	6.7	7.5	7.8	8.1	8.3	7.9	8.2	7.0	7.2	6.7	6.7	7.0	7.0	7.3	7.1	7.2
Education (secondary)	3.7	3.8	3.7	3.9	4.4	4.6	4.5	4.4	4.5	4.4	4.5	4.6	4.7	4.5	4.9	4.6	5.0	4.8	4.9	5.1	5.1
Education (elementary)	4.5	4.9	4.9	4.8	5.6	5.6	5.3	5.4	5.5	5.5	5.6	5.7	6.2	6.3	6.3	5.5	5.7	5.3	5.1	5.1	4.8
Engineer	9.0	8.5	8.0	8.7	8.7	9.5	8.9	8.9	7.7	7.2	8.3	8.4	7.1	7.6	7.3	7.3	7.1	6.9	7.5	6.6	6.3
Farmer or forester	0.6	0.6	0.6	0.8	0.8	0.8	0.9	1.1	1.1	1.0	0.9	0.8	0.9	0.7	0.6	0.5	0.5	0.5	0.5	0.5	0.5
Health professional	4.9	4.9	5.2	5.2	5.3	6.3	7.4	8.3	8.2	8.4	7.8	7.7	7.4	6.2	5.4	5.2	5.7	6.3	7.5	7.1	7.0
Homemaker	0.1	0.1	0.1	0.1	0.1	0.1	0.1	0.1	0.1	0.1	0.1	0.1	0.1	0.1	0.1	0.1	0.1	0.1	0.1	0.1	0.1
Lawyer	5.0	5.6	6.5	6.5	6.4	5.9	5.4	5.0	5.2	4.1	3.8	3.8	3.7	4.1	4.1	4.0	4.3	4.3	4.1	4.1	3.9
Military	1.8	1.4	1.2	1.1	1.2	1.2	0.7	0.6	0.8	0.7	1.2	0.9	0.7	0.8	0.8	1.0	1.1	1.3	1.0	0.9	1.2
Nurse	2.0	1.7	1.7	1.7	2.3	3.1	3.4	3.4	3.1	2.7	2.4	2.2	2.2	2.2	2.1	2.4	2.7	3.5	3.9	3.9	4.1
Research scientist	1.8	1.7	1.8	2.0	1.9	2.0	2.2	2.3	2.2	2.4	2.2	2.3	2.0	2.1	1.8	1.8	1.8	1.7	1.9	1.8	1.8
Social worker	1.1	1.1	1.3	1.1	1.0	1.1	1.1	1.2	1.3	1.3	1.2	1.2	1.1	1.1	1.1	1.0	0.9	0.8	0.9	0.9	1.0
Skilled worker	0.2	0.3	0.5	0.3	0.4	0.4	0.4	0.4	0.3	0.4	0.4	0.4	0.4	0.4	0.4	0.3	0.3	0.3	0.3	0.3	0.3
Other career	13.7	13.7	14.3	15.2	16.1	15.8	16.0	16.4	16.2	17.3	18.0	17.9	19.1	19.6	19.7	20.2	19.6	19.4	17.8	17.4	17.1
Undecided	12.7	12.7	12.0	12.6	12.4	12.4	12.9	12.5	12.9	12.7	12.7	12.2	12.6	12.5	13.0	14.8	14.7	14.5	14.1	14.1	14.0

PLANS, GOALS, AND EXPECTATIONS
ALL FRESHMEN

ITEM	1966	1967	1968	1969	1970	1971	1972	1973	1974	1975	1976	1977	1978	1979	1980	1981	1982	1983	1984	1985
Your probable major field [2]																				
Agriculture	1.7	1.5	1.6	1.4	1.4	1.9	2.1	2.0	2.6	2.6	2.4	2.2	1.6	1.8	1.5	1.6	1.3	1.0	1.1	1.0
Biological Science	4.0	4.3	4.3	3.9	4.1	5.0	5.4	8.9	8.3	8.0	8.0	5.6	5.6	4.8	4.4	4.4	4.3	4.7	4.8	4.6
Business	11.4	11.6	11.5	11.0	11.1	10.7	10.8	13.4	14.0	14.8	16.5	18.6	20.5	21.2	21.0	21.9	21.9	22.2	24.7	24.6
Education	10.9	11.1	12.1	11.9	12.6	9.8	8.5	13.2	11.5	11.3	10.7	9.9	8.8	9.3	8.4	7.0	6.5	6.5	6.5	6.8
Engineering	9.3	8.9	9.8	9.5	9.1	7.5	6.5	5.8	7.7	8.5	8.4	9.4	10.2	10.3	11.3	11.0	11.9	11.5	11.0	11.0
English	5.0	4.8	4.4	4.4	3.6	2.8	2.1	2.0	1.6	1.4	1.4	1.3	1.3	1.1	1.1	1.2	1.1	1.2	1.4	1.4
Health Professional	4.7	4.5	4.5	4.7	5.9	12.2	14.1	5.8	7.0	7.1	7.3	10.6	10.8	10.3	10.8	10.2	10.3	11.2	10.6	9.6
History or Political Science	7.5	7.8	7.7	7.4	6.4	5.4	4.9	6.0	5.0	4.7	4.4	4.2	4.1	3.7	3.7	3.6	3.5	3.5	3.9	4.7
Humanities	5.4	5.3	4.3	4.4	4.0	4.9	5.1	4.4	4.0	3.5	3.4	3.0	2.7	2.6	2.5	2.6	2.5	2.2	2.3	2.5
Fine Arts	8.3	8.7	8.7	8.9	9.1	6.9	6.5	5.5	6.2	5.6	5.5	5.3	5.5	5.3	5.2	4.9	4.5	4.3	4.1	3.9
Mathematics or Statistics	5.4	5.3	5.0	4.7	4.2	3.7	2.9	3.5	2.0	1.5	1.4	1.1	1.2	0.9	0.9	0.9	1.0	1.2	1.2	1.1
Physical Sciences	3.8	3.8	3.3	3.2	3.0	2.7	2.5	3.5	3.4	3.4	3.4	2.9	3.0	2.6	2.3	2.4	2.2	2.2	2.1	2.2
Social Sciences	8.5	8.8	9.3	10.1	9.8	10.1	9.1	8.3	7.8	7.3	6.8	6.3	6.2	6.1	5.4	5.1	4.6	4.8	5.5	5.8
Other Technical	1.5	1.6	2.0	1.9	2.8	3.4	3.9	5.2	5.4	5.9	5.5	4.8	4.8	5.6	7.1	8.7	10.1	9.6	6.9	5.6
Other Non-technical	10.7	10.2	9.5	10.2	10.7	10.6	10.7	8.7	8.5	8.8	9.8	8.8	8.2	9.0	8.5	8.0	8.5	7.8	7.8	8.3
Undecided	1.7	1.7	2.0	2.4	2.2	2.4	4.9	5.1	4.9	5.5	5.1	5.6	5.4	5.4	5.6	5.8	5.8	6.1	6.2	6.8
Where do you plan to live during the fall term?																				
With parents or relatives	—	—	—	—	—	—	—	21.3	22.1	21.8	24.1	26.6	23.2	21.5	22.0	19.8	20.7	22.3	21.6	18.5
Other private home, apartment, room	—	—	—	—	—	—	—	2.2	3.0	3.4	3.3	4.1	3.4	4.2	4.3	3.2	3.6	2.7	2.8	2.7
College dormitory	—	—	—	—	—	—	—	73.9	72.5	71.9	69.5	66.3	70.6	71.4	70.6	73.9	72.7	72.3	72.9	76.0
Fraternity or sorority house	—	—	—	—	—	—	—	0.7	1.1	0.8	0.8	0.7	1.4	0.9	0.9	1.0	0.8	0.7	0.6	0.6
Other campus student housing	—	—	—	—	—	—	—	1.4	1.0	1.7	1.7	1.7	1.4	1.5	1.8	1.7	1.6	1.6	1.7	1.8
Other	—	—	—	—	—	—	—	0.5	0.4	0.5	0.5	0.6	0.6	0.5	0.6	0.5	0.7	0.4	0.3	0.4
Student's Estimates: Chances are very good that he/she will																				
Be elected to an academic honor society	—	3.6	3.2	3.0	3.2	4.0	5.5	6.0	6.5	6.8	8.2	8.4	9.2	9.0	9.5	9.1	8.2	8.7	8.8	9.4
Be elected to a student office	—	2.6	2.5	2.2	2.0	1.5	2.2	2.3	2.2	2.3	2.6	2.9	2.9	3.3	3.5	3.3	3.4	3.4	3.7	4.2
Be satisfied with your college	—	—	—	—	66.9	57.4	62.3	58.8	56.8	56.1	54.3	56.2	57.8	56.7	56.3	57.8	57.6	57.4	57.1	56.4
Change career choice	—	19.7	17.3	20.2	19.0	15.6	19.8	16.4	14.0	14.7	13.4	14.2	14.2	13.8	13.8	13.7	13.2	13.6	14.1	15.0
Change major field	—	18.8	16.6	19.6	18.6	15.3	19.1	17.1	14.4	14.8	13.8	14.6	14.7	14.4	14.2	14.3	14.2	14.6	15.0	15.7
Drop out permanently (exclude transferring)	—	0.6	0.5	0.5	0.7	0.8	1.0	1.1	1.0	1.0	0.9	0.9	0.8	1.0	0.9	1.0	0.8	0.8	0.8	0.8
Drop out of this college temporarily (exclude transferring)	—	1.1	0.9	1.2	1.4	1.6	2.0	2.0	1.8	1.8	1.6	1.5	1.3	1.3	1.2	1.2	1.1	1.1	1.1	1.2
Fail one or more courses	—	2.9	2.0	2.5	3.4	2.1	2.7	2.3	1.9	2.2	1.7	2.0	1.7	1.8	1.8	1.8	1.5	1.3	1.4	1.5
Get a bachelor's degree (B.A., B.S., etc.)	—	—	—	—	—	—	75.2	76.5	73.4	76.7	76.2	75.7	77.5	75.0	75.1	76.2	77.1	77.3	78.0	78.1
Get a job to help pay for college expenses	8.4	—	—	—	—	—	—	—	—	—	41.2	43.8	42.2	40.8	40.0	42.3	40.3	38.4	39.0	39.1
Get married while in college	—	7.2	6.6	8.4	7.8	8.9	8.0	6.9	6.5	6.3	5.8	5.6	5.2	5.3	5.5	5.5	4.9	4.7	4.7	4.8
Graduate with honors	—	4.1	4.2	4.7	5.2	5.6	8.5	10.4	11.0	11.5	12.2	12.6	13.0	12.8	13.3	12.5	13.2	13.3	12.9	13.7
Join a social fraternity, sorority, or club	—	34.7	29.7	25.5	22.8	26.7	35.8	38.3	40.4	42.2	44.1	42.8	—	—	—	—	—	—	—	—
Join a social fraternity or sorority	—	—	—	—	—	—	—	—	—	—	—	—	21.3	20.5	20.7	21.4	20.3	20.4	20.5	22.1
Make at least a "B" average	—	—	—	—	—	—	—	—	—	—	—	—	44.6	42.4	43.8	43.4	44.4	44.0	43.4	43.8
Need extra time to complete your degree requirements	—	—	—	—	—	3.5	4.1	4.2	4.0	4.5	4.3	4.8	4.7	4.9	5.0	5.7	5.3	5.2	5.6	6.4
Participate in student government	—	—	—	—	—	—	—	—	—	—	—	—	—	—	—	—	—	—	—	—
Participate in student protests or demonstrations	—	5.2	4.6	—	—	—	—	—	—	—	—	—	3.5	4.3	5.0	4.1	4.8	4.2	4.7	5.7

70

PLANS, GOALS, AND EXPECTATIONS
ALL FRESHMEN

ITEM	1986	1987	1988	1989	1990	1991	1992	1993	1994	1995	1996	1997	1998	1999	2000	2001	2002	2003	2004	2005	2006
Your probable major field [2]																					
Agriculture	0.8	0.7	0.7	0.8	0.8	0.9	0.9	1.1	1.2	1.1	1.2	1.1	1.1	1.0	0.7	0.6	0.7	0.5	0.7	0.5	0.6
Biological Science	4.6	4.4	4.4	4.5	4.8	5.7	6.5	7.1	7.9	8.3	8.2	8.0	7.1	7.2	6.8	6.9	7.1	7.2	7.7	7.6	8.3
Business	25.3	25.7	24.9	23.5	21.0	17.8	15.8	14.8	15.3	15.5	15.6	15.7	16.5	16.6	16.8	16.6	16.2	15.8	16.1	17.4	18.0
Education	8.4	8.8	8.6	8.7	10.3	10.3	9.8	9.9	10.3	10.0	10.2	10.2	11.1	10.6	11.0	10.0	10.6	10.1	9.7	9.9	9.5
Engineering	10.2	9.4	8.7	9.9	9.7	10.8	10.0	10.0	8.8	8.1	9.7	9.7	8.2	9.0	8.7	9.1	9.6	9.2	9.5	8.3	7.8
English	1.6	1.6	1.7	1.8	1.8	1.8	1.7	1.8	1.8	1.8	1.9	1.8	1.8	1.8	1.7	1.7	1.7	1.7	1.8	1.9	2.0
Health Professional	8.4	7.6	8.3	8.7	9.6	11.6	13.6	14.5	13.6	13.4	12.3	12.2	11.7	10.4	9.3	9.8	10.1	11.8	12.7	12.2	11.5
History or Political Science	4.4	4.6	5.3	5.3	5.2	4.8	4.6	4.5	4.3	3.9	3.9	3.8	3.7	3.9	3.9	4.3	4.6	4.8	4.6	5.0	5.1
Humanities	2.6	2.8	2.6	2.5	2.5	2.6	2.5	2.4	2.6	2.6	2.7	2.8	3.1	3.0	3.5	3.4	3.5	3.3	3.2	3.5	3.6
Fine Arts	4.6	5.0	4.5	4.5	4.6	4.6	5.0	4.5	4.7	5.0	4.4	4.7	5.2	5.1	5.3	5.5	5.5	5.5	5.2	5.3	4.6
Mathematics or Statistics	1.0	0.9	0.8	0.8	0.8	0.8	0.8	0.8	0.8	0.7	0.7	0.7	0.7	0.6	0.7	0.7	0.8	0.8	0.8	0.8	0.8
Physical Sciences	2.0	1.8	1.9	2.0	2.0	2.1	2.3	2.5	2.1	2.3	2.1	2.1	1.8	1.9	1.8	1.9	2.0	2.1	2.3	2.3	2.4
Social Sciences	6.1	6.5	7.2	7.0	7.0	6.6	7.1	7.2	7.3	7.2	7.1	6.8	7.0	6.9	7.2	7.2	7.2	7.3	7.0	7.2	7.8
Other Technical	4.3	3.6	4.0	3.6	3.5	3.6	3.4	3.4	3.6	4.2	4.9	5.4	5.7	6.1	6.2	5.9	4.1	3.6	3.3	2.7	2.7
Other Non-technical	8.2	8.6	9.0	8.5	8.8	8.1	7.8	7.5	7.4	7.6	7.3	7.0	7.5	7.9	8.1	7.9	8.1	8.2	7.9	8.0	8.3
Undecided	7.6	7.8	7.3	7.8	7.6	7.8	8.0	8.0	8.4	8.2	7.9	8.0	8.0	8.0	8.3	8.5	8.4	8.0	7.4	7.3	7.2
Where do you plan to live during the fall term?																					
With parents or relatives	17.1	15.1	16.5	16.2	15.5	16.3	14.9	14.7	15.1	15.5	16.0	15.4	14.6	15.4	17.6	17.4	16.9	16.4	14.8	15.5	14.3
Other private home, apartment, room	3.8	3.5	3.8	3.8	2.9	2.9	3.2	3.0	2.8	3.0	2.9	3.6	3.0	3.1	4.4	4.1	4.3	3.6	4.2	2.6	3.6
College dormitory	75.6	78.3	76.2	77.0	79.1	78.0	79.4	79.8	79.5	79.1	78.2	79.0	79.8	79.0	75.4	75.9	75.5	77.4	77.7	79.3	79.1
Fraternity or sorority house	0.8	0.9	0.8	0.5	0.4	0.5	0.6	0.7	0.7	0.6	1.0	0.2	0.6	0.7	0.5	0.4	0.5	0.4	0.5	0.3	0.3
Other campus student housing	2.2	2.0	2.3	2.2	1.8	1.8	1.5	1.5	1.6	1.4	1.6	1.4	1.7	1.5	1.7	1.9	2.3	1.9	2.4	2.1	2.5
Other	0.4	0.3	0.3	0.3	0.3	0.5	0.4	0.3	0.3	0.3	0.3	0.4	0.3	0.3	0.3	0.3	0.4	0.3	0.3	0.2	0.3
Student's Estimates: Chances are very good that he/she will																					
Be elected to an academic honor society	8.1	8.7	8.4	9.1	9.7	10.0	9.8	10.5	10.7	10.7	11.3	11.6	10.3	10.1	—	—	—	—	—	—	—
Be elected to a student office	3.9	3.9	3.7	3.7	4.0	3.5	3.4	3.7	3.9	3.6	3.8	3.8	3.5	3.6	—	—	—	—	—	—	—
Be satisfied with your college	55.1	54.8	53.4	52.5	52.9	53.8	53.8	51.8	50.4	48.8	50.8	51.9	50.4	50.1	48.7	48.5	51.8	52.0	51.3	52.4	53.4
Change career choice	14.4	15.2	14.7	14.2	13.9	13.7	13.8	13.7	13.6	13.9	13.8	13.5	13.4	13.8	13.9	13.7	13.6	13.3	13.4	13.2	13.3
Change major field	15.3	16.1	15.9	15.3	14.9	14.5	14.5	14.6	14.5	14.4	14.4	14.2	14.1	14.6	14.9	14.7	14.8	14.4	14.2	13.9	13.9
Drop out permanently (exclude transferring)	0.8	0.7	0.7	0.8	0.8	0.7	0.7	0.7	0.7	0.7	0.7	0.6	0.6	0.6	0.7	0.7	—	—	—	—	—
Drop out of this college temporarily (exclude transferring)	1.2	1.0	1.0	1.0	1.0	1.0	1.0	0.9	0.9	0.9	0.9	0.8	0.9	0.9	1.0	0.9	—	—	—	—	—
Fail one or more courses	1.4	1.4	1.3	1.3	1.4	1.4	1.3	1.0	1.1	1.1	1.1	1.1	1.0	1.1	—	—	—	—	—	—	—
Get a bachelor's degree (B.A., B.S., etc.)	78.2	78.6	77.5	77.0	76.8	77.4	76.0	77.1	76.8	76.3	77.2	77.1	76.2	76.3	77.6	76.5	79.5	79.5	77.7	79.3	79.1
Get a job to help pay for college expenses	37.8	37.7	36.0	35.3	37.3	38.0	38.7	40.0	39.4	41.1	40.4	41.3	39.3	38.7	42.5	44.8	47.1	47.0	47.2	46.8	44.1
Get married while in college	4.5	4.1	4.1	4.8	5.1	5.9	5.9	5.4	5.5	5.3	5.0	4.8	4.7	4.6	—	—	—	—	—	—	—
Graduate with honors	12.6	13.3	13.3	14.2	14.6	15.6	16.3	17.8	18.1	18.3	19.6	20.5	19.3	18.3	20.7	20.8	—	—	—	—	—
Join a social fraternity, sorority, or club	21.8	22.5	21.4	21.6	21.2	21.1	20.2	20.3	19.9	18.7	19.5	18.9	18.2	18.5	—	—	—	—	—	—	—
Join a social fraternity or sorority	—	—	—	—	—	—	—	—	—	—	—	—	—	—	11.5	10.7	11.1	9.8	9.5	10.4	10.1
Make at least a "B" average	43.0	42.3	43.8	44.4	44.1	45.5	47.0	49.1	50.0	50.8	52.5	54.4	52.6	52.0	58.1	57.5	60.2	59.4	59.6	60.8	60.6
Need extra time to complete your degree requirements	6.7	7.2	7.3	7.6	8.9	8.8	9.2	7.5	8.8	7.9	7.8	7.3	6.9	6.5	6.7	6.3	7.6	7.3	7.2	7.7	6.6
Participate in student government	—	—	—	—	—	—	—	—	—	—	—	—	—	—	7.3	7.4	7.6	7.3	7.2	7.7	7.5
Participate in student protests or demonstrations	5.8	6.8	6.4	7.6	8.4	7.1	8.6	7.5	6.2	5.7	5.5	4.9	4.8	4.7	5.1	5.2	5.6	6.3	6.0	6.5	5.8

PLANS, GOALS, AND EXPECTATIONS
ALL FRESHMEN

ITEM	1966	1967	1968	1969	1970	1971	1972	1973	1974	1975	1976	1977	1978	1979	1980	1981	1982	1983	1984	1985
Student's Estimates: Chances are very good that he/she will																				
Participate in volunteer or community service work	—	—	—	—	—	—	—	—	—	—	—	—	—	—	—	—	—	16.4	16.9	16.6
Play varsity/intercollegiate athletics	—	—	—	—	—	7.1	6.9	6.0	5.7	5.8	4.4	4.8	4.7	4.9	4.7	4.4	4.0	4.2	3.7	4.4
Seek personal counseling	—	—	—	—	—	—	—	—	—	—	—	—	—	—	—	—	—	—	—	—
Transfer to another college before graduating	—	10.6	10.3	11.6	10.5	10.8	12.1	11.8	11.8	12.3	11.8	10.9	9.9	10.2	9.6	9.8	8.8	8.9	9.5	8.9
Work full time while attending college	—	—	—	—	—	—	—	—	—	—	—	—	—	—	—	—	2.9	2.9	3.2	3.0
Objectives considered to be essential or very important																				
Becoming accomplished in one of the performing arts (acting, dancing, etc.)	11.2	12.3	9.3	12.2	13.5	13.2	12.9	—	12.4	13.0	12.9	15.0	14.2	13.4	13.5	12.9	13.4	13.2	12.3	12.4
Becoming a community leader	28.1	26.0	22.7	19.3	16.0	14.6	16.6	—	—	—	—	—	—	—	—	—	—	—	—	—
Becoming an authority in my field	67.2	70.0	60.2	60.6	67.4	60.7	61.7	63.9	64.2	71.3	71.3	76.6	74.7	74.4	75.2	74.8	75.3	74.8	75.3	73.2
Becoming involved in programs to clean up the environment	—	—	—	—	—	43.7	45.9	33.6	26.1	29.4	28.2	30.2	27.9	26.4	26.5	24.7	23.2	21.3	20.6	19.9
Becoming successful in a business of my own	51.4	44.5	43.0	42.7	41.3	38.3	42.5	39.6	36.5	41.4	43.4	46.2	46.7	47.9	48.3	48.9	49.5	49.3	51.2	50.4
Being very well off financially	42.2	41.9	39.5	42.2	36.2	37.2	38.7	—	43.7	46.9	50.2	56.2	58.5	61.1	62.5	64.0	68.0	68.7	70.4	69.2
Creating artistic work (painting, sculpture, decorating, etc.)	15.1	16.0	13.9	15.9	16.8	16.3	18.1	—	14.4	15.0	14.4	16.4	14.8	14.6	14.3	13.6	13.0	12.3	11.9	11.9
Developing a meaningful philosophy of life	—	85.8	85.0	84.9	79.1	72.6	74.9	72.4	65.2	68.3	65.2	63.0	60.3	56.3	54.2	52.8	50.6	47.9	48.0	46.9
Having administrative responsibility for the work of others	28.2	24.3	22.0	22.6	19.9	18.4	22.7	25.3	24.6	29.5	30.6	34.1	35.3	37.2	38.9	39.7	41.0	41.0	42.9	43.0
Helping others who are in difficulty	69.7	63.7	60.6	67.2	71.7	64.2	68.6	65.7	63.2	68.1	65.5	66.9	67.4	66.3	66.7	65.2	64.0	64.5	64.0	65.0
Influencing social values	—	—	—	35.7	35.3	29.9	31.9	32.2	28.4	31.2	31.2	32.4	32.9	33.5	34.2	33.0	33.1	32.4	34.1	34.1
Influencing the political structure	—	—	—	18.1	20.0	15.9	17.4	15.9	13.9	15.9	16.9	17.7	16.7	17.3	18.2	16.7	16.8	15.7	17.2	17.7
Integrating spirituality into my life	—	—	—	—	—	—	—	—	—	—	—	—	—	—	—	—	—	—	—	—
Keeping up to date with political affairs	60.3	54.5	55.4	56.2	57.2	46.7	53.3	46.2	41.0	42.7	42.6	44.6	41.9	42.6	45.2	44.1	43.7	40.5	43.2	—
Making a theoretical contribution to science	14.2	12.9	11.7	11.0	11.2	10.1	11.5	—	14.3	14.6	15.0	15.6	15.9	15.6	16.0	15.5	15.2	15.6	14.7	15.2
Obtaining recognition from my colleagues for contributions to my special field	43.6	43.2	38.4	41.5	40.0	38.2	37.5	—	40.2	44.6	47.0	50.1	52.3	53.9	56.5	56.3	57.8	57.7	57.9	57.5
Participating in a community action program	—	—	—	—	31.1	27.5	31.3	—	30.1	33.0	31.6	32.0	29.1	28.5	29.6	26.1	25.3	24.4	24.3	24.7
Participating in an organization like the Peace Corps or AmeriCorps/VISTA	22.2	—	—	—	—	17.3	16.5	—	—	—	—	—	—	—	—	—	—	—	—	—
Helping to promote racial understanding	—	—	—	—	—	—	—	—	—	—	—	39.0	37.1	35.1	35.7	33.6	34.2	33.5	34.5	35.2
Raising a family	—	—	—	71.5	67.0	—	—	—	—	—	—	58.8	62.3	65.3	64.0	67.4	68.1	67.5	69.8	70.6
Writing original works (poems, novels, short stories, etc.)	15.4	15.9	14.5	15.5	15.5	15.1	15.6	—	13.4	13.7	14.2	15.6	14.4	14.0	13.7	13.2	13.1	12.7	12.6	13.5

PLANS, GOALS, AND EXPECTATIONS
ALL FRESHMEN

ITEM	1986	1987	1988	1989	1990	1991	1992	1993	1994	1995	1996	1997	1998	1999	2000	2001	2002	2003	2004	2005	2006
Student's Estimates: Chances are very good that he/she will																					
Participate in volunteer or community service work	—	—	—	—	16.9	17.8	20.5	22.3	21.3	22.3	22.7	23.6	24.2	24.1	23.8	24.0	25.2	25.3	24.1	26.3	26.8
Play varsity/intercollegiate athletics	15.9	16.6	16.0	15.8	16.2	16.8	16.7	16.8	16.1	16.9	17.0	16.7	16.4	15.8	15.3	15.0	15.1	15.9	15.7	16.3	16.5
Seek personal counseling	3.8	4.0	3.9	3.5	4.1	3.7	—	—	—	—	5.9	5.4	4.8	4.7	6.4	6.6	7.1	7.6	7.1	7.5	7.8
Transfer to another college before graduating	8.8	8.6	9.2	9.1	9.0	8.7	8.2	8.4	8.0	8.1	7.2	7.1	6.7	6.5	6.6	6.7	7.3	7.1	7.1	6.4	7.0
Work full time while attending college	3.2	2.5	2.7	3.0	3.2	3.4	3.3	3.6	3.9	4.1	4.0	4.1	4.0	4.1	4.5	5.9	6.2	6.0	6.3	6.4	5.6
Objectives considered to be essential or very important																					
Becoming accomplished in one of the performing arts (acting, dancing, etc.)	12.0	14.4	—	11.8	11.8	11.6	11.9	12.0	12.5	12.6	12.9	13.5	14.2	13.7	14.5	14.8	16.1	15.9	15.1	16.2	15.7
Becoming a community leader	—	—	—	—	—	—	34.5	—	34.9	33.5	35.3	35.0	34.4	31.5	30.9	32.0	31.6	32.1	30.7	33.9	35.2
Becoming an authority in my field	73.7	78.7	—	67.6	66.7	70.1	70.2	68.6	67.5	66.5	65.7	64.7	62.9	60.1	59.7	59.9	60.2	60.3	58.3	59.1	58.2
Becoming involved in programs to clean up the environment	15.7	18.1	—	27.0	35.8	33.1	35.2	29.7	25.4	22.9	21.0	19.5	19.4	18.2	17.5	17.0	17.1	17.4	17.5	20.3	22.2
Becoming successful in a business of my own	48.4	49.8	—	43.7	41.6	41.9	41.4	40.4	39.7	39.7	39.2	39.2	38.5	38.0	39.3	39.9	39.5	40.4	41.0	42.6	41.9
Being very well off financially	71.9	74.1	—	73.8	72.3	72.7	71.4	71.9	71.8	72.8	72.9	73.3	72.9	72.1	73.4	73.6	73.2	73.8	73.6	74.5	73.4
Creating artistic work (painting, sculpture, decorating, etc.)	11.8	13.7	—	12.7	12.3	11.9	12.8	13.1	13.2	13.5	13.2	13.5	13.9	14.0	14.8	15.4	16.1	16.3	15.6	16.5	16.2
Developing a meaningful philosophy of life	44.0	43.1	—	43.8	45.9	47.5	48.9	47.8	46.6	45.4	44.5	44.5	44.1	43.0	42.4	43.1	40.6	39.3	42.1	45.0	46.3
Having administrative responsibility for the work of others	44.9	45.5	—	43.5	42.8	41.7	40.9	40.7	39.8	38.6	39.1	38.6	37.9	36.0	36.9	37.2	38.4	39.1	38.5	40.4	41.0
Helping others who are in difficulty	59.1	60.4	—	60.8	63.2	62.9	64.9	65.4	64.2	62.9	63.6	63.8	63.5	61.9	61.7	61.4	63.2	63.7	62.4	66.3	66.7
Influencing social values	34.3	38.1	—	43.3	44.8	42.9	46.1	44.3	42.3	40.7	40.3	39.1	38.3	37.3	37.6	37.7	38.8	38.6	38.3	41.3	42.5
Influencing the political structure	16.4	18.6	—	21.6	22.2	20.5	22.3	22.5	20.8	18.7	18.8	17.6	17.5	17.1	17.6	19.0	19.6	20.1	19.7	21.8	22.7
Integrating spirituality into my life	—	—	—	—	—	—	—	—	—	—	—	—	—	46.4	45.1	42.6	41.5	40.4	39.5	40.5	—
Keeping up to date with political affairs	—	—	—	44.4	46.6	43.5	44.6	42.1	36.5	32.3	32.8	30.1	30.2	28.6	28.1	31.4	32.9	33.9	34.3	36.4	37.2
Making a theoretical contribution to science	13.7	13.4	—	17.9	18.6	17.5	19.3	20.0	18.5	18.2	18.5	18.1	16.6	16.3	16.0	16.5	16.8	17.1	17.8	18.9	19.7
Obtaining recognition from my colleagues for contributions to my special field	56.8	60.5	—	56.7	56.7	55.9	57.7	56.4	56.3	56.2	54.8	54.7	52.5	51.3	51.2	51.3	52.6	52.7	51.8	54.2	53.8
Participating in a community action program	20.4	21.7	—	25.2	28.2	26.4	29.0	28.2	27.2	25.8	25.8	25.3	24.7	23.3	22.7	22.6	22.4	22.8	21.5	25.6	27.0
Participating in an organization like the Peace Corps or AmeriCorps/VISTA	—	—	—	—	—	—	—	—	—	—	—	—	—	—	—	—	—	—	—	—	11.3
Helping to promote racial understanding	30.1	32.2	—	38.2	42.3	38.8	46.4	43.4	38.5	35.8	36.1	33.7	32.3	30.0	30.8	31.5	31.1	30.5	29.7	33.3	34.0
Raising a family	68.3	—	—	69.8	70.2	69.9	71.8	71.7	72.3	72.5	73.3	74.5	74.4	73.6	73.1	72.3	73.6	74.8	75.1	75.9	75.5
Writing original works (poems, novels, short stories, etc.)	13.0	14.3	—	13.8	13.5	13.6	13.9	14.4	14.1	14.3	14.5	14.4	14.6	14.1	14.7	14.7	15.4	15.4	15.1	16.0	16.2

STUDENT VIEWS
ALL FRESHMEN

ITEM	1966	1967	1968	1969	1970	1971	1972	1973	1974	1975	1976	1977	1978	1979	1980	1981	1982	1983	1984	1985
Student agrees strongly or somewhat																				
A national health care plan is needed to cover everybody's medical costs	—	—	—	—	—	—	—	—	—	—	—	58.8	58.1	58.9	55.0	52.7	55.2	57.5	59.1	57.8
Abortion should be legalized]	—	—	—	78.8	85.7	—	—	—	—	—	—	55.6	56.3	53.7	53.7	54.5	55.7	56.0	55.4	56.4
Affirmative action in college admissions should be abolished	—	—	—	—	—	—	—	—	—	—	—	—	—	—	—	—	—	—	—	—
College officials have the right to ban persons with extreme views from speaking on campus	—	37.2	29.6	29.5	30.2	25.0	22.6	20.9	20.3	22.2	23.2	23.8	23.8	24.2	24.7	24.6	23.2	23.4	20.1	23.6
Colleges should prohibit racist/sexist speech on campus	—	—	—	—	—	—	—	—	—	—	—	—	—	—	—	—	—	—	—	—
Employers should be allowed to require drug testing of employees or job applicants	—	—	—	—	—	—	—	—	—	—	—	—	—	—	—	—	—	—	—	—
Federal military spending should be increased	—	—	—	—	—	—	—	—	—	—	—	—	—	—	—	—	37.3	35.7	31.0	25.7
Grading in the high schools has become too easy	—	—	—	—	—	—	—	—	—	—	60.3	63.7	66.6	61.6	61.9	59.3	56.3	60.0	56.2	52.2
If two people really like each other, it's all right for them to have sex even if they've known each other for only a very short time	—	—	—	—	—	—	—	—	44.3	47.7	46.8	48.6	46.8	47.8	45.9	44.9	46.1	47.1	46.2	—
It is important to have laws prohibiting homosexual relationships	—	—	—	—	—	—	—	—	—	—	43.6	46.6	44.5	45.1	47.5	46.1	44.2	45.5	44.7	44.2
Just because a man thinks that a woman has "led him on" does not entitle him to have sex with her	—	—	—	—	—	—	—	—	—	—	—	—	—	—	—	—	—	—	—	—
Marijuana should be legalized	—	—	20.3	26.2	40.6	40.4	47.6	48.3	45.6	46.1	47.3	51.3	47.8	44.6	37.1	32.5	27.8	24.5	22.7	21.4
Only volunteers should serve in the armed forces	—	—	—	—	—	—	—	—	33.3	31.5	30.8	31.4	31.4	32.7	31.2	31.0	—	—	—	—
People should not obey laws which violate their personal values	—	—	—	—	—	—	—	—	—	—	—	—	—	—	—	—	—	—	—	—
Racial discrimination is no longer a major problem in America	—	—	—	—	—	—	—	—	—	—	—	—	—	—	—	—	—	—	—	—
Realistically, an individual can do little to bring about change in our society	32.3	—	31.3	35.1	38.0	41.9	41.4	39.6	41.6	46.5	42.3	42.6	—	—	—	—	—	—	—	—
Same sex couples should have the right to legal marital status	—	—	—	—	—	—	—	—	—	—	—	—	—	—	—	—	—	—	—	35.3
The activities of married women are best confined to the home and family	—	53.5	—	—	44.5	38.4	33.2	27.1	27.3	25.9	26.3	26.1	25.8	26.4	25.3	25.3	23.8	22.3	21.1	20.7
The chief benefit of a college education is that it increases one's earning power	—	—	50.4	47.2	60.6	52.7	52.5	48.3	—	—	—	—	—	—	—	—	—	—	—	68.3
The death penalty should be abolished	—	—	53.0	56.4	59.4	60.2	—	—	—	—	—	—	33.6	35.6	34.8	30.7	29.2	29.7	26.8	27.6
The federal government is not doing enough to control environmental pollution	—	—	—	—	—	91.7	90.6	88.7	83.1	82.4	82.9	81.4	81.9	80.4	79.2	77.5	78.7	80.5	78.1	78.4
The federal government should do more to control the sale of handguns	—	—	—	—	—	—	—	—	—	—	—	—	—	—	—	—	—	—	—	—

STUDENT VIEWS
ALL FRESHMEN

ITEM	1986	1987	1988	1989	1990	1991	1992	1993	1994	1995	1996	1997	1998	1999	2000	2001	2002	2003	2004	2005	2006
Student agrees strongly or somewhat																					
A national health care plan is needed to cover everybody's medical costs	59.4	—	—	74.1	72.6	75.4	77.6	75.7	68.8	70.3	70.7	70.8	—	—	—	—	—	—	—	73.6	73.0
Abortion should be legal[ized]	60.3	60.3	59.2	65.7	65.5	64.6	67.2	64.1	60.9	59.9	57.7	53.7	54.3	53.2	53.9	55.0	53.6	54.5	53.9	55.2	56.8
Affirmative action in college admissions should be abolished	—	—	—	—	—	—	—	—	—	51.5	51.3	53.0	—	50.1	49.9	49.0	49.0	52.8	50.4	48.5	47.1
College officials have the right to ban persons with extreme views from speaking on campus	24.1	—	—	—	—	—	—	—	—	—	—	—	—	—	—	—	—	—	—	—	40.5
Colleges should prohibit racist/sexist speech on campus	—	—	—	—	—	—	58.9	60.6	60.6	61.9	63.2	62.5	60.7	62.3	61.8	60.4	60.0	58.4	58.6	59.1	—
Employers should be allowed to require drug testing of employees or job applicants	—	—	70.4	77.4	79.9	80.4	80.3	79.5	80.3	77.7	79.4	79.8	78.5	78.2	76.5	75.0	—	—	—	—	—
Federal military spending should be increased	26.2	25.2	24.5	22.4	21.8	23.2	17.7	21.4	—	—	—	—	—	—	—	—	45.0	38.4	35.4	34.2	32.3
Grading in the high schools has become too easy	50.4	—	—	—	—	—	51.0	—	—	—	—	—	—	—	—	—	—	—	—	50.6	—
If two people really like each other, it's all right for them to have sex even if they've known each other for only a very short time	—	50.6	49.7	48.5	50.1	49.2	44.9	44.9	42.4	41.9	40.3	39.4	38.6	38.8	41.8	42.2	—	—	46.2	44.9	—
It is important to have laws prohibiting homosexual relationships	48.7	50.4	46.4	42.4	40.6	38.6	32.9	32.8	30.8	27.9	31.7	31.2	29.5	28.1	27.2	24.9	24.8	26.1	29.9	27.4	25.6
Just because a man thinks that a woman has "led him on" does not entitle him to have sex with her	—	—	85.3	88.0	88.1	88.7	90.3	90.8	90.6	90.2	—	89.4	89.2	88.9	—	—	—	—	—	—	—
Marijuana should be legalized	20.8	19.1	19.8	16.7	18.8	21.2	24.8	29.3	32.7	33.4	32.4	33.1	32.7	32.4	34.2	36.5	39.7	38.8	37.2	37.7	37.1
Only volunteers should serve in the armed forces	—	—	53.6	51.6	—	—	—	—	—	—	—	—	—	—	—	—	—	—	—	63.1	63.2
People should not obey laws which violate their personal values	—	—	—	—	—	—	—	—	35.8	36.6	35.3	35.9	—	—	—	—	35.3	34.5	—	—	—
Racial discrimination is no longer a major problem in America	—	—	—	—	18.0	17.5	12.7	12.5	15.6	17.3	15.4	17.6	19.3	21.4	20.5	19.5	21.8	22.4	22.7	21.0	19.1
Realistically, an individual can do little to bring about change in our society	—	—	—	—	—	27.7	28.5	29.7	30.4	31.0	29.2	29.6	28.7	28.9	27.2	26.2	27.5	28.1	26.8	27.3	27.0
Same sex couples should have the right to legal marital status	—	—	—	—	—	—	—	—	—	—	—	50.9	52.4	53.9	56.0	57.9	59.3	59.4	56.7	57.9	61.2
The activities of married women are best confined to the home and family	19.2	24.0	23.4	23.8	23.2	23.2	23.2	22.1	23.3	22.6	22.5	22.8	—	26.0	22.2	21.5	21.7	21.7	21.0	20.3	—
The chief benefit of a college education is that it increases one's earning power	67.1	65.9	66.1	67.4	66.6	66.8	65.7	—	—	—	—	—	—	—	—	—	—	—	—	—	66.5
The death penalty should be abolished	26.0	24.3	23.7	22.0	23.1	22.4	22.8	22.8	21.2	22.0	23.0	24.4	24.1	26.7	31.2	32.2	32.1	32.6	33.2	33.3	34.5
The federal government is not doing enough to control environmental pollution	78.4	81.4	84.1	87.4	88.8	86.4	89.2	84.9	84.1	83.9	82.0	81.0	—	—	—	—	—	—	78.7	77.1	77.9
The federal government should do more to control the sale of handguns	—	—	—	79.8	79.5	80.9	82.4	83.0	81.6	82.8	82.9	83.2	84.1	83.8	82.0	80.8	77.8	76.5	78.7	78.7	73.8

STUDENT VIEWS
ALL FRESHMEN

ITEM	1966	1967	1968	1969	1970	1971	1972	1973	1974	1975	1976	1977	1978	1979	1980	1981	1982	1983	1984	1985
Student agrees strongly or somewhat																				
The federal government should do more to discourage energy consumption	—	—	—	—	—	—	—	—	—	82.8	80.6	82.9	82.6	83.9	83.5	80.3	78.3	75.9	73.6	72.1
The federal government should raise taxes to reduce the deficit	—	—	—	—	—	—	—	—	—	—	—	—	—	—	—	—	—	—	—	24.9
There is too much concern in the courts for the rights of criminals	—	—	—	53.8	50.7	46.0	47.7	47.9	49.6	52.5	58.1	62.4	64.4	61.3	65.0	68.1	69.3	68.1	—	—
Wealthy people should pay a larger share of taxes than they do now	—	—	—	—	—	—	73.0	72.8	75.8	75.7	75.3	74.4	72.3	69.3	68.7	69.4	70.6	68.8	68.2	72.4
How would you characterize your political views?																				
Far left	—	—	—	—	2.9	3.0	2.6	2.1	2.1	1.9	1.9	1.8	1.6	1.8	1.7	1.6	1.7	1.7	1.9	1.7
Liberal	—	—	—	—	35.7	37.9	35.0	34.3	30.3	30.7	27.4	26.2	24.8	23.8	21.0	19.4	20.2	20.9	21.3	22.4
Middle of the road	—	—	—	—	43.4	44.1	46.0	48.6	52.6	51.9	53.3	54.3	55.3	55.9	57.0	56.6	57.0	57.2	55.0	53.1
Conservative	—	—	—	—	17.3	14.5	15.7	14.4	14.4	15.0	16.4	16.9	17.6	17.5	19.0	21.3	20.0	19.0	20.6	21.3
Far right	—	—	—	—	0.8	0.6	0.7	0.5	0.7	0.6	1.0	0.8	0.8	0.9	1.2	1.1	1.1	1.1	1.2	1.5

STUDENT VIEWS
ALL FRESHMEN

ITEM	1986	1987	1988	1989	1990	1991	1992	1993	1994	1995	1996	1997	1998	1999	2000	2001	2002	2003	2004	2005	2006
Student agrees strongly or somewhat																					
The federal government should do more to discourage energy consumption	70.5	—	—	—	—	80.9	80.7	77.0	73.2	—	—	—	—	—	—	—	75.1	—	—	—	—
The federal government should raise taxes to reduce the deficit	25.2	25.8	29.9	30.6	31.9	27.9	29.9	35.3	26.9	27.4	25.2	23.6	—	—	—	—	—	—	—	—	26.7
There is too much concern in the courts for the rights of criminals	—	68.0	68.2	68.1	65.1	64.5	65.2	67.1	72.4	73.2	71.7	70.8	72.3	71.2	66.5	64.4	64.0	61.1	58.1	57.9	55.9
Wealthy people should pay a larger share of taxes than they do now	71.2	—	—	—	—	—	71.9	71.3	66.2	66.4	65.0	62.4	58.2	54.6	52.2	51.6	50.1	53.1	55.5	58.1	58.0
How would you characterize your political views?																					
Far left	1.8	2.1	2.2	1.8	1.9	2.0	2.3	2.3	2.2	2.3	2.4	2.5	2.4	2.4	2.9	3.0	2.5	2.8	3.4	3.4	2.8
Liberal	23.4	23.8	23.7	23.3	24.6	25.9	27.4	26.6	24.5	22.9	22.8	23.1	23.3	23.6	24.8	26.9	25.3	24.2	26.1	27.1	28.4
Middle of the road	52.9	53.1	51.0	50.7	51.7	50.3	49.4	47.4	49.4	51.3	51.0	52.0	53.1	53.4	51.9	49.5	50.8	50.3	46.4	45.0	43.3
Conservative	20.6	19.6	21.5	22.7	20.6	20.6	19.5	22.1	22.3	21.8	22.0	21.0	19.9	19.3	18.9	19.1	20.0	21.1	21.9	22.6	23.9
Far right	1.3	1.4	1.6	1.5	1.2	1.2	1.3	1.6	1.6	1.6	1.7	1.5	1.4	1.3	1.4	1.6	1.3	1.6	2.2	1.9	1.7

77

SOURCES OF STUDENT FUNDS
ALL FRESHMEN

ITEM	1966	1967	1968	1969	1970	1971	1972	1973	1974	1975	1976	1977	1978	1979	1980	1981	1982	1983	1984	1985
Students receiving funds to cover educational expenses (room, board, tuition, and fees) from:																				
Parents, other relatives or friends	—	—	—	—	—	—	—	—	—	—	—	—	76.9	74.1	74.7	73.9	74.7	75.2	74.0	75.1
Spouse	—	—	—	—	—	—	—	—	—	—	—	—	0.6	0.5	0.5	0.6	0.6	0.6	0.6	0.6
Savings from summer work	—	—	—	—	—	—	—	—	—	—	—	—	50.7	47.9	46.8	47.3	44.0	44.6	49.1	52.4
Other savings	—	—	—	—	—	—	—	—	—	—	—	—	21.5	19.6	19.5	20.2	19.1	19.9	21.6	24.0
Part time job on campus	—	—	—	—	—	—	—	—	—	—	—	—	—	—	—	—	—	—	—	—
Part time job off campus	—	—	—	—	—	—	—	—	—	—	—	—	22.7	20.3	21.3	21.6	20.9	21.2	28.2	30.3
Full time job while in college	—	—	—	—	—	—	—	—	—	—	—	—	1.7	1.6	1.7	1.6	1.6	1.5	1.7	2.0
Pell Grant	—	—	—	—	—	—	—	—	—	—	—	—	20.7	31.0	30.3	24.2	22.8	25.6	18.7	18.2
Supplemental Educational Opportunity Grant (SEOG)	—	—	—	—	—	—	—	—	—	—	—	—	6.3	7.9	8.9	6.4	6.2	7.3	6.0	5.6
State scholarship or grant	—	—	—	—	—	—	—	—	—	—	—	—	15.7	16.3	16.7	14.4	14.4	16.2	14.2	15.1
College Work-Study Grant	—	—	—	—	—	—	—	—	—	—	—	—	12.8	14.3	17.0	14.6	14.5	16.3	11.7	12.4
College grant/scholarship (other than above)	—	—	—	—	—	—	—	—	—	—	—	—	15.9	14.6	16.5	14.7	15.5	17.3	21.5	23.9
Other private grant	—	—	—	—	—	—	—	—	—	—	—	—	8.5	8.2	8.4	7.9	8.4	8.9	7.4	7.1
Other government aid (ROTC, BIA, GI/ military benefits, etc.)	—	—	—	—	—	—	—	—	—	—	—	—	5.9	5.8	6.0	5.9	3.8	3.2	3.3	2.8
Stafford Loan (GSL)	—	—	—	—	—	—	—	—	—	—	—	—	10.5	15.2	22.6	27.4	20.8	21.8	23.6	23.0
Perkins Loan (NDSL)	—	—	—	—	—	—	—	—	—	—	—	—	8.9	9.3	10.6	8.4	6.9	7.9	7.1	7.1
Other college loan	—	—	—	—	—	—	—	—	—	—	—	—	3.6	3.9	4.6	4.0	3.6	4.0	3.9	3.9
Other loan	—	—	—	—	—	—	—	—	—	—	—	—	3.7	3.8	4.2	4.4	4.2	4.2	4.0	3.9
Other than above	—	—	—	—	—	—	—	—	—	—	—	—	4.4	4.5	4.3	4.1	3.4	4.0	2.7	2.7
Students receiving funds to cover educational expenses (room, board, tuition, and fees) from:																				
Family resources (parents, relatives, spouse, etc.)	—	—	—	—	—	—	—	—	—	—	—	—	—	—	—	—	—	—	—	—
My own resources (savings from work, work-study, other income)	—	—	—	—	—	—	—	—	—	—	—	—	—	—	—	—	—	—	—	—
Aid which need not be repaid (grants, scholarships, military funding, etc.)	—	—	—	—	—	—	—	—	—	—	—	—	—	—	—	—	—	—	—	—
Aid which must be repaid (loans, etc.)	—	—	—	—	—	—	—	—	—	—	—	—	—	—	—	—	—	—	—	—
Other than above	—	—	—	—	—	—	—	—	—	—	—	—	—	—	—	—	—	—	—	—
Do you have any concern about your ability to finance your college education?																				
None (I am confident that I will have sufficient funds)	34.4	33.7	33.9	32.4	31.7	31.7	33.7	34.5	36.7	35.0	33.2	33.0	34.4	32.9	31.6	31.1	30.4	32.8	33.5	35.3
Some (but I probably will have enough funds)	57.3	57.5	57.3	57.1	57.1	56.7	50.7	48.1	47.7	47.9	49.9	49.5	50.0	51.8	52.3	51.5	51.0	51.3	51.5	50.5
Major (not sure I will have enough funds)	8.3	8.5	8.7	10.6	11.2	11.6	15.6	17.3	15.6	17.2	16.9	17.5	15.7	15.2	16.0	17.4	18.6	15.9	15.0	14.2

SOURCES OF STUDENT FUNDS
ALL FRESHMEN

ITEM	1986	1987	1988	1989	1990	1991	1992	1993	1994	1995	1996	1997	1998	1999	2000	2001	2002	2003	2004	2005	2006
Students receiving funds to cover educational expenses (room, board, tuition, and fees) from:																					
Parents, other relatives or friends	78.9	83.1	83.5	84.3	82.6	82.1	84.4	83.5	83.6	82.9	82.4	82.2	83.1	84.6	82.5	—	—	—	—	—	82.1
Spouse	0.9	0.7	0.9	0.7	0.8	0.9	0.7	0.6	0.6	0.7	0.6	0.6	0.6	0.6	0.7	—	—	—	—	—	1.2
Savings from summer work	54.3	58.5	58.4	58.2	58.6	52.1	55.2	53.7	53.5	54.2	53.6	52.3	52.7	55.5	49.0	—	—	—	—	—	48.1
Other savings	27.9	30.2	31.2	30.5	33.7	29.8	32.3	31.3	32.8	32.5	33.5	32.4	33.7	38.0	32.0	—	—	—	—	—	38.3
Part time job on campus	—	22.0	23.4	23.4	23.8	23.2	25.5	25.0	25.3	26.8	26.8	27.2	27.3	29.4	25.8	—	—	—	—	—	29.0
Part time job off campus	32.5	19.2	20.2	20.5	19.1	17.3	18.3	17.8	18.9	19.9	19.8	20.0	19.8	23.6	21.9	—	—	—	—	—	24.3
Full time job while in college	2.2	1.4	1.7	1.7	1.8	1.8	1.9	1.4	2.2	2.3	2.4	2.3	2.5	3.4	2.7	—	—	—	—	—	4.7
Pell Grant	14.7	15.9	19.0	19.4	20.0	21.3	21.2	19.9	19.2	18.8	19.0	18.9	19.2	18.3	16.9	—	—	—	—	—	16.1
Supplemental Educational Opportunity Grant (SEOG)	5.7	6.4	6.0	6.4	6.7	6.5	7.2	6.2	6.3	6.4	6.8	5.9	6.5	6.8	5.8	—	—	—	—	—	7.3
State scholarship or grant	14.1	17.9	15.5	16.2	16.7	14.9	16.3	16.2	17.3	17.2	17.8	17.9	19.1	20.9	21.9	—	—	—	—	—	—
College Work-Study Grant	12.3	11.8	11.5	11.7	12.4	13.2	15.2	15.2	15.5	15.8	15.1	15.0	15.3	15.8	13.2	—	—	—	—	—	14.3
College grant/scholarship (other than above)	22.6	16.3	24.3	25.4	26.3	27.6	29.9	30.2	31.4	32.7	34.9	34.3	34.7	35.9	32.5	—	—	—	—	—	30.7
Other private grant	8.3	11.5	10.8	10.9	11.8	11.4	12.1	11.4	11.8	11.3	12.5	12.0	12.8	13.3	11.7	—	—	—	—	—	11.4
Other government aid (ROTC, BIA, GI/ military benefits, etc.)	1.1	2.9	2.6	2.7	3.0	2.8	2.4	2.4	2.6	2.7	3.2	2.5	2.6	3.0	2.8	—	—	—	—	—	—
Stafford Loan (GSL)	24.6	21.8	22.4	22.0	21.8	23.9	26.9	31.6	31.4	31.0	29.7	27.7	28.5	28.7	26.2	—	—	—	—	—	25.8
Perkins Loan (NDSL)	7.1	5.1	3.4	2.6	8.2	8.2	10.1	9.8	10.2	10.5	11.1	10.5	11.0	10.7	9.5	—	—	—	—	—	10.2
Other college loan	4.3	5.8	6.4	8.3	6.1	5.8	6.7	7.2	8.5	10.6	11.1	11.9	12.4	13.1	11.4	—	—	—	—	—	14.7
Other loan	4.1	5.2	5.7	6.5	6.1	5.8	6.4	6.2	7.0	7.6	7.6	7.5	8.2	8.7	8.0	—	—	—	—	—	9.9
Other than above	2.8	3.9	3.0	3.4	3.2	3.1	3.2	3.9	4.3	4.5	5.0	5.7	5.6	6.1	5.2	—	—	—	—	—	5.9
Students receiving funds to cover educational expenses (room, board, tuition, and fees) from:																					
Family resources (parents, relatives, spouse, etc.)															—	79.9	79.4	80.1	81.2	78.8	—
My own resources (savings from work, work-study, other income)															—	61.1	59.4	59.2	60.7	56.8	—
Aid which need not be repaid (grants, scholarships, military funding, etc.)															—	63.9	63.9	63.6	65.1	64.5	—
Aid which must be repaid (loans, etc.)															—	44.8	45.0	48.0	49.5	48.6	—
Other than above															—	5.0	4.5	4.9	5.2	5.2	—
Do you have any concern about your ability to finance your college education?																					
None (I am confident that I will have sufficient funds)	37.6	37.7	36.8	35.5	—	—	29.6	—	29.2	27.8	30.6	31.4	34.0	34.5	36.3	35.3	34.7	34.3	34.5	34.0	35.8
Some (but I probably will have enough funds)	48.6	48.7	48.8	51.1	—	—	53.9	—	52.2	53.1	52.2	53.3	52.3	52.7	51.6	52.2	52.7	52.6	52.5	52.7	52.5
Major (not sure I will have enough funds)	13.7	13.6	14.4	13.4	—	—	16.6	—	18.7	19.1	17.2	15.3	13.7	12.8	12.1	12.4	12.6	13.0	13.0	13.2	11.6

79

DISAGGREGATED RESPONSES
ALL FRESHMEN

ITEM	1966	1967	1968	1969	1970	1971	1972	1973	1974	1975	1976	1977	1978	1979	1980	1981	1982	1983	1984	1985
Your probable career/occupation																				
Accountant or actuary	—	—	—	—	—	2.7	3.0	—	—	—	5.4	5.6	5.9	5.5	5.7	5.6	5.9	5.8	6.2	6.3
Actor or entertainer	—	—	—	—	—	0.8	0.8	—	—	—	1.1	1.0	1.1	1.1	1.1	1.0	1.1	1.0	1.0	1.1
Architect	—	—	—	—	—	1.2	1.4	—	—	—	1.3	1.3	1.3	1.3	1.3	1.0	0.9	0.8	1.1	1.0
Artist	—	—	—	—	—	1.9	1.9	—	—	—	1.9	2.1	1.7	1.8	1.9	1.9	1.8	1.9	1.6	1.5
Business (clerical)	—	—	—	—	—	1.4	1.2	—	—	—	0.9	1.0	0.9	1.1	0.8	0.9	0.8	0.7	0.7	0.8
Business executive (mgmt, administrator)	—	—	—	—	—	4.6	4.4	—	—	—	6.9	8.2	9.2	9.8	10.1	10.6	10.4	11.0	12.1	12.7
Business owner or proprietor	—	—	—	—	—	0.8	1.0	—	—	—	1.6	1.9	2.1	2.2	2.1	2.3	2.2	2.3	2.8	2.9
Business salesperson or buyer	—	—	—	—	—	0.5	0.5	—	—	—	0.7	0.9	1.1	1.2	1.1	1.0	1.1	1.1	1.2	1.4
Clergy (minister, priest)	—	—	—	—	—	0.5	0.5	—	—	—	0.5	0.4	0.4	0.3	0.3	0.3	0.3	0.3	0.2	0.3
Clergy (other religious)	—	—	—	—	—	0.3	0.2	—	—	—	0.2	0.2	0.2	0.2	0.2	0.2	0.1	0.1	0.1	0.2
Clinical psychologist	—	—	—	—	—	1.6	1.5	—	—	—	1.3	1.2	1.3	1.3	1.2	1.2	1.1	1.2	1.4	1.4
College administrator/staff	—	—	—	—	—	—	—	—	—	—	—	—	—	—	—	—	—	—	—	—
College teacher	—	—	—	—	—	0.9	0.8	—	—	—	0.5	0.4	0.4	0.3	0.3	0.3	0.3	0.3	0.3	0.3
Computer programmer or analyst	—	—	—	—	—	1.1	1.0	—	—	—	1.8	2.1	2.9	3.5	4.7	6.6	8.3	7.7	5.4	4.0
Conservationist or forester	—	—	—	—	—	1.4	1.5	—	—	—	1.3	1.5	1.0	0.9	0.7	0.7	0.5	0.4	0.4	0.3
Dentist (including orthodontist)	—	—	—	—	—	1.0	1.3	—	—	—	1.5	1.2	1.2	1.1	0.9	0.6	0.8	0.8	0.7	0.7
Dietitian or home economist	—	—	—	—	—	0.8	0.7	—	—	—	0.7	0.6	0.3	0.4	0.4	0.3	0.3	0.2	0.3	0.2
Engineer	—	—	—	—	—	5.3	5.6	—	—	—	7.5	8.3	8.8	8.9	10.1	10.0	11.1	10.3	10.0	10.1
Farmer or rancher	—	—	—	—	—	0.6	0.7	—	—	—	0.9	0.7	0.6	0.8	0.7	0.7	0.6	0.4	0.5	0.5
Foreign service worker (incl diplomat)	—	—	—	—	—	0.7	0.7	—	—	—	0.7	0.7	0.8	0.7	0.7	0.7	0.7	0.8	0.9	1.4
Homemaker (full-time)	—	—	—	—	—	0.5	0.4	—	—	—	0.2	0.2	0.1	0.2	0.1	0.2	0.1	0.1	0.1	0.1
Interior decorator (including designer)	—	—	—	—	—	0.7	0.6	—	—	—	0.6	0.6	0.6	0.6	0.5	0.6	0.5	0.4	0.5	0.6
Interpreter (translator)	—	—	—	—	—	0.6	0.5	—	—	—	0.3	0.3	0.2	0.3	0.2	0.2	0.2	0.2	0.3	0.2
Lab technician or hygienist	—	—	—	—	—	1.3	1.5	—	—	—	1.5	1.5	1.2	1.1	1.0	0.9	0.8	0.9	0.7	0.5
Law enforcement officer	—	—	—	—	—	0.6	0.8	—	—	—	1.4	1.5	1.3	1.1	0.8	0.5	1.0	0.6	0.8	0.7
Lawyer (attorney) or judge	—	—	—	—	—	5.5	6.1	—	—	—	5.9	6.0	5.9	5.6	5.6	5.2	5.8	5.2	5.2	5.1
Military service (career)	—	—	—	—	—	1.9	2.0	—	—	—	1.3	1.4	1.6	1.5	1.4	1.5	1.2	1.6	1.6	1.4
Musician (performer, composer)	—	—	—	—	—	1.5	1.5	—	—	—	1.7	1.8	1.7	1.6	1.5	1.5	1.4	1.3	1.1	1.2
Nurse	—	—	—	—	—	3.2	3.4	—	—	—	4.2	3.6	3.6	3.4	3.8	3.6	3.7	4.0	3.6	2.7
Optometrist	—	—	—	—	—	0.1	0.2	—	—	—	0.3	0.3	0.3	0.3	0.3	0.2	0.2	0.3	0.3	0.3
Pharmacist	—	—	—	—	—	0.9	1.0	—	—	—	1.1	0.9	0.8	0.8	0.6	0.6	0.5	0.7	0.8	0.8
Physician	—	—	—	—	—	4.8	5.7	—	—	—	5.5	4.7	5.1	4.9	5.1	4.9	5.2	5.7	5.4	6.0
Policymaker/government	—	—	—	—	—	—	—	—	—	—	—	—	—	—	—	—	—	—	—	—
School counselor	—	—	—	—	—	0.5	0.4	—	—	—	0.4	0.3	0.2	0.3	0.2	0.2	0.2	0.2	0.3	0.2
School principal or superintendent	—	—	—	—	—	0.1	0.1	—	—	—	0.1	0.0	0.0	0.0	0.0	0.0	0.0	0.0	0.0	0.0
Scientific researcher	—	—	—	—	—	3.3	3.0	—	—	—	3.1	2.8	2.7	2.2	2.0	1.9	1.7	1.8	1.8	1.9
Social, welfare or recreation worker	—	—	—	—	—	3.4	2.9	—	—	—	2.7	2.5	2.3	2.2	1.9	1.5	1.1	1.2	1.2	1.1
Statistician	—	—	—	—	—	0.1	0.1	—	—	—	0.1	0.1	0.1	0.1	0.1	0.1	0.1	0.1	0.1	0.1
Therapist (physical, occupational, speech)	—	—	—	—	—	1.9	2.4	—	—	—	2.6	2.4	2.4	2.4	2.5	2.5	2.2	2.5	2.5	2.1
Teacher or administrator (elementary)	—	—	—	—	—	7.7	6.5	—	—	—	5.0	4.7	4.1	4.4	4.1	4.0	3.3	3.4	3.4	3.7
Teacher or administrator (secondary)	—	—	—	—	—	9.6	7.3	—	—	—	4.3	3.6	3.2	3.0	2.5	2.4	2.1	2.3	2.4	2.8
Veterinarian	—	—	—	—	—	1.1	1.5	—	—	—	1.6	1.3	1.3	1.2	1.2	1.0	1.0	1.0	1.0	1.0
Writer or journalist	—	—	—	—	—	1.8	2.0	—	—	—	2.6	2.4	2.3	2.7	2.6	2.7	2.7	2.6	2.6	2.8
Skilled trades	—	—	—	—	—	0.5	0.5	—	—	—	0.4	1.0	0.5	0.6	0.7	0.6	0.4	0.3	0.3	0.3
Other	—	—	—	—	—	5.8	5.6	—	—	—	5.4	5.6	5.7	6.0	5.7	5.6	5.1	5.0	5.2	5.3
Undecided	—	—	—	—	—	14.5	15.2	—	—	—	11.1	10.8	11.7	11.2	11.3	11.5	11.0	11.2	11.9	12.0

DISAGGREGATED RESPONSES
ALL FRESHMEN

ITEM	1986	1987	1988	1989	1990	1991	1992	1993	1994	1995	1996	1997	1998	1999	2000	2001	2002	2003	2004	2005	2006
Your probable career/occupation																					
Accountant or actuary	5.7	5.7	5.7	5.7	5.2	4.9	4.2	4.0	3.8	3.6	3.1	2.8	2.7	2.4	2.3	2.1	2.2	2.0	2.2	2.5	2.6
Actor or entertainer	1.2	1.3	1.2	1.1	1.1	1.2	1.2	1.2	1.2	1.3	1.3	1.5	1.7	1.7	2.0	1.8	1.7	1.6	1.4	1.5	1.4
Architect	1.1	1.2	1.2	1.4	1.4	1.5	1.5	1.4	1.5	1.5	1.2	1.2	1.3	1.4	1.3	1.0	1.0	1.2	1.3	1.1	0.7
Artist	1.9	2.2	1.9	1.7	1.6	1.6	2.0	1.7	1.5	1.9	1.5	1.7	1.8	1.8	2.0	2.2	2.3	2.2	1.9	2.1	2.1
Business (clerical)	0.5	0.5	0.5	0.5	0.6	0.5	0.5	0.5	0.5	0.5	0.5	0.6	0.6	0.6	0.7	0.7	0.6	0.6	0.5	0.6	0.7
Business executive (mgmt, administrator)	13.1	13.3	12.8	11.5	9.9	8.0	7.2	6.8	7.1	7.5	7.6	8.0	8.5	8.7	8.8	8.2	7.7	7.4	7.5	7.9	8.4
Business owner or proprietor	3.5	3.7	3.6	3.2	2.7	2.4	2.3	2.2	2.3	2.6	2.6	2.7	2.7	2.8	3.0	3.0	2.8	3.0	3.3	3.6	3.5
Business salesperson or buyer	1.6	1.6	1.3	1.3	1.3	1.0	0.9	0.9	0.9	0.9	0.9	1.0	1.1	1.1	1.1	1.1	1.1	1.1	0.9	1.0	1.1
Clergy (minister, priest)	0.2	0.2	0.2	0.2	0.2	0.2	0.3	0.2	0.2	0.3	0.3	0.3	0.3	0.3	0.3	0.2	0.3	0.2	0.3	0.3	0.2
Clergy (other religious)	0.1	0.1	0.1	0.1	0.1	0.1	0.1	0.1	0.1	0.1	0.2	0.2	0.2	0.2	0.2	0.1	0.2	0.1	0.1	0.1	0.1
Clinical psychologist	1.7	1.7	2.0	1.8	1.7	1.8	1.9	2.0	1.9	1.8	1.8	1.7	1.7	1.7	1.8	1.7	1.6	1.6	1.5	1.5	1.5
College administrator/staff	—	—	—	—	—	—	—	—	—	—	0.1	0.0	0.1	0.0	0.0	0.0	0.0	0.0	0.1	0.0	0.0
College teacher	0.4	0.4	0.5	0.5	0.5	0.6	0.6	0.6	0.6	0.6	0.6	0.6	0.6	0.5	0.5	0.5	0.5	0.5	0.5	0.5	0.5
Computer programmer or analyst	3.0	2.4	2.3	2.3	2.2	2.2	2.0	2.1	2.4	2.9	3.6	3.9	4.6	5.1	5.2	4.5	3.5	2.7	2.2	1.8	1.7
Conservationist or forester	0.3	0.3	0.3	0.5	0.5	0.5	0.6	0.7	0.6	0.6	0.5	0.5	0.5	0.4	0.3	0.3	0.3	0.3	0.2	0.2	0.3
Dentist (including orthodontist)	0.7	0.6	0.6	0.6	0.6	0.6	0.5	0.6	0.6	0.7	0.7	0.8	0.7	0.7	0.7	0.7	0.8	0.9	1.1	1.1	1.2
Dietitian or home economist	0.2	0.2	0.2	0.2	0.2	0.2	0.2	0.2	0.3	0.3	0.3	0.3	0.3	0.3	0.2	0.2	0.2	0.2	0.4	0.4	0.4
Engineer	9.0	8.5	8.0	8.7	8.7	9.5	8.9	8.9	7.7	7.2	8.3	8.4	7.1	7.6	7.3	7.3	7.1	6.9	7.5	6.6	6.3
Farmer or rancher	0.3	0.3	0.3	0.3	0.3	0.3	0.3	0.4	0.5	0.4	0.4	0.3	0.4	0.3	0.3	0.2	0.2	0.2	0.2	0.2	0.3
Foreign service worker (incl diplomat)	1.3	1.4	1.4	1.2	1.1	1.0	0.8	0.8	0.8	0.6	0.6	0.6	0.7	0.7	0.6	0.6	0.6	0.7	0.7	0.8	0.8
Homemaker (full-time)	0.1	0.1	0.1	0.1	0.1	0.4	0.1	0.1	0.1	0.1	0.1	0.1	0.1	0.1	0.1	0.1	0.1	0.1	0.1	0.1	0.1
Interior decorator (including designer)	0.6	0.6	0.5	0.5	0.5	0.4	0.4	0.3	0.3	0.3	0.3	0.3	0.4	0.4	0.6	0.5	0.5	0.5	0.5	0.5	0.4
Interpreter (translator)	0.3	0.2	0.3	0.2	0.2	0.2	0.2	0.2	0.2	0.1	—	—	—	—	—	—	—	—	—	—	—
Lab technician or hygienist	0.4	0.4	0.4	0.3	0.2	0.2	0.3	0.3	0.3	0.3	0.3	0.3	0.2	0.2	0.2	0.2	0.2	0.2	0.2	0.2	0.2
Law enforcement officer	0.7	0.8	0.9	0.7	1.1	1.1	1.3	1.2	1.2	1.3	1.2	1.1	1.2	1.1	1.0	1.0	1.1	1.2	1.2	1.1	1.2
Lawyer (attorney) or judge	5.0	5.6	6.5	6.5	6.4	5.9	5.4	5.0	5.2	4.1	3.8	3.8	3.7	4.1	4.1	4.0	4.3	4.3	4.1	4.1	3.9
Military service (career)	1.8	1.4	1.2	1.1	1.2	1.2	0.7	0.6	0.8	0.7	1.2	0.9	0.7	0.8	0.8	1.0	1.1	1.3	1.0	0.9	1.2
Musician (performer, composer)	1.3	1.3	1.2	1.1	1.2	1.2	1.3	1.2	1.3	1.3	1.5	1.5	1.5	1.5	1.6	1.5	1.5	1.5	1.4	1.7	1.5
Nurse	2.0	1.7	1.7	1.7	2.3	3.1	3.4	3.4	3.1	2.7	2.4	2.2	2.2	2.2	2.1	2.4	2.7	3.5	3.9	3.9	4.1
Optometrist	0.2	0.3	0.3	0.3	0.3	0.3	0.3	0.3	0.4	0.4	0.3	0.3	0.3	0.3	0.2	0.2	0.2	0.3	0.3	0.3	0.3
Pharmacist	0.8	0.8	1.2	1.1	1.1	1.2	1.1	1.4	1.2	1.4	1.2	1.2	1.0	0.8	1.0	1.2	1.6	2.0	2.4	2.3	2.1
Physician	5.0	4.7	4.9	5.0	5.2	6.1	7.0	7.2	7.4	7.6	7.2	7.4	6.3	6.4	6.0	6.0	5.9	6.1	6.2	6.0	6.1
Policymaker/government	—	—	—	—	—	—	—	—	—	0.8	0.9	0.9	0.9	0.8	0.8	0.9	1.0	1.0	1.0	1.0	1.0
School counselor	0.3	0.3	0.3	0.3	0.4	0.4	0.4	0.4	0.4	0.3	0.3	0.3	0.3	0.3	0.4	0.3	0.3	0.3	0.3	0.3	0.3
School principal or superintendent	0.1	0.0	0.1	0.1	0.1	0.1	0.1	0.1	0.1	0.1	0.1	0.1	0.1	0.1	0.1	0.1	0.1	0.0	0.1	0.1	0.0
Scientific researcher	1.8	1.7	1.8	2.0	1.9	2.0	2.2	2.3	2.2	2.4	2.2	2.3	2.0	2.1	1.8	1.8	1.8	1.7	1.9	1.8	1.8
Social, welfare or recreation worker	1.1	1.1	1.3	1.1	1.0	1.1	1.1	1.2	1.3	1.3	1.2	1.2	1.1	1.1	1.1	1.0	0.9	0.8	1.0	0.9	1.0
Statistician	0.1	0.1	0.1	0.1	0.1	0.1	0.1	0.1	0.1	0.1	—	—	—	—	—	—	—	—	—	—	—
Therapist (physical, occupational, speech)	2.3	2.4	2.3	2.5	2.6	3.4	4.5	4.9	4.6	4.6	4.2	4.2	4.2	3.1	2.6	2.4	2.5	2.6	3.0	3.0	2.9
Teacher or administrator (elementary)	4.5	4.9	4.9	4.8	5.6	5.6	5.3	5.4	5.5	5.5	5.6	5.7	6.2	6.3	6.3	5.5	5.7	5.3	5.1	5.1	4.8
Teacher or administrator (secondary)	3.3	3.5	3.4	3.5	4.0	4.1	4.1	4.0	4.1	4.0	4.2	4.3	4.4	4.2	4.5	4.3	4.6	4.4	4.6	4.8	4.8
Veterinarian	0.9	0.9	0.8	0.8	0.8	1.0	1.0	1.2	1.4	1.5	1.5	1.5	1.4	1.5	1.1	1.1	1.1	1.1	1.2	1.0	1.2
Writer or journalist	2.9	2.9	3.1	2.8	2.6	2.5	2.4	2.6	2.6	2.7	2.5	2.4	2.5	2.5	2.7	2.4	2.6	2.5	2.6	2.6	2.9
Skilled trades	0.2	0.3	0.5	0.3	0.4	0.4	0.4	0.4	0.3	0.4	0.4	0.4	0.4	0.4	0.4	0.3	0.3	0.3	0.3	0.3	0.3
Other	5.5	5.9	6.3	7.5	8.3	8.0	8.3	8.7	8.2	8.1	8.6	8.4	8.7	8.7	8.9	10.5	10.7	11.1	9.8	9.5	10.1
Undecided	12.7	12.7	12.0	12.6	12.4	12.4	12.9	12.5	12.9	12.7	12.7	12.2	12.6	12.5	13.0	14.8	14.7	14.5	14.1	14.1	14.0

DISAGGREGATED RESPONSES
ALL FRESHMEN

ITEM	1966	1967	1968	1969	1970	1971	1972	1973	1974	1975	1976	1977	1978	1979	1980	1981	1982	1983	1984	1985
Your probable undergraduate field																				
Arts and Humanities																				
Art, fine and applied	—	—	—	—	—	2.9	2.5	2.4	2.5	2.4	2.4	2.6	2.2	2.4	2.4	2.4	2.2	2.2	2.0	1.9
English (language and literature)	—	—	—	—	—	2.8	2.1	2.0	1.6	1.4	1.4	1.3	1.3	1.1	1.1	1.2	1.1	1.2	1.4	1.4
History	—	—	—	—	—	2.9	2.3	1.9	1.6	1.4	1.2	1.0	0.9	0.8	0.8	0.8	0.8	0.7	0.9	1.0
Journalism	—	—	—	—	—	1.5	1.6	1.6	1.6	1.6	1.8	1.6	1.6	2.0	1.9	1.9	2.0	1.8	1.8	1.9
Language and Literature (except English)	—	—	—	—	—	2.2	1.8	1.5	1.3	1.0	0.9	0.7	0.7	0.7	0.6	0.6	0.6	0.6	0.7	0.7
Music	—	—	—	—	—	2.6	2.8	2.1	2.3	2.0	2.0	1.9	1.9	1.7	1.7	1.7	1.5	1.4	1.2	1.2
Philosophy	—	—	—	—	—	0.5	0.4	0.4	0.3	0.2	0.2	0.2	0.2	0.2	0.2	0.2	0.2	0.2	0.2	0.2
Speech or Theater	—	—	—	—	—	1.1	1.1	1.1	1.0	1.0	1.1	1.0	—	—	—	—	—	—	—	—
Theater or Drama	—	—	—	—	—	—	—	—	—	—	—	—	1.0	0.9	0.9	0.9	0.9	0.8	0.7	0.8
Speech	—	—	—	—	—	—	—	—	—	—	—	—	0.2	0.2	0.1	0.2	0.2	0.2	0.2	0.1
Theology or Religion	—	—	—	—	—	0.5	0.5	0.6	0.7	0.6	0.6	0.4	0.4	0.3	0.3	0.3	0.2	0.2	0.2	0.2
Other Arts and Humanities	—	—	—	—	—	0.5	1.2	0.8	0.7	0.7	0.7	0.6	0.5	0.5	0.5	0.6	0.6	0.5	0.5	0.7
Biological Science																				
Biology (general)	—	—	—	—	—	2.4	2.2	4.3	3.9	3.8	3.8	2.5	2.5	2.2	2.1	2.1	2.1	2.4	2.4	2.5
Biochemistry or Biophysics	—	—	—	—	—	0.6	0.6	1.0	1.0	1.0	1.0	0.6	0.7	0.6	0.6	0.6	0.6	0.7	0.7	0.7
Botany	—	—	—	—	—	0.1	0.2	0.2	0.2	0.2	0.2	0.2	0.1	0.1	0.1	0.1	0.1	0.0	0.0	0.0
Environmental Science	—	—	—	—	—	0.5	0.5	—	—	—	—	—	—	—	—	—	—	—	—	—
Marine (life) Science	—	—	—	—	—	—	—	0.9	0.8	0.9	0.8	0.9	0.7	0.6	0.5	0.5	0.4	0.4	0.5	0.4
Microbiology or Bacteriology	—	—	—	—	—	—	—	0.5	0.4	0.4	0.5	0.3	0.3	0.3	0.3	0.3	0.3	0.3	0.3	0.2
Zoology	—	—	—	—	—	0.6	0.6	1.0	1.0	0.8	0.7	0.5	0.5	0.4	0.4	0.4	0.4	0.4	0.4	0.3
Other Biological Science	—	—	—	—	—	0.7	1.3	0.9	0.9	0.9	0.9	0.7	0.7	0.6	0.5	0.6	0.5	0.6	0.6	0.4
Business																				
Accounting	—	—	—	—	—	3.0	3.1	4.1	4.9	5.1	5.7	5.9	6.3	6.0	6.2	6.1	6.4	6.3	6.7	6.4
Business Administration (general)	—	—	—	—	—	5.8	5.5	4.3	4.4	4.8	5.3	6.2	6.6	7.0	7.1	7.4	7.0	6.9	7.4	6.8
Finance	—	—	—	—	—	—	—	0.6	0.5	0.5	0.5	0.7	0.8	0.9	0.8	1.0	1.2	1.3	1.6	1.9
International Business	—	—	—	—	—	—	—	—	—	—	—	—	—	—	—	—	—	—	—	—
Marketing	—	—	—	—	—	—	—	0.8	0.8	0.9	1.0	1.3	1.7	1.9	1.9	2.0	2.0	2.2	2.6	2.9
Management	—	—	—	—	—	—	—	1.9	1.9	2.1	2.5	2.9	3.5	3.7	3.7	3.9	3.9	4.0	4.7	5.0
Secretarial Studies	—	—	—	—	—	1.3	1.1	1.2	1.0	0.9	0.8	0.9	0.7	0.9	0.6	0.6	0.5	0.5	0.5	0.5
Other Business	—	—	—	—	—	0.6	1.1	0.6	0.5	0.6	0.6	0.7	0.8	0.9	0.9	0.9	0.9	1.0	1.2	1.1
Education																				
Business Education	—	—	—	—	—	—	—	0.3	0.3	0.3	0.2	0.3	0.2	0.2	0.2	0.1	0.2	0.2	0.1	0.3
Elementary Education	—	—	—	—	—	—	—	4.4	3.8	3.3	3.2	3.0	2.5	2.7	2.6	2.7	2.4	2.6	2.7	3.0
Music or Art Education	—	—	—	—	—	—	—	0.7	0.8	0.7	0.7	0.6	0.6	0.5	0.5	0.4	0.5	0.4	0.4	0.4
Physical Education or Recreation	—	—	—	—	—	3.0	2.8	2.6	2.4	2.7	2.7	2.4	2.2	2.4	1.8	1.5	1.2	1.1	1.2	1.0
Secondary Education	—	—	—	—	—	—	—	1.6	1.4	1.1	1.2	1.0	0.8	0.8	0.8	0.8	0.8	0.9	1.0	1.2
Special Education	—	—	—	—	—	—	—	3.0	2.4	2.6	2.3	2.3	2.1	2.3	2.1	1.7	1.2	1.1	0.9	0.7
Other Education	—	—	—	—	—	7.8	5.7	0.6	0.5	0.5	0.5	0.4	0.4	0.4	0.4	0.3	0.3	0.2	0.2	0.3
Engineering																				
Aeronautical or Astronautical Eng	—	—	—	—	—	0.8	0.7	0.6	0.7	0.8	0.6	0.8	1.1	1.2	1.3	1.4	1.4	1.3	1.4	1.4
Civil Engineering	—	—	—	—	—	1.0	1.1	1.0	1.5	1.4	1.4	1.2	1.2	1.2	1.2	1.1	0.9	0.8	1.0	0.9
Chemical Engineering	—	—	—	—	—	0.6	0.5	0.5	0.8	1.1	1.0	0.9	1.1	1.2	1.2	1.3	1.2	1.0	0.8	0.9
Electrical or Electronic Engineering	—	—	—	—	—	1.7	1.9	1.7	2.0	2.2	2.2	3.1	3.0	2.9	3.5	3.2	3.7	4.1	4.0	3.9
Industrial Engineering	—	—	—	—	—	0.4	0.3	0.3	0.3	0.3	0.3	0.4	0.4	0.5	0.5	0.4	0.5	0.4	0.4	0.4
Mechanical Engineering	—	—	—	—	—	1.4	1.2	1.0	1.3	1.4	1.4	1.6	1.8	1.8	1.9	1.9	2.0	1.8	2.0	2.0
Other Engineering	—	—	—	—	—	0.6	0.8	0.8	1.2	1.4	1.5	1.4	1.6	1.6	1.6	1.9	2.2	1.9	1.4	1.5

DISAGGREGATED RESPONSES
ALL FRESHMEN

ITEM	1986	1987	1988	1989	1990	1991	1992	1993	1994	1995	1996	1997	1998	1999	2000	2001	2002	2003	2004	2005	2006
Your probable undergraduate field																					
Arts and Humanities																					
Art, fine and applied	2.3	2.6	2.4	2.1	2.1	2.0	2.3	2.0	2.0	2.3	1.9	2.1	2.4	2.2	2.5	2.9	3.0	2.9	2.4	2.6	2.5
English (language and literature)	1.6	1.6	1.7	1.8	1.8	1.8	1.7	1.8	1.8	1.8	1.9	1.8	1.8	1.8	1.7	1.7	1.7	1.7	1.9	1.9	2.0
History	1.0	1.0	1.1	1.1	1.2	1.2	1.2	1.1	1.1	1.1	1.1	1.1	1.1	1.1	1.1	1.2	1.2	1.3	1.3	1.4	1.6
Journalism	1.9	1.9	1.9	1.7	1.6	1.4	1.3	1.6	1.7	1.9	1.5	1.5	1.6	1.6	1.7	1.6	1.6	1.7	1.7	1.7	1.9
Language and Literature (except English)	0.8	0.7	0.8	0.7	0.6	0.6	0.6	0.6	0.5	0.5	0.5	0.5	0.5	0.5	0.4	0.5	0.5	0.5	0.6	0.6	0.7
Music	1.3	1.3	1.1	1.1	1.2	1.2	1.3	1.2	1.3	1.2	1.4	1.5	1.5	1.5	1.5	1.6	1.5	1.4	1.4	1.6	1.4
Philosophy	0.2	0.2	0.2	0.2	0.2	0.2	0.2	0.2	0.2	0.3	0.2	0.2	0.3	0.2	0.3	0.3	0.3	0.3	0.3	0.3	0.3
Speech or Theater	—	—	—	—	—	—	—	—	—	—	—	—	—	—	—	—	—	—	—	—	—
Theater or Drama	0.8	0.9	0.8	0.8	0.8	0.9	0.9	0.9	0.9	0.9	1.0	1.0	1.2	1.1	1.3	1.2	1.2	1.1	1.0	1.2	1.2
Speech	0.1	0.2	0.1	0.1	0.2	0.2	0.1	0.1	0.2	0.2	0.1	0.1	0.2	0.1	0.1	0.2	0.1	0.1	0.1	0.1	0.1
Theology or Religion	0.2	0.2	0.2	0.2	0.2	0.2	0.3	0.2	0.3	0.3	0.3	0.4	0.4	0.4	0.4	0.3	0.4	0.3	0.3	0.3	0.3
Other Arts and Humanities	0.6	0.7	0.7	0.6	0.6	0.6	0.6	0.5	0.7	0.7	0.7	0.7	0.8	0.8	1.1	1.1	1.1	1.0	1.0	1.1	1.1
Biological Science																					
Biology (general)	2.4	2.3	2.2	2.2	2.5	3.0	3.4	4.0	4.0	4.3	4.2	4.2	3.8	3.9	3.6	4.0	4.1	4.2	4.5	4.5	4.7
Biochemistry or Biophysics	0.7	0.6	0.6	0.6	0.6	0.6	0.7	0.8	0.8	0.8	0.8	0.8	0.7	0.7	0.7	0.7	0.9	1.0	1.1	1.1	1.2
Botany	0.0	0.0	0.0	0.0	0.0	0.0	0.1	0.1	0.1	0.1	0.1	0.1	0.1	0.1	0.0	0.0	0.0	0.0	0.0	0.0	0.0
Environmental Science	—	—	—	—	—	—	—	—	1.0	0.9	0.9	0.7	0.7	0.7	0.5	0.5	0.5	0.5	0.5	0.5	0.5
Marine (life) Science	0.5	0.5	0.5	0.7	0.6	0.8	0.9	0.9	0.7	0.8	0.8	0.7	0.4	0.6	0.4	0.4	0.4	0.3	0.3	0.4	0.4
Microbiology or Bacteriology	0.3	0.2	0.2	0.2	0.2	0.4	0.2	0.2	0.3	0.3	0.3	0.4	0.3	0.3	0.4	0.3	0.3	0.3	0.3	0.2	0.3
Zoology	0.3	0.3	0.3	0.4	0.4	0.4	0.4	0.4	0.4	0.5	0.5	0.5	0.4	0.4	0.4	0.4	0.4	0.4	0.3	0.3	0.4
Other Biological Science	0.5	0.5	0.5	0.5	0.6	0.6	0.7	0.8	0.6	0.6	0.6	0.6	0.6	0.5	0.6	0.6	0.6	0.6	0.7	0.6	0.8
Business																					
Accounting	6.0	6.1	5.9	6.0	5.6	5.3	4.5	4.2	4.0	3.8	3.3	3.0	2.8	2.5	2.3	2.2	2.4	2.2	2.2	2.6	2.7
Business Administration (general)	7.1	7.0	6.8	6.3	5.2	4.3	3.9	3.6	3.3	3.5	3.8	3.8	4.0	3.9	4.1	3.8	3.8	3.6	3.7	4.0	4.0
Finance	2.4	2.5	2.4	2.2	1.9	1.4	1.2	1.2	1.2	1.1	1.2	1.3	1.5	1.6	1.7	1.7	1.6	1.4	1.4	1.6	1.7
International Business	—	—	—	—	—	—	—	—	1.5	1.5	1.5	1.6	1.6	1.6	1.5	1.5	1.4	1.3	1.3	1.4	1.5
Marketing	3.2	3.4	3.3	3.2	3.0	2.3	2.1	2.0	1.9	1.9	2.1	2.2	2.5	2.6	2.7	2.7	2.7	2.7	2.7	2.9	2.9
Management	5.0	5.0	4.7	4.2	3.9	3.1	2.9	2.6	2.6	2.8	2.8	2.8	3.0	3.1	3.3	3.6	3.4	3.7	3.8	3.9	4.0
Secretarial Studies	0.2	0.2	0.2	0.1	0.2	0.1	0.1	0.1	0.1	0.1	0.1	0.0	0.0	0.0	0.0	0.0	0.0	0.0	0.0	0.0	0.0
Other Business	1.4	1.5	1.6	1.4	1.3	1.2	1.1	1.1	0.7	0.7	0.8	0.9	1.0	1.1	1.1	1.1	0.9	1.0	0.9	0.9	1.1
Education																					
Business Education	0.3	0.2	0.3	0.2	0.2	0.2	0.1	0.2	0.3	0.2	0.2	0.2	0.2	0.2	0.2	0.2	0.2	0.2	0.2	0.2	0.2
Elementary Education	3.8	4.3	4.3	4.3	5.1	5.0	4.8	4.8	4.9	4.9	5.0	5.0	5.5	5.5	5.6	5.1	5.2	4.9	4.6	4.4	4.2
Music or Art Education	0.4	0.4	0.4	0.4	0.6	0.5	0.6	0.5	0.6	0.6	0.7	0.7	0.7	0.6	0.7	0.7	0.7	0.7	0.6	0.8	0.7
Physical Education or Recreation	1.3	1.2	0.9	0.9	1.0	1.1	1.0	1.1	1.0	1.1	0.9	1.0	1.1	0.9	0.9	0.8	0.8	0.8	0.9	1.0	1.0
Secondary Education	1.5	1.7	1.8	2.0	2.2	2.3	2.3	2.1	2.2	2.2	2.3	2.2	2.4	2.3	2.5	2.4	2.7	2.6	2.4	2.5	2.4
Special Education	0.8	0.7	0.6	0.6	0.8	0.8	0.7	0.8	0.8	0.7	0.7	0.7	0.8	0.7	0.7	0.6	0.6	0.6	0.6	0.7	0.6
Other Education	0.3	0.3	0.3	0.3	0.4	0.4	0.4	0.4	0.4	0.4	0.4	0.4	0.4	0.4	0.4	0.3	0.4	0.3	0.3	0.4	0.4
Engineering																					
Aeronautical or Astronautical Eng	1.8	1.7	1.7	1.8	1.6	1.6	1.1	0.7	0.6	0.5	0.7	0.6	0.6	0.8	0.9	1.0	0.9	1.0	0.9	0.8	0.6
Civil Engineering	0.8	0.8	0.8	1.0	1.1	1.1	1.3	1.4	1.3	1.2	1.2	1.1	0.9	1.0	0.9	0.9	0.9	1.1	1.1	1.1	1.1
Chemical Engineering	0.7	0.6	0.6	0.8	0.8	1.1	1.2	1.4	1.1	0.9	0.9	1.1	0.8	0.8	0.6	0.6	0.6	0.6	0.7	0.6	0.7
Electrical or Electronic Engineering	3.4	3.0	2.5	2.7	2.3	2.5	2.2	2.2	2.0	1.9	2.4	2.3	1.9	2.1	2.0	2.0	1.3	1.2	1.3	1.0	1.0
Industrial Engineering	0.4	0.3	0.3	0.3	0.3	0.4	0.3	0.3	0.2	0.2	0.3	0.2	0.3	0.3	0.2	0.3	0.2	0.2	0.3	0.2	0.2
Mechanical Engineering	1.8	1.7	1.7	1.9	2.1	2.3	2.2	2.1	1.8	1.8	2.0	2.2	1.8	2.0	1.9	2.1	2.3	2.3	2.6	2.2	2.1
Other Engineering	1.2	1.3	1.1	1.3	1.5	1.8	1.8	2.0	1.7	1.6	2.1	2.1	1.9	2.0	2.2	2.2	3.3	2.9	2.7	2.5	2.3

DISAGGREGATED RESPONSES
ALL FRESHMEN

ITEM	1966	1967	1968	1969	1970	1971	1972	1973	1974	1975	1976	1977	1978	1979	1980	1981	1982	1983	1984	1985
Your probable undergraduate field																				
Physical Science																				
Astronomy	—	—	—	—	—	—	—	0.2	0.1	0.1	0.1	0.1	0.1	0.1	0.1	0.1	0.1	0.1	0.1	0.1
Atmospheric Science (incl Meteorology)	—	—	—	—	—	—	—	0.1	0.1	0.1	0.1	0.1	0.1	0.1	0.1	0.1	0.1	0.0	0.0	0.1
Chemistry	—	—	—	—	—	1.2	1.1	1.6	1.5	1.6	1.7	1.1	1.2	1.1	1.0	1.0	0.9	1.0	1.0	1.0
Earth Science	—	—	—	—	—	0.4	0.3	0.3	0.3	0.3	0.3	0.3	0.4	0.3	0.2	0.3	0.3	0.2	0.2	0.1
Marine Science	—	—	—	—	—	—	—	0.5	0.4	0.4	0.3	0.4	0.4	0.3	0.2	0.2	0.1	0.2	0.2	0.1
Mathematics	—	—	—	—	—	3.6	2.9	2.3	1.9	1.5	1.3	1.1	1.2	0.9	0.9	0.9	0.9	1.1	1.1	1.1
Physics	—	—	—	—	—	0.9	0.7	0.7	0.7	0.7	0.7	0.6	0.6	0.6	0.5	0.5	0.5	0.5	0.5	0.6
Statistics	—	—	—	—	—	0.0	0.0	0.0	0.0	0.0	0.1	0.0	0.0	0.0	0.0	0.0	0.0	0.0	0.0	0.0
Other Physical Science	—	—	—	—	—	0.3	0.3	0.2	0.2	0.2	0.2	0.2	0.2	0.2	0.2	0.2	0.2	0.1	0.1	0.1
Professional																				
Architecture or Urban Planning	—	—	—	—	—	1.3	1.3	1.1	1.4	1.2	1.0	1.0	1.1	1.0	1.0	0.7	0.7	0.5	0.8	0.8
Home Economics	—	—	—	—	—	2.2	1.9	1.6	1.6	1.3	1.2	1.2	0.9	0.9	0.8	0.6	0.5	0.4	0.5	0.5
Health Technology (medical, dental, laboratory)	—	—	—	—	—	1.7	2.2	3.5	3.4	3.5	3.6	1.9	1.6	1.5	1.5	1.4	1.2	1.3	1.1	1.0
Library or Archival Science	—	—	—	—	—	0.2	0.2	0.2	0.1	0.1	0.1	0.1	0.1	0.0	0.0	0.0	0.0	0.0	0.0	0.0
Medical, Dental, Veterinary	—	—	—	—	—	6.3	7.4	3.2	4.2	4.2	4.2	4.4	4.5	4.3	4.5	4.0	4.1	4.3	4.0	4.4
Nursing	—	—	—	—	—	3.2	3.5	3.2	3.7	3.5	3.0	3.5	3.6	3.3	3.8	3.6	3.8	4.1	3.6	2.7
Pharmacy	—	—	—	—	—	0.9	0.9	0.9	1.1	0.8	1.0	0.8	0.7	0.7	0.5	0.5	0.5	0.6	0.7	0.7
Therapy (occupational, physical, speech)	—	—	—	—	—	1.9	2.3	1.7	1.7	2.1	2.1	1.9	1.9	1.9	2.0	2.2	1.9	2.2	2.3	1.9
Other Professional	—	—	—	—	—	0.6	1.3	2.5	2.6	2.5	2.7	1.4	1.4	1.5	1.4	1.3	1.2	1.2	1.2	1.1
Social Science																				
Anthropology	—	—	—	—	—	0.4	0.4	0.4	0.3	0.2	0.2	0.1	0.1	0.1	0.1	0.1	0.1	0.1	0.1	0.1
Economics	—	—	—	—	—	0.5	0.5	0.5	0.5	0.5	0.5	0.5	0.5	0.6	0.5	0.5	0.6	0.6	0.6	0.7
Ethnic Studies	—	—	—	—	—	0.0	0.0	0.1	—	0.0	0.1	0.0	0.0	0.1	0.0	—	0.0	0.0	0.0	0.0
Geography	—	—	—	—	—	0.0	0.0	0.1	0.1	0.0	0.1	0.0	0.0	0.1	0.0	0.0	0.0	0.0	0.0	0.0
Political science (gov't, int'l relations)	—	—	—	—	—	2.5	2.7	4.1	3.4	3.3	3.2	3.2	3.1	2.8	2.9	2.7	2.7	2.8	3.1	3.7
Psychology	—	—	—	—	—	4.7	4.2	4.0	3.7	3.5	3.0	2.9	3.0	3.0	2.7	2.7	2.6	2.8	3.3	3.6
Social Work	—	—	—	—	—	2.5	2.0	1.8	1.9	1.9	1.9	1.7	1.6	1.5	1.3	1.1	0.8	0.8	0.8	0.8
Sociology	—	—	—	—	—	1.8	1.6	1.2	1.1	0.9	0.8	0.7	0.6	0.5	0.5	0.4	0.3	0.3	0.4	0.4
Women's Studies	—	—	—	—	—	—	—	—	—	—	—	—	—	—	—	—	0.0	0.0	0.0	0.0
Other Social Science	—	—	—	—	—	0.3	0.4	0.3	0.3	0.3	0.3	0.3	0.3	0.3	0.2	0.2	0.2	0.1	0.2	0.1
Technical																				
Building Trades	—	—	—	—	—	0.3	0.2	0.1	0.1	0.1	0.1	0.1	0.1	0.1	0.1	0.1	0.1	0.0	0.0	0.1
Data Processing or Computer Programming	—	—	—	—	—	0.4	0.3	0.4	0.5	0.6	0.6	0.8	1.0	1.3	1.7	2.4	3.1	2.8	1.8	1.7
Drafting or Design	—	—	—	—	—	—	—	0.1	0.2	0.2	0.1	0.2	0.2	0.3	0.3	0.4	0.3	0.2	0.2	0.3
Electronics	—	—	—	—	—	0.2	0.3	0.4	0.2	0.6	0.1	0.7	0.4	0.4	0.7	0.5	0.4	0.2	0.1	0.1
Mechanics	—	—	—	—	—	—	—	0.1	0.1	0.1	0.1	0.1	0.0	0.1	0.1	0.1	0.1	0.1	0.1	0.1
Other Technical	—	—	—	—	—	0.4	0.3	0.1	0.2	0.1	0.1	0.2	0.1	0.1	0.2	0.2	0.1	0.1	0.1	0.1
Other																				
Agriculture	—	—	—	—	—	1.0	1.2	1.3	1.6	1.4	1.7	1.2	1.1	1.2	1.1	1.1	0.9	0.7	0.9	0.9
Communications (radio, TV, etc.)	—	—	—	—	—	0.8	0.7	0.9	1.0	1.3	1.5	1.7	1.8	2.1	2.4	2.5	2.5	2.5	2.4	2.8
Computer Science	—	—	—	—	—	0.7	0.7	0.5	0.8	0.8	0.9	1.0	1.5	1.8	2.6	3.8	4.9	4.9	3.5	2.4
Forestry	—	—	—	—	—	0.9	0.9	0.7	1.0	1.2	0.6	0.9	0.5	0.5	0.4	0.4	0.4	0.3	0.2	0.2
Law Enforcement	—	—	—	—	—	—	—	1.0	0.8	1.2	1.5	1.8	1.5	1.4	1.1	0.6	1.3	1.0	1.0	1.0
Military Science	—	—	—	—	—	0.5	0.2	0.3	0.2	0.2	0.1	0.2	0.2	0.1	0.1	0.1	0.1	0.2	0.1	0.2
Other field	—	—	—	—	—	4.4	4.4	0.6	0.6	0.7	0.8	0.8	0.7	0.8	0.7	0.8	0.7	0.7	0.8	0.8
Undecided	—	—	—	—	—	2.4	4.9	5.1	4.9	5.5	5.1	5.6	5.4	5.4	5.6	5.8	5.8	6.1	6.2	6.8

DISAGGREGATED RESPONSES
ALL FRESHMEN

ITEM	1986	1987	1988	1989	1990	1991	1992	1993	1994	1995	1996	1997	1998	1999	2000	2001	2002	2003	2004	2005	2006
Your probable undergraduate field																					
Physical Science																					
Astronomy	0.1	0.1	0.1	0.1	0.1	0.1	0.1	0.1	0.1	0.1	0.1	0.1	0.1	0.1	0.1	0.1	0.1	0.1	0.1	0.1	0.1
Atmospheric Science (incl Meteorology)	0.1	0.1	0.1	0.1	0.1	0.1	0.1	0.1	0.1	0.1	0.1	0.1	0.1	0.1	0.1	0.1	0.1	0.1	0.1	0.2	0.1
Chemistry	0.9	0.8	0.8	0.7	0.8	0.8	0.9	1.0	1.1	1.0	0.9	0.9	0.8	0.7	0.8	0.8	0.9	0.9	1.1	1.1	1.2
Earth Science	0.1	0.1	0.1	0.2	0.2	0.2	0.3	0.3	0.1	0.1	0.1	0.1	0.1	0.1	0.1	0.1	0.1	0.1	0.1	0.1	0.1
Marine Science	0.1	0.1	0.1	0.2	0.2	0.3	0.3	0.3	0.2	0.1	0.3	0.3	0.2	0.2	0.2	0.2	0.1	0.1	0.1	0.1	0.1
Mathematics	0.9	0.8	0.8	0.8	0.8	0.8	0.8	0.7	0.8	0.4	0.7	0.6	0.6	0.6	0.7	0.7	0.7	0.7	0.7	0.8	0.8
Physics	0.6	0.5	0.5	0.6	0.5	0.5	0.5	0.5	0.4	0.7	0.5	0.5	0.4	0.4	0.5	0.5	0.5	0.5	0.6	0.5	0.5
Statistics	0.0	0.0	0.0	0.0	0.0	0.0	0.0	0.0	0.0	0.5	0.0	0.0	0.0	0.0	0.0	0.0	0.0	0.0	0.0	0.0	0.0
Other Physical Science	0.1	0.1	0.1	0.1	0.1	0.2	0.2	0.2	0.1	0.2	0.1	0.1	0.1	0.0	0.1	0.1	0.2	0.2	0.2	0.2	0.2
Professional																					
Architecture or Urban Planning	0.8	0.9	0.9	1.1	1.1	1.3	1.3	1.2	1.3	1.3	1.0	1.0	1.1	1.2	1.1	0.9	0.9	1.1	1.1	1.0	0.5
Home Economics	0.4	0.4	0.3	0.3	0.3	0.2	0.2	0.1	0.1	0.1	0.1	0.1	0.1	0.1	0.1	0.1	0.1	0.1	0.0	0.2	0.2
Health Technology (medical, dental, laboratory)	0.7	0.7	0.8	0.7	0.7	0.8	0.8	0.8	0.8	0.8	0.8	0.8	0.6	0.5	0.4	0.5	0.5	0.5	0.5	0.5	0.6
Library or Archival Science	0.0	0.0	0.0	0.0	0.0	0.0	0.0	0.0	0.0	0.0	0.0	0.0	0.0	0.0	0.0	0.0	0.0	0.0	0.0	0.0	0.0
Medical, Dental, Veterinary	3.8	3.3	3.5	3.8	3.9	4.3	4.9	5.1	5.2	5.2	4.9	5.1	4.8	5.0	4.4	4.3	4.2	4.4	4.4	4.1	3.9
Nursing	2.0	1.6	1.7	1.8	2.4	3.2	3.5	3.5	3.2	2.7	2.5	2.3	2.3	2.3	2.1	2.6	2.7	3.7	4.0	4.0	4.1
Pharmacy	0.7	0.7	1.1	1.0	1.1	1.1	1.0	1.3	1.1	1.2	1.1	1.1	0.9	0.6	0.8	1.0	1.3	1.7	2.0	1.9	1.5
Therapy (occupational, physical, speech)	1.9	2.0	2.0	2.2	2.3	3.1	4.1	4.6	4.2	4.2	3.9	3.7	3.7	2.5	1.9	1.9	1.9	2.1	2.3	2.2	2.0
Other Professional	1.1	1.1	1.2	1.2	1.2	1.1	1.0	1.0	1.1	1.0	1.0	1.0	1.0	0.9	0.8	0.7	0.7	0.7	0.8	0.7	0.7
Social Science																					
Anthropology	0.1	0.2	0.2	0.2	0.2	0.2	0.3	0.3	0.3	0.3	0.3	0.3	0.3	0.3	0.3	0.3	0.3	0.3	0.3	0.3	0.4
Economics	0.6	0.7	0.7	0.6	0.6	0.5	0.4	0.4	0.4	0.4	0.4	0.4	0.4	0.5	0.5	0.5	0.5	0.5	0.5	0.6	0.7
Ethnic Studies	0.0	0.0	0.0	0.0	0.0	0.0	0.1	0.0	0.0	0.0	0.0	0.0	0.0	0.0	0.0	0.0	0.0	0.0	0.0	0.1	0.1
Geography	0.0	0.0	0.0	0.0	0.1	0.1	0.1	0.1	0.0	0.0	0.0	0.0	0.0	0.0	0.0	0.0	0.0	0.0	0.0	0.0	0.0
Political science (gov't, int'l relations)	3.4	3.6	4.2	4.1	4.0	3.6	3.4	3.4	3.1	2.8	2.8	2.7	2.6	2.8	2.8	3.1	3.3	3.5	3.3	3.5	3.5
Psychology	4.0	4.3	4.7	4.7	4.5	4.4	4.7	4.7	4.7	4.6	4.6	4.3	4.5	4.5	4.8	4.8	4.8	4.7	4.6	4.6	4.8
Social Work	0.7	0.7	0.8	0.7	0.8	0.7	0.9	0.8	1.0	1.0	1.0	0.8	0.8	0.8	0.8	0.7	0.6	0.6	0.6	0.7	0.7
Sociology	0.4	0.4	0.4	0.5	0.5	0.5	0.5	0.6	0.6	0.5	0.5	0.5	0.6	0.5	0.5	0.6	0.6	0.6	0.6	0.6	0.7
Women's Studies	0.0	0.0	0.0	0.0	0.0	0.0	0.0	0.0	0.0	0.0	0.0	0.0	0.0	0.0	0.0	0.0	0.0	0.0	0.0	0.0	0.0
Other Social Science	0.2	0.2	0.2	0.2	0.3	0.2	0.3	0.2	0.3	0.3	0.3	0.3	0.3	0.3	0.3	0.3	0.3	0.3	0.3	0.3	0.3
Technical																					
Building Trades	0.0	0.0	0.1	0.0	0.0	0.1	0.0	0.0	0.0	0.0	0.0	0.1	0.1	0.0	0.0	0.0	0.0	0.1	0.1	0.1	0.1
Data Processing or Computer Programming	1.1	0.7	0.7	0.7	0.7	0.6	0.5	0.5	0.6	0.8	0.9	1.1	1.2	1.4	1.5	1.4	0.9	0.7	0.6	0.5	0.5
Drafting or Design	0.3	0.3	0.3	0.2	0.2	0.2	0.3	0.2	0.2	0.2	0.2	0.3	0.3	0.3	0.3	0.4	0.3	0.4	0.3	0.3	0.3
Electronics	0.1	0.2	0.1	0.1	0.1	0.1	0.1	0.1	0.1	0.1	0.1	0.1	0.1	0.1	0.1	0.1	0.1	0.1	0.2	0.1	0.1
Mechanics	0.0	0.0	0.3	0.1	0.0	0.1	0.0	0.1	0.0	0.0	0.0	0.0	0.0	0.0	0.0	0.0	0.0	0.0	0.1	0.1	0.0
Other Technical	0.1	0.1	0.3	0.1	0.1	0.1	0.1	0.1	0.1	0.0	0.1	0.1	0.0	0.1	0.1	0.2	0.1	0.2	0.2	0.1	0.1
Other																					
Agriculture	0.6	0.6	0.6	0.6	0.6	0.7	0.6	0.7	1.0	0.8	0.9	0.8	0.9	0.9	0.6	0.5	0.6	0.4	0.6	0.4	0.5
Communications (radio, TV, etc.)	3.0	3.2	3.2	3.0	2.9	2.5	2.5	2.2	1.9	1.8	2.1	2.1	2.2	2.4	2.7	2.6	2.5	2.4	1.9	2.0	2.2
Computer Science	1.9	1.6	1.6	1.6	1.7	1.8	1.6	1.6	1.9	2.2	2.7	3.0	3.4	3.7	3.7	3.3	2.2	1.7	1.4	1.1	1.1
Forestry	0.2	0.1	0.1	0.2	0.2	0.3	0.3	0.4	0.3	0.3	0.2	0.3	0.2	0.1	0.1	0.1	0.1	0.1	0.1	0.1	0.1
Law Enforcement	0.9	0.9	1.1	1.0	1.3	1.4	1.4	1.2	1.3	1.4	1.3	1.2	1.3	1.2	1.1	1.1	1.2	1.4	1.4	1.2	1.2
Military Science	0.1	0.1	0.1	0.1	0.1	0.1	0.1	0.1	0.1	0.1	0.1	0.0	0.1	0.1	0.1	0.1	0.1	0.1	0.1	0.1	0.1
Other field	0.8	1.0	1.1	1.2	1.4	1.3	1.2	1.3	1.1	1.2	1.2	1.2	1.2	1.6	1.3	1.3	1.8	1.9	2.1	1.9	1.8
Undecided	7.6	7.8	7.3	7.8	7.6	7.8	8.0	8.0	8.4	8.2	7.9	8.0	8.0	8.0	8.3	8.5	8.4	8.0	7.4	7.3	7.2

DISAGGREGATED RESPONSES
ALL FRESHMEN

ITEM	1966	1967	1968	1969	1970	1971	1972	1973	1974	1975	1976	1977	1978	1979	1980	1981	1982	1983	1984	1985
Your father's occupation																				
Accountant or actuary	—	—	—	—	—	2.5	2.6	—	—	—	2.7	2.6	2.7	2.5	2.5	2.6	2.6	2.5	2.7	2.7
Actor or entertainer	—	—	—	—	—	0.0	0.1	—	—	—	0.1	0.1	0.1	0.0	0.1	0.1	0.1	0.1	0.1	0.1
Architect	—	—	—	—	—	0.6	0.5	—	—	—	0.7	0.7	0.6	0.7	0.7	0.7	0.7	0.7	0.8	0.8
Artist	—	—	—	—	—	0.3	0.3	—	—	—	0.3	0.3	0.3	0.3	0.3	0.3	0.3	0.3	0.3	0.3
Business (clerical)	—	—	—	—	—	1.3	1.4	—	—	—	0.9	0.9	0.9	0.9	0.9	0.8	0.8	0.7	0.8	0.7
Business executive (mgmt, administrator)	—	—	—	—	—	14.6	15.6	—	—	—	14.8	14.5	15.1	14.6	14.9	14.6	14.9	14.6	14.3	14.8
Business owner or proprietor	—	—	—	—	—	8.0	8.2	—	—	—	8.0	7.7	7.8	8.0	8.1	8.2	8.6	8.5	8.7	8.7
Business salesperson or buyer	—	—	—	—	—	6.5	6.3	—	—	—	6.3	6.2	6.3	6.2	5.8	5.9	5.9	5.9	5.8	5.4
Clergy (minister, priest)	—	—	—	—	—	0.9	1.0	—	—	—	1.2	1.1	1.3	1.1	1.1	1.1	1.0	1.0	0.9	1.0
Clergy (other religious)	—	—	—	—	—	0.1	0.1	—	—	—	0.2	0.2	0.2	0.2	0.2	0.2	0.2	0.2	0.2	0.1
Clinical psychologist	—	—	—	—	—	0.1	0.1	—	—	—	0.1	0.1	0.1	0.1	0.1	0.1	0.1	0.1	0.1	0.2
College administrator/staff	—	—	—	—	—	—	—	—	—	—	—	—	—	—	—	—	—	—	—	—
College teacher	—	—	—	—	—	1.0	1.1	—	—	—	1.2	1.1	1.2	1.2	1.2	1.2	1.2	1.2	1.2	1.4
Computer programmer or analyst	—	—	—	—	—	0.5	0.5	—	—	—	0.9	1.0	1.2	1.2	1.4	1.5	1.6	1.8	1.9	2.1
Conservationist or forester	—	—	—	—	—	0.2	0.3	—	—	—	0.2	0.2	0.2	0.2	0.2	0.2	0.2	0.1	0.2	0.2
Dentist (including orthodontist)	—	—	—	—	—	0.6	0.7	—	—	—	0.8	0.7	0.7	0.7	0.7	0.7	0.7	0.7	0.6	0.6
Dietitian or home economist	—	—	—	—	—	0.0	0.1	—	—	—	0.1	0.1	0.1	0.0	0.1	0.0	0.1	0.1	0.1	0.1
Engineer	—	—	—	—	—	8.2	8.4	—	—	—	9.0	8.7	9.4	8.7	8.6	8.7	8.7	8.6	8.8	9.1
Farmer or rancher	—	—	—	—	—	5.1	4.7	—	—	—	3.9	3.4	3.0	3.0	3.5	3.8	3.4	3.1	3.0	3.5
Foreign service worker (incl diplomat)	—	—	—	—	—	0.2	0.2	—	—	—	0.1	0.1	0.1	0.1	0.1	0.2	0.1	0.1	0.1	0.2
Homemaker (full-time)	—	—	—	—	—	0.2	0.0	—	—	—	0.1	0.1	0.1	0.1	0.1	0.1	0.1	0.1	0.1	0.1
Interior decorator (including designer)	—	—	—	—	—	0.1	0.1	—	—	—	0.1	0.1	0.1	0.1	0.1	0.1	0.1	0.1	0.1	0.1
Interpreter (translator)	—	—	—	—	—	0.0	0.0	—	—	—	0.0	0.0	0.0	0.0	0.1	0.0	0.0	0.0	0.0	0.0
Lab technician or hygienist	—	—	—	—	—	0.4	0.4	—	—	—	0.4	0.4	0.4	0.4	0.4	0.4	0.4	0.3	0.4	0.4
Law enforcement officer	—	—	—	—	—	0.9	1.0	—	—	—	1.1	1.2	1.1	1.1	1.2	1.1	1.3	1.2	1.4	1.3
Lawyer (attorney) or judge	—	—	—	—	—	1.6	1.8	—	—	—	1.9	1.9	1.9	2.0	2.0	2.1	2.2	2.0	2.0	2.2
Military service (career)	—	—	—	—	—	2.2	2.0	—	—	—	2.2	2.3	2.2	2.0	2.0	2.1	2.0	2.1	1.9	1.7
Musician (performer, composer)	—	—	—	—	—	0.1	0.1	—	—	—	0.1	0.1	0.1	0.1	0.1	0.1	0.2	0.2	0.1	0.1
Nurse	—	—	—	—	—	0.1	0.1	—	—	—	0.1	0.1	0.1	0.1	0.1	0.1	0.1	0.1	0.1	0.1
Optometrist	—	—	—	—	—	0.1	0.1	—	—	—	0.1	0.1	0.1	0.1	0.1	0.1	0.1	0.1	0.1	0.1
Pharmacist	—	—	—	—	—	0.4	0.4	—	—	—	0.5	0.5	0.5	0.5	0.5	0.5	0.4	0.5	0.5	0.5
Physician	—	—	—	—	—	2.0	2.0	—	—	—	2.4	2.2	2.4	2.3	2.4	2.4	2.5	2.5	2.3	2.5
Policymaker/government	—	—	—	—	—	—	—	—	—	—	—	—	—	—	—	—	—	—	—	—
School counselor	—	—	—	—	—	0.1	0.2	—	—	—	0.2	0.1	0.2	0.2	0.2	0.2	0.2	0.2	0.2	0.2
School principal or superintendent	—	—	—	—	—	0.8	0.9	—	—	—	0.7	0.7	0.7	0.7	0.7	0.7	0.7	0.7	0.6	0.6
Scientific researcher	—	—	—	—	—	0.8	0.8	—	—	—	0.8	0.7	0.8	0.7	0.8	0.7	0.7	0.8	0.7	0.8
Social, welfare or recreation worker	—	—	—	—	—	0.3	0.3	—	—	—	0.4	0.4	0.4	0.4	0.4	0.4	0.4	0.4	0.5	0.4
Statistician	—	—	—	—	—	0.1	0.1	—	—	—	0.1	0.1	0.1	0.1	0.1	0.1	0.1	0.1	0.1	0.1
Therapist (physical, occupational, speech)	—	—	—	—	—	0.1	0.1	—	—	—	0.1	0.1	0.1	0.1	0.1	0.1	0.1	0.1	0.1	0.1
Teacher or administrator (elementary)	—	—	—	—	—	0.4	0.4	—	—	—	0.6	0.6	0.6	0.6	0.6	0.6	0.7	0.7	0.7	0.8
Teacher or administrator (secondary)	—	—	—	—	—	1.6	1.8	—	—	—	2.6	2.4	2.6	2.7	2.6	2.9	3.0	2.9	2.9	3.2
Veterinarian	—	—	—	—	—	0.2	0.2	—	—	—	0.2	0.2	0.2	0.2	0.3	0.2	0.2	0.2	0.2	0.2
Writer or journalist	—	—	—	—	—	0.3	0.3	—	—	—	0.4	0.3	0.4	0.3	0.3	0.3	0.4	0.3	0.4	0.3
Skilled trades	—	—	—	—	—	11.0	10.8	—	—	—	9.4	9.9	9.3	9.5	9.5	9.4	9.3	9.1	9.3	8.2
Laborer (unskilled)	—	—	—	—	—	3.5	3.5	—	—	—	3.3	3.3	2.9	3.1	3.2	2.9	2.8	2.7	2.8	2.7
Semi skilled worker	—	—	—	—	—	6.6	5.8	—	—	—	4.9	5.3	4.4	4.7	4.6	4.2	4.1	4.4	4.1	4.1
Other occupation	—	—	—	—	—	14.4	13.0	—	—	—	14.0	15.1	15.1	15.9	14.9	15.6	15.0	15.2	15.6	14.8
Unemployed	—	—	—	—	—	1.2	1.8	—	—	—	2.0	2.2	2.1	2.2	2.4	1.9	2.0	2.7	2.4	2.3

DISAGGREGATED RESPONSES
ALL FRESHMEN

ITEM	1986	1987	1988	1989	1990	1991	1992	1993	1994	1995	1996	1997	1998	1999	2000	2001	2002	2003	2004	2005	2006
Your father's occupation																					
Accountant or actuary	2.7	2.8	2.7	2.7	2.7	2.6	2.7	2.8	2.7	2.7	2.7	2.6	2.7	2.7	2.8	2.7	2.7	2.8	2.8	2.8	2.8
Actor or entertainer	0.1	0.1	0.1	0.1	0.1	0.1	0.1	0.1	0.1	0.1	0.1	0.1	0.1	0.1	0.1	0.1	0.1	0.1	0.1	0.1	0.1
Architect	0.9	0.9	0.9	0.9	0.8	0.8	0.9	0.8	0.8	0.9	0.8	0.9	1.0	1.1	1.1	1.1	1.0	1.0	1.1	1.0	1.0
Artist	0.3	0.3	0.3	0.3	0.3	0.3	0.3	0.3	0.3	0.3	0.3	0.3	0.3	0.3	0.3	0.3	0.3	0.4	0.3	0.3	0.4
Business (clerical)	0.7	0.8	0.7	0.7	0.7	0.7	0.7	0.7	0.8	0.8	0.7	0.8	0.9	0.9	1.0	1.1	1.1	1.1	1.1	1.1	1.2
Business executive (mgmt, administrator)	15.3	15.6	14.4	14.5	13.6	12.9	13.0	12.7	12.5	12.1	11.9	12.0	12.4	12.2	12.4	12.5	12.3	12.2	12.0	11.9	12.0
Business owner or proprietor	9.4	9.4	9.2	9.2	8.8	8.6	8.7	8.7	8.8	8.9	8.8	9.1	9.1	9.4	9.4	9.3	9.2	9.5	9.7	9.4	9.3
Business salesperson or buyer	5.7	5.6	5.2	5.2	4.8	4.8	5.0	4.8	4.7	4.8	4.8	4.9	4.7	4.8	4.7	4.7	4.6	4.7	4.6	4.6	4.7
Clergy (minister, priest)	1.0	0.9	0.9	1.1	1.1	1.1	1.1	1.0	1.1	1.0	1.2	1.1	1.1	1.1	1.0	0.9	1.0	0.9	0.8	0.9	0.8
Clergy (other religious)	0.2	0.2	0.1	0.1	0.1	0.1	0.1	0.1	0.1	0.1	0.1	0.1	0.1	0.1	0.1	0.1	0.1	0.1	0.1	0.1	0.1
Clinical psychologist	0.2	0.2	0.2	0.2	0.2	0.2	0.2	0.2	0.2	0.2	0.2	0.2	0.2	0.2	0.2	0.2	0.2	0.2	0.2	0.1	0.1
College administrator/staff	—	—	0.2	0.2	0.2	0.2	0.2	0.2	0.2	0.2	0.2	0.2	0.2	0.3	0.4	0.4	0.3	0.4	0.4	0.4	0.3
College teacher	1.3	1.3	1.2	1.1	1.0	1.0	1.0	0.9	0.9	0.8	0.8	0.8	0.8	0.8	0.8	0.8	0.8	0.8	0.8	0.7	0.8
Computer programmer or analyst	2.1	2.3	2.2	2.4	2.3	2.3	2.5	2.5	2.6	2.7	2.8	2.8	3.1	3.2	3.3	3.5	3.4	3.5	3.5	3.5	3.6
Conservationist or forester	0.2	0.2	0.2	0.2	0.2	0.2	0.2	0.2	0.2	0.2	0.2	0.2	0.2	0.2	0.2	0.2	0.2	0.2	0.2	0.2	0.2
Dentist (including orthodontist)	0.7	0.7	0.7	0.6	0.6	0.6	0.6	0.6	0.6	0.6	0.6	0.6	0.6	0.6	0.6	0.6	0.6	0.6	0.6	0.6	0.6
Dietitian or home economist	0.1	0.0	0.0	0.0	0.1	0.1	0.1	0.1	0.0	0.1	0.1	0.1	0.0	0.0	0.1	0.0	0.1	0.1	0.1	0.1	0.1
Engineer	8.8	8.6	8.3	8.2	8.0	8.0	8.1	8.1	7.9	7.9	8.0	7.9	8.1	8.2	8.1	8.4	8.3	8.6	8.7	8.5	8.5
Farmer or rancher	2.6	2.5	2.4	2.6	2.8	2.7	2.4	2.7	3.0	3.0	2.6	2.7	2.4	2.5	2.2	1.9	1.8	1.5	1.7	1.4	1.3
Foreign service worker (incl diplomat)	0.1	0.2	0.2	0.1	0.2	0.1	0.2	0.1	0.1	0.1	0.1	0.2	0.1	0.1	0.1	0.1	0.1	0.1	0.1	0.1	0.1
Homemaker (full-time)	0.1	0.1	0.1	0.1	0.2	0.2	0.2	0.2	0.1	0.2	0.1	0.2	0.2	0.2	0.2	0.2	0.2	0.2	0.2	0.2	0.2
Interior decorator (including designer)	0.0	0.0	0.1	0.1	0.1	0.0	0.0	0.0	0.1	0.0	0.0	0.1	0.0	0.0	0.1	0.1	0.0	0.0	0.0	0.1	0.1
Interpreter (translator)	0.0	0.0	0.0	—	0.0	0.0	0.0	0.0	0.0	0.0	—	—	0.0	—	—	0.1	0.0	—	—	—	—
Lab technician or hygienist	0.4	0.4	0.4	0.4	0.4	0.4	0.4	0.4	0.4	0.3	0.4	0.4	0.4	0.4	0.4	0.4	0.4	0.4	0.4	0.3	0.3
Law enforcement officer	1.3	1.4	1.4	1.5	1.6	1.5	1.6	1.6	1.7	1.6	1.6	1.6	1.6	1.6	1.6	1.7	1.6	1.6	1.5	1.6	1.7
Lawyer (attorney) or judge	2.3	2.4	2.4	2.2	2.1	2.0	2.1	2.2	2.2	2.2	2.2	2.4	2.2	2.3	2.3	2.3	2.4	2.4	2.3	2.4	2.5
Military service (career)	2.0	1.9	2.0	2.1	2.0	2.3	2.2	1.8	1.8	1.7	1.7	1.5	1.6	1.6	1.5	1.7	1.7	1.6	1.5	1.5	1.5
Musician (performer, composer)	0.1	0.1	0.1	0.1	0.1	0.2	0.1	0.2	0.1	0.1	0.2	0.2	0.2	0.2	0.2	0.2	0.2	0.2	0.2	0.2	0.2
Nurse	0.1	0.1	0.1	0.1	0.1	0.2	0.2	0.2	0.2	0.3	0.3	0.4	0.4	0.4	0.4	0.4	0.5	0.5	0.5	0.5	0.5
Optometrist	0.1	0.1	0.1	0.1	0.1	0.1	0.1	0.1	0.1	0.1	0.1	0.2	0.1	0.1	0.2	0.1	0.1	0.1	0.1	0.1	0.1
Pharmacist	0.5	0.5	0.5	0.4	0.4	0.4	0.4	0.4	0.5	0.4	0.5	0.5	0.5	0.4	0.4	0.5	0.5	0.5	0.5	0.5	0.4
Physician	2.5	2.6	2.5	2.4	2.3	2.2	2.2	2.2	2.2	2.2	2.1	2.4	2.2	2.3	2.4	2.5	2.4	2.4	2.4	2.4	2.4
Policymaker/government	—	—	—	—	—	—	—	—	—	0.9	0.9	0.8	0.9	0.9	0.9	0.9	0.9	0.8	0.8	0.8	0.8
School counselor	0.2	0.2	0.2	0.2	0.2	0.2	0.2	0.2	0.2	0.2	0.1	0.1	0.1	0.1	0.1	0.1	0.1	0.1	0.1	0.1	0.1
School principal or superintendent	0.6	0.6	0.6	0.6	0.6	0.6	0.5	0.6	0.6	0.5	0.5	0.5	0.4	0.4	0.4	0.3	0.3	0.3	0.3	0.2	0.2
Scientific researcher	0.8	0.7	0.7	0.6	0.6	0.7	0.6	0.6	0.6	0.6	0.6	0.6	0.6	0.6	0.6	0.7	0.7	0.7	0.7	0.7	0.7
Social, welfare or recreation worker	0.4	0.5	0.5	0.5	0.5	0.6	0.5	0.6	0.6	0.6	0.6	0.6	0.6	0.6	0.6	0.6	0.6	0.6	0.5	0.6	0.6
Statistician	0.1	0.2	0.1	0.1	0.1	0.1	0.1	0.1	0.1	0.1	0.1	0.2	0.1	0.1	0.2	0.1	0.1	0.1	0.1	0.1	0.2
Therapist (physical, occupational, speech)	0.1	0.2	0.1	0.1	0.1	0.2	0.2	0.2	0.1	0.2	0.2	0.2	0.2	0.2	0.2	0.3	0.3	0.3	0.3	0.3	0.3
Teacher or administrator (elementary)	0.8	0.9	1.0	1.0	1.0	1.0	1.1	1.1	1.1	1.1	1.2	1.1	1.1	1.1	1.0	0.9	0.9	0.9	0.8	0.8	0.7
Teacher or administrator (secondary)	3.4	3.4	3.5	3.5	3.3	3.4	3.5	3.4	3.3	3.3	3.2	3.1	2.8	2.8	2.6	2.5	2.4	2.3	2.2	2.1	2.1
Veterinarian	0.2	0.2	0.2	0.2	0.2	0.2	0.2	0.2	0.2	0.2	0.1	0.2	0.2	0.2	0.1	0.1	0.2	0.1	0.2	0.1	0.2
Writer or journalist	0.3	0.4	0.4	0.3	0.3	0.3	0.3	0.3	0.3	0.2	0.3	0.3	0.3	0.3	0.3	0.3	0.3	0.3	0.3	0.3	0.3
Skilled trades	8.4	8.3	8.8	8.8	9.0	9.0	8.4	9.2	8.6	8.5	8.4	8.4	8.4	7.9	7.7	8.3	8.2	7.9	8.0	7.6	7.6
Laborer (unskilled)	2.3	2.1	2.5	2.4	2.8	2.9	2.6	2.9	2.7	2.6	2.7	2.5	2.7	2.5	2.6	3.1	3.1	3.1	3.1	3.3	3.0
Semi skilled worker	3.4	3.2	3.6	3.6	3.8	4.0	3.6	3.5	3.6	3.6	3.4	3.4	3.3	3.1	3.0	3.2	3.1	3.0	3.0	3.0	2.8
Other occupation	14.8	15.0	16.1	16.2	17.8	17.4	17.8	17.5	18.2	18.3	18.4	18.5	18.4	18.7	18.8	18.0	18.2	18.6	18.7	19.7	20.0
Unemployed	2.2	1.9	2.0	2.0	2.2	2.8	2.9	2.9	2.9	2.7	2.9	2.5	2.4	2.2	2.4	2.0	2.4	2.6	2.5	2.6	2.5

DISAGGREGATED RESPONSES
ALL FRESHMEN

ITEM	1966	1967	1968	1969	1970	1971	1972	1973	1974	1975	1976	1977	1978	1979	1980	1981	1982	1983	1984	1985
Your mother's occupation																				
Accountant or actuary	—	—	—	—	—	1.5	1.6	—	—	—	1.5	1.7	1.8	1.8	2.0	2.2	2.2	2.3	2.3	2.4
Actor or entertainer	—	—	—	—	—	0.0	0.0	—	—	—	0.0	0.1	0.1	0.1	0.1	0.1	0.1	0.1	0.1	0.1
Architect	—	—	—	—	—	0.0	0.0	—	—	—	0.0	0.0	0.0	0.0	0.1	0.1	0.1	0.1	0.1	0.1
Artist	—	—	—	—	—	0.4	0.4	—	—	—	0.5	0.6	0.6	0.5	0.6	0.6	0.7	0.7	0.7	0.7
Business (clerical)	—	—	—	—	—	8.7	10.7	—	—	—	9.7	9.7	10.0	10.4	10.9	11.0	11.1	10.8	11.3	10.5
Business executive (mgmt, administrator)	—	—	—	—	—	1.2	1.4	—	—	—	2.0	2.1	2.4	2.7	3.1	3.3	3.7	4.1	4.4	4.8
Business owner or proprietor	—	—	—	—	—	1.0	1.4	—	—	—	1.4	1.5	1.6	1.9	1.9	2.2	2.2	2.4	2.6	2.8
Business salesperson or buyer	—	—	—	—	—	1.0	1.3	—	—	—	1.5	1.6	1.8	1.8	1.9	2.1	2.1	2.1	2.1	2.9
Clergy (minister, priest)	—	—	—	—	—	0.0	0.0	—	—	—	0.0	0.0	0.0	0.1	0.0	0.0	0.1	0.1	0.1	0.1
Clergy (other religious)	—	—	—	—	—	0.0	0.1	—	—	—	0.0	0.1	0.1	0.1	0.1	0.1	0.1	0.1	0.1	0.1
Clinical psychologist	—	—	—	—	—	0.1	0.1	—	—	—	0.1	0.1	0.1	0.1	0.1	0.1	0.1	0.1	0.2	0.2
College administrator/staff	—	—	—	—	—	0.3	0.4	—	—	—	0.4	0.4	0.4	0.4	0.4	0.4	0.4	0.4	—	—
College teacher	—	—	—	—	—	0.2	0.2	—	—	—	0.4	0.4	0.4	0.4	0.4	0.4	0.4	0.4	0.4	0.5
Computer programmer or analyst	—	—	—	—	—	0.2	0.2	—	—	—	0.3	0.4	0.4	0.4	0.5	0.6	0.8	0.8	0.9	1.0
Conservationist or forester	—	—	—	—	—	0.0	0.0	—	—	—	0.0	0.0	0.0	0.0	0.0	0.0	0.0	0.0	0.0	0.0
Dentist (including orthodontist)	—	—	—	—	—	0.0	0.0	—	—	—	0.1	0.1	0.1	0.1	0.1	0.1	0.1	0.1	0.1	0.1
Dietitian or home economist	—	—	—	—	—	0.4	0.5	—	—	—	0.5	0.5	0.5	0.5	0.5	0.5	0.5	0.5	0.5	0.5
Engineer	—	—	—	—	—	0.1	0.0	—	—	—	0.1	0.1	0.1	0.1	0.1	0.1	0.1	0.1	0.1	0.2
Farmer or rancher	—	—	—	—	—	0.1	0.0	—	—	—	0.2	0.2	0.2	0.2	0.2	0.2	0.3	0.2	0.2	0.3
Foreign service worker (incl diplomat)	—	—	—	—	—	0.0	0.1	—	—	—	0.1	0.1	0.1	0.1	0.1	0.1	0.1	0.1	0.0	0.0
Homemaker (full-time)	—	—	—	—	—	52.4	35.6	—	—	—	35.1	32.6	31.9	29.4	27.9	23.6	22.7	24.9	23.6	21.9
Interior decorator (including designer)	—	—	—	—	—	0.2	0.2	—	—	—	0.3	0.3	0.3	0.3	0.3	0.4	0.4	0.4	0.4	0.5
Interpreter (translator)	—	—	—	—	—	0.0	0.0	—	—	—	0.0	0.0	0.0	0.0	0.0	0.0	0.0	0.0	0.0	0.0
Lab technician or hygienist	—	—	—	—	—	0.4	0.5	—	—	—	0.6	0.5	0.5	0.6	0.6	0.7	0.7	0.7	0.8	0.8
Law enforcement officer	—	—	—	—	—	0.0	0.1	—	—	—	0.0	0.1	0.1	0.1	0.1	0.1	0.1	0.1	0.1	0.1
Lawyer (attorney) or judge	—	—	—	—	—	0.1	0.1	—	—	—	0.1	0.1	0.1	0.1	0.1	0.2	0.2	0.2	0.2	0.3
Military service (career)	—	—	—	—	—	0.0	0.0	—	—	—	0.0	0.0	0.0	0.0	0.0	0.0	0.0	0.0	0.1	0.0
Musician (performer, composer)	—	—	—	—	—	0.1	0.2	—	—	—	0.2	0.2	0.2	0.2	0.2	0.2	0.3	0.2	0.2	0.2
Nurse	—	—	—	—	—	4.6	4.9	—	—	—	6.3	6.5	6.5	6.7	6.8	7.4	7.5	7.4	7.5	7.4
Optometrist	—	—	—	—	—	0.0	0.0	—	—	—	0.1	0.1	0.0	0.1	0.1	0.1	0.1	0.2	0.1	0.1
Pharmacist	—	—	—	—	—	0.1	0.0	—	—	—	0.1	0.1	0.1	0.1	0.1	0.1	0.1	0.1	0.1	0.1
Physician	—	—	—	—	—	0.1	0.1	—	—	—	0.2	0.1	0.2	0.2	0.2	0.2	0.2	0.2	0.2	0.3
Policymaker/government	—	—	—	—	—	—	0.3	—	—	—	0.3	0.3	0.3	0.3	0.3	0.3	0.3	0.3	0.3	0.3
School counselor	—	—	—	—	—	0.2	0.3	—	—	—	0.1	0.3	0.3	0.3	0.3	0.3	0.3	0.3	0.3	0.3
School principal or superintendent	—	—	—	—	—	0.1	0.1	—	—	—	0.1	0.1	0.1	0.1	0.1	0.1	0.1	0.1	0.1	0.1
Scientific researcher	—	—	—	—	—	0.1	0.1	—	—	—	0.1	0.1	0.1	0.1	0.1	0.1	0.1	0.2	0.1	0.2
Social, welfare or recreation worker	—	—	—	—	—	0.7	0.9	—	—	—	1.2	1.2	1.1	1.3	1.2	1.3	1.3	1.3	1.4	1.3
Statistician	—	—	—	—	—	0.1	0.2	—	—	—	0.1	0.1	0.1	0.2	0.1	0.2	0.2	0.2	0.2	0.1
Therapist (physical, occupational, speech)	—	—	—	—	—	0.1	0.2	—	—	—	0.3	0.3	0.3	0.3	0.4	0.4	0.4	0.4	0.4	0.5
Teacher or administrator (elementary)	—	—	—	—	—	4.8	5.4	—	—	—	6.3	6.2	6.5	6.4	6.3	6.7	6.9	6.3	6.3	6.8
Teacher or administrator (secondary)	—	—	—	—	—	2.3	2.6	—	—	—	2.8	2.7	2.9	2.9	2.9	3.3	3.4	3.2	3.3	3.9
Veterinarian	—	—	—	—	—	0.0	0.0	—	—	—	0.0	0.0	0.0	0.0	0.0	0.0	0.0	0.0	0.0	0.0
Writer or journalist	—	—	—	—	—	0.2	0.2	—	—	—	0.3	0.3	0.3	0.3	0.3	0.3	0.3	0.3	0.3	0.4
Skilled trades	—	—	—	—	—	1.3	1.8	—	—	—	1.5	1.6	1.7	1.7	1.7	1.8	1.9	1.8	1.9	1.8
Laborer (unskilled)	—	—	—	—	—	1.5	1.9	—	—	—	1.9	2.0	1.8	2.0	2.1	2.0	1.9	1.8	1.8	1.8
Semi skilled worker	—	—	—	—	—	2.6	3.0	—	—	—	2.9	3.1	2.7	2.9	3.0	3.0	2.9	2.9	2.7	2.6
Other occupation	—	—	—	—	—	9.5	12.1	—	—	—	12.4	13.5	13.8	14.4	14.3	15.8	15.8	15.0	15.3	14.9
Unemployed	—	—	—	—	—	3.1	11.2	—	—	—	8.4	8.7	8.1	8.3	8.1	8.1	7.5	6.7	6.1	6.3

DISAGGREGATED RESPONSES
ALL FRESHMEN

ITEM	1986	1987	1988	1989	1990	1991	1992	1993	1994	1995	1996	1997	1998	1999	2000	2001	2002	2003	2004	2005	2006
Your mother's occupation																					
Accountant or actuary	2.6	2.7	2.6	2.6	2.6	2.5	2.6	2.6	2.7	2.7	2.9	3.0	3.3	3.6	3.7	4.0	4.3	4.4	4.6	4.7	4.9
Actor or entertainer	0.1	0.1	0.1	0.1	0.1	0.1	0.1	0.0	0.1	0.1	0.0	0.0	0.0	0.1	0.1	0.1	0.1	0.1	0.1	0.1	0.1
Architect	0.1	0.1	0.1	0.1	0.1	0.1	0.1	0.1	0.1	0.1	0.1	0.1	0.1	0.1	0.2	0.2	0.2	0.2	0.2	0.2	0.2
Artist	0.7	0.7	0.7	0.7	0.6	0.6	0.7	0.6	0.6	0.7	0.6	0.6	0.7	0.6	0.6	0.7	0.7	0.7	0.7	0.7	0.7
Business (clerical)	11.1	11.2	10.6	10.6	10.1	9.6	9.2	8.8	8.4	8.1	7.7	7.5	7.7	7.2	7.0	6.8	6.2	5.9	5.3	5.0	5.0
Business executive (mgmt, administrator)	5.3	5.7	5.7	6.0	5.7	5.6	5.6	5.5	5.5	5.5	5.2	5.5	5.8	6.0	5.9	6.3	6.2	6.1	6.2	6.3	6.3
Business owner or proprietor	3.0	3.2	3.2	3.3	3.3	3.2	3.1	3.0	3.2	3.1	3.1	3.2	3.2	3.3	3.2	3.3	3.3	3.4	3.4	3.4	3.3
Business salesperson or buyer	3.0	3.1	2.9	2.8	2.7	2.6	2.5	2.4	2.2	2.2	2.1	2.2	2.1	2.1	2.2	2.2	2.2	2.2	2.2	2.2	2.2
Clergy (minister, priest)	0.1	0.1	0.1	0.1	0.1	0.1	0.1	0.1	0.1	0.1	0.1	0.1	0.1	0.1	0.1	0.1	0.1	0.1	0.1	0.1	0.2
Clergy (other religious)	0.1	0.1	0.1	0.1	0.1	0.1	0.1	0.1	0.1	0.1	0.1	0.1	0.1	0.1	0.1	0.1	0.1	0.1	0.1	0.1	0.1
Clinical psychologist	0.2	0.2	0.2	0.2	0.2	0.2	0.2	0.2	0.2	0.2	0.2	0.2	0.2	0.2	0.2	0.2	0.2	0.2	0.2	0.2	0.2
College administrator/staff	—	—	—	—	—	—	—	—	—	—	0.6	0.6	0.6	0.6	0.6	0.6	0.6	0.6	0.6	0.6	0.6
College teacher	0.5	0.5	0.5	0.5	0.5	0.6	0.6	0.6	0.6	0.6	0.5	0.5	0.6	0.6	0.6	0.6	0.6	0.5	0.6	0.6	0.5
Computer programmer or analyst	1.1	1.2	1.4	1.4	1.5	1.4	1.4	1.3	1.3	1.3	1.2	1.2	1.3	1.3	1.3	1.4	1.3	1.4	1.4	1.4	1.5
Conservationist or forester	0.0	0.0	0.0	0.0	0.0	0.0	0.0	0.0	0.0	0.0	0.0	0.0	0.0	0.0	0.0	0.0	0.0	0.0	0.0	0.0	0.1
Dentist (including orthodontist)	0.2	0.2	0.2	0.2	0.2	0.2	0.2	0.2	0.3	0.2	0.3	0.3	0.3	0.4	0.4	0.4	0.4	0.5	0.5	0.5	0.6
Dietitian or home economist	0.4	0.4	0.4	0.4	0.4	0.5	0.4	0.4	0.4	0.4	0.3	0.3	0.4	0.4	0.4	0.3	0.4	0.3	0.4	0.4	0.4
Engineer	0.2	0.2	0.2	0.2	0.2	0.2	0.3	0.3	0.3	0.3	0.4	0.3	0.4	0.4	0.4	0.5	0.6	0.6	0.7	0.7	0.8
Farmer or rancher	0.2	0.3	0.2	0.2	0.3	0.3	0.3	0.3	0.4	0.4	0.3	0.4	0.3	0.3	0.3	0.2	0.2	0.2	0.2	0.2	0.2
Foreign service worker (incl diplomat)	0.1	0.1	0.1	0.0	0.0	0.1	0.1	0.1	0.1	0.1	0.1	0.1	0.1	0.1	0.1	0.1	0.1	0.1	0.1	0.1	0.1
Homemaker (full-time)	20.1	17.9	16.9	16.0	14.9	14.7	14.0	13.5	12.9	11.9	11.7	11.1	11.1	11.0	11.4	10.9	10.5	10.4	10.2	9.5	8.9
Interior decorator (including designer)	0.5	0.5	0.5	0.5	0.5	0.4	0.4	0.4	0.4	0.4	0.4	0.4	0.4	0.4	0.4	0.4	0.4	0.4	0.4	0.4	0.4
Interpreter (translator)	0.0	0.0	0.0	0.0	0.0	0.1	0.0	0.1	0.1	0.1	—	—	—	—	—	—	—	—	—	—	—
Lab technician or hygienist	0.8	0.8	0.7	0.8	0.8	0.8	0.8	0.9	0.9	0.9	0.9	0.9	0.9	0.9	0.9	0.9	0.9	0.9	0.9	0.8	0.8
Law enforcement officer	0.1	0.1	0.1	0.1	0.1	0.1	0.2	0.1	0.2	0.2	0.2	0.2	0.2	0.2	0.2	0.2	0.2	0.2	0.2	0.3	0.3
Lawyer (attorney) or judge	0.3	0.3	0.3	0.3	0.3	0.3	0.3	0.3	0.4	0.4	0.4	0.4	0.4	0.5	0.6	0.6	0.7	0.7	0.8	0.9	1.0
Military service (career)	0.0	0.0	0.1	0.1	0.1	0.1	0.1	0.1	0.1	0.1	0.1	0.1	0.1	0.1	0.2	0.2	0.2	0.2	0.2	0.2	0.2
Musician (performer, composer)	0.2	0.2	0.2	0.2	0.2	0.2	0.2	0.2	0.2	0.2	0.2	0.2	0.2	0.2	0.2	0.2	0.2	0.2	0.2	0.2	0.2
Nurse	7.4	7.5	7.6	7.8	7.8	7.9	8.0	8.2	8.2	8.6	8.5	8.8	8.7	8.7	8.6	8.6	8.8	8.8	8.9	8.8	8.8
Optometrist	0.1	0.1	0.1	0.1	0.1	0.1	0.1	0.1	0.1	0.1	0.1	0.1	0.1	0.1	0.1	0.1	0.1	0.2	0.1	0.1	0.2
Pharmacist	0.1	0.1	0.1	0.2	0.2	0.2	0.2	0.2	0.2	0.2	0.2	0.3	0.3	0.3	0.4	0.4	0.4	0.4	0.4	0.4	0.5
Physician	0.3	0.3	0.3	0.3	0.3	0.3	0.3	0.4	0.4	0.4	0.4	0.5	0.5	0.6	0.6	0.7	0.7	0.7	0.8	0.8	0.8
Policymaker/government	—	—	—	—	—	—	—	—	—	0.4	0.4	0.4	0.5	0.5	0.5	0.5	0.5	0.5	0.5	0.6	0.6
School counselor	0.3	0.3	0.4	0.3	0.3	0.4	0.4	0.4	0.5	0.4	0.4	0.4	0.4	0.4	0.4	0.4	0.4	0.4	0.4	0.4	0.4
School principal or superintendent	0.2	0.2	0.2	0.2	0.2	0.2	0.2	0.2	0.2	0.2	0.2	0.3	0.2	0.3	0.3	0.3	0.3	0.3	0.2	0.2	0.2
Scientific researcher	0.2	0.2	0.2	0.2	0.2	0.2	0.2	0.3	0.2	0.2	0.2	0.2	0.2	0.2	0.2	0.3	0.3	0.3	0.3	0.4	0.4
Social, welfare or recreation worker	1.4	1.5	1.6	1.5	1.5	1.7	1.6	1.7	1.7	1.8	1.8	1.8	1.9	1.8	1.9	1.9	1.8	1.8	1.7	1.9	1.9
Statistician	0.1	0.1	0.1	0.1	0.1	0.1	0.1	0.1	0.1	0.1	—	—	—	—	—	—	—	—	—	—	—
Therapist (physical, occupational, speech)	0.5	0.6	0.6	0.6	0.6	0.6	0.7	0.7	0.8	0.8	0.8	1.0	0.9	1.0	1.1	1.1	1.2	1.3	1.3	1.2	1.4
Teacher or administrator (elementary)	7.1	7.5	7.7	7.9	8.0	8.7	9.3	9.7	10.1	10.2	10.8	11.0	10.8	10.7	10.3	10.1	9.9	9.5	8.9	8.8	8.5
Teacher or administrator (secondary)	4.0	4.1	4.2	4.2	4.2	4.5	4.7	4.8	5.0	5.0	5.2	5.0	4.9	4.9	4.7	4.6	4.6	4.4	4.4	4.3	4.3
Veterinarian	0.0	0.0	0.0	0.0	0.0	0.0	0.0	0.0	0.0	0.0	0.0	0.0	0.0	0.1	0.1	0.1	0.1	0.1	0.1	0.1	0.1
Writer or journalist	0.3	0.4	0.4	0.3	0.3	0.3	0.3	0.3	0.3	0.3	0.3	0.3	0.3	0.4	0.4	0.4	0.4	0.4	0.4	0.4	0.4
Skilled trades	1.9	2.0	1.9	2.0	2.1	2.1	1.9	2.1	1.9	1.9	1.8	1.7	1.7	1.7	1.6	1.8	1.7	1.6	1.6	1.5	1.5
Laborer (unskilled)	1.5	1.4	1.6	1.6	1.8	1.8	1.7	2.1	1.7	1.6	1.6	1.5	1.5	1.5	1.5	1.8	1.8	1.7	1.7	1.8	1.7
Semi skilled worker	2.4	2.3	2.3	2.5	2.6	2.6	2.4	2.4	2.4	2.4	2.3	2.2	2.1	2.0	1.9	2.2	2.1	2.0	2.0	2.0	1.8
Other occupation	15.3	15.7	16.8	17.3	18.9	18.2	19.1	19.0	19.3	19.8	19.7	19.8	19.5	19.5	19.6	18.9	19.5	20.1	20.5	21.3	21.7
Unemployed	5.8	5.7	5.5	5.2	5.2	5.6	5.4	5.2	5.3	5.1	5.5	5.0	4.8	4.6	4.9	4.3	4.5	4.9	5.0	5.4	5.4

DISAGGREGATED RESPONSES
ALL FRESHMEN

ITEM	1966	1967	1968	1969	1970	1971	1972	1973	1974	1975	1976	1977	1978	1979	1980	1981	1982	1983	1984	1985
Your religious preference [3]																				
Baptist	—	—	—	11.2	12.6	—	—	13.1	13.2	14.0	12.4	14.1	13.8	—	—	—	—	—	15.3	15.2
Buddhist	—	—	—	—	—	—	—	—	—	—	—	—	—	—	—	—	—	—	0.2	0.4
Congregational (UCC)	—	—	—	3.6	2.5	—	—	2.0	2.2	1.9	2.0	2.2	2.0	—	—	—	—	—	1.8	1.7
Eastern Orthodox	—	—	—	—	0.5	—	—	0.6	0.6	0.5	0.5	0.6	0.6	—	—	—	—	—	0.6	0.6
Episcopal	—	—	—	4.0	3.8	—	—	3.9	3.4	3.6	3.4	3.3	3.5	—	—	—	—	—	—	3.0
Jewish	—	—	—	4.6	5.4	—	—	5.2	4.1	4.4	4.7	4.0	4.4	—	—	—	—	—	3.4	3.6
Latter Day Saints (Mormon)	—	—	—	0.8	0.2	—	—	0.2	0.2	0.2	0.2	0.2	0.2	—	—	—	—	—	0.2	0.2
Lutheran	—	—	—	6.8	6.6	—	—	6.0	6.7	6.1	6.9	5.9	5.6	—	—	—	—	—	6.0	6.0
Methodist	—	—	—	11.4	11.8	—	—	11.3	11.4	11.2	9.7	10.4	10.6	—	—	—	—	—	10.2	9.1
Muslim (Islamic)	—	—	—	0.0	0.0	—	—	0.1	0.1	0.2	0.2	0.2	0.2	—	—	—	—	—	0.2	0.2
Presbyterian	—	—	—	6.7	6.9	—	—	6.8	6.1	6.7	5.8	5.8	6.2	—	—	—	—	—	—	5.1
Quaker (Society of Friends)	—	—	—	0.4	0.4	—	—	0.3	0.2	0.2	0.2	0.2	0.2	—	—	—	—	—	0.2	0.2
Roman Catholic	—	—	—	27.4	28.2	—	—	30.3	30.8	29.6	31.6	32.9	33.4	—	—	—	—	—	36.5	34.5
Seventh Day Adventist	—	—	—	0.3	0.3	—	—	0.4	0.4	0.7	0.7	0.4	0.6	—	—	—	—	—	0.2	0.2
Unitarian Universalist	—	—	—	0.9	0.7	—	—	0.5	0.5	0.5	0.4	0.4	0.4	—	—	—	—	—	0.3	—
Other Christian (Protestant)	—	—	—	5.2	5.9	—	—	5.0	5.5	5.3	6.2	6.1	6.2	—	—	—	—	—	10.5	5.4
Other religion	—	—	—	3.3	2.9	—	—	3.4	3.6	4.1	4.7	4.2	3.9	—	—	—	—	—	5.4	5.1
None	—	—	—	13.6	10.7	—	—	10.8	10.9	10.9	10.2	9.1	8.3	—	—	—	—	—	8.8	9.4
Your father's religious preference [3]																				
Baptist	—	—	—	—	—	—	—	13.3	13.6	14.1	12.4	14.0	13.7	—	—	—	—	—	15.0	14.6
Buddhist	—	—	—	—	—	—	—	—	—	—	—	—	—	—	—	—	—	—	0.3	0.5
Congregational (UCC)	—	—	—	—	—	—	—	2.3	2.4	2.1	2.2	2.3	2.0	—	—	—	—	—	1.8	1.7
Eastern Orthodox	—	—	—	—	—	—	—	0.7	0.7	0.7	0.7	0.8	0.7	—	—	—	—	—	0.8	0.7
Episcopal	—	—	—	—	—	—	—	4.3	3.9	3.9	3.7	3.6	3.7	—	—	—	—	—	—	3.1
Jewish	—	—	—	—	—	—	—	6.2	4.9	5.1	5.4	4.6	5.0	—	—	—	—	—	4.0	4.2
Latter Day Saints (Mormon)	—	—	—	—	—	—	—	0.2	0.2	0.2	0.2	0.2	0.2	—	—	—	—	—	0.2	0.2
Lutheran	—	—	—	—	—	—	—	6.6	7.3	6.7	7.6	6.4	6.0	—	—	—	—	—	6.4	6.4
Methodist	—	—	—	—	—	—	—	12.8	12.5	12.3	10.5	11.3	11.4	—	—	—	—	—	10.7	9.5
Muslim (Islamic)	—	—	—	—	—	—	—	0.1	0.1	0.2	0.2	0.2	0.2	—	—	—	—	—	0.3	0.3
Presbyterian	—	—	—	—	—	—	—	8.0	7.1	7.7	6.7	6.5	6.9	—	—	—	—	—	—	5.6
Quaker (Society of Friends)	—	—	—	—	—	—	—	0.2	0.2	0.2	0.2	0.2	0.2	—	—	—	—	—	0.2	0.2
Roman Catholic	—	—	—	—	—	—	—	30.9	31.2	29.6	31.7	33.0	32.9	—	—	—	—	—	35.9	34.0
Seventh Day Adventist	—	—	—	—	—	—	—	0.4	0.4	0.6	0.6	0.3	0.5	—	—	—	—	—	0.2	0.2
Unitarian Universalist	—	—	—	—	—	—	—	0.5	0.5	0.5	0.5	0.5	0.4	—	—	—	—	—	0.3	—
Other Christian (Protestant)	—	—	—	—	—	—	—	5.1	5.4	5.4	6.3	6.2	6.3	—	—	—	—	—	11.2	5.7
Other religion	—	—	—	—	—	—	—	2.0	2.3	2.8	3.4	3.1	3.0	—	—	—	—	—	4.6	4.3
None	—	—	—	—	—	—	—	6.4	7.4	8.0	7.8	7.1	6.9	—	—	—	—	—	8.1	8.9

DISAGGREGATED RESPONSES
ALL FRESHMEN

ITEM	1986	1987	1988	1989	1990	1991	1992	1993	1994	1995	1996	1997	1998	1999	2000	2001	2002	2003	2004	2005	2006
Your religious preference [3]																					
Baptist	—	14.3	14.9	16.1	17.6	17.6	16.9	15.4	15.0	13.3	14.2	14.1	14.1	14.2	11.6	12.1	11.6	11.1	11.8	12.4	11.0
Buddhist	—	0.4	0.4	0.4	0.4	0.4	0.4	0.4	0.7	0.8	0.7	0.7	0.8	0.9	1.0	1.1	1.1	1.2	1.1	1.1	1.1
Congregational (UCC)	—	1.6	1.3	1.3	1.3	2.1	2.1	1.9	1.8	1.8	1.6	1.6	1.6	1.6	1.5	1.4	1.5	1.5	0.9	0.9	1.0
Eastern Orthodox	—	0.5	0.5	0.5	0.6	0.5	0.5	0.6	0.6	0.6	0.6	0.6	0.6	0.5	0.7	0.6	0.6	0.7	0.7	0.7	0.6
Episcopal	—	3.2	2.9	2.8	2.5	2.4	2.4	2.2	2.1	2.0	2.0	2.0	1.9	1.9	1.7	1.8	1.8	1.8	1.7	1.7	1.6
Jewish	—	3.4	3.4	3.0	2.8	2.2	2.4	2.5	2.4	2.5	2.4	2.2	2.2	2.1	2.8	2.6	2.4	2.4	2.5	2.6	2.6
Latter Day Saints (Mormon)	—	0.3	0.3	0.3	0.3	0.4	0.4	0.4	0.4	0.5	0.4	0.4	1.5	1.5	1.5	1.5	0.3	0.6	1.6	0.3	0.3
Lutheran	—	6.7	6.3	6.4	6.4	5.9	6.1	6.7	6.9	7.4	5.9	6.5	5.0	5.7	5.8	5.2	4.9	4.9	5.4	4.1	4.0
Methodist	—	9.2	8.7	9.4	8.5	8.4	8.4	8.1	8.0	7.3	7.3	7.5	7.5	7.2	6.4	6.1	6.0	5.8	5.8	5.8	5.2
Muslim (Islamic)	—	0.2	0.3	0.3	0.4	0.4	0.5	0.5	0.5	0.6	0.6	0.6	0.6	0.7	0.9	0.9	0.7	0.8	0.9	0.9	0.8
Presbyterian	—	5.1	5.0	5.1	4.5	4.5	4.9	4.5	4.4	4.1	4.3	4.3	4.2	4.2	4.0	3.8	4.0	4.1	3.8	4.0	3.4
Quaker (Society of Friends)	—	0.2	0.2	0.2	0.2	0.2	0.2	0.2	0.2	0.2	0.3	0.2	0.2	0.2	0.2	0.2	0.2	0.2	0.2	0.2	0.2
Roman Catholic	—	33.5	32.2	31.1	32.1	31.7	30.4	32.4	30.2	31.0	29.8	30.3	29.0	28.5	30.5	30.3	30.1	29.7	27.8	28.0	27.7
Seventh Day Adventist	—	0.2	0.3	0.4	0.2	0.3	0.3	0.3	0.3	0.2	0.3	0.2	0.3	0.3	0.3	0.3	0.3	0.3	0.3	0.4	0.2
Unitarian Universalist	—	—	—	—	—	—	—	—	—	—	—	—	—	0.3	0.3	—	0.3	0.3	0.3	0.3	—
Other Christian (Protestant)	—	5.1	5.0	5.2	4.5	4.7	5.0	4.7	9.4	10.1	11.8	11.8	12.1	12.5	12.7	12.6	13.5	13.4	14.4	15.7	17.2
Other religion	—	5.0	5.4	5.1	5.5	5.4	5.5	5.8	3.6	3.6	3.8	3.9	3.8	3.6	3.6	3.8	3.9	3.4	3.4	3.5	3.7
None	—	11.0	13.0	12.3	12.3	12.8	13.4	13.5	13.4	14.0	14.0	13.2	14.6	14.3	14.9	15.8	17.2	17.6	17.5	17.4	19.1
Your father's religious preference [3]																					
Baptist	—	14.3	14.7	15.3	16.5	16.6	16.2	14.5	14.3	12.6	13.3	13.2	13.5	13.6	11.0	11.8	11.3	10.7	11.1	11.9	10.9
Buddhist	—	0.5	0.6	0.5	0.6	0.7	0.7	0.7	1.1	1.2	1.2	1.5	1.1	1.4	1.5	1.5	1.5	1.6	1.5	1.6	1.5
Congregational (UCC)	—	1.6	1.3	1.4	1.3	2.0	2.0	1.8	1.7	1.7	1.5	1.5	1.6	1.5	1.3	1.3	1.3	1.5	1.0	0.9	1.0
Eastern Orthodox	—	0.6	0.6	0.7	0.7	0.6	0.7	0.8	0.7	0.7	0.8	0.7	0.7	0.6	0.8	0.8	0.7	0.7	0.8	0.8	0.8
Episcopal	—	3.3	3.0	2.9	2.6	2.6	2.6	2.4	2.3	2.2	2.2	2.2	2.2	2.1	1.9	2.0	2.0	2.1	1.9	2.0	1.9
Jewish	—	4.1	4.1	3.7	3.5	2.8	3.0	3.2	3.1	3.2	3.1	2.9	2.8	2.7	3.5	3.3	3.1	3.1	3.3	3.3	3.4
Latter Day Saints (Mormon)	—	0.3	0.3	0.3	0.3	0.4	0.4	0.4	0.5	0.5	0.5	0.4	1.5	1.5	1.5	1.5	0.4	0.7	1.7	0.3	0.3
Lutheran	—	7.2	6.9	7.2	7.0	6.8	6.8	7.5	7.7	8.4	6.8	7.4	5.7	6.4	6.6	6.0	5.7	5.7	6.1	4.7	4.7
Methodist	—	9.7	9.2	10.1	8.9	9.0	9.1	8.7	8.8	8.1	8.0	8.1	8.0	7.8	6.9	6.5	6.5	6.3	6.2	6.2	5.7
Muslim (Islamic)	—	0.3	0.4	0.4	0.5	0.5	0.6	0.6	0.7	0.7	0.8	0.8	0.9	0.9	1.2	1.2	1.0	1.0	1.1	1.2	1.1
Presbyterian	—	5.6	5.5	5.7	5.1	5.1	5.4	5.0	5.1	4.8	4.9	4.9	4.8	4.8	4.6	4.4	4.6	4.6	4.4	4.5	3.9
Quaker (Society of Friends)	—	0.2	0.2	0.2	0.2	0.2	0.2	0.2	0.2	0.3	0.3	0.2	0.2	0.2	0.2	0.2	0.2	0.3	0.2	0.2	0.2
Roman Catholic	—	33.4	32.2	32.3	33.2	33.0	31.7	34.2	31.5	33.0	32.0	32.0	30.7	30.1	32.5	32.4	32.6	32.2	30.1	30.4	30.4
Seventh Day Adventist	—	0.2	0.2	0.4	0.3	0.3	0.3	0.3	0.3	0.2	0.3	0.2	0.3	0.3	0.3	0.3	0.3	0.3	0.3	0.3	0.2
Unitarian Universalist	—	—	—	—	—	—	—	—	—	—	—	—	—	—	—	—	—	0.3	0.3	0.3	—
Other Christian (Protestant)	—	5.4	5.3	5.4	4.9	5.1	5.3	5.0	8.4	9.3	10.5	10.6	10.9	11.2	11.4	11.2	12.1	12.1	13.0	14.3	16.1
Other religion	—	4.1	4.5	4.1	4.5	4.4	4.4	4.7	3.0	3.0	3.2	3.2	3.2	3.0	3.0	3.1	3.2	3.1	2.9	2.9	2.9
None	—	9.2	10.9	9.3	9.9	10.0	10.5	10.0	10.6	10.0	10.6	10.5	11.9	11.9	11.9	12.4	13.5	13.9	14.2	13.9	14.9

DISAGGREGATED RESPONSES
ALL FRESHMEN

ITEM	1966	1967	1968	1969	1970	1971	1972	1973	1974	1975	1976	1977	1978	1979	1980	1981	1982	1983	1984	1985
Your mother's religious preference [3]																				
Baptist	—	—	—	—	13.6	—	—	13.9	14.2	15.0	13.1	14.9	14.4	—	—	—	—	—	15.7	15.3
Buddhist	—	—	—	—	—	—	—	—	—	—	—	—	—	—	—	—	—	—	0.3	0.5
Congregational (UCC)	—	—	—	—	3.0	—	—	2.4	2.6	2.2	2.3	2.5	2.2	—	—	—	—	—	2.0	1.8
Eastern Orthodox	—	—	—	—	0.7	—	—	0.6	0.7	0.6	0.6	0.7	0.7	—	—	—	—	—	0.7	0.6
Episcopal	—	—	—	—	4.8	—	—	4.7	4.2	4.3	4.1	4.0	4.1	—	—	—	—	—	—	3.4
Jewish	—	—	—	—	6.5	—	—	6.0	4.7	4.9	5.2	4.4	4.8	—	—	—	—	—	3.8	4.0
Latter Day Saints (Mormon)	—	—	—	—	0.2	—	—	0.2	0.2	0.2	0.2	0.2	0.2	—	—	—	—	—	0.2	0.3
Lutheran	—	—	—	—	7.4	—	—	6.8	7.5	6.9	7.7	6.5	6.1	—	—	—	—	—	6.6	6.6
Methodist	—	—	—	—	13.6	—	—	13.2	13.0	12.9	11.1	11.6	11.9	—	—	—	—	—	11.1	10.0
Muslim (Islamic)	—	—	—	—	0.1	—	—	0.1	0.1	0.1	0.2	0.2	0.2	—	—	—	—	—	0.2	0.2
Presbyterian	—	—	—	—	8.4	—	—	8.2	7.2	7.9	6.9	6.6	7.1	—	—	—	—	—	—	5.8
Quaker (Society of Friends)	—	—	—	—	0.2	—	—	0.3	0.2	0.2	0.2	0.2	0.2	—	—	—	—	—	0.2	0.2
Roman Catholic	—	—	—	—	29.7	—	—	32.3	32.7	31.1	33.4	34.3	34.3	—	—	—	—	—	37.2	35.4
Seventh Day Adventist	—	—	—	—	0.3	—	—	0.4	0.4	0.7	0.8	0.4	0.6	—	—	—	—	—	0.2	0.3
Unitarian Universalist	—	—	—	—	0.6	—	—	0.6	0.6	0.6	0.5	0.5	0.5	—	—	—	—	—	0.4	—
Other Christian (Protestant)	—	—	—	—	6.2	—	—	5.2	5.6	5.5	6.4	6.3	6.4	—	—	—	—	—	11.6	5.9
Other religion	—	—	—	—	2.0	—	—	2.1	2.5	3.1	3.7	3.4	3.3	—	—	—	—	—	5.3	4.8
None	—	—	—	—	3.1	—	—	3.1	3.5	3.8	3.7	3.4	3.3	—	—	—	—	—	4.5	4.9

DISAGGREGATED RESPONSES
ALL FRESHMEN

ITEM	1986	1987	1988	1989	1990	1991	1992	1993	1994	1995	1996	1997	1998	1999	2000	2001	2002	2003	2004	2005	2006
Your mother's religious preference [3]																					
Baptist	—	14.8	15.4	16.0	17.2	17.4	16.9	15.1	14.9	13.3	14.0	13.9	14.3	14.3	11.6	12.6	12.0	11.3	11.9	12.8	11.5
Buddhist	—	0.5	0.7	0.6	0.7	0.8	0.8	0.8	1.2	1.3	1.3	1.2	1.1	1.4	1.5	1.6	1.5	1.7	1.6	1.7	1.6
Congregational (UCC)	—	1.8	1.5	1.5	1.4	2.2	2.2	2.0	1.9	1.9	1.7	1.6	1.7	1.6	1.5	1.5	1.5	1.6	1.1	1.1	1.2
Eastern Orthodox	—	0.6	0.6	0.6	0.6	0.6	0.6	0.7	0.6	0.6	0.7	0.7	0.7	0.6	0.8	0.7	0.7	0.7	0.8	0.8	0.8
Episcopal	—	3.7	3.3	3.4	2.9	2.9	2.9	2.8	2.6	2.5	2.5	2.4	2.4	2.4	2.1	2.3	2.3	2.3	2.2	2.2	2.1
Jewish	—	3.9	3.9	3.5	3.3	2.6	2.8	2.9	2.8	2.9	2.8	2.6	2.6	2.5	3.3	3.1	2.9	2.9	3.0	3.0	3.2
Latter Day Saints (Mormon)	—	0.3	0.3	0.3	0.4	0.4	0.4	0.5	0.5	0.5	0.5	0.4	1.5	1.5	1.5	1.5	0.4	0.7	1.7	0.3	0.4
Lutheran	—	7.5	7.1	7.2	7.1	6.7	6.9	7.6	7.7	8.5	6.8	7.5	5.8	6.5	6.7	6.1	5.8	5.8	6.2	4.8	4.9
Methodist	—	10.3	9.8	10.7	9.7	9.6	9.7	9.3	9.4	8.6	8.5	8.7	8.8	8.4	7.6	7.1	7.2	6.8	6.9	6.8	6.3
Muslim (Islamic)	—	0.2	0.3	0.3	0.4	0.4	0.5	0.5	0.5	0.5	0.7	0.6	0.7	0.7	0.9	0.9	0.8	0.8	0.9	1.0	0.9
Presbyterian	—	5.9	5.9	6.0	5.3	5.4	5.8	5.3	5.4	5.1	5.3	5.2	5.1	5.1	4.8	4.6	4.8	5.0	4.7	4.8	4.3
Quaker (Society of Friends)	—	0.2	0.2	0.3	0.2	0.2	0.3	0.2	0.2	0.3	0.3	0.2	0.3	0.2	0.2	0.2	0.2	0.3	0.2	0.3	0.2
Roman Catholic	—	34.8	34.0	33.5	34.4	34.3	33.0	35.6	33.0	34.4	33.3	33.5	32.1	31.7	34.0	34.0	34.2	33.9	31.7	32.0	32.0
Seventh Day Adventist	—	0.2	0.3	0.4	0.3	0.4	0.4	0.4	0.4	0.3	0.4	0.3	0.3	0.3	0.3	0.3	0.4	0.3	0.3	0.4	0.3
Unitarian Universalist	—	—	—	—	—	—	—	—	—	—	—	—	—	—	—	—	—	0.4	0.4	0.4	—
Other Christian (Protestant)	—	5.6	5.5	5.7	5.0	5.2	5.6	5.2	9.3	10.2	11.4	11.6	12.0	12.4	12.4	12.4	13.3	13.2	14.2	15.6	17.0
Other religion	—	4.6	5.1	4.6	5.0	4.9	4.9	5.1	3.1	3.1	3.3	3.2	3.3	3.1	3.1	3.2	3.3	3.1	2.9	2.9	3.0
None	—	5.1	6.3	5.6	6.0	6.2	6.6	6.1	6.4	6.2	6.5	6.4	7.3	7.3	7.4	7.8	8.7	9.1	9.2	9.1	9.8

Forty Year Trends
for Freshman Men

NOTES

These notes refer to report items that are followed by numbers or asterisks in [brackets].

[*] Changes in the question text and/or the text of the response options have occurred over the years. The text used in this report reflects the most recent year the question was asked. The text changes were deemed by HERI to have had no significant effect on the results for this item.

[1] Percentages will total more than 100.0 if any respondents marked more than one response.

[2] Disaggregated responses for this item can be found at the end of this report.

[3] See Appendix D for special circumstances affecting this item.

[4] Based on curriculum recommendations of the National Commission on Excellence in Education.

[5] Percentage responding "frequently" only. Results for other items in this group represent the percentage responding "frequently" or "occasionally."

DEMOGRAPHICS
FRESHMAN MEN

ITEM	1966	1967	1968	1969	1970	1971	1972	1973	1974	1975	1976	1977	1978	1979	1980	1981	1982	1983	1984	1985
How old will you be on December 31 of this year?																				
16 or younger	—	0.3	0.1	0.2	0.1	0.1	0.1	0.1	0.1	0.1	0.1	0.1	0.1	0.1	0.1	0.1	0.1	0.0	0.0	0.1
17	—	4.9	4.5	3.9	3.9	3.3	3.4	3.7	3.0	2.9	3.0	2.5	2.5	2.1	2.1	1.9	2.0	2.0	2.2	2.3
18	—	78.1	77.5	77.4	78.4	76.5	76.7	76.9	76.0	75.2	75.4	74.3	75.1	72.8	72.1	72.5	73.1	72.2	72.4	72.1
19	—	13.5	13.5	14.0	13.6	15.8	16.1	16.4	17.2	18.1	17.8	19.2	19.2	21.0	21.8	22.1	21.6	22.5	22.2	22.5
20	—	1.3	1.6	1.4	1.2	1.4	1.6	1.4	1.8	1.7	1.8	1.9	1.5	2.0	1.9	1.8	1.7	1.6	1.8	1.7
21 or older	—	2.0	2.9	3.1	2.8	2.9	2.0	1.5	1.9	2.0	1.8	2.0	1.7	2.0	2.1	1.7	1.6	1.7	1.3	1.4
Are you: (mark all that apply) [1,3]																				
White/Caucasian	—	—	—	—	—	91.8	89.6	90.5	89.7	88.0	87.2	86.5	87.2	86.0	85.5	87.0	86.3	86.5	86.2	86.0
African American/Black	—	—	—	—	—	6.6	8.1	7.1	7.4	8.9	9.2	9.6	9.1	9.7	10.8	9.6	9.7	9.6	9.8	9.2
American Indian	—	—	—	—	—	0.9	0.9	0.9	0.7	0.8	1.0	0.7	0.8	0.9	0.8	1.1	1.1	1.2	1.2	1.1
Asian American/Asian	—	—	—	—	—	0.6	0.9	0.8	1.1	1.3	1.2	1.4	1.3	1.6	1.6	1.5	1.9	2.0	2.0	2.9
Mexican American/Chicano	—	—	—	—	—	0.3	0.4	0.6	0.7	0.8	0.7	0.8	1.0	0.9	0.6	0.8	0.9	0.7	0.7	0.8
Puerto Rican American	—	—	—	—	—	0.3	0.6	0.4	0.5	0.7	0.5	1.0	0.8	1.1	0.9	0.6	1.1	0.5	0.5	0.5
Other Latino	—	—	—	—	—	—	—	—	—	—	—	—	—	—	—	—	—	—	—	—
Other	—	—	—	—	—	1.0	1.4	1.1	1.5	1.6	1.5	1.8	1.8	2.0	1.8	1.8	1.7	1.5	1.4	1.3
Is English your native language?																				
Yes	—	—	—	—	—	—	—	—	—	—	—	—	—	—	—	—	—	—	—	—
No	—	—	—	—	—	—	—	—	—	—	—	—	—	—	—	—	—	—	—	—
Are you presently married? [*]																				
No	—	—	—	—	—	98.2	99.0	99.2	99.2	99.1	99.2	99.3	99.3	99.4	99.3	99.4	99.5	99.5	99.6	99.5
Yes	—	—	—	—	—	1.8	1.0	0.8	0.8	0.9	0.8	0.7	0.7	0.6	0.7	0.6	0.5	0.5	0.4	0.5
Citizenship status																				
Yes	—	—	—	98.3	98.5	—	98.4	98.6	—	—	—	—	—	—	—	—	97.2	97.6	97.4	97.5
No	—	—	—	1.7	1.5	—	1.6	1.4	—	—	—	—	—	—	—	—	2.8	2.4	2.6	2.5
U.S. Citizen	—	—	—	—	—	—	—	—	—	—	—	—	—	—	—	—	—	—	—	—
Permanent resident (green card)	—	—	—	—	—	—	—	—	—	—	—	—	—	—	—	—	—	—	—	—
Neither	—	—	—	—	—	—	—	—	—	—	—	—	—	—	—	—	—	—	—	—
Do you have a disability? [3]																				
Hearing	—	—	—	—	—	—	—	—	—	—	—	—	—	—	—	—	—	0.8	0.9	0.9
Speech	—	—	—	—	—	—	—	—	—	—	—	—	—	—	—	—	—	0.3	0.3	0.4
Orthopedic	—	—	—	—	—	—	—	—	—	—	—	—	—	—	—	—	—	0.8	0.9	0.8
Learning disability	—	—	—	—	—	—	—	—	—	—	—	—	—	—	—	—	—	0.7	0.9	0.9
Health related	—	—	—	—	—	—	—	—	—	—	—	—	—	—	—	—	—	0.8	0.9	0.9
Partially sighted or blind	—	—	—	—	—	—	—	—	—	—	—	—	—	—	—	—	—	2.4	2.3	2.3
Other	—	—	—	—	—	—	—	—	—	—	—	—	—	—	—	—	—	1.2	1.3	1.2
Which of the following statements applies to you?																				
I was born in the United States	—	—	—	—	—	—	—	—	—	—	—	—	—	—	—	—	—	—	—	—
I came to the U.S. before age 6	—	—	—	—	—	—	—	—	—	—	—	—	—	—	—	—	—	—	—	—
I came to the U.S. between ages 6–12	—	—	—	—	—	—	—	—	—	—	—	—	—	—	—	—	—	—	—	—
I came to the U.S. after age 12	—	—	—	—	—	—	—	—	—	—	—	—	—	—	—	—	—	—	—	—

DEMOGRAPHICS
FRESHMAN MEN

ITEM	1986	1987	1988	1989	1990	1991	1992	1993	1994	1995	1996	1997	1998	1999	2000	2001	2002	2003	2004	2005	2006
How old will you be on December 31 of this year?																					
16 or younger	0.1	0.1	0.0	0.1	0.0	0.1	0.0	0.0	0.0	0.1	0.0	0.0	0.0	0.0	0.0	0.1	0.0	0.0	0.0	0.0	0.0
17	2.1	2.2	2.1	2.0	1.9	1.9	1.9	1.9	1.9	1.6	1.7	1.5	1.5	1.5	1.6	1.4	1.3	1.3	1.3	1.4	1.4
18	72.1	72.2	72.5	70.0	68.0	67.9	68.3	67.2	66.8	66.2	65.5	65.0	65.3	63.2	63.4	62.4	62.3	63.2	61.7	64.3	63.8
19	22.6	22.9	22.8	25.0	26.7	26.2	26.5	27.9	28.3	29.2	30.1	30.7	30.7	32.9	32.5	33.8	34.1	33.5	34.6	32.3	32.7
20	1.6	1.5	1.5	1.7	2.0	2.1	1.7	1.6	1.8	1.8	1.7	1.7	1.5	1.5	1.5	1.4	1.4	1.3	1.4	1.3	1.3
21 or older	1.6	1.1	1.0	1.2	1.3	1.8	1.6	1.3	1.3	1.2	0.9	1.0	1.0	0.8	1.0	1.0	0.8	0.6	0.9	0.6	0.7
Are you: (mark all that apply) [1,3]																					
White/Caucasian	86.4	86.6	83.3	84.4	82.1	80.9	82.1	82.0	79.9	80.2	79.3	80.1	79.6	78.6	77.2	75.0	77.2	76.7	77.2	75.7	77.8
African American/Black	8.0	8.0	10.2	9.1	10.5	10.4	9.2	9.2	9.4	9.2	9.5	9.3	9.7	8.9	9.3	9.4	8.8	8.2	8.8	10.0	9.6
American Indian	0.9	0.9	0.9	0.8	1.2	1.6	1.7	1.8	2.0	2.1	2.2	2.9	1.9	2.2	1.8	0.9	1.1	1.1	1.7	1.5	2.2
Asian American/Asian	3.2	3.2	3.7	3.7	4.0	4.5	4.5	4.7	6.5	6.0	6.4	6.5	5.9	7.2	7.5	7.8	8.0	9.1	9.4	9.5	9.2
Mexican American/Chicano	1.2	1.0	1.5	1.4	1.7	2.2	2.3	2.1	2.1	2.3	2.3	1.9	2.7	3.2	3.5	4.1	3.1	3.4	3.3	3.5	2.9
Puerto Rican American	0.6	0.6	0.6	0.6	0.6	0.7	0.6	0.7	0.7	0.7	0.8	0.9	1.0	0.9	1.0	0.8	0.8	0.8	1.1	1.1	1.3
Other Latino	—	—	—	—	—	—	1.1	1.2	1.4	1.6	1.7	1.7	1.6	1.8	2.0	2.0	1.9	2.0	2.2	2.7	3.1
Other	1.6	1.6	1.8	1.7	1.9	2.2	1.8	1.7	2.1	2.2	2.7	3.0	2.7	3.4	3.6	3.1	2.8	2.7	2.8	2.6	3.4
Is English your native language?																					
Yes	—	95.5	95.3	95.4	94.8	94.3	94.5	94.4	92.8	92.7	92.4	93.4	94.0	93.3	92.4	92.2	93.0	92.5	92.6	92.1	92.8
No	—	4.5	4.7	4.6	5.2	5.7	5.5	5.6	7.2	7.3	7.6	6.6	6.0	6.7	7.6	7.8	7.0	7.5	7.4	7.9	7.2
Are you presently married? [*]																					
No	99.6	—	—	—	—	—	—	99.4	—	—	—	—	—	—	99.6	99.6	—	—	—	—	—
Yes	0.4	—	—	—	—	—	—	0.6	—	—	—	—	—	—	0.4	0.4	—	—	—	—	—
Citizenship status																					
Yes	97.4	98.1	98.1	97.3	—	—	—	—	—	—	—	—	—	—	—	—	—	—	—	—	—
No	2.6	1.9	1.9	2.7	—	—	—	—	—	—	—	—	—	—	—	—	—	—	—	—	—
U.S. Citizen	—	—	—	—	97.0	96.5	96.8	96.8	95.7	95.6	95.3	96.1	96.2	95.8	95.5	95.8	96.4	96.4	96.1	96.3	96.4
Permanent resident (green card)	—	—	—	—	2.1	2.4	2.2	2.2	3.1	3.2	3.5	2.7	2.7	2.9	3.0	2.8	2.3	2.3	2.4	2.2	2.1
Neither	—	—	—	—	0.9	1.1	1.0	1.1	1.1	1.2	1.2	1.1	1.1	1.3	1.4	1.4	1.3	1.3	1.4	1.5	1.5
Do you have a disability? [3]																					
Hearing	0.6	0.7	0.8	—	—	0.9	0.9	—	0.9	—	0.8	—	—	—	0.6	—	0.6	—	0.6	—	—
Speech	0.2	0.2	0.3	—	—	0.5	0.4	—	0.4	—	0.3	—	0.7	—	0.3	—	0.3	—	0.3	—	—
Orthopedic	0.6	0.7	0.8	—	—	1.0	0.8	—	0.8	—	0.7	—	0.7	—	0.5	—	0.4	—	0.5	—	—
Learning disability	0.0	1.3	1.3	—	—	1.7	2.2	—	2.5	—	2.9	—	3.0	—	3.0	—	3.3	—	3.3	—	—
Health related	0.7	0.8	0.9	—	—	1.0	1.1	—	1.3	—	1.2	—	1.3	—	0.8	—	0.9	—	0.9	—	—
Partially sighted or blind	2.0	2.2	2.2	—	—	2.6	2.4	—	2.5	—	2.1	—	1.3	—	1.1	—	1.1	—	1.2	—	—
Other	0.9	1.1	1.4	—	—	1.7	1.5	—	1.7	—	1.7	—	—	—	1.2	—	1.3	—	1.4	—	—
Which of the following statements applies to you?																					
I was born in the United States	—	—	—	—	—	—	—	—	93.1	—	—	—	—	—	—	—	—	93.0	—	92.9	—
I came to the U.S. before age 6	—	—	—	—	—	—	—	—	3.1	—	—	—	—	—	—	—	—	3.0	—	3.1	—
I came to the U.S. between ages 6–12	—	—	—	—	—	—	—	—	1.7	—	—	—	—	—	—	—	—	1.9	—	1.9	—
I came to the U.S. after age 12	—	—	—	—	—	—	—	—	2.1	—	—	—	—	—	—	—	—	2.1	—	2.2	—

DEMOGRAPHICS
FRESHMAN MEN

ITEM	1966	1967	1968	1969	1970	1971	1972	1973	1974	1975	1976	1977	1978	1979	1980	1981	1982	1983	1984	1985
Your religious preference [2,3]																				
Protestant (Christian)	52.7	48.5	44.5	49.4	49.6	40.1	38.8	48.4	49.0	49.0	46.9	47.6	47.9	36.3	36.4	35.8	34.2	32.7	44.0	45.2
Roman Catholic	27.7	29.0	30.0	26.8	28.8	28.3	28.4	31.2	31.0	29.7	31.4	33.1	33.6	34.4	33.8	34.8	36.0	36.5	36.2	34.3
Jewish	5.2	6.6	5.3	4.5	5.7	3.7	4.2	5.1	4.3	4.5	4.9	4.3	4.7	4.3	3.9	4.0	4.0	3.8	3.7	4.0
Other	6.2	6.5	8.4	3.5	2.9	10.7	12.1	3.5	3.7	4.4	5.1	4.3	4.1	15.3	16.2	16.3	16.8	17.0	5.7	5.6
None	8.3	9.5	11.9	15.7	11.9	17.2	16.5	11.9	11.9	12.5	11.7	10.7	9.6	9.7	9.7	9.1	9.1	10.0	10.3	11.0
Do you consider yourself a born-again Christian?																				
No	—	—	—	—	—	—	—	—	—	—	—	—	—	—	—	—	—	—	—	76.7
Yes	—	—	—	—	—	—	—	—	—	—	—	—	—	—	—	—	—	—	—	23.3
Which of your parents were born in the U.S.?																				
Both	—	—	—	—	—	—	—	—	—	—	—	—	—	—	—	—	—	—	—	—
Father only	—	—	—	—	—	—	—	—	—	—	—	—	—	—	—	—	—	—	—	—
Mother only	—	—	—	—	—	—	—	—	—	—	—	—	—	—	—	—	—	—	—	—
Neither	—	—	—	—	—	—	—	—	—	—	—	—	—	—	—	—	—	—	—	—
What is the best estimate of your parents' total income last year? Consider income from all sources before taxes. [3]																				
Less than $6,000	17.9	—	14.3	11.5	9.3	9.5	10.1	7.8	7.8	7.9	7.9	7.6	6.2	5.7	5.5	4.5	4.0	3.9	4.0	3.5
$6,000 to $9,999	34.5	—	31.2	27.6	21.9	19.6	16.5	12.7	11.7	9.3	8.9	8.1	6.6	6.2	5.5	4.7	4.3	3.9	3.7	3.1
Less than $10,000	—	—	—	—	—	—	—	—	—	—	—	—	—	—	—	—	—	—	—	—
$10,000 to $14,999	25.1	—	28.4	29.9	33.0	32.6	30.4	28.3	27.5	23.0	20.6	18.2	15.1	12.4	11.3	9.7	8.3	8.4	7.7	5.7
$15,000 to $19,999	9.4	—	11.9	13.7	14.8	15.9	16.7	18.4	18.0	18.5	17.8	17.1	15.3	12.9	11.2	9.2	7.9	7.7	6.6	5.7
$20,000 to $24,999	4.7	—	5.7	7.0	8.4	9.2	10.4	12.5	13.2	14.2	14.7	15.8	16.6	16.8	16.1	14.2	12.4	11.2	10.2	7.4
$25,000 to $29,999	2.5	—	2.9	3.3	4.0	4.5	5.2	6.3	6.9	8.2	8.6	9.9	10.9	11.5	11.4	11.6	11.1	10.3	9.6	7.9
$30,000 or more	5.8	—	5.9	7.0	—	—	—	—	—	—	—	—	—	—	—	—	—	—	—	—
$30,000 to $39,999	—	—	—	—	—	—	—	—	—	—	—	—	—	—	—	—	—	—	—	—
$30,000 to $34,999	—	—	—	—	2.6	2.7	3.4	4.3	4.6	5.8	6.5	7.3	9.0	9.7	10.3	11.1	11.6	11.5	10.9	10.4
$35,000 to $39,999	—	—	—	—	1.4	1.5	2.0	2.5	2.7	3.5	4.1	4.3	5.3	6.4	7.2	8.5	8.9	9.1	9.1	9.3
$40,000 or more	—	—	—	—	4.4	4.5	—	—	—	—	—	—	—	—	—	—	—	—	—	—
$40,000 to $49,999	—	—	—	—	—	—	2.0	2.5	2.7	3.4	3.9	4.2	5.4	7.3	8.7	10.6	12.2	13.1	14.1	12.9
$50,000 or more	—	—	—	—	—	—	3.5	4.6	5.0	6.1	6.9	7.6	9.5	8.4	9.6	12.0	14.6	16.0	18.1	—
$50,000 to $59,999	—	—	—	—	—	—	—	—	—	—	—	—	—	—	—	—	—	—	—	11.3
$60,000 to $74,999	—	—	—	—	—	—	—	—	—	—	—	—	—	—	—	—	—	—	—	8.7
$75,000 to $99,999	—	—	—	—	—	—	—	—	—	—	—	—	—	—	—	—	—	—	—	5.7
$100,000 or more	—	—	—	—	—	—	—	—	—	—	—	—	—	2.8	3.2	3.9	4.9	4.9	6.0	—
$100,000 to $149,999	—	—	—	—	—	—	—	—	—	—	—	—	—	—	—	—	—	—	—	4.4
$150,000 or more	—	—	—	—	—	—	—	—	—	—	—	—	—	—	—	—	—	—	—	4.0
$150,000 to $199,999	—	—	—	—	—	—	—	—	—	—	—	—	—	—	—	—	—	—	—	—
$200,000 or more	—	—	—	—	—	—	—	—	—	—	—	—	—	—	—	—	—	—	—	—
$200,000 to $249,999	—	—	—	—	—	—	—	—	—	—	—	—	—	—	—	—	—	—	—	—
$250,000 or more	—	—	—	—	—	—	—	—	—	—	—	—	—	—	—	—	—	—	—	—
MEDIAN INCOME (in thousands of dollars)	9.7	—	10.8	11.8	12.8	13.2	13.8	15.3	15.8	17.7	18.5	19.7	22.0	23.8	25.2	28.3	30.9	32.0	33.8	38.4
Are your parents:																				
Both alive and living with each other?	—	—	—	—	—	—	85.6	—	—	—	—	—	—	—	—	—	—	—	—	—
Both alive, divorced or living apart?	—	—	—	—	—	—	7.4	—	—	—	—	—	—	—	—	—	—	—	—	—
One or both deceased?	—	—	—	—	—	—	7.0	—	—	—	—	—	—	—	—	—	—	—	—	—

DEMOGRAPHICS
FRESHMAN MEN

ITEM	1986	1987	1988	1989	1990	1991	1992	1993	1994	1995	1996	1997	1998	1999	2000	2001	2002	2003	2004	2005	2006
Your religious preference [2,3]																					
Protestant (Christian)	31.4	44.5	42.7	45.5	45.2	45.0	45.5	43.4	47.2	45.2	47.0	47.4	47.5	48.0	44.5	43.7	42.7	42.5	44.9	44.2	43.0
Roman Catholic	33.2	33.3	32.3	31.1	31.8	31.7	30.1	32.3	29.6	30.8	29.1	29.3	28.4	28.1	29.8	29.6	29.3	29.3	26.7	27.6	27.1
Jewish	3.6	3.6	3.7	3.2	3.0	2.3	2.7	2.7	2.7	2.7	2.7	2.5	2.4	2.4	3.1	2.8	2.5	2.6	2.7	2.9	2.9
Other	19.4	5.5	6.0	5.6	6.0	6.1	6.2	6.5	5.1	5.2	5.4	5.5	5.3	5.4	5.7	5.9	5.7	5.5	5.6	5.6	5.8
None	12.4	13.0	15.3	14.5	14.0	14.9	15.5	15.2	15.4	16.1	15.8	15.3	16.4	16.1	16.9	18.0	19.8	20.1	20.1	19.7	21.2
Do you consider yourself a born-again Christian?																					
No	—	—	78.3	74.2	74.0	73.5	73.5	75.5	74.4	76.1	73.1	73.1	—	—	—	77.1	—	—	77.3	—	—
Yes	—	—	21.7	25.8	26.0	26.5	26.5	24.5	25.6	23.9	26.9	26.9	—	—	—	22.9	—	—	22.7	—	—
Which of your parents were born in the U.S.?																					
Both	—	—	—	—	—	—	—	—	84.3	—	—	—	—	—	—	—	—	80.3	—	—	—
Father only	—	—	—	—	—	—	—	—	2.8	—	—	—	—	—	—	—	—	3.0	—	—	—
Mother only	—	—	—	—	—	—	—	—	2.4	—	—	—	—	—	—	—	—	3.1	—	—	—
Neither	—	—	—	—	—	—	—	—	10.5	—	—	—	—	—	—	—	—	13.6	—	—	—
What is the best estimate of your parents' total income last year? Consider income from all sources before taxes. [3]																					
Less than $6,000	2.7	2.3	2.3	2.0	2.2	2.5	2.2	2.2	2.0	1.9	1.8	1.6	1.7	1.6	1.7	1.6	—	—	—	—	—
$6,000 to $9,999	2.5	2.1	2.0	1.8	2.0	2.1	1.9	1.8	1.8	1.7	1.7	1.5	1.5	1.4	1.4	1.3	—	—	—	—	—
Less than $10,000	—	—	—	—	—	—	—	—	—	—	—	—	—	—	—	—	2.4	2.5	2.7	2.6	2.5
$10,000 to $14,999	4.9	3.9	3.6	3.6	3.4	3.6	3.3	3.3	3.2	2.9	3.0	2.5	2.5	2.4	2.3	2.2	2.1	2.1	2.2	2.3	2.0
$15,000 to $19,999	4.9	4.7	4.5	4.1	4.1	4.1	3.7	3.4	3.4	3.2	3.1	2.9	2.7	2.5	2.3	2.2	2.0	2.3	2.0	2.1	2.0
$20,000 to $24,999	6.8	6.2	6.0	5.7	5.7	5.6	5.0	4.8	4.7	4.4	4.2	4.0	3.9	3.8	3.4	3.3	3.0	3.2	3.1	3.1	2.9
$25,000 to $29,999	7.2	6.4	6.1	6.0	5.9	5.9	5.8	5.6	5.3	5.1	4.5	4.6	4.6	4.1	3.7	3.4	3.3	3.0	3.1	2.9	2.8
$30,000 or more	—	—	—	—	—	—	—	—	—	—	—	—	—	—	—	—	—	—	—	—	—
$30,000 to $39,999	—	—	—	—	—	12.9	11.9	11.4	10.6	10.6	9.8	9.4	8.9	8.1	7.8	7.1	6.4	5.9	5.8	6.0	5.3
$30,000 to $34,999	9.8	8.8	8.2	8.1	7.6	—	—	—	—	—	—	—	—	—	—	—	—	—	—	—	—
$35,000 to $39,999	9.5	9.0	8.6	8.1	8.0	—	—	—	—	—	—	—	—	—	—	—	—	—	—	—	—
$40,000 or more	—	—	—	—	—	—	—	—	—	—	—	—	—	—	—	—	—	—	—	—	—
$40,000 to $49,999	13.3	13.1	12.8	12.8	12.7	13.1	13.2	12.3	12.1	11.7	10.9	10.5	10.3	9.9	8.9	8.2	8.0	7.4	7.5	7.1	6.6
$50,000 or more	—	—	—	—	—	—	—	—	—	—	—	—	—	—	—	—	—	—	—	—	—
$50,000 to $59,999	11.5	12.2	12.4	12.8	12.4	12.4	12.6	12.3	12.3	12.3	12.0	11.9	11.7	11.0	10.5	9.8	9.8	9.5	9.3	8.7	8.6
$50,000 to $99,999	—	—	—	—	—	—	—	—	—	—	—	—	—	—	—	—	—	—	—	—	—
$60,000 to $74,999	10.2	11.6	12.5	12.4	13.0	13.2	14.0	14.2	14.3	14.4	14.5	14.9	14.5	14.5	14.0	13.4	13.2	12.7	12.3	11.8	11.8
$75,000 to $99,999	7.0	8.2	8.7	9.6	9.9	10.5	11.3	12.1	12.5	13.2	14.0	14.4	15.2	16.0	16.0	16.9	17.0	16.8	16.3	16.0	16.0
$100,000 or more	—	—	—	—	—	—	—	—	—	—	—	—	—	—	—	—	—	—	—	—	—
$100,000 to $149,999	5.0	5.8	6.4	6.7	6.8	7.4	8.1	8.9	9.7	10.1	11.4	12.1	12.9	13.8	15.6	17.0	17.7	18.3	18.6	18.9	19.4
$150,000 or more	4.9	5.7	5.9	6.3	6.2	—	—	—	—	—	—	—	—	—	—	—	—	—	—	—	—
$150,000 to $199,999	—	—	—	—	—	2.7	2.8	3.1	3.3	3.6	3.9	4.1	4.1	4.8	5.4	5.9	6.4	6.9	7.1	7.6	8.2
$200,000 or more	—	—	—	—	—	3.9	4.2	4.6	4.7	4.8	5.2	5.6	5.4	6.2	7.0	7.6	—	—	—	—	—
$200,000 to $249,999	—	—	—	—	—	—	—	—	—	—	—	—	—	—	—	—	2.9	3.2	3.3	3.7	4.1
$250,000 or more	—	—	—	—	—	—	—	—	—	—	—	—	—	—	—	—	5.6	6.1	6.7	7.2	7.9
MEDIAN INCOME (in thousands of dollars)	**41.3**	**45.0**	**46.8**	**48.3**	**48.7**	**50.2**	**52.4**	**54.2**	**55.6**	**56.9**	**59.2**	**61.2**	**62.4**	**65.7**	**69.1**	**73.0**	**75.8**	**77.1**	**78.1**	**80.3**	**83.6**
Are your parents:																					
Both alive and living with each other?	77.4	77.2	75.1	74.9	74.3	74.0	74.1	74.8	74.5	74.8	74.6	75.2	74.5	75.3	75.2	74.5	74.8	75.2	74.2	73.9	73.4
Both alive, divorced or living apart?	18.0	18.4	20.4	20.9	21.4	21.7	21.8	21.2	21.7	21.5	21.7	21.2	21.9	21.2	21.2	22.1	22.0	21.5	22.3	22.7	23.1
One or both deceased?	4.6	4.4	4.4	4.2	4.3	4.3	4.1	4.0	3.8	3.7	3.7	3.6	3.7	3.5	3.6	3.4	3.3	3.3	3.4	3.4	3.5

DEMOGRAPHICS
FRESHMAN MEN

ITEM	1966	1967	1968	1969	1970	1971	1972	1973	1974	1975	1976	1977	1978	1979	1980	1981	1982	1983	1984	1985
WHAT IS THE HIGHEST LEVEL OF FORMAL EDUCATION OBTAINED BY:																				
Your father?																				
Grammar school or less	9.0	8.9	8.9	8.3	7.5	7.5	6.9	5.6	6.0	5.6	5.6	5.6	4.6	4.8	4.7	4.2	3.8	3.7	3.6	2.9
Some high school	14.8	14.0	15.2	14.1	13.6	13.7	12.6	10.8	10.7	10.8	10.3	10.3	9.1	9.1	9.3	8.5	7.9	7.9	7.3	6.7
High school graduate	29.0	28.5	29.9	29.0	29.0	29.1	28.9	25.3	26.5	26.0	25.6	26.4	24.6	25.5	25.5	24.9	25.0	24.9	24.8	23.1
Postsecondary school other than college	—	—	—	—	—	—	4.3	4.3	4.3	4.0	3.9	4.0	4.1	3.9	4.0	3.9	4.1	4.5	4.6	4.6
Some college	18.4	18.2	18.3	18.1	17.8	17.3	16.6	15.1	14.2	14.1	13.5	13.6	14.3	13.8	13.6	14.0	13.9	14.1	14.2	14.1
College degree	17.8	18.3	17.6	19.4	20.3	20.8	18.6	20.3	20.2	20.8	21.4	21.1	22.1	21.9	21.7	22.7	22.8	22.4	22.7	22.5
Some graduate school	—	—	—	—	—	—	3.1	2.9	2.9	2.9	2.9	3.2	3.2	3.0	2.9	3.0	3.0	3.0	2.9	3.6
Graduate degree	11.0	12.1	10.2	11.3	11.7	11.7	13.4	15.7	15.1	16.0	16.6	16.1	18.0	18.0	18.2	18.7	19.5	19.5	19.8	22.5
Your mother?																				
Grammar school or less	5.5	5.2	5.5	5.1	4.8	4.5	4.2	3.3	3.7	3.4	3.4	3.7	3.1	3.3	3.2	2.5	2.6	2.5	2.3	2.1
Some high school	12.3	11.5	12.9	11.9	11.8	11.7	10.3	9.2	9.0	9.2	8.8	8.7	7.7	8.0	7.5	7.0	6.5	6.3	5.7	5.4
High school graduate	43.4	43.2	44.4	43.7	44.1	44.5	43.9	40.5	40.6	40.7	39.8	40.8	39.3	39.1	38.6	38.4	36.9	36.4	35.9	33.6
Postsecondary school other than college	—	—	—	—	—	—	7.0	7.0	7.0	6.5	6.8	6.7	6.7	6.7	6.4	6.4	7.1	7.4	7.5	7.3
Some college	19.3	19.9	19.4	19.7	19.2	18.5	18.8	16.1	15.6	15.2	15.0	15.0	15.6	15.3	15.9	15.9	16.1	16.2	16.5	17.0
College degree	16.4	16.7	15.0	16.2	16.6	17.2	15.6	16.2	16.6	16.9	17.8	16.8	18.1	17.9	18.5	19.7	20.1	19.8	20.1	20.9
Some graduate school	—	—	—	—	—	—	2.7	2.6	2.5	2.4	2.6	2.4	2.7	2.7	2.7	2.6	2.7	2.9	2.9	3.5
Graduate degree	3.1	3.3	2.9	3.4	3.5	3.7	4.5	5.1	5.1	5.7	5.9	6.0	6.8	7.0	7.1	7.5	8.0	8.6	9.0	10.2
Your father's occupation [2,3]																				
Artist	—	0.9	0.8	0.9	0.8	0.8	0.8	—	—	—	1.0	0.9	0.9	0.9	0.9	1.0	1.0	1.0	1.0	0.9
Business	—	34.5	32.5	32.6	33.5	31.9	33.0	—	—	—	32.5	31.9	33.0	32.6	32.6	32.8	33.1	32.6	32.7	32.8
Clerical	—	1.1	0.8	1.0	1.1	1.4	1.6	—	—	—	1.1	1.0	1.0	1.1	1.1	0.9	1.0	0.9	0.9	0.9
Clergy	—	0.8	0.8	0.9	0.8	1.0	1.0	—	—	—	1.2	1.3	1.4	1.3	1.2	1.3	1.3	1.2	1.2	1.2
College teacher	—	3.1	2.5	2.6	2.6	2.5	1.1	—	—	—	1.2	1.1	1.2	1.1	1.2	1.2	1.1	1.1	1.3	1.4
Doctor (MD or DDS)	—	2.2	2.2	2.3	2.5	2.4	2.6	—	—	—	3.3	2.9	3.2	3.1	3.2	3.2	3.3	3.4	3.2	3.4
Education (secondary)	—	0.3	0.3	0.3	0.3	0.4	2.7	—	—	—	3.5	3.3	3.5	3.8	3.6	4.0	4.1	4.0	3.9	4.2
Education (elementary)	—	0.3	0.3	0.3	0.3	0.4	0.4	—	—	—	0.6	0.6	0.6	0.6	0.6	0.7	0.7	0.7	0.6	0.9
Engineer	—	7.1	7.4	7.8	8.0	8.1	8.4	—	—	—	8.9	8.7	9.4	8.8	8.7	8.7	8.6	8.7	8.6	9.1
Farmer or forester	—	6.2	6.1	5.3	4.7	5.4	4.8	—	—	—	3.9	3.1	2.7	3.0	3.3	3.5	3.3	3.1	3.1	3.5
Health professional	—	1.1	1.1	1.3	1.3	1.3	1.3	—	—	—	1.5	1.5	1.5	1.6	1.4	1.5	1.3	1.4	1.3	1.4
Homemaker	—	—	—	—	—	—	0.0	—	—	—	0.1	0.1	0.1	0.1	0.1	0.1	0.1	0.1	0.1	0.1
Lawyer	—	1.6	1.3	1.5	1.6	1.5	1.7	—	—	—	1.9	1.8	1.9	2.0	2.0	2.0	2.2	2.1	2.1	2.3
Military	—	1.8	1.9	2.1	2.1	2.5	2.3	—	—	—	2.5	2.5	2.3	2.2	2.2	2.3	2.1	2.2	2.0	1.7
Nurse	—	—	—	—	—	0.1	0.0	—	—	—	0.1	0.1	0.1	0.1	0.1	0.1	0.1	0.1	0.1	0.1
Research scientist	—	0.6	0.6	0.7	0.6	0.7	0.7	—	—	—	0.9	0.7	0.8	0.8	0.8	0.8	0.7	0.8	0.7	0.9
Social worker	—	—	—	0.3	0.3	0.3	0.4	—	—	—	0.4	0.4	0.4	0.4	0.4	0.4	0.4	0.5	0.5	0.5
Skilled worker	—	11.9	12.6	12.9	12.0	11.9	11.7	—	—	—	9.8	10.6	9.9	10.0	10.2	10.1	9.9	9.7	9.9	8.8
Semi skilled worker	—	7.5	8.5	7.4	7.2	7.3	6.4	—	—	—	5.2	5.8	4.8	5.1	4.9	4.5	4.4	4.6	4.4	4.5
Laborer	—	3.2	3.5	3.4	3.3	3.4	3.4	—	—	—	3.3	3.3	3.0	2.8	3.0	2.7	2.7	2.7	2.8	2.6
Unemployed	—	0.7	0.9	1.0	1.1	1.0	1.7	—	—	—	1.8	1.9	1.9	1.8	1.9	1.5	1.7	2.3	2.0	2.1
Other occupation	—	15.2	16.1	16.4	15.8	15.0	13.9	—	—	—	15.2	16.4	16.2	16.8	16.3	16.8	16.6	16.9	17.6	16.7

DEMOGRAPHICS
FRESHMAN MEN

ITEM	1986	1987	1988	1989	1990	1991	1992	1993	1994	1995	1996	1997	1998	1999	2000	2001	2002	2003	2004	2005	2006
WHAT IS THE HIGHEST LEVEL OF FORMAL EDUCATION OBTAINED BY:																					
Your father?																					
Grammar school or less	2.6	2.4	2.5	2.2	2.9	2.7	2.2	2.1	2.4	3.0	3.0	2.5	1.9	2.6	2.5	2.4	1.9	2.2	2.4	2.3	2.8
Some high school	5.8	5.2	5.2	5.0	5.0	5.1	4.3	4.3	4.1	3.9	4.0	3.5	3.9	3.7	3.8	3.9	3.7	3.6	3.7	4.1	3.7
High school graduate	21.9	21.3	21.7	21.7	22.7	22.0	20.2	21.7	20.8	20.8	19.7	19.8	20.6	19.2	19.6	19.4	19.3	19.2	19.5	20.1	19.4
Postsecondary school other than college	4.6	4.9	4.8	4.7	4.9	4.8	5.0	4.9	4.3	4.6	3.9	4.2	4.1	4.0	3.9	3.7	3.7	3.8	3.8	3.4	3.6
Some college	14.5	14.2	14.5	14.9	15.1	15.2	16.0	15.1	14.9	15.1	15.2	15.1	15.2	15.3	15.1	15.2	15.2	14.5	14.2	14.2	14.1
College degree	23.5	24.1	23.7	24.7	23.8	24.2	25.7	25.3	27.1	27.5	27.9	28.6	28.4	28.5	28.6	28.6	29.2	29.7	29.6	29.4	29.6
Some graduate school	3.6	3.7	3.5	3.2	3.1	3.2	3.3	2.9	3.0	2.6	2.7	2.7	2.6	2.4	2.2	2.3	2.2	2.3	2.2	2.1	2.2
Graduate degree	23.5	24.3	24.1	23.5	22.5	22.8	23.3	23.7	23.5	22.5	23.5	23.7	23.2	24.3	24.3	24.6	24.7	24.7	24.6	24.4	24.6
Your mother?																					
Grammar school or less	1.7	1.8	1.8	1.8	2.3	2.1	1.9	1.7	2.1	2.8	2.8	2.3	1.7	2.4	2.3	2.1	1.7	2.0	2.2	2.1	2.4
Some high school	4.6	3.8	4.0	3.8	3.9	4.2	3.6	3.3	3.3	3.1	3.1	2.7	2.9	2.8	2.9	3.1	2.7	2.7	2.7	3.1	2.7
High school graduate	31.4	30.5	29.9	29.6	29.7	28.7	26.7	27.6	25.8	25.5	24.6	23.6	24.1	22.5	22.4	21.4	21.0	20.4	20.2	20.0	19.5
Postsecondary school other than college	7.8	7.9	7.5	7.6	7.5	7.1	7.3	7.1	6.4	6.2	5.6	5.5	5.3	4.9	4.9	4.6	4.3	4.6	4.3	3.8	4.0
Some college	17.8	17.3	17.7	18.0	17.5	17.8	18.3	17.1	17.4	17.0	17.1	17.2	17.2	16.8	16.8	17.3	17.3	16.5	16.7	16.3	15.9
College degree	22.1	23.1	22.7	23.4	23.2	23.4	25.0	25.3	26.6	27.5	28.2	29.4	29.4	30.5	30.2	30.9	32.4	32.8	32.9	33.4	33.6
Some graduate school	3.8	3.8	3.9	3.7	3.6	3.7	3.8	3.6	3.7	3.3	3.4	3.3	3.4	3.1	3.0	2.9	2.8	3.0	2.7	2.8	2.9
Graduate degree	10.8	11.7	12.3	12.3	12.5	12.8	13.5	14.3	14.6	14.6	15.5	16.1	16.0	17.0	17.4	17.6	17.7	18.0	18.4	18.6	19.0
Your father's occupation [2,3]																					
Artist	1.0	1.0	1.0	0.8	0.8	0.9	0.8	0.8	0.8	0.9	0.9	0.9	0.9	0.9	1.1	1.0	1.1	1.0	1.0	1.1	1.1
Business	34.3	34.8	32.9	33.2	31.5	30.4	30.4	30.3	29.8	29.8	29.8	29.9	30.1	30.2	30.6	30.3	30.2	30.2	30.2	29.8	30.1
Clerical	0.9	0.9	0.8	0.8	0.8	0.8	0.8	0.8	0.9	0.9	0.9	0.9	1.0	1.0	1.1	1.2	1.2	1.2	1.3	1.3	1.4
Clergy	1.3	1.2	1.1	1.2	1.2	1.2	1.3	1.1	1.3	1.1	1.4	1.3	1.3	1.0	1.1	1.0	1.2	1.1	1.0	1.0	0.9
College teacher	1.4	1.3	1.2	1.1	1.1	1.1	1.0	0.9	1.0	0.9	0.8	0.8	0.8	0.8	0.9	0.9	0.9	0.8	0.8	0.8	0.8
Doctor (MD or DDS)	3.3	3.5	3.5	3.3	3.1	2.9	3.1	3.1	3.1	3.1	3.0	3.2	3.1	3.3	3.3	3.5	3.3	3.4	3.4	3.3	3.2
Education (secondary)	4.4	4.4	4.6	4.5	4.3	4.4	4.5	4.4	4.2	4.4	4.1	4.0	3.6	3.6	3.4	3.1	3.0	2.9	2.8	2.7	2.6
Education (elementary)	1.0	0.9	1.0	1.1	1.1	1.1	1.2	1.2	1.2	1.2	1.4	1.2	1.2	1.3	1.1	1.0	1.1	1.1	0.9	0.9	0.9
Engineer	8.7	8.9	8.6	8.3	8.3	8.3	8.5	8.3	8.3	8.1	8.1	8.3	8.4	8.6	8.4	8.6	8.5	8.8	9.0	8.6	8.7
Farmer or forester	2.7	2.6	2.6	2.8	2.9	2.7	2.6	3.0	3.1	2.9	2.6	2.8	2.5	2.6	2.4	2.1	1.9	1.6	1.8	1.5	1.4
Health professional	1.4	1.5	1.5	1.5	1.4	1.4	1.4	1.3	1.5	1.4	1.5	1.6	1.6	1.6	1.6	1.6	1.6	1.6	1.5	1.6	1.5
Homemaker	0.2	0.1	0.1	0.1	0.2	0.2	0.2	0.2	0.2	0.2	0.2	0.2	0.2	0.2	0.2	0.2	0.2	0.2	0.2	0.3	0.3
Lawyer	2.3	2.5	2.5	2.4	2.2	2.1	2.3	2.4	2.4	2.2	2.4	2.6	2.3	2.6	2.5	2.5	2.7	2.6	2.5	2.5	2.7
Military	2.0	2.0	2.1	2.1	2.1	2.3	2.2	1.8	1.9	1.8	1.7	1.5	1.8	1.7	1.4	1.7	1.7	1.5	1.5	1.5	1.5
Nurse	0.1	0.1	0.2	0.2	0.2	0.2	0.3	0.3	0.3	0.4	0.3	0.4	0.4	0.5	0.5	0.5	0.6	0.5	0.5	0.5	0.6
Research scientist	0.8	0.8	0.8	0.7	0.6	0.7	0.7	0.7	0.7	0.6	0.6	0.7	0.7	0.7	0.7	0.7	0.7	0.8	0.8	0.7	0.7
Social worker	0.5	0.6	0.6	0.5	0.5	0.6	0.6	0.6	0.6	0.6	0.6	0.6	0.6	0.6	0.7	0.6	0.7	0.6	0.6	0.6	0.6
Skilled worker	8.9	8.5	9.2	9.3	9.5	9.6	8.8	9.7	8.8	8.9	8.7	8.8	9.0	8.5	8.5	8.9	8.5	8.5	8.6	8.3	8.1
Semi skilled worker	3.6	3.4	3.8	3.7	3.9	4.3	3.8	3.6	3.8	3.8	3.6	3.5	3.5	3.3	3.1	3.3	3.2	3.1	3.1	3.1	2.9
Laborer	2.3	2.1	2.2	2.3	2.6	2.6	2.4	2.8	2.6	2.7	2.6	2.4	2.5	2.3	2.5	2.8	2.9	2.9	3.0	3.2	2.9
Unemployed	1.8	1.6	1.6	1.7	1.8	2.4	2.5	2.6	2.6	2.3	2.5	2.2	2.0	1.8	1.9	1.6	1.9	2.1	2.0	2.1	2.0
Other occupation	16.9	17.3	18.2	18.3	19.9	19.6	20.6	20.2	20.8	21.7	22.3	22.3	22.3	22.7	23.1	22.8	22.9	23.4	23.4	24.5	24.8

103

DEMOGRAPHICS
FRESHMAN MEN

ITEM	1966	1967	1968	1969	1970	1971	1972	1973	1974	1975	1976	1977	1978	1979	1980	1981	1982	1983	1984	1985
Your mother's occupation [2,3]																				
Artist	—	—	—	—	—	0.8	0.9	—	—	—	1.3	1.4	1.3	1.3	1.4	1.5	1.6	1.7	1.7	1.9
Business	—	—	—	—	—	5.0	6.0	—	—	—	6.5	6.9	7.8	8.2	9.1	9.9	10.2	10.6	11.3	12.7
Clerical	—	—	—	—	—	7.6	10.1	—	—	—	8.7	8.9	9.4	9.6	10.2	10.4	10.5	10.5	10.8	10.1
Clergy	—	—	—	—	—	0.1	0.1	—	—	—	0.1	0.1	0.1	0.1	0.1	0.1	0.1	0.1	0.2	0.2
College teacher	—	—	—	—	—	0.3	0.3	—	—	—	0.4	0.4	0.4	0.4	0.4	0.4	0.4	0.4	0.4	0.5
Doctor (MD or DDS)	—	—	—	—	—	0.1	0.1	—	—	—	0.2	0.2	0.2	0.3	0.3	0.3	0.4	0.4	0.4	0.5
Education (secondary)	—	—	—	—	—	2.4	3.0	—	—	—	3.2	3.2	3.4	3.5	3.4	3.9	4.2	3.8	4.0	4.5
Education (elementary)	—	—	—	—	—	4.6	5.1	—	—	—	6.3	6.2	6.4	6.2	6.5	7.0	7.0	6.5	6.5	6.9
Engineer	—	—	—	—	—	0.1	0.0	—	—	—	0.1	0.1	0.1	0.1	0.1	0.1	0.1	0.1	0.2	0.2
Farmer or forester	—	—	—	—	—	0.1	0.2	—	—	—	0.2	0.2	0.2	0.2	0.2	0.3	0.3	0.2	0.2	0.3
Health professional	—	—	—	—	—	1.0	1.2	—	—	—	1.5	1.5	1.5	1.6	1.6	1.8	1.8	1.8	1.9	2.0
Homemaker	—	—	—	—	—	53.4	34.5	—	—	—	35.6	32.8	32.1	30.3	28.3	23.8	23.1	25.4	23.9	21.6
Lawyer	—	—	—	—	—	0.1	0.1	—	—	—	0.1	0.1	0.1	0.1	0.1	0.2	0.2	0.2	0.3	0.3
Military	—	—	—	—	—	0.0	0.0	—	—	—	0.0	0.0	0.0	0.0	0.0	0.0	0.0	0.0	0.1	0.1
Nurse	—	—	—	—	—	4.5	4.9	—	—	—	6.0	6.3	6.3	6.6	6.6	7.4	7.4	7.4	7.5	7.6
Research scientist	—	—	—	—	—	0.1	0.1	—	—	—	0.1	0.1	0.1	0.1	0.1	0.1	0.2	0.2	0.1	0.1
Social worker	—	—	—	—	—	0.7	1.0	—	—	—	1.2	1.3	1.2	1.4	1.3	1.3	1.3	1.4	1.4	1.4
Skilled worker	—	—	—	—	—	1.4	1.9	—	—	—	1.6	1.8	1.8	1.8	1.8	2.0	2.0	2.0	2.2	2.0
Semi skilled worker	—	—	—	—	—	2.9	3.4	—	—	—	3.2	3.5	3.1	3.4	3.3	3.3	3.3	3.2	2.9	3.0
Laborer	—	—	—	—	—	1.6	2.1	—	—	—	1.9	2.1	1.9	1.9	2.2	2.1	2.0	1.9	1.8	1.8
Unemployed	—	—	—	—	—	3.7	12.9	—	—	—	9.2	9.4	9.0	8.6	8.3	8.3	7.8	6.9	6.3	6.6
Other occupation	—	—	—	—	—	9.5	12.2	—	—	—	12.5	13.6	13.7	14.2	14.5	15.8	15.9	15.2	16.0	15.7
Your father's religious preference [2,3]																				
Protestant (Christian)	—	—	—	—	—	—	—	54.0	54.0	53.9	51.3	51.6	51.6	39.1	39.4	38.4	36.7	35.7	46.7	47.6
Roman Catholic	—	—	—	—	—	—	—	32.0	31.6	30.2	32.1	33.6	33.6	34.5	33.7	34.3	35.4	35.4	36.0	34.2
Jewish	—	—	—	—	—	—	—	6.1	5.1	5.2	5.6	5.0	5.4	4.9	4.5	4.5	4.6	4.4	4.2	4.6
Other	—	—	—	—	—	—	—	2.1	2.5	3.0	3.8	3.1	3.1	15.0	15.5	15.8	16.5	16.6	5.1	5.0
None	—	—	—	—	—	—	—	5.8	6.8	7.7	7.3	6.7	6.4	6.5	6.9	7.0	6.8	7.4	7.9	8.6
Your mother's religious preference [2,3]																				
Protestant (Christian)	—	—	—	—	57.8	—	—	—	—	—	53.3	53.5	53.3	40.0	40.0	39.0	37.5	36.1	48.4	49.2
Roman Catholic	—	—	—	—	30.9	—	—	—	—	—	33.6	34.9	34.7	35.9	35.2	35.9	37.0	37.8	37.1	35.9
Jewish	—	—	—	—	6.6	—	—	—	—	—	5.4	4.8	5.2	4.7	4.3	4.4	4.4	4.2	4.1	4.4
Other	—	—	—	—	1.9	—	—	—	—	—	3.9	3.4	3.5	15.6	16.3	16.5	17.1	17.4	5.6	5.4
None	—	—	—	—	2.8	—	—	—	—	—	3.8	3.5	3.3	3.8	4.1	4.1	3.9	4.4	4.7	5.2
How many persons are currently dependent on your parents?																				
One	—	—	—	—	—	—	—	—	—	—	—	—	4.4	5.2	4.9	4.7	5.1	5.5	5.7	6.2
Two	—	—	—	—	—	—	—	—	—	—	—	—	7.9	9.2	9.1	9.7	10.5	11.5	12.2	12.9
Three	—	—	—	—	—	—	—	—	—	—	—	—	18.9	19.4	19.8	20.0	20.6	23.2	23.1	21.0
Four	—	—	—	—	—	—	—	—	—	—	—	—	26.3	25.7	26.8	27.3	27.8	29.7	30.1	29.3
Five	—	—	—	—	—	—	—	—	—	—	—	—	23.1	22.0	22.3	22.1	21.1	18.9	18.8	18.8
Six or more	—	—	—	—	—	—	—	—	—	—	—	—	19.4	18.4	17.0	16.2	14.9	11.2	10.2	11.8

DEMOGRAPHICS
FRESHMAN MEN

ITEM	1986	1987	1988	1989	1990	1991	1992	1993	1994	1995	1996	1997	1998	1999	2000	2001	2002	2003	2004	2005	2006
Your mother's occupation [2,3]																					
Artist	2.0	1.9	2.0	1.8	1.6	1.7	1.7	1.6	1.7	1.6	1.6	1.6	1.7	1.7	1.7	1.8	1.8	1.9	1.9	1.9	1.9
Business	13.7	14.6	14.4	14.8	14.2	13.9	13.9	13.4	13.6	13.5	13.4	13.8	14.6	15.0	15.1	15.8	16.0	16.1	16.7	16.6	16.7
Clerical	10.8	10.7	10.1	10.2	9.8	9.1	8.6	8.4	7.9	7.7	7.2	7.1	7.3	6.7	6.5	6.5	5.9	5.5	4.9	4.9	4.8
Clergy	0.2	0.2	0.2	0.2	0.2	0.2	0.2	0.2	0.2	0.2	0.3	0.3	0.3	0.3	0.3	0.3	0.3	0.3	0.3	0.2	0.3
College teacher	0.5	0.5	0.5	0.6	0.6	0.6	0.6	0.6	0.6	0.6	0.6	0.6	0.6	0.6	0.6	0.6	0.6	0.6	0.6	0.5	0.6
Doctor (MD or DDS)	0.5	0.5	0.6	0.5	0.6	0.6	0.7	0.6	0.8	0.8	0.8	0.9	1.0	1.1	1.2	1.2	1.3	1.4	1.4	1.5	1.6
Education (secondary)	4.7	4.9	5.3	5.1	5.2	5.5	5.8	5.9	6.2	6.2	6.3	6.3	6.1	6.2	5.9	5.7	5.7	5.4	5.4	5.3	5.4
Education (elementary)	7.3	7.8	8.0	8.2	8.6	9.2	9.9	10.2	10.9	10.8	11.4	11.7	11.5	11.6	11.2	10.9	10.6	10.1	9.5	9.3	9.1
Engineer	0.2	0.2	0.2	0.2	0.2	0.3	0.3	0.3	0.3	0.4	0.4	0.4	0.4	0.5	0.5	0.6	0.6	0.6	0.7	0.7	0.8
Farmer or forester	0.3	0.3	0.3	0.4	0.4	0.4	0.3	0.4	0.4	0.4	0.4	0.4	0.3	0.4	0.3	0.3	0.3	0.3	0.3	0.2	0.3
Health professional	1.9	2.0	2.0	2.1	2.2	2.2	2.2	2.3	2.4	2.4	2.4	2.6	2.7	2.8	3.0	3.1	3.0	3.2	3.4	3.2	3.3
Homemaker	20.0	17.8	16.8	15.6	14.3	14.2	13.5	13.0	12.5	11.5	11.3	11.0	10.8	10.7	10.6	10.5	10.1	10.0	9.5	8.8	8.1
Lawyer	0.3	0.4	0.4	0.4	0.1	0.4	0.3	0.4	0.4	0.4	0.4	0.5	0.5	0.6	0.7	0.7	0.8	0.8	0.9	1.0	1.1
Military	0.1	0.0	0.1	0.1	0.1	0.1	0.1	0.1	0.1	0.1	0.1	0.1	0.2	0.1	0.1	0.2	0.2	0.2	0.2	0.2	0.2
Nurse	7.5	7.6	7.7	7.9	7.9	8.1	8.2	8.4	8.3	8.9	8.7	8.9	8.7	9.0	8.9	8.7	8.9	9.0	9.2	9.0	9.0
Research scientist	0.2	0.2	0.2	0.2	0.2	0.2	0.2	0.2	0.2	0.2	0.2	0.2	0.2	0.3	0.3	0.3	0.3	0.4	0.4	0.4	0.4
Social worker	1.5	1.6	1.6	1.6	1.6	1.8	1.7	1.8	1.8	1.8	1.9	1.8	1.9	1.9	1.9	1.9	1.8	1.8	1.8	1.9	1.9
Skilled worker	2.1	2.2	2.1	2.4	2.4	2.3	2.1	2.4	2.1	2.2	2.1	2.0	2.0	2.3	1.8	2.0	1.9	1.7	1.8	1.6	1.7
Semi skilled worker	2.8	2.5	2.5	2.8	2.8	3.0	2.7	2.8	2.7	2.8	2.6	2.5	2.4	2.3	2.2	2.3	2.3	2.2	2.2	2.2	2.1
Laborer	1.6	1.4	1.5	1.5	1.7	1.7	1.6	1.9	1.7	1.7	1.6	1.4	1.5	1.5	1.4	1.7	1.8	1.7	1.8	1.8	1.5
Unemployed	6.3	6.1	5.9	5.7	5.7	6.1	5.7	5.5	5.5	5.4	5.8	5.4	5.1	4.8	5.2	4.3	4.5	4.9	5.0	5.5	5.5
Other occupation	15.6	16.5	17.6	17.8	19.2	18.4	19.5	19.3	19.5	20.2	20.6	20.5	20.2	20.3	20.7	20.5	21.1	21.9	22.0	23.2	23.7
Your father's religious preference [2,3]																					
Protestant (Christian)	34.3	47.9	46.2	48.9	48.0	47.9	49.0	46.4	49.9	48.5	49.2	49.3	49.7	49.9	46.6	46.2	45.3	45.1	47.2	46.7	45.8
Roman Catholic	33.5	33.9	33.1	32.9	33.0	33.4	31.8	34.6	31.4	33.3	31.6	31.8	30.6	30.2	32.4	32.3	32.5	32.3	29.6	30.3	30.3
Jewish	4.2	4.2	4.5	4.0	3.7	3.4	3.3	3.5	3.4	3.4	3.4	3.2	3.2	3.0	3.9	3.6	3.3	3.4	3.6	3.7	3.8
Other	19.4	4.8	5.6	4.9	5.5	5.7	5.5	5.9	5.0	5.0	5.4	5.2	5.1	5.5	5.7	5.9	5.5	5.7	5.7	5.8	5.6
None	8.7	9.0	10.7	9.3	9.8	10.0	10.3	9.7	10.4	9.8	10.4	10.4	11.5	11.4	11.5	12.0	13.3	13.5	13.9	13.5	14.5
Your mother's religious preference [2,3]																					
Protestant (Christian)	35.2	49.7	48.2	50.8	50.0	49.9	51.0	48.4	52.3	50.6	51.7	52.0	52.6	52.7	49.1	48.9	48.4	47.7	50.4	49.5	49.1
Roman Catholic	35.0	35.5	34.9	34.1	34.4	34.8	33.2	35.9	32.8	34.7	33.0	33.1	32.0	31.6	33.9	33.8	34.1	34.1	31.1	32.0	31.8
Jewish	4.1	4.2	4.3	3.8	3.5	2.8	3.1	3.2	3.2	3.2	3.1	3.0	2.9	2.9	3.7	3.4	3.1	3.2	3.4	3.4	3.5
Other	20.0	5.1	5.9	5.3	5.7	6.0	5.7	6.1	5.0	4.9	5.3	5.2	5.0	5.4	5.6	5.8	5.5	5.7	5.5	5.7	5.5
None	5.7	5.5	6.8	6.1	6.4	6.5	7.0	6.4	6.8	6.5	6.9	6.7	7.5	7.4	7.6	8.1	8.9	9.3	9.5	9.4	10.1
How many persons are currently dependent on your parents?																					
One	6.5	7.9	—	—	—	—	—	—	—	—	8.7	8.8	—	—	—	—	—	—	—	—	10.9
Two	14.3	17.3	—	—	—	—	—	—	—	—	17.7	17.4	—	—	—	—	—	—	—	—	19.4
Three	21.9	22.2	—	—	—	—	—	—	—	—	21.3	21.7	—	—	—	—	—	—	—	—	22.2
Four	29.3	28.1	—	—	—	—	—	—	—	—	28.1	28.7	—	—	—	—	—	—	—	—	27.6
Five	17.6	16.0	—	—	—	—	—	—	—	—	15.7	15.5	—	—	—	—	—	—	—	—	13.7
Six or more	10.4	8.5	—	—	—	—	—	—	—	—	8.5	8.0	—	—	—	—	—	—	—	—	6.3

HIGH SCHOOL EXPERIENCES
FRESHMAN MEN

ITEM	1966	1967	1968	1969	1970	1971	1972	1973	1974	1975	1976	1977	1978	1979	1980	1981	1982	1983	1984	1985
From what kind of secondary school did you graduate? [*]																				
Public	81.4	—	—	81.1	80.8	—	81.6	—	—	—	—	—	—	82.1	82.1	—	—	80.8	80.2	—
Private, denominational	13.2	—	—	14.1	15.6	—	13.2	—	—	—	—	—	—	13.2	13.0	—	—	13.6	14.2	—
Private, nondenominational	5.4	—	—	5.0	3.7	—	5.2	—	—	—	—	—	—	4.6	4.9	—	—	5.6	5.6	—
In what year did you graduate from high school?																				
This year	—	—	—	—	—	—	—	95.9	94.7	94.6	95.1	94.7	95.5	94.2	94.6	95.4	95.6	95.7	95.9	96.0
One year ago	—	—	—	—	—	—	—	2.3	2.8	2.8	2.4	2.8	2.4	3.1	2.9	2.3	2.2	2.3	2.3	2.1
Two years ago	—	—	—	—	—	—	—	0.5	0.7	0.7	0.7	0.6	0.6	0.8	0.7	0.6	0.6	0.6	0.6	0.6
Three or more years ago	—	—	—	—	—	—	—	0.9	1.2	1.3	1.2	1.2	0.9	1.2	1.2	1.0	1.0	1.1	0.8	0.6
Did not graduate but passed G.E.D. test	—	—	—	—	—	—	—	0.3	0.4	0.4	0.4	0.5	0.4	0.6	0.6	0.5	0.5	0.3	0.3	0.3
Never completed high school	—	—	—	—	—	—	—	0.2	0.2	0.2	0.2	0.2	0.2	0.2	0.1	0.1	0.1	0.1	0.1	0.1
HOW WOULD YOU DESCRIBE THE RACIAL COMPOSITION OF THE:																				
High school you last attended																				
Completely non-White	—	—	—	—	—	—	—	—	—	—	—	—	—	—	—	—	—	1.2	—	—
Mostly non-White	—	—	—	—	—	—	—	—	—	—	—	—	—	—	—	—	—	4.2	—	—
Roughly half non-White	—	—	—	—	—	—	—	—	—	—	—	—	—	—	—	—	—	14.5	—	—
Mostly White	—	—	—	—	—	—	—	—	—	—	—	—	—	—	—	—	—	61.5	—	—
Completely White	—	—	—	—	—	—	—	—	—	—	—	—	—	—	—	—	—	18.4	—	—
Neighborhood where you grew up																				
Completely non-White	—	—	—	—	—	—	—	—	—	—	—	—	—	—	—	—	—	3.6	—	—
Mostly non-White	—	—	—	—	—	—	—	—	—	—	—	—	—	—	—	—	—	5.3	—	—
Roughly half non-White	—	—	—	—	—	—	—	—	—	—	—	—	—	—	—	—	—	5.1	—	—
Mostly White	—	—	—	—	—	—	—	—	—	—	—	—	—	—	—	—	—	40.8	—	—
Completely White	—	—	—	—	—	—	—	—	—	—	—	—	—	—	—	—	—	45.1	—	—
Did your high school require community service for graduation?																				
No	—	—	—	—	—	—	—	—	—	—	—	—	—	—	—	—	—	—	—	—
Yes	—	—	—	—	—	—	—	—	—	—	—	—	—	—	—	—	—	—	—	—
Did you meet or exceed recommended years of high school (grades 9–12) study in the following subjects [4]																				
English (4 years)	—	—	—	—	—	—	—	—	—	—	—	—	—	—	—	—	—	—	93.5	93.8
Mathematics (3 years)	—	—	—	—	—	—	—	—	—	—	—	—	—	—	—	—	—	—	91.9	92.2
Foreign language (2 years)	—	—	—	—	—	—	—	—	—	—	—	—	—	—	—	—	—	—	69.1	70.1
Physical science (2 years)	—	—	—	—	—	—	—	—	—	—	—	—	—	—	—	—	—	—	62.4	65.8
Biological science (2 years)	—	—	—	—	—	—	—	—	—	—	—	—	—	—	—	—	—	—	33.3	34.9
History/American govt. (1 year)	—	—	—	—	—	—	—	—	—	—	—	—	—	—	—	—	—	—	99.0	99.3
Computer science (1/2 year)	—	—	—	—	—	—	—	—	—	—	—	—	—	—	—	—	—	—	61.4	66.5
Arts and/or music (1 year)	—	—	—	—	—	—	—	—	—	—	—	—	—	—	—	—	—	—	55.3	55.4
Have you had any special tutoring or remedial work in:																				
English	—	—	—	—	—	—	—	—	—	—	—	—	—	6.7	7.0	5.7	5.8	—	6.0	—
Reading	—	—	—	—	—	—	—	—	—	—	—	—	—	6.7	7.0	5.4	5.7	—	5.5	—
Mathematics	—	—	—	—	—	—	—	—	—	—	—	—	—	7.8	8.2	6.9	7.5	—	8.6	—
Social studies	—	—	—	—	—	—	—	—	—	—	—	—	—	5.6	6.8	4.3	4.5	—	4.3	—
Science	—	—	—	—	—	—	—	—	—	—	—	—	—	5.2	5.9	4.3	4.4	—	4.5	—
Foreign language	—	—	—	—	—	—	—	—	—	—	—	—	—	4.2	4.3	3.5	3.9	—	4.2	—

HIGH SCHOOL EXPERIENCES
FRESHMAN MEN

ITEM	1986	1987	1988	1989	1990	1991	1992	1993	1994	1995	1996	1997	1998	1999	2000	2001	2002	2003	2004	2005	2006
From what kind of secondary school did you graduate? [*]																					
Public	—	—	—	—	—	81.7	—	81.6	—	—	—	—	81.6	—	—	81.2	—	—	—	—	—
Private, denominational	—	—	—	—	—	13.0	—	13.2	—	—	—	—	14.1	—	—	15.0	—	—	—	—	—
Private, nondenominational	—	—	—	—	—	5.3	—	5.2	—	—	—	—	4.3	—	—	4.8	—	—	—	—	—
In what year did you graduate from high school?																					
this year	95.8	96.6	96.7	96.1	96.0	95.8	96.5	96.6	96.9	96.9	97.2	97.2	97.3	97.2	97.4	97.2	97.5	97.9	97.4	97.8	97.5
one year ago	2.2	2.0	1.8	2.1	2.3	1.9	1.7	1.8	1.6	1.8	1.6	1.6	1.4	1.6	1.3	1.5	1.3	1.2	1.4	1.3	1.6
two years ago	0.6	0.5	0.5	0.5	0.6	0.6	0.4	0.4	0.4	0.4	0.3	0.4	0.3	0.3	0.3	0.4	0.4	0.3	0.3	0.3	0.4
three or more years ago	1.1	0.7	0.8	0.9	0.9	1.2	1.1	0.8	0.8	0.7	0.6	0.6	0.7	0.6	0.6	0.6	0.5	0.4	0.6	0.4	0.4
did not graduate but passed G.E.D. test	0.2	0.2	0.2	0.2	0.2	0.4	0.3	0.2	0.2	0.2	0.2	0.2	0.2	0.3	0.3	0.2	0.2	0.2	0.2	0.2	0.1
never completed high school	0.1	0.1	0.0	0.0	0.1	0.1	0.1	0.1	0.1	0.1	0.0	0.0	0.0	0.0	0.0	0.1	0.0	0.0	0.0	0.0	0.0
HOW WOULD YOU DESCRIBE THE RACIAL COMPOSITION OF THE:																					
High school you last attended																					
Completely non-White	—	—	1.6	—	1.7	—	—	—	—	—	—	—	—	—	—	—	—	—	—	—	2.3
Mostly non-White	—	—	5.4	—	6.1	—	—	—	—	—	—	—	—	—	—	—	—	—	—	—	9.9
Roughly half non-White	—	—	15.7	—	16.8	—	—	—	—	—	—	—	—	—	—	—	—	—	—	—	21.7
Mostly White	—	—	61.0	—	61.1	—	—	—	—	—	—	—	—	—	—	—	—	—	—	—	56.1
Completely White	—	—	16.2	—	14.3	—	—	—	—	—	—	—	—	—	—	—	—	—	—	—	10.0
Neighborhood where you grew up																					
Completely non-White	—	—	3.7	—	4.6	—	—	—	—	—	—	—	—	—	—	—	—	—	—	—	4.8
Mostly non-White	—	—	6.3	—	6.4	—	—	—	—	—	—	—	—	—	—	—	—	—	—	—	9.1
Roughly half non-White	—	—	6.4	—	6.9	—	—	—	—	—	—	—	—	—	—	—	—	—	—	—	11.8
Mostly White	—	—	44.8	—	45.3	—	—	—	—	—	—	—	—	—	—	—	—	—	—	—	50.6
Completely White	—	—	38.9	—	36.9	—	—	—	—	—	—	—	—	—	—	—	—	—	—	—	23.7
Did your high school require community service for graduation?																					
No	—	—	—	—	—	—	—	—	—	—	—	—	76.5	75.2	72.1	71.6	70.5	68.2	69.2	67.9	—
Yes	—	—	—	—	—	—	—	—	—	—	—	—	23.5	24.8	27.9	28.4	29.5	31.8	30.8	32.1	—
Did you meet or exceed recommended years of high school (grades 9–12) study in the following subjects [4]																					
English (4 years)	94.9	96.2	95.5	—	96.8	—	97.5	—	97.4	—	97.4	—	97.8	—	—	97.6	—	—	97.3	—	97.5
Mathematics (3 years)	93.9	94.9	95.0	—	96.0	—	97.2	—	97.7	—	97.9	—	98.1	—	—	98.1	—	—	98.1	—	98.5
Foreign language (2 years)	73.9	78.8	79.3	—	81.8	—	86.4	—	87.7	—	88.6	—	90.3	—	—	91.2	—	—	90.7	—	92.2
Physical science (2 years)	63.3	59.4	59.0	—	58.1	—	58.3	—	59.7	—	60.0	—	57.6	—	—	62.2	—	—	62.6	—	63.7
Biological science (2 years)	35.8	33.0	34.5	—	34.7	—	37.5	—	39.8	—	40.6	—	39.9	—	—	41.5	—	—	41.4	—	44.8
History/American govt. (1 year)	99.3	99.4	99.3	—	99.2	—	99.1	—	99.0	—	98.9	—	98.8	—	—	98.8	—	—	98.6	—	98.8
Computer science (1/2 year)	67.6	65.4	63.9	—	59.5	—	59.3	—	61.3	—	63.1	—	64.1	—	—	67.7	—	—	68.3	—	67.2
Arts and/or music (1 year)	56.8	58.4	61.0	—	67.3	—	69.6	—	71.0	—	70.9	—	72.3	—	—	75.2	—	—	74.9	—	75.9
Have you had any special tutoring or remedial work in:																					
English	—	—	—	6.1	—	6.4	—	5.3	—	5.9	—	5.7	—	6.8	7.0	6.7	6.3	6.0	—	7.1	—
Reading	—	—	—	5.4	—	5.9	—	4.8	—	5.1	—	4.8	—	5.6	5.9	5.7	5.3	4.9	—	5.8	—
Mathematics	—	—	—	9.4	—	10.1	—	9.5	—	9.8	—	9.9	—	10.7	11.1	10.9	11.1	9.9	—	10.9	—
Social studies	—	—	—	4.4	—	4.7	—	3.6	—	3.8	—	3.5	—	4.2	4.4	4.2	3.8	3.6	—	4.1	—
Science	—	—	—	4.9	—	5.1	—	4.1	—	4.5	—	4.3	—	5.0	5.2	5.0	4.7	4.4	—	4.9	—
Foreign language	—	—	—	5.1	—	5.5	—	4.9	—	5.1	—	5.0	—	5.8	5.7	5.7	5.5	4.8	—	5.4	—

HIGH SCHOOL EXPERIENCES
FRESHMAN MEN

ITEM	1966	1967	1968	1969	1970	1971	1972	1973	1974	1975	1976	1977	1978	1979	1980	1981	1982	1983	1984	1985
Do you feel you will need any special tutoring or remedial work in:																				
English	—	—	—	—	—	19.1	—	—	—	—	—	14.0	14.8	12.6	12.0	11.4	11.5	—	11.9	—
Reading	—	—	—	—	—	12.0	—	—	—	—	—	7.6	8.6	5.6	5.4	4.3	4.3	—	4.2	—
Mathematics	—	—	—	—	—	31.2	—	—	—	—	—	20.6	20.0	18.6	18.3	17.3	18.5	—	19.2	—
Social studies	—	—	—	—	—	2.9	—	—	—	—	—	1.8	3.5	2.1	2.3	2.1	2.2	—	2.2	—
Science	—	—	—	—	—	16.5	—	—	—	—	—	7.5	10.1	7.4	7.2	6.7	7.4	—	8.1	—
Foreign language	—	—	—	—	—	27.3	—	—	—	—	—	13.9	16.2	10.4	11.2	9.6	9.6	—	10.7	—
What was your average grade in high school? [3]																				
A or A+	5.5	5.6	4.8	5.0	6.0	6.6	7.5	9.1	9.4	9.5	10.4	9.9	11.7	10.6	10.3	10.3	10.8	10.6	10.5	11.6
A-	9.2	9.5	8.8	9.5	10.2	10.0	11.6	11.1	12.7	12.2	13.1	12.0	14.0	12.5	12.5	12.2	12.3	11.9	11.7	14.1
B+	16.8	17.2	16.2	17.2	18.7	18.0	20.0	21.7	19.9	20.5	21.5	20.0	20.1	18.4	18.7	18.7	19.4	18.9	18.4	19.6
B	22.5	22.8	22.7	24.3	24.3	24.2	25.6	25.2	25.0	24.3	25.1	24.8	24.3	24.3	24.6	24.3	24.2	23.6	23.9	23.1
B-	16.4	16.6	17.1	17.1	17.5	17.6	15.4	15.8	13.9	15.0	13.3	14.5	13.2	14.4	14.3	15.1	14.5	15.0	14.9	13.9
C+	16.6	15.9	16.9	15.6	14.4	14.4	12.6	9.9	11.9	11.0	10.3	11.4	10.4	12.5	12.0	12.0	11.9	12.4	12.5	10.8
C	12.1	11.7	12.6	10.8	8.3	8.7	6.9	6.9	7.0	7.2	5.9	6.6	5.9	7.0	7.3	6.9	6.6	7.2	7.7	6.8
D	0.8	0.7	0.7	0.5	0.4	0.4	0.3	0.3	0.3	0.3	0.3	0.4	0.2	0.3	0.3	0.4	0.3	0.3	0.5	0.3
Indicate which activities you did during the past year																				
Asked teacher for advice after class [5]	—	27.0	21.8	25.3	23.2	22.4	—	—	—	—	—	—	—	—	—	—	—	—	—	24.1
Attended a public recital or concert [5]	59.3	—	—	—	—	—	—	—	—	—	—	—	81.4	79.8	—	78.7	76.7	75.0	72.5	76.3
Attended a religious service [5]	59.0	—	90.0	89.2	87.4	85.1	—	—	—	—	—	—	84.9	84.8	—	85.5	85.2	84.5	84.9	83.9
Came late to class [5]	49.9	58.9	54.5	59.8	60.5	54.7	—	—	—	—	—	—	—	—	—	—	—	—	—	—
Checked out a book or journal from the school library [5]	46.5	49.9	44.6	44.5	40.1	38.2	—	—	—	—	—	—	—	—	—	—	—	—	—	—
Communicated via e-mail [5]	—	—	—	—	—	—	—	—	—	—	—	—	—	—	—	—	—	—	—	—
Discussed politics [5]	—	30.6	36.2	33.9	34.8	27.9	—	—	—	—	—	—	—	—	—	—	—	—	—	—
Discussed religion [5]	—	30.0	25.3	25.7	24.7	23.8	—	—	—	—	—	—	—	—	—	—	—	—	—	—
Drank beer [5]	64.2	64.6	61.7	64.8	66.5	68.8	—	—	—	—	—	—	78.8	79.2	—	79.5	78.9	76.7	74.5	71.7
Drank wine or liquor [5]	43.9	—	—	—	—	—	—	—	—	—	—	—	—	—	—	—	—	—	—	—
Felt depressed [5]	—	—	—	—	—	—	—	—	—	—	—	—	—	—	—	—	—	—	—	6.4
Felt overwhelmed by all I had to do [5]	—	—	—	—	—	—	—	—	—	—	—	—	—	—	—	—	—	—	—	13.4
Overslept and missed a class or appointment [5]	22.4	23.8	20.5	25.6	24.8	23.1	—	—	—	—	—	—	15.6	17.3	—	18.9	20.2	25.1	28.4	29.5
Participated in organized demonstrations [5]	16.6	17.5	—	—	—	—	—	—	—	—	—	—	—	—	—	—	—	19.8	—	—
Performed community service as part of a class [5]	—	—	—	—	—	—	—	—	—	—	—	—	—	—	—	—	—	—	—	—
Performed volunteer work [5]	—	—	—	—	—	—	—	—	—	—	—	—	—	—	—	—	—	—	70.5	71.3
Played a musical instrument [5]	—	41.8	38.0	39.2	38.2	37.0	—	—	—	—	—	—	41.0	40.0	—	40.0	42.7	41.0	40.9	41.1
Smoked cigarettes [5]	—	17.0	15.4	14.2	13.5	13.6	—	—	—	—	—	—	8.1	8.0	—	6.7	6.4	5.8	5.4	4.7
Socialized with someone of another racial/ethnic group [5]	—	—	—	—	—	—	—	—	—	—	—	—	—	—	—	—	—	—	—	—
Studied with other students [5]	—	90.1	—	—	—	—	—	—	—	—	—	—	—	—	—	—	—	—	—	89.0
Tutored another student [5]	—	50.0	49.3	48.0	49.3	46.4	—	—	—	—	—	—	—	—	—	—	—	—	—	48.0
Used a personal computer [5]	—	—	—	—	—	—	—	—	—	—	—	—	—	—	—	—	—	—	—	31.4
Used the Internet for research or homework [5]	—	—	—	—	—	—	—	—	—	—	—	—	—	—	—	—	—	—	—	—
Visited an art gallery or museum	—	69.4	67.9	69.3	66.5	64.7	—	—	—	—	—	—	—	—	—	—	—	—	—	—

HIGH SCHOOL EXPERIENCES
FRESHMAN MEN

ITEM	1986	1987	1988	1989	1990	1991	1992	1993	1994	1995	1996	1997	1998	1999	2000	2001	2002	2003	2004	2005	2006
Do you feel you will need any special tutoring or remedial work in:																					
English	—	—	—	11.1	—	12.8	—	11.7	—	11.8	—	10.7	—	11.1	10.1	10.5	9.9	11.3	—	10.6	—
Reading	—	—	—	4.1	—	5.5	—	4.7	—	5.4	—	4.8	—	5.0	4.9	5.2	4.8	5.3	—	5.1	—
Mathematics	—	—	—	19.9	—	22.7	—	21.8	—	20.4	—	19.9	—	19.7	19.5	19.7	18.4	19.5	—	19.3	—
Social studies	—	—	—	2.3	—	3.1	—	2.7	—	3.0	—	2.5	—	2.8	2.6	2.8	2.5	2.8	—	2.9	—
Science	—	—	—	8.0	—	9.4	—	9.4	—	8.8	—	8.2	—	8.4	7.8	7.9	7.6	8.4	—	8.2	—
Foreign language	—	—	—	11.4	—	12.8	—	12.6	—	12.3	—	12.0	—	12.3	11.5	11.2	11.4	11.3	—	11.1	—
What was your average grade in high school? [3]																					
A or A+	12.9	12.6	12.7	12.7	12.2	13.0	13.4	14.1	14.9	14.7	16.4	17.4	16.5	18.0	18.0	18.8	19.7	19.8	19.7	19.1	18.3
A–	13.5	12.4	13.9	14.8	14.3	14.6	15.2	15.9	16.8	16.4	17.5	18.5	18.3	19.6	19.5	20.2	20.7	21.1	21.3	21.3	21.7
B+	18.2	19.2	17.9	19.0	18.5	19.0	19.5	19.6	19.4	19.1	19.7	19.9	19.8	20.1	20.1	20.2	20.2	20.3	20.4	20.8	21.2
B	22.4	20.6	22.6	23.9	23.8	23.3	23.5	23.3	23.7	23.6	22.9	22.6	23.6	22.9	23.0	22.3	22.9	22.6	22.6	22.4	23.2
B–	14.5	17.0	14.5	14.0	14.3	13.8	13.5	12.9	12.4	12.9	11.6	11.0	11.1	10.4	10.3	9.8	9.1	9.0	8.9	8.7	9.1
C+	11.7	9.8	11.3	10.1	10.8	10.6	9.6	9.3	8.4	8.7	7.8	6.9	7.1	6.1	6.1	5.8	4.7	4.6	4.3	5.2	4.6
C	6.6	8.0	6.9	5.3	5.9	5.4	5.0	4.6	4.2	4.4	3.9	3.5	3.5	2.8	2.9	2.8	2.5	2.5	2.7	2.4	1.9
D	0.3	0.3	0.3	0.2	0.3	0.3	0.2	0.2	0.2	0.2	0.2	0.2	0.1	0.1	0.2	0.1	0.1	0.1	0.1	0.1	0.1
Indicate which activities you did during the past year																					
Asked teacher for advice after class [5]	76.6	78.6	—	—	27.8	18.3	19.3	18.7	19.6	19.5	21.7	21.4	21.6	21.8	20.7	21.3	21.0	20.8	21.5	21.5	22.5
Attended a public recital or concert	—	—	—	—	—	—	78.0	—	—	—	—	—	74.7	74.1	75.1	75.7	75.6	—	—	—	—
Attended a religious service	82.7	82.2	79.3	80.8	82.0	82.3	82.4	82.3	82.4	81.5	81.9	82.5	81.9	81.7	80.2	80.7	79.0	77.6	77.5	76.8	74.3
Came late to class	—	—	—	—	61.0	60.1	59.6	59.3	59.4	—	—	—	64.4	64.8	65.0	65.8	64.2	63.6	64.6	63.8	62.3
Checked out a book or journal from the school library [5]	—	—	—	—	24.2	—	—	—	—	—	—	—	17.0	15.9	—	—	—	—	—	—	—
Communicated via e-mail [5]	—	—	—	—	—	—	—	—	—	—	—	—	41.4	54.2	62.1	65.0	62.1	57.8	—	—	—
Discussed politics [5]	—	—	25.4	—	—	28.1	32.5	25.8	22.4	21.3	22.2	19.7	19.6	20.2	19.9	25.1	23.9	27.0	29.3	—	36.8
Discussed religion [5]	—	—	20.5	—	—	—	—	—	22.2	—	—	—	27.8	27.7	27.7	28.6	28.6	27.9	32.7	32.7	29.8
Drank beer	71.9	71.8	71.7	66.1	63.2	61.2	58.9	58.8	56.7	52.2	53.2	53.6	54.8	53.4	53.3	52.6	51.9	49.9	51.0	49.1	48.5
Drank wine or liquor	—	65.2	64.6	59.0	55.2	54.0	52.6	52.8	50.9	52.2	53.3	53.3	54.0	52.3	53.3	53.4	52.1	50.4	52.2	50.9	49.6
Felt depressed [5]	6.5	6.6	7.5	6.5	6.2	6.1	6.2	6.2	7.1	6.9	7.0	6.5	6.6	6.5	6.1	5.9	5.8	5.6	5.7	5.2	5.3
Felt overwhelmed by all I had to do [5]	14.3	15.9	15.9	14.0	13.8	14.2	15.3	15.7	16.9	17.2	19.3	18.9	19.5	19.9	17.9	17.4	16.4	15.9	16.3	15.9	17.3
Overslept and missed a class or appointment	31.8	31.8	32.9	36.2	37.3	36.9	39.0	36.1	38.5	38.8	40.2	40.9	43.9	44.5	43.4	45.8	44.3	44.1	47.1	46.7	47.0
Participated in organized demonstrations	—	—	—	—	—	—	—	—	31.7	34.7	35.0	33.6	35.5	35.9	36.3	36.8	35.5	33.7	—	—	—
Performed community service as part of a class	—	—	—	—	—	—	—	—	—	—	—	—	—	50.5	51.2	53.0	49.4	48.7	49.4	50.9	50.0
Performed volunteer work	69.7	—	62.6	62.6	62.6	65.1	66.2	68.0	70.1	69.9	72.0	74.0	74.8	76.3	76.0	78.1	78.1	78.3	77.5	78.5	77.5
Played a musical instrument	41.3	41.6	—	37.6	37.6	37.5	37.9	38.2	38.4	38.9	39.1	39.7	39.9	40.7	42.0	43.3	44.7	44.6	45.8	46.8	45.5
Smoked cigarettes [5]	5.3	5.8	6.7	6.7	6.7	7.6	8.1	8.6	9.3	10.6	10.7	11.0	12.0	10.0	9.6	8.2	7.1	6.2	6.6	5.8	5.7
Socialized with someone of another racial/ethnic group [5]	—	—	—	—	—	—	56.3	—	—	—	—	—	63.2	63.8	65.1	67.6	67.7	67.0	65.8	68.4	65.7
Studied with other students	88.5	89.2	88.1	85.8	85.5	85.9	86.0	86.1	85.9	85.3	86.0	85.6	83.8	84.0	84.0	83.8	83.4	82.9	82.9	82.8	81.7
Tutored another student	46.5	48.4	49.3	50.3	50.3	50.8	53.4	53.5	54.3	52.5	52.3	51.5	50.8	51.3	50.4	53.1	52.0	51.0	52.0	50.7	49.7
Used a personal computer [5]	30.2	30.8	32.4	35.1	—	43.7	—	—	—	56.6	—	65.8	—	69.4	79.5	82.8	84.7	85.5	85.6	85.4	—
Used the Internet for research or homework [5]	—	—	—	—	—	—	—	—	—	—	—	—	45.4	57.2	65.6	71.8	75.4	78.2	73.2	75.2	—
Visited an art gallery or museum	—	—	—	55.8	54.1	—	—	—	59.9	—	—	—	55.2	54.1	55.7	56.3	54.4	53.4	—	—	—

HIGH SCHOOL EXPERIENCES
FRESHMAN MEN

ITEM	1966	1967	1968	1969	1970	1971	1972	1973	1974	1975	1976	1977	1978	1979	1980	1981	1982	1983	1984	1985
Indicate which activities you did during the past year																				
Voted in a student election [5]	69.5	42.1	76.4	68.3	68.0	63.9	—	—	—	—	—	—	—	—	—	—	—	—	—	—
Was bored in class [5]	—	38.5	—	—	—	—	—	—	—	—	—	—	—	—	—	—	30.4	—	30.4	29.4
Was a guest in a teacher's home	—	—	—	—	—	—	—	—	—	—	—	—	—	—	—	—	—	—	—	35.2
Worked in a local, state or national political campaign	—	—	—	—	—	14.2	—	—	—	—	—	—	10.5	9.9	—	10.2	9.2	8.9	10.0	—
DURING YOUR LAST YEAR IN HIGH SCHOOL, HOW MUCH TIME DID YOU SPEND IN A TYPICAL WEEK DOING THE FOLLOWING ACTIVITIES?																				
Studying/homework																				
None	—	—	—	—	—	—	—	—	—	—	—	—	—	—	—	—	—	—	—	—
Less than one hour	—	—	—	—	—	—	—	—	—	—	—	—	—	—	—	—	—	—	—	—
1 to 2 hours	—	—	—	—	—	—	—	—	—	—	—	—	—	—	—	—	—	—	—	—
3 to 5 hours	—	—	—	—	—	—	—	—	—	—	—	—	—	—	—	—	—	—	—	—
6 to 10 hours	—	—	—	—	—	—	—	—	—	—	—	—	—	—	—	—	—	—	—	—
11 to 15 hours	—	—	—	—	—	—	—	—	—	—	—	—	—	—	—	—	—	—	—	—
16 to 20 hours	—	—	—	—	—	—	—	—	—	—	—	—	—	—	—	—	—	—	—	—
Over 20 hours	—	—	—	—	—	—	—	—	—	—	—	—	—	—	—	—	—	—	—	—
Socializing with friends																				
None	—	—	—	—	—	—	—	—	—	—	—	—	—	—	—	—	—	—	—	—
Less than one hour	—	—	—	—	—	—	—	—	—	—	—	—	—	—	—	—	—	—	—	—
1 to 2 hours	—	—	—	—	—	—	—	—	—	—	—	—	—	—	—	—	—	—	—	—
3 to 5 hours	—	—	—	—	—	—	—	—	—	—	—	—	—	—	—	—	—	—	—	—
6 to 10 hours	—	—	—	—	—	—	—	—	—	—	—	—	—	—	—	—	—	—	—	—
11 to 15 hours	—	—	—	—	—	—	—	—	—	—	—	—	—	—	—	—	—	—	—	—
16 to 20 hours	—	—	—	—	—	—	—	—	—	—	—	—	—	—	—	—	—	—	—	—
Over 20 hours	—	—	—	—	—	—	—	—	—	—	—	—	—	—	—	—	—	—	—	—
Talking with teachers outside of class																				
None	—	—	—	—	—	—	—	—	—	—	—	—	—	—	—	—	—	—	—	—
Less than one hour	—	—	—	—	—	—	—	—	—	—	—	—	—	—	—	—	—	—	—	—
1 to 2 hours	—	—	—	—	—	—	—	—	—	—	—	—	—	—	—	—	—	—	—	—
3 to 5 hours	—	—	—	—	—	—	—	—	—	—	—	—	—	—	—	—	—	—	—	—
6 to 10 hours	—	—	—	—	—	—	—	—	—	—	—	—	—	—	—	—	—	—	—	—
11 to 15 hours	—	—	—	—	—	—	—	—	—	—	—	—	—	—	—	—	—	—	—	—
16 to 20 hours	—	—	—	—	—	—	—	—	—	—	—	—	—	—	—	—	—	—	—	—
Over 20 hours	—	—	—	—	—	—	—	—	—	—	—	—	—	—	—	—	—	—	—	—
Exercising or sports																				
None	—	—	—	—	—	—	—	—	—	—	—	—	—	—	—	—	—	—	—	—
Less than one hour	—	—	—	—	—	—	—	—	—	—	—	—	—	—	—	—	—	—	—	—
1 to 2 hours	—	—	—	—	—	—	—	—	—	—	—	—	—	—	—	—	—	—	—	—
3 to 5 hours	—	—	—	—	—	—	—	—	—	—	—	—	—	—	—	—	—	—	—	—
6 to 10 hours	—	—	—	—	—	—	—	—	—	—	—	—	—	—	—	—	—	—	—	—
11 to 15 hours	—	—	—	—	—	—	—	—	—	—	—	—	—	—	—	—	—	—	—	—
16 to 20 hours	—	—	—	—	—	—	—	—	—	—	—	—	—	—	—	—	—	—	—	—
Over 20 hours	—	—	—	—	—	—	—	—	—	—	—	—	—	—	—	—	—	—	—	—

HIGH SCHOOL EXPERIENCES
FRESHMAN MEN

ITEM	1986	1987	1988	1989	1990	1991	1992	1993	1994	1995	1996	1997	1998	1999	2000	2001	2002	2003	2004	2005	2006
Indicate which activities you did during the past year																					
Voted in a student election [5]	—	—	—	—	—	31.2	31.3	—	—	24.7	25.4	23.8	23.4	22.7	21.5	23.6	21.5	20.7	20.6	20.8	19.1
Was bored in class [5]	33.2	34.1	36.2	36.1	—	34.2	33.9	35.8	37.5	37.4	38.3	39.9	40.6	42.5	41.8	43.1	43.1	42.6	44.6	42.2	43.0
Was a guest in a teacher's home	35.6	—	31.8	31.1	31.2	30.4	29.3	29.6	29.2	28.6	29.3	30.5	29.1	29.5	27.6	28.4	27.5	24.8	24.5	23.8	23.4
Worked in a local, state or national political campaign	—	—	10.2	—	—	—	9.1	—	—	9.5	8.1	9.8	—	—	—	—	—	—	9.6	11.6	—
DURING YOUR LAST YEAR IN HIGH SCHOOL, HOW MUCH TIME DID YOU SPEND IN A TYPICAL WEEK DOING THE FOLLOWING ACTIVITIES?																					
Studying/homework																					
None	—	1.9	2.0	1.6	2.0	2.0	2.2	2.6	2.9	3.2	3.2	3.4	3.7	3.9	3.9	4.0	4.7	4.6	4.1	4.7	4.3
Less than one hour	—	9.7	9.8	9.8	10.0	11.4	11.4	14.3	12.3	14.2	12.9	13.8	14.5	15.9	15.9	15.7	17.5	17.5	16.1	18.1	16.4
1 to 2 hours	—	17.4	19.3	19.3	19.7	20.6	20.5	23.5	21.1	22.1	21.5	22.2	22.5	23.2	23.5	24.3	24.3	24.0	24.7	25.3	25.2
3 to 5 hours	—	29.5	29.2	29.1	29.1	28.9	29.6	27.6	27.9	27.4	28.2	27.9	28.0	26.8	27.2	27.5	26.6	26.5	27.3	26.0	27.2
6 to 10 hours	—	24.2	23.1	23.2	22.9	21.7	21.5	19.0	20.8	19.2	20.0	18.7	18.2	17.2	17.0	16.8	15.8	15.9	16.1	15.2	15.9
11 to 15 hours	—	10.2	9.8	10.0	9.8	9.2	9.0	7.7	8.8	8.1	8.2	8.2	7.6	7.3	7.0	6.6	6.2	6.5	6.5	6.0	6.2
16 to 20 hours	—	4.2	4.1	4.3	3.9	3.7	3.6	3.2	3.6	3.4	3.5	3.3	3.3	3.2	3.2	2.9	2.8	2.9	2.9	2.6	2.7
Over 20 hours	—	2.8	2.6	2.7	2.6	2.6	2.3	2.2	2.6	2.5	2.6	2.5	2.3	2.6	2.3	2.1	2.1	2.2	2.2	2.0	2.1
Socializing with friends																					
None	—	0.2	0.3	0.2	0.2	0.3	0.2	0.2	0.4	0.3	0.3	0.3	0.3	0.4	0.3	0.4	0.4	0.4	0.5	0.4	0.5
Less than one hour	—	0.9	1.0	1.3	1.0	1.0	0.9	1.1	1.1	1.1	1.1	1.1	1.0	1.1	1.2	1.2	1.3	1.4	1.3	1.5	1.3
1 to 2 hours	—	3.4	4.6	4.9	4.2	4.2	3.9	4.5	4.4	4.5	4.4	4.7	4.5	4.5	4.5	4.9	5.3	5.2	5.2	5.6	5.7
3 to 5 hours	—	12.0	13.7	13.9	13.2	13.4	13.0	14.0	14.3	13.6	13.8	14.1	13.9	14.2	13.9	15.1	15.6	15.7	16.0	17.0	17.2
6 to 10 hours	—	22.5	22.6	22.0	22.7	23.0	23.0	23.3	23.1	22.2	23.2	23.5	22.3	22.4	22.3	23.8	23.8	23.8	24.0	24.8	25.3
11 to 15 hours	—	20.3	19.8	19.2	19.9	19.4	20.0	20.4	19.8	19.0	19.7	19.4	19.5	18.7	18.7	18.6	18.3	18.6	19.4	18.5	18.6
16 to 20 hours	—	14.4	14.3	14.1	14.7	14.2	14.5	13.8	13.5	13.7	13.7	13.2	14.0	13.3	13.4	13.0	12.6	12.7	12.9	11.8	11.8
Over 20 hours	—	26.1	23.7	24.3	24.0	24.5	24.4	22.8	23.3	25.6	23.9	23.8	24.5	25.4	25.7	23.0	22.7	22.3	20.8	20.4	19.6
Talking with teachers outside of class																					
None	—	7.3	8.3	7.2	8.7	9.0	9.3	10.0	11.0	11.6	11.0	12.0	11.8	11.5	11.8	11.1	12.1	12.3	12.7	13.2	13.0
Less than one hour	—	39.0	36.6	33.3	42.8	43.6	42.4	44.2	44.0	44.0	43.8	45.0	43.8	43.6	43.1	43.1	44.2	44.5	44.2	45.2	43.3
1 to 2 hours	—	32.4	32.8	29.7	32.1	31.4	32.0	29.9	30.2	29.4	29.9	28.6	29.6	29.8	29.8	30.7	29.4	28.9	28.9	28.1	29.5
3 to 5 hours	—	14.9	14.1	14.9	11.9	11.3	11.6	11.0	10.6	10.6	11.0	10.2	10.4	10.5	10.6	10.5	10.0	9.8	10.0	9.4	10.0
6 to 10 hours	—	4.1	4.7	6.8	3.0	3.0	3.2	3.2	2.8	2.9	2.8	2.7	2.8	2.8	2.9	2.8	2.8	2.8	2.7	2.5	2.7
11 to 15 hours	—	1.2	1.7	3.5	0.9	1.0	0.8	1.0	0.8	0.9	0.8	0.8	0.8	0.9	1.0	0.9	0.8	0.8	0.8	0.8	0.8
16 to 20 hours	—	0.5	0.8	2.1	0.3	0.4	0.4	0.4	0.3	0.3	0.3	0.3	0.4	0.4	0.4	0.3	0.4	0.3	0.3	0.3	0.3
Over 20 hours	—	0.5	0.9	2.5	0.4	0.4	0.3	0.4	0.4	0.4	0.4	0.4	0.4	0.5	0.5	0.4	0.5	0.5	0.5	0.5	0.5
Exercising or sports																					
None	—	2.3	2.3	2.2	2.4	2.4	2.3	2.1	2.8	2.9	2.8	3.1	2.8	3.2	3.2	3.2	3.7	3.7	3.3	3.3	3.0
Less than one hour	—	5.5	5.2	5.0	5.5	5.1	5.1	5.2	5.7	5.4	5.3	6.0	5.9	6.3	6.3	6.5	7.3	6.7	6.4	6.8	6.4
1 to 2 hours	—	11.1	12.0	11.5	11.6	11.4	11.3	10.9	11.7	11.3	11.5	11.7	12.1	12.3	12.4	12.9	13.0	12.6	12.4	12.9	13.0
3 to 5 hours	—	18.1	18.7	18.7	17.9	18.0	17.4	16.6	18.3	17.4	17.7	17.3	18.1	17.4	17.7	18.4	18.2	18.2	18.2	18.4	18.8
6 to 10 hours	—	20.4	20.4	21.1	20.4	19.7	20.6	19.9	19.9	19.3	19.7	19.0	19.1	18.7	18.4	19.1	18.9	18.8	19.0	19.1	19.5
11 to 15 hours	—	17.3	17.2	17.4	17.5	17.5	17.4	17.7	17.1	16.8	16.9	16.6	16.1	16.1	15.3	15.6	15.2	15.1	15.8	15.4	15.5
16 to 20 hours	—	10.2	10.4	10.6	10.8	10.7	11.1	11.2	10.2	10.4	10.8	10.7	10.6	10.1	10.1	9.8	9.4	9.9	10.2	9.5	9.7
Over 20 hours	—	15.1	13.7	13.4	14.0	15.2	14.8	17.0	14.3	16.4	15.3	15.7	15.3	15.9	16.6	14.4	14.2	14.9	14.7	14.6	14.2

111

HIGH SCHOOL EXPERIENCES
FRESHMAN MEN

ITEM	1966	1967	1968	1969	1970	1971	1972	1973	1974	1975	1976	1977	1978	1979	1980	1981	1982	1983	1984	1985
DURING YOUR LAST YEAR IN HIGH SCHOOL, HOW MUCH TIME DID YOU SPEND IN A TYPICAL WEEK DOING THE FOLLOWING ACTIVITIES?																				
Partying																				
None	—	—	—	—	—	—	—	—	—	—	—	—	—	—	—	—	—	—	—	—
Less than one hour	—	—	—	—	—	—	—	—	—	—	—	—	—	—	—	—	—	—	—	—
1 to 2 hours	—	—	—	—	—	—	—	—	—	—	—	—	—	—	—	—	—	—	—	—
3 to 5 hours	—	—	—	—	—	—	—	—	—	—	—	—	—	—	—	—	—	—	—	—
6 to 10 hours	—	—	—	—	—	—	—	—	—	—	—	—	—	—	—	—	—	—	—	—
11 to 15 hours	—	—	—	—	—	—	—	—	—	—	—	—	—	—	—	—	—	—	—	—
16 to 20 hours	—	—	—	—	—	—	—	—	—	—	—	—	—	—	—	—	—	—	—	—
Over 20 hours	—	—	—	—	—	—	—	—	—	—	—	—	—	—	—	—	—	—	—	—
Working (for pay)																				
None	—	—	—	—	—	—	—	—	—	—	—	—	—	—	—	—	—	—	—	—
Less than one hour	—	—	—	—	—	—	—	—	—	—	—	—	—	—	—	—	—	—	—	—
1 to 2 hours	—	—	—	—	—	—	—	—	—	—	—	—	—	—	—	—	—	—	—	—
3 to 5 hours	—	—	—	—	—	—	—	—	—	—	—	—	—	—	—	—	—	—	—	—
6 to 10 hours	—	—	—	—	—	—	—	—	—	—	—	—	—	—	—	—	—	—	—	—
11 to 15 hours	—	—	—	—	—	—	—	—	—	—	—	—	—	—	—	—	—	—	—	—
16 to 20 hours	—	—	—	—	—	—	—	—	—	—	—	—	—	—	—	—	—	—	—	—
Over 20 hours	—	—	—	—	—	—	—	—	—	—	—	—	—	—	—	—	—	—	—	—
Volunteer work																				
None	—	—	—	—	—	—	—	—	—	—	—	—	—	—	—	—	—	—	—	—
Less than one hour	—	—	—	—	—	—	—	—	—	—	—	—	—	—	—	—	—	—	—	—
1 to 2 hours	—	—	—	—	—	—	—	—	—	—	—	—	—	—	—	—	—	—	—	—
3 to 5 hours	—	—	—	—	—	—	—	—	—	—	—	—	—	—	—	—	—	—	—	—
6 to 10 hours	—	—	—	—	—	—	—	—	—	—	—	—	—	—	—	—	—	—	—	—
11 to 15 hours	—	—	—	—	—	—	—	—	—	—	—	—	—	—	—	—	—	—	—	—
16 to 20 hours	—	—	—	—	—	—	—	—	—	—	—	—	—	—	—	—	—	—	—	—
Over 20 hours	—	—	—	—	—	—	—	—	—	—	—	—	—	—	—	—	—	—	—	—
Student clubs/groups																				
None	—	—	—	—	—	—	—	—	—	—	—	—	—	—	—	—	—	—	—	—
Less than one hour	—	—	—	—	—	—	—	—	—	—	—	—	—	—	—	—	—	—	—	—
1 to 2 hours	—	—	—	—	—	—	—	—	—	—	—	—	—	—	—	—	—	—	—	—
3 to 5 hours	—	—	—	—	—	—	—	—	—	—	—	—	—	—	—	—	—	—	—	—
6 to 10 hours	—	—	—	—	—	—	—	—	—	—	—	—	—	—	—	—	—	—	—	—
11 to 15 hours	—	—	—	—	—	—	—	—	—	—	—	—	—	—	—	—	—	—	—	—
16 to 20 hours	—	—	—	—	—	—	—	—	—	—	—	—	—	—	—	—	—	—	—	—
Over 20 hours	—	—	—	—	—	—	—	—	—	—	—	—	—	—	—	—	—	—	—	—
Watching TV																				
None	—	—	—	—	—	—	—	—	—	—	—	—	—	—	—	—	—	—	—	—
Less than one hour	—	—	—	—	—	—	—	—	—	—	—	—	—	—	—	—	—	—	—	—
1 to 2 hours	—	—	—	—	—	—	—	—	—	—	—	—	—	—	—	—	—	—	—	—
3 to 5 hours	—	—	—	—	—	—	—	—	—	—	—	—	—	—	—	—	—	—	—	—
6 to 10 hours	—	—	—	—	—	—	—	—	—	—	—	—	—	—	—	—	—	—	—	—
11 to 15 hours	—	—	—	—	—	—	—	—	—	—	—	—	—	—	—	—	—	—	—	—
16 to 20 hours	—	—	—	—	—	—	—	—	—	—	—	—	—	—	—	—	—	—	—	—
Over 20 hours	—	—	—	—	—	—	—	—	—	—	—	—	—	—	—	—	—	—	—	—

HIGH SCHOOL EXPERIENCES
FRESHMAN MEN

ITEM	1986	1987	1988	1989	1990	1991	1992	1993	1994	1995	1996	1997	1998	1999	2000	2001	2002	2003	2004	2005	2006
DURING YOUR LAST YEAR IN HIGH SCHOOL, HOW MUCH TIME DID YOU SPEND IN A TYPICAL WEEK DOING THE FOLLOWING ACTIVITIES?																					
Partying																					
None	—	10.2	10.6	11.5	12.4	13.2	14.1	13.2	15.1	15.1	16.0	15.9	15.5	16.1	15.7	16.3	18.6	19.9	20.2	21.2	21.7
Less than one hour	—	11.5	11.5	12.5	12.5	12.9	13.6	14.4	13.6	13.4	13.6	13.4	12.8	13.0	12.9	13.5	14.4	14.7	14.6	14.9	14.2
1 to 2 hours	—	15.8	16.8	17.4	17.4	17.4	17.7	17.7	17.5	17.0	17.5	17.4	17.5	17.2	17.1	18.0	17.7	17.7	17.7	18.0	18.1
3 to 5 hours	—	23.3	23.8	23.9	23.2	22.2	22.3	21.4	21.5	21.0	21.1	21.2	21.2	21.1	21.2	21.1	20.4	20.1	20.0	19.9	20.4
6 to 10 hours	—	18.8	18.5	17.8	17.4	17.0	16.3	16.1	15.6	15.7	15.3	15.3	15.8	15.7	15.5	15.0	14.1	13.7	13.8	13.1	13.3
11 to 15 hours	—	9.3	8.9	7.9	8.2	7.8	7.6	8.0	7.8	7.9	7.4	7.7	7.9	7.9	8.1	7.7	7.0	6.5	6.6	6.2	6.0
16 to 20 hours	—	4.5	4.4	3.9	4.0	4.1	3.8	4.0	3.8	4.1	3.7	3.8	4.1	4.0	4.2	3.7	3.4	3.3	3.3	2.9	2.8
Over 20 hours	—	6.6	5.5	5.0	4.9	5.3	4.6	5.1	5.2	5.9	5.3	5.3	5.3	5.1	5.4	4.6	4.5	4.1	3.8	3.7	3.5
Working (for pay)																					
None	—	26.5	26.7	27.5	28.4	30.4	31.5	28.3	30.3	28.3	29.7	29.1	28.0	28.7	28.0	29.1	30.6	32.5	32.0	32.9	32.4
Less than one hour	—	3.0	3.0	2.9	2.8	3.1	3.1	3.6	3.0	2.7	2.6	2.7	2.5	2.7	2.7	2.7	3.2	3.2	3.3	3.6	3.3
1 to 2 hours	—	3.9	3.9	3.9	3.7	4.0	4.2	4.2	3.9	3.6	3.7	3.5	3.6	3.6	3.6	3.7	3.7	4.1	4.3	4.5	4.7
3 to 5 hours	—	6.3	6.7	6.1	6.0	6.6	6.5	6.5	6.3	6.2	6.1	6.3	5.9	6.1	6.3	6.3	6.4	7.0	7.1	7.1	7.4
6 to 10 hours	—	10.2	10.1	10.3	10.6	10.7	10.8	10.5	10.5	10.6	10.4	10.5	10.4	10.5	10.5	10.8	11.0	11.1	11.1	11.2	11.1
11 to 15 hours	—	10.9	11.0	11.4	11.5	11.2	11.6	12.0	11.7	11.6	11.7	11.7	12.0	11.6	11.7	12.3	11.9	11.6	11.7	11.4	11.5
16 to 20 hours	—	14.9	15.2	15.0	15.3	14.1	14.0	14.1	14.5	15.1	14.8	15.1	15.3	15.0	15.2	14.9	14.5	13.2	13.2	12.3	12.7
Over 20 hours	—	24.3	23.4	22.9	21.7	20.0	18.4	20.7	19.9	21.8	20.9	21.0	22.3	22.0	22.1	20.1	18.7	17.4	17.4	17.1	16.8
Volunteer work																					
None	—	56.6	56.3	48.4	49.2	47.0	46.3	41.9	43.1	43.9	42.4	39.7	37.9	37.4	37.8	36.4	36.9	36.3	35.1	36.3	35.9
Less than one hour	—	17.1	17.6	21.5	21.3	21.8	21.5	23.7	22.8	22.4	23.0	24.2	24.0	23.9	23.7	24.3	24.6	24.4	25.1	24.6	23.8
1 to 2 hours	—	14.2	14.5	17.2	16.6	17.0	17.6	18.8	18.7	18.2	18.9	19.6	20.6	20.7	20.2	21.3	20.4	20.7	22.0	20.7	21.6
3 to 5 hours	—	7.1	7.0	7.8	7.7	8.5	8.7	9.2	9.1	9.1	9.2	9.7	10.3	10.4	10.5	10.7	10.3	10.7	10.7	10.5	10.8
6 to 10 hours	—	2.7	2.6	2.8	2.8	3.1	3.3	3.5	3.3	3.4	3.5	3.5	3.8	3.9	4.1	4.0	4.1	4.0	3.9	4.1	4.2
11 to 15 hours	—	0.9	0.8	0.9	0.9	1.0	1.0	1.2	1.2	1.2	1.2	1.4	1.4	1.4	1.4	1.4	1.5	1.5	1.4	1.6	1.6
16 to 20 hours	—	0.5	0.4	0.5	0.5	0.5	0.6	0.6	0.6	0.6	0.6	0.6	0.7	0.8	0.8	0.8	0.8	0.8	0.7	0.8	0.8
Over 20 hours	—	0.9	0.8	0.8	0.9	1.1	1.0	1.1	1.1	1.2	1.2	1.2	1.3	1.4	1.5	1.3	1.4	1.6	1.1	1.5	1.4
Student clubs/groups																					
None	—	33.3	33.7	30.4	31.8	30.7	32.0	31.6	33.1	35.9	35.6	35.0	34.5	33.6	35.4	34.8	35.3	35.7	35.1	36.9	35.6
Less than one hour	—	13.9	14.1	15.2	14.9	15.2	15.2	16.9	15.7	15.8	15.4	16.1	16.0	16.2	15.5	15.8	16.7	16.5	15.9	15.9	15.6
1 to 2 hours	—	23.4	24.2	24.9	24.6	24.5	24.6	23.5	24.4	22.8	23.8	23.2	23.8	23.5	22.6	23.3	23.0	22.7	22.5	22.7	22.9
3 to 5 hours	—	16.6	15.6	16.5	16.3	16.1	15.5	15.1	14.9	14.0	14.0	14.3	14.3	14.5	14.1	14.5	13.8	14.2	13.8	13.8	14.1
6 to 10 hours	—	7.1	6.8	7.1	6.8	7.1	7.0	7.0	6.5	6.1	6.0	6.1	5.9	6.3	6.3	6.2	5.8	5.7	5.8	6.0	6.2
11 to 15 hours	—	2.7	2.6	2.8	2.6	2.9	2.7	2.8	2.5	2.5	2.4	2.5	2.4	2.6	2.7	2.5	2.4	2.5	2.4	2.5	2.4
16 to 20 hours	—	1.2	1.3	1.3	1.3	1.3	1.2	1.2	1.1	1.1	1.0	1.1	1.2	1.2	1.3	1.2	1.1	1.1	1.1	1.3	1.2
Over 20 hours	—	1.8	1.7	1.8	1.8	2.2	1.8	1.9	1.8	1.8	1.7	1.7	1.7	2.0	2.0	1.8	1.8	1.8	1.6	1.8	1.9
Watching TV																					
None	—	5.0	4.9	4.6	3.9	3.9	3.8	4.2	4.6	4.9	4.5	4.9	4.6	4.9	4.8	4.9	5.3	5.2	5.2	5.6	6.3
Less than one hour	—	10.9	11.2	11.1	10.3	10.5	10.5	12.0	11.7	12.5	11.7	12.7	11.8	12.1	12.0	12.6	13.6	12.7	12.3	13.1	12.9
1 to 2 hours	—	19.8	20.0	20.0	19.2	19.2	19.8	20.7	20.5	20.8	21.2	21.4	21.2	21.7	21.3	22.0	22.2	21.9	21.9	22.1	22.7
3 to 5 hours	—	27.6	27.5	27.6	27.1	26.4	27.1	26.1	27.1	26.2	26.9	26.5	27.1	26.6	26.8	27.1	26.8	26.6	27.4	26.6	27.4
6 to 10 hours	—	20.0	19.6	19.7	20.3	20.3	19.9	19.1	18.9	18.6	18.8	18.2	18.4	18.1	18.2	17.6	17.1	17.8	17.8	17.5	17.1
11 to 15 hours	—	8.3	8.3	8.4	9.0	9.2	8.9	8.7	8.2	8.2	8.1	8.0	8.0	8.0	7.9	7.7	7.0	7.6	7.6	7.2	6.8
16 to 20 hours	—	3.6	3.8	3.8	4.5	4.2	4.2	3.8	3.8	3.6	3.6	3.5	3.6	3.6	3.6	3.4	3.2	3.4	3.4	3.2	2.9
Over 20 hours	—	4.7	4.7	4.8	5.8	6.3	5.9	5.3	5.2	5.3	5.1	4.8	5.2	5.0	5.3	4.8	4.7	4.8	4.5	4.7	4.0

HIGH SCHOOL EXPERIENCES
FRESHMAN MEN

ITEM	1966	1967	1968	1969	1970	1971	1972	1973	1974	1975	1976	1977	1978	1979	1980	1981	1982	1983	1984	1985
DURING YOUR LAST YEAR IN HIGH SCHOOL, HOW MUCH TIME DID YOU SPEND IN A TYPICAL WEEK DOING THE FOLLOWING ACTIVITIES?																				
Housework/childcare																				
None	—	—	—	—	—	—	—	—	—	—	—	—	—	—	—	—	—	—	—	—
Less than one hour	—	—	—	—	—	—	—	—	—	—	—	—	—	—	—	—	—	—	—	—
1 to 2 hours	—	—	—	—	—	—	—	—	—	—	—	—	—	—	—	—	—	—	—	—
3 to 5 hours	—	—	—	—	—	—	—	—	—	—	—	—	—	—	—	—	—	—	—	—
6 to 10 hours	—	—	—	—	—	—	—	—	—	—	—	—	—	—	—	—	—	—	—	—
11 to 15 hours	—	—	—	—	—	—	—	—	—	—	—	—	—	—	—	—	—	—	—	—
16 to 20 hours	—	—	—	—	—	—	—	—	—	—	—	—	—	—	—	—	—	—	—	—
Over 20 hours	—	—	—	—	—	—	—	—	—	—	—	—	—	—	—	—	—	—	—	—
Prayer/meditation																				
None	—	—	—	—	—	—	—	—	—	—	—	—	—	—	—	—	—	—	—	—
Less than one hour	—	—	—	—	—	—	—	—	—	—	—	—	—	—	—	—	—	—	—	—
1 to 2 hours	—	—	—	—	—	—	—	—	—	—	—	—	—	—	—	—	—	—	—	—
3 to 5 hours	—	—	—	—	—	—	—	—	—	—	—	—	—	—	—	—	—	—	—	—
6 to 10 hours	—	—	—	—	—	—	—	—	—	—	—	—	—	—	—	—	—	—	—	—
11 to 15 hours	—	—	—	—	—	—	—	—	—	—	—	—	—	—	—	—	—	—	—	—
16 to 20 hours	—	—	—	—	—	—	—	—	—	—	—	—	—	—	—	—	—	—	—	—
Over 20 hours	—	—	—	—	—	—	—	—	—	—	—	—	—	—	—	—	—	—	—	—
Reading for pleasure																				
None	—	—	—	—	—	—	—	—	—	—	—	—	—	—	—	—	—	—	—	—
Less than one hour	—	—	—	—	—	—	—	—	—	—	—	—	—	—	—	—	—	—	—	—
1 to 2 hours	—	—	—	—	—	—	—	—	—	—	—	—	—	—	—	—	—	—	—	—
3 to 5 hours	—	—	—	—	—	—	—	—	—	—	—	—	—	—	—	—	—	—	—	—
6 to 10 hours	—	—	—	—	—	—	—	—	—	—	—	—	—	—	—	—	—	—	—	—
11 to 15 hours	—	—	—	—	—	—	—	—	—	—	—	—	—	—	—	—	—	—	—	—
16 to 20 hours	—	—	—	—	—	—	—	—	—	—	—	—	—	—	—	—	—	—	—	—
Over 20 hours	—	—	—	—	—	—	—	—	—	—	—	—	—	—	—	—	—	—	—	—
Playing video games																				
None	—	—	—	—	—	—	—	—	—	—	—	—	—	—	—	—	—	—	—	—
Less than one hour	—	—	—	—	—	—	—	—	—	—	—	—	—	—	—	—	—	—	—	—
1 to 2 hours	—	—	—	—	—	—	—	—	—	—	—	—	—	—	—	—	—	—	—	—
3 to 5 hours	—	—	—	—	—	—	—	—	—	—	—	—	—	—	—	—	—	—	—	—
6 to 10 hours	—	—	—	—	—	—	—	—	—	—	—	—	—	—	—	—	—	—	—	—
11 to 15 hours	—	—	—	—	—	—	—	—	—	—	—	—	—	—	—	—	—	—	—	—
16 to 20 hours	—	—	—	—	—	—	—	—	—	—	—	—	—	—	—	—	—	—	—	—
Over 20 hours	—	—	—	—	—	—	—	—	—	—	—	—	—	—	—	—	—	—	—	—
Playing video/computer games																				
None	—	—	—	—	—	—	—	—	—	—	—	—	—	—	—	—	—	—	—	—
Less than one hour	—	—	—	—	—	—	—	—	—	—	—	—	—	—	—	—	—	—	—	—
1 to 2 hours	—	—	—	—	—	—	—	—	—	—	—	—	—	—	—	—	—	—	—	—
3 to 5 hours	—	—	—	—	—	—	—	—	—	—	—	—	—	—	—	—	—	—	—	—
6 to 10 hours	—	—	—	—	—	—	—	—	—	—	—	—	—	—	—	—	—	—	—	—
11 to 15 hours	—	—	—	—	—	—	—	—	—	—	—	—	—	—	—	—	—	—	—	—
16 to 20 hours	—	—	—	—	—	—	—	—	—	—	—	—	—	—	—	—	—	—	—	—
Over 20 hours	—	—	—	—	—	—	—	—	—	—	—	—	—	—	—	—	—	—	—	—

HIGH SCHOOL EXPERIENCES
FRESHMAN MEN

ITEM	1986	1987	1988	1989	1990	1991	1992	1993	1994	1995	1996	1997	1998	1999	2000	2001	2002	2003	2004	2005	2006
DURING YOUR LAST YEAR IN HIGH SCHOOL, HOW MUCH TIME DID YOU SPEND IN A TYPICAL WEEK DOING THE FOLLOWING ACTIVITIES?																					
Housework/childcare																					
None	—	—	—	—	—	—	—	22.0	29.1	28.3	29.6	30.2	29.2	30.0	31.1	29.1	30.0	29.8	28.8	28.0	27.8
Less than one hour	—	—	—	—	—	—	—	21.1	20.0	25.1	24.0	25.6	23.9	24.8	21.1	21.5	23.0	22.4	21.1	22.3	20.6
1 to 2 hours	—	—	—	—	—	—	—	28.5	27.2	26.6	27.0	26.2	27.4	26.1	26.8	27.9	26.9	27.1	27.6	27.6	28.6
3 to 5 hours	—	—	—	—	—	—	—	18.4	16.0	13.5	13.4	12.3	13.5	13.0	14.0	14.8	13.8	14.0	15.1	14.7	15.5
6 to 10 hours	—	—	—	—	—	—	—	6.3	4.9	4.1	3.8	3.6	3.8	3.9	4.2	4.2	3.9	4.1	4.6	4.6	4.8
11 to 15 hours	—	—	—	—	—	—	—	1.9	1.5	1.3	1.2	1.1	1.3	1.2	1.4	1.3	1.3	1.3	1.4	1.5	1.4
16 to 20 hours	—	—	—	—	—	—	—	0.7	0.5	0.5	0.4	0.4	0.4	0.5	0.5	0.4	0.4	0.5	0.6	0.5	0.5
Over 20 hours	—	—	—	—	—	—	—	1.1	0.8	0.7	0.6	0.6	0.7	0.7	0.9	0.8	0.7	0.8	0.8	0.8	0.9
Prayer/meditation																					
None	—	—	—	—	—	—	—	—	—	—	36.8	35.4	35.9	34.8	35.8	37.9	38.5	39.3	41.0	40.2	—
Less than one hour	—	—	—	—	—	—	—	—	—	—	34.6	35.5	34.2	34.5	34.4	33.6	34.0	33.1	32.4	33.8	—
1 to 2 hours	—	—	—	—	—	—	—	—	—	—	19.1	19.2	19.6	19.8	19.4	18.4	17.7	17.1	17.1	16.7	—
3 to 5 hours	—	—	—	—	—	—	—	—	—	—	5.9	6.2	6.4	6.8	6.4	6.2	5.9	6.0	5.8	5.7	—
6 to 10 hours	—	—	—	—	—	—	—	—	—	—	2.0	1.9	2.2	2.2	2.1	2.2	2.1	2.0	2.0	2.0	—
11 to 15 hours	—	—	—	—	—	—	—	—	—	—	0.6	0.6	0.7	0.7	0.8	0.7	0.7	0.7	0.7	0.7	—
16 to 20 hours	—	—	—	—	—	—	—	—	—	—	0.3	0.4	0.3	0.4	0.4	0.3	0.3	0.3	0.3	0.3	—
Over 20 hours	—	—	—	—	—	—	—	—	—	—	0.7	0.7	0.8	0.8	0.8	0.7	0.8	0.7	0.7	0.7	—
Reading for pleasure																					
None	—	—	—	—	—	—	—	—	24.4	28.3	28.3	30.4	30.6	30.8	30.3	30.2	31.4	31.6	31.7	32.0	31.5
Less than one hour	—	—	—	—	—	—	—	—	25.9	26.1	26.1	27.0	26.2	26.5	26.7	26.5	26.7	26.2	25.6	26.2	25.0
1 to 2 hours	—	—	—	—	—	—	—	—	24.5	22.6	23.6	22.2	23.0	22.6	22.6	23.0	21.6	21.6	21.7	21.3	22.0
3 to 5 hours	—	—	—	—	—	—	—	—	14.7	13.5	13.1	12.2	12.1	12.3	12.4	12.4	12.1	12.4	12.6	12.5	12.9
6 to 10 hours	—	—	—	—	—	—	—	—	6.4	5.9	5.5	5.1	5.0	4.8	4.9	4.9	5.0	4.9	5.2	4.9	5.2
11 to 15 hours	—	—	—	—	—	—	—	—	2.1	2.0	1.9	1.8	1.6	1.7	1.7	1.7	1.8	1.8	1.8	1.7	1.8
16 to 20 hours	—	—	—	—	—	—	—	—	0.8	0.8	0.7	0.7	0.6	0.6	0.6	0.7	0.6	0.6	0.7	0.7	0.7
Over 20 hours	—	—	—	—	—	—	—	—	1.1	0.9	0.8	0.7	0.9	0.7	0.8	0.8	0.8	0.8	0.8	0.8	0.8
Playing video games																					
None	—	—	—	—	—	—	—	—	—	37.8	40.0	36.7	27.1	24.7	—	—	—	—	—	—	—
Less than one hour	—	—	—	—	—	—	—	—	—	25.5	24.2	25.0	24.3	24.4	—	—	—	—	—	—	—
1 to 2 hours	—	—	—	—	—	—	—	—	—	17.8	17.5	18.4	21.5	22.1	—	—	—	—	—	—	—
3 to 5 hours	—	—	—	—	—	—	—	—	—	10.6	10.5	11.3	14.9	15.6	—	—	—	—	—	—	—
6 to 10 hours	—	—	—	—	—	—	—	—	—	4.5	4.3	4.9	6.8	7.3	—	—	—	—	—	—	—
11 to 15 hours	—	—	—	—	—	—	—	—	—	1.8	1.7	1.8	2.7	2.9	—	—	—	—	—	—	—
16 to 20 hours	—	—	—	—	—	—	—	—	—	0.7	0.6	0.8	1.2	1.2	—	—	—	—	—	—	—
Over 20 hours	—	—	—	—	—	—	—	—	—	1.3	1.1	1.1	1.6	1.9	—	—	—	—	—	—	—
Playing video/computer games																					
None	—	—	—	—	—	—	—	—	—	—	—	—	—	—	18.5	18.0	18.1	16.4	16.3	16.8	17.5
Less than one hour	—	—	—	—	—	—	—	—	—	—	—	—	—	—	22.7	22.2	21.7	19.9	19.0	19.4	19.2
1 to 2 hours	—	—	—	—	—	—	—	—	—	—	—	—	—	—	23.5	23.3	22.4	22.9	22.4	21.8	21.9
3 to 5 hours	—	—	—	—	—	—	—	—	—	—	—	—	—	—	18.2	18.4	18.8	19.8	20.1	19.7	19.5
6 to 10 hours	—	—	—	—	—	—	—	—	—	—	—	—	—	—	9.0	9.3	9.7	10.6	11.2	11.0	11.0
11 to 15 hours	—	—	—	—	—	—	—	—	—	—	—	—	—	—	3.7	4.1	4.4	4.7	5.1	5.1	4.9
16 to 20 hours	—	—	—	—	—	—	—	—	—	—	—	—	—	—	1.8	1.8	1.9	2.1	2.3	2.3	2.3
Over 20 hours	—	—	—	—	—	—	—	—	—	—	—	—	—	—	2.7	2.8	3.0	3.4	3.4	3.9	3.8

HIGH SCHOOL EXPERIENCES
FRESHMAN MEN

ITEM	1966	1967	1968	1969	1970	1971	1972	1973	1974	1975	1976	1977	1978	1979	1980	1981	1982	1983	1984	1985
Student rated self above average or highest 10% as compared with the average person of his/her age in:																				
Academic ability	63.8	—	—	—	—	63.0	—	—	64.4	—	64.0	—	—	—	62.2	—	—	—	—	69.8
Artistic ability	15.9	—	—	—	—	16.6	—	—	18.3	—	20.5	—	—	—	22.6	—	—	—	—	26.1
Athletic ability	45.1	—	—	—	—	36.8	—	—	39.8	—	41.2	—	—	—	43.1	—	—	—	—	—
Competitiveness	—	—	—	—	—	—	—	—	—	—	—	—	—	—	—	—	—	—	—	—
Computer skills	—	—	—	—	—	—	—	—	—	—	—	—	—	—	—	—	—	—	—	—
Cooperativeness	—	—	—	—	—	—	—	—	—	—	—	—	—	—	—	—	—	—	—	—
Creativity	59.6	—	—	—	—	56.9	—	—	64.9	—	67.7	—	—	—	68.8	—	—	—	—	68.4
Drive to achieve	—	—	—	—	—	—	—	—	—	—	—	—	—	—	—	—	—	—	—	68.1
Emotional health	—	—	—	—	—	—	—	—	—	—	—	—	—	—	—	—	—	—	—	61.3
Leadership ability	43.8	—	—	—	—	44.4	—	—	51.3	—	54.4	—	—	—	56.4	—	—	—	—	53.9
Mathematical ability	48.2	—	—	—	—	46.1	—	—	47.8	—	48.4	—	—	—	47.7	—	—	—	—	74.4
Physical health	—	—	—	—	—	—	—	—	—	—	—	—	—	—	—	—	—	—	—	—
Popularity	36.8	—	—	—	—	35.3	—	—	37.6	—	39.5	—	—	—	42.0	—	—	—	—	52.3
Public speaking ability	26.4	—	—	—	—	25.7	—	—	27.5	—	29.7	—	—	—	30.9	—	—	—	—	—
Self confidence (intellectual)	44.1	—	—	—	—	46.5	—	—	53.1	—	56.0	—	—	—	58.5	—	—	—	—	68.6
Self confidence (social)	40.6	—	—	—	—	32.5	—	—	39.9	—	43.4	—	—	—	47.0	—	—	—	—	53.4
Self understanding	—	—	—	—	—	—	—	—	—	—	—	—	—	—	—	—	—	—	—	—
Spirituality	—	—	—	—	—	—	—	—	—	—	—	—	—	—	—	—	—	—	—	—
Understanding of others	56.8	—	—	—	—	61.3	—	—	63.9	—	64.8	—	—	—	67.8	—	—	—	—	—
Writing ability	28.8	—	—	—	—	31.9	—	—	34.1	—	36.6	—	—	—	36.2	—	—	—	—	42.8

COLLEGE CHOICE
FRESHMAN MEN

ITEM	1966	1967	1968	1969	1970	1971	1972	1973	1974	1975	1976	1977	1978	1979	1980	1981	1982	1983	1984	1985
Reasons noted as very important in deciding to go to college																				
A mentor/role model encouraged me to go	—	—	—	—	—	—	—	—	—	—	—	—	—	—	—	—	—	—	—	—
I could not find a job	—	—	—	—	—	—	—	—	—	—	4.1	4.6	3.2	3.9	4.8	4.4	5.6	4.6	3.9	—
My parents wanted me to go	—	—	—	—	—	21.8	—	—	—	—	29.0	28.2	27.3	28.8	31.0	31.0	31.9	29.5	28.5	—
There was nothing better to do	—	—	—	—	—	2.2	—	—	—	—	2.9	2.6	2.0	2.1	2.3	2.4	2.5	2.5	2.3	2.6
To be able to get a better job	—	—	—	—	—	73.9	—	—	—	—	69.0	74.6	73.2	76.4	74.9	73.7	74.6	72.3	72.1	70.8
To be able to make more money	—	—	—	—	—	52.7	—	—	—	—	56.4	64.9	63.7	67.7	66.4	68.4	70.5	68.7	69.3	—
To get training for a specific career	—	—	—	—	—	—	—	—	—	—	—	—	—	—	—	—	—	—	—	—
To gain a general education and appreciation of ideas	—	—	—	—	—	55.9	—	—	—	—	60.5	68.1	64.8	64.7	62.3	64.1	62.9	59.0	60.3	57.1
To improve my reading and study skills	—	—	—	—	—	20.2	—	—	—	—	32.8	41.4	36.0	36.5	37.0	37.6	37.9	38.4	37.7	36.3
To learn more about things that interest me	—	—	—	—	—	65.3	—	—	—	—	68.9	76.6	70.1	69.8	69.9	70.0	69.2	67.2	67.9	69.2
To make me a more cultured person	—	—	—	—	—	24.8	—	—	—	—	29.6	35.9	30.8	30.6	31.0	30.9	31.4	28.7	30.3	29.2
To prepare for graduate or professional school	—	—	—	—	—	—	—	—	—	—	46.6	49.0	47.6	46.4	46.8	46.3	46.6	47.2	47.1	46.4
Wanted to get away from home	—	—	—	—	—	40.6	—	—	—	—	10.5	10.1	7.9	8.9	9.6	9.9	10.9	11.3	12.3	—

HIGH SCHOOL EXPERIENCES
FRESHMAN MEN

ITEM	1986	1987	1988	1989	1990	1991	1992	1993	1994	1995	1996	1997	1998	1999	2000	2001	2002	2003	2004	2005	2006
Student rated self above average or highest 10% as compared with the average person of his/her age in:																					
Academic ability	68.7	68.1	69.3	70.5	68.4	67.3	68.0	68.2	69.2	68.6	70.4	71.2	69.7	71.1	70.5	71.6	73.3	73.0	—	72.5	71.9
Artistic ability	26.5	28.5	28.2	28.5	28.8	28.5	29.8	28.5	29.5	29.0	29.4	29.6	30.5	29.6	29.9	30.6	29.7	29.7	—	29.0	28.4
Athletic ability	—	—	—	—	—	—	—	—	—	—	—	—	42.6	—	—	—	—	—	—	—	—
Competitiveness	—	—	71.5	71.5	71.8	71.9	71.9	73.1	72.3	72.3	71.4	71.9	71.0	71.2	69.5	69.1	—	—	—	—	—
Computer skills	—	—	—	—	—	—	—	—	—	—	—	—	—	44.1	46.4	47.6	51.2	52.4	—	50.3	48.5
Cooperativeness	—	—	—	—	70.3	70.8	69.2	69.9	70.0	70.6	70.4	71.3	69.7	71.8	70.8	71.1	70.1	70.9	71.9	71.1	72.0
Creativity	—	—	—	—	—	—	—	57.6	56.7	58.3	57.5	58.7	58.9	60.3	59.6	59.0	59.1	59.1	—	58.0	57.8
Drive to achieve	67.7	65.5	71.1	72.1	71.5	72.2	71.9	70.0	69.8	70.4	69.8	70.6	69.6	70.7	69.4	69.4	66.9	68.1	—	68.4	69.3
Emotional health	67.6	65.6	66.4	66.2	66.2	65.7	65.0	64.2	63.2	63.3	62.7	64.3	62.6	62.7	60.2	60.4	60.5	61.2	—	60.8	62.2
Leadership ability	62.4	60.6	61.5	61.2	60.1	59.5	59.6	60.4	60.5	62.4	61.5	63.3	63.4	64.4	63.9	64.2	63.7	63.9	—	64.5	64.5
Mathematical ability	55.0	54.7	54.6	54.7	52.1	51.0	51.5	51.1	52.8	52.8	53.4	53.9	53.1	54.3	53.8	54.4	55.4	54.9	—	53.8	53.1
Physical health	74.8	72.9	72.8	72.8	72.6	70.8	70.3	71.2	66.6	66.4	69.2	69.8	69.6	69.0	67.7	66.8	67.2	67.6	—	66.8	67.2
Popularity	54.6	53.7	54.2	53.2	52.7	50.0	48.9	49.4	46.6	47.0	47.8	49.6	48.2	48.7	48.5	46.5	45.4	44.9	—	—	—
Public speaking ability	—	36.3	36.3	36.4	34.8	34.6	34.2	35.0	35.0	35.1	35.4	37.0	37.9	40.2	40.3	39.8	39.5	39.3	—	39.7	40.5
Self confidence (intellectual)	69.2	63.0	64.2	65.3	63.1	65.5	65.6	67.1	65.1	65.7	67.1	68.7	68.4	70.2	69.1	68.4	69.6	69.2	—	68.5	68.8
Self confidence (social)	56.0	51.7	52.2	52.2	51.8	53.6	53.4	55.0	52.3	53.7	54.9	56.5	57.3	58.3	57.3	56.1	55.0	54.7	—	56.8	57.7
Self understanding	—	—	—	—	—	—	—	—	—	—	62.3	63.3	62.3	62.9	61.7	60.9	60.6	60.2	—	59.7	62.4
Spirituality	—	—	—	—	—	—	—	—	—	—	42.5	43.7	44.4	45.3	43.3	38.0	37.3	36.6	—	35.9	35.8
Understanding of others	—	—	—	—	66.2	65.9	65.7	65.7	65.5	65.7	62.1	62.5	62.3	63.9	62.7	63.5	63.0	63.0	—	63.8	64.5
Writing ability	44.7	44.0	44.9	45.6	43.4	44.2	44.4	44.6	42.4	42.1	44.4	44.8	43.9	45.2	44.3	44.8	45.1	45.2	—	45.5	45.7

COLLEGE CHOICE
FRESHMAN MEN

ITEM	1986	1987	1988	1989	1990	1991	1992	1993	1994	1995	1996	1997	1998	1999	2000	2001	2002	2003	2004	2005	2006
Reasons noted as very important in deciding to go to college																					
A mentor/role model encouraged me to go	—	—	—	—	—	—	12.9	13.4	13.0	14.0	13.5	13.3	15.1	12.2	12.6	12.8	13.1	12.8	—	14.7	16.0
I could not find a job	—	—	—	5.4	5.3	5.1	5.6	6.5	5.6	5.3	5.6	4.7	5.8	4.0	4.6	4.7	5.1	5.4	5.8	5.9	5.2
My parents wanted me to go	—	—	—	31.1	33.1	31.3	31.4	31.8	32.1	31.8	35.9	32.6	36.9	31.5	33.2	31.6	33.0	33.0	38.9	40.5	43.3
There was nothing better to do	—	2.9	3.1	3.1	3.2	3.5	3.4	3.8	4.4	4.6	4.4	4.1	—	4.2	4.6	4.7	5.4	5.3	5.2	5.1	—
To be able to get a better job	—	—	—	73.4	75.5	74.9	75.5	79.8	74.5	75.0	75.5	72.8	75.4	71.9	72.0	71.0	71.6	70.8	71.9	72.1	70.4
To be able to make more money	71.2	72.3	74.7	73.8	75.2	74.7	74.1	75.8	73.7	74.0	74.8	74.1	76.4	73.7	74.4	74.3	74.0	73.2	72.9	73.5	71.9
To get training for a specific career	—	—	—	—	—	—	—	—	—	—	—	—	—	68.2	68.5	68.3	67.5	66.2	70.1	64.8	64.8
To gain a general education and appreciation of ideas	57.1	56.1	54.6	56.7	57.6	55.5	57.5	60.1	54.6	58.6	58.3	56.0	58.5	56.3	58.0	60.0	59.4	59.1	57.6	58.3	57.5
To improve my reading and study skills	36.3	36.1	34.9	35.6	38.6	34.3	36.7	37.1	37.1	39.0	39.5	36.7	38.5	35.9	37.7	38.3	37.2	36.8	—	—	—
To learn more about things that interest me	69.9	68.6	69.9	68.6	69.1	69.9	70.4	72.5	70.5	71.7	72.8	72.6	—	71.0	72.7	74.2	73.7	73.0	72.0	73.1	72.1
To make me a more cultured person	29.2	30.3	31.2	32.4	36.6	34.9	35.9	39.1	33.9	36.6	34.9	33.7	—	33.9	34.6	35.8	35.7	34.2	33.3	35.3	34.7
To prepare for graduate or professional school	46.1	46.2	48.2	49.7	51.2	52.4	51.9	55.9	52.4	—	—	—	—	49.7	50.2	50.8	50.9	50.5	49.8	51.3	51.0
Wanted to get away from home	—	—	—	16.7	17.3	17.4	18.5	19.7	20.1	19.8	19.8	19.8	20.5	20.1	21.2	20.7	21.9	21.1	21.4	21.1	21.1

COLLEGE CHOICE
FRESHMAN MEN

ITEM	1966	1967	1968	1969	1970	1971	1972	1973	1974	1975	1976	1977	1978	1979	1980	1981	1982	1983	1984	1985
Reasons noted as very important in influencing student's decision to attend this particular college																				
A college rep. recruited me	—	—	—	—	—	—	—	—	—	5.8	5.6	6.6	6.4	6.4	7.1	6.8	6.8	3.7	4.0	4.5
A friend suggested attending	—	—	—	—	—	—	—	—	—	6.7	6.8	7.6	6.2	6.4	6.3	6.6	6.9	6.4	6.3	6.6
I wanted to go to a school about the size of this college	—	—	—	—	—	—	—	—	—	—	—	—	—	—	—	—	—	—	—	—
I wanted to live at home	—	—	—	—	—	8.0	6.9	7.7	6.8	8.2	6.6	7.9	7.2	6.5	6.7	6.4	6.7	—	—	—
I wanted to live near home	—	—	—	—	—	—	—	—	—	—	—	—	—	—	—	—	—	14.1	13.7	12.3
I was admitted through an Early Action or Early Decision program	—	—	—	—	—	—	—	—	—	—	—	—	—	—	—	—	—	—	—	—
I was attracted by the religious affiliation/orientation of the college	—	—	—	—	—	—	20.4	19.4	20.7	20.1	17.2	17.9	16.5	17.5	18.0	16.6	18.6	22.6	21.4	22.0
I was offered financial assistance	—	—	—	—	—	5.9	5.9	8.4	8.6	7.1	6.6	7.3	6.3	6.4	6.5	6.1	6.4	6.8	6.5	6.3
Information from a website	—	—	—	—	—	—	—	—	—	—	—	—	—	—	—	—	—	—	—	—
My guidance counselor advised me	—	—	—	—	—	—	—	—	—	—	—	—	—	—	—	—	—	—	—	—
High school guidance counselor advised me	—	—	—	—	—	—	—	—	—	—	—	—	—	—	—	—	—	—	—	—
Private college counselor advised me	—	—	—	—	—	—	—	—	—	—	—	—	—	—	—	—	—	—	—	—
My relatives wanted me to come here	—	—	—	—	—	6.1	—	5.5	5.5	6.5	5.8	5.8	5.1	5.2	5.8	5.5	5.7	5.6	5.7	5.6
My teacher advised me	—	—	—	—	—	—	—	5.0	5.3	4.6	4.2	4.2	3.9	3.9	4.3	3.8	3.8	3.9	3.7	3.9
Not accepted anywhere else	—	—	—	—	—	2.9	3.0	—	—	—	—	—	2.5	2.7	2.8	2.9	2.7	—	—	—
Not offered aid by first choice	—	—	—	—	—	—	—	—	—	—	—	—	—	—	—	—	—	—	4.3	4.5
Rankings in national magazines	—	—	—	—	—	—	—	—	—	—	—	—	—	—	—	—	—	7.7	7.7	7.8
The athletic dept. recruited me	—	—	—	—	—	—	—	—	—	—	—	—	—	—	—	—	—	—	—	—
This college's graduates gain admission to top graduate/professional schools	—	—	—	—	—	—	—	—	—	—	—	—	—	—	—	—	—	26.4	25.9	27.6
This college's graduates get good jobs	—	—	—	—	—	—	—	—	—	—	—	—	—	—	—	—	—	46.4	45.9	47.2
This college has a good reputation for its social activities	—	—	—	—	—	—	—	—	—	—	—	—	—	—	—	—	—	22.6	24.3	24.6
This college has low tuition	—	—	—	—	—	14.7	15.0	19.4	20.7	18.0	12.3	15.6	14.3	13.2	13.1	13.8	15.9	17.5	18.1	17.9
The cost of attending this college	—	—	—	—	—	—	—	—	—	—	—	—	—	—	—	—	—	—	—	—
This college has a very good academic reputation	—	—	—	—	—	—	54.8	55.6	56.5	53.1	49.7	51.9	54.0	52.6	53.3	54.0	55.9	53.9	55.9	58.5
This college offers special educational programs	—	—	—	—	—	29.7	24.9	24.6	25.1	23.6	21.8	25.4	21.9	22.9	23.0	22.3	21.7	18.0	17.8	17.8
Is this college your:																				
First choice?	—	—	—	—	—	—	—	—	77.0	79.1	76.4	74.8	75.2	74.5	74.4	73.5	72.6	71.5	71.6	72.0
Second choice?	—	—	—	—	—	—	—	—	17.9	16.7	17.6	18.9	18.8	19.0	19.3	19.1	20.5	21.6	21.3	20.9
Less than second choice?	—	—	—	—	—	—	—	—	5.1	4.2	6.0	6.3	5.9	6.5	6.3	6.6	6.9	—	—	—
Third choice?	—	—	—	—	—	—	—	—	—	—	—	—	—	—	—	—	—	4.7	4.8	4.7
Less than third choice	—	—	—	—	—	—	—	—	—	—	—	—	—	—	—	—	—	2.0	2.1	2.4
How many miles is this college from your permanent home? [*]																				
10 or less	—	—	—	15.0	15.2	16.6	14.9	15.0	—	15.2	16.0	17.5	17.0	15.7	16.1	14.7	14.6	14.4	13.8	12.3
11 to 50	—	—	—	19.4	19.9	21.0	19.1	18.9	—	20.1	21.4	21.3	21.8	19.7	20.7	19.1	19.7	22.6	23.7	21.5
51 to 100	—	—	—	15.2	15.3	14.6	16.1	15.9	—	15.2	15.7	16.2	15.1	16.6	16.5	17.9	17.9	18.1	16.4	18.0
101 to 500	—	—	—	35.6	37.0	35.2	36.3	36.8	—	36.0	34.2	33.3	33.2	35.2	33.9	35.8	35.3	32.0	33.2	34.6
More than 500	—	—	—	14.7	12.7	12.6	13.7	13.4	—	13.6	12.7	11.6	12.9	12.7	12.8	12.6	12.5	12.9	12.8	13.6

COLLEGE CHOICE
FRESHMAN MEN

ITEM	1986	1987	1988	1989	1990	1991	1992	1993	1994	1995	1996	1997	1998	1999	2000	2001	2002	2003	2004	2005	2006
Reasons noted as very important in influencing student's decision to attend this particular college																					
A college rep. recruited me	4.8	4.3	4.3	4.6	5.0	5.3	5.4	5.6	5.4	5.5	5.9	5.5	—	—	—	—	—	—	—	—	—
A friend suggested attending	7.9	7.7	7.9	7.5	8.5	8.4	8.0	8.7	8.6	8.3	8.7	8.8	—	—	—	—	—	—	—	—	—
I wanted to go to a school about the size of this college	—	—	—	29.2	31.6	32.1	33.2	35.4	32.1	30.4	31.4	31.5	29.8	28.8	28.2	28.3	27.0	26.6	28.2	31.1	31.2
I wanted to live near home	13.1	11.8	12.6	12.7	13.4	13.2	13.0	12.4	13.0	13.1	13.7	13.7	13.4	12.5	13.7	13.8	14.2	13.4	13.2	14.6	14.4
I was admitted through an Early Action or Early Decision program	—	—	—	—	—	—	—	—	—	—	—	—	—	6.3	6.4	7.0	7.9	8.0	7.8	8.8	9.6
I was attracted by the religious affiliation/orientation of the college	—	—	—	4.4	4.9	5.0	5.0	5.4	5.5	5.1	6.2	6.1	6.3	6.0	5.9	5.2	4.7	4.4	5.2	5.6	5.9
I was offered financial assistance	22.8	21.3	21.6	23.5	24.4	27.7	28.2	30.3	28.6	30.0	32.8	32.2	30.7	29.7	28.9	29.7	30.7	29.9	29.6	31.2	30.7
Information from a website	—	—	—	—	—	—	—	—	—	—	—	—	—	—	6.2	7.7	9.6	10.2	10.6	12.3	13.4
My guidance counselor advised me	7.2	6.0	6.8	6.0	6.6	6.6	6.3	7.7	—	—	—	—	—	—	—	—	—	—	—	—	—
High school guidance counselor advised me	—	—	—	—	—	—	—	—	6.3	6.4	6.3	6.6	5.8	6.0	6.1	6.5	6.4	6.3	7.1	7.9	8.4
Private college counselor advised me	—	—	—	—	—	—	—	1.9	2.3	2.2	2.2	1.9	2.0	2.1	2.3	2.3	2.2	2.4	2.6	2.8	3.1
My relatives wanted me to come here	7.1	6.5	6.0	7.3	7.8	7.5	7.4	7.8	7.9	7.5	8.3	7.6	7.4	6.9	7.3	7.1	8.3	8.2	8.8	9.7	10.9
My teacher advised me	4.3	3.7	4.0	3.4	4.0	3.9	3.9	4.0	4.2	3.8	4.1	3.6	3.7	3.7	3.8	4.2	4.5	4.4	4.9	5.5	6.1
Not accepted anywhere else	—	—	—	—	—	2.4	2.8	2.5	2.6	2.8	2.9	2.8	3.3	3.5	4.0	4.1	—	—	—	—	—
Not offered aid by first choice	5.1	4.5	4.9	5.4	—	—	—	—	—	—	—	—	—	—	—	—	—	—	—	—	—
Rankings in national magazines	—	—	—	—	—	—	—	—	—	5.6	5.6	4.9	5.4	5.2	5.1	5.3	5.3	5.3	5.3	5.7	5.8
The athletic dept. recruited me	8.6	8.1	7.9	8.2	8.5	9.4	9.5	9.6	9.5	10.3	9.8	10.0	9.9	9.8	10.1	11.8	13.8	13.6	14.5	16.1	16.1
This college's graduates gain admission to top graduate/professional schools	25.4	27.1	24.2	24.2	24.7	23.9	24.5	26.3	27.2	26.1	29.1	29.4	26.6	26.3	26.2	26.8	—	—	24.5	27.1	26.3
This college's graduates get good jobs	45.3	46.4	35.8	44.0	44.2	44.3	42.8	46.9	45.9	45.7	50.6	51.9	48.6	48.9	49.1	49.4	—	—	45.3	47.4	46.1
This college has a good reputation for its social activities	29.6	29.3	25.2	24.6	25.2	25.3	26.8	28.9	25.4	25.2	26.6	28.3	26.8	26.0	26.9	27.1	28.0	26.7	27.3	29.7	30.7
This college has low tuition	19.5	17.1	17.8	19.0	21.4	22.5	22.3	24.4	22.2	21.5	22.1	22.7	20.3	19.0	18.4	19.2	19.6	18.5	—	—	—
The cost of attending this college	—	—	—	—	—	—	—	—	—	—	—	—	—	—	—	—	—	—	27.3	28.8	28.7
This college has a very good academic reputation	58.6	56.9	56.9	54.0	53.9	54.4	54.0	55.8	53.7	52.5	54.8	55.6	51.4	51.2	51.1	52.5	51.4	51.3	52.1	53.5	52.4
This college offers special educational programs	18.5	17.4	19.0	16.6	17.6	17.7	18.4	18.8	17.7	17.0	18.3	16.9	15.7	16.5	16.8	17.2	16.1	16.3	—	—	—
Is this college your:																					
First choice?	70.4	68.0	66.2	68.9	71.3	71.9	71.5	71.8	73.0	72.2	71.2	71.1	71.1	71.5	70.4	69.7	69.2	68.9	69.2	70.2	67.9
Second choice?	21.9	23.4	23.7	22.8	21.4	20.8	21.4	20.7	19.7	20.1	20.6	20.4	20.4	20.0	20.7	21.2	21.1	21.5	21.3	20.6	22.3
Less than second choice?	—	—	—	—	—	—	—	—	—	—	—	—	—	—	—	—	—	—	—	—	—
Third choice?	5.2	5.7	6.7	5.5	5.1	4.7	4.8	5.0	4.8	5.1	5.2	5.4	5.4	5.4	5.6	5.7	6.0	5.9	5.9	5.8	6.0
Less than third choice	2.5	2.9	3.3	2.8	2.2	2.6	2.3	2.5	2.5	2.7	3.0	3.1	3.1	3.1	3.4	3.4	3.7	3.7	3.6	3.4	3.8
How many miles is this college from your permanent home? [*]																					
10 or less	11.5	10.1	9.8	10.4	9.7	10.4	9.7	9.7	9.9	10.4	10.2	9.8	10.3	10.0	11.5	11.1	11.5	10.4	10.0	10.6	10.4
11 to 50	21.7	21.3	21.0	20.5	22.3	21.2	20.0	20.1	21.4	21.9	21.5	22.0	22.9	22.5	24.0	25.4	23.6	25.6	24.2	26.7	24.2
51 to 100	17.1	18.8	16.2	16.1	17.8	16.4	16.1	16.5	16.3	16.1	16.3	16.6	17.7	16.9	16.4	16.0	16.6	16.6	16.8	17.6	18.5
101 to 500	34.4	35.3	37.1	37.6	35.8	37.7	40.2	39.4	38.1	37.9	37.9	36.6	37.2	37.7	35.2	34.6	35.7	34.6	36.1	32.3	33.2
More than 500	15.4	14.4	16.0	15.4	14.5	14.3	14.1	14.3	14.3	13.6	14.2	14.9	11.9	12.9	13.0	12.9	12.7	12.7	12.9	12.9	13.6

119

COLLEGE CHOICE
FRESHMAN MEN

ITEM	1966	1967	1968	1969	1970	1971	1972	1973	1974	1975	1976	1977	1978	1979	1980	1981	1982	1983	1984	1985
To how many colleges other than this one did you apply for admission this year?																				
None	—	40.6	43.2	41.7	—	—	36.9	39.1	—	39.9	36.1	34.0	32.4	32.2	32.8	31.1	30.4	28.8	27.4	27.0
One	—	20.6	20.6	20.8	—	—	19.2	19.7	—	20.3	18.0	17.8	16.7	16.5	15.7	16.7	16.1	16.2	15.5	17.4
Two	—	16.7	15.8	16.6	—	—	17.5	16.9	—	15.4	16.3	17.9	18.0	17.5	17.4	18.0	17.6	18.3	18.4	17.1
Three	—	11.1	10.5	10.3	—	—	11.9	10.9	—	10.9	13.5	14.4	15.2	15.8	15.4	15.5	15.7	16.4	16.7	16.1
Four	—	5.8	5.2	5.5	—	—	6.9	6.4	—	6.2	7.3	7.3	7.9	8.0	8.3	8.4	8.8	8.9	9.7	9.2
Five	—	3.1	2.6	2.9	—	—	3.9	3.6	—	3.5	4.2	4.3	4.8	5.0	5.1	4.8	5.3	5.4	5.6	5.8
Six or more	—	2.4	2.0	2.3	—	—	3.7	3.4	—	3.7	4.6	4.5	5.0	5.1	5.3	5.7	6.2	6.0	6.6	7.5
Six	—	—	—	—	—	—	—	—	—	—	—	—	—	—	—	—	—	—	—	—
Seven to ten	—	—	—	—	—	—	—	—	—	—	—	—	—	—	—	—	—	—	—	—
Eleven or more	—	—	—	—	—	—	—	—	—	—	—	—	—	—	—	—	—	—	—	—
How many other acceptances did you receive this year?																				
None	—	35.1	37.1	—	—	—	—	—	—	21.3	19.9	19.2	17.0	16.8	16.5	16.1	—	13.4	12.8	13.0
One	—	29.6	29.5	—	—	—	—	—	—	32.6	29.4	29.9	29.0	28.4	27.9	28.5	—	27.6	26.9	26.2
Two	—	20.8	19.5	—	—	—	—	—	—	22.6	23.0	24.4	24.2	24.6	24.8	25.2	—	25.3	25.0	24.8
Three	—	9.3	9.1	—	—	—	—	—	—	12.7	15.4	14.9	16.5	16.8	17.0	16.6	—	18.2	18.8	19.0
Four	—	3.3	3.1	—	—	—	—	—	—	6.0	6.7	6.3	7.1	7.3	7.6	7.6	—	8.5	8.8	9.0
Five	—	1.2	1.1	—	—	—	—	—	—	2.3	2.8	2.7	3.2	3.2	3.2	3.0	—	3.6	3.9	3.9
Six or more	—	0.7	0.7	—	—	—	—	—	—	2.5	2.8	2.5	3.0	2.9	3.1	3.0	—	3.6	3.8	4.1
Six	—	—	—	—	—	—	—	—	—	—	—	—	—	—	—	—	—	—	—	—
Seven to ten	—	—	—	—	—	—	—	—	—	—	—	—	—	—	—	—	—	—	—	—
Eleven or more	—	—	—	—	—	—	—	—	—	—	—	—	—	—	—	—	—	—	—	—
Prior to this term, have you ever taken courses for credit at this institution?																				
No	—	—	—	—	—	—	97.6	98.1	98.2	97.6	97.3	97.5	97.3	97.4	97.4	97.7	97.4	97.4	97.4	97.5
Yes	—	—	—	—	—	—	2.4	1.9	1.8	2.4	2.7	2.5	2.7	2.6	2.6	2.3	2.6	2.6	2.6	2.5

PLANS, GOALS, AND EXPECTATIONS
FRESHMAN MEN

ITEM	1966	1967	1968	1969	1970	1971	1972	1973	1974	1975	1976	1977	1978	1979	1980	1981	1982	1983	1984	1985
What is the highest academic degree you intend to obtain anywhere?																				
None	4.2	2.2	2.5	0.6	0.5	—	1.4	—	2.2	2.1	1.9	1.7	1.5	1.2	1.7	1.6	1.5	1.7	1.3	1.6
Vocational certificate	—	—	—	—	—	—	—	—	—	—	—	—	—	—	—	—	—	0.3	0.4	0.3
Associate (A.A.) or equivalent	1.5	0.9	1.5	0.7	0.9	—	1.0	—	1.1	1.2	1.1	1.6	1.2	1.6	1.4	1.4	1.6	0.9	0.8	0.5
Bachelor's (B.A., B.S., etc.)	30.6	28.9	30.4	30.2	31.3	—	32.8	—	33.1	30.9	30.9	31.7	32.3	31.9	33.8	34.2	33.7	32.7	33.8	33.1
Master's degree (M.A., M.S., etc.)	33.7	36.1	35.7	37.9	34.7	—	28.6	—	28.5	29.5	30.5	31.6	32.9	34.4	32.7	34.5	34.5	34.3	34.9	35.1
Ph.D. or Ed.D.	16.3	18.1	17.8	18.0	15.7	—	13.4	—	12.9	13.0	12.9	13.0	12.2	11.8	11.1	11.2	11.1	11.7	12.2	13.5
M.D., D.D.S., D.V.M. or D.O.	8.9	8.8	7.7	8.0	8.3	—	12.2	—	12.1	11.6	11.6	9.7	10.1	9.4	9.4	8.5	8.7	9.3	8.4	8.8
LL.B. or J.D. (law)	3.1	3.0	2.8	3.2	7.0	—	8.4	—	7.6	8.3	8.2	7.7	7.2	6.9	6.5	6.1	6.4	5.9	5.7	5.1
B.D. or M.Div. (divinity)	0.4	0.5	0.3	0.4	0.6	—	0.6	—	0.7	0.8	0.8	0.7	0.6	0.7	0.7	0.6	0.7	0.7	0.6	0.5
Other	1.5	1.2	1.3	1.2	1.1	—	1.5	—	1.7	2.4	2.3	2.3	1.9	2.0	2.7	1.9	1.8	2.4	1.8	1.4

120

COLLEGE CHOICE
FRESHMAN MEN

ITEM	1986	1987	1988	1989	1990	1991	1992	1993	1994	1995	1996	1997	1998	1999	2000	2001	2002	2003	2004	2005	2006
To how many colleges other than this one did you apply for admission this year?																					
None	27.0	25.2	23.4	23.8	23.0	24.7	22.2	20.7	23.1	24.1	23.1	23.9	22.6	21.8	20.4	20.3	20.7	18.3	19.5	18.0	18.5
One	15.4	14.6	13.4	13.6	14.5	13.8	13.9	14.0	13.4	13.5	13.2	14.1	13.5	13.2	12.5	12.4	12.8	11.9	12.4	11.9	10.7
Two	16.9	16.8	16.8	16.9	17.5	17.5	17.5	17.6	17.2	16.4	16.6	16.3	16.2	15.9	16.0	15.9	16.1	15.5	15.5	15.3	14.9
Three	16.5	16.9	17.4	17.0	17.2	17.1	17.9	18.0	17.0	16.5	16.4	16.5	17.1	17.4	17.6	17.5	16.9	17.1	16.7	16.9	17.0
Four	10.1	10.9	11.5	11.1	11.2	10.8	11.7	11.9	11.8	11.3	11.7	10.8	11.7	12.0	12.4	12.5	12.3	12.7	12.1	12.6	12.8
Five	6.4	6.9	7.6	7.6	7.3	7.2	7.4	8.1	7.5	7.5	7.9	7.2	7.4	7.8	7.9	8.3	8.0	8.9	8.2	8.7	9.2
Six or more	7.7	8.7	9.9	10.0	9.3	8.9	9.4	9.8	10.1	10.6	11.1	—	—	—	—	—	—	—	—	—	—
Six	—	—	—	—	—	—	—	—	—	—	—	4.6	4.7	4.7	5.3	5.2	5.3	5.9	5.6	5.8	6.1
Seven to ten	—	—	—	—	—	—	—	—	—	—	—	5.4	5.6	6.0	6.3	6.5	6.6	7.9	8.0	8.7	8.7
Eleven or more	—	—	—	—	—	—	—	—	—	—	—	1.2	1.1	1.1	1.4	1.5	1.4	1.7	1.9	2.0	2.1
How many other acceptances did you receive this year?																					
None	13.7	12.8	11.3	10.8	—	—	—	—	—	8.9	8.6	9.9	9.7	—	—	—	—	—	—	—	—
One	25.8	25.5	25.0	24.2	—	—	—	—	—	22.0	21.9	22.9	22.5	—	—	—	—	—	—	—	—
Two	24.4	24.7	24.8	24.6	—	—	—	—	—	23.7	23.7	22.9	22.9	—	—	—	—	—	—	—	—
Three	18.3	19.1	19.3	19.4	—	—	—	—	—	19.7	20.0	19.3	19.9	—	—	—	—	—	—	—	—
Four	9.3	9.6	10.3	10.6	—	—	—	—	—	12.0	12.1	11.3	11.7	—	—	—	—	—	—	—	—
Five	4.2	4.2	4.6	5.1	—	—	—	—	—	6.3	6.4	6.3	6.1	—	—	—	—	—	—	—	—
Six or more	4.3	4.1	4.6	5.4	—	—	—	—	—	7.4	7.3	—	—	—	—	—	—	—	—	—	—
Six	—	—	—	—	—	—	—	—	—	—	—	3.2	3.1	—	—	—	—	—	—	—	—
Seven to ten	—	—	—	—	—	—	—	—	—	—	—	3.5	3.3	—	—	—	—	—	—	—	—
Eleven or more	—	—	—	—	—	—	—	—	—	—	—	0.7	0.7	—	—	—	—	—	—	—	—
Prior to this term, have you ever taken courses for credit at this institution?																					
No	97.2	96.7	97.0	96.6	96.8	96.8	96.9	96.9	96.5	96.8	95.8	96.5	95.7	96.0	96.0	95.9	96.0	96.6	96.2	96.6	96.3
Yes	2.8	3.3	3.0	3.4	3.2	3.2	3.1	3.1	3.5	3.2	4.2	3.5	4.3	4.0	4.0	4.1	4.0	3.4	3.8	3.4	3.7

PLANS, GOALS, AND EXPECTATIONS
FRESHMAN MEN

ITEM	1986	1987	1988	1989	1990	1991	1992	1993	1994	1995	1996	1997	1998	1999	2000	2001	2002	2003	2004	2005	2006
What is the highest academic degree you intend to obtain anywhere?																					
None	1.6	1.3	1.4	0.8	1.2	1.0	2.5	0.7	0.7	0.7	0.7	0.7	0.8	0.7	—	0.7	0.9	0.9	1.3	0.9	1.0
Vocational certificate	0.2	0.2	0.2	0.2	0.2	0.2	0.2	0.1	0.1	0.1	0.2	0.1	0.2	0.1	—	0.1	0.2	0.2	0.2	0.2	0.1
Associate (A.A.) or equivalent	0.7	0.6	0.9	0.7	0.7	0.6	0.6	0.5	0.5	0.5	0.6	0.5	0.6	0.5	—	0.5	0.5	0.4	0.5	0.5	0.5
Bachelor's (B.A., B.S., etc.)	33.1	31.8	28.9	28.4	28.4	26.5	29.7	25.5	25.5	26.7	25.2	25.1	26.7	25.9	—	25.5	25.8	26.4	25.7	26.1	25.5
Master's degree (M.A., M.S., etc.)	37.0	38.3	38.8	39.9	39.1	39.2	39.0	39.6	38.8	39.1	40.3	40.6	42.1	42.0	—	42.8	42.0	41.0	40.6	41.1	41.7
Ph.D. or Ed.D.	13.4	13.7	14.7	14.9	15.1	16.7	13.7	17.1	17.6	16.8	17.7	18.1	16.4	16.5	—	17.2	17.2	17.2	17.3	16.3	16.4
M.D., D.D.S., D.V.M. or D.O.	7.4	6.8	6.9	6.9	7.4	8.3	8.3	9.8	10.0	9.7	9.1	8.9	7.3	7.3	—	6.7	6.9	7.1	7.4	7.7	7.7
LL.B. or J.D. (law)	4.7	5.5	6.4	6.3	5.9	5.4	4.4	5.1	5.1	4.3	4.2	4.2	3.9	4.6	—	4.8	5.0	4.9	5.0	5.2	4.9
B.D. or M.Div. (divinity)	0.4	0.4	0.4	0.4	0.5	0.5	0.4	0.4	0.5	0.5	0.5	0.5	0.5	0.6	—	0.4	0.4	0.4	0.4	0.4	0.5
Other	1.5	1.3	1.4	1.5	1.5	1.4	1.3	1.2	1.3	1.4	1.6	1.4	1.5	1.8	—	1.2	1.2	1.4	1.6	1.6	1.7

PLANS, GOALS, AND EXPECTATIONS
FRESHMAN MEN

ITEM	1966	1967	1968	1969	1970	1971	1972	1973	1974	1975	1976	1977	1978	1979	1980	1981	1982	1983	1984	1985
What is the highest academic degree you intend to obtain at this institution?																				
None	—	—	—	—	—	—	4.1	3.8	4.4	5.0	4.7	4.1	3.7	3.4	3.5	3.4	3.2	2.8	3.0	2.5
Vocational certificate	—	—	—	—	—	—	—	—	—	—	—	—	—	—	—	—	—	0.5	0.4	0.4
Associate (A.A.) or equivalent	—	—	—	—	—	—	2.2	2.1	3.1	3.1	2.6	3.4	2.9	4.0	3.5	3.5	3.2	2.9	2.8	1.8
Bachelor's (B.A., B.S., etc.)	—	—	—	—	—	—	72.2	71.4	69.8	68.5	69.3	68.3	68.9	68.5	68.8	69.7	69.0	69.1	70.2	71.1
Master's degree (M.A., M.S., etc.)	—	—	—	—	—	—	13.2	13.2	13.8	13.6	14.0	14.9	15.5	15.7	15.1	15.4	16.3	15.4	15.7	16.6
Ph.D. or Ed.D.	—	—	—	—	—	—	2.4	2.6	2.5	2.5	2.5	2.4	2.5	2.4	2.2	2.3	2.4	2.4	2.5	2.6
M.D., D.D.S., D.V.M. or D.O.	—	—	—	—	—	—	2.6	3.3	3.0	3.0	2.8	2.6	2.8	2.4	2.8	2.3	2.6	2.8	2.2	2.5
LL.B. or J.D. (law)	—	—	—	—	—	—	1.8	2.1	1.8	1.9	1.7	1.8	1.8	1.7	1.7	1.6	1.7	1.6	1.4	1.2
B.D. or M.Div. (divinity)	—	—	—	—	—	—	0.2	0.2	0.2	0.4	0.6	0.5	0.4	0.3	0.4	0.3	0.4	0.6	0.4	0.2
Other	—	—	—	—	—	—	1.4	1.3	1.4	2.1	1.8	2.0	1.6	1.7	2.2	1.5	1.3	2.0	1.4	1.1
Your probable career/occupation [2,3]																				
Artist	4.4	4.2	4.1	4.3	4.7	5.1	4.8	—	—	—	6.0	6.1	5.5	6.3	6.2	6.1	6.0	5.9	5.7	5.9
Business	17.3	16.3	15.3	15.3	15.5	13.8	14.0	—	—	—	19.6	21.3	22.6	22.6	21.9	22.3	21.2	22.1	24.5	25.7
Clerical	1.3	1.9	1.1	1.5	1.4	0.3	0.3	—	—	—	0.2	0.3	0.2	0.3	0.2	0.3	0.3	0.2	0.3	0.3
Clergy	2.4	1.7	1.5	1.6	1.4	1.3	1.2	—	—	—	1.3	1.0	0.9	0.8	0.8	0.9	0.6	0.7	0.5	0.7
College teacher	1.8	1.7	1.6	1.5	1.4	1.2	0.9	—	—	—	0.5	0.4	0.4	0.3	0.3	0.3	0.3	0.3	0.3	0.4
Doctor (MD or DDS)	8.9	8.4	7.3	6.8	7.7	9.0	10.3	—	—	—	9.4	7.6	8.1	7.3	7.5	6.9	7.1	7.7	7.1	7.5
Education (secondary)	10.6	11.2	12.1	10.5	9.3	7.3	5.6	—	—	—	3.8	2.9	2.6	2.6	2.4	2.0	1.9	2.2	2.2	2.5
Education (elementary)	0.8	0.7	0.8	0.8	0.8	0.9	0.8	—	—	—	0.9	0.7	0.5	0.6	0.5	0.6	0.4	0.4	0.4	0.5
Engineer	16.1	15.2	15.5	15.1	15.3	10.0	10.2	—	—	—	13.1	14.6	15.4	15.7	17.4	17.3	18.6	17.5	17.1	17.0
Farmer or forester	2.9	2.2	2.2	2.2	2.4	3.4	3.6	—	—	—	3.3	3.2	3.5	2.5	2.1	2.2	1.8	1.5	1.6	1.3
Health professional	2.9	2.3	2.5	2.3	2.8	3.6	4.3	—	—	—	4.3	3.8	3.5	3.2	3.1	2.7	2.6	3.0	3.0	2.8
Homemaker	—	—	—	—	—	0.0	0.0	—	—	—	0.0	0.0	0.0	0.0	0.0	0.0	0.0	0.0	0.0	0.0
Lawyer	7.8	7.4	6.7	7.7	7.8	8.9	9.2	—	—	—	7.6	7.4	7.1	6.8	6.5	6.1	6.5	5.7	5.8	5.4
Military	—	0.0	0.1	0.0	0.0	3.6	3.7	—	—	—	2.3	2.4	2.6	2.6	2.4	2.6	2.1	2.9	2.9	2.5
Nurse	0.1	0.0	0.1	0.0	0.0	0.1	0.1	—	—	—	0.2	0.2	0.1	0.1	0.2	0.2	0.2	0.2	0.2	0.1
Research scientist	5.8	5.0	4.9	4.3	4.5	4.4	4.0	—	—	—	3.9	3.6	3.3	2.8	2.6	2.4	2.1	2.2	2.2	2.2
Social worker	—	—	—	—	—	1.4	1.2	—	—	—	0.9	0.7	0.6	0.5	0.6	0.3	0.3	0.4	0.5	0.3
Skilled worker	—	—	—	—	—	0.9	0.8	—	—	—	0.7	1.7	0.8	1.0	1.2	1.1	0.8	0.5	0.5	0.5
Other career	14.3	13.3	14.4	15.1	15.0	11.5	11.2	—	—	—	12.0	12.7	13.3	13.9	14.4	16.0	18.2	17.2	15.3	14.3
Undecided	4.7	10.3	11.3	12.0	11.6	13.7	14.1	—	—	—	10.1	9.4	10.1	9.9	9.6	9.7	9.1	9.4	9.9	10.0

PLANS, GOALS, AND EXPECTATIONS
FRESHMAN MEN

ITEM	1986	1987	1988	1989	1990	1991	1992	1993	1994	1995	1996	1997	1998	1999	2000	2001	2002	2003	2004	2005	2006
What is the highest academic degree you intend to obtain at this institution?																					
None	2.8	2.3	2.5	2.7	2.6	2.7	—	2.1	2.1	2.1	1.7	1.7	1.9	1.6	—	1.6	2.0	1.5	2.0	1.5	1.7
Vocational certificate	0.2	0.3	0.3	0.3	0.3	0.4	—	0.2	0.2	0.3	0.3	0.2	0.2	0.3	—	0.2	0.3	0.4	0.2	0.2	0.2
Associate (A.A.) or equivalent	1.9	1.9	2.4	2.1	2.1	2.4	—	1.9	1.8	1.7	1.6	1.7	1.7	1.6	—	1.7	1.5	1.3	1.7	1.6	1.6
Bachelor's (B.A., B.S., etc.)	72.5	70.9	68.7	71.1	69.5	68.6	—	68.3	67.7	68.3	67.5	68.2	66.9	70.4	—	68.5	69.1	70.5	67.9	69.2	66.7
Master's degree (M.A., M.S., etc.)	16.1	17.8	18.7	17.0	18.2	18.8	—	19.7	20.0	19.6	20.7	20.3	21.7	19.3	—	21.5	20.6	19.2	20.6	20.2	21.4
Ph.D. or Ed.D.	2.3	2.6	2.6	2.6	2.6	2.7	—	3.1	3.5	3.3	3.3	3.4	3.2	2.5	—	3.2	3.1	3.1	3.6	3.3	3.8
M.D., D.D.S., D.V.M. or D.O.	1.8	1.8	1.9	1.5	1.7	1.8	—	2.3	2.1	2.2	2.2	2.1	1.9	1.4	—	1.4	1.4	1.4	1.4	1.7	1.9
LL.B. or J.D. (law)	1.0	1.1	1.4	1.2	1.1	1.0	—	1.0	1.1	0.9	0.8	0.8	0.7	0.9	—	0.7	0.8	0.9	0.8	0.8	1.0
B.D. or M.Div. (divinity)	0.3	0.3	0.3	0.2	0.3	0.2	—	0.2	0.3	0.3	0.3	0.2	0.3	0.4	—	0.2	0.2	0.3	0.3	0.2	0.2
Other	1.1	1.1	1.1	1.2	1.5	1.3	—	1.1	1.3	1.2	1.5	1.3	1.4	1.6	—	1.0	1.0	1.3	1.5	1.2	1.5
Your probable career/occupation [2,3]																					
Artist	6.4	7.2	6.8	6.1	6.0	6.1	6.9	6.5	6.7	7.1	6.4	6.9	7.5	7.1	7.7	7.2	7.4	7.3	6.9	7.4	7.2
Business	26.9	28.1	27.1	25.4	22.6	19.0	17.6	17.0	17.6	18.0	17.6	18.2	19.0	18.5	19.2	18.2	17.4	17.3	18.0	19.7	20.6
Clerical	0.3	0.3	0.3	0.3	0.3	0.4	0.4	0.4	0.4	0.4	0.5	0.4	0.6	0.5	0.6	0.6	0.5	0.6	0.5	0.6	0.8
Clergy	0.6	0.6	0.5	0.5	0.6	0.6	0.7	0.5	0.6	0.6	0.7	0.8	0.8	0.8	0.7	0.6	0.7	0.6	0.6	0.6	0.5
College teacher	0.4	0.5	0.5	0.5	0.6	0.6	0.6	0.6	0.6	0.7	0.6	0.6	0.6	0.6	0.6	0.5	0.6	0.6	0.6	0.6	0.6
Doctor (MD or DDS)	6.2	5.7	5.9	5.9	6.0	6.8	7.9	8.0	8.2	8.0	7.2	7.3	6.2	6.3	5.5	5.5	5.5	5.9	6.3	6.5	6.4
Education (secondary)	3.1	3.1	3.2	3.2	3.7	4.1	4.0	4.1	4.3	4.3	4.1	4.4	4.4	4.1	4.5	4.2	4.4	4.4	4.6	4.8	4.8
Education (elementary)	0.6	0.7	0.6	0.7	0.9	1.1	1.2	1.5	1.6	1.6	1.6	1.6	1.6	1.6	1.6	1.3	1.3	1.3	1.1	1.1	1.0
Engineer	15.6	14.8	14.1	15.1	15.0	16.2	15.1	15.3	13.3	12.8	14.6	14.8	12.7	13.8	13.0	13.2	13.1	12.6	13.9	12.3	11.7
Farmer or forester	1.1	1.0	1.0	1.3	1.3	1.3	1.4	1.6	1.7	1.5	1.3	1.3	1.3	1.1	0.9	0.8	0.8	0.7	0.8	0.7	0.8
Health professional	3.0	2.8	3.2	3.3	3.6	4.4	5.0	5.7	5.5	5.4	4.6	4.5	4.0	3.3	3.0	2.8	3.4	3.9	4.8	4.7	4.6
Homemaker	0.0	0.0	0.0	0.0	0.0	0.0	0.0	0.0	0.1	0.0	0.1	0.0	0.0	0.0	0.0	0.0	0.0	0.0	0.1	0.0	0.1
Lawyer	5.0	5.7	6.7	6.5	6.2	5.6	5.1	4.8	5.0	3.7	3.5	3.5	3.4	4.0	3.9	3.9	4.1	4.0	3.8	3.9	3.8
Military	3.2	2.5	2.3	2.1	2.1	2.2	1.3	1.2	1.5	1.3	2.1	1.5	1.3	1.6	1.6	1.9	2.0	2.5	1.9	1.8	2.1
Nurse	0.1	0.1	0.1	0.2	0.3	0.5	0.5	0.6	0.6	0.5	0.4	0.3	0.3	0.2	0.2	0.3	0.4	0.6	0.7	0.7	0.8
Research scientist	2.2	2.1	2.2	2.2	2.2	2.2	2.5	2.6	2.3	2.4	2.3	2.4	2.0	2.0	1.8	1.9	1.9	1.8	2.0	1.9	2.0
Social worker	0.3	0.3	0.3	0.3	0.3	0.3	0.3	0.3	0.4	0.4	0.3	0.3	0.3	0.3	0.3	0.3	0.2	0.2	0.2	0.3	0.3
Skilled worker	0.4	0.4	0.9	0.6	0.6	0.7	0.6	0.6	0.6	0.6	0.7	0.6	0.7	0.7	0.7	0.6	0.6	0.6	0.6	0.5	0.5
Other career	13.7	13.4	14.1	14.9	16.4	16.5	16.7	17.2	17.1	19.0	19.8	19.8	21.8	22.5	22.9	23.1	22.1	21.5	19.4	18.4	18.0
Undecided	10.8	10.7	10.2	10.8	11.2	11.3	12.2	11.5	12.1	11.8	11.5	10.7	11.5	10.8	11.2	13.1	13.6	13.5	13.2	13.5	13.5

PLANS, GOALS, AND EXPECTATIONS
FRESHMAN MEN

ITEM	1966	1967	1968	1969	1970	1971	1972	1973	1974	1975	1976	1977	1978	1979	1980	1981	1982	1983	1984	1985
Your probable major field [2]																				
Agriculture	3.1	2.6	2.6	2.6	2.3	3.4	3.6	3.2	4.1	3.9	3.5	3.2	2.4	2.7	2.4	2.5	2.1	1.7	1.8	1.6
Biological Science	4.5	4.8	4.8	4.5	4.7	6.1	6.4	10.7	9.5	9.1	8.9	6.0	5.8	5.0	4.7	4.8	4.6	5.1	4.9	4.5
Business	15.7	16.6	16.3	16.0	16.1	14.7	15.0	18.9	19.1	19.2	21.2	22.8	24.6	24.9	23.6	24.1	23.3	23.5	26.5	26.4
Education	4.2	4.4	5.4	4.5	4.9	4.4	3.7	5.1	4.9	4.9	5.1	4.2	3.8	4.2	3.8	3.0	2.7	2.9	2.9	3.1
Engineering	17.5	16.3	17.5	17.4	17.3	12.3	12.2	11.0	14.0	15.2	15.0	16.8	18.1	18.4	19.8	19.5	20.4	19.9	19.2	18.9
English	2.3	2.2	2.0	2.0	1.7	1.4	1.1	1.3	1.1	0.9	0.8	0.8	0.9	0.7	0.7	0.8	0.8	0.8	1.0	0.9
Health Professional	1.3	1.2	1.1	1.2	1.8	10.8	12.0	1.4	1.8	1.6	1.6	6.5	6.7	6.1	6.2	5.5	5.6	5.9	5.8	5.9
History or Political Science	8.6	8.7	8.8	8.6	7.5	6.7	6.3	7.9	6.3	5.7	5.3	5.0	4.6	4.3	4.3	4.2	4.1	4.0	4.5	5.2
Humanities	2.5	2.8	2.1	2.5	2.4	3.1	3.1	2.8	3.0	2.6	2.7	2.2	2.1	2.0	1.9	2.0	1.8	1.8	1.6	2.0
Fine Arts	6.3	6.5	6.6	6.8	7.0	6.0	5.6	4.8	5.7	5.2	5.2	5.2	4.9	4.9	4.9	4.5	4.2	4.0	4.1	3.9
Mathematics or Statistics	5.4	5.2	4.8	4.9	4.5	3.5	2.9	2.5	2.2	1.6	1.6	1.3	1.3	1.3	1.0	0.9	0.9	1.2	1.0	1.1
Physical Sciences	5.8	5.8	5.1	5.1	5.0	4.2	5.2	5.5	5.2	5.3	5.2	4.2	4.4	3.8	3.4	3.6	3.1	3.1	3.3	3.1
Social Sciences	5.2	5.6	6.0	6.6	6.5	6.5	5.9	5.3	5.2	4.5	4.1	3.6	3.4	3.4	3.0	2.8	2.6	2.9	3.3	3.5
Other Technical	2.5	2.2	2.9	2.3	3.6	3.2	3.5	6.4	5.9	6.7	6.1	5.1	5.1	6.1	8.2	10.0	11.6	11.3	8.4	7.1
Other Non-technical	0.6	13.0	12.0	13.2	14.0	11.3	10.5	8.6	7.8	8.6	9.2	8.2	7.5	8.2	7.7	7.1	7.6	7.2	6.9	7.3
Undecided	14.5	1.8	2.0	2.4	2.0	2.3	4.4	4.7	4.4	4.9	4.5	4.8	4.5	4.4	4.5	4.7	4.5	4.9	4.9	5.5
Where do you plan to live during the fall term?																				
With parents or relatives	—	—	—	—	—	—	—	22.6	22.3	23.1	25.0	27.2	25.1	22.1	22.5	20.0	21.1	22.5	21.9	18.9
Other private home, apartment, room	—	—	—	—	—	—	—	3.1	3.3	4.6	3.7	5.2	4.3	5.2	5.5	4.1	4.6	3.1	3.2	2.9
College dormitory	—	—	—	—	—	—	—	70.7	70.9	68.4	67.6	63.5	67.0	68.7	67.6	71.4	70.2	71.1	71.5	74.8
Fraternity or sorority house	—	—	—	—	—	—	—	1.3	1.8	1.3	1.4	1.2	1.6	1.7	1.6	1.9	1.4	1.2	1.1	1.0
Other campus student housing	—	—	—	—	—	—	—	1.7	1.2	2.0	1.7	2.0	1.7	1.7	2.1	2.0	1.9	1.7	1.9	1.9
Other	—	—	—	—	—	—	—	0.7	0.5	0.6	0.6	0.8	0.7	0.6	0.7	0.6	0.8	0.4	0.4	0.4
Student's Estimates: Chances are very good that he/she will																				
Be elected to an academic honor society	—	3.6	3.2	3.0	3.2	3.9	5.6	6.1	6.8	7.1	8.5	8.8	9.3	9.2	9.1	8.9	8.0	8.3	8.3	9.2
Be elected to a student office	—	3.0	2.9	2.8	2.5	1.8	2.6	2.7	2.7	2.6	2.8	3.2	3.3	3.7	3.5	3.3	3.5	3.5	3.6	4.4
Be satisfied with your college	—	—	—	—	64.5	53.3	58.3	53.8	52.0	51.7	49.7	51.9	53.2	51.8	51.3	52.6	52.5	51.9	51.9	51.9
Change career choice	—	19.2	16.6	19.6	18.0	14.3	18.8	15.3	12.7	13.5	12.1	12.7	12.6	11.9	11.9	11.6	11.3	11.7	11.8	12.8
Change major field	—	18.0	15.8	18.8	17.6	14.1	18.5	16.5	13.9	14.2	12.7	13.5	13.7	13.3	13.0	12.9	12.9	13.3	13.5	14.0
Drop out permanently (exclude transferring)	—	0.4	0.4	0.3	0.5	0.7	0.9	1.0	0.9	1.0	0.9	0.9	0.8	1.2	0.9	1.1	0.9	0.9	0.9	0.9
Drop out of this college temporarily (exclude transferring)	—	0.9	0.8	1.0	1.3	1.4	1.8	1.7	1.5	1.7	1.5	1.4	1.2	1.4	1.2	1.2	1.1	1.2	1.3	1.3
Fail one or more courses	—	3.5	2.5	3.1	4.1	2.5	3.2	2.6	2.3	2.5	1.9	2.2	1.9	2.0	2.1	2.0	1.8	1.6	1.7	1.8
Get a bachelor's degree (B.A., B.S., etc.)	—	—	—	—	—	—	74.5	74.9	72.2	74.9	74.8	74.6	75.9	73.5	72.5	74.6	74.5	74.6	75.6	76.7
Get a job to help pay for college expenses	—	—	—	—	—	—	—	—	—	—	40.3	43.2	40.9	39.0	37.6	39.9	38.0	35.4	35.7	36.1
Get married while in college	7.2	6.2	5.7	7.0	6.4	7.4	7.0	5.9	5.4	5.4	4.8	4.4	4.1	4.1	4.1	4.3	3.8	3.5	3.5	3.7
Graduate with honors	—	4.8	4.9	5.5	6.1	6.4	9.8	11.9	12.4	13.2	13.6	14.3	14.6	14.3	14.0	13.7	14.2	14.1	13.7	14.7
Join a social fraternity, sorority, or club	33.9	33.9	29.1	25.4	22.1	14.9	—	—	—	—	—	—	—	—	—	—	—	—	—	—
Join a social fraternity or sorority	—	—	—	—	—	—	18.8	16.4	15.0	16.8	16.6	18.7	18.8	17.5	17.4	18.1	16.4	16.8	17.2	18.7
Make at least a "B" average	—	—	—	—	—	26.3	35.9	38.5	40.0	42.8	44.6	43.4	45.1	42.1	42.9	42.9	43.6	42.6	42.3	43.1
Need extra time to complete your degree requirements	—	—	—	—	—	—	—	—	—	—	—	—	4.6	4.8	5.2	5.9	5.3	5.2	5.5	6.4
Participate in student government	—	—	—	—	—	—	—	—	—	—	—	—	—	—	—	—	—	—	—	—
Participate in student protests or demonstrations	—	5.6	4.7	—	—	3.5	4.3	4.4	4.1	4.7	4.4	4.6	3.6	4.5	5.2	4.4	4.8	4.2	4.9	5.9

124

PLANS, GOALS, AND EXPECTATIONS
FRESHMAN MEN

ITEM	1986	1987	1988	1989	1990	1991	1992	1993	1994	1995	1996	1997	1998	1999	2000	2001	2002	2003	2004	2005	2006
Your probable major field [2]																					
Agriculture	1.2	1.0	1.1	1.4	1.3	1.5	1.4	1.6	1.8	1.6	1.6	1.4	1.5	1.3	1.0	0.8	0.8	0.6	0.8	0.6	0.8
Biological Science	4.6	4.6	4.6	4.6	4.9	5.5	6.4	7.2	7.6	7.6	7.3	7.0	6.1	6.0	5.5	5.7	5.9	6.1	6.7	6.8	7.3
Business	28.2	29.7	28.5	27.2	24.7	20.6	19.0	17.9	18.8	18.8	19.1	19.4	20.6	20.4	21.0	21.0	20.4	20.3	20.5	22.7	23.5
Education	4.0	3.9	3.9	3.9	4.9	5.4	5.3	5.7	6.2	6.2	6.0	5.8	6.3	5.7	6.1	5.4	5.8	5.8	5.5	5.9	5.7
Engineering	17.9	16.8	15.6	17.4	17.1	18.9	17.3	17.3	15.4	14.6	17.3	17.2	14.8	16.5	15.9	16.7	17.8	17.2	17.8	15.6	14.6
English	1.1	1.2	1.3	1.2	1.3	1.3	1.2	1.2	1.3	1.3	1.3	1.4	1.2	1.2	1.2	1.1	1.3	1.2	1.3	1.3	1.5
Health Professional	5.4	4.8	5.3	5.6	6.2	7.5	8.8	9.4	8.8	8.4	7.3	7.2	6.7	5.7	5.2	5.1	5.4	6.4	6.9	7.0	6.2
History or Political Science	4.8	4.9	5.7	5.6	5.5	4.9	4.8	4.8	4.7	4.3	4.4	4.2	4.0	5.7	4.3	4.8	5.0	5.4	5.0	5.4	5.7
Humanities	2.0	2.2	2.0	2.0	2.0	2.2	2.2	2.0	2.3	2.4	2.4	2.6	2.8	2.6	3.0	2.9	3.0	3.0	2.8	3.0	3.2
Fine Arts	4.5	4.9	4.6	4.7	4.8	5.1	5.8	5.1	5.4	5.7	4.7	5.0	5.5	5.3	5.4	5.2	5.3	5.4	5.1	5.4	4.4
Mathematics or Statistics	1.1	0.9	0.8	0.9	0.9	0.9	0.9	0.8	0.9	0.8	0.7	0.7	0.7	0.7	0.8	0.7	0.9	0.9	0.9	0.9	1.0
Physical Sciences	2.9	2.7	2.7	2.8	2.9	2.9	3.1	3.2	2.8	2.8	2.6	2.7	2.3	2.4	2.3	2.4	2.6	2.6	2.9	2.8	3.0
Social Sciences	3.5	3.7	4.0	3.8	4.0	3.8	4.2	4.4	4.2	4.0	3.9	3.7	3.9	3.7	3.9	3.9	4.1	4.2	4.2	4.2	5.1
Other Technical	5.6	4.9	5.4	4.8	4.6	4.8	4.7	4.8	5.4	6.4	7.6	8.5	9.1	10.1	10.4	10.2	7.0	6.2	5.6	4.4	4.3
Other Non-technical	7.0	7.6	8.5	7.6	8.4	7.8	7.7	7.4	7.0	7.5	6.9	6.5	7.3	7.2	7.2	7.1	7.4	7.7	7.6	7.2	7.4
Undecided	6.2	6.3	6.2	6.5	6.6	6.9	7.2	7.2	7.6	7.6	6.9	6.8	7.1	6.8	6.9	6.9	7.2	6.9	6.4	6.6	6.4
Where do you plan to live during the fall term?																					
With parents or relatives	17.4	15.5	16.5	16.2	15.6	16.6	14.7	15.1	15.5	16.0	16.6	15.5	15.0	15.6	17.9	17.4	17.3	16.2	14.7	15.4	14.2
Other private home, apartment, room	4.3	4.1	4.4	4.2	3.1	3.0	3.5	3.2	2.7	3.1	3.1	4.0	3.1	3.2	4.8	4.2	4.6	3.6	4.5	2.7	3.7
College dormitory	74.1	76.3	74.8	76.0	78.2	77.0	78.8	78.6	78.3	77.9	76.5	77.9	78.9	78.3	74.4	75.7	74.6	77.5	77.3	79.1	78.9
Fraternity or sorority house	1.3	1.7	1.4	0.9	0.8	0.8	1.0	1.3	1.4	1.2	1.6	0.4	1.0	1.2	1.0	0.7	0.8	0.5	0.7	0.5	0.6
Other campus student housing	2.2	2.1	2.5	2.3	2.0	2.0	1.6	1.6	1.7	1.5	1.7	1.6	1.6	1.4	1.6	1.8	2.2	1.8	2.3	1.9	2.3
Other	0.5	0.3	0.4	0.4	0.4	0.5	0.4	0.3	0.4	0.4	0.4	0.5	0.3	0.3	0.4	0.3	0.5	0.4	0.4	0.3	0.3
Student's Estimates: Chances are very good that he/she will																					
Be elected to an academic honor society	8.0	8.8	8.5	8.9	9.2	9.7	9.3	10.0	9.8	9.6	10.1	10.5	9.3	9.2	—	—	—	—	—	—	—
Be elected to a student office	4.0	4.2	3.8	3.9	3.9	3.4	3.5	3.8	3.9	3.6	3.8	3.8	3.5	3.7	—	—	—	—	—	—	—
Be satisfied with your college	50.2	50.4	48.8	47.5	48.2	48.7	48.6	47.0	44.9	43.9	46.4	47.2	45.6	45.5	44.3	44.5	47.5	47.3	46.5	47.6	48.9
Change career choice	12.2	13.0	12.6	12.2	12.2	12.2	12.6	12.3	12.1	12.4	12.1	11.6	11.7	11.8	11.6	11.4	11.7	11.6	11.5	11.4	11.7
Change major field	13.9	14.7	14.3	13.9	13.7	13.6	13.8	13.6	13.6	13.4	13.1	12.7	13.0	12.9	13.0	12.8	13.3	13.0	12.9	12.6	12.7
Drop out permanently (exclude transferring)	0.9	0.8	0.9	0.9	1.0	0.9	1.0	0.9	1.0	0.9	0.9	0.8	0.9	0.8	0.9	0.9	—	—	—	—	—
Drop out of this college temporarily (exclude transferring)	1.5	1.2	1.2	1.2	1.3	1.2	1.3	1.2	1.2	1.2	1.1	1.0	1.2	1.2	1.4	1.3	—	—	—	—	—
Fail one or more courses	1.7	1.8	1.5	1.6	1.7	1.7	1.6	1.3	1.5	1.5	1.4	1.4	1.4	1.4	—	—	—	—	—	—	—
Get a bachelor's degree (B.A., B.S., etc.)	76.1	76.7	75.7	74.9	74.4	75.0	73.2	74.3	73.9	73.3	74.5	74.7	73.3	73.8	74.5	73.8	76.8	76.2	—	—	—
Get a job to help pay for college expenses	34.2	34.2	32.3	31.1	33.3	33.9	34.2	35.3	34.1	35.9	34.7	35.8	33.9	33.1	36.4	38.1	40.0	39.2	39.6	39.2	36.5
Get married while in college	3.5	3.0	3.0	3.6	3.9	4.4	4.7	3.9	4.2	4.0	3.7	3.8	3.8	3.7	—	—	—	—	—	—	—
Graduate with honors	13.5	14.5	14.6	15.1	15.3	16.3	16.5	18.1	18.3	18.2	19.4	20.4	18.9	18.1	20.2	19.9	—	—	—	—	—
Join a social fraternity, sorority, or club	17.9	19.6	18.7	18.6	18.3	18.0	17.7	17.6	16.4	15.1	15.9	14.8	14.4	14.4	—	—	—	—	—	—	—
Join a social fraternity or sorority	—	—	—	—	—	—	—	—	—	—	—	—	—	—	9.6	8.9	8.7	7.4	7.5	7.8	7.8
Make at least a "B" average	42.4	42.6	44.7	44.5	44.1	45.2	46.5	48.5	49.5	50.1	51.7	53.8	51.5	51.0	57.0	56.4	58.9	57.6	58.0	59.3	58.8
Need extra time to complete your degree requirements	6.7	7.2	7.0	7.4	8.6	8.1	8.8	7.4	8.5	7.8	7.4	7.0	6.7	6.2	6.4	6.0	6.0	5.7	5.6	6.1	6.1
Participate in student government	—	—	—	—	—	—	—	—	—	—	—	—	—	—	5.9	6.1	6.0	5.7	5.6	6.1	5.9
Participate in student protests or demonstrations	5.6	6.4	5.6	6.3	6.7	5.8	6.8	5.8	5.0	4.7	4.5	4.3	4.4	4.4	4.8	5.0	5.3	5.7	5.5	5.7	5.2

PLANS, GOALS, AND EXPECTATIONS
FRESHMAN MEN

ITEM	1966	1967	1968	1969	1970	1971	1972	1973	1974	1975	1976	1977	1978	1979	1980	1981	1982	1983	1984	1985
Student's Estimates: Chances are very good that he/she will																				
Participate in volunteer or community service work	—	—	—	—	—	—	—	—	—	—	—	—	—	—	—	—	—	22.1	22.6	22.1
Play varsity/intercollegiate athletics	—	—	—	—	—	7.4	7.0	6.6	5.8	6.1	4.4	5.0	4.7	4.8	4.5	4.2	3.7	4.0	3.5	3.9
Seek personal counseling	—	9.8	9.6	11.0	9.3	9.5	10.5	10.0	10.2	11.2	10.9	9.9	9.1	9.7	9.0	9.2	8.4	8.7	9.5	8.5
Transfer to another college before graduating	—	—	—	—	—	—	—	—	—	—	—	—	—	—	—	—	—	—	—	—
Work full time while attending college	—	—	—	—	—	—	—	—	—	—	—	—	—	—	—	—	3.0	3.0	3.5	3.2
Objectives considered to be essential or very important																				
Becoming accomplished in one of the performing arts (acting, dancing, etc.)	8.9	9.5	7.2	10.1	11.3	10.8	10.5	—	10.2	10.9	10.9	12.5	12.1	11.9	11.8	11.2	11.8	11.5	10.8	11.2
Becoming a community leader	32.8	30.6	27.0	22.9	19.2	17.9	19.6	—	—	—	—	—	—	—	—	—	—	—	—	—
Becoming an authority in my field	71.3	73.4	63.4	64.7	72.1	65.4	65.6	67.7	67.6	74.0	73.9	78.8	76.6	76.3	76.1	75.9	76.4	75.4	76.3	74.5
Becoming involved in programs to clean up the environment	—	—	—	—	—	44.4	46.3	34.3	27.7	30.7	29.7	31.2	28.7	27.4	27.5	26.4	25.3	23.4	22.7	22.4
Becoming successful in a business of my own	62.7	55.8	53.3	52.4	51.0	49.1	52.4	48.6	45.5	49.8	51.7	53.9	53.7	54.5	53.7	54.4	53.9	53.8	55.7	54.6
Being very well off financially	53.2	53.5	50.4	52.3	45.8	47.5	48.1	—	52.6	55.3	58.3	63.8	66.1	67.5	68.4	69.4	72.4	73.0	74.9	74.0
Creating artistic work (painting, sculpture, decorating, etc.)	9.7	10.0	9.4	10.9	11.7	11.2	12.5	—	10.3	11.0	10.5	12.5	11.2	11.6	11.6	11.3	11.1	11.1	10.7	10.8
Developing a meaningful philosophy of life	—	—	81.7	82.0	76.2	68.5	71.3	68.0	61.2	64.9	62.3	60.6	57.6	54.2	52.2	51.1	49.4	46.6	47.3	47.3
Having administrative responsibility for the work of others	34.7	30.9	27.7	29.2	25.9	24.4	29.0	30.5	28.7	33.3	34.2	37.6	38.7	40.2	40.9	42.1	42.9	42.6	44.9	45.5
Helping others who are in difficulty	60.5	54.5	51.3	59.8	58.8	56.6	61.6	57.4	54.9	60.4	57.5	59.4	59.7	58.4	58.7	57.2	56.1	56.5	55.9	57.4
Influencing social values	—	—	—	33.7	33.9	28.5	30.3	29.9	26.1	29.4	29.4	30.5	30.7	31.5	31.4	30.6	30.4	29.9	31.5	32.0
Influencing the political structure	—	—	—	22.4	23.7	19.7	20.7	19.3	16.8	19.4	20.3	21.3	20.2	21.1	22.2	20.5	20.0	18.9	20.3	21.2
Integrating spirituality into my life	—	—	—	—	—	—	—	—	—	—	—	—	—	—	—	—	—	—	—	—
Keeping up to date with political affairs	60.8	56.2	55.5	57.7	58.9	49.3	55.2	47.7	43.0	45.9	45.9	49.0	46.3	47.8	50.5	49.6	48.9	45.8	48.6	—
Making a theoretical contribution to science	19.8	18.2	16.3	15.5	15.0	13.9	15.0	—	17.2	18.1	18.4	19.3	19.4	19.1	19.6	19.3	19.2	19.5	18.1	19.2
Obtaining recognition from my colleagues for contributions to my special field	49.2	48.9	43.4	46.7	45.6	43.5	42.2	—	44.3	48.1	50.4	53.3	55.1	56.3	58.3	57.9	59.4	58.9	59.0	59.2
Participating in a community action program	—	—	—	—	28.1	24.7	28.3	—	26.6	29.1	28.0	28.4	25.7	25.2	25.7	23.3	22.7	21.8	21.7	21.9
Participating in an organization like the Peace Corps or AmeriCorps/VISTA	—	—	—	—	—	—	—	—	—	—	—	—	—	—	—	—	—	—	—	—
Helping to promote racial understanding	—	—	—	—	—	—	—	—	—	—	—	35.0	32.9	31.8	32.8	31.4	32.4	31.7	32.7	34.0
Raising a family	—	—	—	66.6	63.3	—	—	—	—	—	—	59.1	63.2	65.9	64.3	67.8	68.2	66.9	69.7	70.8
Writing original works (poems, novels, short stories, etc.)	12.8	13.4	12.4	13.4	13.5	13.2	13.2	—	11.6	11.9	12.1	13.3	12.2	12.2	12.0	12.3	12.4	12.2	12.0	13.2

PLANS, GOALS, AND EXPECTATIONS
FRESHMAN MEN

ITEM	1986	1987	1988	1989	1990	1991	1992	1993	1994	1995	1996	1997	1998	1999	2000	2001	2002	2003	2004	2005	2006
Student's Estimates: Chances are very good that he/she will																					
Participate in volunteer or community service work	—	—	—	—	10.8	11.6	13.2	14.2	13.0	13.8	14.0	14.4	15.0	15.0	14.8	14.9	15.6	15.5	14.4	16.5	17.0
Play varsity/intercollegiate athletics	21.5	22.0	21.4	21.2	22.1	23.1	22.5	22.6	21.6	22.5	22.0	21.8	21.3	20.3	19.7	19.3	19.0	20.1	19.7	20.4	20.9
Seek personal counseling	3.6	3.4	3.4	3.0	3.6	3.0	—	—	—	—	5.0	4.6	4.1	3.9	5.0	5.0	5.3	5.8	5.4	5.9	6.1
Transfer to another college before graduating	8.6	8.4	8.8	8.6	8.8	8.7	8.2	8.2	7.7	7.7	6.9	6.8	6.7	6.2	6.5	6.6	6.9	6.8	7.0	6.2	6.8
Work full time while attending college	3.5	2.7	2.7	3.0	3.2	3.3	3.2	3.3	3.9	3.8	3.6	3.8	3.8	3.8	4.3	5.1	5.5	5.1	5.2	5.1	4.9
Objectives considered to be essential or very important																					
Becoming accomplished in one of the performing arts (acting, dancing, etc.)	10.7	12.6	—	11.1	11.2	10.5	11.5	11.3	12.0	12.1	12.1	12.7	13.5	13.1	13.3	13.4	14.8	14.7	14.4	15.3	15.0
Becoming a community leader	—	—	—	—	—	—	35.4	—	35.3	33.9	35.8	35.6	34.8	32.7	31.4	32.3	32.0	32.6	31.0	34.3	35.3
Becoming an authority in my field	73.8	79.7	—	69.0	68.2	70.7	71.2	69.5	68.7	67.7	67.0	66.5	64.7	62.8	61.6	62.0	61.9	61.5	59.6	60.5	59.9
Becoming involved in programs to clean up the environment	17.7	20.6	—	28.8	34.4	31.1	33.3	27.4	23.9	21.6	20.1	18.8	18.5	18.0	17.4	17.1	16.9	17.0	17.1	19.6	21.1
Becoming successful in a business of my own	52.5	54.5	—	48.6	46.7	46.7	47.0	46.3	45.8	45.6	45.1	45.6	44.5	43.8	45.1	45.4	44.3	45.4	45.9	47.3	46.7
Being very well off financially	75.9	78.3	—	78.1	76.9	76.9	75.3	76.0	75.3	75.6	75.7	76.2	76.1	75.4	76.3	76.3	75.3	75.4	75.2	75.9	74.6
Creating artistic work (painting, sculpture, decorating, etc.)	10.8	12.7	—	12.3	12.2	11.6	13.3	13.3	13.6	13.8	13.2	13.4	13.5	13.5	13.7	13.9	14.6	14.8	14.2	15.2	14.8
Developing a meaningful philosophy of life	44.0	43.4	—	43.3	44.6	46.1	48.2	46.7	46.3	44.6	44.0	44.7	44.1	43.1	43.1	44.1	41.7	40.4	41.9	45.1	46.7
Having administrative responsibility for the work of others	46.7	48.3	—	45.4	44.6	43.0	42.7	42.1	41.3	40.2	41.1	41.0	40.4	39.4	39.4	40.2	40.2	41.3	40.4	42.6	42.8
Helping others who are in difficulty	50.6	52.6	—	51.0	52.9	53.3	55.2	55.2	54.4	53.2	54.3	54.7	54.2	53.4	52.8	52.8	54.6	55.1	53.4	58.4	58.9
Influencing social values	31.3	35.0	—	37.2	38.4	36.8	39.7	37.8	36.8	35.4	35.4	34.5	33.9	33.5	34.1	34.1	35.3	35.3	34.2	37.4	39.2
Influencing the political structure	19.3	22.0	—	24.3	24.3	22.3	24.2	24.2	22.8	21.1	21.3	20.4	20.3	20.4	20.4	22.1	22.8	23.3	22.3	24.1	25.5
Integrating spirituality into my life	—	—	—	—	—	—	—	—	—	—	—	—	—	43.1	41.3	38.8	37.5	36.2	35.6	36.8	—
Keeping up to date with political affairs	—	—	—	48.2	49.9	46.1	46.7	44.0	39.0	35.0	35.7	33.2	33.3	32.5	31.8	35.4	37.5	38.1	37.4	39.3	40.1
Making a theoretical contribution to science	17.3	17.2	—	21.6	22.4	20.4	22.2	22.8	21.0	20.6	21.0	20.7	18.9	19.1	18.9	19.4	19.9	19.9	20.6	21.5	22.3
Obtaining recognition from my colleagues for contributions to my special field	57.0	61.6	—	57.4	57.7	56.2	57.9	56.3	56.2	56.4	54.9	55.4	53.1	52.5	51.7	52.3	53.0	52.8	52.0	54.6	54.1
Participating in a community action program	17.6	18.9	—	21.7	23.7	21.4	23.9	22.5	21.6	20.8	20.9	20.4	19.4	19.0	18.5	18.5	18.3	18.7	17.7	21.0	22.4
Participating in an organization like the Peace Corps or AmeriCorps/VISTA	—	—	—	—	—	—	—	—	—	—	—	—	—	—	—	—	—	—	—	—	8.8
Helping to promote racial understanding	28.0	30.7	—	35.3	37.9	34.6	41.9	38.3	33.8	31.4	31.9	30.4	29.1	27.7	28.1	28.5	28.4	28.0	27.1	30.5	31.5
Raising a family	68.3	—	—	70.0	69.9	69.4	71.6	71.4	72.2	72.8	74.0	75.0	74.4	73.8	72.7	72.2	72.6	73.7	73.6	75.2	74.7
Writing original works (poems, novels, short stories, etc.)	12.8	14.4	—	13.6	13.6	13.5	14.3	14.6	14.6	14.6	14.8	14.9	15.0	14.5	15.2	15.1	16.1	16.2	15.7	16.3	16.6

STUDENT VIEWS
FRESHMAN MEN

Student agrees strongly or somewhat

ITEM	1966	1967	1968	1969	1970	1971	1972	1973	1974	1975	1976	1977	1978	1979	1980	1981	1982	1983	1984	1985
A national health care plan is needed to cover everybody's medical costs	—	—	—	—	—	—	—	—	—	—	—	57.7	55.4	56.7	51.5	49.2	52.0	54.4	55.8	54.9
Abortion should be legal[ized]	—	—	—	80.9	86.8	—	—	—	—	—	—	55.6	56.0	53.7	53.4	53.5	54.2	55.6	54.8	55.3
Affirmative action in college admissions should be abolished	—	—	—	—	—	—	—	—	—	—	—	—	—	—	—	—	—	—	—	—
College officials have the right to ban persons with extreme views from speaking on campus	—	40.0	32.0	31.7	32.4	27.3	25.3	23.7	22.6	24.3	25.6	25.5	25.7	26.2	26.6	26.6	25.0	25.6	22.5	25.7
Colleges should prohibit racist/sexist speech on campus	—	—	—	—	—	—	—	—	—	—	—	—	—	—	—	—	—	—	—	—
Employers should be allowed to require drug testing of employees or job applicants	—	—	—	—	—	—	—	—	—	—	—	—	—	—	—	—	—	—	—	—
Federal military spending should increased	—	—	—	—	—	—	—	—	—	—	—	—	—	—	—	—	46.5	45.1	39.5	33.7
Grading in the high schools has become too easy	—	—	—	—	—	—	—	—	—	—	60.3	63.6	66.0	61.6	63.5	60.5	56.7	59.8	55.4	52.4
If two people really like each other, it's all right for them to have sex even if they've known each other for only a very short time	—	—	—	—	—	—	—	—	58.9	62.6	62.2	64.9	63.5	64.4	62.4	61.0	62.3	63.2	62.2	—
It is important to have laws prohibiting homosexual relationships	—	—	—	—	—	—	—	—	—	—	51.6	54.2	52.5	53.3	56.3	55.1	53.6	54.5	54.7	54.1
Just because a man thinks that a woman has "led him on" does not entitle him to have sex with her	—	—	—	—	—	—	—	—	—	—	—	—	—	—	—	—	—	—	—	—
Marijuana should be legalized	—	—	—	28.7	43.1	43.4	50.3	50.9	48.2	49.4	49.4	55.0	50.4	47.4	39.7	35.4	30.7	27.3	25.5	24.4
Only volunteers should serve in the armed forces	—	—	—	—	—	—	—	—	—	—	—	—	—	—	—	—	—	—	—	—
People should not obey laws which violate their personal values	—	—	—	—	—	—	—	—	34.4	33.0	32.7	33.1	33.1	34.9	33.3	33.6	—	—	—	—
Racial discrimination is no longer a major problem in America	—	—	—	—	—	—	—	—	—	—	—	—	—	—	—	—	—	—	—	—
Realistically, an individual can do little to bring about change in our society	—	34.7	34.5	38.5	41.0	45.2	44.7	43.3	45.7	50.5	45.3	45.4	—	—	—	—	—	—	—	—
Same sex couples should have the right to legal marital status	—	—	—	—	—	—	—	—	—	—	—	—	—	—	—	—	—	—	—	37.8
The activities of married women are best confined to the home and family	—	64.1	—	—	53.8	48.1	43.3	37.4	36.7	34.8	34.7	33.7	33.8	34.1	32.9	32.9	31.6	29.6	28.1	27.3
The chief benefit of a college education is that it increases one's earning power	—	58.5	60.3	53.9	65.5	60.3	59.0	54.6	—	—	—	—	—	—	—	—	—	—	—	71.6
The death penalty should be abolished	—	—	—	52.1	56.1	55.6	—	—	—	—	—	—	27.5	28.8	28.1	25.2	24.0	24.8	22.7	23.4
The federal government is not doing enough to control environmental pollution	—	—	—	—	—	91.3	90.4	87.3	81.4	80.2	80.9	79.4	79.2	76.5	75.1	73.0	75.1	78.0	75.2	—
The federal government should do more to control the sale of handguns	—	—	—	—	—	—	—	—	—	—	—	—	—	—	—	—	—	—	—	76.2

STUDENT VIEWS
FRESHMAN MEN

ITEM	1986	1987	1988	1989	1990	1991	1992	1993	1994	1995	1996	1997	1998	1999	2000	2001	2002	2003	2004	2005	2006
Student agrees strongly or somewhat																					
A national health care plan is needed to cover everybody's medical costs	56.1	—	—	70.1	68.1	71.5	73.8	70.5	63.8	65.3	66.0	65.5	—	—	—	—	—	—	—	69.3	68.7
Abortion should be legal[ized]	59.2	59.9	58.9	64.1	64.2	63.3	65.9	62.4	59.4	58.4	56.8	53.2	53.7	53.3	54.5	55.1	54.2	55.0	54.6	55.8	57.3
Affirmative action in college admissions should be abolished	—	—	—	—	—	—	—	—	—	58.3	58.6	59.9	—	57.3	56.2	55.3	55.4	58.4	56.1	54.0	52.7
College officials have the right to ban persons with extreme views from speaking on campus	26.5	—	—	—	—	—	—	—	—	—	—	—	—	—	—	—	—	—	—	—	43.8
Colleges should prohibit racist/sexist speech on campus	—	—	—	—	—	—	54.7	55.3	55.6	57.2	58.7	57.3	56.1	57.2	56.4	55.0	54.3	53.5	54.5	55.7	—
Employers should be allowed to require drug testing of employees or job applicants	—	—	69.1	76.2	78.5	79.3	79.3	77.7	78.3	74.9	76.9	76.6	75.4	75.3	73.3	71.6	—	—	—	—	—
Federal military spending should increased	34.6	32.5	31.5	28.6	26.1	26.9	20.0	24.6	—	—	—	—	—	—	—	—	50.7	43.5	39.9	37.6	35.5
Grading in the high schools has become too easy	51.2	—	—	—	—	—	53.1	—	—	—	—	—	—	—	—	—	—	—	—	53.5	—
If two people really like each other, it's all right for them to have sex even if they've known each other for only a very short time	—	65.1	—	63.7	64.8	63.6	59.2	58.3	55.4	54.9	52.3	52.0	51.3	51.1	54.6	55.2	—	59.8	—	58.1	—
It is important to have laws prohibiting homosexual relationships	58.7	60.1	57.0	54.1	52.1	49.8	43.4	44.1	41.9	39.1	42.5	41.5	38.9	37.6	36.0	33.5	32.6	34.6	38.0	35.2	33.4
Just because a man thinks that a woman has "led him on" does not entitle him to have sex with her	—	—	76.8	81.0	81.2	82.6	84.9	85.5	85.3	84.8	—	83.9	83.9	83.7	—	—	—	—	—	—	—
Marijuana should be legalized	24.2	22.8	23.4	19.9	21.7	24.1	28.2	32.6	36.4	37.1	36.1	36.7	37.7	37.2	40.4	42.9	45.8	44.3	43.1	42.8	42.0
Only volunteers should serve in the armed forces	—	—	52.9	52.3	—	—	—	—	40.2	41.0	39.8	40.7	—	—	—	—	40.1	39.0	—	—	—
People should not obey laws which violate their personal values	—	—	—	—	—	—	—	—	—	—	—	—	—	—	—	—	—	—	—	—	—
Racial discrimination is no longer a major problem in America	—	—	—	—	20.9	20.3	15.4	15.8	19.9	21.6	19.3	21.4	23.0	24.8	24.4	23.7	26.0	27.4	27.9	25.9	23.8
Realistically, an individual can do little to bring about change in our society	—	—	—	—	—	32.2	33.5	35.4	36.1	35.8	34.1	34.1	33.3	33.1	31.6	30.3	31.6	32.3	31.4	31.4	31.0
Same sex couples should have the right to legal marital status	—	—	—	—	—	—	—	—	—	—	—	41.3	43.1	44.9	47.2	48.8	50.8	50.2	48.3	50.1	52.9
The activities of married women are best confined to the home and family	25.4	30.2	29.6	29.7	29.1	29.3	28.3	28.0	29.5	28.9	28.9	29.3	—	32.5	28.7	28.5	27.7	28.1	27.4	26.2	—
The chief benefit of a college education is that it increases one's earning power	70.9	71.0	71.5	72.7	72.8	72.3	72.0	—	—	—	—	—	—	—	—	—	—	—	—	—	69.7
The death penalty should be abolished	21.7	20.6	20.2	18.9	19.6	19.4	19.9	19.6	18.5	19.1	19.4	20.9	20.6	23.0	27.4	28.2	28.1	28.8	29.5	29.7	30.7
The federal government is not doing enough to control environmental pollution	76.2	79.5	82.2	85.5	87.4	84.7	86.7	81.3	79.9	80.2	78.1	76.4	75.1	74.6	72.6	71.6	69.1	67.6	70.1	73.9	74.4
The federal government should do more to control the sale of handguns	—	—	—	69.7	68.9	71.0	73.0	73.3	71.9	73.2	74.0	73.6	—	—	—	—	—	—	—	71.0	65.6

129

STUDENT VIEWS
FRESHMAN MEN

ITEM	1966	1967	1968	1969	1970	1971	1972	1973	1974	1975	1976	1977	1978	1979	1980	1981	1982	1983	1984	1985
Student agrees strongly or somewhat																				
The federal government should do more to discourage energy consumption	—	—	—	—	—	—	—	—	—	80.6	77.9	80.8	80.0	81.9	80.4	76.9	75.2	71.9	69.8	68.5
The federal government should raise taxes to reduce the deficit	—	—	—	—	—	—	—	—	—	—	—	—	—	—	—	—	—	—	—	28.7
There is too much concern in the courts for the rights of criminals	—	—	—	60.0	56.3	52.0	54.6	54.1	55.5	59.0	63.8	67.5	69.5	66.7	69.7	73.4	73.8	72.2	—	—
Wealthy people should pay a larger share of taxes than they do now	—	—	—	—	—	—	75.8	75.3	78.0	77.9	77.4	75.7	73.6	70.4	69.4	69.5	71.0	68.6	68.3	72.2
How would you characterize your political views?																				
Far left	—	—	—	—	3.6	3.7	3.1	2.6	2.6	2.3	2.3	2.1	1.8	2.1	2.0	1.9	2.1	2.1	2.3	2.2
Liberal	—	—	—	—	37.5	39.9	36.0	35.1	31.2	31.6	28.5	26.9	25.2	24.7	21.9	19.2	19.8	20.5	20.5	21.9
Middle of the road	—	—	—	—	40.0	40.3	42.9	45.9	49.1	48.1	48.6	50.5	51.1	51.3	52.2	52.0	52.7	53.2	50.7	47.9
Conservative	—	—	—	—	18.1	15.3	17.1	15.7	16.2	17.1	19.2	19.6	20.8	20.8	22.2	25.4	23.9	22.7	24.7	25.8
Far right	—	—	—	—	1.1	0.9	0.9	0.8	0.9	0.9	1.3	1.0	1.1	1.1	1.7	1.6	1.5	1.5	1.8	2.1

STUDENT VIEWS
FRESHMAN MEN

ITEM	1986	1987	1988	1989	1990	1991	1992	1993	1994	1995	1996	1997	1998	1999	2000	2001	2002	2003	2004	2005	2006
Student agrees strongly or somewhat																					
The federal government should do more to discourage energy consumption	67.0	—	—	—	—	79.8	79.0	74.4	70.3	—	—	—	—	—	—	—	73.7	—	—	—	—
The federal government should raise taxes to reduce the deficit	29.7	30.0	33.9	34.7	37.4	31.8	34.0	37.4	29.3	30.0	27.6	25.6	—	—	—	—	—	—	—	—	31.0
There is too much concern in the courts for the rights of criminals	—	71.2	71.4	71.2	68.5	67.2	67.5	69.4	74.1	74.1	73.2	71.4	73.5	72.5	67.8	65.8	65.8	63.3	61.0	60.7	59.1
Wealthy people should pay a larger share of taxes than they do now	71.4	—	—	—	—	—	71.7	68.9	64.6	65.0	63.7	61.7	58.6	55.4	53.0	51.4	50.0	52.6	54.9	57.3	57.8
How would you characterize your political views?																					
Far left	2.5	2.7	2.6	2.3	2.3	2.5	2.9	2.7	2.8	2.9	3.0	3.1	3.1	3.1	3.6	3.8	3.2	3.4	4.0	3.9	3.3
Liberal	22.6	22.9	21.9	20.7	21.4	22.8	24.0	21.7	20.7	19.3	19.7	20.3	21.1	22.0	23.2	24.7	23.7	22.5	23.6	24.1	24.5
Middle of the road	47.9	48.0	46.5	46.3	48.5	47.5	47.4	45.7	47.0	48.8	48.7	49.7	51.3	51.0	49.8	47.4	48.2	47.5	45.0	44.8	43.6
Conservative	25.0	24.2	26.6	28.5	25.8	25.3	23.7	27.3	27.0	26.5	26.0	24.5	22.4	22.0	21.3	21.7	23.0	24.3	24.4	24.5	26.2
Far right	2.0	2.2	2.4	2.3	1.9	2.0	2.0	2.6	2.5	2.5	2.6	2.4	2.2	1.9	2.1	2.4	1.9	2.4	3.1	2.7	2.4

SOURCES OF STUDENT FUNDS
FRESHMAN MEN

ITEM	1966	1967	1968	1969	1970	1971	1972	1973	1974	1975	1976	1977	1978	1979	1980	1981	1982	1983	1984	1985
Students receiving funds to cover educational expenses (room, board, tuition, and fees) from:																				
Parents, other relatives or friends	—	—	—	—	—	—	—	—	—	—	—	—	74.7	72.4	72.8	72.1	73.2	73.2	72.2	73.2
Spouse	—	—	—	—	—	—	—	—	—	—	—	—	0.5	0.5	0.5	0.6	0.6	0.6	0.7	0.7
Savings from summer work	—	—	—	—	—	—	—	—	—	—	—	—	51.4	48.3	46.8	47.6	44.9	45.1	49.8	52.5
Other savings	—	—	—	—	—	—	—	—	—	—	—	—	21.5	19.4	19.0	19.9	18.9	19.6	21.3	23.6
Part time job on campus	—	—	—	—	—	—	—	—	—	—	—	—	—	—	—	—	—	—	—	—
Part time job off campus	—	—	—	—	—	—	—	—	—	—	—	—	23.9	21.2	22.4	22.1	21.1	20.6	26.4	28.2
Full time job while in college	—	—	—	—	—	—	—	—	—	—	—	—	2.2	2.0	2.1	2.0	2.0	1.8	2.0	2.4
Pell Grant	—	—	—	—	—	—	—	—	—	—	—	—	20.1	29.5	29.1	23.5	22.0	24.7	17.4	17.2
Supplemental Educational Opportunity Grant (SEOG)	—	—	—	—	—	—	—	—	—	—	—	—	6.1	7.8	8.6	6.3	6.1	7.0	5.7	5.3
State scholarship or grant	—	—	—	—	—	—	—	—	—	—	—	—	15.2	15.5	16.0	13.7	13.8	15.6	13.6	14.0
College Work-Study Grant	—	—	—	—	—	—	—	—	—	—	—	—	11.4	13.1	15.3	12.8	13.4	14.8	10.1	10.9
College grant/scholarship (other than above)	—	—	—	—	—	—	—	—	—	—	—	—	15.8	14.1	16.1	14.1	15.0	16.8	19.9	22.4
Other private grant	—	—	—	—	—	—	—	—	—	—	—	—	7.7	7.5	7.8	7.3	8.0	8.2	7.0	6.6
Other government aid (ROTC, BIA, GI/ military benefits, etc.)	—	—	—	—	—	—	—	—	—	—	—	—	5.5	5.5	5.8	5.6	3.5	4.1	4.3	3.7
Stafford Loan (GSL)	—	—	—	—	—	—	—	—	—	—	—	—	11.0	16.0	23.7	28.0	21.2	21.8	23.5	22.3
Perkins Loan (NDSL)	—	—	—	—	—	—	—	—	—	—	—	—	8.4	8.8	10.0	7.8	6.6	7.2	6.6	6.8
Other college loan	—	—	—	—	—	—	—	—	—	—	—	—	3.6	3.9	4.7	4.1	3.7	4.0	4.1	4.0
Other loan	—	—	—	—	—	—	—	—	—	—	—	—	3.4	3.5	3.9	4.2	4.0	3.8	3.7	3.7
Other than above	—	—	—	—	—	—	—	—	—	—	—	—	4.9	5.2	4.8	4.5	3.9	4.3	2.7	2.3
Students receiving funds to cover educational expenses (room, board, tuition, and fees) from:																				
Family resources (parents, relatives, spouse, etc.)	—	—	—	—	—	—	—	—	—	—	—	—	—	—	—	—	—	—	—	—
My own resources (savings from work, work-study, other income)	—	—	—	—	—	—	—	—	—	—	—	—	—	—	—	—	—	—	—	—
Aid which need not be repaid (grants, scholarships, military funding, etc.)	—	—	—	—	—	—	—	—	—	—	—	—	—	—	—	—	—	—	—	—
Aid which must be repaid (loans, etc.)	—	—	—	—	—	—	—	—	—	—	—	—	—	—	—	—	—	—	—	—
Other than above	—	—	—	—	—	—	—	—	—	—	—	—	—	—	—	—	—	—	—	—
Do you have any concern about your ability to finance your college education?																				
None (I am confident that I will have sufficient funds)	34.6	34.0	34.3	34.1	33.3	33.7	35.9	37.1	40.3	38.9	36.8	36.7	38.6	37.5	36.2	35.6	35.0	37.8	38.6	40.5
Some (but I probably will have enough funds)	57.9	58.1	57.7	56.5	56.7	56.0	49.9	47.1	45.7	45.9	48.0	47.8	47.7	49.4	49.8	49.5	49.0	48.4	48.7	47.5
Major (not sure I will have enough funds)	7.6	7.9	8.0	9.4	10.1	10.3	14.2	15.8	14.0	15.3	15.2	15.5	13.7	13.1	14.0	14.9	15.9	13.8	12.7	12.0

132

SOURCES OF STUDENT FUNDS
FRESHMAN MEN

ITEM	1986	1987	1988	1989	1990	1991	1992	1993	1994	1995	1996	1997	1998	1999	2000	2001	2002	2003	2004	2005	2006
Students receiving funds to cover educational expenses (room, board, tuition, and fees) from:																					
Parents, other relatives or friends	76.5	82.1	82.2	83.2	81.6	81.2	83.5	82.2	82.7	81.8	81.4	80.9	82.2	83.2	81.3	—	—	—	—	—	81.1
Spouse	1.0	0.9	1.0	0.7	0.8	0.9	0.8	0.7	0.7	0.8	0.6	0.7	0.8	1.0	0.8	—	—	—	—	—	1.6
Savings from summer work	54.1	58.9	59.1	58.2	58.2	52.2	54.8	52.9	52.7	53.2	52.1	51.0	51.4	54.3	48.0	—	—	—	—	—	47.3
Other savings	27.2	29.9	30.9	30.1	32.7	29.0	31.8	30.4	31.6	31.2	31.5	30.8	32.4	36.4	30.4	—	—	—	—	—	36.4
Part time job on campus	—	20.0	21.1	21.2	21.5	20.9	23.2	22.6	22.9	23.9	23.3	24.2	24.4	26.5	22.9	—	—	—	—	—	26.3
Part time job off campus	30.5	18.4	19.0	19.1	18.6	16.9	17.7	17.3	18.3	18.7	18.7	19.2	18.9	22.3	20.5	—	—	—	—	—	22.1
Full time job while in college	2.7	1.6	1.8	1.8	2.0	2.0	2.0	1.6	2.3	2.4	2.5	2.5	2.6	3.6	2.8	—	—	—	—	—	4.7
Pell Grant	13.9	15.1	17.2	18.2	18.6	19.5	19.7	18.6	17.9	17.3	17.7	17.1	17.4	16.8	15.2	—	—	—	—	—	14.7
Supplemental Educational Opportunity Grant (SEOG)	5.5	6.2	5.5	6.1	6.2	6.0	6.7	5.8	5.9	5.9	6.5	5.5	6.2	6.4	5.5	—	—	—	—	—	7.1
State scholarship or grant	13.6	17.3	14.6	15.2	15.6	13.9	14.9	15.2	16.1	15.9	16.4	16.4	17.8	19.3	20.0	—	—	—	—	—	—
College Work-Study Grant	10.9	10.2	9.7	10.0	10.7	11.4	13.3	13.1	13.4	13.5	12.7	12.7	13.1	13.4	11.0	—	—	—	—	—	12.2
College grant/scholarship (other than above)	21.6	15.9	22.3	23.5	23.9	25.5	27.5	27.8	28.9	29.8	32.2	31.3	32.0	32.9	29.5	—	—	—	—	—	27.6
Other private grant	7.9	10.9	10.2	10.2	11.0	10.8	11.6	10.8	11.1	10.7	11.6	11.5	12.1	12.7	11.1	—	—	—	—	—	10.8
Other government aid (ROTC, BIA, GI/ military benefits, etc.)	1.6	4.3	4.0	4.0	4.3	4.0	3.2	3.3	3.5	3.7	4.2	3.3	3.4	4.0	3.7	—	—	—	—	—	—
Stafford Loan (GSL)	24.0	21.3	21.7	21.2	21.0	22.7	25.7	30.2	29.8	29.0	28.3	26.1	26.7	26.7	24.5	—	—	—	—	—	24.2
Perkins Loan (NDSL)	6.7	5.1	3.4	2.7	7.9	7.9	9.8	9.3	9.7	10.0	10.6	10.1	10.4	10.0	9.0	—	—	—	—	—	10.0
Other college loan	4.6	5.9	6.5	8.3	6.2	5.9	6.7	7.2	8.4	10.3	10.7	11.4	12.0	12.7	10.8	—	—	—	—	—	13.8
Other loan	4.1	4.9	5.3	6.0	5.8	5.4	6.0	5.7	6.5	7.0	6.8	6.7	7.6	8.1	7.4	—	—	—	—	—	8.8
Other than above	2.5	3.3	2.6	3.3	2.8	2.6	2.8	3.3	3.7	3.7	4.6	5.0	4.9	5.5	4.8	—	—	—	—	—	5.6
Students receiving funds to cover educational expenses (room, board, tuition, and fees) from:																					
Family resources (parents, relatives, spouse, etc.)	—	—	—	—	—	—	—	—	—	—	—	—	—	—	—	78.9	78.7	79.2	80.6	78.0	—
My own resources (savings from work, work-study, other income)	—	—	—	—	—	—	—	—	—	—	—	—	—	—	—	60.0	58.6	57.7	59.9	55.8	—
Aid which need not be repaid (grants, scholarships, military funding, etc.)	—	—	—	—	—	—	—	—	—	—	—	—	—	—	—	60.8	61.0	60.2	61.9	61.4	—
Aid which must be repaid (loans, etc.)	—	—	—	—	—	—	—	—	—	—	—	—	—	—	—	42.6	42.3	45.0	46.9	46.0	—
Other than above	—	—	—	—	—	—	—	—	—	—	—	—	—	—	—	5.5	5.0	5.4	5.5	5.6	—
Do you have any concern about your ability to finance your college education?																					
None (I am confident that I will have sufficient funds)	43.0	43.1	42.3	39.9	—	—	34.2	—	35.4	33.6	37.4	37.7	40.8	40.7	43.1	42.1	41.7	41.7	41.6	41.0	42.5
Some (but I probably will have enough funds)	45.5	45.7	45.7	48.9	—	—	52.0	—	49.6	50.8	49.0	49.9	48.2	48.8	47.2	47.8	48.3	48.2	48.2	48.7	48.6
Major (not sure I will have enough funds)	11.5	11.2	12.1	11.3	—	—	13.8	—	15.0	15.6	13.5	12.4	11.0	10.5	9.7	10.0	10.2	10.2	10.2	10.3	8.9

DISAGGREGATED RESPONSES
FRESHMAN MEN

ITEM	1966	1967	1968	1969	1970	1971	1972	1973	1974	1975	1976	1977	1978	1979	1980	1981	1982	1983	1984	1985
Your probable career/occupation																				
Accountant or actuary	—	—	—	—	—	4.0	4.3	—	—	—	6.6	6.4	6.5	5.8	5.7	5.4	5.4	5.3	5.7	5.8
Actor or entertainer	—	—	—	—	—	0.7	0.6	—	—	—	1.0	0.9	0.9	1.0	1.0	0.8	0.9	0.9	0.8	1.0
Architect	—	—	—	—	—	2.1	2.3	—	—	—	2.0	2.2	2.1	2.1	1.9	1.5	1.5	1.2	1.7	1.7
Artist	—	—	—	—	—	1.2	1.1	—	—	—	1.2	1.5	1.1	1.4	1.4	1.4	1.4	1.6	1.5	1.3
Business (clerical)	—	—	—	—	—	0.3	0.3	—	—	—	0.2	0.3	0.2	0.3	0.2	0.3	0.3	0.2	0.3	0.3
Business executive (mgmt, administrator)	—	—	—	—	—	7.7	7.3	—	—	—	9.5	10.7	11.6	11.9	11.8	12.4	11.5	12.3	13.5	14.5
Business owner or proprietor	—	—	—	—	—	1.5	1.8	—	—	—	2.7	3.3	3.5	3.7	3.3	3.6	3.3	3.4	4.1	4.2
Business salesperson or buyer	—	—	—	—	—	0.6	0.6	—	—	—	0.8	1.0	1.1	1.2	1.1	1.0	1.0	1.0	1.2	1.2
Clergy (minister, priest)	—	—	—	—	—	0.9	0.9	—	—	—	1.0	0.8	0.7	0.6	0.6	0.6	0.5	0.6	0.4	0.5
Clergy (other religious)	—	—	—	—	—	0.3	0.3	—	—	—	0.3	0.2	0.2	0.2	0.2	0.2	0.1	0.2	0.2	0.2
Clinical psychologist	—	—	—	—	—	1.0	0.9	—	—	—	0.8	0.6	0.7	0.6	0.5	0.6	0.4	0.5	0.6	0.6
College administrator/staff	—	—	—	—	—	—	—	—	—	—	0.5	0.4	0.4	0.3	0.3	0.3	0.3	0.3	0.3	0.4
College teacher	—	—	—	—	—	1.0	0.9	—	—	—	1.0	0.8	0.6	0.5	0.4	0.3	0.3	0.3	0.3	0.4
Computer programmer or analyst	—	—	—	—	—	1.2	1.2	—	—	—	2.1	2.5	3.4	4.1	5.4	7.7	9.8	9.5	6.9	5.3
Conservationist or forester	—	—	—	—	—	2.3	2.3	—	—	—	1.8	2.0	1.3	1.2	0.9	1.0	0.7	0.7	0.6	0.5
Dentist (including orthodontist)	—	—	—	—	—	1.9	2.2	—	—	—	2.4	1.8	1.8	1.6	1.6	1.3	1.2	1.1	1.0	0.9
Dietitian or home economist	—	—	—	—	—	0.0	0.0	—	—	—	0.1	0.1	0.1	0.1	0.1	0.1	0.1	0.0	0.1	0.1
Engineer	—	—	—	—	—	10.0	10.2	—	—	—	13.1	14.6	15.4	15.7	17.4	17.3	18.6	17.5	17.1	17.0
Farmer or rancher	—	—	—	—	—	1.1	1.2	—	—	—	1.4	1.1	0.9	1.3	1.2	1.2	1.0	0.8	1.0	0.8
Foreign service worker (incl diplomat)	—	—	—	—	—	0.6	0.5	—	—	—	0.4	0.5	0.5	0.4	0.5	0.5	0.6	0.6	0.7	1.0
Homemaker (full-time)	—	—	—	—	—	0.0	0.0	—	—	—	0.0	0.0	0.0	0.0	0.0	0.0	0.0	0.0	0.0	0.0
Interior decorator (including designer)	—	—	—	—	—	0.1	0.1	—	—	—	0.1	0.1	0.1	0.1	0.1	0.1	0.1	0.1	0.1	0.1
Interpreter (translator)	—	—	—	—	—	0.1	0.1	—	—	—	0.1	0.1	0.1	0.1	0.1	0.1	0.1	0.1	0.1	0.2
Lab technician or hygienist	—	—	—	—	—	0.5	0.5	—	—	—	0.6	0.6	0.5	0.4	0.4	0.3	0.3	0.4	0.3	0.2
Law enforcement officer	—	—	—	—	—	1.0	1.3	—	—	—	2.0	2.2	1.8	1.5	1.2	0.8	1.5	1.0	1.2	1.2
Lawyer (attorney) or judge	—	—	—	—	—	8.9	9.2	—	—	—	7.6	7.4	7.1	6.8	6.5	6.1	6.5	5.7	5.8	5.4
Military service (career)	—	—	—	—	—	3.6	3.7	—	—	—	2.3	2.4	2.6	2.6	2.4	2.6	2.1	2.9	2.9	2.5
Musician (performer, composer)	—	—	—	—	—	1.7	1.5	—	—	—	1.8	1.9	1.8	1.8	1.8	1.8	1.7	1.5	1.3	1.5
Nurse	—	—	—	—	—	0.1	0.1	—	—	—	0.2	0.2	0.1	0.1	0.2	0.2	0.2	0.2	0.2	0.1
Optometrist	—	—	—	—	—	0.2	0.4	—	—	—	0.4	0.4	0.4	0.4	0.3	0.2	0.3	0.3	0.3	0.3
Pharmacist	—	—	—	—	—	1.0	1.1	—	—	—	1.1	1.0	0.8	0.7	0.6	0.5	0.4	0.5	0.6	0.6
Physician	—	—	—	—	—	7.1	8.1	—	—	—	7.0	5.8	6.3	5.7	5.9	5.6	5.9	6.5	6.2	6.7
Policymaker/government	—	—	—	—	—	—	—	—	—	—	0.2	0.2	0.1	0.2	0.1	0.1	0.1	0.1	0.2	0.1
School counselor	—	—	—	—	—	0.2	0.2	—	—	—	0.1	0.0	0.0	0.0	0.0	0.0	0.1	0.1	0.0	0.0
School principal or superintendent	—	—	—	—	—	0.1	0.1	—	—	—	0.0	0.0	0.0	0.0	0.0	0.0	0.0	0.0	0.0	0.0
Scientific researcher	—	—	—	—	—	4.4	4.0	—	—	—	3.9	3.6	3.3	2.8	2.6	2.4	2.1	2.2	2.2	2.2
Social, welfare or recreation worker	—	—	—	—	—	1.4	1.2	—	—	—	0.9	0.7	0.6	0.5	0.6	0.3	0.3	0.4	0.4	0.3
Statistician	—	—	—	—	—	0.2	0.2	—	—	—	0.2	0.1	0.1	0.1	0.1	0.1	0.1	0.1	0.1	0.1
Therapist (physical, occupational, speech)	—	—	—	—	—	0.4	0.5	—	—	—	0.7	0.5	0.6	0.7	0.7	0.7	0.6	0.8	0.9	0.7
Teacher or administrator (elementary)	—	—	—	—	—	0.9	0.8	—	—	—	0.9	0.7	0.5	0.6	0.5	0.6	0.4	0.4	0.4	0.5
Teacher or administrator (secondary)	—	—	—	—	—	7.0	5.3	—	—	—	3.6	2.7	2.5	2.5	2.3	1.9	1.7	2.1	2.0	2.3
Veterinarian	—	—	—	—	—	1.4	1.8	—	—	—	1.6	1.2	1.2	1.0	1.0	0.9	0.9	0.9	0.7	0.8
Writer or journalist	—	—	—	—	—	1.5	1.6	—	—	—	1.9	1.8	1.6	2.0	1.9	2.1	2.0	1.9	2.0	2.0
Skilled trades	—	—	—	—	—	0.9	0.8	—	—	—	0.7	1.7	0.8	1.0	1.2	1.1	0.8	0.5	0.5	0.5
Other	—	—	—	—	—	5.3	4.7	—	—	—	4.4	4.6	4.6	5.0	4.7	4.8	4.3	4.1	4.1	4.3
Undecided	—	—	—	—	—	13.7	14.1	—	—	—	10.1	9.4	10.1	9.9	9.6	9.7	9.1	9.4	9.9	10.0

DISAGGREGATED RESPONSES
FRESHMAN MEN

ITEM	1986	1987	1988	1989	1990	1991	1992	1993	1994	1995	1996	1997	1998	1999	2000	2001	2002	2003	2004	2005	2006
Your probable career/occupation																					
Accountant or actuary	5.2	5.5	5.4	5.4	5.1	4.5	4.0	3.8	3.7	3.4	2.9	2.6	2.6	2.2	2.3	2.0	2.3	2.2	2.4	3.0	3.2
Actor or entertainer	1.1	1.2	1.1	1.0	0.9	1.1	1.1	1.1	1.3	1.3	1.3	1.4	1.7	1.6	1.8	1.6	1.5	1.5	1.4	1.4	1.4
Architect	1.7	1.8	1.9	2.2	2.1	2.4	2.3	2.1	2.3	2.4	1.8	1.8	2.0	2.0	1.8	1.4	1.4	1.6	1.7	1.6	1.0
Artist	1.6	2.0	1.8	1.6	1.6	1.6	2.3	1.9	1.6	2.0	1.4	1.7	1.8	1.6	1.9	1.9	1.9	2.0	1.7	1.8	1.7
Business (clerical)	0.3	0.3	0.3	0.3	0.3	0.4	0.4	0.4	0.4	0.4	0.5	0.4	0.6	0.5	0.6	0.6	0.5	0.6	0.5	0.6	0.8
Business executive (mgmt, administrator)	15.1	15.7	15.0	14.0	12.0	9.8	8.9	8.6	8.9	9.4	9.3	10.1	10.9	10.8	11.3	10.5	9.9	9.6	9.6	10.5	11.1
Business owner or proprietor	5.0	5.4	5.4	4.8	4.2	3.9	3.6	3.6	3.9	4.3	4.3	4.4	4.2	4.3	4.5	4.5	4.2	4.5	5.0	5.2	5.2
Business salesperson or buyer	1.6	1.5	1.3	1.3	1.3	1.0	1.1	1.0	1.1	1.0	1.1	1.1	1.3	1.2	1.1	1.2	1.1	1.0	1.0	1.1	1.2
Clergy (minister, priest)	0.4	0.4	0.3	0.4	0.4	0.5	0.5	0.4	0.5	0.5	0.5	0.6	0.6	0.6	0.5	0.4	0.5	0.5	0.4	0.5	0.4
Clergy (other religious)	0.2	0.2	0.1	0.1	0.1	0.2	0.2	0.1	0.1	0.1	0.2	0.2	0.2	0.2	0.2	0.1	0.2	0.1	0.1	0.1	0.1
Clinical psychologist	0.7	0.7	0.8	0.6	0.7	0.7	0.8	0.8	0.8	0.8	0.7	0.6	0.7	0.6	0.7	0.7	0.6	0.6	0.6	0.6	0.7
College administrator/staff	—	—	—	—	—	—	—	—	—	—	0.0	0.0	0.1	0.1	0.0	0.0	0.0	0.0	0.1	0.0	0.1
College teacher	0.4	0.5	0.5	0.5	0.6	0.6	0.6	0.6	0.6	0.7	0.6	0.6	0.6	0.6	0.6	0.5	0.6	0.6	0.6	0.6	0.6
Computer programmer or analyst	4.4	3.5	3.2	3.2	3.1	3.1	3.0	3.3	4.0	4.9	6.1	6.8	7.9	9.2	9.3	8.3	6.7	5.3	4.4	3.6	3.4
Conservationist or forester	0.5	0.5	0.5	0.7	0.7	0.7	0.8	0.9	0.8	0.8	0.7	0.7	0.6	0.6	0.4	0.4	0.4	0.3	0.3	0.3	0.4
Dentist (including orthodontist)	0.9	0.8	0.7	0.7	0.7	0.7	0.7	0.8	0.8	0.8	0.8	0.8	0.7	0.8	0.7	0.7	0.7	0.8	1.1	1.2	1.1
Dietitian or home economist	0.0	0.0	0.0	0.0	0.0	0.1	0.1	0.1	0.1	0.1	0.0	0.0	0.1	0.1	0.1	0.0	0.1	0.1	0.2	0.1	0.1
Engineer	15.6	14.8	14.1	15.1	15.0	16.2	15.1	15.3	13.3	12.8	14.6	14.8	12.7	13.8	13.0	13.2	13.1	12.6	13.9	12.3	11.7
Farmer or rancher	0.5	0.5	0.5	0.6	0.6	0.6	0.6	0.7	0.9	0.7	0.6	0.6	0.7	0.6	0.5	0.4	0.4	0.3	0.4	0.4	0.4
Foreign service worker (incl diplomat)	0.9	0.9	0.9	0.8	0.7	0.7	0.6	0.6	0.6	0.4	0.3	0.3	0.4	0.4	0.3	0.4	0.3	0.4	0.4	0.5	0.5
Homemaker (full-time)	0.0	0.0	0.0	0.0	0.0	0.0	0.0	0.0	0.1	0.0	0.1	0.0	0.0	0.0	0.0	0.0	0.0	0.0	0.1	0.0	0.1
Interior decorator (including designer)	0.1	0.1	0.1	0.1	0.1	0.1	0.1	0.1	0.0	0.1	0.0	0.0	0.0	0.0	0.0	0.0	0.0	0.0	0.1	0.1	0.0
Interpreter (translator)	0.1	0.1	0.1	—	—	0.1	0.1	0.0	0.1	0.1	0.2	—	0.1	0.1	0.1	0.1	0.1	0.1	0.2	0.1	0.1
Lab technician or hygienist	0.2	0.2	0.2	0.2	0.2	0.2	0.2	0.2	0.2	0.2	0.2	0.2	0.1	0.1	0.1	0.1	0.1	0.1	0.2	0.1	0.1
Law enforcement officer	1.1	1.2	1.4	1.2	1.9	1.9	2.2	2.0	1.9	2.2	2.1	1.9	1.9	1.9	1.7	1.5	1.8	1.9	2.0	1.7	2.0
Lawyer (attorney) or judge	5.0	5.7	6.7	6.5	6.2	5.6	5.1	4.8	5.0	3.7	3.5	3.5	3.4	4.0	3.9	3.9	4.1	4.0	3.9	3.9	3.8
Military service (career)	3.2	2.5	2.3	2.1	2.1	2.2	1.3	1.2	1.5	1.3	2.1	1.5	1.3	1.6	1.6	1.9	2.0	2.5	1.9	1.8	2.1
Musician (performer, composer)	1.6	1.7	1.5	1.4	1.5	1.5	1.6	1.5	1.7	1.6	1.8	1.9	2.0	1.9	2.0	2.0	2.1	2.0	1.9	2.4	2.1
Nurse	0.1	0.1	0.1	0.2	0.3	0.5	0.5	0.6	0.6	0.5	0.4	0.3	0.3	0.2	0.2	0.3	0.4	0.6	0.7	0.7	0.8
Optometrist	0.2	0.3	0.4	0.3	0.3	0.3	0.3	0.3	0.3	0.4	0.3	0.3	0.2	0.2	0.2	0.2	0.2	0.2	0.2	0.2	0.2
Pharmacist	0.7	0.6	0.9	0.8	0.9	0.9	0.8	1.1	1.0	1.1	1.0	1.0	0.7	0.5	0.7	0.8	1.2	1.7	2.1	2.0	1.9
Physician	5.4	5.0	5.1	5.2	5.3	6.1	7.2	7.3	7.3	7.2	6.4	6.5	5.5	5.6	4.8	4.8	4.8	5.0	5.2	5.3	5.3
Policymaker/government	—	—	—	—	—	—	—	—	—	1.0	1.1	1.1	1.1	1.0	1.0	1.1	1.1	1.2	1.2	1.2	1.2
School counselor	0.1	0.0	0.1	0.1	0.2	0.1	0.2	0.2	0.2	0.1	0.1	0.1	0.1	0.1	0.1	0.1	0.1	0.1	0.1	0.1	0.1
School principal or superintendent	0.0	0.0	0.1	0.1	0.1	0.1	0.1	0.1	0.1	0.1	0.1	0.1	0.1	0.1	0.1	0.1	0.1	0.1	0.1	0.1	0.1
Scientific researcher	2.2	2.1	2.2	2.2	2.2	2.2	2.5	2.6	2.3	2.4	2.3	2.4	2.0	2.0	1.8	1.9	1.8	1.8	2.0	1.9	2.0
Social, welfare or recreation worker	0.3	0.3	0.3	0.3	0.3	0.3	0.3	0.3	0.4	0.4	0.3	0.3	0.3	0.3	0.3	0.3	0.2	0.2	0.2	0.3	0.3
Statistician	0.1	0.1	0.1	0.1	0.1	0.1	0.1	0.1	0.1	0.1	—	—	—	—	—	—	—	—	—	—	—
Therapist (physical, occupational, speech)	1.1	1.0	1.1	1.3	1.6	2.2	2.9	3.1	2.9	2.8	2.3	2.1	2.1	1.7	1.4	1.2	1.3	1.5	1.7	1.8	1.7
Teacher or administrator (elementary)	0.6	0.7	0.6	0.7	0.9	1.1	1.2	1.5	1.6	1.6	1.6	1.6	1.6	1.6	1.6	1.3	1.3	1.3	1.1	1.1	1.0
Teacher or administrator (secondary)	2.9	2.9	3.0	3.0	3.5	3.8	3.8	3.9	4.0	4.1	4.0	4.2	4.2	4.0	4.3	4.1	4.3	4.3	4.4	4.7	4.6
Veterinarian	0.8	0.7	0.6	0.6	0.6	0.7	0.7	0.9	1.0	0.9	0.9	0.8	0.7	0.7	0.6	0.5	0.5	0.4	0.5	0.4	0.5
Writer or journalist	2.0	2.1	2.4	2.0	1.9	1.9	1.8	2.0	2.1	2.0	1.9	1.8	1.9	1.9	1.9	1.7	1.8	1.8	1.9	1.9	2.1
Skilled trades	0.4	0.4	0.9	0.6	0.6	0.7	0.6	0.6	0.6	0.6	0.7	0.6	0.7	0.7	0.7	0.6	0.6	0.6	0.6	0.5	0.5
Other	4.7	5.0	5.7	6.7	7.8	7.6	7.7	8.1	7.3	7.1	7.6	7.3	7.8	7.4	7.9	9.7	10.0	10.4	8.9	9.1	9.3
Undecided	10.8	10.7	10.2	10.8	11.2	11.3	12.2	11.5	12.1	11.8	11.5	10.7	11.5	10.8	11.2	13.1	13.6	13.5	13.2	13.5	13.5

DISAGGREGATED RESPONSES
FRESHMAN MEN

ITEM	1966	1967	1968	1969	1970	1971	1972	1973	1974	1975	1976	1977	1978	1979	1980	1981	1982	1983	1984	1985
Your probable undergraduate field																				
Arts and Humanities																				
Art, fine and applied	—	—	—	—	—	1.4	1.2	1.1	1.4	1.4	1.5	1.7	1.3	1.6	1.6	1.6	1.5	1.7	1.6	1.4
English (language and literature)	—	—	—	—	—	1.4	1.1	1.3	1.1	0.9	0.8	0.8	0.9	0.7	0.7	0.8	0.8	0.8	1.0	0.9
History	—	—	—	—	—	3.3	2.7	2.4	2.0	1.7	1.6	1.3	1.2	1.1	1.2	1.1	1.1	1.0	1.2	1.3
Journalism	—	—	—	—	—	1.2	1.2	1.4	1.3	1.3	1.4	1.1	1.1	1.5	1.4	1.5	1.5	1.3	1.3	1.4
Language and Literature (except English)	—	—	—	—	—	0.6	0.5	0.4	0.4	0.2	0.3	0.2	0.3	0.2	0.2	0.2	0.2	0.3	0.2	0.3
Music	—	—	—	—	—	2.3	2.2	1.8	2.1	2.0	2.0	1.8	1.8	1.7	1.7	1.8	1.5	1.4	1.2	1.3
Philosophy	—	—	—	—	—	0.7	0.5	0.5	0.4	0.3	0.3	0.3	0.2	0.2	0.2	0.2	0.2	0.2	0.2	0.3
Speech or Theater	—	—	—	—	—	0.7	0.6	0.7	0.7	0.7	0.8	0.7	—	—	—	—	—	—	—	—
Theater or Drama	—	—	—	—	—	—	—	—	—	—	—	—	0.7	0.7	0.7	0.6	0.6	0.6	0.6	0.6
Speech	—	—	—	—	—	—	—	—	—	—	—	—	0.1	0.2	0.1	0.1	0.1	0.1	0.1	0.1
Theology or Religion	—	—	—	—	—	0.8	0.7	0.7	1.0	0.9	0.9	0.7	0.6	0.5	0.5	0.5	0.4	0.4	0.3	0.4
Other Arts and Humanities	—	—	—	—	—	0.4	0.7	0.6	0.5	0.5	0.4	0.4	0.3	0.3	0.3	0.4	0.4	0.4	0.3	0.5
Biological Science																				
Biology (general)	—	—	—	—	—	2.8	2.5	5.2	4.5	4.4	4.3	2.6	2.6	2.3	2.3	2.2	2.2	2.6	2.3	2.3
Biochemistry or Biophysics	—	—	—	—	—	0.8	0.8	1.5	1.2	1.2	1.3	0.7	0.8	0.7	0.7	0.7	0.7	0.8	0.8	0.8
Botany	—	—	—	—	—	0.2	0.2	0.2	0.2	0.2	0.2	0.2	0.1	0.1	0.1	0.1	0.1	0.0	0.0	0.0
Environmental Science	—	—	—	—	—	0.8	0.6	—	—	—	—	—	—	—	—	—	—	—	—	—
Marine (life) Science	—	—	—	—	—	—	—	1.2	1.1	1.2	1.1	1.2	0.9	0.7	0.6	0.6	0.5	0.4	0.6	0.4
Microbiology or Bacteriology	—	—	—	—	—	—	—	0.4	0.4	0.3	0.3	0.3	0.2	0.2	0.2	0.2	0.3	0.3	0.2	0.2
Zoology	—	—	—	—	—	0.7	0.6	1.1	1.1	0.8	0.7	0.5	0.5	0.4	0.4	0.4	0.4	0.3	0.4	0.3
Other Biological Science	—	—	—	—	—	0.9	1.7	1.1	1.0	1.0	1.0	0.6	0.7	0.6	0.5	0.6	0.4	0.6	0.5	0.4
Business																				
Accounting	—	—	—	—	—	4.4	4.6	6.0	6.8	6.4	7.2	6.8	7.2	6.6	6.4	6.0	6.1	5.8	6.2	6.1
Business Administration (general)	—	—	—	—	—	9.6	8.9	6.8	6.7	7.0	7.5	8.5	8.7	9.0	8.5	8.8	8.1	8.1	8.7	7.8
Finance	—	—	—	—	—	—	—	1.0	0.8	0.8	0.9	1.0	1.1	1.2	1.0	1.4	1.5	1.8	2.2	2.7
International Business	—	—	—	—	—	—	—	—	—	—	—	—	—	—	—	—	—	—	—	—
Marketing	—	—	—	—	—	—	—	1.0	1.0	1.0	1.1	1.4	1.7	2.0	1.8	1.9	1.9	2.0	2.5	2.8
Management	—	—	—	—	—	—	—	3.3	3.2	3.2	3.8	4.2	4.9	5.2	4.9	5.1	4.7	4.8	5.8	6.1
Secretarial Studies	—	—	—	—	—	0.0	0.0	0.0	0.0	0.0	0.0	0.0	0.0	0.0	0.0	0.0	0.0	0.0	0.0	0.0
Other Business	—	—	—	—	—	0.7	1.5	0.8	0.7	0.8	0.8	0.8	0.9	0.9	0.9	0.9	0.9	1.0	1.1	1.0
Education																				
Business Education	—	—	—	—	—	—	—	0.1	0.1	0.2	0.1	0.1	0.1	0.1	0.1	0.1	0.2	0.1	0.1	0.2
Elementary Education	—	—	—	—	—	—	—	0.5	0.5	0.5	0.5	0.4	0.3	0.3	0.3	0.4	0.2	0.3	0.2	0.4
Music or Art Education	—	—	—	—	—	—	—	0.5	0.5	0.4	0.4	0.4	0.4	0.3	0.4	0.3	0.3	0.3	0.2	0.3
Physical Education or Recreation	—	—	—	—	—	2.8	2.6	2.4	2.3	2.6	2.6	2.2	2.1	2.4	1.9	1.5	1.3	1.3	1.4	1.2
Secondary Education	—	—	—	—	—	—	—	1.1	1.1	0.9	1.0	0.8	0.6	0.6	0.7	0.6	0.5	0.8	0.7	0.9
Special Education	—	—	—	—	—	—	—	0.3	0.3	0.3	0.3	0.3	0.2	0.3	0.2	0.1	0.1	0.1	0.1	0.0
Other Education	—	—	—	—	—	1.6	1.2	0.3	0.2	0.2	0.2	0.1	0.1	0.1	0.2	0.1	0.1	0.1	0.1	0.1
Engineering																				
Aeronautical or Astronautical Eng	—	—	—	—	—	1.5	1.2	1.1	1.3	1.4	1.2	1.6	1.9	2.2	2.3	2.6	2.5	2.4	2.6	2.6
Civil Engineering	—	—	—	—	—	1.9	2.0	1.9	2.7	2.5	2.5	2.1	2.2	2.2	2.2	2.0	1.5	1.5	1.7	1.5
Chemical Engineering	—	—	—	—	—	1.1	0.9	0.8	1.3	1.6	1.6	1.4	1.7	1.8	1.8	1.8	1.8	1.5	1.1	1.2
Electrical or Electronic Engineering	—	—	—	—	—	3.2	3.6	3.3	3.8	4.2	4.1	5.8	5.7	5.5	6.7	6.0	6.7	7.5	7.3	7.1
Industrial Engineering	—	—	—	—	—	0.8	0.6	0.5	0.5	0.4	0.5	0.6	0.7	0.7	0.7	0.6	0.7	0.7	0.5	0.6
Mechanical Engineering	—	—	—	—	—	2.6	2.3	1.9	2.4	2.6	2.7	3.0	3.3	3.3	3.6	3.6	3.7	3.4	3.7	3.7
Other Engineering	—	—	—	—	—	1.1	1.5	1.5	2.0	2.4	2.4	2.3	2.6	2.6	2.4	2.9	3.5	2.9	2.2	2.2

DISAGGREGATED RESPONSES
FRESHMAN MEN

ITEM	1986	1987	1988	1989	1990	1991	1992	1993	1994	1995	1996	1997	1998	1999	2000	2001	2002	2003	2004	2005	2006
Your probable undergraduate field																					
Arts and Humanities																					
Art, fine and applied	1.8	2.1	2.0	1.7	1.8	1.7	2.5	2.0	1.8	2.2	1.6	1.8	2.1	1.8	2.2	2.2	2.3	2.3	1.9	2.0	1.8
English (language and literature)	1.1	1.2	1.3	1.2	1.3	1.3	1.2	1.2	1.3	1.3	1.3	1.4	1.2	1.2	1.2	1.1	1.3	1.2	1.3	1.3	1.5
History	1.4	1.4	1.5	1.5	1.6	1.5	1.5	1.5	1.5	1.4	1.5	1.4	1.4	1.5	1.5	1.6	1.7	1.8	1.7	1.9	2.1
Journalism	1.2	1.3	1.4	1.1	1.1	0.9	0.9	1.2	1.3	1.4	1.1	1.0	1.2	1.1	1.1	1.1	1.1	1.2	1.2	1.1	1.3
Language and Literature (except English)	0.3	0.3	0.3	0.3	0.3	0.3	0.3	0.3	0.3	0.3	0.2	0.2	0.3	0.2	0.2	0.3	0.3	0.3	0.3	0.4	0.4
Music	1.4	1.4	1.2	1.2	1.3	1.3	1.4	1.3	1.5	1.4	1.6	1.6	1.8	1.8	1.7	1.8	1.8	1.7	1.7	2.1	1.9
Philosophy	0.3	0.4	0.3	0.3	0.3	0.3	0.3	0.3	0.4	0.4	0.4	0.3	0.4	0.4	0.4	0.4	0.5	0.5	0.4	0.4	0.5
Speech or Theater	—	—	—	—	—	—	—	—	—	—	—	—	—	—	—	—	—	—	—	—	—
Theater or Drama	0.7	0.7	0.6	0.7	0.6	0.8	0.8	0.7	0.8	0.8	0.8	0.9	1.0	0.9	1.0	1.0	1.0	1.0	0.8	0.9	1.1
Speech	0.1	0.1	0.1	0.1	0.1	0.1	0.1	0.1	0.1	0.1	0.1	0.1	0.1	0.0	0.1	0.1	0.1	0.1	0.1	0.1	0.1
Theology or Religion	0.3	0.4	0.3	0.3	0.3	0.4	0.5	0.3	0.4	0.4	0.5	0.5	0.6	0.5	0.6	0.5	0.6	0.5	0.4	0.4	0.4
Other Arts and Humanities	0.4	0.5	0.5	0.4	0.4	0.4	0.4	0.3	0.5	0.4	0.5	0.6	0.5	0.6	0.8	0.7	0.8	0.8	0.8	0.8	0.8
Biological Science																					
Biology (general)	2.3	2.3	2.2	2.2	2.5	2.8	3.3	3.9	3.8	3.9	3.5	3.5	3.1	3.1	2.8	3.0	3.1	3.3	3.7	3.8	3.9
Biochemistry or Biophysics	0.8	0.7	0.8	0.6	0.6	0.7	0.8	0.8	0.9	0.9	0.9	0.9	0.8	0.8	0.7	0.7	0.9	1.0	1.1	1.1	1.2
Botany	0.0	0.0	0.1	0.0	0.0	0.0	0.1	0.1	0.1	0.0	0.1	0.0	0.0	0.1	0.0	0.0	0.0	0.0	0.0	0.0	0.1
Environmental Science	—	—	—	—	—	—	—	0.8	1.1	1.0	0.9	0.8	0.8	0.7	0.6	0.6	0.5	0.6	0.5	0.5	0.6
Marine (life) Science	0.5	0.5	0.5	0.6	0.6	0.9	0.9	0.8	0.5	0.6	0.6	0.6	0.3	0.4	0.3	0.4	0.3	0.2	0.3	0.3	0.3
Microbiology or Bacteriology	0.2	0.2	0.2	0.1	0.2	0.2	0.2	0.2	0.2	0.3	0.6	0.4	0.3	0.3	0.3	0.2	0.3	0.3	0.3	0.3	0.3
Zoology	0.3	0.3	0.3	0.3	0.3	0.3	0.3	0.4	0.4	0.4	0.4	0.4	0.3	0.3	0.3	0.3	0.3	0.3	0.3	0.3	0.3
Other Biological Science	0.5	0.6	0.5	0.6	0.6	0.6	0.8	0.9	0.6	0.6	0.5	0.5	0.5	0.5	0.5	0.5	0.5	0.5	0.6	0.5	0.7
Business																					
Accounting	5.6	6.0	5.7	5.8	5.4	4.9	4.5	4.1	4.1	3.6	3.3	2.8	2.7	2.4	2.3	2.1	2.5	2.5	2.5	3.1	3.3
Business Administration (general)	8.3	8.4	8.2	7.6	6.6	5.4	5.1	4.7	4.5	4.7	5.0	5.1	5.4	5.3	5.6	5.1	5.2	5.1	5.1	5.7	5.7
Finance	3.4	3.8	3.4	3.4	2.9	2.2	1.9	1.9	1.8	1.7	1.9	2.1	2.4	2.6	2.7	2.8	2.6	2.2	2.1	2.7	2.8
International Business	—	—	—	—	—	—	—	—	1.5	1.5	1.5	1.5	1.5	1.5	1.4	1.4	1.3	1.3	1.4	1.4	1.6
Marketing	3.2	3.5	3.5	3.4	3.3	2.5	2.4	2.4	2.2	2.2	2.4	2.7	2.9	2.8	2.9	2.9	2.7	2.6	2.7	2.9	2.9
Management	6.3	6.4	5.9	5.3	5.0	4.1	4.0	3.6	3.8	4.1	4.0	4.0	4.4	4.5	4.7	5.3	4.9	5.4	5.5	5.8	5.9
Secretarial Studies	0.0	0.0	0.0	0.0	0.0	0.0	0.0	0.0	0.0	0.0	0.0	0.0	0.0	0.0	0.0	0.0	0.0	0.0	0.0	0.0	0.0
Other Business	1.4	1.5	1.7	1.6	1.5	1.3	1.2	1.3	0.9	1.0	1.1	1.2	1.3	1.5	1.4	1.4	1.2	1.3	1.2	1.1	1.4
Education																					
Business Education	0.3	0.2	0.2	0.2	0.2	0.2	0.1	0.2	0.3	0.3	0.2	0.2	0.2	0.2	0.3	0.2	0.3	0.2	0.2	0.2	0.3
Elementary Education	0.4	0.5	0.5	0.5	0.8	0.9	1.1	1.3	1.4	1.4	1.5	1.3	1.4	1.3	1.3	1.1	1.1	1.1	0.9	0.8	0.8
Music or Art Education	0.3	0.3	0.3	0.3	0.5	0.4	0.4	0.4	0.5	0.5	0.5	0.5	0.5	0.5	0.6	0.5	0.5	0.5	0.5	0.7	0.5
Physical Education or Recreation	1.7	1.4	1.3	1.2	1.4	1.6	1.3	1.6	1.5	1.5	1.3	1.4	1.6	1.2	1.4	1.1	1.1	1.2	1.4	1.5	1.6
Secondary Education	1.1	1.3	1.4	1.5	1.7	2.0	2.1	1.8	2.1	2.1	2.2	2.0	2.2	2.1	2.2	2.2	2.5	2.4	2.2	2.2	2.3
Special Education	0.1	0.1	0.1	0.1	0.1	0.1	0.1	0.2	0.2	0.1	0.1	0.2	0.2	0.2	0.2	0.1	0.2	0.2	0.2	0.2	0.2
Other Education	0.1	0.1	0.1	0.1	0.2	0.1	0.2	0.2	0.2	0.2	0.2	0.1	0.2	0.2	0.2	0.1	0.2	0.2	0.2	0.2	0.2
Engineering																					
Aeronautical or Astronautical Eng	3.3	3.1	3.1	3.2	2.8	2.8	1.9	1.3	1.1	0.9	1.2	1.0	1.1	1.6	1.6	1.9	1.7	1.8	1.8	1.5	1.0
Civil Engineering	1.5	1.5	1.4	1.9	1.9	1.9	2.1	2.4	2.3	2.1	2.2	2.0	1.5	1.8	1.6	1.6	1.7	1.9	2.0	2.0	1.9
Chemical Engineering	1.0	0.9	0.8	1.1	1.2	1.5	1.8	1.9	1.5	1.3	1.3	1.6	1.2	1.2	0.9	0.9	0.9	0.9	1.0	0.9	1.0
Electrical or Electronic Engineering	6.2	5.6	4.8	5.1	4.3	4.7	4.2	4.1	4.0	3.8	4.6	4.5	3.7	4.3	4.0	4.1	2.6	2.4	2.6	2.1	2.0
Industrial Engineering	0.6	0.5	0.5	0.4	0.5	0.6	0.4	0.4	0.3	0.3	0.4	0.4	0.4	0.4	0.4	0.4	0.3	0.3	0.4	0.3	0.3
Mechanical Engineering	3.4	3.3	3.3	3.7	4.0	4.4	4.1	4.2	3.4	3.5	4.0	4.3	3.5	3.9	3.7	4.2	4.6	4.7	5.2	4.4	4.2
Other Engineering	1.8	2.0	1.7	2.1	2.4	3.0	2.8	3.1	2.7	2.6	3.6	3.4	3.3	3.3	3.7	3.7	6.1	5.1	4.9	4.4	4.1

DISAGGREGATED RESPONSES
FRESHMAN MEN

ITEM	1966	1967	1968	1969	1970	1971	1972	1973	1974	1975	1976	1977	1978	1979	1980	1981	1982	1983	1984	1985
Your probable undergraduate field																				
Physical Science																				
Astronomy	—	—	—	—	—	—	—	0.2	0.2	0.2	0.2	0.2	0.2	0.1	0.2	0.1	0.1	0.1	0.1	0.1
Atmospheric Science (incl Meteorology)	—	—	—	—	—	—	—	0.1	0.1	0.1	0.1	0.1	0.2	0.2	0.1	0.1	0.1	0.1	0.1	0.1
Chemistry	—	—	—	—	—	1.7	1.5	2.4	2.2	2.2	2.3	1.5	1.6	1.5	1.4	1.3	1.2	1.3	1.3	1.3
Earth Science	—	—	—	—	—	0.6	0.5	0.4	0.4	0.5	0.5	0.4	0.6	0.5	0.3	0.5	0.4	0.3	0.3	0.2
Marine Science	—	—	—	—	—	—	—	0.7	0.7	0.7	0.5	0.6	0.5	0.4	0.2	0.3	0.2	0.2	0.2	0.2
Mathematics	—	—	—	—	—	3.5	2.8	2.4	2.1	1.6	1.5	1.2	1.3	0.9	0.9	0.9	0.9	1.2	1.0	1.1
Physics	—	—	—	—	—	1.5	1.3	1.2	1.3	1.3	1.2	1.1	1.1	1.0	0.9	1.0	0.9	0.9	0.9	1.1
Statistics	—	—	—	—	—	0.1	0.1	0.1	0.1	0.1	0.1	0.1	0.1	0.1	0.0	0.0	0.0	0.1	0.0	0.1
Other Physical Science	—	—	—	—	—	0.4	0.5	0.2	0.2	0.3	0.2	0.2	0.2	0.2	0.2	0.2	0.2	0.2	0.2	0.2
Professional																				
Architecture or Urban Planning	—	—	—	—	—	2.3	2.2	1.8	2.2	1.8	1.6	1.6	1.7	1.5	1.4	1.0	1.1	0.8	1.2	1.2
Home Economics	—	—	—	—	—	0.1	0.0	0.0	0.0	0.0	0.0	0.0	0.0	0.0	0.0	0.0	0.0	0.0	0.0	0.0
Health Technology (medical, dental, laboratory)	—	—	—	—	—	0.8	1.1	3.6	3.1	3.1	3.3	1.1	0.9	0.8	0.8	0.7	0.7	0.8	0.7	0.7
Library or Archival Science	—	—	—	—	—	0.0	0.0	0.0	0.0	0.0	0.0	0.0	0.0	0.0	0.0	0.0	0.0	0.0	0.0	0.0
Medical, Dental, Veterinary	—	—	—	—	—	9.3	10.3	—	—	—	—	5.1	5.4	4.9	5.0	4.3	4.5	4.7	4.2	4.6
Nursing	—	—	—	—	—	0.2	0.1	0.1	0.1	0.2	0.2	0.2	0.1	0.1	0.2	0.1	0.2	0.2	0.2	0.1
Pharmacy	—	—	—	—	—	1.0	1.1	0.9	1.3	0.9	1.0	0.9	0.7	0.6	0.5	0.4	0.4	0.4	0.5	0.5
Therapy (occupational, physical, speech)	—	—	—	—	—	0.4	0.5	0.4	0.4	0.5	0.5	0.4	0.5	0.5	0.6	0.6	0.5	0.7	0.8	0.7
Other Professional	—	—	—	—	—	0.4	1.0	3.2	3.0	2.9	3.1	1.5	1.5	1.6	1.5	1.3	1.2	1.1	1.1	1.0
Social Science																				
Anthropology	—	—	—	—	—	0.3	0.3	0.3	0.2	0.2	0.1	0.1	0.1	0.1	0.1	0.1	0.1	0.1	0.1	0.1
Economics	—	—	—	—	—	0.7	0.7	0.7	0.8	0.7	0.7	0.7	0.7	0.8	0.7	0.7	0.8	0.8	0.8	0.9
Ethnic Studies	—	—	—	—	—	0.0	0.0	0.1	—	0.1	0.1	0.1	0.1	0.1	0.1	—	0.0	0.0	0.0	0.0
Geography	—	—	—	—	—	0.0	0.0	0.1	0.1	0.1	0.1	0.1	0.1	0.1	0.1	0.1	0.0	0.1	0.0	0.1
Political science (gov't, int'l relations)	—	—	—	—	—	3.4	3.6	5.5	4.3	4.0	3.7	3.7	3.4	3.2	3.2	3.1	3.0	3.0	3.3	3.9
Psychology	—	—	—	—	—	3.2	2.8	2.7	2.4	2.3	1.9	1.6	1.6	1.5	1.4	1.3	1.2	1.5	1.7	1.8
Social Work	—	—	—	—	—	0.9	0.7	0.5	0.6	0.5	0.6	0.4	0.4	0.4	0.3	0.2	0.2	0.2	0.2	0.2
Sociology	—	—	—	—	—	1.2	1.0	0.7	0.7	0.5	0.5	0.4	0.3	0.3	0.2	0.2	0.2	0.2	0.3	0.3
Women's Studies	—	—	—	—	—	—	—	—	—	—	—	—	—	—	—	—	0.0	0.0	0.0	0.0
Other Social Science	—	—	—	—	—	0.2	0.3	0.3	0.3	0.3	0.3	0.2	0.2	0.2	0.2	0.2	0.1	0.1	0.2	0.1
Technical																				
Building Trades	—	—	—	—	—	0.5	0.4	0.2	0.2	0.1	0.1	0.3	0.2	0.2	0.3	0.2	0.1	0.1	0.1	0.1
Data Processing or Computer Programming	—	—	—	—	—	0.5	0.4	0.5	0.6	0.7	0.7	1.0	1.2	1.6	2.1	2.9	3.8	3.6	2.4	2.3
Drafting or Design	—	—	—	—	—	—	—	0.2	0.3	0.3	0.2	0.3	0.3	0.5	0.3	0.5	0.3	0.3	0.3	0.4
Electronics	—	—	—	—	—	0.4	0.6	0.9	0.3	1.2	0.3	1.2	0.8	0.8	1.4	1.0	0.9	0.4	0.3	0.3
Mechanics	—	—	—	—	—	—	—	0.2	0.3	0.2	0.2	0.1	0.1	0.2	0.2	0.2	0.2	0.1	0.1	0.1
Other Technical	—	—	—	—	—	0.6	0.4	0.2	0.3	0.2	0.2	0.2	0.1	0.2	0.3	0.3	0.2	0.2	0.1	0.1
Other																				
Agriculture	—	—	—	—	—	1.8	2.0	2.0	2.4	2.0	2.5	1.9	1.6	1.9	1.7	1.8	1.5	1.2	1.4	1.3
Communications (radio, TV, etc.)	—	—	—	—	—	1.2	1.0	1.1	1.3	1.5	1.6	1.9	1.7	2.1	2.3	2.3	2.3	2.4	2.1	2.5
Computer Science	—	—	—	—	—	0.9	0.9	0.6	1.0	0.9	1.2	1.1	1.8	2.1	2.9	4.5	5.5	5.8	4.5	3.2
Forestry	—	—	—	—	—	1.6	1.5	1.2	1.7	1.9	1.0	1.4	0.8	0.8	0.6	0.7	0.6	0.5	0.4	0.3
Law Enforcement	—	—	—	—	—	—	—	1.5	1.1	1.7	2.0	2.4	2.0	1.8	1.4	0.8	1.7	1.3	1.3	1.3
Military Science	—	—	—	—	—	0.9	0.4	0.5	0.3	0.4	0.2	0.3	0.3	0.3	0.3	0.3	0.2	0.3	0.2	0.3
Other field	—	—	—	—	—	6.9	6.4	0.7	0.6	0.6	0.6	0.7	0.6	0.7	0.5	0.7	0.5	0.6	0.7	0.6
Undecided	—	—	—	—	—	2.3	4.4	4.7	4.4	4.9	4.5	4.8	4.5	4.4	4.5	4.7	4.5	4.9	4.9	5.5

DISAGGREGATED RESPONSES
FRESHMAN MEN

ITEM	1986	1987	1988	1989	1990	1991	1992	1993	1994	1995	1996	1997	1998	1999	2000	2001	2002	2003	2004	2005	2006
Your probable undergraduate field																					
Physical Science																					
Astronomy	0.2	0.2	0.2	0.2	0.2	0.1	0.1	0.1	0.1	0.1	0.1	0.1	0.1	0.1	0.1	0.1	0.1	0.1	0.1	0.1	0.1
Atmospheric Science (incl Meteorology)	0.1	0.1	0.2	0.1	0.1	0.1	0.1	0.1	0.1	0.1	0.1	0.1	0.1	0.2	0.2	0.2	0.1	0.1	0.2	0.2	0.1
Chemistry	1.2	1.0	1.0	0.9	1.0	1.0	1.1	1.2	1.3	1.1	1.0	1.1	0.8	0.8	0.8	0.8	0.9	1.0	1.1	1.1	1.2
Earth Science	0.2	0.2	0.1	0.2	0.3	0.3	0.4	0.3	0.2	0.2	0.1	0.2	0.2	0.2	0.1	0.1	0.1	0.1	0.2	0.1	0.2
Marine Science	0.2	0.2	0.2	0.3	0.2	0.3	0.3	0.3	0.2	0.3	0.3	0.3	0.1	0.2	0.1	0.1	0.1	0.1	0.1	0.1	0.1
Mathematics	1.0	0.8	0.8	0.9	0.8	0.8	0.8	0.8	0.9	0.8	0.7	0.7	0.7	0.7	0.8	0.7	0.8	0.9	0.9	0.8	0.9
Physics	1.1	1.0	0.9	1.0	1.0	0.9	0.9	0.9	0.8	0.8	0.8	0.8	0.7	0.8	0.8	0.8	0.9	0.9	1.0	0.9	0.9
Statistics	0.1	0.1	0.1	0.1	0.1	0.0	0.0	0.1	0.0	0.0	0.0	0.0	0.7	0.0	0.0	0.0	0.0	0.0	0.1	0.1	0.0
Other Physical Science	0.1	0.1	0.2	0.2	0.2	0.2	0.2	0.3	0.2	0.2	0.2	0.2	0.2	0.2	0.1	0.2	0.2	0.2	0.2	0.2	0.2
Professional																					
Architecture or Urban Planning	1.3	1.3	1.3	1.7	1.6	2.0	1.9	1.8	2.0	2.0	1.4	1.5	1.6	1.6	1.5	1.2	1.2	1.4	1.5	1.3	0.7
Home Economics	0.0	0.0	0.0	0.0	0.0	0.0	0.0	0.0	0.0	0.0	0.0	0.0	0.0	0.0	0.0	0.0	0.0	0.0	0.0	0.0	0.0
Health Technology (medical, dental, laboratory)	0.5	0.6	0.5	0.6	0.6	0.6	0.8	0.7	0.7	0.7	0.5	0.6	0.4	0.3	0.3	0.3	0.3	0.4	0.4	0.4	0.5
Library or Archival Science	0.0	0.0	0.0	0.0	0.0	0.0	0.0	0.0	0.0	0.0	0.0	0.0	0.0	0.0	0.0	0.0	0.0	0.0	0.0	0.0	0.0
Medical, Dental, Veterinary	3.9	3.4	3.4	3.6	3.6	4.0	4.6	4.7	4.6	4.4	3.8	4.0	3.8	3.7	3.3	3.1	3.0	3.1	3.1	3.2	2.9
Nursing	0.1	0.1	0.1	0.2	0.3	0.6	0.6	0.6	0.7	0.5	0.4	0.3	0.3	0.2	0.2	0.3	0.4	0.6	0.6	0.8	0.7
Pharmacy	0.6	0.5	0.8	0.8	0.8	0.8	0.8	0.9	0.9	0.9	0.8	0.9	0.6	0.4	0.5	0.7	1.0	1.4	1.7	1.6	1.3
Therapy (occupational, physical, speech)	0.9	0.9	1.0	1.1	1.4	2.1	2.9	3.1	2.7	2.7	2.2	2.0	2.0	1.3	1.1	1.0	1.1	1.3	1.4	1.4	1.3
Other Professional	1.0	1.0	1.2	1.1	1.1	0.9	0.9	0.9	0.9	0.8	0.7	0.8	0.7	0.7	0.7	0.6	0.6	0.6	0.7	0.6	0.6
Social Science																					
Anthropology	0.1	0.1	0.2	0.2	0.2	0.2	0.2	0.2	0.2	0.2	0.2	0.3	0.2	0.2	0.2	0.2	0.2	0.2	0.2	0.2	0.3
Economics	0.9	0.9	1.0	0.9	0.8	0.7	0.5	0.6	0.6	0.7	0.5	0.5	0.6	0.7	0.7	0.7	0.8	0.8	0.8	0.9	1.2
Ethnic Studies	0.0	0.0	0.0	0.0	0.0	0.0	0.0	0.0	0.0	0.0	0.0	0.0	0.0	0.0	0.0	0.0	0.0	0.0	0.0	0.0	0.0
Geography	0.1	0.1	0.1	0.1	0.1	0.1	0.1	0.1	0.1	0.1	0.1	0.1	0.1	0.1	0.1	0.1	0.1	0.1	0.1	0.0	0.1
Political science (gov't, int'l relations)	3.4	3.6	4.2	4.1	3.9	3.4	3.3	3.3	3.2	2.9	2.9	2.8	2.5	2.9	2.9	3.3	3.4	3.6	3.3	3.5	3.6
Psychology	1.9	2.0	2.2	2.0	2.1	2.1	2.4	2.6	2.4	2.2	2.2	2.0	2.2	2.0	2.2	2.2	2.3	2.3	2.3	2.2	2.6
Social Work	0.2	0.2	0.2	0.1	0.2	0.2	0.1	0.2	0.3	0.2	0.3	0.1	0.2	0.1	0.1	0.1	0.1	0.1	0.1	0.1	0.1
Sociology	0.2	0.2	0.2	0.3	0.3	0.3	0.4	0.5	0.4	0.4	0.4	0.4	0.4	0.3	0.3	0.4	0.4	0.4	0.4	0.4	0.5
Women's Studies	0.0	0.0	0.0	0.0	0.0	0.0	0.0	0.0	0.0	0.0	0.0	0.0	0.0	0.0	0.0	0.0	0.0	0.0	0.0	0.0	0.0
Other Social Science	0.2	0.1	0.2	0.1	0.2	0.2	0.1	0.2	0.2	0.1	0.2	0.2	0.2	0.2	0.2	0.2	0.2	0.2	0.3	0.3	0.3
Technical																					
Building Trades	0.1	0.1	0.1	0.1	0.0	0.1	0.1	0.1	0.1	0.1	0.1	0.1	0.1	0.1	0.1	0.1	0.1	0.1	0.1	0.1	0.1
Data Processing or Computer Programming	1.6	1.1	1.0	1.0	1.0	0.9	0.9	0.9	1.0	1.4	1.7	2.0	2.1	2.5	2.8	2.7	1.8	1.4	1.3	0.9	0.9
Drafting or Design	0.3	0.3	0.4	0.2	0.3	0.3	0.3	0.3	0.3	0.3	0.3	0.3	0.4	0.3	0.4	0.4	0.5	0.5	0.4	0.3	0.3
Electronics	0.3	0.3	0.2	0.2	0.2	0.2	0.2	0.2	0.1	0.1	0.2	0.2	0.2	0.2	0.2	0.2	0.2	0.2	0.2	0.2	0.2
Mechanics	0.1	0.1	0.5	0.2	0.1	0.1	0.1	0.0	0.0	0.1	0.1	0.1	0.1	0.1	0.1	0.1	0.1	0.1	0.2	0.1	0.1
Other Technical	0.2	0.1	0.5	0.2	0.2	0.2	0.1	0.1	0.1	0.1	0.2	0.2	0.2	0.2	0.2	0.3	0.3	0.3	0.3	0.2	0.2
Other																					
Agriculture	0.9	0.8	0.9	1.0	0.9	1.0	0.9	1.1	1.4	1.2	1.2	1.0	1.1	1.1	0.7	0.7	0.7	0.5	0.6	0.5	0.7
Communications (radio, TV, etc.)	2.6	2.9	2.7	2.6	2.5	2.2	2.4	2.1	1.8	1.7	1.8	1.7	2.0	2.0	2.0	1.9	1.9	1.9	1.5	1.5	1.7
Computer Science	2.6	2.4	2.2	2.4	2.3	2.5	2.4	2.6	3.1	3.7	4.6	5.1	5.8	6.6	6.5	6.1	4.2	3.3	2.8	2.2	2.1
Forestry	0.3	0.2	0.3	0.4	0.4	0.4	0.5	0.6	0.4	0.4	0.4	0.4	0.3	0.2	0.2	0.1	0.1	0.2	0.2	0.2	0.2
Law Enforcement	1.3	1.3	1.5	1.3	2.0	2.0	2.2	1.9	1.9	2.2	2.0	1.8	2.0	1.8	1.6	1.6	1.8	2.0	2.0	1.8	1.8
Military Science	0.3	0.2	0.2	0.2	0.1	0.2	0.1	0.1	0.1	0.1	0.1	0.1	0.1	0.1	0.1	0.2	0.1	0.2	0.2	0.2	0.2
Other field	0.6	0.8	1.1	1.1	1.3	1.4	1.1	1.1	1.0	1.1	1.1	1.0	1.1	1.5	1.2	1.6	1.3	1.4	1.5	1.8	1.4
Undecided	6.2	6.3	6.2	6.5	6.6	6.9	7.2	7.2	7.6	7.6	6.9	6.8	7.1	6.8	6.9	6.9	7.6	7.3	6.8	6.6	6.8

DISAGGREGATED RESPONSES
FRESHMAN MEN

ITEM	1966	1967	1968	1969	1970	1971	1972	1973	1974	1975	1976	1977	1978	1979	1980	1981	1982	1983	1984	1985
Your father's occupation																				
Accountant or actuary	—	—	—	—	—	2.5	2.7	—	—	—	2.8	2.7	2.8	2.5	2.6	2.6	2.7	2.5	2.8	2.9
Actor or entertainer	—	—	—	—	—	0.0	0.1	—	—	—	0.1	0.1	0.1	0.0	0.1	0.1	0.1	0.1	0.1	0.1
Architect	—	—	—	—	—	0.5	0.4	—	—	—	0.6	0.6	0.6	0.6	0.7	0.7	0.7	0.7	0.8	0.8
Artist	—	—	—	—	—	0.3	0.3	—	—	—	0.3	0.3	0.2	0.3	0.3	0.3	0.3	0.4	0.3	0.3
Business (clerical)	—	—	—	—	—	1.4	1.6	—	—	—	1.1	1.0	1.0	1.1	1.1	0.9	1.0	0.9	0.9	0.9
Business executive (mgmt, administrator)	—	—	—	—	—	14.9	15.9	—	—	—	15.5	15.5	16.1	15.7	16.0	15.8	16.0	15.7	15.4	15.9
Business owner or proprietor	—	—	—	—	—	7.8	7.9	—	—	—	7.7	7.5	7.7	7.8	8.0	8.2	8.3	8.4	8.5	8.5
Business salesperson or buyer	—	—	—	—	—	6.7	6.5	—	—	—	6.5	6.3	6.4	6.5	6.0	6.2	6.1	6.0	6.0	5.5
Clergy (minister, priest)	—	—	—	—	—	0.9	0.9	—	—	—	1.3	1.1	1.2	1.1	1.1	1.1	1.1	1.0	0.9	1.1
Clergy (other religious)	—	—	—	—	—	0.1	0.1	—	—	—	0.2	0.2	0.2	0.2	0.2	0.2	0.2	0.2	0.2	0.2
Clinical psychologist	—	—	—	—	—	0.1	0.1	—	—	—	0.1	0.1	0.1	0.1	0.1	0.1	0.1	0.1	0.1	0.1
College administrator/staff	—	—	—	—	—	—	—	—	—	—	—	—	—	—	—	—	—	—	—	—
College teacher	—	—	—	—	—	0.9	1.1	—	—	—	1.2	1.1	1.2	1.1	1.2	1.2	1.2	1.1	1.3	1.4
Computer programmer or analyst	—	—	—	—	—	0.5	0.5	—	—	—	1.0	1.1	1.3	1.2	1.5	1.5	1.6	1.8	1.9	2.0
Conservationist or forester	—	—	—	—	—	0.2	0.3	—	—	—	0.2	0.2	0.2	0.1	0.1	0.2	0.2	0.1	0.2	0.2
Dentist (including orthodontist)	—	—	—	—	—	0.6	0.6	—	—	—	0.8	0.7	0.8	0.7	0.7	0.8	0.7	0.7	0.6	0.7
Dietitian or home economist	—	—	—	—	—	0.0	0.1	—	—	—	0.1	0.1	0.0	0.1	0.1	0.1	0.1	0.1	0.1	0.1
Engineer	—	—	—	—	—	8.1	8.4	—	—	—	8.9	8.7	9.4	8.8	8.7	8.7	8.6	8.7	8.6	9.1
Farmer or rancher	—	—	—	—	—	5.2	4.5	—	—	—	3.7	3.0	2.5	2.8	3.2	3.4	3.2	2.9	2.9	3.3
Foreign service worker (incl diplomat)	—	—	—	—	—	0.1	0.2	—	—	—	0.1	0.2	0.1	0.2	0.2	0.2	0.1	0.1	0.1	0.2
Homemaker (full-time)	—	—	—	—	—	0.2	0.0	—	—	—	0.1	0.1	0.1	0.1	0.1	0.1	0.1	0.1	0.1	0.1
Interior decorator (including designer)	—	—	—	—	—	0.1	0.1	—	—	—	0.1	0.1	0.1	0.1	0.1	0.1	0.1	0.1	0.1	0.1
Interpreter (translator)	—	—	—	—	—	0.0	0.0	—	—	—	0.0	0.0	0.0	0.0	0.0	0.0	0.0	0.0	0.0	0.0
Lab technician or hygienist	—	—	—	—	—	0.4	0.4	—	—	—	0.4	0.4	0.5	0.4	0.4	0.5	0.4	0.4	0.4	0.4
Law enforcement officer	—	—	—	—	—	1.1	1.1	—	—	—	1.3	1.4	1.2	1.2	1.3	1.3	1.4	1.3	1.5	1.3
Lawyer (attorney) or judge	—	—	—	—	—	1.5	1.7	—	—	—	1.9	1.8	1.9	2.0	2.0	2.0	2.2	2.1	2.1	2.3
Military service (career)	—	—	—	—	—	2.5	2.3	—	—	—	2.5	2.5	2.3	2.2	2.2	2.3	2.1	2.2	2.0	1.7
Musician (performer, composer)	—	—	—	—	—	0.1	0.1	—	—	—	0.1	0.1	0.1	0.1	0.1	0.2	0.2	0.1	0.1	0.1
Nurse	—	—	—	—	—	0.1	0.0	—	—	—	0.1	0.1	0.1	0.1	0.1	0.1	0.1	0.1	0.1	0.1
Optometrist	—	—	—	—	—	0.1	0.2	—	—	—	0.2	0.1	0.1	0.2	0.1	0.1	0.1	0.1	0.1	0.1
Pharmacist	—	—	—	—	—	0.4	0.4	—	—	—	0.5	0.6	0.5	0.5	0.5	0.5	0.5	0.5	0.5	0.5
Physician	—	—	—	—	—	1.9	2.0	—	—	—	2.5	2.2	2.4	2.4	2.5	2.5	2.6	2.6	2.5	2.7
Policymaker/government	—	—	—	—	—	—	—	—	—	—	—	—	—	—	—	—	—	—	—	—
School counselor	—	—	—	—	—	0.1	0.2	—	—	—	0.2	0.1	0.2	0.2	0.2	0.2	0.2	0.2	0.2	0.2
School principal or superintendent	—	—	—	—	—	0.7	0.8	—	—	—	0.7	0.7	0.6	0.8	0.7	0.7	0.7	0.7	0.7	0.6
Scientific researcher	—	—	—	—	—	0.7	0.7	—	—	—	0.9	0.7	0.8	0.8	0.8	0.8	0.7	0.8	0.7	0.9
Social, welfare or recreation worker	—	—	—	—	—	0.3	0.4	—	—	—	0.4	0.4	0.4	0.4	0.4	0.4	0.4	0.5	0.5	0.5
Statistician	—	—	—	—	—	0.1	0.1	—	—	—	0.1	0.1	0.1	0.1	0.1	0.1	0.1	0.1	0.1	0.1
Therapist (physical, occupational, speech)	—	—	—	—	—	0.1	0.1	—	—	—	0.1	0.1	0.1	0.1	0.1	0.1	0.1	0.1	0.1	0.1
Teacher or administrator (elementary)	—	—	—	—	—	0.4	0.4	—	—	—	0.6	0.6	0.6	0.6	0.6	0.7	0.7	0.7	0.6	0.9
Teacher or administrator (secondary)	—	—	—	—	—	1.6	1.8	—	—	—	2.6	2.5	2.7	2.9	2.7	3.1	3.1	3.1	3.0	3.4
Veterinarian	—	—	—	—	—	0.2	0.2	—	—	—	0.2	0.2	0.2	0.3	0.3	0.2	0.2	0.2	0.2	0.2
Writer or journalist	—	—	—	—	—	0.3	0.3	—	—	—	0.3	0.4	0.4	0.3	0.3	0.4	0.4	0.3	0.4	0.4
Skilled trades	—	—	—	—	—	11.9	11.7	—	—	—	9.8	10.6	9.9	10.0	10.2	10.1	9.9	9.7	9.9	8.8
Laborer (unskilled)	—	—	—	—	—	3.4	3.4	—	—	—	3.3	3.3	3.0	2.8	3.0	2.7	2.7	2.7	2.8	2.6
Semi skilled worker	—	—	—	—	—	7.3	6.4	—	—	—	5.2	5.8	4.8	5.1	4.9	4.5	4.4	4.6	4.4	4.5
Other occupation	—	—	—	—	—	12.6	11.5	—	—	—	11.9	12.9	12.8	13.4	12.5	13.0	12.5	12.7	13.1	12.2
Unemployed	—	—	—	—	—	1.0	1.7	—	—	—	1.8	1.9	1.9	1.8	1.9	1.5	1.7	2.3	2.0	2.1

DISAGGREGATED RESPONSES
FRESHMAN MEN

ITEM	1986	1987	1988	1989	1990	1991	1992	1993	1994	1995	1996	1997	1998	1999	2000	2001	2002	2003	2004	2005	2006
Your father's occupation																					
Accountant or actuary	2.8	2.9	2.7	2.8	2.7	2.9	2.8	2.9	3.0	2.8	2.9	2.8	2.8	2.8	3.0	2.8	3.0	2.9	2.9	2.9	3.0
Actor or entertainer	0.1	0.1	0.1	0.1	0.1	0.1	0.1	0.1	0.1	0.1	0.1	0.1	0.1	0.1	0.1	0.1	0.1	0.1	0.1	0.1	0.1
Architect	0.9	0.8	0.8	0.9	0.8	0.9	0.9	0.8	0.8	0.9	0.8	1.0	1.0	1.1	1.0	1.1	1.0	1.1	1.1	1.1	1.0
Artist	0.3	0.3	0.3	0.3	0.3	0.3	0.3	0.3	0.3	0.4	0.3	0.3	0.3	0.3	0.3	0.3	0.3	0.4	0.3	0.3	0.3
Business (clerical)	0.9	0.9	0.8	0.8	0.8	0.8	0.8	0.8	0.9	0.9	0.9	0.9	1.0	1.0	1.1	1.2	1.2	1.2	1.3	1.3	1.4
Business executive (mgmt, administrator)	16.4	16.9	15.6	15.8	14.9	14.1	13.9	13.8	13.3	13.1	12.9	13.1	13.5	13.3	13.6	13.8	13.6	13.3	13.2	13.1	13.2
Business owner or proprietor	9.2	9.3	9.2	9.2	8.8	8.4	8.6	8.7	8.7	8.8	8.9	9.0	8.9	9.3	9.3	9.0	8.9	9.2	9.4	9.1	9.1
Business salesperson or buyer	5.9	5.8	5.5	5.4	5.1	5.1	5.1	4.9	4.8	5.1	5.0	5.0	4.9	4.9	4.8	4.7	4.8	4.9	4.7	4.7	4.8
Clergy (minister, priest)	1.1	0.9	1.0	1.0	1.1	1.1	1.1	1.0	1.1	1.0	1.2	1.2	1.2	1.2	1.0	0.9	1.0	0.9	0.9	0.9	0.8
Clergy (other religious)	0.2	0.2	0.1	0.1	0.1	0.1	0.1	0.1	0.1	0.1	0.1	0.1	0.2	0.1	0.2	0.1	0.1	0.1	0.1	0.1	0.1
Clinical psychologist	0.2	0.2	0.2	0.2	0.2	0.2	0.2	0.2	0.2	0.2	0.2	0.2	0.2	0.2	0.2	0.2	0.2	0.2	0.2	0.1	0.2
College administrator/staff	—	—	—	—	—	—	—	—	—	—	0.4	0.4	0.4	0.4	0.4	0.4	0.4	0.3	0.4	0.4	0.4
College teacher	1.4	1.3	1.2	1.1	1.1	1.1	1.0	0.9	1.0	0.9	0.8	0.8	0.8	0.8	0.9	0.9	0.9	0.8	0.8	0.8	0.8
Computer programmer or analyst	2.1	2.2	2.3	2.4	2.4	2.3	2.5	2.6	2.7	2.7	2.8	2.7	3.0	3.2	3.3	3.4	3.4	3.5	3.5	3.4	3.5
Conservationist or forester	0.2	0.2	0.2	0.2	0.2	0.2	0.2	0.2	0.2	0.2	0.2	0.2	0.2	0.2	0.2	0.2	0.2	0.2	0.2	0.2	0.1
Dentist (including orthodontist)	0.7	0.8	0.7	0.7	0.7	0.6	0.6	0.6	0.7	0.6	0.7	0.6	0.7	0.7	0.7	0.7	0.6	0.7	0.7	0.6	0.6
Dietitian or home economist	0.1	0.0	0.1	0.1	0.1	0.1	0.0	0.0	0.0	0.1	0.1	0.0	0.0	0.0	0.1	0.1	0.1	0.1	0.1	0.1	0.1
Engineer	8.7	8.9	8.6	8.3	8.3	8.3	8.5	8.3	8.3	8.1	8.1	8.3	8.4	8.6	8.4	8.6	8.5	8.8	9.0	8.6	8.7
Farmer or rancher	2.6	2.5	2.4	2.6	2.8	2.5	2.4	2.8	2.9	2.7	2.4	2.6	2.3	2.4	2.2	1.9	1.8	1.4	1.6	1.3	1.3
Foreign service worker (incl diplomat)	0.1	0.2	0.2	0.1	0.2	0.1	0.2	0.2	0.2	0.1	0.1	0.1	0.2	0.1	0.1	0.1	0.1	0.1	0.1	0.1	0.1
Homemaker (full-time)	0.2	0.1	0.1	0.1	0.2	0.2	0.2	0.2	0.2	0.2	0.2	0.2	0.2	0.2	0.2	0.2	0.1	0.2	0.2	0.3	0.3
Interior decorator (including designer)	0.1	0.1	0.1	0.1	0.1	0.1	0.1	0.1	0.1	0.2	0.1	0.1	0.0	0.0	0.1	0.1	0.1	0.0	0.1	0.1	0.1
Interpreter (translator)	0.0	0.0	0.0	0.0	0.0	0.0	0.0	0.0	0.0	0.0	—	—	—	—	—	—	—	—	—	—	—
Lab technician or hygienist	0.5	0.4	0.5	0.4	0.4	0.5	0.4	0.4	0.4	0.4	0.4	0.4	0.4	0.5	0.4	0.4	0.4	0.4	0.4	0.4	0.3
Law enforcement officer	1.4	1.5	1.4	1.5	1.6	1.6	1.6	1.6	1.7	1.6	1.7	1.6	1.6	1.7	1.6	1.7	1.6	1.7	1.6	1.7	1.7
Lawyer (attorney) or judge	2.3	2.5	2.5	2.4	2.2	2.1	2.3	2.4	2.4	2.2	2.4	2.6	2.3	2.6	2.5	2.5	2.7	2.6	2.5	2.5	2.7
Military service (career)	2.0	2.0	2.1	2.1	2.1	2.3	2.2	1.8	1.9	1.8	1.7	1.5	1.8	1.7	1.4	1.7	1.7	1.6	1.5	1.5	1.5
Musician (performer, composer)	0.2	0.1	0.1	0.1	0.1	0.2	0.1	0.1	0.1	0.1	0.2	0.1	0.2	0.2	0.2	0.2	0.2	0.2	0.2	0.2	0.2
Nurse	0.1	0.1	0.2	0.2	0.2	0.2	0.3	0.3	0.3	0.4	0.3	0.4	0.4	0.5	0.5	0.5	0.6	0.5	0.5	0.5	0.6
Optometrist	0.1	0.1	0.1	0.1	0.1	0.2	0.1	0.1	0.2	0.1	0.1	0.1	0.1	0.1	0.2	0.1	0.1	0.1	0.1	0.1	0.1
Pharmacist	0.5	0.5	0.5	0.5	0.5	0.4	0.4	0.5	0.5	0.4	0.5	0.5	0.5	0.5	0.5	0.5	0.5	0.5	0.5	0.5	0.5
Physician	2.6	2.7	2.7	2.6	2.5	2.3	2.5	2.4	2.5	2.5	2.3	2.6	2.4	2.6	2.6	2.8	2.7	2.7	2.7	2.7	2.6
Policymaker/government	—	—	—	—	—	—	—	—	—	0.9	0.9	0.8	0.9	0.9	1.0	0.9	0.9	0.8	0.8	0.9	0.8
School counselor	0.2	0.2	0.2	0.2	0.2	0.2	0.2	0.2	0.2	0.2	0.1	0.1	0.1	0.1	0.1	0.1	0.1	0.1	0.1	0.1	0.1
School principal or superintendent	0.6	0.6	0.6	0.6	0.6	0.6	0.5	0.6	0.6	0.5	0.5	0.5	0.4	0.5	0.4	0.3	0.3	0.3	0.3	0.3	0.2
Scientific researcher	0.8	0.8	0.8	0.7	0.6	0.7	0.7	0.7	0.6	0.6	0.6	0.7	0.7	0.7	0.7	0.7	0.7	0.8	0.8	0.7	0.7
Social, welfare or recreation worker	0.5	0.6	0.6	0.5	0.5	0.6	0.6	0.6	0.6	0.6	0.6	0.6	0.6	0.6	0.7	0.6	0.7	0.6	0.6	0.6	0.6
Statistician	0.1	0.1	0.1	0.1	0.1	0.1	0.1	0.1	0.1	0.1	—	—	—	—	—	—	—	—	—	—	—
Therapist (physical, occupational, speech)	0.1	0.2	0.2	0.2	0.1	0.2	0.2	0.2	0.2	0.3	0.2	0.2	0.3	0.3	0.3	0.3	0.3	0.3	0.3	0.3	0.3
Teacher or administrator (elementary)	1.0	0.9	1.0	1.1	1.1	1.1	1.2	1.2	1.2	1.2	1.4	1.2	1.2	1.3	1.1	1.0	1.1	1.1	0.9	0.9	0.9
Teacher or administrator (secondary)	3.6	3.6	3.8	3.7	3.5	3.7	3.8	3.6	3.5	3.7	3.5	3.4	3.0	3.0	2.8	2.7	2.5	2.5	2.3	2.3	2.3
Veterinarian	0.2	0.2	0.2	0.2	0.2	0.2	0.2	0.2	0.2	0.2	0.2	0.2	0.2	0.2	0.2	0.3	0.2	0.2	0.2	0.1	0.2
Writer or journalist	0.4	0.4	0.4	0.3	0.3	0.3	0.3	0.2	0.3	0.3	0.3	0.3	0.3	0.3	0.3	0.3	0.4	0.3	0.3	0.3	0.3
Skilled trades	8.9	8.5	9.2	9.3	9.5	9.6	8.8	9.7	8.8	8.9	8.7	8.8	9.0	8.5	8.5	8.9	8.5	8.5	8.6	8.3	8.1
Laborer (unskilled)	2.3	2.1	2.2	2.3	2.6	2.6	2.4	2.8	2.6	2.7	2.6	2.4	2.5	2.3	2.5	2.8	2.9	2.9	3.0	3.2	2.9
Semi skilled worker	3.6	3.4	3.8	3.7	3.9	4.3	3.8	3.6	3.8	3.8	3.6	3.5	3.5	3.3	3.1	3.3	3.2	3.1	3.1	3.1	2.9
Other occupation	12.2	12.3	13.2	13.1	14.7	14.4	15.2	14.8	15.2	15.2	15.3	15.4	15.1	15.2	15.4	15.1	15.3	15.8	15.8	16.9	17.1
Unemployed	1.8	1.6	1.6	1.7	1.8	2.4	2.5	2.6	2.6	2.3	2.5	2.2	2.0	1.8	1.9	1.6	1.9	2.1	2.0	2.1	2.0

DISAGGREGATED RESPONSES
FRESHMAN MEN

ITEM	1966	1967	1968	1969	1970	1971	1972	1973	1974	1975	1976	1977	1978	1979	1980	1981	1982	1983	1984	1985
Your mother's occupation																				
Accountant or actuary	—	—	—	—	—	1.7	1.9	—	—	—	1.6	1.9	2.0	2.0	2.2	2.4	2.4	2.5	2.4	2.6
Actor or entertainer	—	—	—	—	—	0.0	0.0	—	—	—	0.1	0.1	0.1	0.0	0.1	0.1	0.1	0.1	0.1	0.1
Architect	—	—	—	—	—	0.0	0.0	—	—	—	0.0	0.1	0.0	0.0	0.1	0.1	0.1	0.1	0.1	0.1
Artist	—	—	—	—	—	0.3	0.3	—	—	—	0.5	0.5	0.5	0.5	0.5	0.6	0.6	0.7	0.7	0.8
Business (clerical)	—	—	—	—	—	7.6	10.1	—	—	—	8.7	8.9	9.4	9.6	10.2	10.4	10.5	10.5	10.8	10.1
Business executive (mgmt, administrator)	—	—	—	—	—	1.2	1.4	—	—	—	1.9	2.0	2.4	2.6	2.9	3.1	3.5	3.7	4.1	4.6
Business owner or proprietor	—	—	—	—	—	1.1	1.3	—	—	—	1.4	1.5	1.6	1.8	1.9	2.2	2.1	2.3	2.6	2.7
Business salesperson or buyer	—	—	—	—	—	1.1	1.3	—	—	—	1.6	1.6	1.9	1.8	2.0	2.2	2.2	2.1	2.1	2.9
Clergy (minister, priest)	—	—	—	—	—	0.0	0.0	—	—	—	0.0	0.0	0.0	0.1	0.1	0.0	0.0	0.0	0.1	0.1
Clergy (other religious)	—	—	—	—	—	0.0	0.1	—	—	—	0.1	0.1	0.1	0.1	0.1	0.1	0.1	0.1	0.1	0.1
Clinical psychologist	—	—	—	—	—	0.0	0.1	—	—	—	0.1	0.1	0.1	0.1	0.1	0.1	0.1	0.1	0.1	0.2
College administrator/staff	—	—	—	—	—	—	—	—	—	—	—	—	—	—	—	—	—	—	—	—
College teacher	—	—	—	—	—	0.3	0.3	—	—	—	0.4	0.4	0.4	0.4	0.4	0.4	0.4	0.4	0.4	0.5
Computer programmer or analyst	—	—	—	—	—	0.2	0.2	—	—	—	0.3	0.4	0.4	0.4	0.5	0.6	0.8	0.8	0.9	1.0
Conservationist or forester	—	—	—	—	—	0.0	0.0	—	—	—	0.0	0.0	0.0	0.0	0.0	0.0	0.0	0.0	0.0	0.0
Dentist (including orthodontist)	—	—	—	—	—	0.0	0.0	—	—	—	0.1	0.1	0.1	0.1	0.1	0.1	0.2	0.1	0.2	0.2
Dietitian or home economist	—	—	—	—	—	0.4	0.5	—	—	—	0.5	0.4	0.5	0.5	0.5	0.4	0.5	0.4	0.4	0.5
Engineer	—	—	—	—	—	0.1	0.0	—	—	—	0.1	0.1	0.1	0.1	0.1	0.1	0.1	0.1	0.2	0.2
Farmer or rancher	—	—	—	—	—	0.1	0.2	—	—	—	0.2	0.2	0.1	0.2	0.2	0.2	0.3	0.2	0.2	0.3
Foreign service worker (incl diplomat)	—	—	—	—	—	0.0	0.0	—	—	—	0.1	0.1	0.1	0.1	0.1	0.1	0.0	0.0	0.0	0.1
Homemaker (full-time)	—	—	—	—	—	53.4	34.5	—	—	—	35.6	32.8	32.1	30.3	28.3	23.8	23.1	25.4	23.9	21.6
Interior decorator (including designer)	—	—	—	—	—	0.2	0.2	—	—	—	0.3	0.3	0.3	0.3	0.4	0.4	0.4	0.4	0.4	0.5
Interpreter (translator)	—	—	—	—	—	0.0	0.0	—	—	—	0.0	0.0	0.0	0.0	0.0	0.0	0.0	0.0	0.0	0.0
Lab technician or hygienist	—	—	—	—	—	0.4	0.4	—	—	—	0.5	0.5	0.5	0.6	0.6	0.7	0.7	0.7	0.7	0.8
Law enforcement officer	—	—	—	—	—	0.0	0.1	—	—	—	0.0	0.1	0.1	0.1	0.1	0.1	0.1	0.1	0.1	0.1
Lawyer (attorney) or judge	—	—	—	—	—	0.1	0.1	—	—	—	0.1	0.1	0.1	0.1	0.1	0.2	0.2	0.2	0.3	0.3
Military service (career)	—	—	—	—	—	0.0	0.0	—	—	—	0.0	0.0	0.0	0.0	0.0	0.0	0.0	0.0	0.1	0.1
Musician (performer, composer)	—	—	—	—	—	0.1	0.1	—	—	—	0.2	0.2	0.2	0.2	0.2	0.2	0.2	0.2	0.2	0.2
Nurse	—	—	—	—	—	4.5	4.9	—	—	—	6.0	6.3	6.3	6.6	6.6	7.4	7.4	7.4	7.5	7.6
Optometrist	—	—	—	—	—	0.0	0.0	—	—	—	0.1	0.1	0.0	0.1	0.1	0.1	0.1	0.1	0.2	0.1
Pharmacist	—	—	—	—	—	0.1	0.0	—	—	—	0.1	0.1	0.1	0.1	0.1	0.1	0.1	0.1	0.1	0.1
Physician	—	—	—	—	—	0.1	0.1	—	—	—	0.2	0.1	0.2	0.2	0.2	0.2	0.2	0.2	0.3	0.4
Policymaker/government	—	—	—	—	—	—	—	—	—	—	—	—	—	—	—	—	—	—	—	—
School counselor	—	—	—	—	—	0.2	0.3	—	—	—	0.3	0.3	0.3	0.3	0.3	0.3	0.4	0.3	0.3	0.3
School principal or superintendent	—	—	—	—	—	0.1	0.1	—	—	—	0.1	0.1	0.1	0.1	0.1	0.2	0.1	0.1	0.1	0.1
Scientific researcher	—	—	—	—	—	0.1	0.1	—	—	—	0.1	0.1	0.1	0.1	0.1	0.1	0.2	0.2	0.1	0.1
Social, welfare or recreation worker	—	—	—	—	—	0.7	1.0	—	—	—	1.2	1.3	1.2	1.4	1.3	1.3	1.3	1.4	1.4	1.4
Statistician	—	—	—	—	—	0.2	0.2	—	—	—	0.2	0.2	0.2	0.2	0.2	0.2	0.2	0.3	0.2	0.2
Therapist (physical, occupational, speech)	—	—	—	—	—	0.2	0.2	—	—	—	0.3	0.3	0.3	0.3	0.4	0.4	0.4	0.4	0.5	0.5
Teacher or administrator (elementary)	—	—	—	—	—	4.6	5.1	—	—	—	6.3	6.2	6.4	6.2	6.5	7.0	7.0	6.5	6.5	6.9
Teacher or administrator (secondary)	—	—	—	—	—	2.2	2.6	—	—	—	2.8	2.8	2.9	3.0	3.0	3.4	3.7	3.4	3.5	4.0
Veterinarian	—	—	—	—	—	0.0	0.0	—	—	—	0.0	0.0	0.0	0.0	0.0	0.0	0.0	0.0	0.0	0.0
Writer or journalist	—	—	—	—	—	0.2	0.2	—	—	—	0.2	0.3	0.2	0.3	0.3	0.3	0.3	0.3	0.4	0.4
Skilled trades	—	—	—	—	—	1.4	1.9	—	—	—	1.6	1.8	1.8	1.8	1.8	2.0	2.0	2.0	2.2	2.0
Laborer (unskilled)	—	—	—	—	—	1.6	2.1	—	—	—	1.9	2.1	1.9	1.9	2.2	2.1	2.0	1.9	1.8	1.8
Semi skilled worker	—	—	—	—	—	2.9	3.4	—	—	—	3.2	3.5	3.1	3.4	3.3	3.3	3.3	3.2	2.9	3.0
Other occupation	—	—	—	—	—	8.9	11.6	—	—	—	11.8	12.7	12.8	13.3	13.4	14.6	14.5	13.8	14.4	14.0
Unemployed	—	—	—	—	—	3.7	12.9	—	—	—	9.2	9.4	9.0	8.6	8.3	8.3	7.8	6.9	6.3	6.6

DISAGGGREGATED RESPONSES
FRESHMAN MEN

ITEM	1986	1987	1988	1989	1990	1991	1992	1993	1994	1995	1996	1997	1998	1999	2000	2001	2002	2003	2004	2005	2006
Your mother's occupation																					
Accountant or actuary	2.8	2.9	2.8	2.8	2.8	2.7	2.9	2.7	2.9	3.0	3.2	3.2	3.6	3.9	4.1	4.3	4.7	4.7	5.1	5.0	5.2
Actor or entertainer	0.1	0.1	0.1	0.1	0.1	0.1	0.1	0.1	0.1	0.1	0.1	0.1	0.0	0.1	0.1	0.1	0.1	0.1	0.1	0.1	0.1
Architect	0.1	0.1	0.1	0.1	0.1	0.1	0.1	0.1	0.1	0.1	0.1	0.1	0.1	0.1	0.2	0.2	0.2	0.2	0.2	0.2	0.2
Artist	0.7	0.7	0.7	0.6	0.6	0.6	0.7	0.6	0.6	0.6	0.6	0.7	0.7	0.7	0.6	0.7	0.7	0.8	0.7	0.8	0.7
Business (clerical)	10.8	10.7	10.1	10.2	9.8	9.1	8.6	8.4	7.9	7.7	7.2	7.1	7.3	6.7	6.5	6.5	5.9	5.5	4.9	4.9	4.8
Business executive (mgmt, administrator)	4.9	5.3	5.5	5.6	5.5	5.4	5.3	5.3	5.3	5.2	5.0	5.2	5.7	5.6	5.7	6.0	6.0	5.9	5.9	6.1	6.1
Business owner or proprietor	2.9	3.2	3.1	3.4	3.1	3.2	3.2	3.1	3.1	3.1	3.1	3.1	3.2	3.3	3.1	3.2	3.1	3.3	3.4	3.2	3.2
Business salesperson or buyer	3.1	3.2	2.9	3.0	2.7	2.7	2.5	2.3	2.2	2.2	2.2	2.1	2.1	2.1	2.2	2.2	2.2	2.2	2.3	2.3	2.3
Clergy (minister, priest)	0.1	0.1	0.1	0.1	0.1	0.1	0.1	0.1	0.1	0.1	0.1	0.1	0.2	0.1	0.1	0.1	0.1	0.1	0.1	0.1	0.1
Clergy (other religious)	0.1	0.1	0.1	0.1	0.1	0.1	0.1	0.1	0.1	0.1	0.1	0.1	0.2	0.1	0.2	0.1	0.1	0.1	0.2	0.1	0.1
Clinical psychologist	0.2	0.2	0.2	0.2	0.2	0.2	0.2	0.2	0.2	0.2	0.2	0.2	0.2	0.2	0.3	0.2	0.2	0.2	0.1	0.2	0.2
College administrator/staff	—	—	—	—	—	—	—	—	—	—	0.6	0.6	0.6	0.6	0.7	0.6	0.7	0.7	0.7	0.7	0.7
College teacher	0.5	0.5	0.5	0.6	0.6	0.6	0.6	0.6	0.6	0.6	0.6	0.6	0.6	0.6	0.6	0.6	0.6	0.6	0.6	0.5	0.6
Computer programmer or analyst	1.1	1.1	1.4	1.3	1.5	1.3	1.3	1.4	1.3	1.3	1.2	1.2	1.3	1.3	1.3	1.4	1.4	1.4	1.4	1.4	1.5
Conservationist or forester	0.0	0.0	0.0	0.0	0.0	0.0	0.0	0.0	0.0	0.0	0.0	0.0	0.1	0.0	0.0	0.0	0.1	0.1	0.0	0.0	0.1
Dentist (including orthodontist)	0.2	0.2	0.2	0.2	0.2	0.2	0.3	0.3	0.3	0.3	0.4	0.3	0.4	0.4	0.5	0.5	0.5	0.5	0.6	0.6	0.6
Dietitian or home economist	0.4	0.4	0.4	0.4	0.4	0.4	0.4	0.4	0.3	0.3	0.4	0.3	0.3	0.3	0.3	0.3	0.3	0.3	0.4	0.4	0.4
Engineer	0.2	0.2	0.2	0.2	0.2	0.3	0.3	0.3	0.3	0.4	0.4	0.4	0.4	0.5	0.5	0.6	0.6	0.6	0.7	0.7	0.8
Farmer or rancher	0.3	0.3	0.3	0.4	0.4	0.3	0.3	0.4	0.4	0.4	0.3	0.3	0.3	0.3	0.3	0.2	0.3	0.2	0.3	0.2	0.2
Foreign service worker (incl diplomat)	0.1	0.1	0.1	0.1	0.1	0.1	0.1	0.1	0.1	0.1	0.1	0.1	0.1	0.1	0.1	0.1	0.1	0.1	0.1	0.1	0.1
Homemaker (full-time)	20.0	17.8	16.8	15.6	14.3	14.2	13.5	13.0	12.5	11.5	11.3	11.0	10.8	10.7	10.6	10.5	10.1	10.0	9.5	8.8	8.1
Interior decorator (including designer)	0.6	0.6	0.6	0.5	0.5	0.4	0.4	0.4	0.4	0.4	0.4	0.3	0.4	0.4	0.4	0.4	0.4	0.4	0.4	0.4	0.4
Interpreter (translator)	0.0	0.0	0.0	0.0	0.0	0.1	0.1	0.1	0.1	0.1	—	—	—	—	—	—	—	—	—	—	—
Lab technician or hygienist	0.7	0.8	0.7	0.7	0.8	0.9	0.8	0.9	0.8	0.8	0.9	0.9	0.9	0.9	0.9	0.9	0.8	0.9	0.9	0.8	0.7
Law enforcement officer	0.1	0.1	0.1	0.1	0.1	0.1	0.2	0.2	0.2	0.2	0.2	0.1	0.1	0.2	0.2	0.2	0.2	0.3	0.3	0.3	0.3
Lawyer (attorney) or judge	0.3	0.4	0.4	0.4	0.4	0.4	0.4	0.4	0.4	0.4	0.4	0.5	0.5	0.6	0.7	0.7	0.8	0.8	0.9	1.0	1.1
Military service (career)	0.1	0.0	0.1	0.1	0.1	0.1	0.1	0.1	0.1	0.1	0.1	0.1	0.2	0.1	0.1	0.2	0.2	0.2	0.2	0.2	0.2
Musician (performer, composer)	0.2	0.2	0.2	0.2	0.2	0.2	0.1	0.2	0.2	0.2	0.2	0.2	0.2	0.2	0.2	0.2	0.2	0.2	0.2	0.2	0.2
Nurse	7.5	7.6	7.7	7.9	7.9	8.1	8.2	8.4	8.3	8.9	8.7	8.9	8.7	9.0	8.9	8.7	8.9	9.0	9.2	9.0	9.0
Optometrist	0.1	0.1	0.1	0.1	0.1	0.1	0.1	0.1	0.1	0.1	0.1	0.1	0.1	0.1	0.1	0.1	0.1	0.2	0.1	0.2	0.1
Pharmacist	0.2	0.1	0.2	0.2	0.2	0.2	0.2	0.2	0.2	0.2	0.3	0.3	0.4	0.3	0.4	0.4	0.4	0.4	0.5	0.5	0.5
Physician	0.3	0.4	0.4	0.4	0.4	0.4	0.4	0.4	0.5	0.5	0.5	0.6	0.6	0.7	0.5	0.8	0.8	0.9	0.9	0.9	1.0
Policymaker/government	—	—	—	—	—	—	—	—	—	0.4	0.5	0.4	0.5	0.5	0.6	0.5	0.6	0.5	0.5	0.6	0.6
School counselor	0.3	0.4	0.4	0.4	0.4	0.4	0.4	0.5	0.5	0.5	0.5	0.5	0.5	0.5	0.5	0.4	0.4	0.4	0.4	0.4	0.4
School principal or superintendent	0.2	0.2	0.2	0.2	0.2	0.2	0.3	0.2	0.3	0.2	0.3	0.3	0.3	0.3	0.3	0.3	0.3	0.3	0.2	0.3	0.3
Scientific researcher	2.1	2.2	2.1	2.4	2.4	2.3	2.1	2.4	2.1	2.2	2.1	2.0	2.0	1.9	0.3	0.3	0.3	0.4	0.4	0.4	0.4
Social, welfare or recreation worker	1.5	1.6	1.6	1.6	1.7	1.8	1.7	1.8	1.7	1.7	1.6	1.4	1.5	1.5	1.9	1.9	1.8	1.8	1.8	1.9	1.9
Statistician	0.2	0.2	0.2	0.2	0.2	0.2	0.2	0.2	0.2	0.1	0.2	0.2	0.2	0.2	—	—	—	—	—	—	—
Therapist (physical, occupational, speech)	0.5	0.7	0.7	0.7	0.7	0.7	0.7	0.7	0.8	0.8	0.8	1.0	1.0	1.1	1.2	1.2	1.2	1.3	1.4	1.3	1.4
Teacher or administrator (elementary)	7.3	7.8	8.0	8.2	8.6	9.2	9.9	10.2	10.9	10.8	11.4	11.7	11.5	11.6	11.2	10.9	10.6	10.1	9.4	9.3	9.1
Teacher or administrator (secondary)	4.2	4.3	4.6	4.5	4.6	4.9	5.1	5.2	5.4	5.5	5.5	5.5	5.4	5.4	5.1	5.0	5.0	4.7	4.7	4.6	4.7
Veterinarian	0.0	0.0	0.0	0.0	0.0	0.0	0.0	0.0	0.0	0.1	0.0	0.0	0.1	0.1	0.1	0.1	0.1	0.1	0.1	0.1	0.1
Writer or journalist	0.4	0.4	0.4	0.3	0.4	0.3	0.3	0.4	0.3	0.3	0.3	0.4	0.3	0.4	0.4	0.4	0.4	0.4	0.4	0.4	0.5
Skilled trades	2.1	2.2	2.1	2.4	2.4	2.3	2.1	2.4	2.1	2.2	2.1	2.0	2.0	1.9	1.8	2.0	1.9	1.7	1.8	1.6	1.7
Laborer (unskilled)	1.6	1.4	1.5	1.5	1.7	1.7	1.6	1.9	1.7	1.7	1.6	1.4	1.5	1.5	1.4	1.7	1.8	1.7	1.8	1.8	1.5
Semi skilled worker	2.8	2.5	2.5	2.8	2.8	3.0	2.7	2.8	2.7	2.8	2.6	2.5	2.4	2.3	2.2	2.3	2.3	2.2	2.2	2.2	2.1
Other occupation	13.9	14.5	15.4	15.7	17.1	16.4	17.4	17.2	17.3	17.7	17.6	17.6	17.1	17.2	17.4	17.3	17.8	18.5	18.6	19.8	20.1
Unemployed	6.3	6.1	5.9	5.7	5.7	6.1	5.7	5.5	5.5	5.4	5.8	5.4	5.1	4.8	5.2	4.3	4.5	4.9	5.0	5.5	5.5

DISAGGREGATED RESPONSES
FRESHMAN MEN

ITEM	1966	1967	1968	1969	1970	1971	1972	1973	1974	1975	1976	1977	1978	1979	1980	1981	1982	1983	1984	1985
Your religious preference [3]																				
Baptist	—	—	—	10.8	12.2	—	—	12.8	12.8	13.3	11.7	13.2	13.2	—	—	—	—	—	14.8	14.6
Buddhist	—	—	—	—	—	—	—	—	—	—	—	—	—	—	—	—	—	—	0.4	0.5
Congregational (UCC)	—	—	—	3.4	2.3	—	—	1.9	2.1	1.8	1.9	2.2	2.0	—	—	—	—	—	1.6	1.6
Eastern Orthodox	—	—	—	—	0.5	—	—	0.6	0.6	0.5	0.6	0.7	0.6	—	—	—	—	—	0.7	0.7
Episcopal	—	—	—	3.6	3.4	—	—	3.4	3.2	3.2	3.1	3.1	3.3	—	—	—	—	—	—	2.8
Jewish	—	—	—	4.5	5.7	—	—	5.1	4.3	4.5	4.9	4.3	4.7	—	—	—	—	—	3.7	4.0
Latter Day Saints (Mormon)	—	—	—	0.9	0.1	—	—	0.2	0.2	0.2	0.2	0.2	0.2	—	—	—	—	—	0.2	0.3
Lutheran	—	—	—	6.5	6.6	—	—	6.1	6.7	6.0	6.9	5.8	5.6	—	—	—	—	—	6.0	5.9
Methodist	—	—	—	11.3	11.7	—	—	10.9	11.1	10.8	9.2	10.2	10.1	—	—	—	—	—	9.5	8.5
Muslim (Islamic)	—	—	—	0.2	0.2	—	—	0.1	0.2	0.3	0.3	0.3	0.3	—	—	—	—	—	0.3	0.3
Presbyterian	—	—	—	6.5	6.6	—	—	6.5	5.9	6.5	5.6	5.7	6.0	—	—	—	—	—	—	4.9
Quaker (Society of Friends)	—	—	—	0.4	0.3	—	—	0.2	0.2	0.2	0.2	0.2	0.2	—	—	—	—	—	0.2	0.2
Roman Catholic	—	—	—	26.8	28.8	—	—	31.2	31.0	29.7	31.4	33.1	33.6	—	—	—	—	—	36.2	34.3
Seventh Day Adventist	—	—	—	0.3	0.3	—	—	0.4	0.4	0.7	0.7	0.4	0.5	—	—	—	—	—	0.2	0.2
Unitarian Universalist	—	—	—	0.6	0.6	—	—	0.4	0.4	0.4	0.4	0.4	0.4	—	—	—	—	—	0.3	—
Other Christian (Protestant)	—	—	—	5.1	5.5	—	—	4.9	5.4	5.3	6.4	5.7	5.9	—	—	—	—	—	10.4	5.5
Other religion	—	—	—	3.5	2.9	—	—	3.3	3.5	4.1	4.8	4.0	3.8	—	—	—	—	—	5.1	4.8
None	—	—	—	15.7	11.9	—	—	11.9	11.9	12.5	11.7	10.7	9.6	—	—	—	—	—	10.3	11.0
Your father's religious preference [3]																				
Baptist	—	—	—	—	—	—	—	13.4	13.4	13.8	12.0	13.5	13.6	—	—	—	—	—	14.9	14.5
Buddhist	—	—	—	—	—	—	—	—	—	—	—	—	—	—	—	—	—	—	0.4	0.5
Congregational (UCC)	—	—	—	—	—	—	—	2.3	2.4	2.1	2.1	2.4	2.0	—	—	—	—	—	1.7	1.7
Eastern Orthodox	—	—	—	—	—	—	—	0.7	0.7	0.7	0.7	0.8	0.7	—	—	—	—	—	0.8	0.8
Episcopal	—	—	—	—	—	—	—	4.0	3.6	3.7	3.5	3.4	3.5	—	—	—	—	—	—	2.9
Jewish	—	—	—	—	—	—	—	6.1	5.1	5.2	5.6	5.0	5.4	—	—	—	—	—	4.2	4.6
Latter Day Saints (Mormon)	—	—	—	—	—	—	—	0.2	0.2	0.2	0.2	0.2	0.2	—	—	—	—	—	0.2	0.3
Lutheran	—	—	—	—	—	—	—	6.8	7.5	6.8	7.7	6.4	6.1	—	—	—	—	—	6.4	6.4
Methodist	—	—	—	—	—	—	—	12.5	12.4	12.0	10.3	11.4	11.2	—	—	—	—	—	10.4	9.2
Muslim (Islamic)	—	—	—	—	—	—	—	0.1	0.2	0.2	0.3	0.2	0.3	—	—	—	—	—	0.3	0.3
Presbyterian	—	—	—	—	—	—	—	7.9	7.1	7.8	6.8	6.5	6.9	—	—	—	—	—	—	5.5
Quaker (Society of Friends)	—	—	—	—	—	—	—	0.2	0.2	0.2	0.2	0.2	0.2	—	—	—	—	—	0.2	0.2
Roman Catholic	—	—	—	—	—	—	—	32.0	31.6	30.2	32.1	33.6	33.6	—	—	—	—	—	36.0	34.2
Seventh Day Adventist	—	—	—	—	—	—	—	0.3	0.3	0.6	0.7	0.3	0.5	—	—	—	—	—	0.2	0.2
Unitarian Universalist	—	—	—	—	—	—	—	0.4	0.5	0.4	0.4	0.4	0.4	—	—	—	—	—	0.3	0.3
Other Christian (Protestant)	—	—	—	—	—	—	—	5.3	5.6	5.6	6.7	6.1	6.2	—	—	—	—	—	11.5	5.8
Other religion	—	—	—	—	—	—	—	2.0	2.3	2.8	3.5	2.9	2.9	—	—	—	—	—	4.5	4.2
None	—	—	—	—	—	—	—	5.8	6.8	7.7	7.3	6.7	6.4	—	—	—	—	—	7.9	8.6

DISAGGREGATED RESPONSES
FRESHMAN MEN

ITEM	1986	1987	1988	1989	1990	1991	1992	1993	1994	1995	1996	1997	1998	1999	2000	2001	2002	2003	2004	2005	2006
Your religious preference [3]																					
Baptist	—	13.3	13.3	14.7	16.8	16.5	15.7	14.4	13.7	12.0	13.4	13.1	13.1	13.5	11.0	11.5	10.9	10.3	11.2	11.5	10.5
Buddhist	—	0.5	0.6	0.5	0.5	0.5	0.5	0.5	0.9	1.0	0.9	0.9	0.9	1.2	1.1	1.2	1.2	1.3	1.3	1.2	1.2
Congregational (UCC)	—	1.6	1.3	1.2	1.2	2.0	2.1	1.9	1.8	1.7	1.6	1.6	1.7	1.6	1.5	1.3	1.4	1.5	0.8	0.9	0.9
Eastern Orthodox	—	0.6	0.6	0.6	0.6	0.5	0.5	0.7	0.6	0.7	0.7	0.7	0.6	0.6	0.7	0.7	0.6	0.7	0.7	0.7	0.7
Episcopal	—	2.9	2.7	2.7	2.3	2.3	2.3	2.0	1.9	1.9	1.9	1.9	1.9	1.8	1.6	1.6	1.7	1.7	1.6	1.5	1.5
Jewish	—	3.6	3.7	3.2	3.0	2.3	2.7	2.7	2.7	2.7	2.7	2.5	2.4	2.4	3.1	2.8	2.5	2.6	2.7	2.9	2.9
Latter Day Saints (Mormon)	—	0.3	0.3	0.3	0.3	0.4	0.4	0.4	0.4	0.5	0.4	0.4	1.3	1.3	1.3	1.3	0.4	0.6	1.4	0.3	0.3
Lutheran	—	6.6	6.4	6.5	6.2	5.9	6.2	6.5	6.8	7.1	5.7	6.3	5.1	5.5	5.8	5.3	5.0	4.8	5.3	4.0	4.0
Methodist	—	8.5	8.0	8.7	8.2	7.8	7.8	7.9	7.4	6.7	6.9	7.1	7.0	6.7	6.0	5.8	5.6	5.4	5.3	5.5	4.9
Muslim (Islamic)	—	0.3	0.4	0.4	0.6	0.6	0.6	0.7	0.7	0.7	0.8	0.7	0.8	0.9	1.0	1.0	0.8	0.9	0.9	1.0	0.9
Presbyterian	—	4.8	4.8	5.0	4.5	4.4	4.8	4.4	4.5	4.0	4.4	4.2	4.2	4.2	3.8	3.7	3.9	4.1	3.7	3.9	3.4
Quaker (Society of Friends)	—	0.2	0.2	0.3	0.2	0.2	0.3	0.2	0.2	0.3	0.2	0.2	0.2	0.2	0.2	0.2	0.2	0.2	0.2	0.2	0.2
Roman Catholic	—	33.3	32.3	31.1	31.8	31.7	30.1	32.3	29.6	30.8	29.1	29.3	28.4	28.1	29.8	29.6	29.3	29.3	26.8	27.6	27.1
Seventh Day Adventist	—	0.2	0.3	0.4	0.3	0.3	0.3	0.3	0.3	0.3	0.3	0.2	0.3	0.3	0.3	0.2	0.3	0.2	0.2	0.4	0.2
Unitarian Universalist	—	—	—	—	—	—	—	—	—	—	—	—	—	—	—	—	—	0.2	0.3	0.3	—
Other Christian (Protestant)	—	5.4	4.9	5.3	4.5	4.7	4.9	4.7	9.5	10.1	11.5	11.7	12.0	12.3	12.3	12.2	12.8	12.7	14.1	15.1	16.4
Other religion	—	4.7	5.0	4.7	5.0	5.0	5.1	5.2	3.5	3.5	3.7	3.9	3.6	3.4	3.6	3.7	3.7	3.3	3.5	3.5	3.7
None	—	13.0	15.3	14.5	14.0	14.9	15.5	15.2	15.4	16.1	15.8	15.3	16.4	16.1	16.9	18.0	19.8	20.1	20.0	19.7	21.2
Your father's religious preference [3]																					
Baptist	—	13.6	13.6	14.7	16.3	16.0	15.6	14.1	13.6	12.0	12.9	12.8	13.1	13.2	10.8	11.6	11.0	10.4	11.1	11.5	10.8
Buddhist	—	0.6	0.7	0.6	0.7	0.9	0.7	0.8	1.4	1.3	1.4	1.3	1.2	1.6	1.5	1.6	1.4	1.6	1.6	1.7	1.5
Congregational (UCC)	—	1.7	1.4	1.4	1.3	2.0	2.1	1.9	1.7	1.7	1.7	1.5	1.7	1.5	1.4	1.3	1.4	1.5	0.9	0.9	0.9
Eastern Orthodox	—	0.7	0.7	0.7	0.7	0.6	0.7	0.8	0.7	0.8	0.8	0.8	0.8	0.7	0.8	0.8	0.7	0.8	0.8	0.8	0.8
Episcopal	—	3.2	2.9	2.9	2.6	2.6	2.7	2.3	2.2	2.2	2.3	2.1	2.2	2.1	1.9	2.0	2.0	2.1	2.0	1.9	1.9
Jewish	—	4.4	4.5	4.0	3.7	3.0	3.3	3.5	3.4	3.4	3.4	3.2	3.2	3.0	3.9	3.6	3.3	3.4	3.6	3.7	3.8
Latter Day Saints (Mormon)	—	0.3	0.3	0.4	0.3	0.4	0.4	0.5	0.5	0.5	0.5	0.4	1.3	1.4	1.4	1.4	0.4	0.6	1.5	0.3	0.3
Lutheran	—	7.3	7.0	7.3	7.0	6.7	7.1	7.5	7.8	8.3	6.7	7.4	5.8	6.4	6.8	6.2	5.9	5.7	6.2	4.8	4.8
Methodist	—	9.4	8.8	9.5	8.9	8.5	8.8	8.6	8.6	7.8	7.7	8.0	7.8	7.6	6.7	6.5	6.4	6.2	6.1	6.2	5.7
Muslim (Islamic)	—	0.3	0.5	0.5	0.6	0.6	0.7	0.7	0.8	0.8	1.0	0.9	1.0	1.1	1.3	1.3	1.0	1.1	1.2	1.2	1.1
Presbyterian	—	5.5	5.6	5.7	5.2	5.0	5.5	5.0	5.4	4.8	5.1	4.9	5.0	4.9	4.5	4.4	4.6	4.6	4.4	4.6	4.0
Quaker (Society of Friends)	—	0.2	0.2	0.2	0.2	0.2	0.3	0.3	0.3	0.3	0.3	0.2	0.3	0.2	0.3	0.2	0.2	0.3	0.2	0.3	0.2
Roman Catholic	—	33.9	33.1	32.9	33.0	33.4	31.8	34.6	31.4	33.3	31.6	31.8	30.6	30.2	32.4	32.3	32.5	32.3	29.6	30.3	30.3
Seventh Day Adventist	—	0.2	0.2	0.4	0.3	0.3	0.3	0.3	0.3	0.3	0.3	0.2	0.3	0.3	0.3	0.2	0.3	0.2	0.3	0.3	0.2
Unitarian Universalist	—	—	—	—	—	—	—	—	—	—	—	—	—	—	—	—	—	0.3	0.3	0.3	—
Other Christian (Protestant)	—	5.9	5.5	5.7	5.1	5.3	5.5	5.1	8.9	9.7	10.8	11.0	11.4	11.7	11.7	11.4	12.3	12.3	13.5	14.6	16.3
Other religion	—	3.9	4.3	3.9	4.1	4.3	4.1	4.4	2.8	2.9	3.0	3.1	3.0	2.8	2.9	3.0	3.1	3.0	2.9	2.9	3.0
None	—	9.0	10.7	9.3	9.8	10.0	10.3	9.7	10.4	9.8	10.4	10.4	11.5	11.4	11.5	12.0	13.3	13.5	13.9	13.5	14.5

145

DISAGGREGATED RESPONSES
FRESHMAN MEN

ITEM	1966	1967	1968	1969	1970	1971	1972	1973	1974	1975	1976	1977	1978	1979	1980	1981	1982	1983	1984	1985
Your mother's religious preference [3]																				
Baptist	—	—	—	—	13.5	—	—	13.8	13.9	14.5	12.6	14.3	14.1	—	—	—	—	—	15.4	15.0
Buddhist	—	—	—	—	—	—	—	—	—	—	—	—	—	—	—	—	—	—	0.4	0.6
Congregational (UCC)	—	—	—	—	2.9	—	—	2.4	2.5	2.2	2.2	2.5	2.2	—	—	—	—	—	1.9	1.8
Eastern Orthodox	—	—	—	—	0.6	—	—	0.6	0.7	0.7	0.7	0.7	0.7	—	—	—	—	—	0.8	0.8
Episcopal	—	—	—	—	4.3	—	—	4.2	4.0	4.1	3.8	3.8	3.9	—	—	—	—	—	—	3.3
Jewish	—	—	—	—	6.6	—	—	5.9	4.9	5.0	5.4	4.8	5.2	—	—	—	—	—	4.1	4.4
Latter Day Saints (Mormon)	—	—	—	—	0.2	—	—	0.2	0.2	0.2	0.2	0.2	0.2	—	—	—	—	—	0.3	0.3
Lutheran	—	—	—	—	7.3	—	—	6.9	7.6	6.9	7.8	6.4	6.2	—	—	—	—	—	6.6	6.4
Methodist	—	—	—	—	13.6	—	—	12.8	12.8	12.6	10.7	11.6	11.6	—	—	—	—	—	10.8	9.5
Muslim (Islamic)	—	—	—	—	0.1	—	—	0.1	0.2	0.2	0.3	0.2	0.2	—	—	—	—	—	0.3	0.3
Presbyterian	—	—	—	—	8.2	—	—	8.0	7.2	7.9	6.9	6.7	7.0	—	—	—	—	—	—	5.7
Quaker (Society of Friends)	—	—	—	—	0.3	—	—	0.2	0.2	0.2	0.2	0.2	0.2	—	—	—	—	—	0.3	0.2
Roman Catholic	—	—	—	—	30.9	—	—	33.4	33.3	31.7	33.6	34.9	34.7	—	—	—	—	—	37.1	35.9
Seventh Day Adventist	—	—	—	—	0.2	—	—	0.4	0.4	0.7	0.8	0.4	0.5	—	—	—	—	—	0.3	0.3
Unitarian Universalist	—	—	—	—	0.7	—	—	0.5	0.5	0.5	0.5	0.5	0.5	—	—	—	—	—	0.4	—
Other Christian (Protestant)	—	—	—	—	6.0	—	—	5.3	5.7	5.7	6.8	6.2	6.2	—	—	—	—	—	11.8	6.0
Other religion	—	—	—	—	1.8	—	—	2.1	2.4	3.1	3.7	3.2	3.2	—	—	—	—	—	5.0	4.5
None	—	—	—	—	2.8	—	—	3.0	3.4	3.9	3.8	3.5	3.3	—	—	—	—	—	4.7	5.2

DISAGGREGATED RESPONSES
FRESHMAN MEN

ITEM	1986	1987	1988	1989	1990	1991	1992	1993	1994	1995	1996	1997	1998	1999	2000	2001	2002	2003	2004	2005	2006
Your mother's religious preference [3]																					
Baptist	—	14.0	14.0	15.2	16.8	16.7	16.2	14.5	14.1	12.5	13.5	13.4	13.7	13.8	11.3	12.2	11.7	10.9	11.8	12.2	11.3
Buddhist	—	0.6	0.7	0.6	0.8	0.9	0.8	0.9	1.4	1.5	1.5	1.3	1.2	1.6	1.6	1.6	1.5	1.8	1.7	1.8	1.6
Congregational (UCC)	—	1.8	1.5	1.5	1.4	2.2	2.3	2.1	1.9	1.9	1.8	1.6	1.8	1.7	1.5	1.5	1.6	1.7	1.0	1.0	1.1
Eastern Orthodox	—	0.6	0.6	0.6	0.7	0.6	0.6	0.7	0.7	0.7	0.8	0.8	0.7	0.7	0.8	0.8	0.7	0.8	0.8	0.8	0.8
Episcopal	—	3.5	3.2	3.3	2.9	2.8	2.9	2.7	2.5	2.4	2.5	2.4	2.4	2.4	2.1	2.2	2.3	2.2	2.2	2.1	2.0
Jewish	—	4.2	4.3	3.8	3.5	2.8	3.1	3.2	3.2	3.2	3.1	3.0	2.9	2.9	3.7	3.4	3.1	3.2	3.4	3.4	3.5
Latter Day Saints (Mormon)	—	0.3	0.3	0.4	0.4	0.5	0.5	0.5	0.5	0.6	0.5	0.5	1.4	1.4	1.4	1.4	0.5	0.7	1.5	0.4	0.3
Lutheran	—	7.4	7.2	7.2	7.1	6.7	7.2	7.5	7.8	8.3	6.8	7.4	5.9	6.3	6.9	6.3	6.0	5.8	6.3	4.7	4.9
Methodist	—	9.8	9.2	10.0	9.5	9.0	9.3	9.2	9.0	8.1	8.2	8.3	8.5	8.0	7.3	6.9	6.9	6.6	6.6	6.6	6.1
Muslim (Islamic)	—	0.3	0.4	0.4	0.5	0.5	0.6	0.6	0.6	0.6	0.8	0.7	0.8	0.9	1.1	1.1	0.9	0.9	1.0	1.1	0.9
Presbyterian	—	5.8	5.9	6.0	5.4	5.4	5.8	5.2	5.6	5.0	5.4	5.2	5.2	5.2	4.7	4.6	4.9	5.0	4.7	4.8	4.3
Quaker (Society of Friends)	—	0.2	0.2	0.3	0.3	0.2	0.3	0.2	0.3	0.3	0.3	0.2	0.3	0.3	0.3	0.2	0.2	0.3	0.2	0.3	0.2
Roman Catholic	—	35.5	34.9	34.1	34.4	34.8	33.2	35.9	32.8	34.7	33.0	33.1	32.0	31.6	33.9	33.8	34.1	34.1	31.1	32.0	31.8
Seventh Day Adventist	—	0.2	0.3	0.4	0.3	0.4	0.4	0.4	0.4	0.3	0.4	0.3	0.4	0.3	0.3	0.3	0.4	0.3	0.3	0.4	0.3
Unitarian Universalist	—	—	—	—	—	—	—	—	—	—	—	—	—	—	—	—	—	0.3	0.4	0.4	—
Other Christian (Protestant)	—	6.0	5.7	5.9	5.3	5.4	5.7	5.4	9.6	10.6	11.6	12.0	12.4	12.6	12.5	12.6	13.4	13.2	14.7	15.8	17.8
Other religion	—	4.2	4.7	4.2	4.5	4.6	4.3	4.6	2.9	2.8	3.0	3.1	3.1	2.9	2.9	3.1	3.1	3.0	2.9	2.8	3.0
None	—	5.5	6.8	6.1	6.4	6.5	7.0	6.4	6.8	6.5	6.9	6.7	7.5	7.4	7.6	8.1	8.9	9.3	9.5	9.4	10.1

Forty Year Trends
for Freshman Women

NOTES

These notes refer to report items that are followed by numbers or asterisks in [brackets].

[*] Changes in the question text and/or the text of the response options have occurred over the years. The text used in this report reflects the most recent year the question was asked. The text changes were deemed by HERI to have had no significant effect on the results for this item.

[1] Percentages will total more than 100.0 if any respondents marked more than one response.

[2] Disaggregated responses for this item can be found at the end of this report.

[3] See Appendix D for special circumstances affecting this item.

[4] Based on curriculum recommendations of the National Commission on Excellence in Education.

[5] Percentage responding "frequently" only. Results for other items in this group represent the percentage responding "frequently" or "occasionally."

DEMOGRAPHICS
FRESHMAN WOMEN

ITEM	1966	1967	1968	1969	1970	1971	1972	1973	1974	1975	1976	1977	1978	1979	1980	1981	1982	1983	1984	1985
How old will you be on December 31 of this year?																				
16 or younger	—	0.2	0.1	0.1	0.1	0.1	0.2	0.2	0.2	0.1	0.1	0.2	0.2	0.1	0.1	0.1	0.1	0.1	0.1	0.1
17	—	6.4	6.3	5.6	5.2	5.1	5.8	6.3	5.5	5.1	4.9	4.2	4.2	3.6	3.6	3.3	3.1	3.1	3.2	3.2
18	—	83.6	82.5	82.7	82.8	81.7	80.5	81.1	79.6	80.6	80.5	79.2	80.2	78.9	78.6	79.1	79.6	78.9	79.8	78.8
19	—	8.4	8.8	9.4	9.8	11.1	11.5	11.1	12.6	12.6	12.6	13.7	13.6	14.9	15.4	15.4	15.5	16.0	15.0	16.1
20	—	0.6	0.9	0.7	0.8	0.8	1.1	0.6	1.0	0.7	0.8	1.0	0.8	1.1	1.1	1.0	0.8	0.8	0.9	0.8
21 or older	—	0.8	1.6	1.4	1.5	1.2	1.0	0.7	1.2	0.8	1.1	1.7	1.0	1.4	1.3	1.2	1.0	1.2	1.0	0.9
Are you: (mark all that apply) [1,3]																				
White/Caucasian	—	—	—	—	—	90.0	87.1	89.2	87.7	86.8	85.3	83.7	85.7	83.3	82.7	84.8	83.9	84.1	83.8	84.0
African American/Black	—	—	—	—	—	8.5	10.6	8.7	9.7	10.7	11.7	12.4	10.9	12.6	14.0	12.3	12.4	12.4	12.6	11.7
American Indian	—	—	—	—	—	1.0	1.1	1.0	0.9	0.7	1.0	0.7	0.7	0.9	0.7	1.1	1.0	1.2	1.1	1.1
Asian American/Asian	—	—	—	—	—	0.5	0.8	0.8	0.9	1.1	1.1	1.2	1.2	1.2	1.3	1.3	1.6	1.7	1.7	2.4
Mexican American/Chicano	—	—	—	—	—	0.3	0.3	0.5	0.5	0.6	0.6	0.8	0.9	0.9	0.5	0.6	0.8	0.7	0.7	0.9
Puerto Rican American	—	—	—	—	—	0.2	0.8	0.3	0.6	0.6	0.5	1.1	0.8	1.1	1.0	0.6	1.2	0.5	0.6	0.4
Other Latino	—	—	—	—	—	—	—	—	—	—	—	—	—	—	—	—	—	—	—	—
Other	—	—	—	—	—	1.0	1.4	1.0	1.4	1.3	1.3	1.5	1.4	1.7	1.6	1.3	1.5	1.2	1.2	1.2
Is English your native language?																				
Yes	—	—	—	—	—	—	—	—	—	—	—	—	—	—	—	—	—	—	—	—
No	—	—	—	—	—	—	—	—	—	—	—	—	—	—	—	—	—	—	—	—
Are you presently married? [*]																				
No	—	—	—	—	—	98.6	99.2	99.4	99.1	99.2	99.1	99.0	99.3	99.2	99.2	99.2	99.4	99.2	99.4	99.2
Yes	—	—	—	—	—	1.4	0.8	0.6	0.9	0.8	0.9	1.0	0.7	0.8	0.8	0.8	0.6	0.8	0.6	0.8
Citizenship status																				
Yes	—	—	—	99.1	98.9	—	98.6	99.0	—	—	—	—	—	—	—	—	97.5	98.2	98.1	98.1
No	—	—	—	0.9	1.1	—	1.4	1.0	—	—	—	—	—	—	—	—	2.5	1.8	1.9	1.9
U.S. Citizen	—	—	—	—	—	—	—	—	—	—	—	—	—	—	—	—	—	—	—	—
Permanent resident (green card)	—	—	—	—	—	—	—	—	—	—	—	—	—	—	—	—	—	—	—	—
Neither	—	—	—	—	—	—	—	—	—	—	—	—	—	—	—	—	—	—	—	—
Do you have a disability? [3]																				
Hearing	—	—	—	—	—	—	—	—	—	—	—	—	—	—	—	—	—	0.6	0.7	0.7
Speech	—	—	—	—	—	—	—	—	—	—	—	—	—	—	—	—	—	0.1	0.1	0.1
Orthopedic	—	—	—	—	—	—	—	—	—	—	—	—	—	—	—	—	—	0.9	0.9	0.8
Learning disability	—	—	—	—	—	—	—	—	—	—	—	—	—	—	—	—	—	0.4	0.5	0.5
Health related	—	—	—	—	—	—	—	—	—	—	—	—	—	—	—	—	—	0.9	1.0	1.3
Partially sighted or blind	—	—	—	—	—	—	—	—	—	—	—	—	—	—	—	—	—	2.2	1.8	2.1
Other	—	—	—	—	—	—	—	—	—	—	—	—	—	—	—	—	—	1.0	1.0	0.9
Which of the following statements applies to you?																				
I was born in the United States	—	—	—	—	—	—	—	—	—	—	—	—	—	—	—	—	—	—	—	—
I came to the U.S. before age 6	—	—	—	—	—	—	—	—	—	—	—	—	—	—	—	—	—	—	—	—
I came to the U.S. between ages 6–12	—	—	—	—	—	—	—	—	—	—	—	—	—	—	—	—	—	—	—	—
I came to the U.S. after age 12	—	—	—	—	—	—	—	—	—	—	—	—	—	—	—	—	—	—	—	—

152

DEMOGRAPHICS
FRESHMAN WOMEN

ITEM	1986	1987	1988	1989	1990	1991	1992	1993	1994	1995	1996	1997	1998	1999	2000	2001	2002	2003	2004	2005	2006
How old will you be on December 31 of this year?																					
16 or younger	0.1	0.1	0.1	0.1	0.1	0.1	0.1	0.1	0.1	0.1	0.1	0.0	0.1	0.0	0.1	0.0	0.1	0.1	0.1	0.0	0.0
17	3.4	3.1	2.9	2.6	2.6	2.8	2.7	2.6	2.7	2.5	2.4	2.4	2.3	2.1	2.2	2.1	2.1	2.0	1.9	2.0	2.2
18	79.5	79.8	80.1	78.5	77.2	76.2	77.0	76.4	75.6	75.2	74.9	74.5	74.7	73.2	73.3	72.2	71.7	72.3	70.8	73.0	72.4
19	15.3	15.8	15.5	17.2	18.2	18.6	18.3	19.5	20.1	20.8	21.4	21.8	21.7	23.5	23.3	24.6	25.0	24.7	26.1	24.0	24.5
20	0.8	0.6	0.7	0.8	1.0	1.1	0.9	0.7	0.9	0.8	0.5	0.8	0.7	0.7	0.7	0.7	0.7	0.6	0.7	0.6	0.6
21 or older	0.9	0.5	0.7	0.8	1.1	1.4	1.0	0.7	0.9	0.6	0.5	0.6	0.5	0.6	0.4	0.4	0.5	0.4	0.4	0.2	0.2
Are you: (mark all that apply) [1,3]																					
White/Caucasian	83.8	84.3	80.6	82.1	79.5	78.3	80.6	80.7	79.0	78.6	78.3	79.1	78.3	78.1	75.3	73.1	74.7	74.8	76.0	73.4	75.5
African American/Black	11.0	10.8	13.6	12.3	13.5	13.9	11.4	11.3	12.0	12.0	12.1	11.6	12.0	10.8	11.3	11.5	11.1	10.7	10.4	12.4	11.2
American Indian	1.0	1.0	0.9	1.0	1.4	1.7	1.9	2.0	2.3	2.4	2.5	3.2	2.2	2.4	2.0	1.4	1.5	1.4	2.1	1.8	2.3
Asian American/Asian	2.8	2.7	3.0	3.0	3.6	4.1	3.9	4.2	5.0	5.1	5.0	5.6	5.3	6.0	6.9	7.5	7.6	8.1	8.3	8.5	8.3
Mexican American/Chicano	1.2	1.1	1.6	1.5	1.8	2.0	2.3	2.2	2.2	2.2	2.6	2.1	2.5	3.1	4.0	4.5	3.7	4.0	3.7	4.1	3.9
Puerto Rican American	0.7	0.6	0.6	0.6	0.6	0.7	0.6	0.6	0.7	0.8	0.8	0.8	1.0	0.9	1.1	0.9	1.0	0.9	1.1	1.3	1.5
Other Latino	—	—	—	—	—	—	1.0	1.1	1.4	1.5	1.6	1.8	1.7	1.9	2.4	2.4	2.2	2.3	2.6	3.3	3.6
Other	1.5	1.5	1.7	1.5	1.8	2.2	1.8	1.8	2.0	2.2	2.6	2.9	2.8	3.3	3.6	3.4	3.3	3.3	3.4	3.0	3.8
Is English your native language?																					
Yes	—	96.1	96.0	96.1	95.3	94.8	95.0	94.8	94.2	93.6	93.7	94.0	94.1	93.9	91.9	91.7	92.5	92.2	92.4	91.9	92.2
No	—	3.9	4.0	3.9	4.7	5.2	5.0	5.2	5.8	6.4	6.3	6.0	5.9	6.1	8.1	8.3	7.5	7.8	7.6	8.1	7.8
Are you presently married? [*]																					
No	99.3	—	—	—	—	—	—	99.2	—	—	—	—	—	—	99.7	99.7	—	—	—	—	—
Yes	0.7	—	—	—	—	—	—	0.8	—	—	—	—	—	—	0.3	0.3	—	—	—	—	—
Citizenship status																					
Yes	97.8	98.7	98.7	98.1	—	—	—	—	—	—	—	—	—	—	—	—	—	—	—	—	—
No	2.2	1.3	1.3	1.9	—	—	—	—	—	—	—	—	—	—	—	—	—	—	—	—	—
U.S. Citizen	—	—	—	—	97.5	97.1	97.4	97.3	97.0	96.5	96.6	96.8	96.6	96.6	95.8	96.1	96.5	96.7	96.7	96.6	96.7
Permanent resident (green card)	—	—	—	—	1.8	2.0	1.9	2.0	2.3	2.6	2.6	2.4	2.6	2.5	3.1	2.9	2.5	2.3	2.3	2.3	2.1
Neither	—	—	—	—	0.7	0.8	0.6	0.7	0.7	0.9	0.8	0.8	0.8	0.9	1.1	1.0	1.0	1.0	1.1	1.1	1.2
Do you have a disability? [3]																					
Hearing	0.5	0.5	0.7	—	—	—	—	—	—	—	0.6	—	—	—	0.5	—	0.5	—	0.6	—	—
Speech	0.1	0.1	0.2	—	—	—	—	—	—	—	0.2	—	0.2	—	0.1	—	0.1	—	0.2	—	—
Orthopedic	0.6	0.7	0.9	—	—	—	—	—	—	—	0.8	—	0.7	—	0.4	—	0.5	—	0.5	—	—
Learning disability	0.5	0.7	0.8	—	—	—	—	—	—	—	1.8	—	2.0	—	2.0	—	2.1	—	2.5	—	—
Health related	0.7	0.8	1.1	—	—	—	—	—	—	—	1.6	—	1.6	—	1.0	—	1.1	—	1.2	—	—
Partially sighted or blind	1.7	1.8	1.8	—	—	—	—	—	—	—	1.8	—	0.9	—	0.9	—	1.0	—	1.0	—	—
Other	0.6	0.8	1.1	—	—	—	—	—	—	—	1.3	—	—	—	0.9	—	0.9	—	1.0	—	—
Which of the following statements applies to you?																					
I was born in the United States	—	—	—	—	—	—	—	—	94.7	—	—	—	—	—	—	—	—	93.3	—	93.1	—
I came to the U.S. before age 6	—	—	—	—	—	—	—	—	2.6	—	—	—	—	—	—	—	—	3.0	—	3.3	—
I came to the U.S. between ages 6–12	—	—	—	—	—	—	—	—	1.3	—	—	—	—	—	—	—	—	1.9	—	1.9	—
I came to the U.S. after age 12	—	—	—	—	—	—	—	—	1.4	—	—	—	—	—	—	—	—	1.7	—	1.7	—

DEMOGRAPHICS
FRESHMAN WOMEN

ITEM	1966	1967	1968	1969	1970	1971	1972	1973	1974	1975	1976	1977	1978	1979	1980	1981	1982	1983	1984	1985
Your religious preference [2,3]																				
Protestant (Christian)	57.1	52.9	48.8	59.4	54.6	45.1	43.8	52.0	51.9	52.6	50.1	51.5	51.6	37.7	37.3	37.2	36.1	34.2	46.6	48.2
Roman Catholic	28.8	30.0	30.0	30.4	27.6	27.1	26.3	29.5	30.6	29.4	31.8	32.7	33.2	34.1	34.1	34.5	35.7	36.1	36.8	34.6
Jewish	4.6	5.9	5.6	5.6	5.3	3.5	4.6	5.3	3.9	4.4	4.5	3.7	4.1	4.0	3.8	3.5	3.7	3.5	3.2	3.3
Other	4.5	4.9	7.6	2.1	3.0	10.8	11.9	3.5	3.8	4.2	4.8	4.6	4.1	17.1	18.1	18.6	18.3	19.3	6.0	5.8
None	4.8	6.4	8.0	2.3	9.1	13.4	13.4	9.7	9.8	9.3	8.8	7.5	7.0	7.0	6.7	6.2	6.2	6.8	7.3	8.0
Do you consider yourself a born-again Christian?																				
No	—	—	—	—	—	—	—	—	—	—	—	—	—	—	—	—	—	—	—	74.2
Yes	—	—	—	—	—	—	—	—	—	—	—	—	—	—	—	—	—	—	—	25.8
Which of your parents were born in the U.S.?																				
Both	—	—	—	—	—	—	—	—	—	—	—	—	—	—	—	—	—	—	—	—
Father only	—	—	—	—	—	—	—	—	—	—	—	—	—	—	—	—	—	—	—	—
Mother only	—	—	—	—	—	—	—	—	—	—	—	—	—	—	—	—	—	—	—	—
Neither	—	—	—	—	—	—	—	—	—	—	—	—	—	—	—	—	—	—	—	—
What is the best estimate of your parents' total income last year? Consider income from all sources before taxes. [3]																				
Less than $6,000	18.5	—	15.7	13.3	10.9	11.3	12.8	9.7	10.5	9.7	10.1	10.3	7.9	8.0	7.7	6.4	5.5	5.6	5.7	4.6
$6,000 to $9,999	32.1	—	28.8	27.3	21.2	20.1	16.7	12.7	12.5	10.6	9.8	9.7	8.0	7.9	7.1	5.9	5.3	4.9	4.8	4.1
Less than $10,000	—	—	—	—	—	—	—	—	—	—	—	—	—	—	—	—	—	—	—	—
$10,000 to $14,999	25.6	—	27.2	28.4	30.5	31.0	27.5	26.7	26.2	23.2	21.0	19.2	16.4	14.1	13.0	11.2	10.0	10.1	9.4	6.6
$15,000 to $19,999	10.4	—	12.8	14.1	14.7	14.8	15.3	16.8	16.1	16.4	16.1	15.6	14.3	12.4	11.0	9.6	8.4	7.9	7.7	6.5
$20,000 to $24,999	5.5	—	6.6	7.3	9.1	9.4	10.3	12.6	12.6	13.4	13.9	14.3	15.3	15.5	14.5	13.7	12.1	11.5	10.4	7.6
$25,000 to $29,999	2.8	—	3.2	3.6	4.5	4.7	5.4	6.5	6.7	7.8	7.9	8.5	9.9	10.2	10.4	10.7	10.1	9.6	9.2	7.5
$30,000 or more	5.1	—	5.8	6.1	—	—	—	—	—	—	—	—	—	—	—	—	—	—	—	—
$30,000 to $34,999	—	—	—	—	3.3	3.1	3.8	4.9	4.9	5.6	6.4	6.8	8.7	8.7	9.7	10.2	11.6	11.0	10.6	10.6
$30,000 to $39,999	—	—	—	—	—	—	—	—	—	—	—	—	—	—	—	—	—	—	—	—
$35,000 to $39,999	—	—	—	—	1.8	1.7	2.5	3.0	3.1	3.7	4.2	4.5	5.3	6.2	6.8	8.0	8.6	8.9	9.3	9.8
$40,000 or more	—	—	—	—	4.1	4.0	—	—	—	—	—	—	—	—	—	—	—	—	—	—
$40,000 to $49,999	—	—	—	—	—	—	2.3	2.6	2.7	3.6	4.1	4.2	5.3	7.1	8.2	10.0	11.1	11.9	12.6	11.7
$50,000 or more	—	—	—	—	—	—	3.5	4.7	4.6	6.0	6.5	6.9	8.9	—	—	—	—	—	—	—
$50,000 to $59,999	—	—	—	—	—	—	—	—	—	—	—	—	—	—	—	—	—	—	—	10.4
$50,000 to $99,999	—	—	—	—	—	—	—	—	—	—	—	—	—	7.5	8.8	10.8	13.2	14.3	15.4	—
$60,000 to $74,999	—	—	—	—	—	—	—	—	—	—	—	—	—	—	—	—	—	—	—	8.3
$75,000 to $99,999	—	—	—	—	—	—	—	—	—	—	—	—	—	—	—	—	—	—	—	5.1
$100,000 or more	—	—	—	—	—	—	—	—	—	—	—	—	—	2.5	2.8	3.5	4.1	4.3	4.9	—
$100,000 to $149,999	—	—	—	—	—	—	—	—	—	—	—	—	—	—	—	—	—	—	—	3.6
$150,000 or more	—	—	—	—	—	—	—	—	—	—	—	—	—	—	—	—	—	—	—	3.7
$150,000 to $199,999	—	—	—	—	—	—	—	—	—	—	—	—	—	—	—	—	—	—	—	—
$200,000 or more	—	—	—	—	—	—	—	—	—	—	—	—	—	—	—	—	—	—	—	—
$200,000 to $249,999	—	—	—	—	—	—	—	—	—	—	—	—	—	—	—	—	—	—	—	—
$250,000 or more	—	—	—	—	—	—	—	—	—	—	—	—	—	—	—	—	—	—	—	—
MEDIAN INCOME (in thousands of dollars)	9.9	—	11.0	11.7	12.9	13.0	13.7	15.3	15.2	17.0	17.8	18.5	21.1	22.5	23.9	26.5	29.3	30.2	31.3	36.3
Are your parents:																				
Both alive and living with each other?	—	—	—	—	—	—	84.0	—	—	—	—	—	—	—	—	—	—	—	—	—
Both alive, divorced or living apart?	—	—	—	—	—	—	8.5	—	—	—	—	—	—	—	—	—	—	—	—	—
One or both deceased?	—	—	—	—	—	—	7.5	—	—	—	—	—	—	—	—	—	—	—	—	—

DEMOGRAPHICS
FRESHMAN WOMEN

ITEM	1986	1987	1988	1989	1990	1991	1992	1993	1994	1995	1996	1997	1998	1999	2000	2001	2002	2003	2004	2005	2006
Your religious preference [2,3]																					
Protestant (Christian)	31.3	48.2	47.5	49.6	47.7	48.9	49.0	46.2	50.8	49.5	50.1	50.4	50.3	51.3	47.9	46.8	46.3	46.7	48.5	48.4	46.4
Roman Catholic	34.2	33.8	32.1	31.2	32.5	31.7	30.6	32.5	30.6	31.2	30.4	31.0	29.6	28.9	31.0	31.0	30.8	30.1	28.6	28.4	28.1
Jewish	3.5	3.2	3.1	2.8	2.7	2.0	2.2	2.3	2.2	2.3	2.1	2.0	2.0	1.9	2.6	2.4	2.2	2.3	2.3	2.3	2.5
Other	22.2	5.7	6.3	5.9	6.5	6.5	6.6	6.9	4.6	4.8	5.0	5.0	5.1	5.0	5.3	5.7	5.6	5.3	5.1	5.3	5.6
None	8.8	9.2	10.9	10.4	10.7	10.9	11.6	12.0	11.7	12.3	12.4	11.5	13.0	12.8	13.2	14.1	15.1	15.6	15.5	15.6	17.4
Do you consider yourself a born-again Christian?																					
No	—	—	75.2	70.5	70.9	69.4	68.8	71.7	70.6	72.5	70.1	70.3	—	—	—	73.3	—	—	74.9	—	—
Yes	—	—	24.8	29.5	29.1	30.6	31.2	28.3	29.4	27.5	29.9	29.7	—	—	—	26.7	—	—	25.1	—	—
Which of your parents were born in the U.S.?																					
Both	—	—	—	—	—	—	—	—	86.5	—	—	—	—	—	—	—	—	80.6	—	—	—
Father only	—	—	—	—	—	—	—	—	2.6	—	—	—	—	—	—	—	—	3.0	—	—	—
Mother only	—	—	—	—	—	—	—	—	2.5	—	—	—	—	—	—	—	—	3.2	—	—	—
Neither	—	—	—	—	—	—	—	—	8.5	—	—	—	—	—	—	—	—	13.2	—	—	—
What is the best estimate of your parents' total income last year? Consider income from all sources before taxes. [3]																					
Less than $6,000	3.4	3.3	3.3	2.8	3.0	3.2	2.8	2.8	2.8	2.6	2.6	2.2	2.3	2.1	2.2	2.1	—	—	—	—	—
$6,000 to $9,999	3.3	2.8	2.9	2.8	2.6	2.9	2.6	2.6	2.5	2.4	2.1	2.0	1.9	2.0	2.1	1.7	—	—	—	—	—
Less than $10,000	—	—	—	—	—	—	—	—	—	—	—	—	—	—	—	—	3.4	3.6	3.6	4.0	3.8
$10,000 to $14,999	5.7	5.0	5.1	4.7	4.7	5.0	4.4	4.4	4.3	3.9	3.8	3.6	3.6	3.3	3.2	3.2	3.3	3.3	3.2	3.5	3.1
$15,000 to $19,999	5.6	5.5	5.4	5.0	5.1	4.8	4.7	4.4	4.2	3.9	3.8	3.6	3.5	3.4	3.2	3.0	3.1	3.1	2.9	3.0	2.8
$20,000 to $24,999	7.3	7.1	6.7	6.5	6.4	6.2	5.9	5.6	5.5	5.4	5.1	5.0	4.9	4.7	4.5	4.5	4.3	4.1	4.1	4.0	3.7
$25,000 to $29,999	7.1	6.7	6.7	6.4	6.4	6.8	6.2	6.0	5.9	5.6	5.4	5.2	5.1	4.9	4.5	4.4	4.2	4.0	3.9	3.8	3.6
$30,000 or more	—	—	—	—	—	—	—	—	—	—	—	—	—	—	—	—	—	—	—	—	—
$30,000 to $34,999	9.7	9.0	8.7	8.3	8.4	13.1	12.9	12.0	11.4	11.2	10.9	10.7	10.3	9.6	9.1	8.7	7.8	7.4	7.3	7.5	7.0
$35,000 to $39,999	9.7	9.4	8.8	8.7	8.2	—	—	—	—	—	—	—	—	—	—	—	—	—	—	—	—
$40,000 or more	—	—	—	—	—	—	—	—	—	—	—	—	—	—	—	—	—	—	—	—	—
$40,000 to $49,999	12.1	12.3	12.0	12.3	12.0	13.0	13.0	12.6	12.1	11.9	11.2	10.8	10.8	10.5	9.7	9.2	9.2	8.7	8.8	8.4	8.2
$50,000 or more	—	—	—	—	—	—	—	—	—	—	—	—	—	—	—	—	—	—	—	—	—
$50,000 to $59,999	11.1	11.3	11.6	11.9	11.9	11.8	12.2	12.2	11.9	12.1	12.1	12.0	11.9	11.2	10.6	10.1	10.3	10.0	9.9	9.1	9.2
$50,000 to $99,999	—	—	—	—	—	—	—	—	—	—	—	—	—	—	—	—	—	—	—	—	—
$60,000 to $74,999	10.0	11.0	11.5	12.0	12.1	12.5	13.0	13.2	13.7	13.8	14.1	13.7	13.9	14.0	13.7	13.4	13.0	12.8	12.6	12.1	12.1
$75,000 to $99,999	6.2	6.9	7.4	8.1	8.2	8.8	9.4	10.1	10.7	11.1	11.7	12.5	12.7	13.5	13.5	14.2	14.3	14.7	14.4	14.1	14.1
$100,000 or more	—	—	—	—	—	—	—	—	—	—	—	—	—	—	—	—	—	—	—	—	—
$100,000 to $149,999	4.3	4.8	5.1	5.3	5.7	5.8	6.3	7.3	7.8	8.6	9.3	10.0	10.7	11.4	12.9	13.9	14.3	14.7	14.9	15.1	15.6
$150,000 or more	4.5	4.8	4.9	5.3	5.4	—	—	—	—	—	—	—	—	—	—	—	—	—	—	—	—
$150,000 to $199,999	—	—	—	—	—	2.6	2.8	2.9	3.1	3.3	3.5	4.0	3.9	4.4	5.0	5.3	5.6	5.8	6.0	6.4	6.8
$200,000 or more	—	—	—	—	—	3.6	3.7	3.8	4.0	4.3	4.3	4.8	4.5	5.1	5.8	6.2	—	—	—	—	—
$200,000 to $249,999	—	—	—	—	—	—	—	—	—	—	—	—	—	—	—	—	2.6	2.8	2.9	3.1	3.5
$250,000 or more	—	—	—	—	—	—	—	—	—	—	—	—	—	—	—	—	4.7	5.0	5.3	5.8	6.5
MEDIAN INCOME (in thousands of dollars)	39.1	41.0	42.0	44.0	44.3	46.2	48.1	49.7	51.1	52.6	54.2	55.7	56.4	58.5	61.1	63.7	65.4	67.3	68.0	68.9	71.4
Are your parents:																					
Both alive and living with each other?	74.6	74.0	71.9	71.5	71.3	70.7	71.1	71.7	71.4	70.9	70.7	71.7	70.7	71.2	71.0	70.5	70.3	70.6	70.2	69.3	69.3
Both alive, divorced or living apart?	20.3	21.0	23.2	23.7	23.8	24.5	24.5	24.1	24.5	24.9	25.1	24.4	25.3	24.9	25.1	25.6	25.8	25.7	25.9	26.8	26.9
One or both deceased?	5.1	5.0	4.9	4.8	4.8	4.8	4.4	4.2	4.2	4.2	4.1	3.9	4.0	3.9	3.9	3.9	3.9	3.7	3.9	3.9	3.8

DEMOGRAPHICS
FRESHMAN WOMEN

ITEM	1966	1967	1968	1969	1970	1971	1972	1973	1974	1975	1976	1977	1978	1979	1980	1981	1982	1983	1984	1985
WHAT IS THE HIGHEST LEVEL OF FORMAL EDUCATION OBTAINED BY:																				
Your father?																				
Grammar school or less	7.8	7.6	8.2	7.9	7.2	7.0	7.2	5.6	6.4	5.7	6.1	6.5	5.4	5.9	5.7	5.2	4.8	4.7	4.3	4.1
Some high school	12.8	12.1	13.6	13.2	12.4	13.0	11.7	10.3	10.6	10.4	10.6	10.4	9.2	10.4	9.9	9.2	8.5	8.5	8.0	7.6
High school graduate	27.4	26.6	27.3	27.3	26.7	27.5	26.4	23.0	24.6	24.4	24.7	25.5	24.0	24.7	24.9	25.3	24.9	24.8	25.2	23.5
Postsecondary school other than college	—	—	—	—	—	—	—	5.0	4.9	4.5	4.2	4.5	4.4	4.4	4.3	4.3	4.3	4.6	5.3	4.7
Some college	20.4	19.8	19.4	19.3	18.5	17.8	17.3	15.5	14.6	14.3	13.7	13.9	14.1	13.7	13.7	13.7	14.1	14.2	14.3	14.1
College degree	19.3	20.6	19.6	20.1	22.2	21.9	19.8	19.8	20.4	21.2	21.7	20.5	22.0	20.9	20.9	21.2	21.7	21.3	21.6	21.7
Some graduate school	—	—	—	—	—	—	3.2	3.3	2.8	2.8	2.9	2.7	3.0	2.9	2.9	3.0	2.9	2.9	3.0	3.3
Graduate degree	12.2	13.5	11.7	12.0	13.0	12.8	14.5	16.5	15.6	16.7	16.2	15.9	17.8	17.2	17.7	18.1	18.8	18.9	18.3	21.0
Your mother?																				
Grammar school or less	4.8	4.6	4.9	4.7	4.3	4.0	4.4	3.2	3.8	3.3	3.5	4.2	3.3	3.9	3.4	3.1	3.0	2.8	2.8	2.6
Some high school	11.2	10.3	12.1	11.4	10.6	11.1	10.4	8.5	9.3	8.9	9.3	9.7	8.1	9.1	8.4	8.1	7.0	7.0	6.6	6.5
High school graduate	40.1	39.7	40.5	40.8	40.2	41.0	39.5	36.3	36.5	36.7	36.8	37.3	36.6	36.3	36.4	36.1	35.6	35.3	34.7	32.2
Postsecondary school other than college	—	—	—	—	—	—	—	8.7	8.9	8.0	8.2	7.6	7.8	7.4	7.5	7.4	7.5	8.0	8.2	8.0
Some college	22.9	22.9	21.9	21.9	21.9	21.2	20.6	17.4	16.3	16.5	15.9	15.7	16.4	16.1	16.5	16.7	16.9	16.8	16.9	17.6
College degree	17.8	18.7	17.2	17.5	18.7	18.4	17.0	17.3	17.2	17.5	17.9	16.9	18.1	17.7	17.9	18.5	19.2	18.7	19.4	20.0
Some graduate school	—	—	—	—	—	—	3.0	2.9	2.6	2.8	2.5	2.5	2.8	2.7	2.7	2.7	2.7	2.8	2.9	3.4
Graduate degree	3.2	3.6	3.4	3.8	4.1	4.2	5.2	5.6	5.3	6.2	5.9	6.1	7.0	6.9	7.2	7.5	8.2	8.7	8.5	9.8
Your father's occupation [2,3]																				
Artist	—	1.1	0.8	1.0	—	0.9	0.9	—	—	—	1.0	1.0	1.0	0.9	0.9	0.9	1.0	1.0	0.9	0.9
Business	—	34.4	32.2	31.5	—	31.5	32.5	—	—	—	30.9	29.9	30.7	30.1	30.2	29.9	31.0	30.4	30.3	30.4
Clerical	—	1.3	1.0	1.0	—	1.2	1.1	—	—	—	0.8	0.7	0.8	0.7	0.7	0.7	0.6	0.6	0.7	0.6
Clergy	—	1.0	1.0	1.0	—	1.1	1.1	—	—	—	1.3	1.3	1.4	1.3	1.3	1.2	1.1	1.2	1.1	1.1
College teacher	—	1.0	1.0	1.2	—	1.0	1.2	—	—	—	1.2	1.1	1.3	1.2	1.3	1.3	1.3	1.2	1.2	1.4
Doctor (MD or DDS)	—	3.3	2.7	2.7	—	2.5	2.8	—	—	—	3.1	2.8	3.1	2.9	3.0	3.0	3.1	3.0	2.7	2.9
Education (secondary)	—	2.4	2.3	2.5	—	2.6	2.9	—	—	—	3.4	3.1	3.4	3.4	3.5	3.7	3.6	3.7	3.5	3.8
Education (elementary)	—	0.3	0.3	0.3	—	0.4	0.4	—	—	—	0.6	0.6	0.6	0.6	0.5	0.6	0.6	0.7	0.7	0.7
Engineer	—	7.7	7.9	7.8	—	8.2	8.3	—	—	—	9.1	8.8	9.5	8.7	8.5	8.6	8.8	8.5	8.9	9.1
Farmer or forester	—	6.0	5.7	5.6	—	5.4	5.2	—	—	—	4.3	4.0	3.5	3.4	3.9	4.4	3.8	3.4	3.3	3.8
Health professional	—	1.0	1.2	1.2	—	1.3	1.2	—	—	—	1.3	1.3	1.3	1.3	1.3	1.3	1.3	1.2	1.3	1.3
Homemaker	—	—	—	—	—	0.2	0.0	—	—	—	0.0	0.1	0.1	0.1	0.1	0.1	0.0	0.0	0.1	0.1
Lawyer	—	2.0	1.6	1.6	—	1.6	1.9	—	—	—	1.9	1.9	1.8	2.0	2.0	2.1	2.1	2.0	1.9	2.1
Military	—	1.6	1.6	1.5	—	1.8	1.7	—	—	—	1.9	2.0	2.0	1.7	1.9	2.0	1.9	2.0	1.8	1.7
Nurse	—	—	—	—	—	0.1	0.1	—	—	—	0.1	0.1	0.1	0.1	0.1	0.1	0.1	0.1	0.1	0.1
Research scientist	—	0.7	0.7	0.6	—	0.8	0.8	—	—	—	0.8	0.7	0.8	0.7	0.7	0.7	0.6	0.7	0.7	0.8
Social worker	—	—	—	—	—	0.2	0.3	—	—	—	0.3	0.4	0.3	0.3	0.4	0.4	0.3	0.4	0.5	0.4
Skilled worker	—	10.0	10.5	11.3	—	10.1	9.9	—	—	—	8.9	9.2	8.7	8.9	8.9	8.7	8.6	8.4	8.8	7.7
Semi skilled worker	—	5.7	6.7	6.6	—	5.9	5.2	—	—	—	4.6	4.8	3.9	4.4	4.3	3.8	3.9	4.2	3.8	3.8
Laborer	—	2.9	3.8	3.4	—	3.5	3.7	—	—	—	3.2	3.3	2.9	3.4	3.3	3.0	2.8	2.8	2.8	2.8
Unemployed	—	0.7	1.3	1.2	—	1.4	1.8	—	—	—	2.2	2.6	2.3	2.6	2.8	2.3	2.3	3.1	2.7	2.5
Other occupation	—	17.8	18.8	19.0	—	18.4	17.1	—	—	—	19.0	20.5	20.3	21.4	20.6	21.6	21.2	21.5	22.4	21.9

DEMOGRAPHICS
FRESHMAN WOMEN

ITEM	1986	1987	1988	1989	1990	1991	1992	1993	1994	1995	1996	1997	1998	1999	2000	2001	2002	2003	2004	2005	2006
WHAT IS THE HIGHEST LEVEL OF FORMAL EDUCATION OBTAINED BY:																					
Your father?																					
Grammar school or less	3.3	3.1	3.5	3.0	3.5	3.1	2.8	2.5	2.9	3.3	3.2	2.8	2.2	2.8	3.3	3.1	2.7	2.7	2.9	3.2	3.8
Some high school	6.5	6.1	6.1	5.7	6.1	5.9	5.3	5.1	4.7	4.7	4.5	4.4	4.6	4.5	4.7	5.0	4.7	4.5	4.7	5.1	4.9
High school graduate	22.9	22.9	23.8	23.8	24.3	24.0	21.7	23.3	23.0	22.8	22.3	22.4	22.8	22.6	21.9	21.7	22.0	21.8	22.1	22.3	22.0
Postsecondary school other than college	4.7	5.1	4.9	5.2	5.2	5.3	5.2	5.1	5.0	5.0	4.6	4.8	4.3	4.3	4.3	4.1	4.1	4.3	4.2	3.8	4.0
Some college	14.5	14.5	15.1	15.2	15.6	16.0	16.8	15.6	16.2	16.0	16.2	15.9	16.6	16.1	15.8	16.1	16.1	15.8	15.3	15.3	15.1
College degree	22.6	22.9	21.9	22.9	22.2	22.5	24.3	24.2	25.0	25.5	26.0	26.5	26.7	26.3	26.3	26.1	26.8	26.9	26.9	26.6	26.6
Some graduate school	3.3	3.3	3.2	3.1	2.9	3.0	3.2	2.9	2.9	2.7	2.6	2.6	2.5	2.3	2.2	2.2	2.1	2.1	2.1	2.1	2.2
Graduate degree	22.2	22.1	21.5	21.2	20.2	20.1	20.7	21.2	20.5	19.9	20.5	20.6	20.3	21.0	21.5	21.8	21.6	21.7	21.8	21.7	21.3
Your mother?																					
Grammar school or less	2.4	2.3	2.5	2.1	2.7	2.5	2.1	2.0	2.2	2.9	2.9	2.5	1.9	2.6	3.1	2.9	2.4	2.5	2.6	2.7	3.4
Some high school	5.2	4.6	4.8	4.5	4.9	5.0	4.2	3.8	3.6	3.7	3.5	3.3	3.3	3.3	3.6	3.7	3.4	3.3	3.5	3.7	3.5
High school graduate	30.4	30.5	30.2	29.9	30.0	29.0	27.3	28.5	27.1	26.4	25.6	24.9	24.9	24.2	23.3	22.4	21.9	21.5	21.4	21.2	20.8
Postsecondary school other than college	8.0	8.5	8.1	8.4	8.2	8.0	7.9	7.5	7.3	6.8	6.2	6.3	5.7	5.4	5.4	5.0	4.9	4.9	4.9	4.4	4.5
Some college	19.0	18.0	18.6	18.7	18.6	18.9	19.6	18.3	18.9	17.9	18.5	18.5	18.9	18.7	18.4	18.7	18.9	18.6	18.0	17.8	17.5
College degree	21.0	21.5	21.1	21.4	20.9	21.7	23.3	23.5	24.6	25.5	26.2	27.2	27.9	27.8	27.4	28.3	29.4	30.0	30.2	30.5	30.7
Some graduate school	3.5	3.7	3.6	3.6	3.3	3.4	3.6	3.4	3.3	3.3	3.2	3.1	3.1	2.9	2.9	2.8	2.8	2.9	2.7	2.7	2.8
Graduate degree	10.6	11.1	11.1	11.5	11.2	11.5	12.1	13.0	13.0	13.5	14.0	14.1	14.3	15.2	16.0	16.2	16.3	16.3	16.6	17.0	17.0
Your father's occupation [2,3]																					
Artist	0.9	1.0	0.9	0.9	0.8	0.8	0.8	0.8	0.8	0.8	0.8	0.8	0.9	0.9	1.0	1.0	0.9	0.9	1.0	1.0	1.1
Business	32.0	32.2	30.3	30.1	28.6	27.8	28.6	27.9	27.8	27.5	26.9	27.8	27.8	28.2	28.2	28.2	27.8	28.5	28.1	27.7	27.7
Clerical	0.6	0.6	0.5	0.6	0.6	0.6	0.6	0.6	0.6	0.6	0.6	0.7	0.8	0.9	0.9	0.9	1.0	1.0	1.0	1.0	1.1
Clergy	1.2	1.1	1.0	1.2	1.2	1.2	1.2	1.1	1.1	1.0	1.2	1.1	1.2	1.1	1.0	1.0	1.0	0.9	0.9	1.0	1.1
College teacher	1.3	1.3	1.2	1.2	1.0	1.0	1.0	0.9	0.8	0.8	0.8	0.7	0.7	0.7	0.7	0.7	0.7	0.7	0.7	0.7	0.9
Doctor (MD or DDS)	3.1	3.1	3.0	2.9	2.7	2.6	2.5	2.7	2.6	2.6	2.5	2.8	2.5	2.7	2.7	2.7	2.8	2.7	2.7	2.7	2.7
Education (secondary)	4.0	4.0	4.0	4.1	3.9	3.8	3.9	4.0	3.8	3.6	3.7	3.4	3.2	3.1	2.9	2.8	2.6	2.6	2.5	2.3	2.2
Education (elementary)	0.7	0.8	0.8	0.9	0.8	1.0	1.0	1.1	1.0	1.1	1.0	1.0	1.0	0.9	0.9	0.8	0.8	0.7	0.8	0.7	0.6
Engineer	9.0	8.4	8.1	8.0	7.8	7.8	7.8	8.0	7.6	7.7	7.8	7.6	7.9	7.9	8.2	8.2	8.2	8.4	8.5	8.3	8.4
Farmer or forester	2.7	2.7	2.5	2.8	3.0	3.2	2.6	2.9	3.3	3.4	2.9	3.1	2.7	2.8	2.4	2.1	2.1	1.8	1.9	1.5	1.5
Health professional	1.3	1.3	1.3	1.2	1.1	1.2	1.3	1.2	1.2	1.2	1.3	1.4	1.3	1.3	1.4	1.3	1.4	1.4	1.4	1.3	1.4
Homemaker	0.1	0.1	0.1	0.1	0.2	0.2	0.1	0.1	0.1	0.1	0.1	0.1	0.1	0.1	0.1	0.1	0.2	0.2	0.2	0.2	0.2
Lawyer	2.3	2.3	2.3	2.1	2.0	1.9	2.0	2.1	2.1	2.1	2.0	2.2	2.1	2.0	2.2	2.2	2.2	2.3	2.2	2.2	2.3
Military	1.9	1.9	1.9	2.0	1.9	2.2	2.2	1.9	1.7	1.7	1.7	1.5	1.5	1.6	1.5	1.6	1.6	1.5	1.6	1.6	1.5
Nurse	0.1	0.1	0.1	0.1	0.2	0.2	0.2	0.2	0.3	0.3	0.3	0.4	0.4	0.4	0.4	0.4	0.5	0.5	0.5	0.5	0.5
Research scientist	0.7	0.7	0.7	0.6	0.6	0.6	0.6	0.6	0.6	0.5	0.6	0.5	0.5	0.6	0.5	0.6	0.6	0.7	0.7	0.6	0.6
Social worker	0.4	0.5	0.5	0.4	0.5	0.5	0.5	0.5	0.5	0.6	0.6	0.6	0.6	0.5	0.6	0.6	0.6	0.6	0.5	0.5	0.5
Skilled worker	7.9	8.0	8.5	8.4	8.5	8.4	8.1	8.7	8.4	8.1	8.2	8.0	7.9	7.5	7.1	7.8	7.9	7.4	7.6	7.1	7.2
Semi skilled worker	3.3	3.1	3.4	3.5	3.6	3.8	3.5	3.4	3.4	3.4	3.3	3.2	3.2	2.9	2.9	3.0	3.0	2.9	2.8	2.9	2.7
Laborer	2.3	2.2	2.7	2.5	3.0	3.1	2.8	3.1	2.8	2.6	2.8	2.6	2.8	2.6	3.4	3.4	3.3	3.2	3.2	3.5	3.1
Unemployed	2.5	2.2	2.4	2.4	2.5	3.2	3.3	3.2	3.1	3.1	3.2	2.7	2.7	2.5	2.4	2.4	2.8	3.0	2.8	3.1	3.0
Other occupation	21.8	22.6	23.6	24.1	25.5	25.0	25.5	25.0	26.2	27.1	27.8	27.7	28.5	28.9	29.0	28.0	28.1	28.3	28.4	29.5	30.1

157

DEMOGRAPHICS
FRESHMAN WOMEN

ITEM	1966	1967	1968	1969	1970	1971	1972	1973	1974	1975	1976	1977	1978	1979	1980	1981	1982	1983	1984	1985
Your mother's occupation [2,3]																				
Artist	—	—	—	—	—	1.1	1.2	—	—	—	1.5	1.5	1.5	1.5	1.4	1.6	1.7	1.7	1.6	1.8
Business	—	—	—	—	—	4.5	5.4	—	—	—	6.3	6.8	7.6	8.0	8.9	9.7	10.3	11.0	11.6	13.1
Clerical	—	—	—	—	—	9.9	11.4	—	—	—	10.6	10.5	10.6	11.1	11.4	11.5	11.6	11.2	11.9	10.9
Clergy	—	—	—	—	—	0.1	0.1	—	—	—	0.1	0.1	0.1	0.1	0.1	0.1	0.1	0.1	0.1	0.1
College teacher	—	—	—	—	—	0.4	0.4	—	—	—	0.4	0.4	0.4	0.4	0.4	0.4	0.5	0.4	0.4	0.5
Doctor (MD or DDS)	—	—	—	—	—	0.1	0.1	—	—	—	0.2	0.2	0.2	0.2	0.2	0.3	0.3	0.3	0.3	0.4
Education (secondary)	—	—	—	—	—	2.7	3.0	—	—	—	3.1	2.9	3.1	3.0	3.1	3.6	3.6	3.4	3.5	4.0
Education (elementary)	—	—	—	—	—	5.2	5.8	—	—	—	6.4	6.2	6.6	6.5	6.2	6.4	6.8	6.2	6.2	6.7
Engineer	—	—	—	—	—	0.1	0.0	—	—	—	0.1	0.1	0.1	0.1	0.1	0.1	0.1	0.1	0.1	0.2
Farmer or forester	—	—	—	—	—	0.1	0.2	—	—	—	0.2	0.2	0.2	0.2	0.3	0.2	0.2	0.2	0.3	0.3
Health professional	—	—	—	—	—	1.2	1.3	—	—	—	1.6	1.6	1.6	1.7	1.8	1.8	1.9	2.1	2.0	2.0
Homemaker	—	—	—	—	—	51.3	36.9	—	—	—	34.6	32.4	31.8	28.6	27.5	23.4	22.3	24.4	23.3	22.1
Lawyer	—	—	—	—	—	0.1	0.0	—	—	—	0.1	0.1	0.1	0.1	0.1	0.1	0.2	0.2	0.0	0.3
Military	—	—	—	—	—	0.0	0.0	—	—	—	0.0	0.0	0.0	0.0	0.0	0.0	0.0	0.0	0.0	0.0
Nurse	—	—	—	—	—	4.7	5.0	—	—	—	6.5	6.7	6.6	6.8	7.0	7.4	7.5	7.3	7.5	7.3
Research scientist	—	—	—	—	—	0.1	0.1	—	—	—	0.1	0.1	0.1	0.1	0.1	0.1	0.1	0.2	0.1	0.2
Social worker	—	—	—	—	—	0.7	0.8	—	—	—	1.1	1.1	1.1	1.3	1.2	1.2	1.3	1.2	1.3	1.2
Skilled worker	—	—	—	—	—	1.3	1.7	—	—	—	1.4	1.5	1.6	1.5	1.6	1.6	1.8	1.6	1.6	1.6
Semi skilled worker	—	—	—	—	—	2.3	2.6	—	—	—	2.5	2.7	2.3	2.5	2.7	2.8	2.5	2.7	2.5	2.3
Laborer	—	—	—	—	—	1.4	1.8	—	—	—	1.8	2.0	1.7	2.0	2.0	1.9	1.8	1.7	1.8	1.7
Unemployed	—	—	—	—	—	2.4	9.3	—	—	—	7.6	8.1	7.3	8.0	7.9	7.8	7.3	6.5	6.0	6.1
Other occupation	—	—	—	—	—	10.5	13.2	—	—	—	13.7	15.0	15.5	16.2	16.1	17.9	18.2	17.4	17.5	17.2
Your father's religious preference [2,3]																				
Protestant (Christian)	—	—	—	—	—	—	—	54.9	54.4	54.6	51.7	52.4	52.4	39.1	38.6	38.3	37.2	35.2	46.8	48.1
Roman Catholic	—	—	—	—	—	—	—	29.7	30.7	29.1	31.4	32.3	32.3	33.1	33.0	33.1	34.3	34.7	35.7	33.7
Jewish	—	—	—	—	—	—	—	6.3	4.7	5.0	5.1	4.3	4.6	4.5	4.2	3.9	4.2	4.1	3.8	3.9
Other	—	—	—	—	—	—	—	2.1	2.4	2.9	3.4	3.4	3.2	16.1	16.9	17.6	17.4	18.3	5.3	5.2
None	—	—	—	—	—	—	—	7.1	8.0	8.3	8.4	7.6	7.5	7.2	7.3	7.1	7.0	7.7	8.4	9.1
Your mother's religious preference [2,3]																				
Protestant (Christian)	—	—	—	—	60.3	—	—	57.4	57.3	57.8	54.5	55.3	55.1	40.3	39.6	39.4	38.2	36.3	49.2	51.0
Roman Catholic	—	—	—	—	28.2	—	—	31.2	32.0	30.6	33.1	33.6	33.8	34.6	34.5	34.7	35.8	36.3	37.2	35.0
Jewish	—	—	—	—	6.1	—	—	6.0	4.5	4.8	4.9	4.1	4.4	4.3	4.0	3.8	4.0	3.9	3.5	3.6
Other	—	—	—	—	2.1	—	—	2.2	2.7	3.1	3.8	3.7	3.5	17.1	18.2	18.5	18.4	19.6	5.9	5.7
None	—	—	—	—	3.3	—	—	3.2	3.6	3.7	3.7	3.3	3.2	3.6	3.6	3.7	3.6	3.9	4.2	4.6
How many persons are currently dependent on your parents?																				
One	—	—	—	—	—	—	—	—	—	—	—	—	3.4	4.2	4.0	3.9	4.4	4.9	4.9	5.5
Two	—	—	—	—	—	—	—	—	—	—	—	—	7.1	8.3	8.3	8.9	9.7	10.8	11.5	12.0
Three	—	—	—	—	—	—	—	—	—	—	—	—	18.6	19.2	19.9	20.2	20.5	22.9	23.2	21.1
Four	—	—	—	—	—	—	—	—	—	—	—	—	26.7	26.1	26.8	27.4	28.1	30.0	30.6	29.6
Five	—	—	—	—	—	—	—	—	—	—	—	—	23.4	22.5	22.6	22.5	21.5	19.3	18.9	19.1
Six or more	—	—	—	—	—	—	—	—	—	—	—	—	20.7	19.7	18.3	17.1	15.7	12.1	11.0	12.7

DEMOGRAPHICS
FRESHMAN WOMEN

ITEM	1986	1987	1988	1989	1990	1991	1992	1993	1994	1995	1996	1997	1998	1999	2000	2001	2002	2003	2004	2005	2006
Your mother's occupation [2,3]																					
Artist	1.8	1.9	1.8	1.7	1.6	1.5	1.6	1.4	1.5	1.6	1.4	1.5	1.5	1.5	1.6	1.6	1.6	1.7	1.7	1.7	1.8
Business	14.1	14.7	14.5	14.6	14.1	13.8	13.7	13.6	13.7	13.6	13.2	14.1	14.3	15.0	14.8	15.8	15.8	16.1	16.3	16.6	16.7
Clerical	11.4	11.6	11.1	11.0	10.4	10.0	9.6	9.1	8.9	8.4	8.1	7.9	8.0	7.6	7.5	7.1	6.5	6.1	5.6	5.2	5.1
Clergy	0.2	0.1	0.2	0.2	0.2	0.2	0.2	0.2	0.2	0.2	0.2	0.2	0.2	0.2	0.2	0.2	0.3	0.3	0.2	0.3	0.3
College teacher	0.5	0.5	0.5	0.5	0.5	0.5	0.6	0.5	0.6	0.5	0.5	0.5	0.5	0.5	0.5	0.5	0.5	0.5	0.5	0.5	0.5
Doctor (MD or DDS)	0.4	0.4	0.4	0.4	0.4	0.4	0.4	0.5	0.6	0.5	0.6	0.6	0.7	0.9	0.9	1.0	1.0	1.1	1.2	1.1	1.2
Education (secondary)	4.2	4.4	4.4	4.4	4.3	4.6	4.9	5.0	5.2	5.3	5.5	5.2	5.1	5.1	5.0	4.9	4.9	4.7	4.8	4.5	4.4
Education (elementary)	6.9	7.3	7.5	7.6	7.5	8.2	8.9	9.2	9.5	9.7	10.2	10.4	10.3	10.0	9.6	9.5	9.4	9.0	8.4	8.3	8.0
Engineer	0.2	0.2	0.2	0.2	0.2	0.2	0.2	0.3	0.2	0.3	0.3	0.3	0.4	0.4	0.4	0.5	0.5	0.6	0.6	0.7	0.8
Farmer or forester	0.2	0.2	0.3	0.3	0.3	0.3	0.3	0.3	0.4	0.4	0.4	0.4	0.3	0.4	0.3	0.2	0.3	0.3	0.3	0.2	0.2
Health professional	2.0	2.1	2.0	2.1	2.2	2.1	2.1	2.2	2.3	2.4	2.5	2.6	2.7	2.8	2.9	2.9	3.0	3.1	3.2	3.0	3.2
Homemaker	20.1	18.0	17.1	16.3	15.3	15.1	14.4	13.8	13.3	12.3	12.0	11.2	11.3	11.3	11.5	11.3	10.9	10.7	10.7	10.0	9.5
Lawyer	0.3	0.3	0.3	0.3	0.3	0.3	0.3	0.3	0.3	0.3	0.4	0.4	0.4	0.5	0.6	0.6	0.7	0.6	0.7	0.8	0.9
Military	0.0	0.0	0.1	0.1	0.1	0.1	0.1	0.1	0.1	0.1	0.1	0.1	0.1	0.1	0.2	0.2	0.2	0.2	0.2	0.2	0.2
Nurse	7.4	7.4	7.5	7.7	7.6	7.7	7.8	8.0	8.1	8.4	8.4	8.7	8.6	8.5	8.4	8.5	8.7	8.7	8.8	8.6	8.7
Research scientist	0.2	0.1	0.2	0.2	0.1	0.2	0.2	0.2	0.2	0.2	0.2	0.2	0.2	0.2	0.2	0.3	0.3	0.3	0.3	0.4	0.3
Social worker	1.4	1.4	1.5	1.5	1.5	1.6	1.6	1.7	1.6	1.7	1.7	1.7	1.8	1.7	1.9	1.9	1.8	1.8	1.6	1.8	1.8
Skilled worker	1.7	1.8	1.8	1.7	1.8	1.8	1.8	1.8	1.7	1.6	1.5	1.4	1.5	1.5	1.4	1.6	1.5	1.5	1.4	1.4	1.4
Semi skilled worker	2.0	2.0	2.1	2.2	2.3	2.2	2.1	2.1	2.1	2.0	2.0	1.9	1.8	1.8	1.7	2.0	2.0	1.8	1.8	1.9	1.7
Laborer	1.4	1.4	1.7	1.6	1.8	1.9	1.7	2.2	1.8	1.6	1.5	1.5	1.4	1.5	1.5	1.9	1.7	1.8	1.7	1.7	1.8
Unemployed	5.4	5.3	5.1	4.7	4.8	5.2	5.1	5.0	5.1	4.9	5.2	4.7	4.6	4.4	4.7	4.2	4.4	4.9	4.9	5.3	5.3
Other occupation	18.3	18.7	19.9	20.6	22.5	22.0	22.5	22.4	22.9	23.8	24.1	24.2	24.2	24.3	24.3	23.3	24.0	24.5	25.1	25.7	26.4
Your father's religious preference [2,3]																					
Protestant (Christian)	32.3	48.9	48.1	50.3	47.7	49.3	49.2	46.9	50.2	49.4	49.1	49.7	49.2	50.0	46.4	46.1	45.1	45.3	46.8	46.6	45.6
Roman Catholic	33.3	33.0	31.5	31.8	33.3	32.6	31.6	33.8	31.7	32.8	32.3	32.2	30.9	30.0	32.6	32.4	32.7	32.0	30.4	30.5	30.4
Jewish	4.1	3.8	3.7	3.5	3.3	2.6	2.8	3.0	2.8	2.9	2.8	2.6	2.5	2.5	3.2	3.1	2.9	2.9	3.0	3.0	3.2
Other	21.4	4.9	5.5	5.0	5.7	5.6	5.8	6.1	4.6	4.8	5.1	4.9	5.1	5.1	5.5	5.7	5.7	5.5	5.4	5.7	5.5
None	8.9	9.3	11.2	9.4	9.9	10.0	10.7	10.3	10.8	10.2	10.8	10.6	12.3	12.3	12.2	12.7	13.6	14.3	14.4	14.2	15.3
Your mother's religious preference [2,3]																					
Protestant (Christian)	33.7	51.8	51.2	53.0	50.5	51.7	52.0	49.5	53.3	52.5	52.4	52.8	53.2	53.7	50.1	50.6	48.7	49.1	50.9	51.0	49.9
Roman Catholic	34.8	34.3	33.2	32.9	34.4	33.9	32.8	35.3	33.2	34.1	33.6	33.8	32.2	31.7	34.1	34.2	34.3	33.7	32.1	31.9	32.2
Jewish	3.8	3.6	3.5	3.2	3.1	2.3	2.5	2.7	2.5	2.7	2.5	2.3	2.3	2.3	2.9	2.8	2.7	2.7	2.7	2.7	2.9
Other	22.5	5.6	6.2	5.6	6.4	6.2	6.5	6.6	4.8	4.9	5.2	4.9	5.1	5.2	5.4	4.8	5.8	5.6	5.2	5.5	5.4
None	5.2	4.8	5.9	5.3	5.6	5.8	6.2	5.9	6.1	5.9	6.3	6.2	7.2	7.2	7.2	7.6	8.5	8.9	9.0	8.9	9.6
How many persons are currently dependent on your parents?																					
One	5.7	7.0	—	—	—	—	—	—	—	—	7.6	7.6	—	—	—	—	—	—	—	—	7.3
Two	13.6	16.4	—	—	—	—	—	—	—	—	16.3	16.1	—	—	—	—	—	—	—	—	16.2
Three	21.9	22.5	—	—	—	—	—	—	—	—	21.3	21.9	—	—	—	—	—	—	—	—	22.5
Four	29.9	29.0	—	—	—	—	—	—	—	—	29.2	29.6	—	—	—	—	—	—	—	—	30.7
Five	17.9	16.2	—	—	—	—	—	—	—	—	16.5	16.2	—	—	—	—	—	—	—	—	15.4
Six or more	11.0	8.9	—	—	—	—	—	—	—	—	9.0	8.5	—	—	—	—	—	—	—	—	7.7

159

HIGH SCHOOL EXPERIENCES
FRESHMAN WOMEN

ITEM	1966	1967	1968	1969	1970	1971	1972	1973	1974	1975	1976	1977	1978	1979	1980	1981	1982	1983	1984	1985
From what kind of secondary school did you graduate? [*]																				
Public	81.6	—	—	82.6	82.7	—	83.9	—	—	—	—	—	—	83.8	84.0	—	82.7	82.7	82.3	—
Private, denominational	14.9	—	—	13.8	14.3	—	11.9	—	—	—	—	—	—	12.4	12.1	—	12.4	12.4	12.9	—
Private, nondenominational	3.5	—	—	3.7	3.0	—	4.3	—	—	—	—	—	—	3.7	3.9	—	4.9	4.9	4.8	—
In what year did you graduate from high school?																				
This year	—	—	—	—	—	—	—	97.4	96.2	96.8	96.7	95.9	96.8	96.1	96.2	96.8	97.3	96.8	96.9	97.0
One year ago	—	—	—	—	—	—	—	1.4	2.1	1.9	1.7	1.8	1.7	2.1	1.9	1.5	1.5	1.7	1.7	1.6
Two years ago	—	—	—	—	—	—	—	0.3	0.4	0.4	0.4	0.5	0.4	0.5	0.4	0.4	0.3	0.3	0.4	0.4
Three or more years ago	—	—	—	—	—	—	—	0.4	0.8	0.6	0.7	1.0	0.6	0.7	0.8	0.7	0.6	0.7	0.7	0.6
Did not graduate but passed G.E.D. test	—	—	—	—	—	—	—	0.2	0.2	0.2	0.3	0.5	0.3	0.4	0.5	0.4	0.3	0.3	0.3	0.3
Never completed high school	—	—	—	—	—	—	—	0.3	0.3	0.2	0.2	0.4	0.3	0.3	0.2	0.2	0.1	0.1	0.1	0.1
HOW WOULD YOU DESCRIBE THE RACIAL COMPOSITION OF THE: High school you last attended																				
Completely non-White	—	—	—	—	—	—	—	—	—	—	—	—	—	—	—	—	—	1.3	—	—
Mostly non-White	—	—	—	—	—	—	—	—	—	—	—	—	—	—	—	—	—	5.0	—	—
Roughly half non-White	—	—	—	—	—	—	—	—	—	—	—	—	—	—	—	—	—	16.8	—	—
Mostly White	—	—	—	—	—	—	—	—	—	—	—	—	—	—	—	—	—	59.5	—	—
Completely White	—	—	—	—	—	—	—	—	—	—	—	—	—	—	—	—	—	17.5	—	—
Neighborhood where you grew up																				
Completely non-White	—	—	—	—	—	—	—	—	—	—	—	—	—	—	—	—	—	4.2	—	—
Mostly non-White	—	—	—	—	—	—	—	—	—	—	—	—	—	—	—	—	—	6.2	—	—
Roughly half non-White	—	—	—	—	—	—	—	—	—	—	—	—	—	—	—	—	—	5.4	—	—
Mostly White	—	—	—	—	—	—	—	—	—	—	—	—	—	—	—	—	—	38.0	—	—
Completely White	—	—	—	—	—	—	—	—	—	—	—	—	—	—	—	—	—	46.1	—	—
Did your high school require community service for graduation?																				
No	—	—	—	—	—	—	—	—	—	—	—	—	—	—	—	—	—	—	—	—
Yes	—	—	—	—	—	—	—	—	—	—	—	—	—	—	—	—	—	—	—	—
Did you meet or exceed recommended years of high school (grades 9–12) study in the following subjects [4]																				
English (4 years)	—	—	—	—	—	—	—	—	—	—	—	—	—	—	—	—	—	—	94.8	94.9
Mathematics (3 years)	—	—	—	—	—	—	—	—	—	—	—	—	—	—	—	—	—	—	87.8	88.7
Foreign language (2 years)	—	—	—	—	—	—	—	—	—	—	—	—	—	—	—	—	—	—	75.2	75.6
Physical science (2 years)	—	—	—	—	—	—	—	—	—	—	—	—	—	—	—	—	—	—	50.5	52.9
Biological science (2 years)	—	—	—	—	—	—	—	—	—	—	—	—	—	—	—	—	—	—	37.9	39.6
History/American govt. (1 year)	—	—	—	—	—	—	—	—	—	—	—	—	—	—	—	—	—	—	98.9	99.3
Computer science (1/2 year)	—	—	—	—	—	—	—	—	—	—	—	—	—	—	—	—	—	—	50.1	57.0
Arts and/or music (1 year)	—	—	—	—	—	—	—	—	—	—	—	—	—	—	—	—	—	—	67.2	67.9
Have you had any special tutoring or remedial work in:																				
English	—	—	—	—	—	—	—	—	—	—	—	—	—	4.9	4.8	3.9	4.0	—	4.1	—
Reading	—	—	—	—	—	—	—	—	—	—	—	—	—	5.1	5.1	3.8	4.0	—	4.0	—
Mathematics	—	—	—	—	—	—	—	—	—	—	—	—	—	7.2	7.4	6.6	7.6	—	8.7	—
Social studies	—	—	—	—	—	—	—	—	—	—	—	—	—	4.3	4.9	2.9	3.2	—	3.0	—
Science	—	—	—	—	—	—	—	—	—	—	—	—	—	3.9	4.5	3.0	3.4	—	3.6	—
Foreign language	—	—	—	—	—	—	—	—	—	—	—	—	—	3.5	3.4	2.6	3.1	—	3.3	—

HIGH SCHOOL EXPERIENCES
FRESHMAN WOMEN

ITEM	1986	1987	1988	1989	1990	1991	1992	1993	1994	1995	1996	1997	1998	1999	2000	2001	2002	2003	2004	2005	2006
From what kind of secondary school did you graduate? [*]																					
Public	—	—	—	—	—	83.9	—	84.3	—	—	—	—	84.2	—	—	83.7	—	—	—	—	—
Private, denominational	—	—	—	—	—	11.5	—	11.1	—	—	—	—	12.3	—	—	12.5	—	—	—	—	—
Private, nondenominational	—	—	—	—	—	4.6	—	4.6	—	—	—	—	3.5	—	—	3.8	—	—	—	—	—
In what year did you graduate from high school?																					
this year	97.1	97.9	97.7	97.5	97.2	96.7	97.5	97.9	97.9	97.9	98.2	98.3	98.2	98.2	98.5	98.4	98.4	98.7	98.4	98.7	98.6
one year ago	1.5	1.2	1.3	1.4	1.5	1.5	1.2	1.2	1.1	1.2	1.1	1.0	1.1	1.1	0.9	1.0	1.0	0.8	1.0	0.8	0.9
two years ago	0.4	0.3	0.3	0.3	0.3	0.4	0.3	0.2	0.3	0.3	0.2	0.2	0.2	0.2	0.2	0.2	0.2	0.1	0.2	0.1	0.2
three or more years ago	0.6	0.4	0.5	0.5	0.6	0.9	0.7	0.5	0.5	0.4	0.3	0.3	0.3	0.3	0.3	0.2	0.3	0.2	0.3	0.2	0.2
did not graduate but passed G.E.D. test	0.3	0.2	0.2	0.2	0.3	0.4	0.3	0.2	0.2	0.2	0.1	0.2	0.2	0.2	0.2	0.1	0.1	0.1	0.2	0.1	0.1
never completed high school	0.1	0.1	0.0	0.0	0.1	0.1	0.1	0.1	0.1	0.1	0.1	0.1	0.0	0.0	0.1	0.0	0.0	0.1	0.0	0.0	0.0
HOW WOULD YOU DESCRIBE THE RACIAL COMPOSITION OF THE:																					
High school you last attended																					
Completely non-White	—	—	1.9	—	2.1	—	—	—	—	—	—	—	—	—	—	—	—	—	—	—	2.6
Mostly non-White	—	—	6.6	—	7.2	—	—	—	—	—	—	—	—	—	—	—	—	—	—	—	11.2
Roughly half non-White	—	—	18.4	—	18.1	—	—	—	—	—	—	—	—	—	—	—	—	—	—	—	23.9
Mostly White	—	—	57.7	—	58.8	—	—	—	—	—	—	—	—	—	—	—	—	—	—	—	53.3
Completely White	—	—	15.4	—	13.7	—	—	—	—	—	—	—	—	—	—	—	—	—	—	—	9.0
Neighborhood where you grew up																					
Completely non-White	—	—	4.6	—	5.0	—	—	—	—	—	—	—	—	—	—	—	—	—	—	—	4.9
Mostly non-White	—	—	7.0	—	7.0	—	—	—	—	—	—	—	—	—	—	—	—	—	—	—	9.6
Roughly half non-White	—	—	6.7	—	7.0	—	—	—	—	—	—	—	—	—	—	—	—	—	—	—	12.5
Mostly White	—	—	41.7	—	43.0	—	—	—	—	—	—	—	—	—	—	—	—	—	—	—	50.1
Completely White	—	—	39.9	—	37.9	—	—	—	—	—	—	—	—	—	—	—	—	—	—	—	22.9
Did your high school require community service for graduation?																					
No	—	—	—	—	—	—	—	—	—	—	—	—	78.3	76.5	73.2	71.9	71.0	69.2	70.1	68.5	—
Yes	—	—	—	—	—	—	—	—	—	—	—	—	21.7	23.5	26.8	28.1	29.0	30.8	29.9	31.5	—
Did you meet or exceed recommended years of high school (grades 9–12) study in the following subjects [4]																					
English (4 years)	96.3	97.0	96.9	—	97.3	—	97.9	—	98.0	—	98.1	—	98.3	—	—	98.1	—	—	98.0	—	98.1
Mathematics (3 years)	91.5	92.8	93.5	—	94.6	—	96.6	—	97.4	—	97.9	—	98.2	—	—	98.0	—	—	98.1	—	98.6
Foreign language (2 years)	81.4	84.7	84.7	—	86.5	—	90.2	—	91.3	—	92.5	—	93.8	—	—	94.2	—	—	93.5	—	94.6
Physical science (2 years)	51.1	47.7	46.9	—	47.7	—	49.2	—	50.8	—	52.4	—	50.4	—	—	54.3	—	—	55.4	—	56.7
Biological science (2 years)	38.9	37.2	38.5	—	38.6	—	41.7	—	43.7	—	45.8	—	45.3	—	—	46.2	—	—	46.1	—	48.5
History/American govt. (1 year)	99.3	99.4	99.4	—	99.0	—	99.1	—	99.0	—	98.9	—	98.9	—	—	98.8	—	—	98.7	—	98.8
Computer science (1/2 year)	58.1	55.3	55.5	—	52.1	—	51.9	—	53.1	—	55.0	—	56.3	—	—	57.2	—	—	57.8	—	56.9
Arts and/or music (1 year)	68.2	69.7	70.5	—	76.7	—	76.6	—	78.5	—	78.9	—	80.6	—	—	84.0	—	—	84.3	—	84.4
Have you had any special tutoring or remedial work in:																					
English	—	—	—	4.1	—	4.3	—	3.5	—	4.1	—	3.9	—	4.6	4.7	4.8	4.7	4.3	—	5.1	—
Reading	—	—	—	3.8	—	4.1	—	3.4	—	3.7	—	3.6	—	4.2	4.3	4.4	4.2	3.8	—	4.4	—
Mathematics	—	—	—	10.7	—	12.1	—	11.7	—	12.3	—	12.5	—	13.5	14.1	14.1	14.2	12.9	—	14.2	—
Social studies	—	—	—	2.9	—	3.3	—	2.4	—	2.7	—	2.6	—	2.9	3.1	3.2	3.0	2.6	—	3.1	—
Science	—	—	—	3.8	—	4.4	—	3.7	—	4.2	—	4.2	—	4.6	4.9	4.9	4.8	4.3	—	4.8	—
Foreign language	—	—	—	3.7	—	4.2	—	3.4	—	3.9	—	4.0	—	4.6	4.7	4.8	4.7	4.3	—	4.6	—

HIGH SCHOOL EXPERIENCES
FRESHMAN WOMEN

ITEM	1966	1967	1968	1969	1970	1971	1972	1973	1974	1975	1976	1977	1978	1979	1980	1981	1982	1983	1984	1985
Do you feel you will need any special tutoring or remedial work in:																				
English	—	—	—	—	—	9.8	—	—	—	—	—	10.5	11.1	9.3	9.3	8.7	8.1	—	8.0	—
Reading	—	—	—	—	—	7.8	—	—	—	—	—	6.5	6.5	4.4	4.3	3.5	3.2	—	3.1	—
Mathematics	—	—	—	—	—	38.4	—	—	—	—	—	28.9	26.9	24.2	24.0	23.0	23.6	—	25.2	—
Social studies	—	—	—	—	—	3.9	—	—	—	—	—	3.1	4.2	2.9	3.0	2.5	2.7	—	2.8	—
Science	—	—	—	—	—	28.5	—	—	—	—	—	14.0	15.9	11.9	11.9	10.6	11.1	—	12.1	—
Foreign language	—	—	—	—	—	18.4	—	—	—	—	—	11.6	13.3	8.7	9.0	7.6	7.6	—	8.1	—
What was your average grade in high school? [3]																				
A or A+	9.2	8.9	7.8	7.7	9.0	9.6	11.5	12.5	12.1	13.1	13.6	13.2	15.9	14.0	13.8	14.0	14.7	14.8	14.2	15.1
A-	15.3	14.8	14.4	13.9	14.6	14.9	16.9	16.1	17.2	16.6	17.8	16.4	18.5	16.3	16.5	16.1	15.9	15.4	15.2	16.6
B+	24.2	24.3	23.4	24.0	24.4	25.0	25.9	27.8	25.1	25.4	26.3	25.3	24.0	23.1	22.9	23.0	22.9	22.5	22.4	23.2
B	25.9	26.4	27.1	28.3	27.8	27.1	26.2	25.9	25.8	25.9	24.9	26.0	26.4	25.8	26.4	25.5	25.4	25.2	24.6	24.6
B-	11.8	12.1	12.7	12.5	12.5	12.0	9.8	9.8	9.8	9.9	9.8	9.3	8.6	9.9	9.6	10.3	10.2	10.2	10.7	9.8
C+	8.8	8.5	9.3	8.7	8.1	7.8	6.6	4.8	6.2	5.7	5.8	6.3	5.6	7.2	6.8	7.3	7.3	7.8	8.0	7.0
C	4.7	4.6	5.0	4.3	3.5	3.5	3.0	3.1	3.3	3.3	3.0	3.4	2.9	3.9	4.0	3.7	3.4	4.1	4.1	3.6
D	0.2	0.0	0.2	0.2	0.2	0.1	0.1	0.1	0.1	0.1	0.1	0.1	0.1	0.1	0.1	0.1	0.1	0.1	0.2	0.1
Indicate which activities you did during the past year																				
Asked teacher for advice after class [5]	—	29.9	24.2	27.6	25.4	26.1	—	—	—	—	—	—	—	—	—	—	—	—	—	30.0
Attended a public recital or concert	78.3	—	—	—	—	—	—	—	—	—	—	—	87.0	84.7	—	83.9	83.6	82.3	81.3	83.4
Attended a religious service	74.0	—	93.7	93.0	90.9	89.9	—	—	—	—	—	—	90.0	89.4	—	90.1	90.2	89.9	89.5	89.0
Came late to class	46.2	55.0	51.7	57.5	58.5	52.7	—	—	—	—	—	—	—	—	—	—	—	—	—	—
Checked out a book or journal from the school library [5]	64.8	65.4	60.7	60.6	55.7	52.8	—	—	—	—	—	—	—	—	—	—	—	—	—	—
Communicated via e-mail [5]	—	—	—	—	—	—	—	—	—	—	—	—	—	—	—	—	—	—	—	—
Discussed politics [5]	—	23.7	30.3	26.6	27.4	20.7	—	—	—	—	—	—	—	—	—	—	—	—	—	—
Discussed religion [5]	—	44.9	40.1	38.7	36.0	35.2	—	—	—	—	—	—	—	—	—	—	—	—	—	—
Drank beer	42.2	42.8	38.2	41.5	43.4	46.4	—	—	—	—	—	—	64.5	65.8	—	68.0	68.6	67.1	63.4	61.2
Drank wine or liquor	—	—	—	—	—	—	—	—	—	—	—	—	—	—	—	—	—	—	—	—
Felt depressed [5]	—	—	—	—	—	—	—	—	—	—	—	—	—	—	—	—	—	—	—	10.7
Felt overwhelmed by all I had to do [5]	—	—	—	—	—	—	—	—	—	—	—	—	—	—	—	—	—	—	—	22.6
Overslept and missed a class or appointment	16.6	16.8	14.6	18.9	18.7	17.0	—	—	—	—	—	—	17.4	19.3	—	21.2	23.4	22.7	28.1	—
Participated in organized demonstrations	14.9	15.5	—	—	—	—	—	—	—	—	—	—	—	—	—	—	—	26.3	—	28.1
Performed community service as part of a class	—	—	—	—	—	—	—	—	—	—	—	—	—	—	—	—	—	—	—	—
Performed volunteer work	—	—	—	—	—	—	—	—	—	—	—	—	—	—	—	—	—	—	74.5	75.2
Played a musical instrument [5]	—	55.5	47.3	46.7	45.7	44.9	—	—	—	—	—	—	53.4	50.8	—	49.5	54.1	51.3	50.2	50.1
Smoked cigarettes [5]	—	13.0	10.9	10.9	10.8	11.1	—	—	—	—	—	—	13.5	13.7	—	11.8	11.5	10.6	9.0	8.2
Socialized with someone of another racial/ethnic group [5]	—	—	—	—	—	—	—	—	—	—	—	—	—	—	—	—	—	—	—	—
Studied with other students [5]	—	92.6	—	—	—	—	—	—	—	—	—	—	—	—	—	—	—	—	—	92.8
Tutored another student	—	54.7	54.3	52.5	52.7	52.1	—	—	—	—	—	—	—	—	—	—	—	—	—	50.9
Used a personal computer [5]	—	—	—	—	—	—	—	—	—	—	—	—	—	—	—	—	—	—	—	23.5
Used the Internet for research or homework [5]	—	—	—	—	—	—	—	—	—	—	—	—	—	—	—	—	—	—	—	—
Visited an art gallery or museum	80.3	80.3	78.5	64.7	76.5	74.0	—	—	—	—	—	—	—	—	—	—	—	—	—	—

HIGH SCHOOL EXPERIENCES
FRESHMAN WOMEN

ITEM	1986	1987	1988	1989	1990	1991	1992	1993	1994	1995	1996	1997	1998	1999	2000	2001	2002	2003	2004	2005	2006
Do you feel you will need any special tutoring or remedial work in:																					
English	—	—	—	8.1	—	9.8	—	8.6	—	8.3	—	8.1	—	8.4	7.9	8.2	8.0	9.2	—	8.4	—
Reading	—	—	—	3.2	—	4.2	—	3.3	—	3.6	—	3.3	—	3.4	3.7	3.9	3.6	3.8	—	3.7	—
Mathematics	—	—	—	27.6	—	31.6	—	30.1	—	28.2	—	27.7	—	28.0	28.2	28.2	27.0	28.3	—	28.0	—
Social studies	—	—	—	3.4	—	3.9	—	3.4	—	3.6	—	3.1	—	3.4	3.8	3.7	3.5	3.8	—	3.6	—
Science	—	—	—	12.1	—	14.6	—	14.2	—	13.1	—	12.7	—	12.9	12.7	12.3	12.5	13.3	—	13.1	—
Foreign language	—	—	—	9.8	—	11.0	—	10.7	—	10.4	—	10.7	—	11.4	10.9	10.8	11.0	11.2	—	11.2	—
What was your average grade in high school? [3]																					
A or A+	15.5	15.3	15.6	15.7	15.0	16.2	17.5	18.6	19.8	20.2	22.1	23.4	22.2	23.5	23.9	24.2	25.5	26.0	26.9	25.9	24.9
A−	16.3	15.4	16.4	17.6	17.0	17.4	18.5	19.5	20.3	20.1	21.5	22.2	21.9	23.3	23.5	24.3	24.6	25.3	25.7	25.6	26.0
B+	22.1	23.0	21.0	22.1	21.9	21.7	22.1	22.0	21.9	21.5	21.6	21.3	21.8	21.7	21.4	21.5	21.6	21.3	20.4	21.3	21.9
B	24.6	22.5	24.2	25.2	24.8	24.4	23.7	22.0	22.5	23.0	21.3	20.8	21.4	20.2	20.3	19.5	19.0	18.6	18.3	18.2	18.7
B−	10.7	12.9	10.9	10.2	10.7	10.2	9.5	9.1	8.4	8.5	7.5	7.1	7.3	6.7	6.5	6.2	5.9	5.5	5.4	5.2	5.4
C+	7.3	6.2	7.7	6.5	7.2	7.0	6.2	5.4	5.0	4.8	4.2	3.7	3.9	3.3	3.1	3.1	2.5	2.4	2.3	2.7	2.3
C	3.5	4.6	4.1	2.6	3.2	3.0	2.4	2.0	2.0	1.9	1.6	1.4	1.4	1.2	1.3	1.1	1.0	0.9	1.0	0.9	0.7
D	0.1	0.1	0.1	0.1	0.1	0.1	0.1	0.1	0.1	0.1	0.1	0.0	0.0	0.0	0.0	0.0	0.0	0.0	0.0	0.0	0.0
Indicate which activities you did during the past year																					
Asked teacher for advice after class [5]	—	—	—	—	34.1	23.4	23.4	22.7	23.4	23.6	27.1	26.9	27.6	27.7	26.6	27.5	27.3	26.8	27.6	27.6	28.8
Attended a public recital or concert	83.4	85.4	—	—	—	—	—	—	—	—	—	—	82.2	82.7	83.0	83.2	83.3	—	—	—	—
Attended a religious service	88.1	87.8	85.6	87.0	87.7	88.3	87.9	87.6	87.7	86.9	87.2	87.9	86.6	86.1	85.0	85.1	84.2	82.6	82.8	81.9	78.8
Came late to class	—	—	—	—	59.5	56.3	56.0	56.0	55.4	—	—	—	63.8	64.2	64.0	64.6	62.3	61.7	62.1	61.0	59.2
Checked out a book or journal from the school library [5]	—	—	—	—	33.6	—	—	—	—	—	—	—	25.0	23.6	—	—	—	—	—	—	—
Communicated via e-mail [5]	—	—	—	—	—	—	—	—	—	—	—	—	42.6	58.5	68.5	72.8	71.7	69.3	—	—	—
Discussed politics [5]	—	18.1	—	—	—	22.0	27.1	20.0	16.5	15.0	15.7	13.8	13.9	14.1	13.6	17.5	15.8	18.8	22.4	—	31.3
Discussed religion [5]	—	25.6	25.9	—	—	—	—	—	—	—	—	—	31.0	32.1	31.5	32.1	32.1	30.9	—	36.8	32.5
Drank beer	60.8	58.5	58.5	54.0	51.0	49.8	49.0	48.9	47.4	—	—	—	46.0	44.7	44.3	42.7	42.0	40.7	41.0	38.8	37.3
Drank wine or liquor	—	69.5	—	64.0	59.9	58.2	56.2	56.6	53.8	55.5	55.9	56.0	55.5	53.8	54.4	54.0	52.9	51.0	51.7	50.2	47.8
Felt depressed [5]	10.6	13.4	13.4	11.1	10.8	11.1	11.1	11.0	11.2	10.8	10.9	10.2	10.2	9.9	9.7	9.4	8.9	8.9	9.4	8.4	9.0
Felt overwhelmed by all I had to do [5]	24.5	30.7	—	27.3	28.1	29.3	31.4	32.1	33.8	34.2	38.1	38.3	38.5	39.6	36.4	36.6	35.2	35.1	36.4	35.6	38.0
Overslept and missed a class or appointment	30.6	30.1	—	—	28.1	29.3	—	29.0	28.1	32.6	33.1	32.3	34.1	34.2	34.5	34.6	32.7	31.3	—	—	—
Participated in organized demonstrations	—	—	37.6	38.2	41.6	41.5	42.9	40.6	42.2	43.0	43.6	43.6	47.6	47.9	47.0	48.8	48.8	48.5	50.9	52.1	52.8
Performed community service as part of a class	—	—	—	—	—	—	—	—	—	—	—	—	—	59.0	59.5	60.5	55.4	55.2	55.9	57.6	56.7
Performed volunteer work	74.8	69.1	—	—	69.7	72.2	73.7	76.6	77.8	79.1	80.9	82.9	83.5	85.1	85.1	86.3	86.3	87.0	85.9	87.0	85.8
Played a musical instrument	49.2	48.3	—	—	44.2	43.4	41.5	42.8	42.7	43.1	42.6	42.6	41.4	41.1	41.0	41.4	41.4	41.0	41.1	41.2	38.9
Smoked cigarettes [5]	8.4	8.4	9.1	8.6	8.4	8.6	9.4	9.7	10.0	11.8	12.3	12.5	13.3	11.2	10.3	8.9	7.7	6.4	6.3	5.7	4.9
Socialized with someone of another racial/ethnic group [5]	—	—	—	—	—	—	60.3	—	—	67.1	67.1	68.3	67.6	68.2	69.7	71.9	71.8	70.5	69.4	71.7	68.0
Studied with other students	92.7	92.3	90.8	89.7	89.7	89.2	90.3	90.7	90.5	90.4	91.1	91.0	90.2	90.2	90.2	90.0	90.2	89.9	89.5	89.4	88.6
Tutored another student	49.8	50.4	49.9	51.6	52.9	53.5	56.9	57.3	58.5	57.3	58.8	58.4	57.6	56.9	56.6	58.7	57.9	57.1	58.0	57.1	54.9
Used a personal computer [5]	23.4	24.0	27.2	30.4	—	39.0	—	40.2	—	51.9	—	61.5	—	67.5	77.8	81.3	83.2	83.7	85.8	85.8	—
Used the Internet for research or homework [5]	—	—	—	—	—	—	—	—	—	—	—	—	43.8	58.9	69.0	76.7	80.9	84.5	81.4	83.3	—
Visited an art gallery or museum	—	—	—	61.0	60.1	—	—	66.0	65.1	—	—	—	61.2	60.9	62.4	63.2	61.2	60.2	—	—	—

HIGH SCHOOL EXPERIENCES
FRESHMAN WOMEN

ITEM	1966	1967	1968	1969	1970	1971	1972	1973	1974	1975	1976	1977	1978	1979	1980	1981	1982	1983	1984	1985
Indicate which activities you did during the past year																				
Voted in a student election [5]	76.7	79.2	81.3	75.0	74.8	70.1	—	—	—	—	—	—	—	—	—	—	—	—	—	—
Was bored in class [5]	—	—	—	—	—	—	—	—	—	—	—	—	—	—	—	—	—	—	29.2	29.1
Was a guest in a teacher's home	—	41.3	—	—	—	—	—	—	—	—	—	—	—	—	—	—	—	—	—	36.4
Worked in a local, state or national political campaign	—	—	—	—	—	16.7	—	—	—	—	—	—	10.9	10.0	—	10.3	9.7	9.5	10.7	—
DURING YOUR LAST YEAR IN HIGH SCHOOL, HOW MUCH TIME DID YOU SPEND IN A TYPICAL WEEK DOING THE FOLLOWING ACTIVITIES?																				
Studying/homework																				
None	—	—	—	—	—	—	—	—	—	—	—	—	—	—	—	—	—	—	—	—
Less than one hour	—	—	—	—	—	—	—	—	—	—	—	—	—	—	—	—	—	—	—	—
1 to 2 hours	—	—	—	—	—	—	—	—	—	—	—	—	—	—	—	—	—	—	—	—
3 to 5 hours	—	—	—	—	—	—	—	—	—	—	—	—	—	—	—	—	—	—	—	—
6 to 10 hours	—	—	—	—	—	—	—	—	—	—	—	—	—	—	—	—	—	—	—	—
11 to 15 hours	—	—	—	—	—	—	—	—	—	—	—	—	—	—	—	—	—	—	—	—
16 to 20 hours	—	—	—	—	—	—	—	—	—	—	—	—	—	—	—	—	—	—	—	—
Over 20 hours	—	—	—	—	—	—	—	—	—	—	—	—	—	—	—	—	—	—	—	—
Socializing with friends																				
None	—	—	—	—	—	—	—	—	—	—	—	—	—	—	—	—	—	—	—	—
Less than one hour	—	—	—	—	—	—	—	—	—	—	—	—	—	—	—	—	—	—	—	—
1 to 2 hours	—	—	—	—	—	—	—	—	—	—	—	—	—	—	—	—	—	—	—	—
3 to 5 hours	—	—	—	—	—	—	—	—	—	—	—	—	—	—	—	—	—	—	—	—
6 to 10 hours	—	—	—	—	—	—	—	—	—	—	—	—	—	—	—	—	—	—	—	—
11 to 15 hours	—	—	—	—	—	—	—	—	—	—	—	—	—	—	—	—	—	—	—	—
16 to 20 hours	—	—	—	—	—	—	—	—	—	—	—	—	—	—	—	—	—	—	—	—
Over 20 hours	—	—	—	—	—	—	—	—	—	—	—	—	—	—	—	—	—	—	—	—
Talking with teachers outside of class																				
None	—	—	—	—	—	—	—	—	—	—	—	—	—	—	—	—	—	—	—	—
Less than one hour	—	—	—	—	—	—	—	—	—	—	—	—	—	—	—	—	—	—	—	—
1 to 2 hours	—	—	—	—	—	—	—	—	—	—	—	—	—	—	—	—	—	—	—	—
3 to 5 hours	—	—	—	—	—	—	—	—	—	—	—	—	—	—	—	—	—	—	—	—
6 to 10 hours	—	—	—	—	—	—	—	—	—	—	—	—	—	—	—	—	—	—	—	—
11 to 15 hours	—	—	—	—	—	—	—	—	—	—	—	—	—	—	—	—	—	—	—	—
16 to 20 hours	—	—	—	—	—	—	—	—	—	—	—	—	—	—	—	—	—	—	—	—
Over 20 hours	—	—	—	—	—	—	—	—	—	—	—	—	—	—	—	—	—	—	—	—
Exercising or sports																				
None	—	—	—	—	—	—	—	—	—	—	—	—	—	—	—	—	—	—	—	—
Less than one hour	—	—	—	—	—	—	—	—	—	—	—	—	—	—	—	—	—	—	—	—
1 to 2 hours	—	—	—	—	—	—	—	—	—	—	—	—	—	—	—	—	—	—	—	—
3 to 5 hours	—	—	—	—	—	—	—	—	—	—	—	—	—	—	—	—	—	—	—	—
6 to 10 hours	—	—	—	—	—	—	—	—	—	—	—	—	—	—	—	—	—	—	—	—
11 to 15 hours	—	—	—	—	—	—	—	—	—	—	—	—	—	—	—	—	—	—	—	—
16 to 20 hours	—	—	—	—	—	—	—	—	—	—	—	—	—	—	—	—	—	—	—	—
Over 20 hours	—	—	—	—	—	—	—	—	—	—	—	—	—	—	—	—	—	—	—	—

HIGH SCHOOL EXPERIENCES
FRESHMAN WOMEN

ITEM	1986	1987	1988	1989	1990	1991	1992	1993	1994	1995	1996	1997	1998	1999	2000	2001	2002	2003	2004	2005	2006
Indicate which activities you did during the past year																					
Voted in a student election [5]	—	—	—	—	—	38.3	37.2	—	—	27.5	28.1	25.9	25.7	24.9	23.9	25.1	23.0	22.1	22.5	25.3	24.4
Was bored in class [5]	31.8	32.1	35.6	36.0	—	32.7	32.5	34.8	36.0	35.6	37.0	37.1	37.7	39.0	38.0	39.4	38.1	38.0	41.4	39.2	39.3
Was a guest in a teacher's home	36.5	—	32.4	32.1	31.1	30.9	29.7	30.1	29.8	28.6	30.2	30.9	29.2	30.0	27.8	27.8	27.1	24.4	23.7	23.9	22.5
Worked in a local, state or national political campaign	—	—	10.1	—	—	—	8.9	—	—	9.1	7.4	9.3	—	—	—	—	—	—	8.4	12.2	—
DURING YOUR LAST YEAR IN HIGH SCHOOL, HOW MUCH TIME DID YOU SPEND IN A TYPICAL WEEK DOING THE FOLLOWING ACTIVITIES?																					
Studying/homework																					
None	—	0.5	0.5	0.5	0.6	0.6	0.6	0.7	0.7	0.8	0.8	0.8	0.9	1.0	1.0	1.0	1.2	1.2	1.0	1.4	1.2
Less than one hour		5.2	5.1	4.8	5.1	5.6	5.6	7.3	6.6	7.2	7.1	7.6	7.3	8.5	8.5	8.7	9.8	10.1	8.8	10.9	9.6
1 to 2 hours		13.3	14.9	14.4	15.1	15.5	15.7	18.1	16.5	17.4	17.1	17.4	17.8	18.7	19.2	19.4	20.2	19.7	19.8	21.6	21.2
3 to 5 hours		28.9	29.8	29.2	29.6	30.2	30.3	29.8	29.7	29.3	30.2	29.6	30.3	29.6	29.9	30.8	30.2	29.9	30.5	29.3	30.4
6 to 10 hours		28.1	26.9	27.4	26.8	26.0	26.3	24.1	24.8	24.2	24.1	23.9	23.6	22.6	22.4	22.1	21.1	21.0	21.4	19.8	20.6
11 to 15 hours		14.1	13.1	13.8	13.0	12.4	12.5	11.6	12.3	11.7	11.7	11.5	11.3	10.8	10.3	10.1	9.6	9.9	10.0	9.1	9.4
16 to 20 hours		6.2	6.1	6.3	6.1	6.1	5.6	5.2	5.8	5.6	5.4	5.6	5.3	5.2	5.1	4.9	4.8	5.0	5.1	4.7	4.5
Over 20 hours		3.8	3.6	3.7	3.7	3.7	3.4	3.3	3.7	3.7	3.5	3.6	3.5	3.5	3.5	3.1	3.2	3.2	3.4	3.2	3.1
Socializing with friends																					
None		0.1	0.2	0.2	0.2	0.2	0.2	0.2	0.2	0.3	0.2	0.2	0.2	0.2	0.2	0.2	0.2	0.2	0.2	0.2	0.2
Less than one hour		1.0	1.3	1.3	1.2	1.2	0.9	1.1	1.2	1.2	1.1	1.1	1.1	1.1	1.1	1.2	1.3	1.3	1.3	1.4	1.4
1 to 2 hours		3.9	4.9	5.0	4.9	5.1	4.7	5.1	4.8	5.3	4.8	5.1	4.6	5.0	5.0	5.5	5.7	5.7	5.6	6.2	6.2
3 to 5 hours		14.2	15.2	14.5	15.5	16.1	16.0	16.3	16.3	16.0	16.1	16.2	16.0	16.1	16.4	17.8	18.4	18.2	18.0	19.3	19.5
6 to 10 hours		24.5	24.1	22.5	24.6	24.6	25.4	25.7	25.6	24.5	25.2	25.5	25.3	25.2	25.4	26.2	26.2	26.4	26.3	26.5	27.3
11 to 15 hours		20.7	19.7	19.8	20.4	19.8	20.6	21.2	20.7	20.2	20.7	20.4	20.5	19.9	19.9	19.6	19.1	19.1	19.5	18.5	19.1
16 to 20 hours		14.7	14.7	14.9	14.5	14.0	14.3	13.7	13.7	13.9	13.8	13.6	14.0	13.7	13.7	12.7	12.4	12.5	12.7	11.6	11.4
Over 20 hours		20.8	19.9	21.8	18.8	18.9	17.9	16.8	17.4	18.6	18.1	17.8	18.3	18.9	18.3	16.5	16.6	16.7	16.5	16.2	14.9
Talking with teachers outside of class																					
None		4.7	5.2	4.2	5.3	5.4	5.8	5.9	6.6	7.0	6.6	6.9	6.7	7.0	7.1	6.9	7.1	7.6	7.4	8.2	8.0
Less than one hour		36.3	32.9	29.7	39.0	39.2	38.5	40.6	41.1	41.4	40.9	42.6	41.0	41.0	40.9	40.9	42.6	42.6	42.7	43.1	40.9
1 to 2 hours		33.7	34.4	31.2	35.1	34.2	35.1	33.4	33.3	32.5	33.5	32.7	33.3	33.2	33.2	33.4	32.5	32.1	32.4	31.3	33.1
3 to 5 hours		18.1	18.0	18.9	14.9	15.2	15.0	14.2	13.8	13.5	13.8	12.9	13.9	13.2	13.5	13.7	12.9	12.8	12.7	12.2	13.0
6 to 10 hours		4.9	5.8	8.2	4.0	3.9	3.7	4.0	3.6	3.8	3.4	3.3	3.5	3.5	3.5	3.5	3.2	3.2	3.2	3.2	3.4
11 to 15 hours		1.4	2.0	3.8	1.1	1.2	1.1	1.1	1.0	1.1	1.1	1.0	1.0	1.2	1.1	1.0	1.0	1.0	1.0	1.1	0.9
16 to 20 hours		0.5	0.9	1.9	0.4	0.5	0.5	0.5	0.4	0.5	0.4	0.4	0.4	0.4	0.4	0.4	0.4	0.4	0.4	0.4	0.4
Over 20 hours		0.4	0.8	2.0	0.3	0.4	0.3	0.3	0.3	0.3	0.4	0.4	0.3	0.4	0.3	0.3	0.4	0.3	0.3	0.4	0.3
Exercising or sports																					
None		4.7	4.7	4.5	5.5	5.3	4.6	4.3	5.3	5.5	5.1	5.4	5.2	5.5	6.0	5.9	6.8	6.6	5.8	6.1	5.8
Less than one hour		12.6	12.3	11.7	12.9	12.7	11.8	12.1	12.1	11.4	11.1	11.6	11.5	11.7	11.7	12.4	12.4	12.3	11.6	12.1	11.6
1 to 2 hours		19.3	20.4	20.0	20.1	19.7	19.7	19.5	18.9	18.1	18.3	17.9	18.4	17.7	18.3	18.4	17.5	17.3	17.4	17.9	17.9
3 to 5 hours		23.6	23.9	24.0	22.4	22.0	22.3	21.7	21.7	21.4	21.2	20.9	20.9	20.5	20.2	20.1	19.8	19.5	20.1	20.0	20.6
6 to 10 hours		18.0	17.7	17.8	17.0	17.1	18.0	17.5	17.8	17.4	17.6	18.0	17.4	17.4	17.1	17.3	17.6	17.5	17.8	17.9	17.8
11 to 15 hours		11.1	10.7	11.5	11.4	11.4	12.0	12.2	12.3	12.9	13.2	13.0	13.1	13.1	12.8	12.7	12.7	13.0	13.1	12.3	12.7
16 to 20 hours		5.3	5.2	5.4	5.5	5.7	6.1	6.3	6.0	6.6	6.7	6.7	6.8	6.9	6.8	6.7	6.6	6.9	7.0	6.7	6.8
Over 20 hours		5.4	5.2	5.0	5.3	6.1	5.6	6.5	5.9	6.7	6.7	6.5	6.6	7.1	7.1	6.5	6.6	6.9	7.1	6.9	6.7

HIGH SCHOOL EXPERIENCES
FRESHMAN WOMEN

ITEM	1966	1967	1968	1969	1970	1971	1972	1973	1974	1975	1976	1977	1978	1979	1980	1981	1982	1983	1984	1985
DURING YOUR LAST YEAR IN HIGH SCHOOL, HOW MUCH TIME DID YOU SPEND IN A TYPICAL WEEK DOING THE FOLLOWING ACTIVITIES?																				
Partying																				
None	—	—	—	—	—	—	—	—	—	—	—	—	—	—	—	—	—	—	—	—
Less than one hour	—	—	—	—	—	—	—	—	—	—	—	—	—	—	—	—	—	—	—	—
1 to 2 hours	—	—	—	—	—	—	—	—	—	—	—	—	—	—	—	—	—	—	—	—
3 to 5 hours	—	—	—	—	—	—	—	—	—	—	—	—	—	—	—	—	—	—	—	—
6 to 10 hours	—	—	—	—	—	—	—	—	—	—	—	—	—	—	—	—	—	—	—	—
11 to 15 hours	—	—	—	—	—	—	—	—	—	—	—	—	—	—	—	—	—	—	—	—
16 to 20 hours	—	—	—	—	—	—	—	—	—	—	—	—	—	—	—	—	—	—	—	—
Over 20 hours	—	—	—	—	—	—	—	—	—	—	—	—	—	—	—	—	—	—	—	—
Working (for pay)																				
None	—	—	—	—	—	—	—	—	—	—	—	—	—	—	—	—	—	—	—	—
Less than one hour	—	—	—	—	—	—	—	—	—	—	—	—	—	—	—	—	—	—	—	—
1 to 2 hours	—	—	—	—	—	—	—	—	—	—	—	—	—	—	—	—	—	—	—	—
3 to 5 hours	—	—	—	—	—	—	—	—	—	—	—	—	—	—	—	—	—	—	—	—
6 to 10 hours	—	—	—	—	—	—	—	—	—	—	—	—	—	—	—	—	—	—	—	—
11 to 15 hours	—	—	—	—	—	—	—	—	—	—	—	—	—	—	—	—	—	—	—	—
16 to 20 hours	—	—	—	—	—	—	—	—	—	—	—	—	—	—	—	—	—	—	—	—
Over 20 hours	—	—	—	—	—	—	—	—	—	—	—	—	—	—	—	—	—	—	—	—
Volunteer work																				
None	—	—	—	—	—	—	—	—	—	—	—	—	—	—	—	—	—	—	—	—
Less than one hour	—	—	—	—	—	—	—	—	—	—	—	—	—	—	—	—	—	—	—	—
1 to 2 hours	—	—	—	—	—	—	—	—	—	—	—	—	—	—	—	—	—	—	—	—
3 to 5 hours	—	—	—	—	—	—	—	—	—	—	—	—	—	—	—	—	—	—	—	—
6 to 10 hours	—	—	—	—	—	—	—	—	—	—	—	—	—	—	—	—	—	—	—	—
11 to 15 hours	—	—	—	—	—	—	—	—	—	—	—	—	—	—	—	—	—	—	—	—
16 to 20 hours	—	—	—	—	—	—	—	—	—	—	—	—	—	—	—	—	—	—	—	—
Over 20 hours	—	—	—	—	—	—	—	—	—	—	—	—	—	—	—	—	—	—	—	—
Student clubs/groups																				
None	—	—	—	—	—	—	—	—	—	—	—	—	—	—	—	—	—	—	—	—
Less than one hour	—	—	—	—	—	—	—	—	—	—	—	—	—	—	—	—	—	—	—	—
1 to 2 hours	—	—	—	—	—	—	—	—	—	—	—	—	—	—	—	—	—	—	—	—
3 to 5 hours	—	—	—	—	—	—	—	—	—	—	—	—	—	—	—	—	—	—	—	—
6 to 10 hours	—	—	—	—	—	—	—	—	—	—	—	—	—	—	—	—	—	—	—	—
11 to 15 hours	—	—	—	—	—	—	—	—	—	—	—	—	—	—	—	—	—	—	—	—
16 to 20 hours	—	—	—	—	—	—	—	—	—	—	—	—	—	—	—	—	—	—	—	—
Over 20 hours	—	—	—	—	—	—	—	—	—	—	—	—	—	—	—	—	—	—	—	—
Watching TV																				
None	—	—	—	—	—	—	—	—	—	—	—	—	—	—	—	—	—	—	—	—
Less than one hour	—	—	—	—	—	—	—	—	—	—	—	—	—	—	—	—	—	—	—	—
1 to 2 hours	—	—	—	—	—	—	—	—	—	—	—	—	—	—	—	—	—	—	—	—
3 to 5 hours	—	—	—	—	—	—	—	—	—	—	—	—	—	—	—	—	—	—	—	—
6 to 10 hours	—	—	—	—	—	—	—	—	—	—	—	—	—	—	—	—	—	—	—	—
11 to 15 hours	—	—	—	—	—	—	—	—	—	—	—	—	—	—	—	—	—	—	—	—
16 to 20 hours	—	—	—	—	—	—	—	—	—	—	—	—	—	—	—	—	—	—	—	—
Over 20 hours	—	—	—	—	—	—	—	—	—	—	—	—	—	—	—	—	—	—	—	—

HIGH SCHOOL EXPERIENCES
FRESHMAN WOMEN

ITEM	1986	1987	1988	1989	1990	1991	1992	1993	1994	1995	1996	1997	1998	1999	2000	2001	2002	2003	2004	2005	2006
DURING YOUR LAST YEAR IN HIGH SCHOOL, HOW MUCH TIME DID YOU SPEND IN A TYPICAL WEEK DOING THE FOLLOWING ACTIVITIES?																					
Partying																					
None	—	12.7	13.7	14.7	16.4	16.7	17.9	16.7	19.4	19.4	20.1	20.2	19.7	21.0	19.9	21.0	22.9	25.2	26.6	28.2	28.6
Less than one hour	—	11.6	11.7	12.6	13.0	13.0	13.9	14.7	13.9	13.9	14.0	13.8	13.6	13.6	13.4	14.3	15.1	15.2	15.7	15.7	15.2
1 to 2 hours	—	15.8	16.9	17.1	17.3	17.4	17.9	18.0	17.4	17.5	17.8	17.9	18.2	18.1	18.3	19.0	18.4	18.0	18.0	17.7	17.9
3 to 5 hours	—	25.4	25.2	25.1	23.7	23.7	23.1	22.8	22.7	22.2	22.5	22.5	22.5	22.4	22.7	22.2	21.6	20.5	19.7	19.2	19.4
6 to 10 hours	—	19.4	18.7	17.9	17.1	16.6	15.5	15.9	15.1	15.0	14.6	14.7	14.8	14.5	14.8	13.8	12.7	12.4	11.8	11.0	11.3
11 to 15 hours	—	8.3	7.6	7.0	7.0	6.8	6.5	6.8	6.4	6.5	6.1	6.1	6.2	5.6	5.9	5.4	5.1	4.9	4.7	4.4	4.3
16 to 20 hours	—	3.5	3.3	3.0	3.0	3.1	2.9	2.8	2.7	3.0	2.7	2.6	2.8	2.6	2.7	2.4	2.2	2.2	2.0	2.0	1.8
Over 20 hours	—	3.3	3.0	2.6	2.4	2.7	2.3	2.3	2.4	2.6	2.2	2.3	2.3	2.1	2.2	1.8	1.9	1.7	1.5	1.7	1.5
Working (for pay)																					
None	—	25.7	26.2	26.2	26.6	29.1	30.0	26.9	27.9	26.0	26.7	27.1	26.0	26.1	26.0	26.2	27.9	28.9	28.6	29.0	28.4
Less than one hour	—	1.9	1.9	1.7	1.7	2.1	2.1	2.3	1.9	1.9	1.7	1.9	1.7	1.7	1.7	1.8	2.0	2.2	2.2	2.4	2.3
1 to 2 hours	—	2.9	3.0	2.9	2.7	3.0	3.3	3.3	3.1	3.0	2.9	2.9	2.8	2.9	2.9	2.9	3.1	3.3	3.4	3.6	3.6
3 to 5 hours	—	5.8	6.1	6.0	6.0	6.5	6.5	6.7	6.4	6.3	6.1	6.1	6.3	6.4	6.3	6.5	6.7	7.0	7.2	7.3	7.4
6 to 10 hours	—	10.5	11.2	11.4	11.7	11.8	12.0	11.8	11.9	11.8	12.1	12.4	12.4	12.3	12.5	12.9	13.1	12.9	12.9	12.9	13.0
11 to 15 hours	—	14.5	14.3	14.9	15.1	14.7	15.2	15.2	15.1	15.1	15.5	15.5	15.4	15.3	15.4	15.8	15.4	15.5	15.1	14.3	14.9
16 to 20 hours	—	18.9	18.5	18.6	18.7	16.6	16.4	16.8	17.2	17.9	17.7	17.4	17.8	17.5	17.6	17.6	16.5	15.6	15.7	15.0	15.4
Over 20 hours	—	19.8	18.9	18.4	17.4	16.3	14.7	16.9	16.7	18.1	17.2	16.8	17.6	17.7	17.5	16.3	15.2	14.6	14.9	15.6	15.0
Volunteer work																					
None	—	56.1	54.3	44.6	43.6	40.3	38.8	33.3	34.4	32.7	31.6	28.9	26.7	25.3	25.4	24.1	24.2	23.8	21.2	23.8	23.9
Less than one hour	—	14.1	14.8	18.7	19.0	19.5	19.3	21.6	20.6	20.9	21.0	21.5	20.9	21.2	21.0	22.1	21.9	21.8	22.7	22.3	21.7
1 to 2 hours	—	14.9	16.2	27.1	20.0	21.2	21.9	22.8	22.9	23.2	24.2	24.6	25.9	26.2	26.2	26.4	25.9	26.0	27.9	26.0	26.6
3 to 5 hours	—	9.2	9.2	10.6	10.7	11.7	12.2	13.7	13.6	13.6	13.9	15.2	15.8	16.0	16.0	16.3	16.3	16.4	17.2	16.1	16.3
6 to 10 hours	—	3.3	3.3	3.6	3.9	4.2	4.6	5.0	5.0	5.5	5.3	5.7	6.0	6.4	6.4	6.3	6.5	6.6	6.2	6.3	6.2
11 to 15 hours	—	1.0	1.0	1.1	1.2	1.4	1.5	1.7	1.7	1.9	1.9	1.9	2.2	2.3	2.3	2.1	2.3	2.3	2.2	2.3	2.3
16 to 20 hours	—	0.5	0.5	0.5	0.6	0.7	0.7	0.7	0.8	0.9	0.8	0.9	1.1	1.1	1.2	1.1	1.2	1.2	1.0	1.2	1.2
Over 20 hours	—	0.8	0.8	0.8	0.9	1.0	1.0	1.1	1.1	1.3	1.3	1.3	1.4	1.5	1.6	1.5	1.9	1.8	1.5	2.0	1.7
Student clubs/groups																					
None	—	19.1	19.5	16.2	17.3	16.2	16.7	16.9	17.4	19.3	19.6	18.8	18.7	18.6	20.5	20.5	21.0	20.8	21.5	20.7	21.7
Less than one hour	—	11.0	11.3	11.4	11.5	11.7	12.3	13.4	12.8	13.2	12.8	13.7	13.4	13.6	13.5	13.9	14.7	14.7	14.3	15.0	14.1
1 to 2 hours	—	25.7	26.2	27.1	26.9	26.9	27.9	26.9	27.7	27.2	28.1	27.7	28.3	27.9	27.1	28.0	27.4	27.3	27.9	27.6	27.2
3 to 5 hours	—	23.7	23.2	24.4	24.1	23.7	23.3	22.4	22.8	21.9	21.9	22.1	21.8	21.7	21.0	20.9	20.7	20.7	20.2	20.2	20.5
6 to 10 hours	—	11.6	11.2	11.7	11.4	11.7	11.0	10.9	10.7	10.1	9.8	9.7	9.8	10.0	9.7	9.3	8.9	9.0	8.9	8.9	9.0
11 to 15 hours	—	4.5	4.3	4.4	4.5	4.7	4.3	4.7	4.5	4.1	3.9	4.0	4.0	4.0	4.0	3.6	3.6	3.6	3.6	3.6	3.6
16 to 20 hours	—	2.1	2.0	2.1	2.1	2.3	2.1	2.2	1.9	2.0	1.8	1.9	1.8	1.9	1.9	1.7	1.7	1.7	1.7	1.8	1.8
Over 20 hours	—	2.3	2.3	2.5	2.2	2.8	2.3	2.7	2.2	2.8	2.1	2.2	2.1	2.2	2.3	2.1	2.1	2.1	1.9	2.2	2.1
Watching TV																					
None	—	5.6	6.0	5.9	5.0	5.0	4.9	5.6	6.0	5.4	6.0	6.4	6.2	6.6	6.4	6.6	6.7	6.1	5.4	5.7	6.3
Less than one hour	—	14.0	14.7	15.5	15.0	15.0	15.2	17.5	16.9	17.4	16.9	18.4	17.0	17.7	17.6	18.2	18.9	17.5	16.6	16.5	16.2
1 to 2 hours	—	23.0	23.2	23.4	23.5	23.5	24.4	25.4	24.9	25.3	25.4	25.5	25.7	26.2	26.1	26.2	26.9	25.6	26.1	25.6	26.5
3 to 5 hours	—	29.0	27.9	27.7	28.1	27.7	28.0	27.0	27.5	26.4	27.2	26.3	27.3	26.7	26.8	27.0	26.5	27.7	28.4	28.1	28.3
6 to 10 hours	—	17.1	16.7	16.2	16.4	16.2	16.1	14.6	14.7	14.6	14.8	14.0	14.3	13.6	13.9	13.4	12.8	14.7	14.4	14.3	14.0
11 to 15 hours	—	6.0	6.0	5.8	5.9	6.2	5.8	5.2	5.2	5.0	5.0	5.0	4.9	4.9	4.6	4.4	4.3	4.7	4.8	5.0	4.6
16 to 20 hours	—	2.5	2.6	2.5	2.9	2.8	2.6	2.1	2.1	2.1	2.0	2.0	2.1	2.0	2.0	1.8	1.7	2.0	2.0	2.1	1.8
Over 20 hours	—	2.8	3.0	3.0	3.3	3.6	2.9	2.6	2.7	2.8	2.5	2.5	2.5	2.4	2.4	2.3	2.3	2.4	2.3	2.7	2.2

HIGH SCHOOL EXPERIENCES
FRESHMAN WOMEN

ITEM	1966	1967	1968	1969	1970	1971	1972	1973	1974	1975	1976	1977	1978	1979	1980	1981	1982	1983	1984	1985
DURING YOUR LAST YEAR IN HIGH SCHOOL, HOW MUCH TIME DID YOU SPEND IN A TYPICAL WEEK DOING THE FOLLOWING ACTIVITIES?																				
Housework/childcare																				
None	—	—	—	—	—	—	—	—	—	—	—	—	—	—	—	—	—	—	—	—
Less than one hour	—	—	—	—	—	—	—	—	—	—	—	—	—	—	—	—	—	—	—	—
1 to 2 hours	—	—	—	—	—	—	—	—	—	—	—	—	—	—	—	—	—	—	—	—
3 to 5 hours	—	—	—	—	—	—	—	—	—	—	—	—	—	—	—	—	—	—	—	—
6 to 10 hours	—	—	—	—	—	—	—	—	—	—	—	—	—	—	—	—	—	—	—	—
11 to 15 hours	—	—	—	—	—	—	—	—	—	—	—	—	—	—	—	—	—	—	—	—
16 to 20 hours	—	—	—	—	—	—	—	—	—	—	—	—	—	—	—	—	—	—	—	—
Over 20 hours	—	—	—	—	—	—	—	—	—	—	—	—	—	—	—	—	—	—	—	—
Prayer/meditation																				
None	—	—	—	—	—	—	—	—	—	—	—	—	—	—	—	—	—	—	—	—
Less than one hour	—	—	—	—	—	—	—	—	—	—	—	—	—	—	—	—	—	—	—	—
1 to 2 hours	—	—	—	—	—	—	—	—	—	—	—	—	—	—	—	—	—	—	—	—
3 to 5 hours	—	—	—	—	—	—	—	—	—	—	—	—	—	—	—	—	—	—	—	—
6 to 10 hours	—	—	—	—	—	—	—	—	—	—	—	—	—	—	—	—	—	—	—	—
11 to 15 hours	—	—	—	—	—	—	—	—	—	—	—	—	—	—	—	—	—	—	—	—
16 to 20 hours	—	—	—	—	—	—	—	—	—	—	—	—	—	—	—	—	—	—	—	—
Over 20 hours	—	—	—	—	—	—	—	—	—	—	—	—	—	—	—	—	—	—	—	—
Reading for pleasure																				
None	—	—	—	—	—	—	—	—	—	—	—	—	—	—	—	—	—	—	—	—
Less than one hour	—	—	—	—	—	—	—	—	—	—	—	—	—	—	—	—	—	—	—	—
1 to 2 hours	—	—	—	—	—	—	—	—	—	—	—	—	—	—	—	—	—	—	—	—
3 to 5 hours	—	—	—	—	—	—	—	—	—	—	—	—	—	—	—	—	—	—	—	—
6 to 10 hours	—	—	—	—	—	—	—	—	—	—	—	—	—	—	—	—	—	—	—	—
11 to 15 hours	—	—	—	—	—	—	—	—	—	—	—	—	—	—	—	—	—	—	—	—
16 to 20 hours	—	—	—	—	—	—	—	—	—	—	—	—	—	—	—	—	—	—	—	—
Over 20 hours	—	—	—	—	—	—	—	—	—	—	—	—	—	—	—	—	—	—	—	—
Playing video games																				
None	—	—	—	—	—	—	—	—	—	—	—	—	—	—	—	—	—	—	—	—
Less than one hour	—	—	—	—	—	—	—	—	—	—	—	—	—	—	—	—	—	—	—	—
1 to 2 hours	—	—	—	—	—	—	—	—	—	—	—	—	—	—	—	—	—	—	—	—
3 to 5 hours	—	—	—	—	—	—	—	—	—	—	—	—	—	—	—	—	—	—	—	—
6 to 10 hours	—	—	—	—	—	—	—	—	—	—	—	—	—	—	—	—	—	—	—	—
11 to 15 hours	—	—	—	—	—	—	—	—	—	—	—	—	—	—	—	—	—	—	—	—
16 to 20 hours	—	—	—	—	—	—	—	—	—	—	—	—	—	—	—	—	—	—	—	—
Over 20 hours	—	—	—	—	—	—	—	—	—	—	—	—	—	—	—	—	—	—	—	—
Playing video/computer games																				
None	—	—	—	—	—	—	—	—	—	—	—	—	—	—	—	—	—	—	—	—
Less than one hour	—	—	—	—	—	—	—	—	—	—	—	—	—	—	—	—	—	—	—	—
1 to 2 hours	—	—	—	—	—	—	—	—	—	—	—	—	—	—	—	—	—	—	—	—
3 to 5 hours	—	—	—	—	—	—	—	—	—	—	—	—	—	—	—	—	—	—	—	—
6 to 10 hours	—	—	—	—	—	—	—	—	—	—	—	—	—	—	—	—	—	—	—	—
11 to 15 hours	—	—	—	—	—	—	—	—	—	—	—	—	—	—	—	—	—	—	—	—
16 to 20 hours	—	—	—	—	—	—	—	—	—	—	—	—	—	—	—	—	—	—	—	—
Over 20 hours	—	—	—	—	—	—	—	—	—	—	—	—	—	—	—	—	—	—	—	—

HIGH SCHOOL EXPERIENCES
FRESHMAN WOMEN

ITEM	1986	1987	1988	1989	1990	1991	1992	1993	1994	1995	1996	1997	1998	1999	2000	2001	2002	2003	2004	2005	2006
DURING YOUR LAST YEAR IN HIGH SCHOOL, HOW MUCH TIME DID YOU SPEND IN A TYPICAL WEEK DOING THE FOLLOWING ACTIVITIES?																					
Housework/childcare																					
None	—	—	—	—	—	—	—	8.4	11.8	11.9	12.4	13.1	12.4	13.8	14.7	13.9	14.9	14.2	13.5	14.1	14.2
Less than one hour	—	—	—	—	—	—	—	17.3	18.2	21.3	21.2	22.7	20.9	22.1	20.7	20.9	22.5	22.1	20.1	21.8	20.2
1 to 2 hours	—	—	—	—	—	—	—	31.9	32.3	32.4	33.3	32.6	33.3	32.6	32.4	33.1	32.4	32.2	32.6	32.0	32.5
3 to 5 hours	—	—	—	—	—	—	—	25.2	23.2	21.1	20.6	19.7	20.9	19.7	20.4	20.8	19.5	20.2	21.3	20.1	20.9
6 to 10 hours	—	—	—	—	—	—	—	9.5	8.1	7.6	7.2	6.7	7.1	6.9	6.9	6.5	6.2	6.5	7.2	6.8	7.0
11 to 15 hours	—	—	—	—	—	—	—	3.4	2.8	2.5	2.5	2.3	2.6	2.3	2.2	2.2	2.1	2.2	2.5	2.3	2.4
16 to 20 hours	—	—	—	—	—	—	—	1.6	1.2	1.1	1.1	1.1	1.1	1.1	1.0	0.9	0.9	0.9	1.0	1.1	1.1
Over 20 hours	—	—	—	—	—	—	—	2.7	2.2	2.0	1.9	1.8	1.8	1.7	1.8	1.7	1.5	1.5	1.7	1.8	1.6
Prayer/meditation																					
None	—	—	—	—	—	—	—	—	—	—	30.1	28.1	29.0	28.9	29.5	31.4	31.7	33.6	34.6	35.1	—
Less than one hour	—	—	—	—	—	—	—	—	—	—	34.2	35.9	34.5	34.1	34.8	34.7	35.3	34.3	33.8	34.4	—
1 to 2 hours	—	—	—	—	—	—	—	—	—	—	23.2	23.4	23.2	23.3	22.6	21.6	20.8	20.3	20.2	19.5	—
3 to 5 hours	—	—	—	—	—	—	—	—	—	—	8.1	8.0	8.5	8.7	8.3	7.9	7.8	7.6	7.4	6.8	—
6 to 10 hours	—	—	—	—	—	—	—	—	—	—	2.6	2.6	2.7	2.8	2.7	2.5	2.4	2.4	2.3	2.2	—
11 to 15 hours	—	—	—	—	—	—	—	—	—	—	0.7	0.8	0.8	0.8	0.8	0.7	0.8	0.7	0.7	0.7	—
16 to 20 hours	—	—	—	—	—	—	—	—	—	—	0.4	0.4	0.4	0.4	0.4	0.4	0.4	0.4	0.3	0.4	—
Over 20 hours	—	—	—	—	—	—	—	—	—	—	0.8	0.8	0.9	1.0	0.9	0.8	0.7	0.8	0.7	0.8	—
Reading for pleasure																					
None	—	—	—	—	—	—	—	—	15.6	18.0	18.5	20.2	20.2	20.6	20.1	20.4	21.0	20.3	18.8	19.0	18.7
Less than one hour	—	—	—	—	—	—	—	—	25.0	26.0	27.4	28.2	27.7	28.2	28.3	28.2	27.8	27.0	26.6	26.1	25.0
1 to 2 hours	—	—	—	—	—	—	—	—	27.0	26.7	26.9	26.1	26.8	26.7	26.7	26.6	25.9	25.5	26.3	25.9	26.5
3 to 5 hours	—	—	—	—	—	—	—	—	18.8	17.5	16.4	15.8	15.6	15.2	15.5	15.5	15.5	16.4	16.8	17.2	17.6
6 to 10 hours	—	—	—	—	—	—	—	—	8.1	7.1	6.6	5.8	5.9	5.7	5.7	5.8	5.9	6.4	6.9	7.0	7.2
11 to 15 hours	—	—	—	—	—	—	—	—	3.0	2.7	2.3	2.1	2.0	2.0	1.9	1.9	2.1	2.3	2.5	2.5	2.6
16 to 20 hours	—	—	—	—	—	—	—	—	1.2	1.1	0.9	0.9	0.9	0.8	0.8	0.7	0.9	0.9	1.0	1.1	1.2
Over 20 hours	—	—	—	—	—	—	—	—	1.4	1.1	0.9	0.9	0.9	0.8	0.9	0.9	0.9	1.0	1.0	1.2	1.2
Playing video games																					
None	—	—	—	—	—	—	—	—	—	80.9	83.3	81.8	75.3	75.5	—	—	—	—	—	—	—
Less than one hour	—	—	—	—	—	—	—	—	—	13.3	11.5	12.6	16.5	16.0	—	—	—	—	—	—	—
1 to 2 hours	—	—	—	—	—	—	—	—	—	3.8	3.5	3.8	5.5	5.6	—	—	—	—	—	—	—
3 to 5 hours	—	—	—	—	—	—	—	—	—	1.3	1.1	1.3	1.9	1.9	—	—	—	—	—	—	—
6 to 10 hours	—	—	—	—	—	—	—	—	—	0.4	0.4	0.4	0.6	0.6	—	—	—	—	—	—	—
11 to 15 hours	—	—	—	—	—	—	—	—	—	0.1	0.1	0.1	0.2	0.2	—	—	—	—	—	—	—
16 to 20 hours	—	—	—	—	—	—	—	—	—	0.1	0.0	0.1	0.1	0.1	—	—	—	—	—	—	—
Over 20 hours	—	—	—	—	—	—	—	—	—	0.1	0.1	0.1	0.1	0.1	—	—	—	—	—	—	—
Playing video/computer games																					
None	—	—	—	—	—	—	—	—	—	—	—	—	—	—	51.9	50.4	56.1	56.8	58.9	60.4	59.5
Less than one hour	—	—	—	—	—	—	—	—	—	—	—	—	—	—	25.7	25.7	25.1	24.1	22.7	21.7	20.9
1 to 2 hours	—	—	—	—	—	—	—	—	—	—	—	—	—	—	12.8	13.6	11.2	11.2	10.7	9.7	10.4
3 to 5 hours	—	—	—	—	—	—	—	—	—	—	—	—	—	—	5.9	6.4	4.9	5.0	4.8	4.8	5.4
6 to 10 hours	—	—	—	—	—	—	—	—	—	—	—	—	—	—	2.2	2.4	1.6	1.7	1.7	1.9	2.1
11 to 15 hours	—	—	—	—	—	—	—	—	—	—	—	—	—	—	0.8	0.7	0.6	0.6	0.7	0.7	0.8
16 to 20 hours	—	—	—	—	—	—	—	—	—	—	—	—	—	—	0.3	0.3	0.3	0.3	0.3	0.3	0.4
Over 20 hours	—	—	—	—	—	—	—	—	—	—	—	—	—	—	0.4	0.4	0.3	0.3	0.3	0.4	0.5

HIGH SCHOOL EXPERIENCES
FRESHMAN WOMEN

ITEM	1966	1967	1968	1969	1970	1971	1972	1973	1974	1975	1976	1977	1978	1979	1980	1981	1982	1983	1984	1985
Student rated self above average or highest 10% as compared with the average person of his/her age in:																				
Academic ability	64.8	—	—	—	—	62.0	—	—	63.1	—	61.0	—	—	—	59.8	—	—	—	—	64.9
Artistic ability	21.7	—	—	—	—	21.2	—	—	23.2	—	25.0	—	—	—	24.0	—	—	—	—	23.7
Athletic ability	24.4	—	—	—	—	25.2	—	—	26.9	—	27.8	—	—	—	29.4	—	—	—	—	—
Competitiveness	—	—	—	—	—	—	—	—	—	—	—	—	—	—	—	—	—	—	—	—
Computer skills	—	—	—	—	—	—	—	—	—	—	—	—	—	—	—	—	—	—	—	—
Cooperativeness	—	—	—	—	—	—	—	—	—	—	—	—	—	—	—	—	—	—	—	—
Creativity	—	—	—	—	—	—	—	—	—	—	—	—	—	—	—	—	—	—	—	68.4
Drive to achieve	60.8	—	—	—	—	58.8	—	—	65.8	—	67.7	—	—	—	70.8	—	—	—	—	59.3
Emotional health	—	—	—	—	—	—	—	—	—	—	—	—	—	—	—	—	—	—	—	—
Leadership ability	38.0	—	—	—	—	34.5	—	—	41.9	—	45.8	—	—	—	50.3	—	—	—	—	52.1
Mathematical ability	29.0	—	—	—	—	30.0	—	—	31.4	—	31.4	—	—	—	33.6	—	—	—	—	38.6
Physical health	—	—	—	—	—	—	—	—	—	—	—	—	—	—	—	—	—	—	—	53.9
Popularity	29.7	—	—	—	—	28.0	—	—	30.0	—	31.2	—	—	—	34.8	—	—	—	—	41.3
Public speaking ability	22.4	—	—	—	—	19.9	—	—	21.6	—	24.0	—	—	—	26.5	—	—	—	—	—
Self confidence (intellectual)	33.2	—	—	—	—	35.9	—	—	40.7	—	43.1	—	—	—	47.5	—	—	—	—	53.8
Self confidence (social)	25.9	—	—	—	—	26.2	—	—	33.2	—	36.5	—	—	—	42.0	—	—	—	—	46.6
Self understanding	—	—	—	—	—	—	—	—	—	—	—	—	—	—	—	—	—	—	—	—
Spirituality	—	—	—	—	—	—	—	—	—	—	—	—	—	—	—	—	—	—	—	—
Understanding of others	66.5	—	—	—	—	69.2	—	—	72.9	—	74.6	—	—	—	78.6	—	—	—	—	—
Writing ability	31.2	—	—	—	—	33.4	—	—	37.1	—	40.1	—	—	—	41.0	—	—	—	—	45.9

COLLEGE CHOICE
FRESHMAN WOMEN

ITEM	1966	1967	1968	1969	1970	1971	1972	1973	1974	1975	1976	1977	1978	1979	1980	1981	1982	1983	1984	1985
Reasons noted as very important in deciding to go to college																				
A mentor/role model encouraged me to go	—	—	—	—	—	—	—	—	—	—	4.2	5.3	3.8	4.7	4.8	5.3	6.2	5.0	4.4	—
I could not find a job	—	—	—	—	—	—	—	—	—	—	—	—	—	—	—	—	—	—	—	—
My parents wanted me to go	—	—	—	—	—	24.3	—	—	—	—	30.9	31.8	30.9	33.1	35.2	36.0	37.1	35.7	34.3	—
There was nothing better to do	—	—	—	—	—	2.3	—	—	—	—	2.5	2.4	1.7	2.0	2.0	2.1	2.0	2.0	1.8	2.2
To be able to get a better job	—	—	—	—	—	66.0	—	—	—	—	66.9	74.5	73.0	76.3	74.9	74.3	75.9	74.2	73.9	—
To be able to make more money	—	—	—	—	—	35.8	—	—	—	—	43.3	53.3	52.2	57.1	56.6	60.7	64.6	61.2	62.5	62.7
To get training for a specific career	—	—	—	—	—	—	—	—	—	—	—	—	—	—	—	—	—	—	—	—
To gain a general education and appreciation of ideas	—	—	—	—	—	70.0	—	—	—	—	74.6	79.7	78.0	77.0	76.3	76.5	76.0	73.7	74.1	69.9
To improve my reading and study skills	—	—	—	—	—	21.6	—	—	—	—	37.6	45.6	41.2	41.9	43.9	43.9	44.1	46.2	45.3	42.9
To learn more about things that interest me	—	—	—	—	—	75.9	—	—	—	—	80.8	85.4	80.9	80.1	81.3	79.8	79.7	78.6	78.6	79.2
To make me a more cultured person	—	—	—	—	—	35.2	—	—	—	—	41.8	47.8	42.1	41.9	44.2	42.8	43.9	41.3	42.7	41.3
To prepare for graduate or professional school	—	—	—	—	—	28.7	—	—	—	—	44.0	48.0	47.3	47.3	50.5	49.2	50.0	52.1	52.5	49.1
Wanted to get away from home	—	—	—	—	—	—	—	—	—	—	12.8	11.8	9.5	9.7	10.5	10.9	12.2	12.6	13.4	—

HIGH SCHOOL EXPERIENCES
FRESHMAN WOMEN

ITEM	1986	1987	1988	1989	1990	1991	1992	1993	1994	1995	1996	1997	1998	1999	2000	2001	2002	2003	2004	2005	2006
Student rated self above average or highest 10% as compared with the average person of his/her age in:																					
Academic ability	63.5	61.8	62.0	64.0	61.6	61.4	62.7	62.8	63.0	63.9	64.3	65.6	64.4	65.2	64.8	65.0	66.3	66.9	66.6	67.0	65.9
Artistic ability	24.2	25.6	24.5	24.0	24.4	23.8	24.7	23.5	25.0	25.1	25.8	26.0	28.0	27.3	28.9	30.6	29.7	29.8	30.3	30.2	29.8
Athletic ability	—	—	—	—	—	—	—	—	—	—	—	—	29.9	—	—	—	—	—	—	—	—
Competitiveness	—	—	46.8	47.6	46.8	46.5	47.1	46.9	46.6	47.1	46.0	46.2	45.5	46.0	45.4	45.2	—	—	—	—	—
Computer skills	—	—	—	—	—	—	—	—	—	—	—	—	—	21.7	23.2	23.4	26.4	27.7	26.5	29.2	29.2
Cooperativeness	—	—	—	—	75.6	75.4	74.9	75.3	74.2	75.9	73.7	74.9	74.0	74.4	74.2	73.1	73.8	74.5	69.7	74.3	74.3
Creativity	—	—	—	—	—	—	—	46.9	46.5	48.3	48.2	49.6	52.4	53.0	54.7	54.9	56.2	56.5	55.0	56.9	55.6
Drive to achieve	67.1	64.9	66.8	69.1	71.0	71.9	72.7	70.1	70.3	70.9	70.8	71.8	71.7	72.7	71.7	72.1	73.3	74.4	73.8	75.6	75.4
Emotional health	58.2	55.0	53.5	55.0	55.0	54.4	53.9	52.5	51.9	51.9	51.1	52.2	51.9	51.1	48.6	47.7	48.5	49.1	45.8	49.0	48.5
Leadership ability	53.6	51.8	51.6	52.7	51.8	51.0	51.8	53.3	53.9	56.1	55.0	56.6	57.1	58.7	58.2	56.3	57.3	57.1	57.1	58.7	58.2
Mathematical ability	38.2	38.3	38.1	38.3	36.3	36.0	37.0	36.4	37.5	37.8	37.4	37.6	37.5	36.5	36.5	36.0	36.9	36.9	36.8	36.5	35.9
Physical health	54.7	52.1	50.8	51.6	51.0	50.4	50.9	50.1	47.5	47.3	49.2	49.6	50.1	48.5	47.2	45.8	47.6	47.6	42.6	46.8	46.3
Popularity	43.1	41.3	40.2	40.5	39.8	39.1	37.1	37.3	33.1	33.6	35.2	37.0	35.1	34.4	34.3	32.9	33.3	32.5	—	—	—
Public speaking ability	—	31.5	31.1	32.2	31.2	32.9	31.9	32.9	32.8	33.3	33.2	34.3	34.3	35.2	35.0	33.8	34.3	33.9	32.4	34.1	34.2
Self confidence (intellectual)	53.6	47.3	47.7	50.0	47.8	52.2	51.5	52.6	50.3	51.8	52.5	53.4	53.7	53.9	53.1	51.3	52.4	52.1	50.4	53.2	52.2
Self confidence (social)	47.7	42.6	41.8	43.1	42.7	45.4	45.2	45.8	44.4	45.8	46.6	47.6	48.1	48.4	47.8	46.4	46.5	46.0	45.8	49.2	48.9
Self understanding	—	—	—	—	—	—	—	—	—	—	55.1	55.5	56.0	54.4	53.3	51.1	51.9	51.9	47.9	52.4	53.3
Spirituality	—	—	—	—	—	—	—	—	—	45.2	45.2	46.2	47.7	47.3	46.1	40.3	40.5	39.7	37.8	39.0	37.4
Understanding of others	—	—	—	—	74.4	73.2	73.8	73.6	77.0	77.0	69.9	69.6	69.0	68.4	68.0	67.2	68.2	67.9	66.3	68.8	68.7
Writing ability	47.3	45.0	45.2	46.2	46.1	47.4	46.6	47.1	45.8	46.9	47.9	48.2	47.8	48.2	47.2	46.8	47.4	47.7	47.8	48.8	49.3

COLLEGE CHOICE
FRESHMAN WOMEN

ITEM	1986	1987	1988	1989	1990	1991	1992	1993	1994	1995	1996	1997	1998	1999	2000	2001	2002	2003	2004	2005	2006
Reasons noted as very important in deciding to go to college																					
A mentor/role model encouraged me to go	—	—	—	—	—	—	14.4	14.6	13.9	14.7	14.7	14.3	15.7	13.2	13.9	13.5	14.6	14.0	—	16.7	18.1
I could not find a job	—	—	—	6.3	6.1	5.9	6.3	7.8	6.3	6.3	6.0	5.6	6.2	4.2	5.1	5.1	5.7	5.9	6.2	6.9	5.9
My parents wanted me to go	—	—	—	35.9	37.1	35.7	35.1	33.8	36.4	34.6	38.6	36.0	40.5	34.8	37.7	34.8	37.3	36.8	44.1	46.3	48.9
There was nothing better to do	2.0	1.9	1.9	1.9	1.9	2.3	2.1	2.1	2.5	2.4	2.3	2.3	—	2.3	2.5	2.5	2.8	2.9	2.9	3.1	3.0
To be able to get a better job	—	—	—	74.6	75.8	76.2	76.5	80.8	76.5	76.0	75.5	72.4	75.2	71.3	71.2	69.6	71.6	69.5	71.8	72.2	70.4
To be able to make more money	64.0	64.8	66.5	67.3	67.2	68.3	66.8	68.8	67.4	67.7	67.7	66.5	68.6	65.8	66.5	66.2	67.7	66.4	67.8	69.0	66.6
To get training for a specific career	—	—	—	—	—	—	—	—	—	—	—	—	—	74.5	74.4	73.7	74.0	73.1	78.2	73.1	72.7
To gain a general education and appreciation of ideas	69.5	68.3	66.8	71.2	71.6	69.7	71.3	72.6	68.0	71.1	70.0	68.1	69.6	68.2	69.9	70.4	71.3	70.4	70.2	71.1	69.9
To improve my reading and study skills	43.1	41.7	41.5	44.1	47.5	43.2	44.9	44.7	45.0	47.0	46.2	43.5	45.7	42.1	43.9	44.3	44.3	43.7	—	—	—
To learn more about things that interest me	79.9	77.8	78.4	77.9	78.6	78.2	78.5	79.9	78.9	79.7	79.8	79.3	—	77.8	79.8	80.8	80.6	80.0	80.7	81.4	80.6
To make me a more cultured person	41.5	42.3	43.3	44.4	49.5	48.4	48.3	51.8	46.8	49.4	46.5	45.2	—	44.0	45.3	47.1	47.3	45.9	46.2	48.3	47.4
To prepare for graduate or professional school	50.5	51.1	54.1	56.5	59.0	60.7	60.1	65.9	62.7	—	—	—	—	61.5	62.4	62.7	63.5	63.0	62.2	63.5	63.1
Wanted to get away from home	—	—	—	17.9	18.1	19.0	19.7	20.9	21.6	21.3	20.4	20.7	20.2	20.1	21.6	21.1	22.7	22.0	21.6	22.2	21.0

COLLEGE CHOICE
FRESHMAN WOMEN

ITEM	1966	1967	1968	1969	1970	1971	1972	1973	1974	1975	1976	1977	1978	1979	1980	1981	1982	1983	1984	1985
Reasons noted as very important in influencing student's decision to attend this particular college																				
A college rep. recruited me	—	—	—	—	—	—	—	—	—	3.6	3.8	4.1	3.7	4.1	4.4	4.0	4.1	3.2	3.2	3.7
A friend suggested attending	—	—	—	—	—	—	—	—	—	7.7	7.7	8.8	6.9	7.2	7.4	7.4	7.5	6.9	7.0	7.3
I wanted to go to a school about the size of this college	—	—	—	—	—	—	—	—	—	—	—	—	—	—	—	—	—	—	—	—
I wanted to live at home	—	—	—	—	—	8.1	7.6	7.6	7.5	7.9	7.0	8.6	7.0	7.4	7.4	7.5	7.3	—	—	—
I wanted to live near home	—	—	—	—	—	—	—	—	—	—	—	—	—	—	—	—	—	19.0	18.3	17.2
I was admitted through an Early Action or Early Decision program	—	—	—	—	—	—	—	—	—	—	—	—	—	—	—	—	—	—	—	—
I was attracted by the religious affiliation/orientation of the college	—	—	—	—	—	—	—	—	—	—	—	—	—	—	—	—	—	—	—	—
I was offered financial assistance	—	—	—	—	—	—	18.5	18.3	20.4	19.2	16.0	17.9	16.6	18.1	18.8	17.7	19.8	24.8	23.4	24.4
Information from a website	—	—	—	—	—	—	—	—	—	—	—	—	—	—	—	—	—	—	—	—
My guidance counselor advised me	—	—	—	—	—	5.3	5.5	7.9	7.9	7.5	6.4	7.5	6.8	7.0	7.1	7.0	6.8	7.2	7.0	6.5
High school guidance counselor advised me	—	—	—	—	—	—	—	—	—	—	—	—	—	—	—	—	—	—	—	—
Private college counselor advised me	—	—	—	—	—	—	—	—	—	—	—	—	—	—	—	—	—	—	—	—
My relatives wanted me to come here	—	—	—	—	—	9.1	—	—	—	8.5	7.6	7.4	6.6	6.8	7.2	7.4	7.2	7.1	7.1	6.8
My teacher advised me	—	—	—	—	—	—	—	5.2	5.4	5.1	4.0	4.4	4.0	4.0	4.2	3.9	3.9	4.0	4.1	4.0
Not accepted anywhere else	—	—	—	—	—	2.1	2.5	—	—	—	1.9	2.1	1.6	1.9	2.0	1.9	1.9	—	—	—
Not offered aid by first choice	—	—	—	—	—	—	—	—	—	—	—	—	—	—	—	—	—	—	4.6	4.8
Rankings in national magazines	—	—	—	—	—	—	—	—	—	—	—	—	—	—	—	—	—	2.2	2.1	2.5
The athletic dept. recruited me	—	—	—	—	—	—	—	—	—	—	—	—	—	—	—	—	—	—	—	—
This college's graduates gain admission to top graduate/professional schools	—	—	—	—	—	—	—	—	—	—	—	—	—	—	—	—	—	30.0	29.6	29.9
This college's graduates get good jobs	—	—	—	—	—	—	—	—	—	—	—	—	—	—	—	—	—	49.5	49.5	48.9
This college has a good reputation for its social activities	—	—	—	—	—	15.6	16.0	20.3	21.9	19.3	12.8	16.2	14.4	14.0	14.1	15.2	17.3	19.6	19.8	19.5
This college has low tuition	—	—	—	—	—	—	—	—	—	—	—	—	—	—	—	—	—	—	—	—
The cost of attending this college	—	—	—	—	—	—	—	—	—	—	—	—	—	—	—	—	—	24.4	25.8	25.6
This college has a very good academic reputation	—	—	—	—	—	—	61.0	63.0	63.1	59.9	55.1	58.2	61.4	59.2	60.5	60.9	61.5	62.7	64.9	64.7
This college offers special educational programs	—	—	—	—	—	34.9	30.0	34.9	36.6	33.6	30.8	34.8	31.5	32.7	33.2	31.9	30.5	26.5	25.9	25.3
Is this college your:																				
First choice?	—	—	—	—	—	—	—	—	77.5	80.4	78.2	76.5	77.5	76.0	76.1	75.2	74.3	73.9	73.8	72.9
Second choice?	—	—	—	—	—	—	—	—	18.4	16.2	17.4	18.3	18.1	18.9	18.8	19.5	20.2	20.8	20.8	21.1
Less than second choice?	—	—	—	—	—	—	—	—	4.2	3.4	4.4	5.1	4.4	5.0	5.1	5.3	5.5	—	—	—
Third choice?	—	—	—	—	—	—	—	—	—	—	—	—	—	—	—	—	—	3.9	3.9	4.3
Less than third choice?	—	—	—	—	—	—	—	—	—	—	—	—	—	—	—	—	—	1.4	1.4	1.7
How many miles is this college from your permanent home? [*]																				
10 or less	—	—	—	15.2	15.4	15.9	14.8	13.9	—	14.5	15.7	17.6	15.1	15.2	15.8	14.7	14.5	15.1	14.3	13.1
11 to 50	—	—	—	22.7	21.2	22.1	19.7	19.8	—	20.9	22.5	22.8	22.2	20.7	22.6	21.0	21.3	24.8	25.2	23.6
51 to 100	—	—	—	16.7	16.8	17.0	18.3	17.8	—	17.1	17.4	17.7	17.8	18.8	18.2	18.7	19.0	18.7	18.1	19.6
101 to 500	—	—	—	34.1	35.4	35.9	37.0	38.2	—	36.7	33.9	32.3	34.1	35.1	32.6	35.2	34.0	30.8	31.4	32.3
More than 500	—	—	—	11.3	11.1	9.0	10.1	10.3	—	10.8	10.5	9.6	10.9	10.2	10.8	10.4	11.1	10.6	11.0	11.5

COLLEGE CHOICE
FRESHMAN WOMEN

ITEM	1986	1987	1988	1989	1990	1991	1992	1993	1994	1995	1996	1997	1998	1999	2000	2001	2002	2003	2004	2005	2006
Reasons noted as very important in influencing student's decision to attend this particular college																					
A college rep. recruited me	3.6	3.6	3.6	3.5	3.7	4.1	4.1	4.2	4.1	4.0	3.9	4.0	—	—	—	—	—	—	—	—	—
A friend suggested attending	8.5	8.1	8.1	8.1	8.5	8.9	8.4	9.6	9.1	8.3	8.8	8.8	—	—	—	—	—	—	—	—	—
I wanted to go to a school about the size of this college	—	—	—	40.7	42.7	45.5	46.2	49.2	46.2	44.0	44.4	45.3	42.0	42.5	40.5	40.7	39.0	38.0	41.8	44.6	45.1
I wanted to live at home	18.2	16.9	18.2	18.9	19.2	19.6	19.6	19.1	19.7	19.6	20.6	20.2	19.5	18.9	19.5	19.3	20.3	19.6	20.1	22.0	21.5
I wanted to live near home	—	—	—	—	—	—	—	—	—	—	—	—	—	7.5	7.6	8.2	9.1	9.4	9.3	11.1	12.1
I was admitted through an Early Action or Early Decision program	—	—	—	—	—	—	—	—	—	—	—	—	—	—	—	—	—	—	—	—	—
I was attracted by the religious affiliation/orientation of the college	—	—	—	6.1	7.0	7.0	7.4	7.3	7.5	7.0	8.4	8.3	8.6	8.2	8.4	7.4	6.8	6.6	7.9	7.9	8.4
I was offered financial assistance	24.3	23.8	25.1	26.5	28.2	32.4	33.5	36.0	34.3	36.5	38.4	39.0	37.4	35.9	34.4	36.0	36.9	36.6	37.1	38.9	37.2
Information from a website	—	—	—	—	—	—	—	—	—	—	—	—	—	—	7.3	9.2	12.2	13.6	15.9	18.8	19.9
My guidance counselor advised me	7.4	6.4	7.1	6.1	6.5	7.1	6.6	—	—	—	—	—	—	—	—	—	—	—	—	—	—
High school guidance counselor advised me	—	—	—	—	—	—	—	7.8	6.3	6.3	6.2	6.7	6.0	5.9	6.0	6.3	6.6	6.4	7.7	8.2	8.7
Private college counselor advised me	—	—	—	—	—	—	—	1.5	2.2	2.1	2.0	1.6	1.8	1.9	2.0	1.9	2.1	2.1	2.3	2.5	2.7
My relatives wanted me to come here	8.7	7.8	7.4	8.9	9.2	8.9	8.5	9.2	9.0	8.6	8.9	8.4	8.0	7.7	8.1	7.8	9.6	9.2	9.9	11.3	12.1
My teacher advised me	4.1	3.6	3.8	3.2	3.6	3.7	3.7	4.0	3.5	3.5	3.6	3.3	3.2	3.1	3.5	3.7	4.3	4.1	4.8	5.3	6.0
Not accepted anywhere else	—	—	—	—	—	1.4	1.6	1.5	1.5	1.6	1.8	1.6	2.2	2.1	2.5	2.5	—	—	—	—	—
Not offered aid by first choice	5.1	4.9	5.2	5.7	—	—	—	—	—	—	6.3	6.0	6.6	5.9	5.9	6.3	6.5	6.5	6.6	7.4	7.1
Rankings in national magazines	—	—	—	—	—	—	—	—	—	10.7	11.5	11.9	10.0	9.7	9.6	10.4	12.8	12.6	14.8	16.9	16.7
The athletic dept. recruited me	2.5	2.7	2.7	2.8	2.8	3.2	3.5	3.5	3.8	3.9	4.3	4.4	—	—	—	—	4.7	—	—	—	5.7
This college's graduates gain admission to top graduate/professional schools	29.4	31.8	—	26.9	27.5	28.5	29.5	31.0	33.0	32.6	36.5	37.3	34.6	32.9	32.5	33.1	—	—	32.4	35.0	33.3
This college's graduates get good jobs	48.5	49.8	31.4	45.4	45.8	47.2	46.6	51.2	50.7	51.0	55.6	57.1	54.4	52.8	52.3	52.3	—	—	52.1	54.3	51.8
This college has a good reputation for its social activities	31.1	29.5	23.9	24.5	24.3	25.7	27.1	29.6	26.2	26.6	28.0	29.6	28.3	27.6	28.7	28.5	29.2	28.7	29.1	32.4	33.5
This college has low tuition	21.1	19.2	19.8	22.0	23.5	25.8	26.2	28.7	26.8	26.2	27.7	28.2	24.7	23.0	21.9	22.1	23.5	22.2	—	—	—
The cost of attending this college	—	—	—	—	—	—	—	—	—	—	—	—	—	—	—	—	—	—	33.9	35.4	34.9
This college has a very good academic reputation	66.6	63.5	61.9	59.9	60.2	62.1	62.5	63.6	61.6	61.1	62.9	63.9	60.2	58.2	58.6	59.1	58.6	58.3	60.4	61.5	61.4
This college offers special educational programs	26.7	25.7	25.5	23.4	25.8	26.0	27.0	28.4	26.5	25.4	26.7	26.3	24.6	24.7	24.8	25.2	25.2	25.2	—	—	—
Is this college your:																					
First choice?	71.1	69.6	67.1	69.6	71.4	72.5	72.6	72.3	73.7	72.0	71.7	70.9	71.9	72.4	70.9	69.7	69.2	68.5	69.9	69.3	66.8
Second choice?	22.2	23.0	24.6	23.2	22.1	21.3	21.2	20.9	20.0	20.7	21.0	21.2	20.7	20.0	20.9	21.9	21.7	22.3	21.4	21.7	23.2
Less than second choice?	—	—	—	—	—	—	—	—	—	—	—	—	—	—	—	—	—	—	—	—	—
Third choice?	4.6	5.2	5.7	5.1	4.6	4.4	4.4	4.7	4.3	4.9	4.9	5.3	5.0	5.0	5.4	5.5	5.8	5.8	5.7	5.8	6.4
Less than third choice?	2.1	2.1	2.6	2.1	1.9	1.8	1.8	2.0	2.0	2.4	2.5	2.6	2.4	2.5	2.8	2.9	3.3	3.3	3.0	3.2	3.7
How many miles is this college from your permanent home? [*]																					
10 or less	11.7	10.4	10.5	11.2	10.5	10.9	10.2	10.4	10.5	11.0	10.6	10.6	10.4	10.6	11.4	11.6	11.8	11.5	10.9	11.3	10.8
11 to 50	23.4	21.8	22.6	21.9	23.6	22.9	21.9	21.3	21.8	22.0	21.7	22.6	22.8	22.5	24.1	25.3	23.9	25.5	24.7	27.0	24.8
51 to 100	18.8	20.5	17.8	17.5	19.1	17.6	17.3	18.2	18.1	17.1	17.8	18.0	18.7	17.7	17.3	17.5	18.0	17.1	18.3	18.5	19.0
101 to 500	32.7	34.1	35.0	36.3	34.2	36.1	37.6	37.6	36.7	37.2	37.2	35.8	36.6	37.0	34.9	33.7	34.1	33.7	33.9	30.8	32.0
More than 500	13.4	13.2	14.0	13.1	12.5	12.5	12.9	12.5	12.8	12.6	12.6	13.0	11.5	12.1	12.2	11.9	12.2	12.2	12.2	12.3	13.4

COLLEGE CHOICE
FRESHMAN WOMEN

ITEM	1966	1967	1968	1969	1970	1971	1972	1973	1974	1975	1976	1977	1978	1979	1980	1981	1982	1983	1984	1985
To how many colleges other than this one did you apply for admission this year?																				
None	—	46.0	47.4	46.1	—	—	39.6	40.1	—	41.2	37.8	36.4	35.2	34.2	34.3	33.3	32.3	31.1	30.4	28.4
One	—	21.1	21.7	22.6	—	—	21.0	21.2	—	23.2	21.2	20.1	19.4	19.0	18.5	19.4	18.1	19.4	18.6	21.3
Two	—	15.8	15.3	15.7	—	—	17.2	16.4	—	15.5	16.7	17.8	18.4	18.5	18.2	18.8	18.3	19.1	18.8	17.9
Three	—	9.5	8.7	8.5	—	—	10.5	10.4	—	9.6	11.8	12.3	13.1	13.7	13.8	13.6	14.4	14.2	15.0	14.2
Four	—	4.4	4.0	4.0	—	—	5.5	5.9	—	5.1	5.8	6.2	6.6	6.6	7.0	7.0	7.6	7.5	7.8	7.8
Five	—	2.1	1.9	1.9	—	—	3.4	3.2	—	2.8	3.3	3.7	3.7	4.1	4.2	3.9	4.5	4.2	4.6	4.9
Six or more	—	1.1	1.0	1.2	—	—	3.0	2.8	—	2.7	3.3	3.4	3.5	3.9	4.0	4.1	4.8	4.5	4.9	5.5
Six	—	—	—	—	—	—	—	—	—	—	—	—	—	—	—	—	—	—	—	—
Seven to ten	—	—	—	—	—	—	—	—	—	—	—	—	—	—	—	—	—	—	—	—
Eleven or more	—	—	—	—	—	—	—	—	—	—	—	—	—	—	—	—	—	—	—	—
How many other acceptances did you receive this year?																				
None	—	39.2	40.3	—	—	—	—	—	—	19.0	17.7	17.3	14.4	15.0	14.0	13.7	11.3	11.3	10.8	10.7
One	—	29.9	30.4	—	—	—	—	—	—	36.5	33.6	33.3	32.4	31.8	31.3	32.1	31.2	31.2	30.4	29.8
Two	—	19.1	18.6	—	—	—	—	—	—	23.5	23.8	24.8	25.5	25.3	25.7	26.2	26.3	26.3	26.1	25.9
Three	—	8.2	7.5	—	—	—	—	—	—	12.0	14.3	14.3	15.8	16.2	16.5	15.9	17.2	17.2	17.9	17.8
Four	—	2.5	2.1	—	—	—	—	—	—	5.3	6.0	6.0	6.8	6.6	7.2	7.0	7.6	7.8	8.1	8.6
Five	—	0.7	0.7	—	—	—	—	—	—	2.0	2.6	2.4	2.9	2.9	2.9	2.9	3.3	3.3	3.7	4.0
Six or more	—	0.4	0.3	—	—	—	—	—	—	1.7	2.0	1.9	2.2	2.2	2.4	2.3	3.0	3.0	3.0	3.2
Six	—	—	—	—	—	—	—	—	—	—	—	—	—	—	—	—	—	—	—	—
Seven to ten	—	—	—	—	—	—	—	—	—	—	—	—	—	—	—	—	—	—	—	—
Eleven or more	—	—	—	—	—	—	—	—	—	—	—	—	—	—	—	—	—	—	—	—
Prior to this term, have you ever taken courses for credit at this institution?																				
No	—	—	—	—	—	—	97.3	97.9	97.7	97.4	97.3	97.2	97.4	97.3	97.1	97.4	97.5	97.4	97.4	97.1
Yes	—	—	—	—	—	—	2.7	2.1	2.3	2.6	2.7	2.8	2.6	2.7	2.9	2.6	2.5	2.6	2.6	2.9

PLANS, GOALS, AND EXPECTATIONS
FRESHMAN WOMEN

ITEM	1966	1967	1968	1969	1970	1971	1972	1973	1974	1975	1976	1977	1978	1979	1980	1981	1982	1983	1984	1985
What is the highest academic degree you intend to obtain anywhere?																				
None	3.3	2.4	2.4	1.1	1.1	—	1.6	—	2.1	2.1	2.0	1.6	1.3	1.1	1.3	1.5	1.2	1.4	1.0	1.4
Vocational certificate	—	—	—	—	—	—	—	—	—	—	—	—	—	—	—	—	—	0.4	0.4	0.4
Associate (A.A.) or equivalent	1.8	1.3	1.9	2.1	2.4	—	1.9	—	2.4	1.9	1.9	2.4	1.9	2.7	1.9	1.9	1.9	1.3	1.6	1.1
Bachelor's (B.A., B.S., etc.)	48.4	46.6	46.7	47.1	47.3	—	44.0	—	41.4	38.8	37.7	36.3	38.0	36.3	36.8	37.7	37.6	34.9	35.2	34.9
Master's degree (M.A., M.S., etc.)	36.4	38.6	38.1	38.4	36.0	—	34.3	—	32.5	34.1	34.2	35.5	34.5	36.2	35.1	35.9	35.2	35.9	36.0	36.2
Ph.D. or Ed.D.	6.0	7.0	7.4	7.6	8.0	—	8.6	—	9.2	9.6	9.9	10.3	10.5	9.9	9.6	9.2	9.8	10.5	11.3	11.2
M.D., D.D.S., D.V.M. or D.O.	2.2	2.3	2.0	2.2	2.7	—	5.3	—	6.8	6.8	7.1	6.5	7.0	6.9	7.5	7.0	7.2	7.6	7.6	8.3
LL.B. or J.D. (law)	0.4	0.4	0.4	0.5	1.2	—	2.7	—	3.5	4.1	4.6	4.8	4.8	4.7	5.1	4.6	5.1	5.0	4.8	4.7
B.D. or M.Div. (divinity)	0.0	0.1	0.2	0.2	0.1	—	0.2	—	0.2	0.3	0.4	0.4	0.3	0.5	0.5	0.4	0.3	0.5	0.4	0.3
Other	1.2	1.1	1.1	1.0	1.1	—	1.5	—	1.8	2.2	2.3	2.2	1.8	1.8	2.1	1.8	1.7	2.4	1.8	1.4

COLLEGE CHOICE
FRESHMAN WOMEN

ITEM	1986	1987	1988	1989	1990	1991	1992	1993	1994	1995	1996	1997	1998	1999	2000	2001	2002	2003	2004	2005	2006
To how many colleges other than this one did you apply for admission this year?																					
None	28.4	27.5	25.5	25.6	24.4	26.0	23.4	22.0	24.0	24.5	24.3	24.8	23.0	22.3	20.4	19.6	19.9	18.2	19.2	17.0	17.1
One	17.9	16.7	15.8	15.7	16.2	16.0	16.1	16.5	15.6	15.2	15.0	15.7	14.7	14.4	13.4	13.1	13.2	12.4	12.8	12.1	11.0
Two	17.4	17.4	17.8	17.5	18.2	18.0	18.2	18.3	17.9	17.3	17.3	16.5	16.9	16.8	16.2	16.2	15.8	15.4	15.3	15.0	14.8
Three	15.4	15.7	16.3	15.8	16.1	16.2	16.9	16.7	16.2	15.6	15.7	15.6	16.6	16.4	17.2	16.8	16.7	16.5	16.2	16.6	16.5
Four	8.8	9.5	9.8	9.9	10.0	9.8	10.2	10.7	10.3	10.2	10.4	10.1	11.0	11.3	11.9	12.1	12.1	12.6	11.9	12.4	12.6
Five	5.8	6.0	6.5	6.8	6.7	6.4	6.8	7.0	6.8	7.1	7.2	6.7	7.0	7.5	7.8	8.2	8.3	8.7	8.2	8.8	9.2
Six or more	6.3	7.2	8.3	8.6	8.4	7.8	8.4	8.8	9.2	10.1	10.2	—	—	—	—	—	—	—	—	—	—
Six	—	—	—	—	—	—	—	—	—	—	—	4.4	4.5	4.6	5.2	5.4	5.5	6.1	5.9	6.4	6.6
Seven to ten	—	—	—	—	—	—	—	—	—	—	—	5.3	5.5	5.8	6.6	7.2	7.2	8.3	8.6	9.5	9.9
Eleven or more	—	—	—	—	—	—	—	—	—	—	—	0.8	0.9	1.0	1.2	1.4	1.4	1.8	1.9	2.2	2.3
How many other acceptances did you receive this year?																					
None	11.8	10.8	9.7	9.0	—	—	—	—	—	6.6	6.3	7.0	7.1	—	—	—	—	—	—	—	—
One	28.1	28.4	27.5	26.5	—	—	—	—	—	24.0	23.4	24.5	23.3	—	—	—	—	—	—	—	—
Two	25.4	24.8	25.8	25.1	—	—	—	—	—	24.0	24.3	23.4	23.6	—	—	—	—	—	—	—	—
Three	18.1	18.7	18.8	19.1	—	—	—	—	—	19.5	19.9	19.4	20.1	—	—	—	—	—	—	—	—
Four	9.1	9.3	9.6	10.5	—	—	—	—	—	11.8	11.9	11.5	12.1	—	—	—	—	—	—	—	—
Five	4.2	4.2	4.5	5.1	—	—	—	—	—	6.6	6.8	6.8	6.4	—	—	—	—	—	—	—	—
Six or more	3.5	3.7	4.0	4.8	—	—	—	—	—	7.6	7.4	—	—	—	—	—	—	—	—	—	—
Six	—	—	—	—	—	—	—	—	—	—	—	3.3	3.3	—	—	—	—	—	—	—	—
Seven to ten	—	—	—	—	—	—	—	—	—	—	—	3.6	3.6	—	—	—	—	—	—	—	—
Eleven or more	—	—	—	—	—	—	—	—	—	—	—	0.5	0.4	—	—	—	—	—	—	—	—
Prior to this term, have you ever taken courses for credit at this institution?																					
No	97.2	96.8	96.7	96.9	96.9	96.6	96.9	96.6	96.5	96.5	96.3	96.3	95.6	96.0	96.0	96.0	96.2	96.7	96.3	96.7	96.7
Yes	2.8	3.2	3.3	3.1	3.1	3.4	3.1	3.4	3.5	3.5	3.7	3.7	4.4	4.0	4.0	4.0	3.8	3.3	3.7	3.3	3.3

PLANS, GOALS, AND EXPECTATIONS
FRESHMAN WOMEN

ITEM	1986	1987	1988	1989	1990	1991	1992	1993	1994	1995	1996	1997	1998	1999	2000	2001	2002	2003	2004	2005	2006
What is the highest academic degree you intend to obtain anywhere?																					
None	1.4	1.2	1.3	0.6	0.9	0.8	1.8	0.4	0.5	0.5	0.5	0.4	0.5	0.4	—	0.5	0.8	0.7	0.9	0.6	0.8
Vocational certificate	0.3	0.2	0.3	0.1	0.2	0.2	0.2	0.1	0.1	0.1	0.1	0.1	0.1	0.1	—	0.1	0.1	0.1	0.1	0.1	0.1
Associate (A.A.) or equivalent	1.0	0.7	1.2	0.8	0.8	0.8	0.7	0.6	0.5	0.5	0.6	0.5	0.5	0.5	—	0.4	0.5	0.4	0.6	0.5	0.5
Bachelor's (B.A., B.S., etc.)	33.4	31.8	27.6	27.1	25.8	24.3	28.5	23.1	22.5	22.7	21.2	21.0	22.2	22.3	—	21.6	21.7	22.3	22.1	21.8	21.8
Master's degree (M.A., M.S., etc.)	39.0	39.8	40.6	41.5	41.2	40.6	40.7	41.2	40.6	40.8	41.3	42.0	43.2	42.5	—	43.3	42.8	41.5	41.2	42.2	42.3
Ph.D. or Ed.D.	11.7	12.5	14.3	14.5	15.0	16.3	13.3	17.1	17.3	17.3	18.0	18.3	17.1	17.1	—	17.4	17.5	17.7	17.5	17.5	17.3
M.D., D.D.S., D.V.M. or D.O.	7.3	7.0	7.2	7.6	8.1	9.3	9.0	11.1	11.6	12.1	12.1	11.9	10.7	10.7	—	10.5	10.5	10.6	10.9	10.5	10.4
LL.B. or J.D. (law)	4.6	5.2	5.9	6.1	6.2	5.9	4.7	5.2	5.2	4.5	4.4	4.4	4.0	4.3	—	4.5	4.8	5.0	4.8	5.0	4.6
B.D. or M.Div. (divinity)	0.2	0.2	0.3	0.2	0.3	0.2	0.1	0.2	0.3	0.3	0.3	0.2	0.3	0.4	—	0.3	0.2	0.2	0.2	0.3	0.3
Other	1.4	1.3	1.4	1.4	1.4	1.4	1.1	1.1	1.3	1.2	1.4	1.2	1.3	1.5	—	1.3	1.2	1.4	1.7	1.4	1.8

PLANS, GOALS, AND EXPECTATIONS
FRESHMAN WOMEN

ITEM	1966	1967	1968	1969	1970	1971	1972	1973	1974	1975	1976	1977	1978	1979	1980	1981	1982	1983	1984	1985
What is the highest academic degree you intend to obtain at this institution?																				
None	—	—	—	—	—	—	5.6	4.6	5.8	5.2	5.0	4.2	3.7	3.0	3.3	3.3	2.6	2.5	2.6	2.5
Vocational certificate	—	—	—	—	—	—	—	—	—	—	—	—	—	—	—	—	—	0.5	0.4	0.4
Associate (A.A.) or equivalent	—	—	—	—	—	—	3.4	3.4	4.5	3.8	3.8	4.8	3.7	5.7	4.1	4.6	3.5	3.2	3.7	2.4
Bachelor's (B.A., B.S., etc.)	—	—	—	—	—	—	75.3	74.9	72.2	71.6	72.6	70.9	73.3	70.8	71.4	71.3	71.7	71.9	72.1	72.1
Master's degree (M.A., M.S., etc.)	—	—	—	—	—	—	11.5	12.6	12.2	13.4	12.5	13.7	13.6	14.5	14.2	14.7	15.2	14.3	14.8	15.9
Ph.D. or Ed.D.	—	—	—	—	—	—	1.3	1.5	1.4	1.7	1.6	1.7	1.7	1.8	1.9	1.8	2.1	1.9	2.0	2.2
M.D., D.D.S., D.V.M. or D.O.	—	—	—	—	—	—	1.1	1.3	1.5	1.4	1.6	1.5	1.7	1.7	2.0	1.6	2.0	2.1	1.8	2.1
LL.B. or J.D. (law)	—	—	—	—	—	—	0.5	0.6	0.6	0.8	0.8	1.0	1.0	1.0	1.1	1.1	1.3	1.2	1.1	0.9
B.D. or M.Div. (divinity)	—	—	—	—	—	—	0.1	0.0	0.1	0.2	0.4	0.3	0.2	0.2	0.3	0.2	0.3	0.5	0.2	0.2
Other	—	—	—	—	—	—	1.2	1.0	1.6	1.8	1.7	1.8	1.2	1.4	1.7	1.3	1.2	1.8	1.2	1.3
Your probable career/occupation [2,3]																				
Artist	8.9	8.8	8.4	8.3	8.4	8.4	8.9	—	—	—	9.6	9.8	9.1	9.4	9.1	9.1	9.0	8.4	7.7	8.4
Business	2.6	2.2	2.4	2.4	3.0	3.2	3.5	—	—	—	9.6	11.8	14.1	15.1	16.3	16.9	17.9	18.3	20.3	21.1
Clerical	0.7	0.3	0.1	0.3	0.2	2.6	2.2	—	—	—	1.7	1.8	1.6	1.8	1.3	1.4	1.2	1.2	1.1	1.2
Clergy	—	—	—	—	—	—	0.3	—	—	—	0.3	0.2	0.2	0.2	0.2	0.2	0.1	0.2	0.1	0.2
College teacher	1.6	1.1	1.0	0.9	1.1	0.7	0.7	—	—	—	0.4	0.3	0.4	0.3	0.2	0.2	0.2	0.3	0.3	0.3
Doctor (MD or DDS)	1.8	1.7	1.6	1.5	1.9	2.5	3.5	—	—	—	4.5	4.2	4.5	4.7	4.9	4.8	5.0	5.5	5.3	5.9
Education (secondary)	20.5	21.7	20.9	20.2	17.3	13.3	10.2	—	—	—	5.6	5.0	4.2	4.0	3.1	3.3	2.7	2.8	3.2	3.6
Education (elementary)	16.4	18.6	20.0	20.4	17.9	15.0	12.8	—	—	—	9.2	8.9	7.5	7.9	7.4	7.2	6.1	6.2	6.2	6.6
Engineer	0.2	0.2	0.2	0.4	0.6	0.3	0.4	—	—	—	1.9	1.8	2.5	2.6	3.3	3.2	3.8	3.6	3.4	3.5
Farmer or forester	0.2	0.1	0.1	0.2	0.5	0.5	0.7	—	—	—	1.0	1.1	0.8	0.9	0.6	0.6	0.5	0.3	0.3	0.3
Health professional	6.7	6.3	5.8	5.9	6.7	8.9	10.7	—	—	—	11.3	10.6	9.4	9.0	8.6	8.2	7.6	8.1	8.0	7.0
Homemaker	—	—	—	—	—	1.0	0.9	—	—	—	0.4	0.3	0.3	0.3	0.2	0.3	0.3	0.1	0.1	0.2
Lawyer	0.8	0.8	0.7	1.0	1.4	1.9	2.7	—	—	—	4.2	4.5	4.6	4.5	4.8	4.3	5.2	4.7	4.7	4.7
Military	—	—	—	—	—	—	0.1	—	—	—	0.2	0.4	0.6	0.5	0.3	0.4	0.3	0.4	0.5	0.4
Nurse	4.3	4.1	4.5	4.6	5.8	6.4	7.1	—	—	—	8.2	7.1	7.0	6.5	7.2	6.8	7.1	7.6	6.7	5.2
Research scientist	2.3	2.0	2.1	1.9	2.2	2.1	2.0	—	—	—	2.3	2.0	2.2	1.7	1.5	1.4	1.3	1.5	1.5	1.6
Social worker	—	—	—	—	—	5.5	4.9	—	—	—	4.6	4.4	4.0	3.7	3.1	2.6	1.9	1.9	1.9	1.9
Skilled worker	—	—	—	—	—	0.1	0.1	—	—	—	0.2	0.2	0.1	0.2	0.2	0.2	0.1	0.1	0.1	0.1
Other career	29.0	21.2	20.2	20.0	20.2	12.1	12.2	—	—	—	12.7	13.1	13.9	14.5	14.8	15.8	16.9	15.9	14.9	14.0
Undecided	3.8	10.7	11.8	12.2	13.1	15.3	16.4	—	—	—	12.2	12.3	13.1	12.5	12.8	13.1	12.9	12.8	13.7	13.9

PLANS, GOALS, AND EXPECTATIONS
FRESHMAN WOMEN

ITEM	1986	1987	1988	1989	1990	1991	1992	1993	1994	1995	1996	1997	1998	1999	2000	2001	2002	2003	2004	2005	2006
What is the highest academic degree you intend to obtain at this institution?																					
None	2.3	2.0	2.2	2.3	2.2	2.0	—	1.7	1.7	1.6	1.4	1.4	1.2	1.2	—	1.2	1.4	1.3	1.4	1.1	1.2
Vocational certificate	0.3	0.3	0.3	0.2	0.3	0.3	—	0.2	0.2	0.1	0.2	0.2	0.3	0.2	—	0.2	0.2	0.3	0.2	0.2	0.2
Associate (A.A.) or equivalent	2.1	2.1	3.0	2.4	2.3	2.5	—	1.9	1.9	1.8	1.6	2.1	1.8	2.0	—	1.9	1.9	1.6	1.9	1.7	1.6
Bachelor's (B.A., B.S., etc.)	73.3	73.3	69.7	71.5	70.4	69.6	—	70.1	68.9	69.8	68.6	68.8	67.3	71.4	—	69.6	70.0	71.1	70.4	70.0	67.8
Master's degree (M.A., M.S., etc.)	16.2	16.5	18.1	17.3	18.1	18.8	—	19.2	19.8	19.2	20.2	19.9	21.8	18.7	—	20.2	19.9	18.5	18.7	19.5	20.6
Ph.D. or Ed.D.	2.1	2.0	2.5	2.4	2.6	2.7	—	2.9	3.1	3.0	3.4	3.3	3.2	2.4	—	3.1	3.1	3.2	3.4	3.5	3.7
M.D., D.D.S., D.V.M. or D.O.	1.6	1.6	1.6	1.4	1.6	1.8	—	2.1	2.1	2.4	2.6	2.5	2.3	1.8	—	1.9	1.9	2.0	1.9	2.0	2.4
LL.B. or J.D. (law)	0.9	1.0	1.2	1.1	1.1	1.1	—	1.0	1.1	0.8	0.8	0.8	0.7	0.7	—	0.7	0.7	0.7	0.7	0.8	0.9
B.D. or M.Div. (divinity)	0.2	0.1	0.2	0.1	0.2	0.2	—	0.1	0.1	0.2	0.1	0.1	0.2	0.2	—	0.1	0.1	0.2	0.1	0.1	0.2
Other	1.0	1.0	1.2	1.2	1.2	1.2	—	0.9	1.1	1.1	1.1	1.0	1.1	1.4	—	1.0	0.9	1.1	1.3	1.1	1.4
Your probable career/occupation [2,3]																					
Artist	9.1	9.5	8.8	8.3	7.8	7.5	7.6	7.2	7.4	7.9	7.4	7.7	8.5	8.6	9.7	9.4	9.4	9.1	8.5	9.3	9.1
Business	21.2	20.6	20.2	18.6	16.1	14.0	12.0	11.4	11.3	11.8	11.5	11.6	11.7	12.0	12.0	11.3	10.9	10.5	10.7	11.2	11.6
Clerical	0.8	0.7	0.7	0.7	0.9	0.7	0.6	0.6	0.6	0.6	0.6	0.6	0.7	0.7	0.7	0.7	0.6	0.6	0.5	0.5	0.6
Clergy	0.1	0.1	0.1	0.1	0.1	0.1	0.1	0.1	0.2	0.2	0.2	0.2	0.3	0.2	0.3	0.2	0.3	0.2	0.2	0.2	0.2
College teacher	0.4	0.4	0.4	0.5	0.5	0.5	0.6	0.5	0.6	0.6	0.6	0.5	0.6	0.5	0.5	0.5	0.4	0.4	0.5	0.5	0.4
Doctor (MD or DDS)	5.2	4.9	5.2	5.4	5.7	6.6	7.2	7.6	8.0	8.6	8.5	8.9	7.7	7.9	7.6	7.7	7.7	7.9	8.1	7.7	7.9
Education (secondary)	4.2	4.5	4.2	4.5	5.1	5.0	5.0	4.6	4.7	4.5	4.9	4.8	5.0	4.9	5.3	5.0	5.4	5.0	5.2	5.4	5.4
Education (elementary)	8.0	8.7	8.6	8.4	9.7	9.5	8.9	8.7	8.8	8.8	9.0	9.1	10.0	10.1	10.2	8.9	9.3	8.6	8.4	8.3	7.9
Engineer	3.0	2.8	2.7	3.1	3.1	3.5	3.4	3.6	3.0	2.5	3.1	3.1	2.5	2.6	2.6	2.5	2.3	2.2	2.4	2.0	2.0
Farmer or forester	0.2	0.2	0.2	0.3	0.4	0.4	0.5	0.6	0.6	0.7	0.6	0.4	0.5	0.5	0.3	0.3	0.3	0.3	0.3	0.3	0.3
Health professional	6.6	6.7	7.0	6.9	6.8	8.0	9.5	10.5	10.5	10.9	10.4	10.4	10.1	8.6	7.2	7.1	7.7	8.2	9.7	9.2	9.0
Homemaker	0.2	0.2	0.1	0.2	0.1	0.1	0.1	0.1	0.1	0.2	0.1	0.2	0.2	0.2	0.2	0.1	0.1	0.3	0.2	0.1	0.1
Lawyer	4.9	5.5	6.3	6.4	6.6	6.2	5.6	5.2	5.4	4.4	4.0	4.1	3.9	4.2	4.2	4.1	4.4	4.4	4.2	4.3	4.0
Military	0.4	0.3	0.3	0.2	0.3	0.2	0.2	0.2	0.3	0.2	0.5	0.3	0.2	0.3	0.2	0.3	0.3	0.3	0.3	0.2	0.4
Nurse	3.7	3.0	3.1	3.1	4.1	5.3	5.9	5.7	5.2	4.6	4.1	3.8	3.8	3.8	3.6	4.1	4.5	5.8	6.6	6.5	6.8
Research scientist	1.4	1.5	1.5	1.7	1.6	1.7	1.9	2.0	2.1	2.4	2.2	2.3	1.9	2.1	1.8	1.8	1.6	1.7	1.8	1.6	1.7
Social worker	1.9	1.9	2.1	1.8	1.7	1.8	1.8	2.0	2.0	2.1	2.0	1.9	1.7	1.8	1.8	1.5	1.4	1.4	1.4	1.5	1.5
Skilled worker	0.1	0.1	0.1	0.1	0.1	0.1	0.2	0.2	0.1	0.1	0.1	0.1	0.1	0.2	0.1	0.1	0.1	0.1	0.1	0.1	0.1
Other career	13.7	13.9	14.5	15.4	15.7	15.2	15.3	15.7	15.4	15.8	16.6	16.2	17.0	17.3	17.1	18.0	17.7	17.8	16.3	16.5	16.6
Undecided	14.6	14.4	13.7	14.2	13.5	13.4	13.5	13.4	13.6	13.5	13.7	13.5	13.5	13.8	14.5	16.2	15.6	15.4	14.7	14.6	14.4

PLANS, GOALS, AND EXPECTATIONS
FRESHMAN WOMEN

ITEM	1966	1967	1968	1969	1970	1971	1972	1973	1974	1975	1976	1977	1978	1979	1980	1981	1982	1983	1984	1985
Your probable major field [2]																				
Agriculture	0.1	0.1	0.1	0.2	0.3	0.3	0.5	0.7	1.1	1.3	1.3	1.1	1.0	0.9	0.7	0.8	0.6	0.4	0.5	0.5
Biological Science	3.5	3.7	3.6	3.2	3.5	3.8	4.2	7.1	7.1	6.9	7.1	5.3	5.4	4.6	4.2	4.1	4.1	4.4	4.8	4.7
Business	6.8	5.5	6.1	5.3	5.4	6.4	6.2	7.9	8.9	10.4	11.8	14.4	16.5	17.9	18.7	19.8	20.6	20.9	22.9	22.8
Education	18.3	18.7	20.3	20.5	21.4	17.7	13.8	21.4	18.2	17.7	16.1	15.6	13.6	14.1	12.6	11.9	10.0	9.7	9.8	10.3
Engineering	0.3	0.3	0.3	0.5	0.6	0.3	0.3	0.6	1.3	1.8	1.9	2.1	2.8	2.9	3.6	3.4	4.1	3.8	3.5	3.8
English	8.1	7.9	7.4	7.2	5.6	4.2	3.1	2.7	2.2	1.8	1.9	1.7	1.8	1.6	1.5	1.5	1.4	1.6	1.7	1.8
Health Professional	8.5	8.3	8.6	8.9	10.6	13.8	16.4	10.2	12.4	12.6	12.9	14.7	14.6	14.1	15.1	14.5	14.6	16.1	14.9	13.1
History or Political Science	6.4	6.6	6.4	6.0	5.0	3.9	3.4	4.1	3.7	3.6	3.5	3.5	3.6	3.1	3.2	3.0	2.9	3.1	3.4	4.2
Humanities	8.5	8.3	6.9	6.6	5.7	6.8	7.2	5.9	5.1	4.3	4.2	3.7	3.3	3.2	3.0	3.1	3.2	2.6	2.8	3.0
Fine Arts	10.6	11.4	11.3	11.3	11.3	7.8	7.6	6.3	6.6	6.1	5.9	6.0	6.0	5.6	5.5	5.3	4.9	4.6	4.1	3.8
Mathematics or Statistics	5.4	5.5	5.2	4.9	4.7	3.9	3.0	2.1	1.7	1.4	1.7	1.0	1.1	1.5	0.9	0.9	1.0	1.1	1.2	1.1
Physical Sciences	1.4	1.4	1.1	1.2	1.2	1.1	1.0	1.4	1.5	1.6	1.7	1.5	1.7	1.5	1.3	1.4	1.2	1.3	1.3	1.4
Social Sciences	12.1	12.3	13.2	14.3	13.8	14.0	12.7	11.2	10.7	10.2	9.3	9.0	9.0	8.6	7.7	7.1	6.5	6.6	7.4	8.0
Other Technical	0.6	1.0	0.9	1.2	1.6	3.7	4.3	4.1	4.8	5.1	5.0	4.5	4.6	5.1	6.2	7.6	8.7	8.2	5.5	4.3
Other Non-technical	7.5	7.6	6.7	6.8	6.8	9.8	10.8	8.7	9.2	9.1	10.4	9.4	9.0	9.7	9.3	8.9	9.3	8.5	8.6	9.2
Undecided	1.7	1.6	2.0	2.2	2.4	2.5	5.4	5.5	5.5	6.1	5.8	6.5	6.3	6.4	6.6	6.8	6.9	7.1	7.4	8.0
Where do you plan to live during the fall term?																				
With parents or relatives	—	—	—	—	—	—	—	19.9	21.9	20.4	23.2	26.1	21.5	20.9	21.5	19.6	20.3	22.2	21.2	18.1
Other private home, apartment, room	—	—	—	—	—	—	—	1.3	2.6	2.1	2.9	3.0	2.5	3.2	3.1	2.4	2.7	2.4	2.5	2.5
College dormitory	—	—	—	—	—	—	—	77.2	74.1	75.5	71.5	69.0	74.0	73.8	73.3	76.1	75.0	73.6	74.2	77.2
Fraternity or sorority house	—	—	—	—	—	—	—	0.2	0.3	0.3	0.3	0.2	0.3	0.2	0.2	0.2	0.1	0.2	0.1	0.2
Other campus student housing	—	—	—	—	—	—	—	1.1	0.7	1.3	1.7	1.3	1.2	1.4	1.5	1.4	1.3	1.4	1.6	1.7
Other	—	—	—	—	—	—	—	0.3	0.3	0.4	0.4	0.4	0.5	0.4	0.4	0.4	0.5	0.3	0.3	0.3
Student's Estimates: Chances are very good that he/she will																				
Be elected to an academic honor society	—	3.6	3.3	2.9	3.2	4.1	5.3	5.8	6.2	6.4	8.0	8.0	9.1	8.9	9.8	9.2	8.4	9.0	9.2	9.5
Be elected to a student office	—	2.2	1.9	1.7	1.4	1.1	1.6	1.8	1.8	2.0	2.2	2.5	2.5	2.9	3.4	3.2	3.3	3.3	3.7	4.0
Be satisfied with your college	—	—	—	—	69.8	61.8	66.9	63.9	61.9	60.6	58.9	60.5	62.2	61.2	60.9	62.5	62.4	62.6	62.0	60.5
Change career choice	—	20.4	18.3	20.9	20.2	17.1	20.9	17.6	15.4	16.0	14.8	15.8	15.8	15.5	15.6	15.6	15.1	15.4	16.2	17.0
Change major field	—	19.8	17.9	20.4	20.0	16.6	19.7	17.9	15.0	15.4	14.8	15.7	15.7	15.4	15.4	15.6	15.5	15.7	16.5	17.2
Drop out permanently (exclude transferring)	—	0.7	0.6	0.7	1.0	1.0	1.2	1.2	1.0	1.0	0.9	0.9	0.8	0.9	0.8	1.0	0.7	0.7	0.6	0.7
Drop out of this college temporarily (exclude transferring)	—	1.1	1.1	1.4	1.7	1.8	2.2	2.2	2.0	1.9	1.8	1.6	1.4	1.3	1.1	1.2	1.0	1.0	0.9	1.0
Fail one or more courses	—	2.2	1.4	1.8	2.4	1.8	2.1	1.9	1.5	1.8	1.5	1.8	1.5	1.6	1.6	1.5	1.3	1.1	1.2	1.2
Get a bachelor's degree (B.A., B.S., etc.)	—	—	—	—	—	—	76.1	78.0	74.6	78.5	77.6	76.8	79.0	76.4	77.6	77.7	79.4	79.7	80.2	79.3
Get a job to help pay for college expenses	9.8	—	—	—	—	—	—	—	—	—	42.0	44.5	43.5	42.4	42.2	44.5	42.4	41.2	42.1	42.0
Get married while in college	—	8.3	7.7	10.2	9.3	10.4	9.1	7.9	7.6	7.3	6.8	6.8	6.3	6.4	6.6	6.5	6.1	5.9	5.8	5.8
Graduate with honors	—	3.2	3.4	3.6	4.1	4.7	7.1	8.8	9.6	9.7	10.8	10.9	11.5	11.4	12.6	11.4	12.2	12.6	12.2	12.8
Join a social fraternity, sorority, or club	35.7	35.7	30.6	25.7	23.2	17.4	21.0	18.5	17.1	18.9	21.0	23.0	23.7	23.2	23.8	24.4	23.9	23.7	23.6	25.2
Join a social fraternity or sorority	—	—	—	—	—	27.1	35.7	38.0	40.8	41.6	43.6	42.1	44.2	42.6	44.6	43.9	45.2	45.3	44.4	44.3
Make at least a "B" average	—	—	—	—	—	3.4	4.0	3.9	3.9	4.3	4.3	4.9	4.8	5.1	5.2	5.5	5.3	5.3	5.6	6.4
Need extra time to complete your degree requirements	—	—	—	—	—	—	—	—	—	—	—	—	3.4	4.1	4.8	3.8	4.8	4.3	4.4	5.6
Participate in student government	—	—	—	—	—	—	—	—	—	—	—	—	—	—	—	—	—	—	—	—
Participate in student protests or demonstrations	—	4.7	4.4	—	—	—	—	—	—	—	—	—	—	—	—	—	—	—	—	—

PLANS, GOALS, AND EXPECTATIONS
FRESHMAN WOMEN

ITEM	1986	1987	1988	1989	1990	1991	1992	1993	1994	1995	1996	1997	1998	1999	2000	2001	2002	2003	2004	2005	2006
Your probable major field [2]																					
Agriculture	0.4	0.4	0.3	0.4	0.4	0.4	0.4	0.6	0.7	0.7	0.8	0.8	0.7	0.8	0.4	0.4	0.5	0.5	0.6	0.4	0.5
Biological Science	4.5	4.4	4.3	4.5	4.8	5.8	6.6	7.1	8.1	8.9	8.9	8.9	7.9	8.2	7.5	7.9	8.0	8.1	8.5	8.3	9.2
Business	22.8	22.3	21.7	20.3	17.8	15.4	13.0	12.2	12.4	12.7	12.6	12.6	13.1	13.5	13.4	13.1	12.8	12.1	12.6	13.2	13.5
Education	12.3	13.2	12.8	12.9	15.0	14.5	13.9	13.5	13.7	13.2	13.7	13.7	15.0	14.6	15.0	13.7	14.4	13.6	13.0	13.1	12.5
Engineering	3.2	2.9	2.8	3.3	3.3	3.7	3.6	3.9	3.3	2.7	3.4	3.5	2.8	2.9	3.0	3.0	2.9	2.9	2.9	2.5	2.4
English	2.0	2.0	2.0	2.2	2.2	2.2	2.2	2.2	2.2	2.2	2.3	2.2	2.2	2.2	2.2	2.2	2.1	2.1	2.3	2.3	2.4
Health Professional	11.2	10.2	11.0	11.5	12.5	15.2	17.9	18.8	17.6	17.5	16.4	16.3	15.7	14.1	12.6	13.5	13.8	16.1	17.4	16.4	15.7
History or Political Science	4.1	4.3	5.0	5.0	4.9	4.7	4.3	4.2	3.9	3.5	3.6	3.5	3.5	3.6	3.6	3.9	4.2	4.4	4.3	4.6	4.5
Humanities	3.1	3.3	3.2	2.9	2.9	2.9	2.8	2.7	2.8	2.8	2.9	3.0	3.4	3.3	3.9	3.9	3.8	3.6	3.6	3.9	3.9
Fine Arts	4.7	5.0	4.3	4.3	4.4	4.3	4.3	4.0	4.2	4.4	4.2	4.5	4.9	4.9	5.1	5.7	5.6	5.6	5.2	5.3	4.7
Mathematics or Statistics	0.9	0.8	0.8	0.8	0.8	0.8	0.8	0.7	0.7	0.7	0.6	0.7	0.6	0.6	0.6	0.6	0.7	0.6	0.7	0.7	0.7
Physical Sciences	1.2	1.1	1.2	1.3	1.3	1.5	1.6	1.9	1.6	1.8	1.7	1.6	1.4	1.5	1.5	1.5	1.6	1.6	1.8	1.8	1.9
Social Sciences	8.5	8.9	10.0	9.8	9.6	9.1	9.7	9.6	9.8	9.8	9.7	9.3	9.5	9.5	9.9	9.8	9.7	9.7	9.3	9.7	10.0
Other Technical	3.0	2.6	2.8	2.5	2.6	2.6	2.3	2.3	2.2	2.5	2.7	2.9	2.9	2.8	2.9	2.6	1.8	1.6	1.6	1.3	1.4
Other Non-technical	9.3	9.5	9.5	9.3	9.2	8.3	7.8	7.6	7.7	7.8	7.6	7.5	7.7	8.5	8.8	8.6	8.6	8.6	8.2	8.6	8.9
Undecided	8.8	9.1	8.3	8.9	8.4	8.6	8.7	8.7	9.1	8.8	8.7	8.9	8.7	9.1	9.5	9.7	9.4	8.9	8.3	8.0	7.8
Where do you plan to live during the fall term?																					
With parents or relatives	16.9	14.7	16.6	16.2	15.3	16.1	15.0	14.3	14.8	15.2	15.5	15.2	14.2	15.2	17.4	17.4	16.6	16.5	14.8	15.5	14.3
Other private home, apartment, room	3.4	2.9	3.3	3.3	2.7	2.9	3.0	2.9	2.8	3.0	2.8	3.2	3.0	3.0	4.1	4.0	4.1	3.5	4.0	2.5	3.6
College dormitory	76.9	80.0	77.4	77.9	79.9	78.9	79.9	80.8	80.5	80.1	79.6	79.9	80.6	79.6	76.3	76.2	76.3	77.4	78.0	79.5	79.2
Fraternity or sorority house	0.3	0.3	0.3	0.2	0.1	0.1	0.3	0.3	0.2	0.2	0.4	0.1	0.3	0.4	0.2	0.2	0.3	0.3	0.4	0.2	0.1
Other campus student housing	2.2	1.9	2.2	2.1	1.7	1.6	1.5	1.5	1.5	1.4	1.5	1.2	1.8	1.7	1.8	2.0	2.4	2.0	2.6	2.2	2.6
Other	0.3	0.2	0.2	0.3	0.3	0.4	0.3	0.2	0.3	0.3	0.2	0.3	0.2	0.2	0.2	0.2	0.3	0.2	0.3	0.2	0.2
Student's Estimates: Chances are very good that he/she will																					
Be elected to an academic honor society	8.2	8.7	8.3	9.3	10.1	10.3	10.4	11.0	11.4	11.5	12.2	12.5	11.1	10.8	—	—	—	—	—	—	—
Be elected to a student office	3.9	3.7	3.6	3.5	4.0	3.6	3.4	3.7	3.8	3.6	3.8	3.7	3.6	3.5	—	—	—	—	—	—	—
Be satisfied with your college	59.6	58.8	57.5	56.9	57.1	58.2	58.4	55.9	55.0	52.9	54.5	55.8	54.4	53.8	52.2	51.6	55.3	55.8	55.1	56.4	57.2
Change career choice	16.4	17.2	16.6	16.0	15.4	15.1	14.9	15.0	14.9	15.1	15.3	15.1	14.8	15.4	15.7	15.6	15.2	14.7	14.8	14.6	14.6
Change major field	16.7	17.5	17.2	16.4	15.8	15.4	15.2	15.3	15.2	15.2	15.5	15.4	15.0	15.9	16.5	16.3	16.0	15.4	15.2	15.0	14.9
Drop out permanently (exclude transferring)	0.6	0.6	0.6	0.6	0.6	0.6	0.5	0.6	0.5	0.5	0.5	0.4	0.4	0.4	0.5	0.5	—	—	—	—	—
Drop out of this college temporarily (exclude transferring)	0.9	0.9	0.8	0.8	0.8	0.8	0.7	0.7	0.7	0.7	0.7	0.6	0.6	0.6	0.6	0.6	—	—	—	—	—
Fail one or more courses	1.2	1.1	1.2	1.0	1.1	1.1	1.0	0.8	0.8	0.8	0.9	0.8	0.8	0.7	0.6	0.7	—	—	—	—	—
Get a bachelor's degree (B.A., B.S., etc.)	80.2	80.2	79.1	78.9	79.0	79.5	78.4	79.4	79.2	78.7	79.3	79.1	78.6	78.4	80.0	78.7	81.8	82.1	—	—	—
Get a job to help pay for college expenses	41.0	40.8	39.2	38.9	40.8	41.6	42.8	43.9	43.8	45.4	45.1	45.9	43.8	43.3	47.5	50.1	52.9	53.2	53.3	52.8	50.2
Get married while in college	5.5	5.1	5.1	5.9	6.3	7.2	7.0	6.7	6.5	6.4	6.0	5.6	5.4	5.3	—	—	—	—	—	—	—
Graduate with honors	11.8	12.2	12.1	13.3	14.0	15.0	16.2	17.5	17.9	18.4	19.8	20.6	19.6	18.5	21.1	21.5	—	—	—	—	—
Join a social fraternity, sorority, or club	25.2	25.1	23.8	24.1	23.7	23.8	22.5	22.6	22.7	21.7	22.5	22.2	21.2	21.8	—	—	—	—	—	—	—
Join a social fraternity or sorority	—	—	—	—	—	—	—	—	—	—	—	—	—	—	13.0	12.1	13.0	11.8	11.1	12.5	12.0
Make at least a "B" average	43.5	42.1	43.0	44.2	44.1	45.8	47.5	49.5	50.4	51.5	53.1	54.8	53.4	52.8	59.1	58.3	61.2	60.8	60.9	62.0	62.0
Need extra time to complete your degree requirements	6.8	7.2	7.5	7.8	9.1	9.4	9.5	7.7	9.1	8.1	8.1	7.5	7.0	6.8	6.8	6.6	8.9	8.7	8.4	9.0	7.0
Participate in student government	—	—	—	—	—	—	—	—	—	—	—	—	—	—	8.4	8.5	8.9	8.7	8.4	9.0	8.9
Participate in student protests or demonstrations	6.0	7.2	7.0	8.6	9.9	8.3	10.1	9.0	7.2	6.6	6.2	5.4	5.1	5.0	5.4	5.3	5.8	6.7	6.4	7.0	6.3

PLANS, GOALS, AND EXPECTATIONS
FRESHMAN WOMEN

ITEM	1966	1967	1968	1969	1970	1971	1972	1973	1974	1975	1976	1977	1978	1979	1980	1981	1982	1983	1984	1985
Student's Estimates: Chances are very good that he/she will																				
Participate in volunteer or community service work	—	—	—	—	—	—	—	—	—	—	—	—	—	—	—	—	—	—	—	—
Play varsity/intercollegiate athletics	—	—	—	—	—	—	—	—	—	—	—	—	—	—	—	—	—	11.0	11.6	11.5
Seek personal counseling	—	—	—	—	—	6.9	6.7	5.5	5.6	5.6	4.4	4.7	4.7	4.9	4.9	4.6	4.2	4.5	4.0	4.8
Transfer to another college before graduating	—	11.5	10.9	12.1	11.9	12.2	13.8	13.6	13.4	13.5	12.8	11.8	10.6	10.6	10.1	10.4	9.1	9.0	9.4	9.2
Work full time while attending college	—	—	—	—	—	—	—	—	—	—	—	—	—	—	—	—	2.7	2.7	2.8	2.8
Objectives considered to be essential or very important																				
Becoming accomplished in one of the performing arts (acting, dancing, etc.)	14.0	15.7	11.8	14.8	16.2	15.8	15.7	—	14.7	15.1	14.8	17.6	16.3	14.9	15.1	14.3	15.0	14.7	13.6	13.4
Becoming a community leader	22.9	20.7	17.5	15.3	12.3	11.0	13.2	—	—	—	—	—	—	—	—	—	—	—	—	—
Becoming an authority in my field	62.4	66.3	56.3	56.0	61.6	55.7	57.4	60.0	60.7	68.6	68.7	74.4	72.9	72.6	74.3	73.7	74.4	74.2	74.5	72.0
Becoming involved in programs to clean up the environment	—	—	—	—	—	42.9	45.4	32.8	24.5	28.0	26.6	29.3	27.1	25.5	25.6	23.1	21.2	19.4	18.6	17.6
Becoming successful in a business of my own	38.5	31.4	30.6	31.0	29.9	26.5	31.4	30.3	27.0	32.6	34.9	38.3	40.0	41.8	43.2	43.8	45.3	45.2	47.1	46.5
Being very well off financially	30.0	28.4	26.2	30.4	24.9	26.0	28.2	—	34.3	38.3	42.0	48.6	51.1	55.1	57.0	59.1	63.8	64.7	66.3	64.7
Creating artistic work (painting, sculpture, decorating, etc.)	21.2	23.0	19.4	21.8	22.8	21.7	24.4	—	18.7	19.1	18.4	20.4	18.2	17.4	16.8	15.6	14.8	13.4	13.0	12.9
Developing a meaningful philosophy of life	—	—	89.0	88.1	82.5	77.0	78.9	77.0	69.3	71.8	68.3	65.5	62.8	58.3	56.0	54.4	51.8	49.0	48.7	46.6
Having administrative responsibility for the work of others	20.8	16.6	15.0	14.9	12.6	12.0	15.7	19.9	20.3	25.4	26.9	30.6	32.0	34.4	37.0	37.5	39.1	39.6	41.1	40.6
Helping others who are in difficulty	80.1	74.8	71.6	75.9	75.0	72.4	76.4	74.2	71.9	76.0	73.6	74.5	74.9	73.6	74.2	72.5	71.5	72.0	71.5	72.1
Influencing social values	—	—	—	38.1	37.2	31.4	33.8	34.6	30.7	33.1	33.1	34.5	35.0	35.3	36.7	35.2	35.7	34.7	36.4	36.0
Influencing the political structure	—	—	—	13.1	15.4	11.7	13.6	12.3	10.9	12.3	13.4	14.0	13.3	13.6	14.4	13.1	13.7	12.7	14.3	14.3
Integrating spirituality into my life	—	—	—	—	—	—	—	—	—	—	—	—	—	—	—	—	—	—	—	—
Keeping up to date with political affairs	59.7	52.9	55.3	54.1	55.2	43.9	51.0	44.6	38.8	39.5	39.4	40.2	37.6	37.8	40.3	39.1	38.8	35.6	38.2	—
Making a theoretical contribution to science	7.8	6.7	6.3	5.7	6.5	6.1	7.6	—	11.2	10.9	11.7	11.8	12.7	12.3	12.7	12.0	11.5	12.1	11.5	11.5
Obtaining recognition from my colleagues for contributions to my special field	37.4	36.6	32.5	35.2	33.3	32.4	32.2	—	35.8	41.0	43.7	46.9	49.6	51.8	54.8	54.9	56.3	56.6	56.9	55.9
Participating in a community action program	—	—	—	—	34.8	30.4	34.7	33.7	33.7	37.0	35.2	35.6	32.4	31.6	33.3	28.6	27.8	26.9	26.7	27.3
Participating in an organization like the Peace Corps or AmeriCorps/VISTA	31.4	—	—	—	—	23.2	22.2	—	—	—	—	—	—	—	—	—	—	—	—	—
Helping to promote racial understanding	—	—	—	—	—	—	—	—	—	—	—	43.0	41.0	38.3	38.5	35.7	36.0	35.1	36.2	36.3
Raising a family	—	—	—	77.3	71.6	—	—	—	—	—	—	58.5	61.4	64.8	63.8	67.1	68.1	68.1	69.9	70.3
Writing original works (poems, novels, short stories, etc.)	18.4	18.9	16.9	18.0	17.9	17.1	18.3	—	15.3	15.6	16.3	17.9	16.6	15.6	15.2	14.0	13.7	13.2	13.1	13.9

PLANS, GOALS, AND EXPECTATIONS
FRESHMAN WOMEN

ITEM	1986	1987	1988	1989	1990	1991	1992	1993	1994	1995	1996	1997	1998	1999	2000	2001	2002	2003	2004	2005	2006
Student's Estimates: Chances are very good that he/she will																					
Participate in volunteer or community service work	—	—	—	—	22.1	23.3	27.0	29.1	28.2	29.2	29.8	31.0	31.7	31.4	31.0	31.3	33.0	33.2	31.8	34.3	34.6
Play varsity/intercollegiate athletics	10.9	11.7	11.2	11.1	11.1	11.2	11.6	12.0	11.4	12.2	12.9	12.6	12.4	12.2	11.8	11.6	11.9	12.5	12.5	13.0	13.0
Seek personal counseling	4.0	4.5	4.4	3.9	4.6	4.3	—	—	—	—	6.7	6.1	5.4	5.4	7.5	7.9	8.6	9.1	8.5	8.8	9.1
Transfer to another college before graduating	8.9	8.8	9.5	9.5	9.1	8.6	8.2	8.5	8.3	8.4	7.5	7.3	6.7	6.7	6.7	6.9	7.6	7.4	7.2	6.5	7.0
Work full time while attending college	2.9	2.3	2.8	3.0	3.1	3.4	3.5	3.9	3.9	4.4	4.4	4.4	4.1	4.4	4.7	6.5	6.7	6.7	7.1	7.3	6.3
Objectives considered to be essential or very important																					
Becoming accomplished in one of the performing arts (acting, dancing, etc.)	13.1	16.1	—	12.4	12.4	12.5	12.3	12.6	12.9	13.0	13.6	14.2	14.7	14.2	15.5	15.9	17.2	16.8	15.7	16.9	16.3
Becoming a community leader	—	—	—	—	—	—	33.7	—	34.6	33.3	34.9	34.5	34.1	30.5	31.7	31.7	31.3	31.8	30.5	33.7	35.1
Becoming an authority in my field	73.6	77.7	—	66.4	65.4	69.5	69.3	67.8	66.5	65.5	64.7	63.2	61.5	57.8	58.1	58.1	58.8	59.2	57.2	58.0	56.7
Becoming involved in programs to clean up the environment	13.9	15.8	—	25.5	37.1	34.8	36.9	31.5	26.6	23.9	21.8	20.2	20.0	18.4	17.5	16.9	17.2	17.7	17.7	20.9	23.1
Becoming successful in a business of my own	44.6	45.5	—	39.4	37.2	37.6	36.5	35.4	34.6	34.8	34.3	33.9	33.6	33.3	34.6	35.4	35.7	36.4	37.0	38.7	37.9
Being very well off financially	68.3	70.3	—	70.1	68.3	68.9	68.0	68.5	68.9	70.5	70.5	71.0	70.3	69.4	71.1	71.4	71.5	72.5	72.4	73.4	72.4
Creating artistic work (painting, sculpture, decorating, etc.)	12.8	14.6	—	13.0	12.4	12.2	12.4	12.9	12.9	13.3	13.3	13.6	14.2	14.5	15.7	16.7	17.3	17.5	16.8	17.6	17.4
Developing a meaningful philosophy of life	44.0	42.8	—	44.3	47.1	48.8	49.6	48.6	46.9	46.0	44.9	44.4	44.1	42.5	41.8	42.4	39.7	38.4	42.2	44.9	46.0
Having administrative responsibility for the work of others	43.2	43.0	—	41.8	41.3	40.6	39.3	39.5	38.4	37.3	37.5	36.6	35.8	33.4	34.8	34.7	36.9	37.4	36.9	38.6	39.5
Helping others who are in difficulty	66.9	67.5	—	69.4	72.1	71.4	73.5	73.9	72.3	70.9	71.3	71.3	71.1	68.8	68.8	68.3	70.1	70.7	69.6	72.7	73.1
Influencing social values	37.0	40.9	—	48.5	50.4	48.4	51.8	49.6	47.0	45.0	44.4	42.8	42.0	40.1	40.9	40.6	41.5	41.2	41.6	44.4	45.2
Influencing the political structure	13.8	15.4	—	19.2	20.3	19.0	20.6	21.1	19.1	16.7	16.8	15.4	15.3	14.6	15.3	16.4	17.0	17.6	17.6	19.9	20.5
Integrating spirituality into my life	—	—	—	—	—	—	—	—	—	—	—	—	—	49.3	48.1	45.6	44.7	43.4	42.6	43.5	—
Keeping up to date with political affairs	—	—	—	41.1	43.8	41.2	42.7	40.5	34.5	30.2	30.3	27.6	27.7	25.4	25.1	28.2	29.2	30.5	31.9	34.0	34.8
Making a theoretical contribution to science	10.5	10.0	—	14.6	15.3	15.0	16.8	17.7	16.4	16.2	16.4	15.9	14.7	14.1	13.7	14.2	14.3	14.8	15.6	16.8	17.5
Obtaining recognition from my colleagues for contributions to my special field	56.6	59.4	—	56.1	55.9	55.6	57.6	56.5	56.3	56.1	54.8	54.1	52.1	50.3	50.8	50.5	52.3	52.6	51.6	53.9	53.6
Participating in a community action program	22.9	24.1	—	28.3	32.2	30.8	33.5	33.0	31.9	30.0	29.8	29.3	29.0	26.8	26.1	25.9	25.8	26.1	24.6	29.3	30.8
Participating in an organization like the Peace Corps or AmeriCorps/VISTA	—	—	—	—	—	—	—	—	—	—	—	—	—	—	—	—	—	—	—	—	13.3
Helping to promote racial understanding	32.0	33.5	—	40.7	46.1	42.5	50.3	47.7	42.5	39.5	39.5	36.5	34.9	31.9	32.9	33.9	33.3	32.5	31.8	35.6	36.0
Raising a family	68.3	—	—	69.6	70.6	70.4	72.1	72.0	72.3	72.3	72.8	74.2	74.3	73.3	73.4	72.4	74.4	75.7	76.3	76.4	76.1
Writing original works (poems, novels, short stories, etc.)	13.3	14.3	—	13.9	13.4	13.7	13.6	14.1	13.6	14.0	14.2	14.0	14.4	13.9	14.4	14.4	14.9	14.8	14.5	15.7	15.9

STUDENT VIEWS
FRESHMAN WOMEN

ITEM	1966	1967	1968	1969	1970	1971	1972	1973	1974	1975	1976	1977	1978	1979	1980	1981	1982	1983	1984	1985
Student agrees strongly or somewhat																				
A national health care plan is needed to cover everybody's medical costs	—	—	—	—	—	—	—	—	—	—	—	59.9	60.3	60.9	57.9	55.6	58.2	60.5	62.1	60.6
Abortion should be legal[ized]	—	—	—	76.4	84.1	—	—	—	—	—	—	55.6	56.6	53.8	54.0	55.3	57.2	56.4	55.9	57.3
Affirmative action in college admissions should be abolished	—	—	—	—	—	—	—	—	—	—	—	—	—	—	—	—	—	—	—	—
College officials have the right to ban persons with extreme views from speaking on campus	—	33.9	26.6	26.8	27.6	22.5	19.5	18.0	17.8	19.9	20.7	21.8	21.9	22.1	22.8	22.5	21.4	21.3	17.7	21.6
Colleges should prohibit racist/sexist speech on campus	—	—	—	—	—	—	—	—	—	—	—	—	—	—	—	—	—	—	—	—
Employers should be allowed to require drug testing of employees or job applicants	—	—	—	—	—	—	—	—	—	—	—	—	—	—	—	—	—	—	—	—
Federal military spending should increased	—	—	—	—	—	—	—	—	—	—	—	—	—	—	—	—	28.5	26.7	23.0	18.1
Grading in the high schools has become too easy	—	—	—	—	—	—	—	—	—	—	60.5	63.7	67.0	61.9	60.4	58.3	56.0	60.3	56.9	51.9
If two people really like each other, it's all right for them to have sex even if they've known each other for only a very short time	—	—	—	—	—	—	—	—	28.8	32.1	31.0	31.9	30.4	32.0	30.4	30.0	30.5	31.9	31.2	—
It is important to have laws prohibiting homosexual relationships	—	—	—	—	—	—	—	—	—	—	35.5	38.8	36.8	37.4	39.3	37.9	35.2	37.0	35.4	34.8
Just because a man thinks that a woman has "led him on" does not entitle him to have sex with her	—	—	—	—	—	—	—	—	—	—	—	—	—	—	—	—	—	—	—	—
Marijuana should be legalized	—	—	—	23.4	37.3	37.2	44.6	45.6	42.8	42.7	45.1	47.5	45.1	41.9	34.8	29.9	25.0	21.9	20.1	18.6
Only volunteers should serve in the armed forces	—	—	—	—	—	—	—	—	—	—	—	—	—	—	—	—	—	—	—	—
People should not obey laws which violate their personal values	—	—	—	—	—	—	—	—	32.1	29.9	28.8	29.5	29.8	30.4	28.9	28.5	—	—	—	—
Racial discrimination is no longer a major problem in America	—	—	—	—	—	—	—	—	—	—	—	—	—	—	—	—	—	—	—	—
Realistically, an individual can do little to bring about change in our society	—	29.4	27.4	31.2	34.4	38.3	37.7	35.8	37.3	42.3	39.2	39.7	—	—	—	—	—	—	—	—
Same sex couples should have the right to legal marital status	—	—	—	—	—	—	—	—	—	—	—	—	—	—	—	—	—	—	—	32.9
The activities of married women are best confined to the home and family	—	41.4	—	—	33.3	27.8	22.1	16.4	17.3	16.6	17.8	18.3	18.1	19.3	18.2	18.3	16.3	15.3	14.6	14.4
The chief benefit of a college education is that it increases one's earning power	—	40.9	44.2	39.3	54.6	44.6	45.3	41.9	—	—	—	—	39.5	42.1	41.1	35.8	34.3	34.4	30.7	65.1
The death penalty should be abolished	—	—	—	61.4	63.4	65.3	—	—	—	—	—	—	—	—	—	—	—	—	—	31.6
The federal government is not doing enough to control environmental pollution	—	—	—	92.2	94.8	92.0	90.8	90.2	84.9	84.8	85.1	83.6	84.5	84.1	83.2	81.8	82.3	82.9	80.9	80.6
The federal government should do more to control the sale of handguns	—	—	—	—	—	—	—	—	—	—	—	—	—	—	—	—	—	—	—	—

182

STUDENT VIEWS
FRESHMAN WOMEN

ITEM	1986	1987	1988	1989	1990	1991	1992	1993	1994	1995	1996	1997	1998	1999	2000	2001	2002	2003	2004	2005	2006
Student agrees strongly or somewhat																					
A national health care plan is needed to cover everybody's medical costs	62.5	—	—	77.7	76.5	79.0	81.0	80.2	73.0	74.4	74.5	75.2	—	—	—	—	—	—	—	77.1	76.5
Abortion should be legal[ized]	61.4	60.6	59.4	67.1	66.7	65.7	68.3	65.5	62.1	61.1	58.5	54.1	54.7	53.2	53.5	54.8	53.2	54.1	53.3	54.8	56.3
Affirmative action in college admissions should be abolished	—	—	—	—	—	—	—	—	—	45.7	45.0	47.1	—	44.1	44.7	43.9	43.7	48.2	45.8	44.0	42.4
College officials have the right to ban persons with extreme views from speaking on campus	21.7	—	—	—	—	—	—	—	—	—	—	—	—	—	—	—	—	—	—	—	37.8
Colleges should prohibit racist/sexist speech on campus	—	—	—	—	—	—	62.7	65.0	64.9	65.8	66.9	66.9	64.6	66.5	66.1	64.8	64.6	62.5	61.9	62.0	—
Employers should be allowed to require drug testing of employees or job applicants	—	—	71.5	78.5	81.1	81.3	81.2	80.9	82.0	80.0	81.5	82.4	81.0	80.6	79.2	77.7	—	—	—	—	—
Federal military spending should increased	18.5	18.4	18.2	16.9	17.9	19.9	15.6	18.6	—	—	—	—	—	—	—	—	40.4	34.3	31.7	31.4	29.7
Grading in the high schools has become too easy	49.8	—	—	—	—	—	49.2	—	—	—	—	—	—	—	—	—	—	—	—	48.3	—
If two people really like each other, it's all right for them to have sex even if they've known each other for only a very short time	—	37.2	36.5	35.1	37.2	36.3	32.2	33.5	31.6	31.0	30.3	29.0	28.1	28.7	31.3	31.7	—	35.1	—	34.1	—
It is important to have laws prohibiting homosexual relationships	39.6	41.6	36.9	32.0	30.5	28.7	23.6	23.2	21.6	18.5	22.5	22.7	21.7	20.3	20.1	18.0	18.5	19.2	23.4	21.0	19.3
Just because a man thinks that a woman has "led him on" does not entitle him to have sex with her	—	—	92.8	94.2	94.1	94.2	95.1	95.4	95.1	94.7	—	93.9	93.5	93.1	—	—	—	—	—	—	—
Marijuana should be legalized	17.7	15.7	16.6	13.8	16.2	18.6	21.8	26.5	29.6	30.3	29.4	30.1	28.6	28.4	29.1	31.4	34.7	34.3	32.5	33.6	33.1
Only volunteers should serve in the armed forces	—	—	54.1	51.2	—	—	—	—	—	—	—	—	—	—	—	—	—	—	—	62.2	63.4
People should not obey laws which violate their personal values	—	—	—	—	—	—	—	—	32.1	32.8	31.6	31.8	—	—	—	—	31.5	30.9	—	—	—
Racial discrimination is no longer a major problem in America	—	—	—	—	15.4	15.0	10.2	9.6	12.1	13.7	12.1	14.5	16.3	18.7	17.3	16.2	18.4	18.3	18.5	17.1	15.2
Realistically, an individual can do little to bring about change in our society	—	—	—	—	—	23.7	23.9	24.8	25.7	27.0	25.1	25.8	24.9	25.5	23.6	22.9	24.1	24.6	23.1	23.9	23.7
Same sex couples should have the right to legal marital status	—	—	—	—	—	—	—	—	—	—	—	58.7	60.0	61.2	63.1	65.2	66.3	66.9	63.5	64.3	67.9
The activities of married women are best confined to the home and family	13.5	18.3	17.9	18.6	18.1	17.8	18.7	17.1	18.1	17.3	17.2	17.5	—	—	16.8	15.9	16.5	16.5	15.8	15.5	—
The chief benefit of a college education is that it increases one's earning power	63.6	61.4	61.3	62.6	61.2	61.8	60.1	—	—	—	—	—	—	—	—	—	—	—	—	—	63.8
The death penalty should be abolished	30.0	27.8	26.9	24.9	26.2	25.0	25.4	25.5	23.4	24.4	25.9	27.4	27.0	29.7	34.3	35.5	35.4	35.8	36.2	36.3	37.6
The federal government is not doing enough to control environmental pollution	80.4	83.2	85.8	89.1	90.1	87.9	91.3	88.0	87.7	86.9	85.3	84.8	—	—	—	—	—	—	—	79.8	80.8
The federal government should do more to control the sale of handguns	—	—	—	88.8	88.8	89.8	90.7	91.3	89.7	90.8	90.3	91.2	91.6	91.3	89.6	88.1	84.8	83.7	85.7	84.9	80.6

183

STUDENT VIEWS
FRESHMAN WOMEN

ITEM	1966	1967	1968	1969	1970	1971	1972	1973	1974	1975	1976	1977	1978	1979	1980	1981	1982	1983	1984	1985
Student agrees strongly or somewhat																				
The federal government should do more to discourage energy consumption	—	—	—	—	—	—	—	—	—	85.1	83.5	85.2	85.2	85.8	86.4	83.4	81.3	79.6	77.1	75.6
The federal government should raise taxes to reduce the deficit	—	—	—	—	—	—	—	—	—	—	—	—	—	—	—	—	—	—	—	21.3
There is too much concern in the courts for the rights of criminals	—	—	—	46.4	44.0	39.4	40.0	41.4	43.3	45.7	52.2	57.2	59.4	56.1	60.6	63.2	65.0	64.3	—	—
Wealthy people should pay a larger share of taxes than they do now	—	—	—	—	—	—	69.8	70.2	73.4	73.4	73.1	73.0	71.0	68.2	68.0	69.3	70.1	68.9	68.2	72.6
How would you characterize your political views?																				
Far left	—	—	—	—	2.2	2.2	2.0	1.5	1.6	1.4	1.5	1.5	1.3	1.6	1.5	1.2	1.3	1.4	1.4	1.3
Liberal	—	—	—	—	33.5	35.8	33.9	33.6	29.3	29.7	26.3	25.5	24.4	23.0	20.1	19.5	20.6	21.4	22.1	23.0
Middle of the road	—	—	—	—	47.3	48.2	49.5	51.5	56.2	55.9	58.1	58.3	59.5	60.2	61.7	61.0	61.2	61.1	59.0	58.0
Conservative	—	—	—	—	16.6	13.6	14.2	13.1	12.4	12.8	13.5	14.0	14.4	14.4	16.0	17.6	16.3	15.5	16.7	17.0
Far right	—	—	—	—	0.4	0.3	0.4	0.3	0.4	0.3	0.6	0.6	0.5	0.7	0.8	0.7	0.6	0.7	0.7	0.8

STUDENT VIEWS
FRESHMAN WOMEN

ITEM	1986	1987	1988	1989	1990	1991	1992	1993	1994	1995	1996	1997	1998	1999	2000	2001	2002	2003	2004	2005	2006
Student agrees strongly or somewhat																					
The federal government should do more to discourage energy consumption	73.7	—	—	—	—	82.0	82.2	79.3	75.6	—	—	—	—	—	—	—	76.2	—	—	—	—
The federal government should raise taxes to reduce the deficit	20.9	22.0	26.4	27.0	27.0	24.5	26.2	33.4	24.8	25.2	23.1	21.9	—	—	—	—	—	—	—	—	23.1
There is too much concern in the courts for the rights of criminals	—	65.1	65.4	65.3	62.2	62.0	63.1	65.2	71.1	72.6	70.4	70.3	71.3	70.0	65.5	63.2	62.5	59.3	55.7	55.5	53.3
Wealthy people should pay a larger share of taxes than they do now	71.0	—	—	—	—	—	72.2	73.4	67.5	67.5	66.0	63.0	57.9	53.9	51.5	51.7	50.2	53.5	55.9	58.9	58.2
How would you characterize your political views?																					
Far left	1.3	1.4	1.8	1.4	1.5	1.6	1.7	1.8	1.8	1.8	1.9	1.9	1.8	1.8	2.3	2.4	2.0	2.2	2.8	3.0	2.4
Liberal	24.1	24.8	25.2	25.6	27.4	28.8	30.5	30.8	27.6	26.0	25.5	25.4	25.2	25.0	26.2	28.6	26.7	25.7	28.2	29.6	31.6
Middle of the road	57.5	57.8	55.2	54.6	54.5	52.7	51.3	48.9	51.6	53.4	53.0	53.9	54.5	55.4	53.7	51.1	53.0	52.7	47.7	45.1	42.9
Conservative	16.6	15.3	17.0	17.6	16.0	16.3	15.8	17.6	18.2	17.9	18.6	18.0	17.8	17.1	16.9	16.9	17.5	18.5	19.9	21.0	21.9
Far right	0.6	0.7	0.8	0.8	0.6	0.6	0.7	0.8	0.8	0.9	1.0	0.8	0.7	0.7	0.8	0.9	0.8	0.9	1.4	1.2	1.1

SOURCES OF STUDENT FUNDS
FRESHMAN WOMEN

ITEM	1966	1967	1968	1969	1970	1971	1972	1973	1974	1975	1976	1977	1978	1979	1980	1981	1982	1983	1984	1985
Students receiving funds to cover educational expenses (room, board, tuition, and fees) from:																				
Parents, other relatives or friends	—	—	—	—	—	—	—	—	—	—	—	—	78.7	75.2	75.7	74.7	76.3	77.0	75.6	76.9
Spouse	—	—	—	—	—	—	—	—	—	—	—	—	0.6	0.6	0.6	0.6	0.6	0.6	0.6	0.6
Savings from summer work	—	—	—	—	—	—	—	—	—	—	—	—	49.7	46.8	46.0	46.1	43.1	44.1	48.5	52.3
Other savings	—	—	—	—	—	—	—	—	—	—	—	—	21.5	19.5	19.7	20.1	19.3	20.1	21.9	24.3
Part time job on campus	—	—	—	—	—	—	—	—	—	—	—	—	—	—	—	—	—	—	—	—
Part time job off campus	—	—	—	—	—	—	—	—	—	—	—	—	21.6	19.2	20.0	20.7	20.7	21.7	29.9	32.3
Full time job while in college	—	—	—	—	—	—	—	—	—	—	—	—	1.3	1.3	1.4	1.3	1.3	1.3	1.5	1.7
Pell Grant	—	—	—	—	—	—	—	—	—	—	—	—	21.4	32.9	32.2	25.8	23.6	26.4	20.0	19.2
Supplemental Educational Opportunity Grant (SEOG)	—	—	—	—	—	—	—	—	—	—	—	—	6.4	8.1	9.2	6.6	6.4	7.7	6.3	5.8
State scholarship or grant	—	—	—	—	—	—	—	—	—	—	—	—	16.1	17.0	17.3	15.0	15.0	16.8	14.7	16.1
College Work-Study Grant	—	—	—	—	—	—	—	—	—	—	—	—	14.1	15.5	18.7	16.3	15.6	17.8	13.2	13.8
College grant/scholarship (other than above)	—	—	—	—	—	—	—	—	—	—	—	—	15.9	14.9	16.6	15.0	16.0	17.8	22.9	25.3
Other private grant	—	—	—	—	—	—	—	—	—	—	—	—	9.2	8.7	8.8	8.3	8.9	9.6	7.9	7.5
Other government aid (ROTC, BIA, GI/ military benefits, etc.)	—	—	—	—	—	—	—	—	—	—	—	—	6.3	6.4	6.4	6.6	4.0	2.4	2.3	1.9
Stafford Loan (GSL)	—	—	—	—	—	—	—	—	—	—	—	—	10.0	14.1	21.2	26.2	20.5	21.7	23.7	23.7
Perkins Loan (NDSL)	—	—	—	—	—	—	—	—	—	—	—	—	9.3	9.6	10.9	8.7	7.2	8.5	7.6	7.3
Other college loan	—	—	—	—	—	—	—	—	—	—	—	—	3.7	3.7	4.5	3.8	3.5	3.9	3.7	3.9
Other loan	—	—	—	—	—	—	—	—	—	—	—	—	3.9	4.0	4.4	4.5	4.4	4.5	4.2	4.1
Other than above	—	—	—	—	—	—	—	—	—	—	—	—	3.9	3.7	3.8	3.7	2.9	3.8	2.7	3.1
Students receiving funds to cover educational expenses (room, board, tuition, and fees) from:																				
Family resources (parents, relatives, spouse, etc.)	—	—	—	—	—	—	—	—	—	—	—	—	—	—	—	—	—	—	—	—
My own resources (savings from work, work-study, other income)	—	—	—	—	—	—	—	—	—	—	—	—	—	—	—	—	—	—	—	—
Aid which need not be repaid (grants, scholarships, military funding, etc.)	—	—	—	—	—	—	—	—	—	—	—	—	—	—	—	—	—	—	—	—
Aid which must be repaid (loans, etc.)	—	—	—	—	—	—	—	—	—	—	—	—	—	—	—	—	—	—	—	—
Other than above	—	—	—	—	—	—	—	—	—	—	—	—	—	—	—	—	—	—	—	—
Do you have any concern about your ability to finance your college education?																				
None (I am confident that I will have sufficient funds)	34.3	33.4	34.6	30.4	29.9	29.5	31.3	31.8	32.9	30.9	29.5	29.3	30.3	28.7	27.4	26.9	26.1	28.1	28.7	30.5
Some (but I probably will have enough funds)	56.7	57.0	57.4	57.8	57.8	57.5	51.6	49.2	49.8	50.0	51.9	51.2	52.2	54.1	54.7	53.3	52.9	54.0	54.1	53.3
Major (not sure I will have enough funds)	9.1	9.5	8.0	11.8	12.4	12.9	17.2	18.9	17.3	19.2	18.6	19.5	17.5	17.2	17.9	19.8	21.1	17.9	17.2	16.3

186

SOURCES OF STUDENT FUNDS
FRESHMAN WOMEN

ITEM	1986	1987	1988	1989	1990	1991	1992	1993	1994	1995	1996	1997	1998	1999	2000	2001	2002	2003	2004	2005	2006
Students receiving funds to cover educational expenses (room, board, tuition, and fees) from:																					
Parents, other relatives or friends	81.1	84.0	84.7	85.2	83.5	83.0	85.2	84.6	84.4	83.8	83.2	83.2	83.7	85.6	83.5	—	—	—	—	—	83.2
Spouse	0.8	0.6	0.8	0.7	0.7	0.9	0.7	0.6	0.6	0.6	0.5	0.5	0.5	0.6	0.5	—	—	—	—	—	0.8
Savings from summer work	54.6	58.0	57.7	58.2	59.0	52.1	55.5	54.5	54.2	55.0	54.9	53.3	53.7	56.3	49.8	—	—	—	—	—	48.7
Other savings	28.6	30.5	31.4	30.8	34.5	30.5	32.7	32.1	33.9	33.5	35.3	33.6	34.8	39.4	33.2	—	—	—	—	—	39.9
Part time job on campus	—	23.8	25.5	25.4	25.9	25.3	27.5	27.0	27.4	29.3	29.7	29.6	29.6	31.7	28.2	—	—	—	—	—	31.3
Part time job off campus	34.3	20.0	21.3	21.6	19.6	17.7	18.8	18.4	19.5	21.0	20.8	20.6	20.6	24.7	23.1	—	—	—	—	—	26.1
Full time job while in college	1.8	1.2	1.5	1.6	1.7	1.6	1.7	1.3	2.0	2.1	2.2	2.2	2.3	3.2	2.6	—	—	—	—	—	4.7
Pell Grant	15.4	16.6	20.6	20.5	21.2	22.9	22.5	21.1	20.3	20.1	20.2	20.5	20.8	19.7	18.4	—	—	—	—	—	17.3
Supplemental Educational Opportunity Grant (SEOG)	5.9	6.6	6.5	6.7	7.1	7.0	7.8	6.6	6.6	6.8	7.1	6.3	6.7	7.1	6.1	—	—	—	—	—	7.4
State scholarship or grant	14.6	18.6	16.4	17.0	17.7	15.8	17.6	17.1	18.2	18.4	19.1	19.2	20.2	22.2	23.4	—	—	—	—	—	—
College Work-Study Grant	13.7	13.2	13.1	13.2	13.9	14.8	16.9	17.0	17.2	17.6	17.0	16.9	17.2	17.7	15.1	—	—	—	—	—	16.1
College grant/scholarship (other than above)	23.6	16.7	26.0	27.1	28.4	29.5	32.0	32.4	33.5	35.1	37.2	36.7	36.9	38.4	35.0	—	—	—	—	—	33.2
Other private grant	8.8	12.1	11.3	11.5	12.5	11.9	12.6	12.0	12.3	11.8	13.2	12.4	13.2	13.8	12.3	—	—	—	—	—	11.9
Other government aid (ROTC, BIA, GI/military benefits, etc.)	0.6	1.5	1.4	1.5	1.8	1.7	1.6	1.7	1.9	1.9	2.4	1.9	2.0	2.2	2.1	—	—	—	—	—	—
Stafford Loan (GSL)	25.3	22.3	23.1	22.6	22.5	24.9	28.1	32.8	32.7	32.6	30.8	29.1	29.9	30.4	27.5	—	—	—	—	—	27.1
Perkins Loan (NDSL)	7.4	5.1	3.4	2.5	8.4	8.4	10.4	10.2	10.6	11.0	11.4	10.9	11.5	11.2	10.0	—	—	—	—	—	10.4
Other college loan	4.1	5.7	6.3	8.3	6.0	5.7	6.8	7.2	8.7	10.9	11.5	12.2	12.6	13.4	11.9	—	—	—	—	—	15.5
Other loan	4.2	5.4	6.0	6.9	6.5	6.1	6.7	6.6	7.5	8.2	8.3	8.1	8.6	9.2	8.5	—	—	—	—	—	10.8
Other than above	3.0	4.6	3.3	3.5	3.6	3.4	3.5	4.4	4.8	5.1	5.4	6.2	6.2	6.5	5.6	—	—	—	—	—	6.1
Students receiving funds to cover educational expenses (room, board, tuition, and fees) from:																					
Family resources (parents, relatives, spouse, etc.)																80.6	80.0	80.8	81.6	79.5	—
My own resources (savings from work, work-study, other income)																62.0	60.0	60.5	61.4	57.7	—
Aid which need not be repaid (grants, scholarships, military funding, etc.)																66.5	66.3	66.5	67.7	67.1	—
Aid which must be repaid (loans, etc.)																46.6	47.2	50.3	51.6	50.8	—
Other than above																4.5	4.1	4.5	4.9	4.8	—
Do you have any concern about your ability to finance your college education?																					
None (I am confident that I will have sufficient funds)	32.7	32.8	31.9	31.5	—	—	25.4	—	24.0	23.0	25.0	26.1	28.4	29.5	30.8	29.9	28.4	28.4	28.8	28.4	30.4
Some (but I probably will have enough funds)	51.5	51.4	51.6	53.2	—	—	55.6	—	54.3	55.1	54.8	56.1	55.7	55.8	55.1	55.8	56.2	56.2	55.9	56.0	55.7
Major (not sure I will have enough funds)	15.8	15.8	16.5	15.3	—	—	19.0	—	21.8	21.9	20.2	17.8	15.9	14.7	14.1	14.4	14.7	15.3	15.3	15.6	13.8

DISAGGREGATED RESPONSES
FRESHMAN WOMEN

ITEM	1966	1967	1968	1969	1970	1971	1972	1973	1974	1975	1976	1977	1978	1979	1980	1981	1982	1983	1984	1985
Your probable career/occupation																				
Accountant or actuary	—	—	—	—	—	1.4	1.6	—	—	—	4.1	4.8	5.3	5.3	5.7	5.8	6.3	6.3	6.8	6.7
Actor or entertainer	—	—	—	—	—	1.0	0.9	—	—	—	1.2	1.2	1.2	1.2	1.2	1.2	1.3	1.1	1.1	1.3
Architect	—	—	—	—	—	0.3	0.3	—	—	—	0.5	0.5	0.6	0.6	0.7	0.4	0.4	0.4	0.5	0.4
Artist	—	—	—	—	—	2.7	2.7	—	—	—	2.5	2.8	2.3	2.3	2.4	2.3	2.2	2.1	1.8	1.6
Business (clerical)	—	—	—	—	—	2.6	2.2	—	—	—	1.7	1.8	1.6	1.8	1.3	1.4	1.2	1.2	1.1	1.2
Business executive (mgmt, administrator)	—	—	—	—	—	1.3	1.3	—	—	—	4.3	5.7	6.9	7.8	8.6	9.0	9.3	9.7	10.8	11.1
Business owner or proprietor	—	—	—	—	—	0.1	0.2	—	—	—	0.5	0.5	0.7	0.8	1.0	1.1	1.1	1.2	1.5	1.7
Business salesperson or buyer	—	—	—	—	—	0.4	0.4	—	—	—	0.7	0.9	1.1	1.2	1.0	1.0	1.1	1.1	1.2	1.6
Clergy (minister, priest)	—	—	—	—	—	0.0	0.1	—	—	—	0.1	0.1	0.0	0.0	0.1	0.0	0.0	0.0	0.0	0.0
Clergy (other religious)	—	—	—	—	—	0.2	0.2	—	—	—	0.2	0.2	0.2	0.1	0.1	0.1	0.1	0.1	0.1	0.1
Clinical psychologist	—	—	—	—	—	2.1	2.1	—	—	—	1.9	1.8	1.8	2.0	1.8	1.7	1.7	1.8	2.1	2.1
College administrator/staff	—	—	—	—	—	—	—	—	—	—	—	—	—	—	—	—	—	—	—	—
College teacher	—	—	—	—	—	0.7	0.7	—	—	—	0.4	0.3	0.4	0.3	0.2	0.2	0.2	0.3	0.3	0.3
Computer programmer or analyst	—	—	—	—	—	1.0	0.8	—	—	—	1.4	1.8	2.4	2.9	4.0	5.6	7.0	6.1	4.0	2.7
Conservationist or forester	—	—	—	—	—	0.4	0.5	—	—	—	0.8	0.9	0.6	0.6	0.5	0.4	0.3	0.2	0.2	0.2
Dentist (including orthodontist)	—	—	—	—	—	0.1	0.3	—	—	—	0.6	0.5	0.6	0.6	0.6	0.6	0.5	0.5	0.5	0.5
Dietitian or home economist	—	—	—	—	—	1.6	1.5	—	—	—	1.3	1.2	0.8	0.7	0.7	0.5	0.5	0.4	0.5	0.4
Engineer	—	—	—	—	—	0.3	0.4	—	—	—	1.9	1.8	2.5	2.6	3.3	3.2	3.8	3.6	3.4	3.5
Farmer or rancher	—	—	—	—	—	0.1	0.2	—	—	—	0.3	0.3	0.2	0.3	0.1	0.2	0.1	0.1	0.1	0.1
Foreign service worker (incl diplomat)	—	—	—	—	—	0.9	0.9	—	—	—	1.0	1.0	1.0	0.9	0.9	0.9	0.9	1.0	1.1	1.7
Homemaker (full-time)	—	—	—	—	—	1.0	0.9	—	—	—	0.4	0.3	0.3	0.3	0.2	0.3	0.2	0.1	0.1	0.2
Interior decorator (including designer)	—	—	—	—	—	1.3	1.3	—	—	—	1.1	1.2	1.1	1.1	1.0	1.0	1.0	0.8	0.8	1.0
Interpreter (translator)	—	—	—	—	—	1.1	1.0	—	—	—	0.5	0.5	0.4	0.4	0.3	0.4	0.4	0.3	0.4	0.4
Lab technician or hygienist	—	—	—	—	—	2.1	2.5	—	—	—	2.5	2.5	1.9	1.8	1.6	1.5	1.3	1.3	1.1	0.8
Law enforcement officer	—	—	—	—	—	0.2	0.2	—	—	—	0.8	0.9	0.7	0.6	0.4	0.3	0.4	0.3	0.4	0.3
Lawyer (attorney) or judge	—	—	—	—	—	1.9	2.7	—	—	—	4.2	4.5	4.6	4.5	4.8	4.3	5.2	4.7	4.7	4.7
Military service (career)	—	—	—	—	—	0.0	0.1	—	—	—	0.2	0.4	0.6	0.5	0.3	0.4	0.3	0.4	0.5	0.4
Musician (performer, composer)	—	—	—	—	—	1.3	1.5	—	—	—	1.6	1.6	1.6	1.4	1.3	1.3	1.2	1.1	0.9	0.9
Nurse	—	—	—	—	—	6.4	7.1	—	—	—	8.2	7.1	7.0	6.5	7.2	6.8	7.1	7.6	6.7	5.2
Optometrist	—	—	—	—	—	0.0	0.1	—	—	—	0.2	0.2	0.2	0.2	0.2	0.2	0.2	0.3	0.3	0.2
Pharmacist	—	—	—	—	—	0.8	0.8	—	—	—	1.2	0.9	0.8	0.8	0.7	0.6	0.7	0.9	0.9	1.0
Physician	—	—	—	—	—	2.4	3.2	—	—	—	4.0	3.7	3.9	4.1	4.3	4.2	4.4	4.9	4.8	5.4
Policymaker/government	—	—	—	—	—	—	—	—	—	—	—	—	—	—	—	—	—	—	—	—
School counselor	—	—	—	—	—	0.8	0.7	—	—	—	0.6	0.5	0.4	0.5	0.3	0.4	0.3	0.3	0.4	0.4
School principal or superintendent	—	—	—	—	—	0.0	0.0	—	—	—	0.0	0.0	0.0	0.0	0.0	0.0	0.0	0.0	0.0	0.0
Scientific researcher	—	—	—	—	—	2.1	2.0	—	—	—	2.3	2.0	2.2	1.7	1.5	1.4	1.3	1.5	1.5	1.6
Social, welfare or recreation worker	—	—	—	—	—	5.5	4.9	—	—	—	4.6	4.4	4.0	3.7	3.1	2.6	1.9	1.9	1.9	1.9
Statistician	—	—	—	—	—	0.1	0.1	—	—	—	0.1	0.1	0.2	0.1	0.1	0.1	0.1	0.2	0.1	0.1
Therapist (physical, occupational, speech)	—	—	—	—	—	3.6	4.5	—	—	—	4.6	4.4	4.1	4.1	4.1	4.2	3.7	4.2	3.9	3.4
Teacher or administrator (elementary)	—	—	—	—	—	15.0	12.8	—	—	—	9.2	8.9	7.5	7.9	7.4	7.2	6.1	6.2	6.2	6.6
Teacher or administrator (secondary)	—	—	—	—	—	12.4	9.5	—	—	—	5.0	4.5	3.9	3.5	2.8	2.9	2.4	2.4	2.8	3.2
Veterinarian	—	—	—	—	—	0.8	1.3	—	—	—	1.5	1.5	1.5	1.3	1.3	1.1	1.2	1.1	1.2	1.2
Writer or journalist	—	—	—	—	—	2.1	2.4	—	—	—	3.3	2.9	3.0	3.4	3.2	3.2	3.3	3.2	3.1	3.5
Skilled trades	—	—	—	—	—	0.1	0.1	—	—	—	0.2	0.2	0.1	0.2	0.2	0.2	0.1	0.1	0.1	0.1
Other	—	—	—	—	—	6.4	6.7	—	—	—	6.4	6.6	6.8	7.0	6.6	6.5	6.0	5.9	6.2	6.2
Undecided	—	—	—	—	—	15.3	16.4	—	—	—	12.2	12.3	13.1	12.5	12.8	13.1	12.9	12.8	13.7	13.9

DISAGGREGATED RESPONSES
FRESHMAN WOMEN

ITEM	1986	1987	1988	1989	1990	1991	1992	1993	1994	1995	1996	1997	1998	1999	2000	2001	2002	2003	2004	2005	2006
Your probable career/occupation																					
Accountant or actuary	6.1	5.9	6.0	6.1	5.4	5.4	4.4	4.2	3.9	3.8	3.2	3.0	2.8	2.6	2.4	2.1	2.1	1.9	2.0	2.2	2.2
Actor or entertainer	1.3	1.4	1.3	1.2	1.2	1.3	1.2	1.2	1.2	1.3	1.3	1.5	1.7	1.7	2.2	1.9	1.8	1.7	1.5	1.7	1.4
Architect	0.6	0.6	0.6	0.7	0.7	0.8	0.8	0.8	0.8	0.8	0.6	0.7	0.8	0.9	0.8	0.7	0.7	0.9	0.9	0.8	0.5
Artist	2.1	2.3	2.0	1.8	1.6	1.6	1.7	1.6	1.5	1.7	1.6	1.7	1.9	1.8	2.0	2.4	2.5	2.3	2.0	2.4	2.4
Business (clerical)	0.8	0.7	0.7	0.7	0.9	0.7	0.6	0.6	0.6	0.6	0.6	0.6	0.7	0.7	0.7	0.7	0.6	0.6	0.5	0.5	0.6
Business executive (mgmt, administrator)	11.3	11.1	10.8	9.4	8.0	6.5	5.7	5.3	5.5	5.9	6.2	6.4	6.5	7.0	6.8	6.4	6.0	5.7	5.8	5.8	6.2
Business owner or proprietor	2.1	2.1	2.1	1.8	1.5	1.1	1.1	1.0	1.0	1.2	1.3	1.3	1.4	1.5	1.7	1.7	1.7	1.8	2.0	2.2	2.1
Business salesperson or buyer	1.7	1.6	1.3	1.3	1.3	1.0	0.8	0.8	0.8	0.8	0.8	0.9	1.0	1.0	1.1	1.1	1.1	1.1	0.9	1.0	1.1
Clergy (minister, priest)	0.0	0.0	0.0	0.0	0.0	0.0	0.1	0.0	0.1	0.1	0.1	0.1	0.1	0.1	0.1	0.1	0.1	0.1	0.1	0.1	0.1
Clergy (other religious)	0.1	0.1	0.1	0.1	0.1	0.1	0.1	0.1	0.1	0.1	0.1	0.2	0.2	0.1	0.1	0.1	0.2	0.1	0.1	0.1	0.1
Clinical psychologist	2.5	2.6	3.0	2.8	2.6	2.7	2.8	2.9	2.8	2.7	2.8	2.6	2.6	2.6	2.7	2.5	2.4	2.3	2.2	2.2	2.2
College administrator/staff	—	—	—	—	—	—	—	—	—	—	0.1	0.0	0.1	0.0	0.0	0.0	0.0	0.0	0.0	0.0	0.0
College teacher	0.4	0.4	0.4	0.5	0.5	0.5	0.6	0.5	0.6	0.6	0.6	0.5	0.6	0.5	0.5	0.5	0.4	0.4	0.5	0.4	0.4
Computer programmer or analyst	1.8	1.4	1.5	1.4	1.4	1.5	1.1	1.1	1.0	1.2	1.4	1.5	1.9	1.8	1.8	1.4	0.9	0.6	0.5	0.4	0.4
Conservationist or forester	0.2	0.2	0.2	0.3	0.3	0.3	0.4	0.5	0.5	0.5	0.4	0.3	0.4	0.3	0.3	0.2	0.2	0.2	0.2	0.2	0.2
Dentist (including orthodontist)	0.5	0.4	0.6	0.5	0.5	0.5	0.4	0.5	0.5	0.6	0.6	0.7	0.6	0.7	0.6	0.7	0.8	0.9	1.1	1.1	1.2
Dietitian or home economist	0.3	0.3	0.3	0.3	0.3	0.3	0.3	0.4	0.5	0.5	0.5	0.5	0.5	0.5	0.4	0.3	0.3	0.4	0.6	0.5	0.6
Engineer	3.0	2.8	2.7	3.1	3.1	3.5	3.4	3.6	3.0	2.5	3.1	3.1	2.5	2.6	2.6	2.5	2.3	2.2	2.4	2.0	2.0
Farmer or rancher	0.1	0.1	0.1	0.1	0.1	0.1	0.1	0.1	0.1	0.1	0.2	0.1	0.1	0.1	0.1	0.1	0.1	0.1	0.1	0.1	0.1
Foreign service worker (incl diplomat)	1.7	1.8	1.8	1.6	1.4	1.2	1.0	1.0	1.0	0.7	0.8	0.8	0.9	0.9	0.8	0.8	0.8	0.9	0.9	1.1	1.1
Homemaker (full-time)	0.2	0.2	0.1	0.2	0.1	0.1	0.1	0.1	0.1	0.2	0.1	0.2	0.2	0.2	0.2	0.1	0.1	0.1	0.2	0.1	0.1
Interior decorator (including designer)	1.1	1.2	0.9	0.9	0.9	0.7	0.7	0.5	0.6	0.6	0.4	0.5	0.7	0.8	1.0	1.0	0.9	0.9	0.9	0.9	0.7
Interpreter (translator)	0.4	0.4	0.4	0.4	0.3	0.3	0.3	0.3	0.2	0.2	—	0.4	—	0.3	0.3	0.2	0.2	—	—	—	0.2
Lab technician or hygienist	0.6	0.5	0.5	0.3	0.3	0.3	0.4	0.4	0.4	0.3	0.3	0.4	0.3	0.3	0.3	0.2	0.2	0.6	0.3	0.2	0.2
Law enforcement officer	0.3	0.4	0.4	0.3	0.3	0.4	0.5	0.5	0.5	0.6	0.5	0.6	0.6	0.6	0.5	0.6	0.6	0.6	0.6	0.6	0.5
Lawyer (attorney) or judge	4.9	5.5	6.3	6.4	6.6	6.2	5.6	5.2	5.4	4.4	4.0	4.1	3.9	4.2	4.2	4.1	4.4	4.4	4.3	4.3	4.0
Military service (career)	0.4	0.3	0.3	0.2	0.3	0.2	0.2	0.2	0.3	0.2	0.5	0.3	0.2	0.3	0.2	0.3	0.3	0.3	0.3	0.2	0.4
Musician (performer, composer)	1.0	1.0	0.9	0.9	0.9	0.9	1.0	0.9	1.1	1.0	1.2	1.1	1.2	1.2	1.2	1.2	1.1	1.0	1.0	1.1	1.0
Nurse	3.7	3.0	3.1	3.1	4.1	5.3	5.9	5.7	5.2	4.6	4.1	3.8	3.8	3.8	3.6	4.1	4.5	5.8	6.5	6.5	6.8
Optometrist	0.2	0.2	0.3	0.3	0.2	0.3	0.3	0.3	0.4	0.4	0.3	0.3	0.3	0.3	0.3	0.3	0.3	0.3	0.3	0.3	0.4
Pharmacist	1.0	1.1	1.5	1.4	1.4	1.4	1.4	1.7	1.4	1.7	1.4	1.4	1.2	1.0	1.2	1.5	1.9	2.2	2.6	2.6	2.2
Physician	4.7	4.5	4.6	4.8	5.2	6.1	6.8	7.2	7.5	8.0	7.9	8.2	7.0	7.1	7.0	7.0	6.9	7.0	7.0	6.6	6.7
Policymaker/government	—	—	—	—	0.6	0.5	0.5	0.5	0.5	0.7	0.8	0.8	0.7	0.7	0.7	0.8	0.8	0.9	0.9	0.9	0.8
School counselor	0.5	0.5	0.5	0.5	0.6	0.5	0.5	0.5	0.5	0.5	0.5	0.5	0.4	0.5	0.5	0.5	0.5	0.5	0.4	0.5	0.5
School principal or superintendent	0.1	0.1	0.1	0.0	0.0	0.1	0.1	0.1	0.1	0.0	0.1	0.0	0.0	0.1	0.1	0.0	0.0	0.0	0.1	0.1	0.0
Scientific researcher	1.4	1.5	1.5	1.7	1.6	1.7	1.9	2.0	2.1	2.4	2.2	2.3	1.9	2.1	1.8	1.8	1.6	1.7	1.8	1.6	1.7
Social, welfare or recreation worker	1.9	1.9	2.1	1.8	1.7	1.8	1.8	2.0	2.0	2.1	2.0	1.9	1.7	1.8	1.8	1.5	1.4	1.4	1.4	1.5	1.5
Statistician	0.1	0.1	0.1	0.1	0.1	0.1	0.0	0.0	0.1	0.1	—	—	0.1	0.2	0.1	0.1	0.1	0.1	0.1	0.1	0.1
Therapist (physical, occupational, speech)	3.4	3.6	3.5	3.6	3.5	4.4	5.8	6.4	6.0	6.1	5.8	5.8	5.8	4.3	3.6	3.3	3.4	3.5	4.1	4.0	3.8
Teacher or administrator (elementary)	8.0	8.7	8.6	8.4	9.7	9.5	8.9	8.7	8.8	8.8	9.0	9.1	10.0	10.1	10.2	8.9	9.3	8.6	8.4	8.3	7.9
Teacher or administrator (secondary)	3.7	4.0	3.7	4.0	4.5	4.4	4.4	4.1	4.1	3.9	4.3	4.3	4.5	4.3	4.7	4.4	4.9	4.5	4.7	4.8	4.9
Veterinarian	1.1	1.0	1.0	1.0	1.0	1.2	1.4	1.5	1.8	1.9	2.0	2.0	1.9	2.2	1.6	1.6	1.6	1.6	1.7	1.5	1.7
Writer or journalist	3.6	3.6	3.7	3.6	3.2	3.0	3.0	3.0	3.0	3.3	2.9	2.9	3.0	3.1	3.3	3.0	3.1	3.1	3.1	3.3	3.6
Skilled trades	0.1	0.1	0.1	0.1	0.1	0.1	0.2	0.2	0.1	0.1	0.1	0.1	0.1	0.2	0.1	0.1	0.1	0.1	0.1	0.1	0.1
Other	6.2	6.7	6.7	8.2	8.8	8.3	8.8	9.1	8.9	8.9	9.5	9.2	9.5	9.8	9.7	11.2	11.4	11.7	10.3	10.5	11.1
Undecided	14.6	14.4	13.7	14.2	13.5	13.4	13.5	13.4	13.6	13.5	13.7	13.5	13.5	13.8	14.5	16.2	15.6	15.4	14.7	14.6	14.4

DISAGGREGATED RESPONSES
FRESHMAN WOMEN

ITEM	1966	1967	1968	1969	1970	1971	1972	1973	1974	1975	1976	1977	1978	1979	1980	1981	1982	1983	1984	1985
Your probable undergraduate field																				
Arts and Humanities																				
Art, fine and applied	—	—	—	—	—	4.5	3.8	3.6	3.6	3.5	3.4	3.5	3.2	3.1	3.1	3.2	2.8	2.7	2.3	2.3
English (language and literature)	—	—	—	—	—	4.2	3.1	2.7	2.2	1.8	1.9	1.7	1.8	1.6	1.5	1.5	1.4	1.6	1.7	1.8
History	—	—	—	—	—	2.4	1.8	1.4	1.2	1.0	0.8	0.7	0.7	0.6	0.5	0.5	0.5	0.5	0.5	0.6
Journalism	—	—	—	—	—	1.8	2.0	1.8	1.9	1.9	2.2	2.0	2.0	2.4	2.2	2.3	2.5	2.2	2.2	2.4
Language and Literature (except English)	—	—	—	—	—	3.8	3.2	2.7	2.3	1.7	1.5	1.2	1.2	1.0	0.9	1.0	1.0	0.9	1.0	1.1
Music	—	—	—	—	—	3.0	3.4	2.3	2.5	2.1	2.1	2.1	2.0	1.7	1.6	1.6	1.5	1.4	1.1	1.1
Philosophy	—	—	—	—	—	0.4	0.3	0.3	0.2	0.2	0.1	0.1	0.1	0.1	0.1	0.1	0.1	0.1	0.1	0.1
Speech or Theater	—	—	—	—	—	1.7	1.6	1.6	1.4	1.3	1.3	1.3	—	—	—	—	—	—	—	—
Theater or Drama	—	—	—	—	—	—	—	—	—	—	—	—	1.2	1.2	1.1	1.1	1.2	0.9	0.9	1.0
Speech	—	—	—	—	—	—	—	—	—	—	—	—	0.3	0.3	0.2	0.2	0.2	0.2	0.3	0.1
Theology or Religion	—	—	—	—	—	0.2	0.3	0.4	0.3	0.3	0.3	0.2	0.2	0.1	0.2	0.1	0.1	0.1	0.1	0.1
Other Arts and Humanities	—	—	—	—	—	0.7	1.8	1.0	0.9	0.9	0.9	0.8	0.6	0.7	0.7	0.8	0.8	0.7	0.7	0.8
Biological Science																				
Biology (general)	—	—	—	—	—	2.0	1.9	3.4	3.2	3.3	3.4	2.4	2.4	2.1	2.0	2.0	2.0	2.2	2.4	2.6
Biochemistry or Biophysics	—	—	—	—	—	0.4	0.4	0.6	0.7	0.8	0.8	0.5	0.6	0.5	0.5	0.5	0.6	0.6	0.7	0.6
Botany	—	—	—	—	—	0.1	0.2	0.2	0.3	0.2	0.2	0.2	0.2	0.1	0.0	0.1	0.0	0.0	0.0	0.0
Environmental Science	—	—	—	—	—	0.3	0.3	—	—	—	—	—	—	—	—	—	—	—	—	—
Marine (life) Science	—	—	—	—	—	—	—	0.6	0.6	0.5	0.5	0.6	0.6	0.5	0.3	0.4	0.3	0.3	0.4	0.4
Microbiology or Bacteriology	—	—	—	—	—	—	—	0.6	0.5	0.5	0.6	0.4	0.4	0.4	0.3	0.3	0.3	0.3	0.3	0.2
Zoology	—	—	—	—	—	0.5	0.6	0.9	1.0	0.8	0.7	0.5	0.5	0.4	0.4	0.4	0.4	0.4	0.4	0.4
Other Biological Science	—	—	—	—	—	0.4	0.9	0.8	0.8	0.8	0.9	0.7	0.7	0.6	0.6	0.5	0.5	0.5	0.6	0.5
Business																				
Accounting	—	—	—	—	—	1.5	1.5	2.2	2.9	3.7	4.2	4.9	5.5	5.5	6.0	6.1	6.7	6.8	7.1	6.7
Business Administration (general)	—	—	—	—	—	1.8	1.8	1.8	2.1	2.6	3.2	4.0	4.6	5.1	5.8	6.1	5.9	5.9	6.2	5.9
Finance	—	—	—	—	—	—	—	0.2	0.2	0.2	0.2	0.4	0.4	0.5	0.5	0.6	0.8	0.9	1.1	1.2
International Business	—	—	—	—	—	—	—	—	—	—	—	—	—	—	—	—	—	—	—	—
Marketing	—	—	—	—	—	—	—	0.6	0.6	0.7	0.9	1.2	1.7	1.9	1.9	2.1	2.1	2.3	2.6	2.9
Management	—	—	—	—	—	—	—	0.5	0.7	0.9	1.3	1.6	2.2	2.4	2.7	2.9	3.2	3.2	3.7	3.9
Secretarial Studies	—	—	—	—	—	2.7	2.2	2.3	2.1	1.8	1.6	1.7	1.4	1.7	1.0	1.1	1.0	0.9	0.9	1.0
Other Business	—	—	—	—	—	0.5	0.7	0.3	0.3	0.4	0.5	0.6	0.7	0.8	0.8	0.9	0.9	1.0	1.3	1.1
Education																				
Business Education	—	—	—	—	—	—	—	0.5	0.5	0.5	0.4	0.4	0.3	0.3	0.3	0.2	0.2	0.2	0.2	0.3
Elementary Education	—	—	—	—	—	—	—	8.4	7.1	6.2	5.8	5.6	4.7	4.9	4.7	4.9	4.4	4.7	4.9	5.5
Music or Art Education	—	—	—	—	—	—	—	0.9	1.1	1.1	0.9	0.9	0.8	0.7	0.6	0.6	0.6	0.5	0.5	0.4
Physical Education or Recreation	—	—	—	—	—	3.2	3.1	2.9	2.6	2.9	2.8	2.7	2.4	2.5	1.7	1.5	1.1	0.8	1.0	0.8
Secondary Education	—	—	—	—	—	—	—	2.1	1.8	1.4	1.3	1.1	0.9	1.0	0.9	1.1	1.0	1.0	1.3	1.5
Special Education	—	—	—	—	—	14.5	10.7	5.6	4.4	5.0	4.2	4.2	3.9	4.1	3.8	3.1	2.1	2.0	1.6	1.3
Other Education	—	—	—	—	—	0.5	0.7	0.9	0.8	0.7	0.8	0.7	0.7	0.6	0.6	0.6	0.5	0.4	0.4	0.4
Engineering																				
Aeronautical or Astronautical Eng	—	—	—	—	—	0.0	0.0	0.0	0.0	0.1	0.1	0.1	0.3	0.3	0.3	0.2	0.2	0.2	0.2	0.3
Civil Engineering	—	—	—	—	—	0.0	0.1	0.1	0.2	0.3	0.3	0.3	0.3	0.3	0.3	0.3	0.3	0.2	0.3	0.3
Chemical Engineering	—	—	—	—	—	0.1	0.1	0.1	0.3	0.5	0.4	0.4	0.6	0.6	0.8	0.6	0.7	0.6	0.5	0.6
Electrical or Electronic Engineering	—	—	—	—	—	0.0	0.1	0.1	0.1	0.2	0.4	0.4	0.5	0.5	0.6	0.7	0.9	1.0	1.0	1.0
Industrial Engineering	—	—	—	—	—	0.0	0.0	0.1	0.1	0.1	0.1	0.1	0.2	0.2	0.3	0.1	0.3	0.2	0.2	0.2
Mechanical Engineering	—	—	—	—	—	0.1	0.0	0.1	0.1	0.2	0.2	0.2	0.3	0.3	0.4	0.4	0.5	0.4	0.4	0.4
Other Engineering	—	—	—	—	—	0.1	0.1	0.1	0.3	0.5	0.6	0.5	0.7	0.7	0.8	0.9	1.1	1.0	0.7	0.9

DISAGGREGATED RESPONSES
FRESHMAN WOMEN

ITEM	1986	1987	1988	1989	1990	1991	1992	1993	1994	1995	1996	1997	1998	1999	2000	2001	2002	2003	2004	2005	2006
Your probable undergraduate field																					
Arts and Humanities																					
Art, fine and applied	2.8	3.0	2.7	2.5	2.4	2.2	2.2	2.0	2.1	2.3	2.1	2.3	2.6	2.5	2.8	3.4	3.5	3.4	2.9	3.2	3.1
English (language and literature)	2.0	2.0	2.0	2.2	2.2	2.2	2.2	2.2	2.2	2.2	2.3	2.2	2.2	2.2	2.2	2.2	2.1	2.1	2.3	2.3	2.4
History	0.6	0.7	0.7	0.8	0.8	1.0	1.0	0.8	0.8	0.8	0.8	0.8	0.8	0.8	0.8	0.9	0.9	0.9	1.0	1.1	1.2
Journalism	2.5	2.4	2.3	2.1	2.0	1.8	1.7	1.9	2.0	2.3	1.8	1.8	2.0	2.1	2.1	2.0	2.1	2.1	2.0	2.2	2.5
Language and Literature (except English)	1.2	1.1	1.2	1.0	0.9	0.8	0.9	0.8	0.7	0.7	0.7	0.7	0.7	0.6	0.6	0.7	0.7	0.7	0.8	0.8	0.9
Music	1.2	1.2	1.0	1.0	1.1	1.1	1.2	1.1	1.2	1.1	1.3	1.4	1.3	1.3	1.3	1.4	1.2	1.2	1.2	1.2	1.1
Philosophy	0.1	0.1	0.1	0.2	0.1	0.1	0.1	0.1	0.1	0.1	0.1	0.1	0.2	0.1	0.2	0.2	0.2	0.2	0.2	0.2	0.2
Speech or Theater	—	—	—	—	—	—	—	—	—	—	—	—	—	—	—	—	—	—	—	—	—
Theater or Drama	0.9	1.1	0.9	0.9	0.9	1.1	1.0	1.0	0.9	1.0	1.1	1.1	1.3	1.3	1.6	1.4	1.4	1.3	1.2	1.3	1.3
Speech	0.2	0.2	0.2	0.2	0.2	0.2	0.2	0.2	0.2	0.2	0.2	0.2	0.2	0.2	0.2	0.2	0.2	0.2	0.2	0.2	0.2
Theology or Religion	0.1	0.1	0.1	0.1	0.1	0.1	0.1	0.1	0.2	0.2	0.2	0.2	0.3	0.2	0.2	0.2	0.3	0.2	0.2	0.2	0.2
Other Arts and Humanities	0.8	0.9	0.8	0.8	0.8	0.8	0.7	0.7	0.8	0.9	0.8	0.8	1.0	1.1	1.3	1.3	1.3	1.2	1.2	1.3	1.3
Biological Science																					
Biology (general)	2.5	2.4	2.2	2.2	2.5	3.1	3.5	4.0	4.2	4.7	4.7	4.7	4.5	4.6	4.2	4.7	4.9	5.0	5.2	5.1	5.4
Biochemistry or Biophysics	0.6	0.5	0.5	0.5	0.5	0.6	0.7	0.7	0.7	0.8	0.7	0.8	0.7	0.7	0.7	0.8	0.9	0.9	1.1	1.1	1.2
Botany	0.0	0.0	0.0	0.0	0.0	0.0	0.1	0.1	0.1	0.1	0.1	0.1	0.1	0.1	0.0	0.0	0.0	0.0	0.0	0.0	0.0
Environmental Science	—	—	—	—	—	—	—	—	1.0	0.9	0.8	0.7	0.7	0.7	0.5	0.5	0.4	0.4	0.4	0.4	0.5
Marine (life) Science	0.4	0.4	0.5	0.7	0.6	0.8	0.9	0.9	0.8	0.9	0.9	0.9	0.5	0.7	0.5	0.5	0.4	0.3	0.3	0.4	0.4
Microbiology or Bacteriology	0.3	0.2	0.3	0.2	0.2	0.2	0.2	0.2	0.3	0.3	0.4	0.5	0.4	0.4	0.4	0.3	0.3	0.3	0.3	0.3	0.3
Zoology	0.3	0.3	0.3	0.4	0.4	0.5	0.5	0.4	0.5	0.6	0.6	0.6	0.5	0.5	0.5	0.4	0.4	0.5	0.4	0.4	0.5
Other Biological Science	0.4	0.5	0.5	0.5	0.5	0.6	0.7	0.8	0.6	0.7	0.7	0.7	0.7	0.6	0.7	0.7	0.7	0.7	0.8	0.7	0.9
Business																					
Accounting	6.4	6.1	6.1	6.3	5.7	5.6	4.5	4.4	4.0	3.9	3.3	3.1	2.8	2.6	2.3	2.2	2.2	1.9	1.9	2.2	2.2
Business Administration (general)	6.0	5.8	5.7	5.1	4.1	3.4	2.9	2.7	2.4	2.6	2.8	2.7	2.8	2.9	3.0	2.8	2.7	2.4	2.5	2.7	2.7
Finance	1.5	1.4	1.4	1.2	1.0	0.8	0.7	0.6	0.6	0.6	0.7	0.7	0.8	0.9	0.9	0.9	0.8	0.7	0.7	0.8	0.9
International Business	—	—	—	—	—	—	1.8	1.6	1.5	1.5	1.6	1.7	1.6	1.7	1.6	1.6	1.5	1.3	1.3	1.4	1.5
Marketing	3.2	3.2	3.0	3.0	2.7	2.1	2.1	1.6	1.7	1.7	1.8	1.9	2.2	2.4	2.6	2.6	2.6	2.7	2.8	2.9	3.0
Management	3.9	3.8	3.7	3.2	2.9	2.2	2.0	1.7	1.7	1.8	1.8	1.8	2.0	2.2	2.2	2.2	2.2	2.3	2.5	2.4	2.5
Secretarial Studies	0.4	0.4	0.4	0.3	0.3	0.2	0.1	0.1	0.1	0.1	0.1	0.1	0.1	0.1	0.1	0.0	0.0	0.0	0.0	0.0	0.0
Other Business	1.3	1.4	1.5	1.3	1.2	1.1	1.0	1.0	0.5	0.5	0.7	0.6	0.7	0.8	0.8	0.8	0.7	0.7	0.8	0.7	0.8
Education																					
Business Education	0.3	0.3	0.3	0.2	0.2	0.2	0.1	0.2	0.2	0.2	0.2	0.2	0.2	0.2	0.1	0.1	0.1	0.1	0.1	0.1	0.2
Elementary Education	6.9	7.7	7.6	7.7	8.9	8.7	8.1	7.8	7.8	7.7	8.0	8.0	8.9	8.9	9.1	8.3	8.6	8.0	7.5	7.3	7.0
Music or Art Education	0.5	0.5	0.5	0.5	0.7	0.6	0.6	0.6	0.7	0.6	0.8	0.7	0.8	0.7	0.8	0.8	0.8	0.8	0.7	0.9	0.8
Physical Education or Recreation	1.0	0.9	0.6	0.7	0.6	0.6	0.6	0.6	0.7	0.7	0.6	0.7	0.7	0.6	0.6	0.5	0.5	0.5	0.5	0.5	0.5
Secondary Education	1.8	2.1	2.1	2.4	2.6	2.5	2.5	2.3	2.3	2.2	2.5	2.4	2.5	2.4	2.7	2.5	3.0	2.8	2.6	2.7	2.6
Special Education	1.4	1.2	1.2	1.0	1.3	1.4	1.3	1.4	1.2	1.2	1.2	1.2	1.3	1.1	1.1	1.0	0.9	0.9	1.0	1.0	0.9
Other Education	0.5	0.5	0.5	0.5	0.6	0.6	0.5	0.6	0.6	0.6	0.5	0.6	0.6	0.6	0.5	0.5	0.5	0.5	0.4	0.5	0.5
Engineering																					
Aeronautical or Astronautical Eng	0.5	0.4	0.5	0.5	0.5	0.5	0.4	0.2	0.2	0.2	0.3	0.2	0.2	0.2	0.3	0.3	0.3	0.3	0.3	0.2	0.2
Civil Engineering	0.2	0.2	0.3	0.3	0.4	0.4	0.5	0.6	0.6	0.4	0.5	0.4	0.3	0.4	0.3	0.3	0.3	0.4	0.4	0.3	0.4
Chemical Engineering	0.4	0.4	0.4	0.5	0.5	0.7	0.8	0.9	0.7	0.6	0.6	0.7	0.5	0.5	0.4	0.4	0.4	0.4	0.4	0.4	0.4
Electrical or Electronic Engineering	0.8	0.7	0.6	0.6	0.6	0.6	0.5	0.5	0.5	0.4	0.5	0.5	0.4	0.4	0.4	0.4	0.3	0.2	0.2	0.2	0.2
Industrial Engineering	0.2	0.2	0.1	0.2	0.2	0.2	0.2	0.1	0.1	0.1	0.1	0.1	0.2	0.2	0.1	0.2	0.1	0.1	0.1	0.1	0.1
Mechanical Engineering	0.4	0.3	0.3	0.4	0.4	0.4	0.4	0.5	0.4	0.4	0.4	0.4	0.3	0.4	0.4	0.4	0.4	0.4	0.5	0.4	0.4
Other Engineering	0.7	0.6	0.6	0.7	0.7	0.8	0.9	1.0	0.8	0.7	0.9	1.0	0.8	0.8	1.0	1.0	1.2	1.1	1.0	1.0	0.8

DISAGGREGATED RESPONSES
FRESHMAN WOMEN

ITEM	1966	1967	1968	1969	1970	1971	1972	1973	1974	1975	1976	1977	1978	1979	1980	1981	1982	1983	1984	1985
Your probable undergraduate field																				
Physical Science																				
Astronomy	—	—	—	—	—	—	—	0.1	0.1	0.0	0.0	0.0	0.0	0.0	0.0	0.0	0.0	0.0	0.0	0.1
Atmospheric Science (incl Meteorology)	—	—	—	—	—	—	—	0.0	0.0	0.0	0.0	0.0	0.0	0.0	0.0	0.0	0.0	0.0	0.0	0.0
Chemistry	—	—	—	—	—	0.6	0.6	0.8	0.9	0.9	1.0	0.7	0.8	0.8	0.7	0.7	0.7	0.8	0.8	0.8
Earth Science	—	—	—	—	—	0.1	0.1	0.1	0.1	0.2	0.1	0.2	0.2	0.2	0.1	0.2	0.1	0.1	0.1	0.1
Marine Science	—	—	—	—	—	—	—	0.2	0.1	0.2	0.2	0.3	0.2	0.2	0.1	0.2	0.1	0.1	0.1	0.1
Mathematics	—	—	—	—	—	3.8	3.0	2.1	1.7	1.4	1.1	1.0	1.1	0.8	0.9	0.9	1.0	1.1	1.2	1.1
Physics	—	—	—	—	—	0.2	0.1	0.1	0.1	0.1	0.1	0.2	0.2	0.2	0.2	0.1	0.1	0.2	0.2	0.3
Statistics	—	—	—	—	—	0.0	0.0	0.0	0.0	0.0	0.0	0.0	0.0	0.0	0.0	0.0	0.0	0.0	0.0	0.0
Other Physical Science	—	—	—	—	—	0.1	0.1	0.1	0.1	0.1	0.2	0.2	0.1	0.1	0.1	0.2	0.2	0.1	0.1	0.1
Professional																				
Architecture or Urban Planning	—	—	—	—	—	0.3	0.3	0.3	0.5	0.5	0.4	0.4	0.5	0.5	0.5	0.3	0.3	0.3	0.4	0.4
Home Economics	—	—	—	—	—	4.5	4.0	3.2	3.2	2.6	2.4	2.3	1.7	1.6	1.5	1.1	1.0	0.8	0.9	0.9
Health Technology (medical, dental, laboratory)	—	—	—	—	—	2.7	3.4	3.3	3.6	3.8	3.8	2.8	2.2	2.2	2.2	2.0	1.7	1.8	1.5	1.2
Library or Archival Science	—	—	—	—	—	0.5	0.4	0.3	0.2	0.2	0.1	0.1	0.1	0.1	0.1	0.1	0.0	0.0	0.0	0.0
Medical, Dental, Veterinary	—	—	—	—	—	3.2	4.3	—	—	—	—	3.6	3.7	3.8	4.0	3.7	3.7	4.0	3.8	4.1
Nursing	—	—	—	—	—	6.4	7.1	6.3	8.4	8.2	8.1	6.9	6.8	6.3	7.1	6.7	7.1	7.7	6.7	5.1
Pharmacy	—	—	—	—	—	0.8	0.7	0.8	0.9	0.7	1.1	0.8	0.7	0.7	0.6	0.6	0.6	0.8	0.8	0.8
Therapy (occupational, physical, speech)	—	—	—	—	—	3.4	4.3	3.1	3.0	3.8	3.7	3.4	3.3	3.2	3.4	3.6	3.2	3.6	3.6	3.0
Other Professional	—	—	—	—	—	0.8	1.7	1.8	2.2	2.0	2.4	1.3	1.4	1.5	1.4	1.3	1.3	1.3	1.3	1.2
Social Science																				
Anthropology	—	—	—	—	—	0.5	0.6	0.5	0.4	0.3	0.3	0.2	0.2	0.2	0.1	0.1	0.1	0.1	0.1	0.1
Economics	—	—	—	—	—	0.3	0.2	0.2	0.2	0.3	0.3	0.3	0.3	0.4	0.4	0.4	0.4	0.5	0.4	0.5
Ethnic Studies	—	—	—	—	—	—	—	—	—	—	—	—	0.0	—	—	0.0	0.0	0.0	0.0	0.0
Geography	—	—	—	—	—	0.0	0.0	0.0	0.0	0.0	0.0	0.0	0.0	0.0	0.0	0.0	0.0	0.0	0.0	0.0
Political science (gov't, int'l relations)	—	—	—	—	—	1.5	1.6	2.7	2.5	2.6	2.7	2.7	2.9	2.5	2.7	2.4	2.5	2.6	2.9	3.6
Psychology	—	—	—	—	—	6.2	5.9	5.3	5.0	4.7	4.1	4.1	4.3	4.3	4.0	3.9	3.9	4.1	4.9	5.3
Social Work	—	—	—	—	—	4.3	3.5	3.1	3.2	3.2	3.2	3.0	2.8	2.6	2.2	1.9	1.4	1.3	1.3	1.3
Sociology	—	—	—	—	—	2.5	2.1	1.7	1.4	1.3	1.0	1.1	0.9	0.7	0.7	0.6	0.4	0.4	0.5	0.5
Women's Studies	—	—	—	—	—	—	—	—	—	—	—	—	—	—	—	—	0.0	0.0	0.0	0.0
Other Social Science	—	—	—	—	—	0.3	0.4	0.3	0.4	0.4	0.4	0.3	0.4	0.3	0.3	0.2	0.2	0.1	0.2	0.2
Technical																				
Building Trades	—	—	—	—	—	0.0	0.0	0.0	0.0	0.0	0.0	0.0	0.0	0.0	0.0	0.0	0.0	0.0	0.0	0.0
Data Processing or Computer Programming	—	—	—	—	—	0.3	0.2	0.3	0.4	0.4	0.4	0.6	0.7	1.1	1.4	2.0	2.5	2.1	1.2	1.1
Drafting or Design	—	—	—	—	—	0.5	0.5	0.1	0.1	0.1	0.1	0.1	0.1	0.2	0.2	0.2	0.2	0.2	0.2	0.2
Electronics	—	—	—	—	—	0.1	0.2	0.0	0.0	0.0	0.0	0.1	0.1	0.1	0.1	0.0	0.0	0.0	0.0	0.0
Mechanics	—	—	—	—	—	—	—	0.0	0.0	0.0	0.0	0.0	0.0	0.0	0.0	0.0	0.0	0.0	0.0	0.0
Other Technical	—	—	—	—	—	0.2	0.2	0.1	0.1	0.1	0.0	0.1	0.1	0.1	0.1	0.1	0.1	0.0	0.0	0.0
Other																				
Agriculture	—	—	—	—	—	0.2	0.3	0.5	0.7	0.9	1.0	0.6	0.7	0.6	0.5	0.6	0.4	0.3	0.4	0.4
Communications (radio, TV, etc.)	—	—	—	—	—	0.3	0.3	0.6	0.7	1.0	1.3	1.5	1.8	2.2	2.4	2.6	2.8	2.6	2.7	3.1
Computer Science	—	—	—	—	—	0.5	0.5	0.3	0.6	0.7	0.6	0.8	1.2	1.5	2.3	3.2	4.2	4.1	2.5	1.7
Forestry	—	—	—	—	—	0.1	0.2	0.3	0.4	0.5	0.3	0.5	0.3	0.3	0.2	0.2	0.2	0.1	0.1	0.1
Law Enforcement	—	—	—	—	—	—	—	0.4	0.4	0.7	1.0	1.2	1.1	1.0	0.7	0.5	0.8	0.7	0.6	0.7
Military Science	—	—	—	—	—	0.0	0.0	0.0	0.0	0.0	0.0	0.0	0.1	0.0	0.0	0.0	0.0	0.0	0.0	0.1
Other field	—	—	—	—	—	1.8	2.3	0.6	0.6	0.7	0.9	0.9	0.8	0.9	0.9	0.9	0.9	0.8	0.9	1.0
Undecided	—	—	—	—	—	2.5	5.4	5.5	5.5	6.1	5.8	6.5	6.3	6.4	6.6	6.8	6.9	7.1	7.4	8.0

DISAGGREGATED RESPONSES
FRESHMAN WOMEN

ITEM	1986	1987	1988	1989	1990	1991	1992	1993	1994	1995	1996	1997	1998	1999	2000	2001	2002	2003	2004	2005	2006
Your probable undergraduate field																					
Physical Science																					
Astronomy	0.0	0.1	0.1	0.1	0.1	0.1	0.0	0.1	0.0	0.1	0.1	0.1	0.1	0.1	0.1	0.1	0.1	0.1	0.1	0.1	0.1
Atmospheric Science (incl Meteorology)	0.0	0.0	0.0	0.0	0.0	0.0	0.0	0.0	0.0	0.0	0.1	0.1	0.1	0.1	0.1	0.1	0.1	0.1	0.1	0.1	0.1
Chemistry	0.7	0.6	0.6	0.6	0.6	0.7	0.8	0.9	0.9	0.8	0.9	0.8	0.7	0.7	0.7	0.8	0.8	0.9	1.1	1.0	1.1
Earth Science	0.1	0.0	0.1	0.1	0.1	0.2	0.2	0.2	0.1	0.1	0.1	0.1	0.2	0.1	0.1	0.1	0.1	0.1	0.1	0.1	0.1
Marine Science	0.1	0.1	0.1	0.2	0.2	0.2	0.2	0.3	0.2	0.5	0.3	0.3	0.2	0.3	0.2	0.2	0.1	0.1	0.1	0.2	0.2
Mathematics	0.9	0.8	0.7	0.7	0.8	0.8	0.7	0.7	0.7	0.7	0.6	0.6	0.6	0.6	0.6	0.6	0.7	0.6	0.6	0.7	0.6
Physics	0.2	0.2	0.2	0.2	0.2	0.2	0.2	0.2	0.2	0.2	0.2	0.2	0.2	0.2	0.2	0.2	0.2	0.2	0.2	0.2	0.2
Statistics	0.0	0.0	0.0	0.0	0.0	0.0	0.0	0.0	0.0	0.0	0.0	0.0	0.0	0.0	0.0	0.0	0.0	0.0	0.0	0.0	0.0
Other Physical Science	0.1	0.1	0.1	0.1	0.1	0.0	0.1	0.2	0.1	0.1	0.1	0.0	0.1	0.1	0.1	0.1	0.2	0.2	0.2	0.2	0.2
Professional																					
Architecture or Urban Planning	0.5	0.5	0.4	0.6	0.7	0.7	0.7	0.7	0.7	0.7	0.6	0.6	0.6	0.8	0.8	0.6	0.7	0.8	0.9	0.7	0.4
Home Economics	0.7	0.7	0.5	0.5	0.5	0.4	0.3	0.3	0.2	0.2	0.2	0.1	0.1	0.1	0.2	0.1	0.1	0.1	0.1	0.3	0.3
Health Technology (medical, dental, laboratory)	0.9	0.9	1.0	0.8	0.8	0.9	0.9	0.9	0.9	1.0	0.9	0.9	0.7	0.6	0.6	0.6	0.6	0.6	0.6	0.7	0.7
Library or Archival Science	0.0	0.0	0.0	0.0	0.0	0.0	0.0	0.0	0.0	0.0	0.0	0.0	0.0	0.0	0.0	0.0	0.0	0.0	0.0	0.0	0.0
Medical, Dental, Veterinary	3.8	3.3	3.7	4.0	4.0	4.5	5.3	5.5	5.6	6.0	5.7	6.0	5.7	6.0	5.3	5.3	5.1	5.4	5.4	4.8	4.6
Nursing	3.7	3.0	3.1	3.1	4.2	5.4	6.1	6.0	5.3	4.6	4.2	3.9	3.9	3.9	3.7	4.4	4.6	6.1	6.7	6.6	6.8
Pharmacy	0.8	0.9	1.3	1.3	1.3	1.3	1.3	1.5	1.3	1.4	1.4	1.2	1.1	0.8	1.0	1.2	1.6	1.9	2.2	2.1	1.7
Therapy (occupational, physical, speech)	2.9	2.9	2.9	3.1	3.0	3.9	5.3	5.8	5.4	5.5	5.2	5.1	5.1	3.4	2.6	2.5	2.5	2.7	3.1	2.9	2.6
Other Professional	1.1	1.2	1.2	1.3	1.3	1.2	1.1	1.1	1.3	1.1	1.2	1.2	1.1	1.0	0.9	0.9	0.8	0.8	0.9	0.8	0.8
Social Science																					
Anthropology	0.2	0.2	0.3	0.3	0.3	0.3	0.3	0.3	0.3	0.4	0.4	0.4	0.4	0.4	0.4	0.4	0.4	0.4	0.4	0.4	0.5
Economics	0.4	0.4	0.4	0.4	0.3	0.3	0.2	0.2	0.2	0.3	0.2	0.3	0.3	0.3	0.3	0.3	0.3	0.3	0.3	0.3	0.4
Ethnic Studies	0.0	0.0	0.0	0.0	0.1	0.0	0.1	0.0	0.1	0.1	0.1	0.0	0.0	0.0	0.0	0.1	0.1	0.1	0.1	0.1	0.1
Geography	0.0	0.0	0.0	0.0	0.0	0.0	0.0	0.0	0.0	0.0	0.0	0.0	0.0	0.0	0.0	0.0	0.0	0.0	0.0	0.0	0.0
Political science (gov't, int'l relations)	3.4	3.6	4.3	4.2	4.1	3.7	3.4	3.4	3.1	2.7	2.8	2.7	2.7	2.8	2.8	3.0	3.3	3.4	3.2	3.5	3.3
Psychology	6.0	6.3	7.0	7.0	6.6	6.4	6.8	6.6	6.6	6.5	6.5	6.2	6.4	6.4	6.8	6.9	6.8	6.7	6.4	6.5	6.6
Social Work	1.2	1.2	1.4	1.2	1.4	1.2	1.4	1.4	1.6	1.6	1.5	1.4	1.3	1.3	1.3	1.1	1.1	1.0	1.0	1.1	1.1
Sociology	0.5	0.6	0.6	0.7	0.6	0.6	0.5	0.7	0.7	0.7	0.7	0.6	0.7	0.7	0.7	0.7	0.7	0.7	0.7	0.7	0.8
Women's Studies	0.0	0.0	0.0	0.0	0.0	0.0	0.0	0.0	0.0	0.0	0.0	0.0	0.1	0.0	0.0	0.0	0.0	0.0	0.0	0.0	0.0
Other Social Science	0.2	0.2	0.3	0.2	0.3	0.3	0.3	0.0	0.3	0.0	0.3	0.3	0.3	0.4	0.3	0.3	0.4	0.4	0.4	0.4	0.4
Technical																					
Building Trades	0.0	0.0	0.0	0.0	0.0	0.0	0.0	0.0	0.0	0.0	0.0	0.0	0.0	0.0	0.0	0.0	0.0	0.0	0.0	0.0	0.0
Data Processing or Computer Programming	0.6	0.4	0.5	0.4	0.4	0.3	0.3	0.2	0.2	0.3	0.3	0.4	0.4	0.4	0.5	0.4	0.2	0.1	0.1	0.1	0.1
Drafting or Design	0.2	0.2	0.2	0.2	0.2	0.2	0.0	0.2	0.2	0.2	0.2	0.2	0.3	0.3	0.3	0.4	0.3	0.4	0.3	0.3	0.3
Electronics	0.0	0.0	0.0	0.0	0.0	0.0	0.0	0.0	0.0	0.0	0.0	0.0	0.0	0.0	0.0	0.0	0.0	0.0	0.1	0.0	0.0
Mechanics	0.0	0.0	0.0	0.0	0.0	0.0	0.0	0.0	0.0	0.0	0.0	0.0	0.0	0.0	0.0	0.0	0.0	0.0	0.0	0.0	0.0
Other Technical	0.1	0.0	0.1	0.0	0.1	0.0	0.0	0.0	0.0	0.0	0.0	0.0	0.1	0.1	0.0	0.1	0.1	0.1	0.1	0.0	0.1
Other																					
Agriculture	0.3	0.3	0.3	0.3	0.3	0.3	0.3	0.4	0.6	0.5	0.7	0.7	0.6	0.8	0.4	0.4	0.5	0.4	0.5	0.4	0.4
Communications (radio, TV, etc.)	3.4	3.4	3.5	3.4	3.1	2.8	2.7	2.2	2.1	1.9	2.3	2.4	2.4	2.8	3.2	3.2	2.9	2.8	2.2	2.4	2.6
Computer Science	1.2	1.0	1.0	1.0	1.1	1.2	0.9	0.9	0.9	1.0	1.2	1.3	1.5	1.4	1.4	1.2	0.7	0.4	0.3	0.3	0.3
Forestry	0.1	0.0	0.0	0.1	0.1	0.1	0.1	0.2	0.1	0.1	0.1	0.1	0.1	0.1	0.0	0.0	0.0	0.0	0.0	0.0	0.0
Law Enforcement	0.7	0.7	0.8	0.7	0.8	0.8	0.8	0.7	0.8	0.8	0.8	0.7	0.8	0.7	0.7	0.8	0.7	0.9	0.9	0.8	0.8
Military Science	0.0	0.0	0.0	0.0	0.0	0.0	0.0	0.0	0.0	0.0	0.0	0.0	0.0	0.0	0.0	0.0	0.0	0.0	0.0	0.0	0.0
Other field	0.9	1.1	1.0	1.3	1.5	1.3	1.2	1.3	1.3	1.3	1.3	1.3	1.3	1.7	1.4	1.4	1.5	1.9	1.7	1.9	1.5
Undecided	8.8	9.1	8.3	8.9	8.4	8.6	8.7	8.7	9.1	8.8	8.7	8.9	8.7	9.1	9.5	9.7	9.8	8.9	8.3	8.0	8.2

DISAGGREGATED RESPONSES
FRESHMAN WOMEN

ITEM	1966	1967	1968	1969	1970	1971	1972	1973	1974	1975	1976	1977	1978	1979	1980	1981	1982	1983	1984	1985
Your father's occupation																				
Accountant or actuary	—	—	—	—	—	2.5	2.6	—	—	—	2.5	2.5	2.6	2.5	2.4	2.5	2.6	2.5	2.5	2.6
Actor or entertainer	—	—	—	—	—	0.0	0.0	—	—	—	0.0	0.1	0.1	0.1	0.1	0.0	0.1	0.1	0.1	0.1
Architect	—	—	—	—	—	0.6	0.5	—	—	—	0.8	0.7	0.7	0.7	0.7	0.8	0.8	0.7	0.8	0.9
Artist	—	—	—	—	—	0.3	0.3	—	—	—	0.4	0.3	0.3	0.3	0.3	0.3	0.3	0.3	0.3	0.3
Business (clerical)	—	—	—	—	—	1.2	1.1	—	—	—	0.8	0.7	0.8	0.7	0.7	0.7	0.6	0.6	0.7	0.6
Business executive (mgmt, administrator)	—	—	—	—	—	14.3	15.2	—	—	—	14.1	13.4	14.2	13.6	13.9	13.5	13.9	13.5	13.3	13.7
Business owner or proprietor	—	—	—	—	—	8.2	8.6	—	—	—	8.2	7.9	7.9	8.1	8.3	8.3	8.8	8.7	8.8	8.9
Business salesperson or buyer	—	—	—	—	—	6.4	6.2	—	—	—	6.1	6.0	6.1	6.0	5.6	5.7	5.8	5.7	5.7	5.2
Clergy (minister, priest)	—	—	—	—	—	1.0	1.0	—	—	—	1.1	1.2	1.3	1.2	1.1	1.0	1.0	1.0	0.9	1.0
Clergy (other religious)	—	—	—	—	—	0.1	0.1	—	—	—	0.2	0.1	0.2	0.2	0.2	0.2	0.2	0.1	0.1	0.1
Clinical psychologist	—	—	—	—	—	0.1	0.1	—	—	—	0.1	0.1	0.1	0.1	0.1	0.1	0.1	0.1	0.2	0.2
College administrator/staff	—	—	—	—	—	—	—	—	—	—	—	—	—	—	—	—	—	—	—	—
College teacher	—	—	—	—	—	1.0	1.2	—	—	—	1.2	1.1	1.3	1.2	1.3	1.3	1.3	1.2	1.2	1.4
Computer programmer or analyst	—	—	—	—	—	0.4	0.5	—	—	—	0.9	1.0	1.1	1.2	1.4	1.5	1.6	1.8	1.9	2.1
Conservationist or forester	—	—	—	—	—	0.3	0.2	—	—	—	0.2	0.2	0.2	0.2	0.2	0.2	0.2	0.1	0.2	0.2
Dentist (including orthodontist)	—	—	—	—	—	0.6	0.7	—	—	—	0.8	0.6	0.7	0.7	0.6	0.7	0.7	0.6	0.6	0.6
Dietitian or home economist	—	—	—	—	—	0.0	0.1	—	—	—	0.1	0.1	0.1	0.1	0.1	0.1	0.1	0.1	0.1	0.1
Engineer	—	—	—	—	—	8.2	8.3	—	—	—	9.1	8.8	9.5	8.7	8.5	8.6	8.8	8.5	8.9	9.1
Farmer or rancher	—	—	—	—	—	5.1	4.9	—	—	—	4.1	3.8	3.4	3.2	3.8	4.2	3.6	3.2	3.1	3.6
Foreign service worker (incl diplomat)	—	—	—	—	—	0.2	0.1	—	—	—	0.1	0.1	0.1	0.1	0.1	0.1	0.1	0.2	0.2	0.2
Homemaker (full-time)	—	—	—	—	—	0.2	0.0	—	—	—	0.0	0.1	0.1	0.1	0.1	0.1	0.1	0.0	0.1	0.1
Interior decorator (including designer)	—	—	—	—	—	0.1	0.1	—	—	—	0.1	0.1	0.1	0.1	0.1	0.1	0.1	0.1	0.1	0.1
Interpreter (translator)	—	—	—	—	—	0.0	0.0	—	—	—	0.0	0.0	0.0	0.0	0.0	0.0	0.0	0.0	0.0	0.0
Lab technician or hygienist	—	—	—	—	—	0.4	0.3	—	—	—	0.3	0.3	0.3	0.3	0.3	0.4	0.4	0.3	0.4	0.3
Law enforcement officer	—	—	—	—	—	0.8	1.0	—	—	—	1.0	1.1	0.9	1.0	1.1	1.0	1.1	1.2	1.3	1.3
Lawyer (attorney) or judge	—	—	—	—	—	1.6	1.9	—	—	—	1.9	1.9	1.8	2.0	2.0	2.1	2.1	2.0	1.9	2.1
Military service (career)	—	—	—	—	—	1.8	1.7	—	—	—	1.9	2.0	2.0	1.7	1.9	2.0	1.9	2.0	1.8	1.7
Musician (performer, composer)	—	—	—	—	—	0.1	0.1	—	—	—	0.1	0.1	0.1	0.1	0.1	0.1	0.2	0.2	0.1	0.1
Nurse	—	—	—	—	—	0.1	0.1	—	—	—	0.1	0.1	0.1	0.1	0.1	0.1	0.1	0.1	0.1	0.1
Optometrist	—	—	—	—	—	0.2	0.1	—	—	—	0.1	0.1	0.1	0.1	0.1	0.1	0.1	0.1	0.1	0.1
Pharmacist	—	—	—	—	—	0.5	0.4	—	—	—	0.5	0.4	0.5	0.5	0.4	0.5	0.4	0.5	0.4	0.5
Physician	—	—	—	—	—	2.0	2.1	—	—	—	2.4	2.2	2.4	2.3	2.3	2.3	2.4	2.3	2.1	2.3
Policymaker/government	—	—	—	—	—	—	—	—	—	—	—	—	—	—	—	—	—	—	—	—
School counselor	—	—	—	—	—	0.2	0.2	—	—	—	0.2	0.1	0.2	0.2	0.2	0.2	0.2	0.2	0.2	0.2
School principal or superintendent	—	—	—	—	—	0.8	1.0	—	—	—	0.7	0.7	0.7	0.7	0.7	0.7	0.7	0.7	0.6	0.6
Scientific researcher	—	—	—	—	—	0.8	0.8	—	—	—	0.8	0.7	0.8	0.7	0.7	0.7	0.6	0.7	0.7	0.8
Social, welfare or recreation worker	—	—	—	—	—	0.2	0.3	—	—	—	0.3	0.4	0.3	0.3	0.4	0.4	0.3	0.4	0.5	0.4
Statistician	—	—	—	—	—	0.1	0.1	—	—	—	0.1	0.1	0.0	0.1	0.0	0.1	0.1	0.1	0.1	0.1
Therapist (physical, occupational, speech)	—	—	—	—	—	0.1	0.1	—	—	—	0.1	0.1	0.1	0.1	0.1	0.1	0.1	0.1	0.1	0.1
Teacher or administrator (elementary)	—	—	—	—	—	0.4	0.4	—	—	—	0.6	0.6	0.6	0.6	0.5	0.6	0.6	0.7	0.7	0.7
Teacher or administrator (secondary)	—	—	—	—	—	1.6	1.7	—	—	—	2.5	2.3	2.5	2.5	2.5	2.8	2.7	2.7	2.7	3.0
Veterinarian	—	—	—	—	—	0.2	0.2	—	—	—	0.2	0.2	0.2	0.2	0.2	0.2	0.2	0.2	0.2	0.3
Writer or journalist	—	—	—	—	—	0.3	0.4	—	—	—	0.4	0.3	0.4	0.3	0.3	0.3	0.4	0.4	0.4	0.3
Skilled trades	—	—	—	—	—	10.1	9.9	—	—	—	8.9	9.2	8.7	8.9	8.9	8.7	8.6	8.4	8.8	7.7
Laborer (unskilled)	—	—	—	—	—	3.5	3.7	—	—	—	3.2	3.3	2.9	3.4	3.3	3.0	2.8	2.8	2.8	2.8
Semi skilled worker	—	—	—	—	—	5.9	5.2	—	—	—	4.6	4.8	3.9	4.4	4.3	3.8	3.9	4.2	3.8	3.8
Other occupation	—	—	—	—	—	16.2	14.7	—	—	—	16.0	17.4	17.3	18.3	17.1	18.0	17.4	17.5	18.0	17.3
Unemployed	—	—	—	—	—	1.4	1.8	—	—	—	2.2	2.6	2.3	2.6	2.8	2.3	2.3	3.1	2.7	2.5

DISAGGREGATED RESPONSES
FRESHMAN WOMEN

ITEM	1986	1987	1988	1989	1990	1991	1992	1993	1994	1995	1996	1997	1998	1999	2000	2001	2002	2003	2004	2005	2006
Your father's occupation																					
Accountant or actuary	2.7	2.8	2.7	2.6	2.7	2.5	2.6	2.7	2.5	2.6	2.6	2.5	2.6	2.7	2.7	2.6	2.5	2.7	2.7	2.6	2.6
Actor or entertainer	0.1	0.1	0.1	0.1	0.1	0.1	0.1	0.0	0.1	0.1	0.1	0.0	0.1	0.1	0.1	0.1	0.1	0.1	0.1	0.1	0.1
Architect	0.9	0.9	0.9	0.9	0.8	0.8	0.8	0.8	0.9	0.9	0.8	0.9	1.0	1.0	1.1	1.0	1.0	1.0	1.0	1.0	1.0
Artist	0.3	0.3	0.3	0.3	0.3	0.3	0.3	0.3	0.3	0.3	0.3	0.3	0.3	0.3	0.3	0.3	0.3	0.4	0.3	0.3	0.4
Business (clerical)	0.6	0.6	0.5	0.6	0.6	0.6	0.6	0.6	0.6	0.7	0.6	0.7	0.8	0.9	0.9	1.0	1.0	1.0	1.0	1.0	1.1
Business executive (mgmt, administrator)	14.2	14.5	13.3	13.3	12.5	11.9	12.3	11.7	11.8	11.3	11.1	11.1	11.5	11.4	11.5	11.4	11.3	11.4	10.9	10.9	11.1
Business owner or proprietor	9.6	9.5	9.3	9.2	8.8	8.9	8.8	8.8	8.8	8.9	8.7	9.3	9.2	9.5	9.5	9.5	9.5	9.8	9.9	9.7	9.5
Business salesperson or buyer	5.5	5.5	4.9	5.1	4.6	4.6	4.9	4.7	4.6	4.6	4.6	4.9	4.6	4.7	4.6	4.6	4.4	4.5	4.5	4.5	4.5
Clergy (minister, priest)	1.0	0.9	0.9	1.1	1.1	1.1	1.1	1.0	1.0	0.9	1.1	1.0	1.0	1.0	1.0	0.9	1.0	0.8	0.8	0.8	0.8
Clergy (other religious)	0.1	0.2	0.1	0.1	0.1	0.1	0.1	0.1	0.1	0.1	0.1	0.1	0.1	0.1	0.1	0.1	0.1	0.1	0.1	0.1	0.1
Clinical psychologist	0.2	0.2	0.2	0.2	0.1	0.1	0.2	0.2	0.2	0.2	0.2	0.2	0.2	0.2	0.2	0.2	0.2	0.2	0.2	0.2	0.1
College administrator/staff	—	—	—	—	—	—	—	—	—	—	0.4	0.3	0.4	0.3	0.3	0.3	0.3	0.3	0.2	0.4	0.3
College teacher	1.3	1.3	1.2	1.2	1.0	1.0	1.0	0.9	0.8	0.8	0.8	0.7	0.7	0.7	0.7	0.7	0.7	0.7	0.7	0.7	0.7
Computer programmer or analyst	2.1	2.3	2.2	2.4	2.2	2.2	2.6	2.5	2.6	2.7	2.8	2.8	3.2	3.2	3.3	3.5	3.4	3.5	3.4	3.6	3.6
Conservationist or forester	0.1	0.1	0.2	0.2	0.2	0.2	0.2	0.2	0.2	0.2	0.2	0.2	0.2	0.2	0.3	0.2	0.2	0.2	0.2	0.2	0.2
Dentist (including orthodontist)	0.7	0.7	0.7	0.6	0.6	0.5	0.5	0.6	0.6	0.6	0.5	0.6	0.5	0.5	0.6	0.5	0.6	0.5	0.6	0.5	0.5
Dietitian or home economist	0.0	0.1	0.0	0.1	0.1	0.1	0.1	0.1	0.0	0.0	0.0	0.1	0.1	0.0	0.0	0.0	0.0	0.0	0.1	0.1	0.1
Engineer	9.0	8.4	8.1	8.0	7.8	7.8	7.8	8.0	7.6	7.7	7.8	7.6	7.9	7.9	7.9	8.2	8.2	8.4	8.5	8.3	8.4
Farmer or rancher	2.6	2.6	2.4	2.6	2.7	2.9	2.4	2.6	3.1	3.2	2.7	2.9	2.5	2.5	2.2	1.9	1.9	1.6	1.7	1.4	1.3
Foreign service worker (incl diplomat)	0.1	0.2	0.1	0.1	0.1	0.1	0.1	0.1	0.1	0.1	0.1	0.1	0.1	0.1	0.1	0.1	0.1	0.1	0.1	0.1	0.1
Homemaker (full-time)	0.1	0.1	0.1	0.1	0.1	0.2	0.1	0.1	0.1	0.1	0.1	0.1	0.2	0.1	0.1	0.1	0.1	0.1	0.1	0.1	0.1
Interior decorator (including designer)	0.1	0.1	0.1	0.1	0.0	0.1	0.0	0.1	0.0	0.0	0.0	0.1	0.0	0.0	0.0	0.0	0.0	0.0	0.0	0.0	0.0
Interpreter (translator)	0.0	0.0	0.0	0.0	0.0	0.0	0.0	0.0	0.0	0.0	—	—	—	—	—	—	—	—	—	—	—
Lab technician or hygienist	0.4	0.4	0.4	0.3	0.3	0.4	0.4	0.4	0.3	0.3	0.4	0.3	0.4	0.4	0.4	0.4	0.4	0.3	0.3	0.3	0.3
Law enforcement officer	1.3	1.4	1.4	1.4	1.5	1.4	1.6	1.6	1.7	1.5	1.6	1.5	1.6	1.6	1.6	1.6	1.6	1.6	1.5	1.6	1.6
Lawyer (attorney) or judge	2.3	2.3	2.3	2.1	2.0	1.9	2.0	2.1	2.1	2.1	2.0	2.2	2.1	2.0	2.2	2.2	2.2	2.3	2.2	2.2	2.3
Military service (career)	1.9	1.9	1.9	2.0	1.9	2.2	2.2	1.9	1.7	1.7	1.7	1.5	1.5	1.6	1.5	1.6	1.6	1.5	1.6	1.6	1.5
Musician (performer, composer)	0.1	0.1	0.1	0.1	0.1	0.1	0.2	0.2	0.1	0.1	0.2	0.2	0.2	0.2	0.2	0.2	0.2	0.2	0.2	0.2	0.2
Nurse	0.1	0.1	0.1	0.1	0.2	0.2	0.2	0.2	0.3	0.3	0.3	0.4	0.4	0.4	0.4	0.4	0.5	0.5	0.5	0.5	0.5
Optometrist	0.1	0.1	0.1	0.1	0.1	0.1	0.1	0.1	0.1	0.1	0.1	0.1	0.1	0.1	0.1	0.1	0.1	0.1	0.1	0.1	0.1
Pharmacist	0.5	0.4	0.4	0.4	0.4	0.4	0.4	0.4	0.4	0.4	0.4	0.5	0.4	0.4	0.4	0.4	0.4	0.4	0.5	0.4	0.4
Physician	2.4	2.4	2.4	2.3	2.1	2.0	2.0	2.1	2.1	2.0	2.0	2.2	2.0	2.1	2.2	2.2	2.2	2.2	2.1	2.1	2.2
Policymaker/government	—	—	—	—	—	—	—	—	—	—	0.8	0.8	0.9	0.7	0.9	0.9	0.9	0.8	0.8	0.7	0.8
School counselor	0.2	0.2	0.2	0.2	0.2	0.2	0.2	0.2	0.2	0.1	0.1	0.1	0.1	0.1	0.1	0.1	0.1	0.1	0.1	0.1	0.1
School principal or superintendent	0.6	0.6	0.5	0.6	0.5	0.6	0.5	0.6	0.6	0.5	0.5	0.4	0.4	0.4	0.4	0.3	0.3	0.3	0.3	0.2	0.3
Scientific researcher	0.7	0.7	0.7	0.6	0.6	0.6	0.6	0.6	0.6	0.5	0.6	0.5	0.5	0.6	0.5	0.6	0.6	0.7	0.7	0.6	0.6
Social, welfare or recreation worker	0.4	0.5	0.5	0.4	0.5	0.5	0.5	0.5	0.5	0.6	0.6	0.6	0.6	0.5	0.6	0.6	0.6	0.6	0.5	0.5	0.5
Statistician	0.1	0.1	0.1	0.1	0.1	0.0	0.1	0.1	0.0	0.0	—	—	—	—	—	—	—	—	—	—	—
Therapist (physical, occupational, speech)	0.1	0.1	0.1	0.1	0.2	0.2	0.2	0.2	0.2	0.2	0.2	0.2	0.2	0.2	0.2	0.2	0.3	0.3	0.3	0.3	0.3
Teacher or administrator (elementary)	0.7	0.8	0.8	0.9	0.8	1.0	1.0	1.1	1.0	1.1	1.0	1.0	1.0	0.9	0.9	0.8	0.8	0.8	0.8	0.7	0.6
Teacher or administrator (secondary)	3.2	3.1	3.3	3.3	3.2	3.1	3.2	3.2	3.1	3.0	3.0	2.8	2.6	2.6	2.4	2.3	2.2	2.2	2.1	2.0	1.9
Veterinarian	0.2	0.2	0.2	0.2	0.3	0.2	0.2	0.2	0.2	0.2	0.2	0.2	0.1	0.2	0.1	0.2	0.1	0.1	0.1	0.2	0.2
Writer or journalist	0.3	0.4	0.4	0.3	0.3	0.3	0.3	0.3	0.3	0.3	0.3	0.2	0.3	0.3	0.3	0.3	0.3	0.3	0.3	0.2	0.3
Skilled trades	7.9	8.0	8.5	8.4	8.5	8.4	8.1	8.7	8.4	8.1	8.2	8.0	7.9	7.5	7.1	7.8	7.9	7.4	7.6	7.1	7.2
Laborer (unskilled)	2.3	2.2	2.7	2.5	3.0	3.1	2.8	3.1	2.8	2.6	2.8	2.6	2.8	2.6	2.7	3.4	3.3	3.2	3.2	3.5	3.1
Semi skilled worker	3.3	3.1	3.4	3.5	3.6	3.8	3.5	3.4	3.4	3.4	3.3	3.2	3.2	2.9	2.9	3.0	3.0	2.9	2.8	2.9	2.7
Other occupation	17.1	17.5	18.7	19.0	20.5	20.2	20.1	19.7	20.7	20.9	21.0	21.1	21.2	21.5	21.6	20.3	20.5	20.8	21.1	22.0	22.4
Unemployed	2.5	2.2	2.4	2.4	2.5	3.2	3.3	3.2	3.1	3.1	3.2	2.7	2.7	2.5	2.8	2.4	2.8	3.0	2.8	3.1	3.0

DISAGGREGATED RESPONSES
FRESHMAN WOMEN

ITEM	1966	1967	1968	1969	1970	1971	1972	1973	1974	1975	1976	1977	1978	1979	1980	1981	1982	1983	1984	1985
Your mother's occupation																				
Accountant or actuary	—	—	—	—	—	1.3	1.2	—	—	—	1.4	1.5	1.6	1.6	1.8	1.9	2.0	2.2	2.3	2.2
Actor or entertainer	—	—	—	—	—	0.0	0.0	—	—	—	0.0	0.1	0.1	0.1	0.1	0.1	0.1	0.1	0.1	0.1
Architect	—	—	—	—	—	0.0	0.0	—	—	—	0.0	0.0	0.1	0.1	0.0	0.1	0.1	0.1	0.1	0.1
Artist	—	—	—	—	—	0.4	0.5	—	—	—	0.6	0.6	0.6	0.6	0.6	0.7	0.7	0.7	0.7	0.7
Business (clerical)	—	—	—	—	—	9.9	11.4	—	—	—	10.6	10.5	10.6	11.1	11.4	11.5	11.6	11.2	11.9	10.9
Business executive (mgmt, administrator)	—	—	—	—	—	1.2	1.4	—	—	—	2.0	2.3	2.5	2.8	3.3	3.5	3.9	4.4	4.7	5.0
Business owner or proprietor	—	—	—	—	—	1.0	1.4	—	—	—	1.5	1.5	1.7	1.9	1.8	2.3	2.4	2.4	2.6	2.8
Business salesperson or buyer	—	—	—	—	—	1.0	1.4	—	—	—	1.4	1.5	1.7	1.7	1.9	2.0	2.1	2.1	2.0	3.0
Clergy (minister, priest)	—	—	—	—	—	0.0	0.0	—	—	—	0.0	0.0	0.0	0.0	0.0	0.0	0.1	0.1	0.1	0.0
Clergy (other religious)	—	—	—	—	—	0.0	0.0	—	—	—	0.0	0.0	0.0	0.0	0.0	0.1	0.1	0.1	0.1	0.1
Clinical psychologist	—	—	—	—	—	0.1	0.1	—	—	—	0.1	0.2	0.2	0.2	0.2	0.2	0.1	0.2	0.3	0.2
College administrator/staff	—	—	—	—	—	—	—	—	—	—	0.4	0.4	0.4	0.4	0.4	0.4	0.5	—	0.4	—
College teacher	—	—	—	—	—	0.4	0.4	—	—	—	0.3	0.4	0.4	0.4	0.5	0.6	0.8	0.8	0.9	1.0
Computer programmer or analyst	—	—	—	—	—	0.2	0.2	—	—	—	0.0	0.0	0.0	0.0	0.0	0.0	0.0	0.0	0.0	0.0
Conservationist or forester	—	—	—	—	—	0.0	0.0	—	—	—	0.0	0.0	0.0	0.0	0.1	0.1	0.0	0.0	0.1	0.1
Dentist (including orthodontist)	—	—	—	—	—	0.0	0.0	—	—	—	0.1	0.1	0.1	0.1	0.1	0.1	0.1	0.1	0.1	0.6
Dietitian or home economist	—	—	—	—	—	0.5	0.5	—	—	—	0.6	0.6	0.6	0.5	0.6	0.5	0.5	0.6	0.6	0.6
Engineer	—	—	—	—	—	0.1	0.0	—	—	—	0.1	0.1	0.1	0.1	0.1	0.1	0.1	0.1	0.1	0.2
Farmer or rancher	—	—	—	—	—	0.1	0.1	—	—	—	0.1	0.2	0.2	0.2	0.2	0.2	0.2	0.2	0.3	0.2
Foreign service worker (incl diplomat)	—	—	—	—	—	0.1	0.1	—	—	—	0.1	0.0	0.1	0.1	0.1	0.1	0.0	0.1	0.1	0.0
Homemaker (full-time)	—	—	—	—	—	51.3	36.9	—	—	—	34.6	32.4	31.8	28.6	27.5	23.4	22.3	24.4	23.3	22.1
Interior decorator (including designer)	—	—	—	—	—	0.2	0.2	—	—	—	0.3	0.3	0.3	0.3	0.3	0.4	0.4	0.5	0.4	0.5
Interpreter (translator)	—	—	—	—	—	0.0	0.0	—	—	—	0.0	0.0	0.0	0.0	0.0	0.0	0.0	0.0	0.0	0.0
Lab technician or hygienist	—	—	—	—	—	0.4	0.5	—	—	—	0.6	0.5	0.5	0.6	0.7	0.7	0.7	0.7	0.8	0.8
Law enforcement officer	—	—	—	—	—	0.0	0.1	—	—	—	0.1	0.1	0.1	0.1	0.1	0.1	0.2	0.1	0.1	0.1
Lawyer (attorney) or judge	—	—	—	—	—	0.1	0.1	—	—	—	0.1	0.1	0.1	0.1	0.1	0.1	0.2	0.2	0.2	0.3
Military service (career)	—	—	—	—	—	0.0	0.0	—	—	—	0.0	0.0	0.0	0.0	0.0	0.0	0.0	0.0	0.0	0.0
Musician (performer, composer)	—	—	—	—	—	0.1	0.2	—	—	—	0.2	0.2	0.2	0.2	0.2	0.2	0.2	0.2	0.2	0.2
Nurse	—	—	—	—	—	4.7	5.0	—	—	—	6.5	6.7	6.6	6.8	7.0	7.4	7.5	7.3	7.5	7.3
Optometrist	—	—	—	—	—	0.0	0.0	—	—	—	0.1	0.1	0.0	0.1	0.1	0.1	0.1	0.2	0.1	0.1
Pharmacist	—	—	—	—	—	0.1	0.0	—	—	—	0.1	0.1	0.1	0.1	0.1	0.1	0.1	0.1	0.1	0.1
Physician	—	—	—	—	—	0.1	0.1	—	—	—	0.1	0.1	0.2	0.2	0.2	0.1	0.2	0.2	0.2	0.3
Policymaker/government	—	—	—	—	—	—	—	—	—	—	—	—	—	—	—	—	—	—	—	—
School counselor	—	—	—	—	—	0.2	0.3	—	—	—	0.2	0.2	0.2	0.2	0.2	0.2	0.3	0.2	0.2	0.2
School principal or superintendent	—	—	—	—	—	0.1	0.1	—	—	—	0.1	0.1	0.1	0.1	0.1	0.1	0.1	0.1	0.1	0.1
Scientific researcher	—	—	—	—	—	0.1	0.1	—	—	—	0.1	0.1	0.1	0.1	0.1	0.1	0.1	0.2	0.1	0.2
Social, welfare or recreation worker	—	—	—	—	—	0.7	0.8	—	—	—	1.1	1.1	1.1	1.3	1.2	1.2	1.3	1.2	1.3	1.2
Statistician	—	—	—	—	—	0.1	0.1	—	—	—	0.1	0.1	0.1	0.1	0.1	0.1	0.1	0.1	0.1	0.1
Therapist (physical, occupational, speech)	—	—	—	—	—	0.2	0.2	—	—	—	0.3	0.3	0.3	0.4	0.4	0.3	0.4	0.4	0.4	0.4
Teacher or administrator (elementary)	—	—	—	—	—	5.2	5.8	—	—	—	6.4	6.2	6.6	6.5	6.2	6.4	6.8	6.2	6.2	6.7
Teacher or administrator (secondary)	—	—	—	—	—	2.4	2.6	—	—	—	2.8	2.6	2.8	2.7	2.8	3.3	3.2	3.1	3.2	3.7
Veterinarian	—	—	—	—	—	0.0	0.0	—	—	—	0.0	0.0	0.0	0.0	0.0	0.0	0.0	0.0	0.0	0.0
Writer or journalist	—	—	—	—	—	0.3	0.2	—	—	—	0.3	0.3	0.3	0.3	0.3	0.3	0.3	0.3	0.3	0.3
Skilled trades	—	—	—	—	—	1.3	1.7	—	—	—	1.4	1.5	1.6	1.5	1.6	1.6	1.8	1.6	1.6	1.6
Laborer (unskilled)	—	—	—	—	—	1.4	1.8	—	—	—	1.8	2.0	1.7	2.0	2.0	1.9	1.8	1.7	1.8	1.7
Semi skilled worker	—	—	—	—	—	2.3	2.6	—	—	—	2.5	2.7	2.3	2.5	2.7	2.8	2.5	2.7	2.5	2.3
Other occupation	—	—	—	—	—	10.0	12.6	—	—	—	13.0	14.3	14.7	15.4	15.2	16.9	17.0	16.1	16.1	15.8
Unemployed	—	—	—	—	—	2.4	9.3	—	—	—	7.6	8.1	7.3	8.0	7.9	7.8	7.3	6.5	6.0	6.1

DISAGGREGATED RESPONSES
FRESHMAN WOMEN

ITEM	1986	1987	1988	1989	1990	1991	1992	1993	1994	1995	1996	1997	1998	1999	2000	2001	2002	2003	2004	2005	2006
Your mother's occupation																					
Accountant or actuary	2.4	2.5	2.5	2.4	2.4	2.4	2.4	2.5	2.6	2.5	2.6	2.9	3.1	3.4	3.4	3.7	3.9	4.2	4.2	4.4	4.8
Actor or entertainer	0.1	0.1	0.1	0.0	0.1	0.0	0.0	0.0	0.0	0.1	0.0	0.0	0.0	0.1	0.1	0.1	0.0	0.1	0.1	0.1	0.1
Architect	0.1	0.1	0.1	0.1	0.1	0.1	0.1	0.1	0.1	0.1	0.1	0.1	0.1	0.1	0.1	0.1	0.1	0.2	0.2	0.2	0.2
Artist	0.7	0.7	0.7	0.7	0.7	0.5	0.7	0.6	0.6	0.7	0.6	0.6	0.6	0.6	0.6	0.6	0.7	0.7	0.7	0.7	0.7
Business (clerical)	11.4	11.6	11.1	11.0	10.4	10.0	9.6	9.1	8.9	8.4	8.1	7.9	8.0	7.6	7.5	7.1	6.5	6.1	5.7	5.2	5.1
Business executive (mgmt, administrator)	5.7	6.1	5.9	6.3	5.8	5.7	5.8	5.8	5.7	5.7	5.4	5.7	5.9	6.3	6.1	6.6	6.4	6.3	6.4	6.4	6.5
Business owner or proprietor	3.1	3.2	3.2	3.2	3.4	3.2	3.1	3.0	3.2	3.1	3.1	3.3	3.3	3.3	3.2	3.3	3.4	3.5	3.5	3.6	3.4
Business salesperson or buyer	2.9	3.0	2.9	2.7	2.6	2.5	2.4	2.4	2.2	2.2	2.1	2.2	2.0	2.1	2.1	2.2	2.1	2.2	2.2	2.2	2.1
Clergy (minister, priest)	0.1	0.1	0.1	0.1	0.1	0.1	0.1	0.1	0.1	0.1	0.1	0.1	0.1	0.1	0.1	0.1	0.1	0.1	0.1	0.1	0.2
Clergy (other religious)	0.1	0.1	0.1	0.1	0.1	0.1	0.1	0.1	0.1	0.1	0.1	0.1	0.1	0.1	0.1	0.1	0.1	0.1	0.1	0.1	0.1
Clinical psychologist	0.2	0.2	0.2	0.2	0.2	0.2	0.2	0.2	0.2	0.2	0.2	0.2	0.2	0.2	0.2	0.2	0.2	0.2	0.2	0.2	0.2
College administrator/staff	—	0.5	0.5	—	0.5	0.5	0.6	0.5	0.6	—	0.6	0.6	0.6	0.6	0.6	0.6	0.6	0.6	0.6	0.6	0.6
College teacher	0.5	0.5	0.5	0.5	0.5	0.5	0.6	0.5	0.6	0.5	0.5	0.5	0.5	0.5	0.5	0.5	0.5	0.5	0.5	0.6	0.5
Computer programmer or analyst	1.1	1.3	1.4	1.4	1.6	1.5	1.4	1.3	1.4	1.3	1.2	1.2	1.3	1.3	1.3	1.4	1.3	1.4	1.4	1.4	1.4
Conservationist or forester	0.0	0.0	0.0	0.0	0.0	0.0	0.0	0.0	0.0	0.0	0.0	0.0	0.0	0.0	0.0	0.0	0.0	0.0	0.0	0.0	0.0
Dentist (including orthodontist)	0.1	0.1	0.2	0.2	0.1	0.2	0.2	0.2	0.2	0.2	0.2	0.3	0.3	0.4	0.4	0.4	0.4	0.4	0.5	0.4	0.5
Dietitian or home economist	0.5	0.5	0.5	0.5	0.5	0.5	0.4	0.4	0.4	0.4	0.3	0.4	0.4	0.4	0.4	0.3	0.3	0.3	0.4	0.4	0.4
Engineer	0.2	0.2	0.2	0.2	0.2	0.2	0.2	0.3	0.4	0.3	0.3	0.3	0.4	0.4	0.4	0.5	0.5	0.6	0.6	0.7	0.8
Farmer or rancher	0.2	0.2	0.2	0.3	0.3	0.3	0.3	0.3	0.4	0.4	0.3	0.4	0.3	0.3	0.2	0.2	0.2	0.2	0.2	0.2	0.2
Foreign service worker (incl diplomat)	0.1	0.1	0.0	0.2	0.0	0.1	0.2	0.1	0.1	0.1	0.1	0.1	0.1	0.1	0.1	0.1	0.1	0.1	0.1	0.1	0.1
Homemaker (full-time)	20.1	18.0	17.1	16.3	15.3	15.1	14.4	13.8	13.3	12.3	12.0	11.2	11.3	11.3	11.5	11.3	10.9	10.7	10.7	10.0	9.5
Interior decorator (including designer)	0.5	0.5	0.5	0.5	0.0	0.5	0.5	0.4	0.4	0.4	0.3	0.4	0.4	0.4	0.4	0.4	0.4	0.4	0.4	0.4	0.4
Interpreter (translator)	0.0	0.0	0.0	0.0	0.0	0.1	0.1	0.1	0.0	0.0	—	—	—	—	—	—	—	—	—	—	—
Lab technician or hygienist	0.8	0.8	0.8	0.8	0.9	0.8	0.8	0.9	0.9	0.9	1.0	0.9	1.0	0.9	0.9	0.9	1.0	0.9	0.9	0.9	0.8
Law enforcement officer	0.1	0.1	0.1	0.1	0.2	0.2	0.1	0.1	0.1	0.2	0.2	0.2	0.2	0.2	0.2	0.2	0.3	0.2	0.2	0.2	0.3
Lawyer (attorney) or judge	0.3	0.3	0.3	0.3	0.3	0.3	0.3	0.3	0.3	0.3	0.4	0.4	0.4	0.5	0.6	0.6	0.7	0.6	0.8	0.8	0.9
Military service (career)	0.0	0.0	0.1	0.1	0.1	0.1	0.1	0.1	0.1	0.1	0.1	0.1	0.1	0.1	0.2	0.2	0.2	0.2	0.2	0.2	0.2
Musician (performer, composer)	0.2	0.2	0.2	0.2	0.1	0.2	0.2	0.1	0.2	0.1	0.1	0.1	0.1	0.2	0.2	0.2	0.2	0.2	0.2	0.2	0.2
Nurse	7.4	7.4	7.5	7.7	7.6	7.7	7.8	8.0	8.1	8.4	8.4	8.7	8.6	8.5	8.4	8.5	8.7	8.7	8.8	8.6	8.7
Optometrist	0.1	0.1	0.1	0.1	0.1	0.1	0.1	0.1	0.1	0.1	0.1	0.1	0.1	0.1	0.1	0.1	0.1	0.1	0.1	0.1	0.2
Pharmacist	0.1	0.1	0.1	0.1	0.2	0.1	0.1	0.1	0.2	0.2	0.2	0.3	0.2	0.3	0.3	0.3	0.3	0.4	0.4	0.4	0.5
Physician	0.3	0.2	0.3	0.3	0.3	0.3	0.3	0.3	0.3	0.3	0.4	0.4	0.4	0.5	0.5	0.6	0.6	0.6	0.7	0.7	0.8
Policymaker/government	—	—	0.0	0.0	0.0	0.0	0.0	0.0	—	0.4	0.0	0.4	0.4	0.4	0.5	0.5	0.5	0.5	0.5	0.5	0.5
School counselor	0.3	0.3	0.3	0.3	0.3	0.3	0.4	0.4	0.4	0.4	0.3	0.4	0.4	0.4	0.4	0.3	0.4	0.5	0.5	0.3	0.3
School principal or superintendent	0.1	0.2	0.2	0.2	0.2	0.2	0.2	0.2	0.2	0.2	0.2	0.2	0.2	0.2	0.3	0.3	0.2	0.2	0.2	0.2	0.2
Scientific researcher	0.2	0.1	0.2	0.2	0.1	0.2	0.3	0.2	0.2	0.2	0.2	0.2	0.2	0.2	0.2	0.3	0.3	0.3	0.3	0.4	0.3
Social, welfare or recreation worker	1.4	1.4	1.5	1.5	1.5	1.6	1.6	1.7	1.6	1.7	1.7	1.7	1.8	1.7	1.9	1.9	1.8	1.8	1.6	1.8	1.8
Statistician	0.1	—	0.1	0.1	0.1	0.1	0.1	0.1	0.1	0.1	0.1	—	0.1	0.1	0.2	0.1	0.2	0.1	0.1	0.2	0.2
Therapist (physical, occupational, speech)	0.5	0.6	0.6	0.6	0.6	0.6	0.6	0.7	0.7	0.8	0.8	0.9	0.9	1.0	1.1	1.1	1.1	1.3	1.3	1.2	1.3
Teacher or administrator (elementary)	6.9	7.3	7.5	7.6	7.5	8.2	8.9	9.2	9.5	9.7	10.2	10.4	10.3	10.0	9.6	9.5	9.4	9.0	8.4	8.3	8.0
Teacher or administrator (secondary)	3.8	4.0	3.9	4.0	3.9	4.1	4.3	4.4	4.6	4.7	4.9	4.6	4.5	4.4	4.4	4.4	4.4	4.2	4.2	4.0	3.9
Veterinarian	0.0	0.0	0.0	0.0	0.0	0.0	0.0	0.0	0.0	0.0	0.0	0.0	0.0	0.1	0.0	0.0	0.1	0.1	0.1	0.1	0.1
Writer or journalist	0.3	0.4	0.3	0.3	0.3	0.3	0.3	0.3	0.3	0.3	0.3	0.3	0.3	0.3	0.3	0.3	0.3	0.3	0.4	0.4	0.4
Skilled trades	1.7	1.8	1.8	1.7	1.8	1.8	1.8	1.8	1.7	1.6	1.5	1.4	1.5	1.5	1.4	1.6	1.5	1.5	1.4	1.4	1.4
Laborer (unskilled)	1.4	1.4	1.7	1.6	1.8	1.9	1.7	2.2	1.8	1.6	1.5	1.5	1.4	1.5	1.5	1.9	1.7	1.7	1.7	1.7	1.8
Semi skilled worker	2.0	2.0	2.1	2.2	2.3	2.2	2.1	2.1	2.1	2.0	2.0	1.9	1.8	1.8	1.7	2.0	2.0	1.8	1.8	1.9	1.7
Other occupation	16.6	16.8	17.9	18.7	20.4	19.9	20.6	20.5	21.0	21.5	21.4	21.6	21.4	21.4	21.4	20.1	20.9	21.4	22.0	22.5	23.1
Unemployed	5.4	5.3	5.1	4.7	4.8	5.2	5.1	5.0	5.1	4.9	5.2	4.7	4.6	4.4	4.7	4.2	4.4	4.9	4.9	5.3	5.3

DISAGGREGATED RESPONSES
FRESHMAN WOMEN

ITEM	1966	1967	1968	1969	1970	1971	1972	1973	1974	1975	1976	1977	1978	1979	1980	1981	1982	1983	1984	1985
Your religious preference [3]																				
Baptist	—	—	—	13.2	13.1	—	—	13.5	13.6	14.7	13.2	15.0	14.3	—	—	—	—	—	15.8	15.7
Buddhist	—	—	—	—	—	—	—	—	—	—	—	—	—	—	—	—	—	—	0.2	0.3
Congregational (UCC)	—	—	—	4.3	2.7	—	—	2.1	2.3	2.0	2.2	2.3	2.0	—	—	—	—	—	1.9	1.7
Eastern Orthodox	—	—	—	—	0.5	—	—	0.5	0.6	0.5	0.5	0.6	0.6	—	—	—	—	—	0.6	0.5
Episcopal	—	—	—	4.8	4.5	—	—	4.3	3.7	3.9	3.7	3.5	3.8	—	—	—	—	—	—	3.1
Jewish	—	—	—	5.6	5.3	—	—	5.3	3.9	4.4	4.5	3.7	4.1	—	—	—	—	—	3.2	3.3
Latter Day Saints (Mormon)	—	—	—	0.5	0.2	—	—	0.2	0.2	0.2	0.2	0.2	0.2	—	—	—	—	—	0.2	0.2
Lutheran	—	—	—	7.6	6.8	—	—	5.9	6.7	6.2	6.8	6.0	5.6	—	—	—	—	—	5.9	6.1
Methodist	—	—	—	13.7	11.8	—	—	11.7	11.7	11.6	10.1	10.6	11.1	—	—	—	—	—	10.8	9.7
Muslim (Islamic)	—	—	—	0.0	0.1	—	—	0.1	0.1	0.1	0.1	0.1	0.2	—	—	—	—	—	0.2	0.1
Presbyterian	—	—	—	8.6	7.3	—	—	7.1	6.2	6.8	5.9	5.8	6.3	—	—	—	—	—	—	5.4
Quaker (Society of Friends)	—	—	—	0.2	0.3	—	—	0.3	0.2	0.3	0.2	0.2	0.2	—	—	—	—	—	0.2	0.2
Roman Catholic	—	—	—	30.4	27.6	—	—	29.5	30.6	29.4	31.8	32.7	33.2	—	—	—	—	—	36.8	34.6
Seventh Day Adventist	—	—	—	0.3	0.5	—	—	0.5	0.6	0.7	0.7	0.4	0.6	—	—	—	—	—	0.2	0.3
Unitarian Universalist	—	—	—	0.5	1.0	—	—	0.6	0.6	0.5	0.5	0.4	0.4	—	—	—	—	—	0.3	—
Other Christian (Protestant)	—	—	—	5.8	6.4	—	—	5.2	5.6	5.3	6.0	6.4	6.5	—	—	—	—	—	10.6	5.4
Other religion	—	—	—	2.1	2.7	—	—	3.4	3.8	4.1	4.7	4.5	4.0	—	—	—	—	—	5.7	5.4
None	—	—	—	2.3	9.1	—	—	9.7	9.8	9.3	8.8	7.5	7.0	—	—	—	—	—	7.3	8.0
Your father's religious preference [3]																				
Baptist	—	—	—	—	—	—	—	13.3	13.7	14.4	12.9	14.4	13.9	—	—	—	—	—	15.1	14.7
Buddhist	—	—	—	—	—	—	—	—	—	—	—	—	—	—	—	—	—	—	0.3	0.5
Congregational (UCC)	—	—	—	—	—	—	—	2.4	2.5	2.1	2.2	2.3	2.1	—	—	—	—	—	1.9	1.6
Eastern Orthodox	—	—	—	—	—	—	—	0.7	0.6	0.6	0.6	0.7	0.7	—	—	—	—	—	0.8	0.6
Episcopal	—	—	—	—	—	—	—	4.7	4.1	4.1	3.9	3.7	3.8	—	—	—	—	—	—	3.2
Jewish	—	—	—	—	—	—	—	6.3	4.7	5.0	5.1	4.3	4.6	—	—	—	—	—	3.8	3.9
Latter Day Saints (Mormon)	—	—	—	—	—	—	—	0.2	0.2	0.2	0.2	0.2	0.1	—	—	—	—	—	0.2	0.2
Lutheran	—	—	—	—	—	—	—	6.4	7.1	6.5	7.5	6.4	5.9	—	—	—	—	—	6.3	6.4
Methodist	—	—	—	—	—	—	—	13.0	12.7	12.6	10.7	11.2	11.5	—	—	—	—	—	11.0	9.8
Muslim (Islamic)	—	—	—	—	—	—	—	0.1	0.1	0.1	0.1	0.1	0.2	—	—	—	—	—	0.2	0.2
Presbyterian	—	—	—	—	—	—	—	8.1	7.1	7.6	6.6	6.4	6.9	—	—	—	—	—	—	5.7
Quaker (Society of Friends)	—	—	—	—	—	—	—	0.2	0.2	0.2	0.2	0.2	0.2	—	—	—	—	—	0.2	0.1
Roman Catholic	—	—	—	—	—	—	—	29.7	30.7	29.1	31.4	32.3	32.3	—	—	—	—	—	35.7	33.7
Seventh Day Adventist	—	—	—	—	—	—	—	0.4	0.4	0.6	0.6	0.5	0.5	—	—	—	—	—	0.2	0.2
Unitarian Universalist	—	—	—	—	—	—	—	0.6	0.6	0.5	0.5	0.5	0.4	—	—	—	—	—	0.4	—
Other Christian (Protestant)	—	—	—	—	—	—	—	5.0	5.3	5.1	5.8	6.3	6.3	—	—	—	—	—	10.9	5.6
Other religion	—	—	—	—	—	—	—	2.0	2.3	2.8	3.3	3.3	3.0	—	—	—	—	—	4.8	4.5
None	—	—	—	—	—	—	—	7.1	8.0	8.3	8.4	7.6	7.5	—	—	—	—	—	8.4	9.1

DISAGGREGATED RESPONSES
FRESHMAN WOMEN

ITEM	1986	1987	1988	1989	1990	1991	1992	1993	1994	1995	1996	1997	1998	1999	2000	2001	2002	2003	2004	2005	2006
Your religious preference [3]																					
Baptist	—	15.2	16.3	17.3	18.3	18.6	18.0	16.2	16.1	14.3	14.9	14.8	14.9	14.9	12.1	12.5	12.1	11.7	12.2	13.1	11.5
Buddhist	—	0.3	0.3	0.3	0.3	0.3	0.4	0.3	0.5	0.7	0.6	0.6	0.7	0.7	0.9	1.1	1.0	1.0	0.9	1.0	1.1
Congregational (UCC)	—	1.6	1.3	1.4	1.3	2.1	2.2	1.9	1.8	1.8	1.5	1.6	1.6	1.6	1.5	1.4	1.5	1.6	1.0	1.0	1.1
Eastern Orthodox	—	0.5	0.5	0.5	0.5	0.5	0.5	0.6	0.5	0.5	0.6	0.5	0.6	0.5	0.6	0.6	0.6	0.6	0.7	0.7	0.6
Episcopal	—	3.5	3.1	2.9	2.6	2.6	2.5	2.4	2.3	2.1	2.1	2.1	2.0	2.0	1.8	2.0	1.8	1.9	1.7	1.9	1.7
Jewish	—	3.2	3.1	2.8	2.7	2.0	2.2	2.3	2.2	2.3	2.1	2.0	2.0	1.9	2.6	2.4	2.2	2.3	2.3	2.3	2.5
Latter Day Saints (Mormon)	—	0.2	0.3	0.3	0.3	0.3	0.4	0.4	0.4	0.4	0.4	0.3	0.6	0.6	0.6	0.6	0.3	0.6	1.8	0.3	0.3
Lutheran	—	6.9	6.2	6.4	6.5	6.0	6.0	6.8	6.9	7.7	6.1	6.6	5.0	5.8	5.8	5.1	4.9	5.1	5.4	4.2	4.1
Methodist	—	9.7	9.3	10.1	8.7	8.9	8.9	8.3	8.5	7.8	7.6	7.8	7.8	7.7	6.8	6.4	6.4	6.2	6.2	6.1	5.5
Muslim (Islamic)	—	0.2	0.2	0.2	0.3	0.3	0.3	0.4	0.4	0.4	0.5	0.5	0.5	0.6	0.8	0.7	0.6	0.7	0.8	0.9	0.8
Presbyterian	—	5.3	5.1	5.2	4.5	4.6	4.9	4.6	4.4	4.2	4.3	4.3	4.2	4.2	4.1	3.9	4.0	4.2	3.9	4.0	3.5
Quaker (Society of Friends)	—	0.2	0.2	0.2	0.2	0.2	0.2	0.2	0.2	0.2	0.3	0.2	0.2	0.2	0.2	0.2	0.2	0.2	0.2	0.2	0.2
Roman Catholic	—	33.8	32.1	31.2	32.5	31.7	30.6	32.5	30.6	31.2	30.4	31.0	29.6	28.9	31.0	31.0	30.8	30.1	28.6	28.4	28.1
Seventh Day Adventist	—	0.2	0.2	0.4	0.2	0.3	0.3	0.3	0.3	0.2	0.3	0.2	0.3	0.3	0.3	0.3	0.3	0.3	0.3	0.4	0.2
Unitarian Universalist	—	—	—	—	—	—	—	—	—	—	—	—	—	—	—	—	—	0.3	0.4	0.4	—
Other Christian (Protestant)	—	4.9	5.0	5.1	4.4	4.8	5.0	4.6	9.4	10.1	12.0	11.8	12.2	12.7	13.1	13.0	14.1	14.0	14.6	16.1	17.8
Other religion	—	5.2	5.7	5.4	5.9	5.8	5.9	6.2	3.7	3.7	3.9	3.9	3.9	3.7	3.6	3.9	4.0	3.6	3.4	3.4	3.7
None	—	9.2	10.9	10.4	10.7	10.9	11.6	12.0	11.7	12.3	12.4	11.5	13.0	12.8	13.2	14.1	15.1	15.6	15.5	15.6	17.4
Your father's religious preference [3]																					
Baptist	—	15.0	15.7	15.9	16.7	17.2	16.7	14.8	14.9	13.2	13.6	13.6	13.8	14.0	11.1	12.1	11.5	11.0	11.2	12.2	10.9
Buddhist	—	0.4	0.5	0.5	0.6	0.6	0.7	0.6	0.9	1.1	1.0	1.0	1.0	1.2	1.4	1.5	1.5	1.5	1.4	1.6	1.5
Congregational (UCC)	—	1.5	1.3	1.3	1.3	1.9	1.9	1.7	1.7	1.6	1.4	1.4	1.4	1.4	1.3	1.3	1.3	1.4	1.0	0.9	1.0
Eastern Orthodox	—	0.6	0.6	0.6	0.7	0.6	0.6	0.7	0.7	0.7	0.7	0.7	0.7	0.6	0.7	0.7	0.7	0.7	0.8	0.7	0.8
Episcopal	—	3.4	3.0	2.9	2.6	2.6	2.5	2.5	2.3	2.2	2.1	2.2	2.2	2.1	2.0	2.1	2.0	2.1	1.9	2.0	1.9
Jewish	—	3.8	3.7	3.5	3.3	2.6	2.8	3.0	2.8	2.9	2.8	2.6	2.5	2.5	3.2	3.1	2.9	2.9	3.0	3.0	3.2
Latter Day Saints (Mormon)	—	0.2	0.3	0.3	0.3	0.3	0.4	0.4	0.4	0.4	0.5	0.4	1.6	1.5	1.6	1.6	0.3	0.7	1.9	0.3	0.4
Lutheran	—	7.2	6.7	7.2	7.1	6.8	6.6	7.6	7.7	8.5	6.8	7.5	5.6	6.4	6.4	5.8	5.4	5.6	6.1	4.7	4.7
Methodist	—	9.9	9.5	10.6	8.9	9.3	9.4	8.7	9.0	8.3	8.2	8.3	8.2	8.1	7.1	6.6	6.7	6.3	6.3	6.2	5.8
Muslim (Islamic)	—	0.2	0.3	0.4	0.4	0.3	0.4	0.5	0.6	0.6	0.7	0.7	0.8	0.8	1.0	1.0	0.9	0.9	1.1	1.2	1.1
Presbyterian	—	5.7	5.5	5.8	5.0	5.1	5.3	5.0	4.9	4.9	4.8	4.9	4.7	4.7	4.6	4.3	4.5	4.5	4.3	4.5	3.9
Quaker (Society of Friends)	—	0.2	0.2	0.2	0.2	0.2	0.2	0.2	0.2	0.3	0.3	0.2	0.2	0.2	0.2	0.2	0.3	0.3	0.2	0.2	0.2
Roman Catholic	—	33.0	31.5	31.8	33.3	32.6	31.6	33.8	31.7	32.8	32.3	32.2	30.9	30.0	32.6	32.4	32.7	32.0	30.4	30.5	30.4
Seventh Day Adventist	—	0.2	0.2	0.4	0.2	0.3	0.3	0.3	0.4	0.2	0.3	0.3	0.3	0.3	0.3	0.3	0.3	0.3	0.3	0.4	0.3
Unitarian Universalist	—	—	—	—	—	—	—	—	—	—	—	—	—	—	—	—	—	0.3	0.3	0.3	—
Other Christian (Protestant)	—	5.0	5.1	5.2	4.7	4.8	5.2	4.9	8.0	9.0	10.3	10.2	10.5	10.7	11.1	10.9	12.0	11.9	12.5	14.0	15.9
Other religion	—	4.3	4.7	4.2	4.7	4.6	4.7	4.9	3.1	3.1	3.3	3.2	3.4	3.1	3.1	3.2	3.4	3.1	2.9	2.9	2.9
None	—	9.3	11.2	9.4	9.9	10.0	10.7	10.3	10.8	10.2	10.8	10.6	12.3	12.3	12.2	12.7	13.6	14.3	14.4	14.2	15.3

DISAGGREGATED RESPONSES
FRESHMAN WOMEN

ITEM	1966	1967	1968	1969	1970	1971	1972	1973	1974	1975	1976	1977	1978	1979	1980	1981	1982	1983	1984	1985
Your mother's religious preference [3]																				
Baptist	—	—	—	—	13.8	—	—	13.9	14.5	15.5	13.5	15.5	14.7	—	—	—	—	—	16.1	15.6
Buddhist	—	—	—	—	—	—	—	—	—	—	—	—	—	—	—	—	—	—	0.2	0.4
Congregational (UCC)	—	—	—	—	3.1	—	—	2.5	2.7	2.2	2.4	2.5	2.2	—	—	—	—	—	2.0	1.8
Eastern Orthodox	—	—	—	—	0.5	—	—	0.6	0.6	0.6	0.6	0.7	0.6	—	—	—	—	—	0.6	0.5
Episcopal	—	—	—	—	5.2	—	—	5.2	4.5	4.6	4.3	4.1	4.3	—	—	—	—	—	—	3.6
Jewish	—	—	—	—	6.1	—	—	6.0	4.5	4.8	4.9	4.1	4.4	—	—	—	—	—	3.5	3.6
Latter Day Saints (Mormon)	—	—	—	—	0.2	—	—	0.2	0.2	0.2	0.2	0.2	0.2	—	—	—	—	—	0.2	0.2
Lutheran	—	—	—	—	7.1	—	—	6.6	7.4	6.8	7.5	6.6	6.0	—	—	—	—	—	6.5	6.7
Methodist	—	—	—	—	13.6	—	—	13.5	13.2	13.2	11.4	11.7	12.2	—	—	—	—	—	11.5	10.4
Muslim (Islamic)	—	—	—	—	0.1	—	—	0.1	0.1	0.1	0.1	0.1	0.1	—	—	—	—	—	0.2	0.2
Presbyterian	—	—	—	—	8.5	—	—	8.4	7.3	8.0	6.9	6.5	7.1	—	—	—	—	—	—	5.9
Quaker (Society of Friends)	—	—	—	—	0.2	—	—	0.2	0.2	0.2	0.2	0.2	0.2	—	—	—	—	—	0.2	0.2
Roman Catholic	—	—	—	—	28.2	—	—	31.2	32.0	30.6	33.1	33.6	33.8	—	—	—	—	—	37.2	35.0
Seventh Day Adventist	—	—	—	—	0.5	—	—	0.5	0.5	0.7	0.8	0.4	0.6	—	—	—	—	—	0.2	0.3
Unitarian Universalist	—	—	—	—	0.8	—	—	0.7	0.7	0.6	0.6	0.6	0.5	—	—	—	—	—	0.4	—
Other Christian (Protestant)	—	—	—	—	6.6	—	—	5.1	5.5	5.3	6.0	6.4	6.5	—	—	—	—	—	11.4	5.9
Other religion	—	—	—	—	2.0	—	—	2.2	2.6	3.1	3.7	3.6	3.4	—	—	—	—	—	5.5	5.1
None	—	—	—	—	3.3	—	—	3.2	3.6	3.7	3.7	3.3	3.2	—	—	—	—	—	4.2	4.6

DISAGGREGATED RESPONSES
FRESHMAN WOMEN

ITEM	1986	1987	1988	1989	1990	1991	1992	1993	1994	1995	1996	1997	1998	1999	2000	2001	2002	2003	2004	2005	2006
Your mother's religious preference [3]																					
Baptist	—	15.5	16.6	16.7	17.7	18.0	17.5	15.6	15.6	13.9	14.5	14.3	14.9	14.6	11.9	12.9	12.4	11.7	12.1	13.3	11.7
Buddhist	—	0.5	0.6	0.5	0.6	0.7	0.8	0.7	1.0	1.1	1.1	1.1	1.0	1.3	1.4	1.6	1.6	1.7	1.5	1.6	1.6
Congregational (UCC)	—	1.7	1.5	1.5	1.5	2.1	2.1	2.0	1.9	1.8	1.6	1.6	1.6	1.6	1.5	1.5	1.5	1.6	1.2	1.1	1.2
Eastern Orthodox	—	0.5	0.5	0.5	0.6	0.5	0.6	0.7	0.6	0.6	0.7	0.6	0.7	0.6	0.7	0.7	0.6	0.7	0.8	0.7	0.7
Episcopal	—	3.8	3.4	3.4	2.9	2.9	2.9	2.9	2.6	2.6	2.6	2.5	2.4	2.4	2.2	2.4	2.2	2.3	2.1	2.3	2.2
Jewish	—	3.6	3.5	3.2	3.1	2.3	2.5	2.7	2.5	2.7	2.5	2.3	2.3	2.3	2.9	2.8	2.7	2.7	2.7	2.7	2.9
Latter Day Saints (Mormon)	—	0.2	0.3	0.3	0.3	0.3	0.4	0.5	0.4	0.4	0.4	0.4	1.6	1.6	1.6	1.6	0.4	0.7	1.9	0.3	0.4
Lutheran	—	7.5	6.9	7.1	7.2	6.8	6.6	7.7	7.7	8.7	6.9	7.5	5.7	6.6	6.6	5.9	5.6	5.8	6.2	4.9	4.9
Methodist	—	10.7	10.2	11.3	9.8	10.0	10.0	9.4	9.7	8.9	8.6	9.0	9.0	8.6	7.9	7.3	7.4	7.0	7.1	6.9	6.5
Muslim (Islamic)	—	0.2	0.3	0.2	0.3	0.3	0.4	0.4	0.5	0.5	0.5	0.5	0.6	0.6	0.8	0.8	0.7	0.7	0.9	0.9	0.8
Presbyterian	—	6.0	5.9	6.1	5.2	5.4	5.8	5.3	5.2	5.1	5.1	5.2	5.0	4.9	4.8	4.6	4.8	4.9	4.7	4.7	4.2
Quaker (Society of Friends)	—	0.2	0.2	0.2	0.2	0.2	0.2	0.2	0.2	0.2	0.3	0.2	0.2	0.2	0.2	0.2	0.3	0.3	0.2	0.2	0.2
Roman Catholic	—	34.3	33.2	32.9	34.4	33.9	32.8	35.3	33.2	34.1	33.6	33.8	32.2	31.7	34.1	34.2	34.3	33.7	32.2	31.9	32.2
Seventh Day Adventist	—	0.2	0.3	0.4	0.3	0.4	0.3	0.3	0.4	0.3	0.4	0.3	0.3	0.3	0.3	0.3	0.3	0.4	0.3	0.4	0.3
Unitarian Universalist	—	—	—	—	—	—	—	—	—	—	—	—	—	—	—	—	—	0.4	0.4	0.4	—
Other Christian (Protestant)	—	5.3	5.4	5.5	4.8	5.0	5.5	5.0	9.0	9.8	11.3	11.2	11.7	12.1	12.4	12.2	13.3	13.3	14.1	15.5	17.5
Other religion	—	4.9	5.3	4.9	5.4	5.2	5.3	5.5	3.3	3.3	3.5	3.3	3.5	3.3	3.2	3.3	3.5	3.2	2.9	3.0	3.0
None	—	4.8	5.9	5.3	5.6	5.8	6.2	5.9	6.1	5.9	6.3	6.2	7.2	7.2	7.2	7.6	8.5	8.9	9.0	8.9	9.6

Appendix A

Research Methodology

Appendix A
Research Methodology

The trends data reported here have been weighted to provide a normative picture of the population of American college freshmen attending baccalaureate-granting institutions between 1966 and 2006. It is designed for readers engaged in policy analysis, human resource planning, campus administration, educational research, and guidance and counseling, as well as for the general community of students and parents. This Appendix provides a brief overview of the CIRP methodology and describes the procedures used to weight the annual freshman survey results to produce the national normative estimates.

HISTORICAL OVERVIEW

From 1966 to 1970, approximately 15 percent of the nation's institutions of higher education were selected by sampling procedures and invited to participate in the program. As the academic community became aware of the value of program participation, additional institutions asked to participate. Beginning in 1971, all institutions that have entering freshman classes and that respond to the U.S. Department of Education's (DOE) Higher Education General Information Survey were invited to participate (see 'The National Population' below). A minimal charge plus a unit rate based on the number of forms processed helps to defray the direct costs of the survey.

While the number of institutions included in the national norms has grown over time, the number of two-year colleges has declined to the point where (as of 2000) those institutions are no longer included in the national norms. In order to make comparisons between results in 2000–2006 with earlier years, results for all years in this report were recalculated to refer only to baccalaureate-granting institutions. Thus, results in this report will **not** be the same as those in HERI's first two publications of trends results (i.e. the Twenty- and Thirty-year Trends reports).

THE NATIONAL POPULATION

For the purposes of this report, the population has been defined as all institutions of higher education admitting first-time freshmen and granting a baccalaureate-level degree or higher listed in the Opening Fall Enrollment (OFE) files of the U.S. Department of Education's Higher Education General Information Survey (HEGIS, since 1986 known as IPEDS—Integrated Postsecondary Education Data System). An institution is considered eligible if it was operating at the time of the HEGIS/IPEDS survey and had a first-time full-time (FTFT) freshman class of at least 25 students. In addition, a small number of institutions or their branches are included even though their separate enrollments were not available from the OFE files, because they were part of prior HEGIS/IPEDS populations and are known to be functioning with FTFT students. The 2006 population figures, for example, were obtained from the on-line OFE Survey for Fall, 2005. In 2006, the national population included 1,557 institutions.

It should be noted that the population reflects institutions of "higher education," rather than "postsecondary education." Most proprietary, special vocational or semiprofessional institutions are not included in the population. Beginning with the Fall 1993 survey, only institutions with regional accreditation (including provisional accreditation) were included.

INSTITUTIONAL STRATIFICATION DESIGN

The institutions identified as part of the national population are divided into 26 stratification groups based on institutional race (predominantly non-black vs. predominantly black), type (four-year college, university[1]), control (public, private nonsectarian, Roman Catholic and other religious[2]) and the "selectivity level" of the institution. Selectivity, defined as the average composite SAT score of the entering class, was made an integral part of the stratification design in 1968. The selectivity figures were revised and updated in 1975, and again in 2001. Figure A1 shows the distribution of institutions across the 26 stratification cells for 2006.

	Universities				Four-year institutions							
	Public		Private		Public		Nonsectarian		Catholic		Oth. Relig.	
Dividing Line Between	SAT V+M	ACT	SAT V+M	ACT	SAT V+M	ACT	SAT V+M	ACT	SAT V+M	ACT	SAT V+M	ACT
Low–medium	1085	22.9	—	—	985	20.2	1015	20.9	1020	21.0	1050	22.0
Medium–high	1140	24.3	1175	25.4	1055	22.2	1099	23.2	1075	22.6	1100	23.2
High–Very high	—	—	1310	28.8	—	—	1250	27.2	—	—	—	—

It should be noted that the dividing lines between low, medium and high selectivity levels are different for different types of institutions, as shown in the table below.

---

[1] For stratification purposes, we define a "university" as an institution that awards a certain minimal number of earned doctoral degrees. Institutions that offer postbaccalaureate programs but do not award a sufficient number of earned doctoral degrees are considered four-year colleges. The stratification design presented here is used to group schools to develop population weights and should not be used as a measure of institutional or program quality.

[2] This type of institution was labeled "Protestant" in publications prior to 2000. "Other Religious" more correctly characterizes the institutions that have always been in this group, which include all institutions affiliated with a religion other than Roman Catholic.

Figure A1: 2006 Data Bank Population
(N = 1,557)

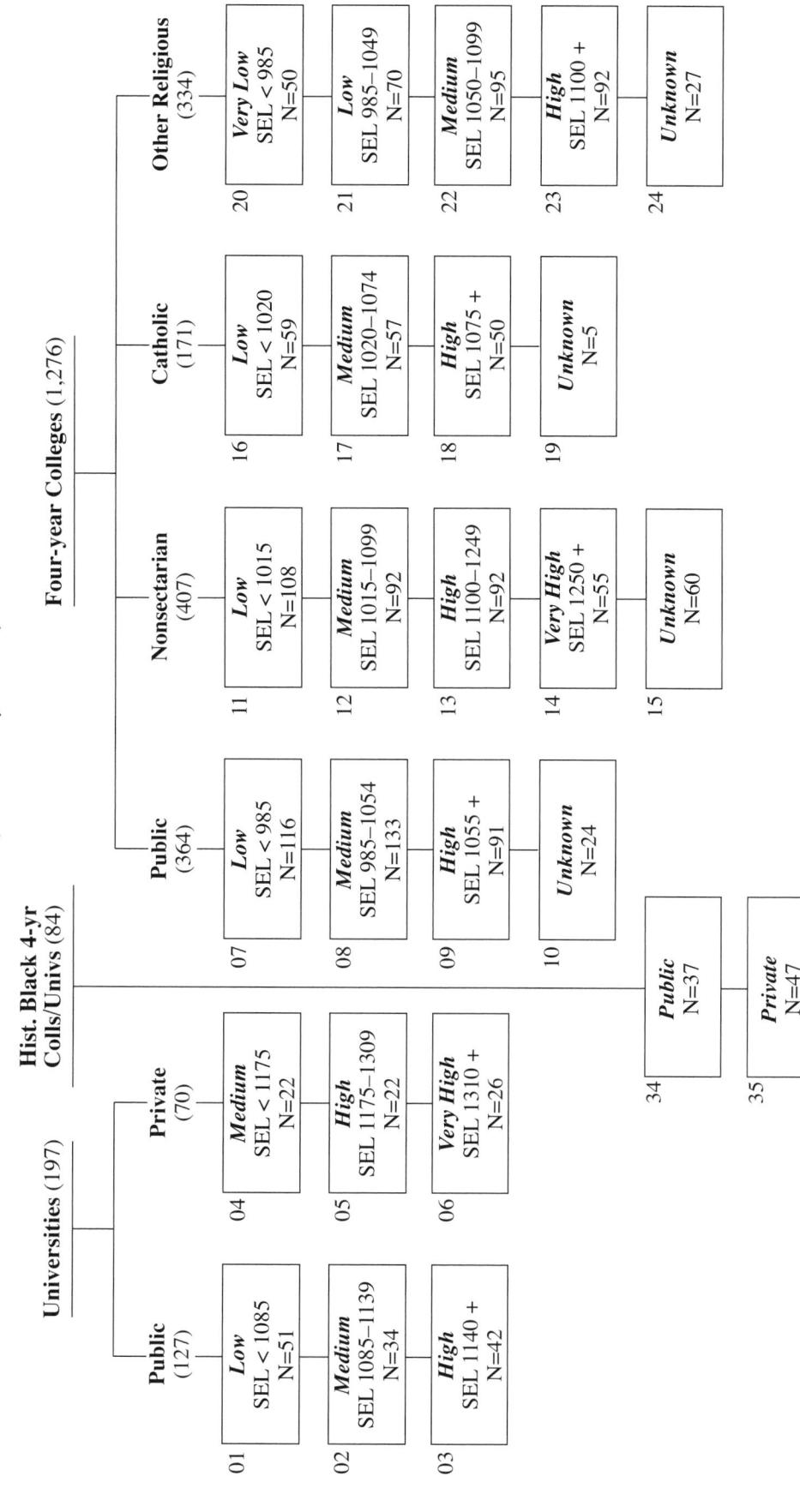

Selectivity (SEL), used to define strata for four-year colleges and universities, is an estimate of the mean score of entering freshmen on the Verbal plus Mathematical portions of the Scholastic Aptitude Test (or the converted SAT Math and Verbal equivalents from the American College Test composite). The method of estimation is described in detail in Astin and Henson (1977).

The stratification design presented here is used to group schools to develop population weights and should not be used as a measure of institutional or program quality.

207

Changes in stratification assignment do occur; institutional requests for review are honored each year. Starting in 2003, HERI will obtain updated information from institutions participating in any HERI survey. Appendix C lists the most recent stratification cell assignment of all institutions that have been included in the CIRP national norms since 1966.

Having defined the population in terms of the stratification cell scheme, the OFE file is used to compute the male and female FTFT population in each cell. These population counts form the target counts of the weighting procedure

IDENTIFYING THE NORMS SAMPLE

Generally speaking, an institution is included in the National Norms sample if it provided a representative sample of its FTFT population. The minimum percentage required of a sample is based on the type of institution from which it was collected. For four-year colleges the minimum is 85 percent, while for universities, the minimum is 75 percent. Institutions whose sample proportions were less than but close to these cutoffs are included if the method used to administer the survey showed no systematic biases in freshman class coverage.

Information about the FTFT population and the method of survey administration is obtained from participating institutions at the time they return their completed surveys. In the event an institution did not return FTFT information, counts from the most recent OFE survey are used. This procedure, although not optimal, is adequate unless the institution experienced a substantial change in its FTFT population changed since the last HEGIS/IPEDS survey.

THE TRENDS DATA

The responses from a total of 8,309,318 first-time full-time freshmen attending 1,201 baccalaureate-granting institutions are included in the results described in this report. Table A1 shows unweighted participant counts and weighted national first-time full-time freshman counts by gender.

The normative data presented here were collected by administering the survey instrument during registration, freshman orientation, or the first few weeks of classes (i.e., before the students have had any substantial experience with college life). The survey is designed to elicit a wide range of biographic and demographic data, as well as data on the student's high school background, career plans, educational aspirations, financial arrangements, high school activities, and current attitudes. In addition to standard biographic and demographic items that have been administered annually to each entering class, the survey also contains other research-oriented items that may have been modified from previous years (e.g., see the list of opinion questions listed under item #32, Appendix B). The inclusion of modified items permits a more thorough coverage of student characteristics but also represents a compromise between two mutually exclusive objectives:

Table A1. Institutional and Respondent Counts for the HERI 40-year Trends Report

| | | Number of First-time Full-time Freshmen | | | | | |
| | | Sample Counts | | | Weighted Estimates of Population | | |
Year	Number of Institutions	Total	Men	Women	Total	Men	Women
1966	222	183,964	98,999	84,965	873,051	462,754	410,297
1967	206	155,603	85,426	70,177	940,106	507,587	432,519
1968	295	207,276	115,775	91,501	1,028,887	563,256	465,631
1969	224	145,670	81,367	64,303	1,052,889	569,028	483,861
1970*	222	147,463	80,777	66,686	1,042,362	570,639	471,723
1971	263	142,826	76,441	66,385	1,018,889	530,702	488,187
1972	287	154,782	84,409	70,373	1,024,126	540,838	483,288
1973	280	157,936	82,039	75,897	973,666	497,176	476,489
1974	289	161,872	83,067	78,805	986,975	508,306	478,668
1975	291	159,526	80,980	78,546	1,018,843	522,854	495,989
1976	305	184,209	92,854	91,355	994,116	502,824	491,292
1977	297	170,940	84,578	86,362	1,065,278	540,433	524,845
1978	303	165,051	79,436	85,615	1,051,242	517,444	533,799
1979	280	168,251	81,810	86,441	1,047,570	512,438	535,131
1980	284	165,544	80,585	84,959	1,031,334	503,700	527,634
1981	295	168,381	80,089	88,292	1,041,532	505,485	536,047
1982	295	167,785	81,003	86,782	1,052,599	516,826	535,773
1983	297	166,548	80,172	86,376	1,054,121	513,222	540,899
1984	294	165,117	78,035	87,082	1,027,880	498,567	529,312
1985	308	172,016	81,465	90,551	1,067,928	521,921	546,007
1986	316	187,283	87,540	99,743	1,023,762	492,130	531,632
1987	331	193,214	88,406	104,808	1,031,968	493,999	537,969
1988	346	207,536	96,074	111,462	1,076,036	508,206	567,830
1989	347	200,535	94,695	105,840	1,028,143	484,298	543,845
1990	347	186,685	86,315	100,370	1,010,548	474,502	536,046
1991	394	202,982	94,405	108,577	1,024,976	485,238	539,738
1992	364	203,093	93,525	109,568	1,060,087	502,018	558,069
1993	385	211,927	96,963	114,964	996,690	460,800	535,890
1994	419	229,930	103,273	126,657	1,017,725	465,715	552,010
1995	432	232,493	102,960	129,533	1,024,550	467,674	556,876
1996	445	240,565	107,094	133,471	1,076,035	492,017	584,018
1997	426	243,040	108,822	134,218	1,054,500	479,912	574,588
1998	440	270,234	117,932	152,302	1,066,679	485,313	581,366
1999	435	254,963	111,719	143,244	1,098,833	497,524	601,309
2000	434	269,413	117,911	151,502	1,101,817	498,173	603,644
2001	421	281,064	124,116	156,948	1,204,240	540,989	663,252
2002	437	282,549	124,014	158,535	1,234,968	555,262	679,706
2003	413	276,449	120,457	155,992	1,196,089	538,896	657,193
2004	440	289,452	128,277	161,175	1,258,333	564,616	693,717
2005	400	263,710	116,074	147,636	1,298,093	584,599	713,494
2006	393	271,441	117,862	153,579	1,320,824	596,203	724,621
TOTAL	1,201	8,309,318	3,927,742	4,381,576	43,598,290	21,074,084	22,524,204

* Raw data are not available for 1966–1970. The gender breakdowns for sample counts and weighted estimates of the population were computed from totals reported in "The American Freshman" for each year.

(1) comparability of information from year to year which is required for assessing trends; and (2) flexibility in item content to meet changing information and research needs

The survey has been developed in collaboration with students, professional associations, participating institutions, government agencies, educational researchers, administrators, policy makers, and members of the CIRP Advisory Committee. It is designed for self-administration under proctored conditions and for processing onto magnetic tape with a mark reflex reader. The SIF content is reviewed annually by the CIRP project staff, with the assistance of the CIRP Advisory Committee as well as others interested in the annual freshman survey program. The 2006 survey instrument can be found in Appendix B.

Four data files are developed from the survey each year: (1) an institutional summary file containing institutional identification numbers and an institutional summary of the responses for men and women; (2) a file containing individual responses and a student identification number, but no names and addresses; (3) a name-and-address file containing a second, independent student identification number; and (4) a "link" file containing *only* the two independent identification numbers. This last file is maintained under an elaborate system developed to ensure strict confidentiality of individual student data and to protect against misuse of the name-and-address file (Astin & Boruch, 1970).

Those data from institutions meeting minimal quality requirements for inclusion in the norms (above) were differentially weighted to represent the population of entering freshmen at all baccalaureate-granting institutions in the United States (see 'Weighting the Sample' below). Part-time students and those who are not first-time college students (i.e., transfers and former enrollees) were excluded from the normative sample. Since the 1972 survey, special care has been taken to define these enrollment statuses; in surveys before 1972, the participating institutions were asked to exclude part-time students, while non-first-time students were excluded during the data processing stage by screening out those who indicated that they had previously attended college. Since that time, all students who did not identify themselves as part-time were included in the national norms if they either graduated from high school in the year of the survey or had never attended any postsecondary institution.

WEIGHTING THE SAMPLE

Those institutions identified as being part of the Norms sample are weighted by a two-step procedure. The first weight is designed to adjust for nonparticipation within institutions. Counts of the male and female FTFT population for each institution are divided by that institution's male and female FTFT respondent count. The resulting weights, when applied to each respondent, bring the male and female respondent counts up to the corresponding counts for the population at that institution.

Table A2. Number of Institutions and Students Used in Computing the Weighted National Norms, Fall 2006

Norm Group	Number of Institutions in the 2006 Norms	Number of Entering First-time, Full-time Freshmen			
		Unweighted Participants	Weighted		
			Number	% Men	% Women
All institutions	393	271,441	1,320,824	45.1	54.9
All universities	65	122,592	530,945	46.9	53.1
All four-year colleges	328	148,849	789,879	44.0	56.0
Black colleges (1)	14	6,333	48,910	41.8	58.2
Public universities	24	70,000	413,545	47.2	52.8
Low selectivity	6	11,631	122,327	45.3	54.7
Medium selectivity	5	15,876	112,859	48.2	51.8
High selectivity	13	42,493	178,359	47.8	52.2
Private universities	41	52,592	117,400	45.8	54.2
Medium selectivity	13	15,827	35,967	41.2	58.8
High selectivity	11	15,496	42,504	45.0	55.0
Very high selectivity	17	21,269	38,929	50.9	49.1
Public four-year colleges	52	44,944	455,532	44.3	55.7
Low selectivity (2)	15	9,271	154,022	43.1	56.9
Medium selectivity	18	18,297	179,388	43.6	56.4
High selectivity	19	17,376	122,122	46.8	53.2
Private four-year colleges	276	103,905	334,347	43.5	56.5
Nonsectarian	120	48,379	157,937	46.1	53.9
Low selectivity (2)	21	6,803	57,214	48.0	52.0
Medium selectivity	24	11,166	35,298	42.6	57.4
High selectivity	41	15,621	39,110	47.5	52.5
Very high selectivity	34	14,789	26,315	44.7	55.3
Catholic	51	21,716	67,100	37.2	62.8
Low selectivity (2)	16	4,934	20,186	32.1	67.9
Medium selectivity	17	6,496	17,559	36.9	63.1
High selectivity	18	10,286	29,355	41.0	59.0
Other Religious	105	33,810	109,310	43.7	56.3
Low selectivity (2)	35	7,992	35,985	45.1	54.9
Medium selectivity	28	8,057	31,340	42.7	57.3
High selectivity	42	17,761	41,985	43.2	56.8
Public Black College	6	3,187	32,020	41.7	58.3
Private Black Colleges	8	3,146	16,890	42.1	57.9
Eastern region	155	108,907	474,771	45.9	54.1
Midwestern region	88	58,316	285,741	47.1	52.9
Southern region	89	55,835	305,374	43.8	56.2
Western region	61	48,383	254,938	43.2	56.8

(1) Black colleges are also included in the appropriate four-year college or university norm group according to their type.
(2) Includes those institutions with unknown selectivity.
NOTE: The weighted counts may not always sum to identical totals due to rounding error.

The second weight is designed to compensate for nonparticipating institutions within each stratification cell. The weighted male and female counts for all participating institutions in each stratification cell are first summed, and then are divided into the national male and female FTFT counts for all institutions in that stratification cell, producing a second set of ("cell") weights. The final weight is simply the product of the first and second weights.

Weighting each respondent using this final weight brings the male and female counts for each stratification cell up to the corresponding national counts for all institutions in that stratification cell.

Appendix B

The CIRP Freshman Survey

Appendix B
The CIRP Freshman Survey

Our trends reports usually only feature the most recent survey instrument, in this case the 2006 CIRP Freshman Survey. This year being the 40th anniversary of the CIRP Freshman Survey, I thought it would be interesting to reprint the 1966 survey instrument alongside its contemporary, giving us an opportunity to observe the similarities and differences over 40 years of research.

The first thing to note is that there is a great deal of similarity between the two instruments. Yes, there are differences, but the same philosophy that guided the creation of the 1996 questionnaire guided the creation of the 2006 questionnaire. We are looking, in both cases, at instruments designed to capture input data on college students that reflect characteristics of the students in order to determine the impact of college. In some cases questions cycled on and off in the intervening years, as theories were tested and either expanded upon or abandoned.

Many of the demographics are the same, although the language is not. Certainly what was common in 1966 for racial categories has changed over time, not only in terms of the language used, but in what groups it was felt necessary to measure (for instance, there was no Hispanic category in 1966). There is a whole series of questions at the bottom of the second page that ask about siblings and twin status that are not a part of the current instrument. We still ask about the education level of students' parents, as well as the parental income level (although the highest income level category was "$30,000 or more" per year in 1966).

Some of the more interesting items are ones that ask about the types of behaviors with which students were involved in high school. Some of the CIRP standards are there, such as "came late to class," and "drank beer," but others that are no longer asked reflect an interest in examining the influence of the arts, such as "acted in plays," or "attended a ballet performance."

Overall, the changes in the instrument over time reflect the changes in American higher education and society as well as the refinements in the theories of student development and the impact of college. But one is also struck by how much of the 1966 instrument is still relevant and might be administered today!

John H. Pryor
Director, Cooperative Institutional Research Program

The 1966 CIRP Freshman Survey

STUDENT INFORMATION FORM

`244985`

YOUR NAME(please print) _____

      First   Middle or Maiden   Last

HOME STREET ADDRESS _____

_____

CITY   STATE   ZIP CODE (if known)

Note: The information in this report is being collected through the American Council on Education as part of a study of this year's entering class. Please complete all items. Your name and address has been requested in order to facilitate mail follow-up studies. Your responses will be used only in group summaries for research purposes, and will <u>not</u> be identified with you individually.

Social Security Number (if known)

If you recently took any of the national achievement tests and happen to remember your score, fill in the appropriate information:

SAT Verbal   Score

ACT Composite   Score

Date of Birth _____ _____ _____

          Month   Day   Year

SAT Math

NMSC Selection Score

DIRECTIONS: Your responses will be read by an automatic scanning device. Your careful observance of these few simple rules will be most appreciated.

Use only black lead pencil (No. 2½ or softer). Make heavy black marks that fill the circle. Erase cleanly any answer you wish to change. Make no stray markings of any kind.

                      Yes   No

Example: Will marks made with ball pen or fountain pen be properly read? ○ ●

---

1. Your Sex: Male○   Female○

2. From what kind of secondary school did you graduate? (Mark one)

Public .... ○
Private (denominational) .... ○
Private (nondenominational) ..... ○
Other .... ○

3. What was your average grade in secondary school? (Mark one)

A or A+ .. ○   B– ... ○
A– ..... ○   C+ ... ○
B+ ..... ○   C .... ○
B ...... ○   D .... ○

4. What is the highest academic degree that you intend to obtain? (Mark one)

None .... ○
Associate (or equivalent) .... ○
Bachelor's degree (B.A., B.S., etc.) .. ○
Master's degree (M.A., M.S., etc.) .... ○
Ph.D. or Ed.D .... ○
M.D., D.D.S., or D.V.M. .... ○
LL.B. or J.D .... ○
B.D. .... ○
Other .... ○

5. The following questions deal with accomplishments that might possibly apply to your high school years. Do not be discouraged by this list; it covers many areas of interest and few students will be able to say "yes" to many items. (Mark all that apply)

Was elected president of one or more student organizations (recognized by the school) .... ○
Received a high rating (Good, Excellent) in a <u>state</u> or <u>regional</u> music contest ○
Participated in a <u>state</u> or <u>regional</u> speech or debate contest .... ○
Had a major part in a play .... ○
Won a varsity letter (sports) .... ○
Won a prize or award in an art competition .... ○
Edited the school paper, yearbook, or literary magazine .... ○
Had poems, stories, essays, or articles published .... ○
Participated in a National Science Foundation summer program .... ○
Placed (first, second, or third) in a <u>state</u> or <u>regional</u> science contest ...... ○
Was a member of a scholastic honor society .... ○
Won a Certificate of Merit or Letter of Commendation in the National Merit Program .... ○

6. Do you have any concern about your ability to finance your college education? (Mark one)

None (I am confident that I will have sufficient funds) .... ○

Some concern (but I will probably have enough funds) .... ○

Major concern (not sure I will be able to complete college) .... ○

7. Through what source do you intend to finance the first year of your undergraduate education?
(Mark one for each item)

	Major Source	Minor Source	Not a Source
Employment during college	○	○	○
Employment during summer	○	○	○
Scholarship	○	○	○
G. I. Bill	○	○	○
Personal savings	○	○	○
Tuition deferment loan from college	○	○	○
Parental aid	○	○	○
Federal government	○	○	○
Commercial loan	○	○	○

8. What is your racial background? (Mark one)

Caucasian .... ○
Negro .... ○
American Indian .... ○
Oriental .... ○
Other .... ○

9. What is the highest level of formal education obtained by your parents? (Mark one in each column)

	Father	Mother
Grammar school or less	○	○
Some high school	○	○
High school graduate	○	○
Some college	○	○
College degree	○	○
Postgraduate degree	○	○

10. What is your best estimate of the total income last year of your parental family (not your own family if you are married)? Consider annual income from all sources before taxes.

Less than $4,000 .. ○ $15,000--$19,999 ... ○
$4,000--$5,999 .... ○ $20,000--$24,999 ... ○
$6,000--$7,999 .... ○ $25,000--$29,999 ... ○
$8,000--$9,999 .... ○ $30,000 or more ... ○
$10,000--$14,999 .. ○

11. Mark one in each column below:

	Religion in Which You Were Reared	Your Present Religious Preference
Protestant	○	○
Roman Catholic	○	○
Jewish	○	○
Other	○	○
None	○	○

12. In deciding where to go to college, through what source did this college first come to your attention?

(Mark one)

Relative .... ○
Friend .... ○
High school counselor or teacher ... ○
Professional counseling or college placement service .... ○
This college or a representative from this college .... ○
Other source .... ○
I cannot recall .... ○

13. To what extent do you think each of the following describes the psychological climate or atmosphere at this college?

(Mark one answer for each item)

	Very Descriptive	In Between	Not at all Descriptive
Intellectual	○	○	○
Snobbish	○	○	○
Social	○	○	○
Victorian	○	○	○
Practical-minded	○	○	○
Warm	○	○	○
Realistic	○	○	○
Liberal	○	○	○

14. Answer each of the following as you think it applies to this college:

	Yes	No
The students are under a great deal of pressure to get high grades	○	○
The student body is apathetic and has little "school spirit"	○	○
Most of the students are of a very high calibre academically	○	○
There is a keen competition among most of the students for high grades	○	○
Freshmen have to take orders from upperclassmen for a period of time	○	○
There isn't much to do except to go to class and study	○	○
I felt "lost" when I first came to the campus	○	○
Being in this college builds poise and maturity	○	○
Athletics are overemphasized	○	○
The classes are usually run in a very informal manner	○	○
Most students are more like "numbers in a book"	○	○

15. Are you:

An only child (Mark and skip to number 20) ○
The first-born (but not an only child) .... ○
The second-born .... ○
The third-born .... ○
Fourth (or later) born .... ○

16. How many brothers and sisters now living do you have? (Mark one)

None (Mark and skip to number 20) .... ○

1 2 3 4 5 6 7 8 or more
○ ○ ○ ○ ○ ○ ○   ○

17. Mark one circle for each of your brothers and sisters between the ages of 13 and 23

	13	14	15	16	17	18	19	20	21	22	23
Brothers	○	○	○	○	○	○	○	○	○	○	○
Sisters	○	○	○	○	○	○	○	○	○	○	○

18. Are you a twin? (Mark one)

No, (Mark and skip to number 20) .. ○
Yes, identical .... ○
Yes, fraternal same sex .... ○
Yes, fraternal opposite sex ...... ○

19. Is your twin attending college?

No .... ○
Yes, the same college ..... ○
Yes, a different college ... ○

218

20.
Mark one in each column:

Your current home state / Your birthplace / Your father's birthplace / Your mother's birthplace

Alabama.......○ ○○○
Alaska ....○ ○○○
Arizona........○ ○○○
Arkansas ......○ ○○○
California......○ ○○○
Colorado.......○ ○○○
Connecticut ....○ ○○○
Delaware.......○ ○○○
D. C...........○ ○○○
Florida ....○ ○○○
Georgia........○ ○○○
Hawaii.........○ ○○○
Idaho..........○ ○○○
Illinois........○ ○○○
Indiana ....○ ○○○
Iowa...........○ ○○○
Kansas ....○ ○○○
Kentucky.......○ ○○○
Louisiana......○ ○○○
Maine..........○ ○○○
Maryland.......○ ○○○
Massachusetts..○ ○○○
Michigan.......○ ○○○
Minnesota......○ ○○○
Mississippi.....○ ○○○
Missouri ....○ ○○○
Montana........○ ○○○
Nebraska.......○ ○○○
Nevada ....○ ○○○
New Hampshire..○ ○○○
New Jersey.....○ ○○○
New Mexico ....○ ○○○
New York ......○ ○○○
North Carolina..○ ○○○
North Dakota ...○ ○○○
Ohio...........○ ○○○
Oklahoma ......○ ○○○
Oregon.........○ ○○○
Pennsylvania...○ ○○○
Rhode Island ...○ ○○○
South Carolina..○ ○○○
South Dakota ...○ ○○○
Tennessee .....○ ○○○
Texas ....○ ○○○
Utah...........○ ○○○
Vermont........○ ○○○
Virginia........○ ○○○
Washington .....○ ○○○
West Virginia...○ ○○○
Wisconsin......○ ○○○
Wyoming ....○ ○○○
Latin America ..○ ○○○
Europe.........○ ○○○
Africa ....○ ○○○
Asia ....○ ○○○
Other..........○ ○○○

21. Below is a list of 66 different undergraduate major fields grouped into general categories.
Mark only three of the 66 fields as follows:

① First choice (your probable major field of study).
② Second choice.
Ⓛ The field of study which is least appealing to you.

Arts and Humanities
Architecture ....① ② Ⓛ
English (literature) ....① ② Ⓛ
Fine arts.............① ② Ⓛ
History ....① ② Ⓛ
Journalism (writing) ...① ② Ⓛ
Language (modern)....① ② Ⓛ
Language (other) ......① ② Ⓛ
Music ....① ② Ⓛ
Philosophy ....① ② Ⓛ
Speech and drama .....① ② Ⓛ
Theology.............① ② Ⓛ
Other ....① ② Ⓛ

Biological Science
Biology (general)......① ② Ⓛ
Biochemistry..........① ② Ⓛ
Biophysics ....① ② Ⓛ
Botany ....① ② Ⓛ
Zoology ....① ② Ⓛ
Other ....① ② Ⓛ

Business
Accounting ....① ② Ⓛ
Business admin. ......① ② Ⓛ
Electronic data
   processing ....① ② Ⓛ
Secretarial studies ....① ② Ⓛ
Other ....① ② Ⓛ

Engineering
Aeronautical ....① ② Ⓛ
Civil ....① ② Ⓛ
Chemical.............① ② Ⓛ
Electrical ....① ② Ⓛ
Industrial ....① ② Ⓛ
Mechanical ....① ② Ⓛ
Other ....① ② Ⓛ

Physical Science
Chemistry ....① ② Ⓛ
Earth science ....① ② Ⓛ
Mathematics ....① ② Ⓛ
Physics ....① ② Ⓛ
Statistics ....① ② Ⓛ
Other ....① ② Ⓛ

Professional
Health Technology
   (medical, dental,
   laboratory)........① ② Ⓛ
Nursing ....① ② Ⓛ
Pharmacy ....① ② Ⓛ
Predentistry ....① ② Ⓛ
Prelaw ....① ② Ⓛ
Premedical ....① ② Ⓛ
Preveterinary ......① ② Ⓛ
Therapy (occupat.,
   physical, speech)..① ② Ⓛ
Other ....① ② Ⓛ

Social Science
Anthropology ......① ② Ⓛ
Economics........① ② Ⓛ
Education ....① ② Ⓛ
History ....① ② Ⓛ
Political science
   (government,
   int. relations) .....① ② Ⓛ
Psychology ....① ② Ⓛ
Social work ....① ② Ⓛ
Sociology ....① ② Ⓛ
Other ....① ② Ⓛ

Other Fields
Agriculture ....① ② Ⓛ
Communications
   (radio, T. V., etc.). ① ② Ⓛ
Electronics
   (technology).......① ② Ⓛ
Forestry..........① ② Ⓛ
Home economics....① ② Ⓛ
Industrial arts......① ② Ⓛ
Library science ....① ② Ⓛ
Military science ....① ② Ⓛ
Physical education
   and recreation .....① ② Ⓛ
Other (technical) ...① ② Ⓛ
Other (nontechnical). ① ② Ⓛ
Undecided ....① ② Ⓛ

Please be sure that only three circles have been marked in the above list.

22. Probable Career Occupation

Note:
Make only three { ① First Choice
responses, one { ② Second Choice
in each column { Ⓛ Least Appealing

Accountant or actuary ....① ② Ⓛ
Actor or entertainer.............① ② Ⓛ
Architect ....① ② Ⓛ
Artist ....① ② Ⓛ
Business (clerical) ....① ② Ⓛ
Business executive
   (management, administrator) ....① ② Ⓛ
Business owner or proprietor .....① ② Ⓛ
Business salesman or buyer......① ② Ⓛ
Clergyman (minister, priest).....① ② Ⓛ
Clergy (other religious).........① ② Ⓛ
Clinical psychologist ....① ② Ⓛ
College teacher ....① ② Ⓛ
Computer programmer..........① ② Ⓛ
Conservationist or forester.......① ② Ⓛ
Dentist (including orthodontist)...① ② Ⓛ
Dietitian or home economist......① ② Ⓛ
Engineer.....................① ② Ⓛ
Farmer or rancher ....① ② Ⓛ
Foreign service worker
   (including diplomat)..........① ② Ⓛ
Housewife ....① ② Ⓛ
Interior decorator
   (including designer)..........① ② Ⓛ
Interpretor (translator)..........① ② Ⓛ
Lab technician or hygienist ......① ② Ⓛ
Law enforcement officer.........① ② Ⓛ
Lawyer (attorney).............① ② Ⓛ
Military service (career) ....① ② Ⓛ
Musician (performer, composer) ...① ② Ⓛ
Nurse ....① ② Ⓛ
Optometrist ....① ② Ⓛ
Pharmacist...................① ② Ⓛ
Physician....................① ② Ⓛ
School counselor...............① ② Ⓛ
School principal or superintendant ① ② Ⓛ
Scientific researcher ....① ② Ⓛ
Social worker.................① ② Ⓛ
Statistician ....① ② Ⓛ
Therapist (physical,
   occupational, speech)..........① ② Ⓛ
Teacher (elementary)...........① ② Ⓛ
Teacher (secondary).............① ② Ⓛ
Veterinarian ....① ② Ⓛ
Writer or journalist ....① ② Ⓛ
Skilled trades.................① ② Ⓛ
Other ....① ② Ⓛ
Undecided ....① ② Ⓛ

23. Below is a general list of things that students sometimes do. Indicate which of these things you did during the past year in school. If you engaged in an activity frequently, Mark "f." If you engaged in an activity one or more times, but not frequently, Mark "o"(occasionally). Mark "n"(not at all) if you have not performed the activity during the past year.

(Mark one for each item)

Frequently / Occasionally / Not at all

Voted in a student election .... (F)(O)(N)
Came late to class .... (F)(O)(N)
Listened to New Orlean's (Dixieland) jazz .... (F)(O)(N)
Gambled with cards or dice .... (F)(O)(N)
Played a musical instrument .... (F)(O)(N)
Took a nap or rest during the day .... (F)(O)(N)
Drove a car .... (F)(O)(N)
Stayed up all night .... (F)(O)(N)
Studied in the library .... (F)(O)(N)
Attended a ballet performance .... (F)(O)(N)
Participated on the speech or debate team .... (F)(O)(N)
Acted in plays .... (F)(O)(N)
Sang in a choir or glee club .... (F)(O)(N)
Argued with other students .... (F)(O)(N)
Called a teacher by his or her first name .... (F)(O)(N)
Wrote an article for the school paper or literary magazine (F)(O)(N)
Had a blind date .... (F)(O)(N)
Wrote a short story or poem (not for a class) .... (F)(O)(N)
Played in a school band .... (F)(O)(N)
Played in a school orchestra .... (F)(O)(N)
Smoked cigarettes .... (F)(O)(N)
Attended Sunday school .... (F)(O)(N)
Checked out a book or journal from the school library .... (F)(O)(N)
Went to the movies .... (F)(O)(N)
Discussed how to make money with other students ...... (F)(O)(N)
Said grace before meals .... (F)(O)(N)
Prayed (not including grace before meals) .... (F)(O)(N)
Listened to folk music .... (F)(O)(N)
Attended a public recital or concert .... (F)(O)(N)
Made wisecracks in class .... (F)(O)(N)
Arranged a date for another student .... (F)(O)(N)
Went to an over-night or week-end party .... (F)(O)(N)
Took weight-reducing or dietary formula .... (F)(O)(N)
Drank beer .... (F)(O)(N)
Overslept and missed a class or appointment .... (F)(O)(N)
Typed a homework assignment .... (F)(O)(N)
Participated in an informal group sing .... (F)(O)(N)
Drank wine .... (F)(O)(N)
Cribbed on an examination .... (F)(O)(N)
Turned in a paper or theme late .... (F)(O)(N)
Tried on clothes in a store without buying anything ..... (F)(O)(N)
Asked questions in class .... (F)(O)(N)
Attended church .... (F)(O)(N)
Participated in organized demonstrations .... (F)(O)(N)

24. Indicate the importance to you personally of each of the following:

(Mark one for each item)

Essential / Very Important / Somewhat Important / Not Important

Becoming accomplished in one of the performing arts (acting, dancing, etc.)............... (E)(V)(S)(N)
Becoming an authority on a special subject in my subject field... (E)(V)(S)(N)
Obtaining recognition from my colleagues for contributions in my special field .... (E)(V)(S)(N)
Becoming an accomplished musician (performer or composer)..... (E)(V)(S)(N)
Becoming an expert in finance and commerce .... (E)(V)(S)(N)
Having administrative responsibility for the work of others .... (E)(V)(S)(N)
Being very well-off financially .... (E)(V)(S)(N)
Helping others who are in difficulty .... (E)(V)(S)(N)
Participating in an organization like the Peace Corps or Vista ... (E)(V)(S)(N)
Becoming an outstanding athlete .... (E)(V)(S)(N)
Becoming a community leader................. (E)(V)(S)(N)
Making a theoretical contribution to science .... (E)(V)(S)(N)
Writing original works (poems, novels, short stories, etc.)........ (E)(V)(S)(N)
Never being obligated to people .... (E)(V)(S)(N)
Creating artistic work (painting, sculpture, decorating, etc.)...... (E)(V)(S)(N)
Keeping up to date with political affairs .... (E)(V)(S)(N)
Being successful in a business of my own............... (E)(V)(S)(N)

25. Rate yourself on each of the following traits as you really think you are when compared with the average student of your own age. We want the most accurate estimate of how you see yourself. (Mark one for each item)

Trait	Highest 10 Percent	Above Average	Average	Below Average	Lowest 10 Percent
Academic ability	O	O	O	O	O
Athletic ability	O	O	O	O	O
Artistic ability	O	O	O	O	O
Cheerfulness	O	O	O	O	O
Defensiveness	O	O	O	O	O
Drive to achieve	O	O	O	O	O
Leadership ability	O	O	O	O	O
Mathematical ability	O	O	O	O	O
Mechanical ability	O	O	O	O	O
Originality	O	O	O	O	O
Political conservatism	O	O	O	O	O
Political liberalism	O	O	O	O	O
Popularity	O	O	O	O	O
Popularity with the opposite sex	O	O	O	O	O
Public speaking ability	O	O	O	O	O
Self-confidence (intellectual)	O	O	O	O	O
Self-confidence (social)	O	O	O	O	O
Sensitivity to criticism	O	O	O	O	O
Stubbornness	O	O	O	O	O
Understanding of others	O	O	O	O	O
Writing ability	O	O	O	O	O

26. How old will you be on December 31 of this year?

(Mark one)

16 or younger .... O
17 .... O
18 .... O
19 .... O
20 .... O
21 .... O
Older than 21 ..... O

27. (If you are married, omit the following question)
What is your best guess as to the chances that you will marry

	While in College?	Within a Year after College?
Very good chance	O	O
Some chance	O	O
Very little chance	O	O
No chance	O	O

Prepared by American Council on Education 1785 Massachusetts Ave., N.W. Washington, D.C.

The 2006 CIRP Freshman Survey

PLEASE PRINT NAME AND PERMANENT/HOME ADDRESS (one letter or number per box)

FIRST · MI · LAST

When were you born?

NAME:

ADDRESS:

CITY: · STATE: · ZIP: · PHONE:

Month (01-12) · Day (01-31) · Year

2006 CIRP FRESHMAN SURVEY

MARKING DIRECTIONS

Your responses will be read by an optical mark reader. Please,

- Use a pencil or black or blue pen.
- Fill in the oval completely.
- Erase cleanly any answer you wish to change or "X" out mark if in pen.

CORRECT MARK · INCORRECT MARKS

PLEASE PROVIDE YOUR ID NUMBER (as instructed) · **Mark here if directed** · GROUP CODE A · GROUP CODE B

1. Your sex: ○ Male ○ Female

2. How old will you be on December 31 of this year? (Mark one)
16 or younger . . ○   21-24 . . . . . ○
17 . . . . ○   25-29 . . . . . . ○
18 . . . . ○   30-39 . . . . . . ○
19 . . . . ○   40-54 . . . . . . ○
20 . . . . ○   55 or older . . ○

3. Is English your native language?
○ Yes ○ No

4. In what year did you graduate from high school? (Mark one)
2006 . . . . ○   Did not graduate but
2005 . . . . ○   passed G.E.D. test . ○
2004 . . . . ○   Never completed
2003 or earlier. ○   high school . . . . ○

5. Are you enrolled (or enrolling) as a:
(Mark one)   Full-time student? . . . . ○
  Part-time student? . . . ○

6. How many miles is this college from your permanent home? (Mark one)
5 or less ○   11-50 ○   101-500 ○
6-10 ○   51-100 ○   Over 500 ○

7. What was your average grade in high school? (Mark one)
A or A+ ○   B ○   C ○
A– ○   B– ○   D ○
B+ ○   C+ ○

8. What were your scores on the SAT I and/or ACT?
SAT VERBAL . . . .
SAT MATH . . . .
ACT Composite . . . .

9. Citizenship status:
○ U.S. citizen
○ Permanent resident (green card)
○ Neither

10. Prior to this term, have you ever taken courses for credit at this institution?
○ Yes ○ No

11. Since leaving high school, have you ever taken courses, whether for credit or not for credit, at any other institution (university, 4- or 2-year college, technical, vocational, or business school)?
○ Yes ○ No

12. Where do you plan to live during the fall term? (Mark one)
With my family or other relatives . . . . ○
Other private home, apartment, or room . ○
College residence hall . . . . ○
Fraternity or sorority house . . . . ○
Other campus student housing . . . . ○
Other . . . . ○

13. Is this college your: (Mark one)
First choice? . . . . . . ○   Less than third
Second choice? . . . ○   choice? . . . . . . ○
Third choice? . . . . . ○

14. If this college was not your first choice, were you accepted by your first choice college?
○ Yes ○ No

15. To how many colleges other than this one did you apply for admission this year?
None ○   1 ○   4 ○   7-10 ○
  2 ○   5 ○   11 or more ○
  3 ○   6 ○

16. Are your parents: (Mark one)
Both alive and living with each other? . . . ○
Both alive, divorced or living apart? . . . . ○
One or both deceased? . . . . ○

17. During high school (grades 9-12) how many years did you study each of the following subjects? (Mark one for each item)

	None	1/2	1	2	3	4	5 or more
English	○	○	○	○	○	○	○
Mathematics	○	○	○	○	○	○	○
Foreign Language	○	○	○	○	○	○	○
Physical Science	○	○	○	○	○	○	○
Biological Science	○	○	○	○	○	○	○
History/Am. Govt.	○	○	○	○	○	○	○
Computer Science	○	○	○	○	○	○	○
Arts and/or Music	○	○	○	○	○	○	○

18. How many Advanced Placement courses or exams did you take in high school? (Mark one in each row)

	Not offered at my high school	None	1-4	5-9	10-14	15+
AP Courses	○	○	○	○	○	○
AP Exams	○	○	○	○	○	○

19. What is the highest academic degree that you intend to obtain? (Mark one in each column)

	Highest Planned	Highest Planned At This College
None	○	○
Vocational certificate	○	○
Associate (A.A. or equivalent)	○	○
Bachelor's degree (B.A., B.S., etc.)	○	○
Master's degree (M.A., M.S., etc.)	○	○
Ph.D. or Ed.D.	○	○
M.D., D.O., D.D.S., or D.V.M.	○	○
J.D. (Law)	○	○
B.D. or M.DIV. (Divinity)	○	○
Other	○	○

20. How would you describe the racial composition of the high school you last attended and the neighborhood where you grew up? (Mark one in each row)

	Completely non-White	Mostly non-White	Roughly half non-White	Mostly White	Completely White
High school I last attended	○	○	○	○	○
Neighborhood where I grew up	○	○	○	○	○

21. Did either of your parents or legal guardians attend the institution that you are now attending?
○ Neither
○ Mother or female legal guardian only
○ Father or male legal guardian only
○ Both

221

22. How much of your first year's educational expenses (room, board, tuition, and fees) do you expect to cover from each of the sources listed below? (Mark one answer for each possible source)

Columns: None / Less than $1,000 / $1,000 to 2,999 / $3,000 to 5,999 / $6,000 to 9,999 / over $10,000

a. My Own or Family Resources

Parents, other relatives or friends .... ○○○○○○
Spouse .... ○○○○○○
Savings from summer work .. ○○○○○○
Other savings .... ○○○○○○
Part-time job on campus..... ○○○○○○
Part-time job off campus..... ○○○○○○
Full-time job while in college.. ○○○○○○

b. Aid Which Need Not Be Repaid

Pell Grant .... ○○○○○
Supplemental Educational Opportunity Grant .... ○○○○○
State Scholarship or Grant
Merit-based .... ○○○○○
Need-based .... ○○○○○
College Work-Study Grant ... ○○○○○
College Grant/Scholarship (other than above) .... ○○○○○
Other private grant .... ○○○○○
Government Aid
GI military benefits .... ○○○○○
ROTC .... ○○○○○
Other Government Aid..... ○○○○○

c. Aid Which Must Be Repaid

Stafford Loan (GSL) .... ○○○○○
Perkins Loan .... ○○○○○
Other College Loan........ ○○○○○
Other Loan................ ○○○○○

d. Other Than Above .... ○○○○○

23. How many individuals in your household are dependent on your parents for financial support? (Include yourself and your parents)

○ 1 ○ 4
○ 2 ○ 5
○ 3 ○ 6 or more

24. What is your best estimate of your parents' total income last year? Consider income from all sources before taxes. (Mark one)

○ Less than $10,000 ○ $50,000-59,999
○ $10,000-14,999 ○ $60,000-74,999
○ $15,000-19,999 ○ $75,000-99,999
○ $20,000-24,999 ○ $100,000-149,999
○ $25,000-29,999 ○ $150,000-199,999
○ $30,000-39,999 ○ $200,000-249,999
○ $40,000-49,999 ○ $250,000 or more

25. Do you have any concern about your ability to finance your college education? (Mark one)

None (I am confident that I will have sufficient funds)..................... ○
Some (but I probably will have enough funds) . ○
Major (not sure I will have enough funds to complete college) .... ○

26. Current religious preference: (Mark one in each column)

Columns: Yours / Father's / Mother's

Baptist .... Ⓨ Ⓕ Ⓜ
Buddhist .... Ⓨ Ⓕ Ⓜ
Church of Christ .... Ⓨ Ⓕ Ⓜ
Eastern Orthodox .... Ⓨ Ⓕ Ⓜ
Episcopalian .... Ⓨ Ⓕ Ⓜ
Hindu .... Ⓨ Ⓕ Ⓜ
Islamic .... Ⓨ Ⓕ Ⓜ
Jewish .... Ⓨ Ⓕ Ⓜ
LDS (Mormon) .... Ⓨ Ⓕ Ⓜ
Lutheran .... Ⓨ Ⓕ Ⓜ
Methodist .... Ⓨ Ⓕ Ⓜ
Presbyterian .... Ⓨ Ⓕ Ⓜ
Quaker .... Ⓨ Ⓕ Ⓜ
Roman Catholic .... Ⓨ Ⓕ Ⓜ
Seventh Day Adventist .... Ⓨ Ⓕ Ⓜ
United Church of Christ/ Congregational .... Ⓨ Ⓕ Ⓜ
Other Christian .... Ⓨ Ⓕ Ⓜ
Other Religion .... Ⓨ Ⓕ Ⓜ
None .... Ⓨ Ⓕ Ⓜ

27. For the activities below, indicate which ones you did during the past year. If you engaged in an activity frequently, mark Ⓕ. If you engaged in an activity one or more times, but not frequently, mark Ⓞ (Occasionally). Mark Ⓝ (Not at all) if you have not performed the activity during the past year. (Mark one for each item)

Columns: Frequently / Occasionally / Not at all

Attended a religious service..... Ⓕ Ⓞ Ⓝ
Was bored in class .... Ⓕ Ⓞ Ⓝ
Participated in organized demonstrations .... Ⓕ Ⓞ Ⓝ
Tutored another student .... Ⓕ Ⓞ Ⓝ
Studied with other students ..... Ⓕ Ⓞ Ⓝ
Was a guest in a teacher's home .. Ⓕ Ⓞ Ⓝ
Smoked cigarettes .... Ⓕ Ⓞ Ⓝ
Drank beer.................... Ⓕ Ⓞ Ⓝ
Drank wine or liquor .... Ⓕ Ⓞ Ⓝ
Felt overwhelmed by all I had to do. Ⓕ Ⓞ Ⓝ
Felt depressed .... Ⓕ Ⓞ Ⓝ
Performed volunteer work ...... Ⓕ Ⓞ Ⓝ
Played a musical instrument .... Ⓕ Ⓞ Ⓝ
Asked a teacher for advice after class .... Ⓕ Ⓞ Ⓝ
Voted in a student election..... Ⓕ Ⓞ Ⓝ
Socialized with someone of another racial/ethnic group .... Ⓕ Ⓞ Ⓝ
Came late to class .... Ⓕ Ⓞ Ⓝ
Used the Internet:
For research or homework ..... Ⓕ Ⓞ Ⓝ
To read news sites .... Ⓕ Ⓞ Ⓝ
To read blogs .... Ⓕ Ⓞ Ⓝ
Performed community service as part of a class .... Ⓕ Ⓞ Ⓝ
Discussed religion............. Ⓕ Ⓞ Ⓝ
Discussed politics .... Ⓕ Ⓞ Ⓝ
Read a newspaper for:
National and global news ...... Ⓕ Ⓞ Ⓝ
Local news and information ... Ⓕ Ⓞ Ⓝ
Schoolwork.................. Ⓕ Ⓞ Ⓝ

28. Rate yourself on each of the following traits as compared with the average person your age. We want the most accurate estimate of how you see yourself. (Mark one in each row)

Columns: Highest 10% / Above Average / Average / Below Average / Lowest 10%

Academic ability ...... ○ ○ ○ ○ ○
Artistic ability .... ○ ○ ○ ○ ○
Computer skills ...... ○ ○ ○ ○ ○
Cooperativeness ..... ○ ○ ○ ○ ○
Creativity............ ○ ○ ○ ○ ○
Drive to achieve ..... ○ ○ ○ ○ ○
Emotional health ..... ○ ○ ○ ○ ○
Leadership ability..... ○ ○ ○ ○ ○
Mathematical ability ... ○ ○ ○ ○ ○
Physical health .... ○ ○ ○ ○ ○
Public speaking ability . ○ ○ ○ ○ ○
Religiousness........ ○ ○ ○ ○ ○
Self-confidence (intellectual)........ ○ ○ ○ ○ ○
Self-confidence (social) . ○ ○ ○ ○ ○
Self-understanding .... ○ ○ ○ ○ ○
Spirituality .... ○ ○ ○ ○ ○
Understanding of others . ○ ○ ○ ○ ○
Writing ability .... ○ ○ ○ ○ ○

29. What is the highest level of formal education obtained by your parents? (Mark one in each column)

Columns: Father / Mother

Grammar school or less ..... ○ ○
Some high school .... ○ ○
High school graduate .... ○ ○
Postsecondary school other than college.......... ○ ○
Some college............... ○ ○
College degree .... ○ ○
Some graduate school ...... ○ ○
Graduate degree........... ○ ○

30. In deciding to go to college, how important to you was each of the following reasons? (Mark one answer for each possible reason)

Columns: Very Important / Somewhat Important / Not Important

My parents wanted me to go.. Ⓥ Ⓢ Ⓝ
I could not find a job .... Ⓥ Ⓢ Ⓝ
Wanted to get away from home. Ⓥ Ⓢ Ⓝ
To be able to get a better job.. Ⓥ Ⓢ Ⓝ
To gain a general education and appreciation of ideas .. Ⓥ Ⓢ Ⓝ
There was nothing better to do . Ⓥ Ⓢ Ⓝ
To make me a more cultured person .... Ⓥ Ⓢ Ⓝ
To be able to make more money . Ⓥ Ⓢ Ⓝ
To learn more about things that interest me .... Ⓥ Ⓢ Ⓝ
To prepare myself for graduate or professional school ..... Ⓥ Ⓢ Ⓝ
A mentor/role model encouraged me to go ..... Ⓥ Ⓢ Ⓝ
To get training for a specific career .... Ⓥ Ⓢ Ⓝ

222

31. Mark only three responses, one in each column.

- Ⓜ Your mother's occupation
- Ⓕ Your father's occupation
- Ⓨ Your probable career occupation

NOTE: If your father or mother is deceased, please indicate his or her last occupation.

Accountant or actuary	Ⓨ	Ⓕ	Ⓜ
Actor or entertainer	Ⓨ	Ⓕ	Ⓜ
Architect or urban planner	Ⓨ	Ⓕ	Ⓜ
Artist	Ⓨ	Ⓕ	Ⓜ
Business (clerical)	Ⓨ	Ⓕ	Ⓜ
Business executive (management, administrator)	Ⓨ	Ⓕ	Ⓜ
Business owner or proprietor	Ⓨ	Ⓕ	Ⓜ
Business salesperson or buyer	Ⓨ	Ⓕ	Ⓜ
Clergy (minister, priest)	Ⓨ	Ⓕ	Ⓜ
Clergy (other religious)	Ⓨ	Ⓕ	Ⓜ
Clinical psychologist	Ⓨ	Ⓕ	Ⓜ
College administrator/staff	Ⓨ	Ⓕ	Ⓜ
College teacher	Ⓨ	Ⓕ	Ⓜ
Computer programmer or analyst	Ⓨ	Ⓕ	Ⓜ
Conservationist or forester	Ⓨ	Ⓕ	Ⓜ
Dentist (including orthodontist)	Ⓨ	Ⓕ	Ⓜ
Dietitian or nutritionist	Ⓨ	Ⓕ	Ⓜ
Engineer	Ⓨ	Ⓕ	Ⓜ
Farmer or rancher	Ⓨ	Ⓕ	Ⓜ
Foreign service worker (including diplomat)	Ⓨ	Ⓕ	Ⓜ
Homemaker (full-time)	Ⓨ	Ⓕ	Ⓜ
Interior decorator (including designer)	Ⓨ	Ⓕ	Ⓜ
Lab technician or hygienist	Ⓨ	Ⓕ	Ⓜ
Law enforcement officer	Ⓨ	Ⓕ	Ⓜ
Lawyer (attorney) or judge	Ⓨ	Ⓕ	Ⓜ
Military service (career)	Ⓨ	Ⓕ	Ⓜ
Musician (performer, composer)	Ⓨ	Ⓕ	Ⓜ
Nurse	Ⓨ	Ⓕ	Ⓜ
Optometrist	Ⓨ	Ⓕ	Ⓜ
Pharmacist	Ⓨ	Ⓕ	Ⓜ
Physician	Ⓨ	Ⓕ	Ⓜ
Policymaker/Government	Ⓨ	Ⓕ	Ⓜ
School counselor	Ⓨ	Ⓕ	Ⓜ
School principal or superintendent	Ⓨ	Ⓕ	Ⓜ
Scientific researcher	Ⓨ	Ⓕ	Ⓜ
Social, welfare, or recreation worker	Ⓨ	Ⓕ	Ⓜ
Therapist (physical, occupational, speech)	Ⓨ	Ⓕ	Ⓜ
Teacher or administrator (elementary)	Ⓨ	Ⓕ	Ⓜ
Teacher or administrator (secondary)	Ⓨ	Ⓕ	Ⓜ
Veterinarian	Ⓨ	Ⓕ	Ⓜ
Writer or journalist	Ⓨ	Ⓕ	Ⓜ
Skilled trades	Ⓨ	Ⓕ	Ⓜ
Laborer (unskilled)	Ⓨ	Ⓕ	Ⓜ
Semi-skilled worker	Ⓨ	Ⓕ	Ⓜ
Unemployed	Ⓨ	Ⓕ	Ⓜ
Other	Ⓨ	Ⓕ	Ⓜ
Undecided	Ⓨ		

32. Mark one in each row:

① Disagree Strongly
② Disagree Somewhat
③ Agree Somewhat
④ Agree Strongly

There is too much concern in the courts for the rights of criminals	④	③	②	①
Abortion should be legal	④	③	②	①
The death penalty should be abolished	④	③	②	①
Marijuana should be legalized	④	③	②	①
It is important to have laws prohibiting homosexual relationships	④	③	②	①
Racial discrimination is no longer a major problem in America	④	③	②	①
Realistically, an individual can do little to bring about changes in our society	④	③	②	①
Wealthy people should pay a larger share of taxes than they do now	④	③	②	①
Same-sex couples should have the right to legal marital status	④	③	②	①
Affirmative action in college admissions should be abolished	④	③	②	①
Federal military spending should be increased	④	③	②	①
The federal government should do more to control the sale of handguns	④	③	②	①
Only volunteers should serve in the armed forces	④	③	②	①
The federal government is not doing enough to control environmental pollution	④	③	②	①
A national health care plan is needed to cover everybody's medical costs	④	③	②	①
Undocumented immigrants should be denied access to public education	④	③	②	①
Through hard work, everybody can succeed in American society	④	③	②	①
Dissent is a critical component of the political process	④	③	②	①
Colleges have the right to ban extreme speakers from campus	④	③	②	①
The chief benefit of a college education is that it increases one's earning power	④	③	②	①
The federal government should raise taxes to reduce the deficit	④	③	②	①

33. During your last year in high school, how much time did you spend during a typical week doing the following activities?

Hours per week:	None	Less than 1 hour	1-2	3-5	6-10	11-15	16-20	Over 20
Studying/homework	○	○	○	○	○	○	○	○
Socializing with friends	○	○	○	○	○	○	○	○
Talking with teachers outside of class	○	○	○	○	○	○	○	○
Exercise or sports	○	○	○	○	○	○	○	○
Partying	○	○	○	○	○	○	○	○
Working (for pay)	○	○	○	○	○	○	○	○
Volunteer work	○	○	○	○	○	○	○	○
Student clubs/groups	○	○	○	○	○	○	○	○
Watching TV	○	○	○	○	○	○	○	○
Household/childcare duties	○	○	○	○	○	○	○	○
Reading for pleasure	○	○	○	○	○	○	○	○
Playing video/computer games	○	○	○	○	○	○	○	○

34. Are you: (Mark all that apply)

- White/Caucasian ○
- African American/Black ○
- American Indian/Alaska Native ○
- Asian American/Asian ○
- Native Hawaiian/Pacific Islander ○
- Mexican American/Chicano ○
- Puerto Rican ○
- Other Latino ○
- Other ○

35. How would you characterize your political views? (Mark one)

- ○ Far left
- ○ Liberal
- ○ Middle-of-the-road
- ○ Conservative
- ○ Far right

36. Below are some reasons that might have influenced your decision to attend this particular college. How important was each reason in your decision to come here? (Mark one answer for each possible reason)

Ⓥ Very Important
Ⓢ Somewhat Important
Ⓝ Not Important

My relatives wanted me to come here	Ⓥ	Ⓢ	Ⓝ
My teacher advised me	Ⓥ	Ⓢ	Ⓝ
This college has a very good academic reputation	Ⓥ	Ⓢ	Ⓝ
This college has a good reputation for its social activities	Ⓥ	Ⓢ	Ⓝ
I was offered financial assistance	Ⓥ	Ⓢ	Ⓝ
The cost of attending this college	Ⓥ	Ⓢ	Ⓝ
High school counselor advised me	Ⓥ	Ⓢ	Ⓝ
Private college counselor advised me	Ⓥ	Ⓢ	Ⓝ
I wanted to live near home	Ⓥ	Ⓢ	Ⓝ
Not offered aid by first choice	Ⓥ	Ⓢ	Ⓝ
Could not afford first choice	Ⓥ	Ⓢ	Ⓝ
This college's graduates gain admission to top graduate/professional schools	Ⓥ	Ⓢ	Ⓝ
This college's graduates get good jobs	Ⓥ	Ⓢ	Ⓝ
I was attracted by the religious affiliation/orientation of the college	Ⓥ	Ⓢ	Ⓝ
I wanted to go to a school about the size of this college	Ⓥ	Ⓢ	Ⓝ
Rankings in national magazines	Ⓥ	Ⓢ	Ⓝ
Information from a website	Ⓥ	Ⓢ	Ⓝ
I was admitted through an Early Action or Early Decision program	Ⓥ	Ⓢ	Ⓝ
The athletic department recruited me	Ⓥ	Ⓢ	Ⓝ
A visit to the campus	Ⓥ	Ⓢ	Ⓝ

223

37. Below is a list of different undergraduate major fields grouped into general categories. Mark only one oval to indicate your probable field of study.

ARTS AND HUMANITIES
- Art, fine and applied ①
- English (language and literature) ②
- History ③
- Journalism ④
- Language and Literature (except English) ⑤
- Music ⑥
- Philosophy ⑦
- Speech ⑧
- Theater or Drama ⑨
- Theology or Religion ⑩
- Other Arts and Humanities ⑪

BIOLOGICAL SCIENCE
- Biology (general) ⑫
- Biochemistry or Biophysics ⑬
- Botany ⑭
- Environmental Science ⑮
- Marine (Life) Science ⑯
- Microbiology or Bacteriology ⑰
- Zoology ⑱
- Other Biological Science ⑲

BUSINESS
- Accounting ⑳
- Business Admin. (general) ㉑
- Finance ㉒
- International Business ㉓
- Marketing ㉔
- Management ㉕
- Secretarial Studies ㉖
- Other Business ㉗

EDUCATION
- Business Education ㉘
- Elementary Education ㉙
- Music or Art Education ㉚
- Physical Education or Recreation ㉛
- Secondary Education ㉜
- Special Education ㉝
- Other Education ㉞

ENGINEERING
- Aeronautical or Astronautical Eng ㉟
- Civil Engineering ㊱
- Chemical Engineering ㊲
- Computer Engineering ㊳
- Electrical or Electronic Engineering ㊴
- Industrial Engineering ㊵
- Mechanical Engineering ㊶
- Other Engineering ㊷

PHYSICAL SCIENCE
- Astronomy ㊸
- Atmospheric Science (incl. Meteorology) ㊹
- Chemistry ㊺
- Earth Science ㊻
- Marine Science (incl. Oceanography) ㊼
- Mathematics ㊽
- Physics ㊾
- Statistics ㊿
- Other Physical Science (51)

PROFESSIONAL
- Architecture or Urban Planning (52)
- Family & Consumer Sciences (53)
- Health Technology (medical, dental, laboratory) (54)
- Library or Archival Science (55)
- Medicine, Dentistry, Veterinary Medicine (56)
- Nursing (57)
- Pharmacy (58)
- Therapy (occupational, physical, speech) (59)
- Other Professional (60)

SOCIAL SCIENCE
- Anthropology (61)
- Economics (62)
- Ethnic Studies (63)
- Geography (64)
- Political Science (gov't., international relations) (65)
- Psychology (66)
- Social Work (67)
- Sociology (68)
- Women's Studies (69)
- Other Social Science (70)

TECHNICAL
- Building Trades (71)
- Data Processing or Computer Programming (72)
- Drafting or Design (73)
- Electronics (74)
- Mechanics (75)
- Other Technical (76)

OTHER FIELDS
- Agriculture (77)
- Communications (78)
- Computer Science (79)
- Forestry (80)
- Kinesiology (81)
- Law Enforcement (82)
- Military Science (83)
- Other Field (84)
- Undecided (85)

DO NOT WRITE IN THIS AREA

38. Please indicate the importance to you personally of each of the following:
(Mark one for each item)

Ⓝ Not Important / Ⓢ Somewhat Important / Ⓥ Very Important / Ⓔ Essential

	E	V	S	N
Becoming accomplished in one of the performing arts (acting, dancing, etc.)	Ⓔ	Ⓥ	Ⓢ	Ⓝ
Becoming an authority in my field	Ⓔ	Ⓥ	Ⓢ	Ⓝ
Obtaining recognition from my colleagues for contributions to my special field	Ⓔ	Ⓥ	Ⓢ	Ⓝ
Influencing the political structure	Ⓔ	Ⓥ	Ⓢ	Ⓝ
Influencing social values	Ⓔ	Ⓥ	Ⓢ	Ⓝ
Raising a family	Ⓔ	Ⓥ	Ⓢ	Ⓝ
Having administrative responsibility for the work of others	Ⓔ	Ⓥ	Ⓢ	Ⓝ
Being very well off financially	Ⓔ	Ⓥ	Ⓢ	Ⓝ
Helping others who are in difficulty	Ⓔ	Ⓥ	Ⓢ	Ⓝ
Making a theoretical contribution to science	Ⓔ	Ⓥ	Ⓢ	Ⓝ
Writing original works (poems, novels, short stories, etc.)	Ⓔ	Ⓥ	Ⓢ	Ⓝ
Creating artistic work (painting, sculpture, decorating, etc.)	Ⓔ	Ⓥ	Ⓢ	Ⓝ
Becoming successful in a business of my own	Ⓔ	Ⓥ	Ⓢ	Ⓝ
Becoming involved in programs to clean up the environment	Ⓔ	Ⓥ	Ⓢ	Ⓝ
Developing a meaningful philosophy of life	Ⓔ	Ⓥ	Ⓢ	Ⓝ
Participating in a community action program	Ⓔ	Ⓥ	Ⓢ	Ⓝ
Helping to promote racial understanding	Ⓔ	Ⓥ	Ⓢ	Ⓝ
Keeping up to date with political affairs	Ⓔ	Ⓥ	Ⓢ	Ⓝ
Becoming a community leader	Ⓔ	Ⓥ	Ⓢ	Ⓝ
Improving my understanding of other countries and cultures	Ⓔ	Ⓥ	Ⓢ	Ⓝ
Participating in an organization like the Peace Corps or AmeriCorps/VISTA	Ⓔ	Ⓥ	Ⓢ	Ⓝ

39. What is your best guess as to the chances that you will:
(Mark one for each item)

Ⓝ No Chance / Ⓛ Very Little Chance / Ⓢ Some Chance / Ⓥ Very Good Chance

	V	S	L	N
Change major field?	Ⓥ	Ⓢ	Ⓛ	Ⓝ
Change career choice?	Ⓥ	Ⓢ	Ⓛ	Ⓝ
Participate in student government?	Ⓥ	Ⓢ	Ⓛ	Ⓝ
Get a job to help pay for college expenses?	Ⓥ	Ⓢ	Ⓛ	Ⓝ
Work full-time while attending college?	Ⓥ	Ⓢ	Ⓛ	Ⓝ
Join a social fraternity or sorority?	Ⓥ	Ⓢ	Ⓛ	Ⓝ
Play varsity/intercollegiate athletics?	Ⓥ	Ⓢ	Ⓛ	Ⓝ
Make at least a "B" average?	Ⓥ	Ⓢ	Ⓛ	Ⓝ
Need extra time to complete your degree requirements?	Ⓥ	Ⓢ	Ⓛ	Ⓝ
Participate in student protests or demonstrations?	Ⓥ	Ⓢ	Ⓛ	Ⓝ
Transfer to another college before graduating?	Ⓥ	Ⓢ	Ⓛ	Ⓝ
Be satisfied with your college?	Ⓥ	Ⓢ	Ⓛ	Ⓝ
Participate in volunteer or community service work?	Ⓥ	Ⓢ	Ⓛ	Ⓝ
Seek personal counseling?	Ⓥ	Ⓢ	Ⓛ	Ⓝ
Communicate regularly with your professors?	Ⓥ	Ⓢ	Ⓛ	Ⓝ
Socialize with someone of another racial/ethnic group?	Ⓥ	Ⓢ	Ⓛ	Ⓝ
Participate in student clubs/groups?	Ⓥ	Ⓢ	Ⓛ	Ⓝ
Participate in a study abroad program?	Ⓥ	Ⓢ	Ⓛ	Ⓝ

40. Do you give the Higher Education Research Institute (HERI) permission to include your ID number should your college request the data for additional research analyses? HERI maintains strict standards of confidentiality and would require your college to sign a pledge of confidentiality. ◯ Yes ◯ No

The remaining ovals are provided for questions specifically designed by your college rather than the Higher Education Research Institute. If your college has chosen to use the ovals, please observe carefully the supplemental directions given to you.

41. Ⓐ Ⓑ Ⓒ Ⓓ Ⓔ	47. Ⓐ Ⓑ Ⓒ Ⓓ Ⓔ	53. Ⓐ Ⓑ Ⓒ Ⓓ Ⓔ
42. Ⓐ Ⓑ Ⓒ Ⓓ Ⓔ	48. Ⓐ Ⓑ Ⓒ Ⓓ Ⓔ	54. Ⓐ Ⓑ Ⓒ Ⓓ Ⓔ
43. Ⓐ Ⓑ Ⓒ Ⓓ Ⓔ	49. Ⓐ Ⓑ Ⓒ Ⓓ Ⓔ	55. Ⓐ Ⓑ Ⓒ Ⓓ Ⓔ
44. Ⓐ Ⓑ Ⓒ Ⓓ Ⓔ	50. Ⓐ Ⓑ Ⓒ Ⓓ Ⓔ	56. Ⓐ Ⓑ Ⓒ Ⓓ Ⓔ
45. Ⓐ Ⓑ Ⓒ Ⓓ Ⓔ	51. Ⓐ Ⓑ Ⓒ Ⓓ Ⓔ	57. Ⓐ Ⓑ Ⓒ Ⓓ Ⓔ
46. Ⓐ Ⓑ Ⓒ Ⓓ Ⓔ	52. Ⓐ Ⓑ Ⓒ Ⓓ Ⓔ	58. Ⓐ Ⓑ Ⓒ Ⓓ Ⓔ

THANK YOU!

Data Recognition Corp.-6G6044-6754-54321

Appendix C

Institutional Participation, 1966–2006

INSTITUTIONS INCLUDED IN THE CIRP FRESHMAN SURVEY
NATIONAL NORMS SAMPLE, 1966–2006

Institution	Strat Cell	# of Years	-200x-- 6543210	---199x--- 9876543210	---198x--- 9876543210	---197x--- 9876543210	196x 9876
Abilene Christian University	23	28	XXXXXXX	XXXXXXX-X-	XXXXX-----	XXXX--X--X	XX--
Adelphi University	04	18	XXXXXXX	XXXXX-XXX-	----------	-------XX	-X--
Adrian College	22	35	X-XXXXX	XXXXX--XX-	XXXXXXXXX-	XXXXXXXX-X	XXXX
Agnes Scott College	23	21	X-X--XX	XX--XXXXXX	XXXXX----	-XXX------	----
Alabama A & M University	34	22	XXX---X	--XXXXXXXX	X---------	--XXX-XX-X	-XXX
Alabama State University	34	8	-------	----------	-------XX	X----XXXXX	----
Alaska Pacific University	11	5	XX--XX-	----------	X---------	----------	----
Albertson College of Idaho	13	13	-X--XXX	XXXXX-XXXX	----------	----------	----
Albertus Magnus College	16	29	--XXXXX	XXXXXXXX-	XXXXXXXXXX	XXXXX-----	----
Albion College	23	18	-X-XXXX	XX-XXXXXX-	-XXXX-X---	----------	----
Albright College	22	12	XXXXXXX	-XXXX-X---	----------	----------	----
Alderson-Broaddus College	20	1	-------	----------	----------	---X------	----
Alfred University	13	13	X-XX--X	-----XX-X-	----------	--X------X	XXXX
Alice Lloyd College	11	10	-------	----------	-------X	XXXXXXXXX-	----
Allegheny College	13	39	--XXXXX	XXXXXXXXXX	XXXXXXXXXX	XXXXXXXXXX	XXXX
Alliance College	11	2	-------	----------	----------	XX-------	----
Alliant International U	11	2	------X	X---------	----------	----------	----
Alma College	23	27	-XX-X-X	-XXXXXXXX	XXXXXXXXX	XXXX------	----
Alvernia College	16	12	XXXXXXX	X--XXXX---	----------	----------	----
American Intercontinental U (CA)	15	1	-------	--X-------	----------	----------	----
American International College	11	1	-------	----------	X---------	----------	----
American University	05	32	XXXX-XX	XXXXXXX--X	XXXXXXXXXX	XXX-X-----	XXXX
Amherst College	14	32	X-XXXXX	XXXX------	X-XXX-XXXX	XXXXXXXXXX	XXXX
Anderson College	22	23	XX-X---	----XXXXXX	XXXX-X-X-	X-X-X-XXXX	----
Anderson University	22	4	----X--	---X-X----	----------	-----X----	----
Andrews University	22	7	-------	----------	-------XX	XXX--XX---	----
Anna Maria College	17	5	-----XX	XXX-------	----------	----------	----
Antioch University	13	9	XX-----	--------XX	X-X-XXX---	----------	----
Appalachian State University	09	8	-------	----------	----------	XXX-XXXXX-	----
Aquinas College (MI)	18	39	--XXXXX	XXXXXXXXXX	XXXXXXXXXX	XXXXXXXXXX	XXXX
Aquinas College at Newton	18	6	-------	----------	----------	-------X-X	XXXX
Arcadia University	22	9	-------	----------	-XX-------	-XXXXX-X--	----
Arizona State University	01	2	-------	----------	----------	----------	--XX
Arkansas State University	08	1	X------	----------	----------	----------	----
Art Center College of Design	12	3	XX--X--	----------	----------	----------	----
Asbury College	13	5	--X-X-X	-X---X----	----------	----------	----
Ashford University	17	8	-------	--X-------	-X-X-XXXXX	----------	----
Ashland University	20	4	-------	--XX-XX---	----------	----------	----
Assumption College	18	7	XXXXXX-	----------	----------	-----X----	----
Athens State University	20	3	-------	----------	----------	-------X-	XX--
Atlanta Christian College	15	1	-------	----------	X---------	----------	----
Atlanta College of Art	12	7	--XXXX-	-------X--	-X-X------	----------	----
Auburn University	03	1	-----X	----------	----------	----------	----
Augsburg College	23	24	--X-XXX	X-XXXX----	--XXXXXXX-	-XXX-----X	XXXX
Augustana College (IL)	23	32	XXXXXXX	XXX---X-XX	XXXXXXXXXX	XXXXXXXX-X	----
Augustana College (SD)	23	29	-------	XXXXXX-XX-	XXXXXXXXXX	XXXXXXXXXX	X---
Aurora University	11	4	-X-X-X-	--X-------	----------	----------	----
Austin College	23	41	XXXXXXX	XXXXXXXXXX	XXXXXXXXXX	XXXXXXXXXX	XXXX
Austin Peay State University	08	12	-X-----	----------	----X-X-XX	-XXXXX--XX	----
Averett University	20	21	XX-XX--	-----XXXXX	XX------XX	--XXXX---X	-XXX
Avila University	17	13	-XXXXX	XXXXXX---	----------	----------	----
Azusa Pacific University	12	8	XX-X---	-XX------X	----------	-XX-------	----
Babson College	14	21	XXXXXXX	-XXXXXXXX	XXXX-----	----------	----
Bacone College	24	1	-------	----------	----------	X--------	----
Baker University	22	7	-------	-------X--	-----X-X-X	XX---X----	----

Institutions whose results for first-time full-time freshmen were included in the National Norms sample for a particular year are indicated by an "X".

Please note that the mark (–) shows only that the institution was not included in the Norms sample for a particular year. It may well have participated in the survey. In addition, institutions that were never included in the Norms and all two-year colleges are not included in this report. For a full record of CIRP Freshman Survey participation, please refer to Appendix D of "The American Freshman: National Norms for Fall, 2006.

Institution	Strat Cell	# of Years	-200x-- 6543210	---199x--- 9876543210	---198x--- 9876543210	---197x--- 9876543210	196x 9876
Baldwin-Wallace College	23	7	-------	--XX-XXX-X	-X-------	----------	----
Baptist Bible College & Seminary	21	8	-------	----------	----------	----XXXXXX	XX--
Barat College	17	2	-------	----------	---------X	---X------	----
Bard College	14	31	XXXXXXX	XXXXXXXXXX	XXXXXXXX--	-XX--X-XXX	----
Barnard College	14	21	XXXXXXX	XXXXXXX--	-----XXXX	-XX-------	----
Barrington College	12	3	-------	----------	----------	-X-X-X----	----
Barry University	16	6	--XXX--	--------X-	--X-------	-----X----	----
Barton College	20	8	-XX----	XXXXX-----	-------X--	----------	----
Bates College	14	28	XXXX-XX	XXX-------	----XXXXXX	XXXXXX-XXX	XXXX
Baylor University	05	30	XXXX-X-	--XX-X-XXX	XXX-XXXX--	-XXXXXXX-X	XXXX
Belhaven College	22	1	-------	-------X--	----------	----------	----
Bellarmine University	18	5	XXX----	----X---X-	----------	----------	----
Bellarmine-Ursuline College	18	4	-------	----------	----------	----------	XXXX
Belmont Abbey College	16	2	-------	----------	X--------	----X-----	----
Belmont University	23	6	X-XXXX-	X---------	----------	----------	----
Beloit College	13	38	XXXXXXX	XXXXXXXXXX	XXXXXXXXXX	XXX--XXXX-	XXXX
Benedict College	35	7	-------	----------	----XXXX-X	-XX-------	----
Benedictine College	17	29	XXXXXX-	-XXXXXXXX-	-XXXXXXXX	-X-XXXXX--	----
Benedictine University	18	6	X-X----	---X-X----	----X-X---	----------	----
Bennett College for Women	35	8	XX-----	--------X	XXX-----XX	----------	----
Bennington College	13	10	X------	----------	----------	----X-XXXX	XXXX
Bentley College	13	9	-X-X-X-	X--XXX----	----------	---X-X----	----
Berea College	12	30	X-X-X--	-----XXXX	X--XXXXXX	XXXXXXXXX-	XXXX
Bernard M Baruch College	09	4	-X-----	----------	----------	---------X	-XX-
Berry College	13	28	XXXXXXX	XXXXXXXXXX	XXXXXX-XXX	--X----X--	----
Bethany College (KS)	22	8	-------	--XXXX----	----XX----	--XX------	----
Bethany College (WV)	13	22	XX-XXXX	XXX-XXXXX-	XX-XXXXXX-	----------	----
Bethany Lutheran College	22	36	XX-----	XXXXXXXXXX	XXXXXXXXXX	XXXXXXXXXX	XXXX
Bethel College (IN)	22	13	XXXXXXX	XXXXX-----	----------	----------	----
Bethel College (KS)	22	17	XXXXXXX	XXXXXXXXXX	----------	----------	----
Bethel College	20	3	--X----	---XX-----	----------	----------	----
Bethel University	23	2	------X	-X--------	----------	----------	----
Bethune-Cookman College	35	1	X------	----------	----------	----------	----
Biola University	04	6	--X-X--	---X-X-X-X	----------	----------	----
Birmingham-Southern College	23	8	-------	-------X-X	XX-----X--	--XXX-----	----
Bishop College	35	1	-------	----------	----------	-------X--	----
Black Hills State University	08	1	-------	----X-----	----------	----------	----
Blackburn College	12	5	-------	-X--------	---------X	-X-XX-----	----
Bloomfield College	20	8	-------	-X--------	--XX-XX---	-XX-X-----	----
Bloomsburg U of Pennsylvania	08	21	---XXXX	X----XXXX	XXXXX-XXXX	XX--------	----
Bluffton College	22	19	XXXXXXX	XXXXXXXXX-	----------	-----X-XX-	----
Boston College	05	18	XXXXXXX	XXXXXX-X--	----------	----------	-XXX
Boston University	05	5	-------	----------	-------X--	X-XX--X---	----
Bowdoin College	14	30	XXXXXXX	X-XXX-XX-X	----XXX---	XX-XXXXXX	XXXX
Bowie State University	34	14	--X----	-X-----XX	X------X--	-XX--XXXX-	-X-X
Bowling Green State University	01	9	-------	----XX----	----------	XXXXXXX---	----
Bradford College	11	13	-------	XXX-XX----	XXX-----X-	----XXX-X-	----
Bradley University	04	33	XXXXXXX	XXXXXXXXXX	X---X----X	XXXXX-XXX	XXXX
Brandeis University	06	31	X-----X	XXXXXXX-X	X---XXXXXX	XXXXXXXXXX	-XXX
Brenau University	12	9	-----X-	--X-----XX	XXX---X---	-----X----	----
Brevard College	20	33	X-XXXXX	-XXXXXXX--	XXXXXXXXXX	XXXXXXXXXX	----
Briarcliffe College	12	5	-------	----------	----------	-----X----	XXXX
Bridgewater College	21	5	--X----	-X--X-----	XX--------	----------	----
Bridgewater State College	08	14	XXXXXXX	XXXXXXX---	----------	----------	----
Brigham Young University	05	1	-------	----------	---X------	----------	----
Brooklyn College	08	1	-------	----X-----	----------	----------	----
Brown University	06	8	X-X---X	---X------	-X---X----	-X-X------	----
Bryan College	12	2	-------	----------	----------	----X--X--	----
Bryant College	12	11	XXX-XXX	----XXXX--	----------	------X---	----
Bryn Athyn Coll of the New Church	23	10	-X---XX	-XXXXXn--X	----------	----------	----
Bryn Mawr College	14	28	X--XXXX	XXXXXXXXXX	XXXXXXXXXX	-XX-X-----	----
Bucknell University	14	10	XXXXXXX	XXX-------	----------	----------	----
Buena Vista University	22	34	XXXXXXX	XXX-XXXX-X	XX-X--XXXX	--XXXXXXXX	XXXX
Butler University	04	22	XXXXXXX	XXXXXXXXXX	X------XX	XX--------	----
Cabrini College	16	12	X--XXX-	XXXXXX-XX-	----------	----------	----
Cal Poly State U-Pomona	08	8	-XXX---	X-XXXX----	----------	------X---	----
Cal Poly State U-San Luis Obispo	09	5	--XXX--	XX--------	----------	----------	----

Institution	Strat Cell	# of Years	-200x-- 6543210	---199x--- 9876543210	---198x--- 9876543210	---197x--- 9876543210	196x 9876
Caldwell College	16	12	-------	XXXXXXX--	XXXX------	----------	----
California Baptist University	20	13	XXXXXXX	XXXX----XX	----------	----------	----
California College of the Arts	11	9	--XXX--	----X-XXX-	X-X-------	----------	----
California Institute of Technology	06	38	XXXXXXX	XXXXXXXXXX	---XXXXXXX	XXXXXXXXXX	XXXX
California Lutheran University	22	8	-------	------X-X-	XXX-X-X---	-------X--	----
California State U-Bakersfield	07	3	-------	-------X----	----------	---XX-----	----
California State U-Channel Islands	10	2	X--X---	----------	----------	----------	----
California State U-Chico	08	2	-------	----------	----------	---XX-----	----
California State U-Dominguez Hills	07	2	---X---	----------	--X-------	----------	----
California State U-Fresno	07	1	-------	----------	----------	----------	---X
California State U-Fullerton	07	10	-------	----------	----------	-XXX--XX-X	XXXX
California State U-Hayward	08	2	-------	X---X-----	----------	----------	----
California State U-Long Beach	07	8	---XXXX	XXX-------	---X------	----------	----
California State U-Los Angeles	07	5	-X---XX	---XX-----	----------	----------	----
California State U-San Marcos	07	8	XXXXXXX	X---------	----------	----------	----
California State U-Stanislaus	07	4	-------	----------	----------	-----X----	X-XX
California U of Pennsylvania	07	2	-------	----------	----------	--------X	-X--
Calvin College	23	34	XX----X	XXXXXXXXXX	XXXXXXXXXX	-XXXXXXX-X	XXX-
Campbell University	22	1	-------	-X--------	----------	----------	----
Campbellsville University	21	3	-------	------X-XX	----------	----------	----
Canisius College	18	19	-----XX	X-XXX-XXXX	XXXX-X-X-	XX--------	----
Capital University	22	3	-------	-------XX-	------X---	----------	----
Cardinal Stritch University	17	17	--XX-X-	--X-------	-X---X----	XXXXX-X--	XXXX
Carleton College	14	38	XXXXXXX	XXXXXXXXXX	XX-XXXXXXX	XXXXXXXXXX	XX--
Carlow College	16	21	XXX-XXX	--X-X-----	XXXXXXXXXX	XXX-------	----
Carnegie-Mellon University	06	22	XXXXXXX	XXXXXX----	XXXX-----	--XX------	-X--
Carroll College (MT)	18	5	-------	-----X----	----------	-X--XX--X-	----
Carroll College (WI)	22	37	--X--XX	XXXXXXXXXX	XXXXXXXXXX	XXXXXXXXXX	XXXX
Carson-Newman College	22	16	-----XX	-XXXX-----	--XXX-X---	--XXXX--XX	----
Carthage College	23	6	XXX-X--	----------	X---------	X---------	----
Cascade College	11	1	-------	----------	----------	----------	-X--
Case Western Reserve University	06	6	--X----	-XX-------	---XX-----	----------	-X--
Castleton State College	07	2	X------	----------	--X-------	----------	----
Catawba College	21	23	XX-XXXX	XXXXXXXXXX	XXXXX-XX--	----------	----
Catholic University of America	04	20	-------	XXXXXXXXXX	-XXXX--XXX	XX-----X--	----
Cazenovia College	11	12	-------	----------	------XXX	XXXXX--XX	-X--
Cedar Crest College	12	25	XXX--X-	--X-XXX-XX	XXXXXXXX--	XXXXXXX---	----
Cedarville University	23	5	-----XX	---XXX----	----------	----------	----
Centenary College	20	6	-XX----	----X---X-	----------	-------XX-	----
Centenary College of Louisiana	23	7	--XX-XX	-X--------	X-X-------	----------	----
Central College	23	4	-XX----	----XX----	----------	----------	----
Central Methodist University	20	5	-------	-------X--	----------	--XXX--X-	----
Central Michigan University	08	3	-----X-	XX--------	----------	----------	----
Central Missouri State University	09	2	-X---X-	----------	----------	----------	----
Central State University	34	4	---XX-X	X---------	----------	----------	----
Central Washington University	07	3	-------	------XXX	----------	----------	----
Centre College	13	34	XXXXXXX	XXXXXXX-XX	-XXXXXXXXX	XXXXXXXXX-	----
Chadron State College	08	1	-------	--X-------	----------	----------	----
Chaminade University of Honolulu	16	5	--X--X-	X-X-------	----------	------X---	----
Champlain College	11	10	-------	----X---X-	--X-------	-XXXXXX---	X---
Chapman University	13	13	-XXX-X-	------X---	------X---	XX---X-X--	-XXX
Charleston Southern University	22	2	--X-X--	----------	----------	----------	----
Chatham College	12	30	--XXX-X	XX------X-	XXXXXXX-XX	XXXXXXXXXX	XXXX
Chestnut Hill College	16	1	-------	----------	----------	--------X-	----
Cheyney U of Pennsylvania	34	8	--X--XX	-X-----X-X	XX--------	----------	----
Chicago State University	34	5	-------	----------	----------	----X-XX--	XX--
Chowan College	20	32	XX---X-	X--XXXXXXX	XXXXXXXXXX	XXXXXXXXXX	X---
Christian Brothers University	18	8	XXXXXXX	X---------	----------	----------	----
Christopher Newport University	09	2	----XX-	----------	----------	----------	----
Citadel	09	2	X------	---X------	----------	----------	----
City College	09	10	-------	----------	---------X	X-X--X-X-X	XXXX
Claflin University	35	1	-------	----------	X---------	----------	----
Claremont McKenna College	14	34	XXXXXXX	XXXXXXXXXX	XXX-X-X-X-	XXX-XXXXXX	XX--
Clarion U of Pennsylvania	08	4	-------	-X--------	----------	-X-X------	X---
Clark Atlanta University	35	20	----X-X	-----X--X-	XXXX-XXXXX	X-XXXXXX--	----
Clark University	13	23	XXXXXXX	XXXXXXXXXX	XXXX-----	----------	-X--
Clarke College	18	10	----XXX	X-X-X-X---	----------	----XX-X--	----
Clarkson University	05	11	XXXXXXX	--X--XX---	---------	------X---	----

229

Institution	Strat Cell	# of Years	-200x-- 6543210	---199x--- 9876543210	---198x--- 9876543210	---197x--- 9876543210	196x 9876
Clearwater Christian College	11	1	X------	----------	----------	----------	----
Clemson University	03	1	-------	----------	----------	-----X----	----
Cleveland Institute of Art	12	4	-------	----------	-X-X----X-	-------X--	----
Cleveland Institute of Music	14	4	-------	-----XXXX-	----------	----------	----
Coastal Carolina University	08	19	-X---XX	X-XXX-XXX-	X--X-----X	XX-X--XXX-	----
Coe College	13	14	XXXXXXX	XXXX------	--------X-	-XX-------	----
Cogswell Polytechnical College	11	2	-------	----------	----------	--XX------	----
Coker College	11	2	-------	----------	----------	----XX----	----
Colby College	14	27	-XXXXXX	XXXX-XX-XX	XXXXX-XX-X	-------XX-	-XXX
Colby-Sawyer College	11	6	-------	XXXXX-----	----------	-------X--	----
Colgate University	14	18	-XXXX-X	XX--X-X-X-	--X-X-X-X-	X---X-X-X-	----
College Misericordia	16	9	--X-XX-	----------	XXX----X-	----XX----	----
College for Creative Studies	11	7	XXXX---	----X-----	XX--------	----------	----
College of Charleston	09	18	XXX----	--X-XXXXX-	XXXX------	--------X-	XXXX
College of Mount Saint Joseph	17	5	-------	--X-------	------XXX-	----X-----	----
College of Mount Saint Vincent	16	38	X-XX-XX	XXXXXXXXXX	XXXXXXX-XX	XXXXXXXXXX	XXXX
College of New Jersey	09	20	-X-X-XX	XXXXXXXXXX	XXXXX-----	-------X--	----
College of New Rochelle	16	19	-X-X-XX	XX---X-X-X	--X-XXXX--	----X-----	XXXX
College of Notre Dame of Maryland	17	7	-XX--XX	XX--------	--------X	----------	----
College of Our Lady of the Elms	16	5	----X-X	--X-------	----------	-------XX-	----
College of Saint Benedict	18	31	---XXXX	X-XXXXX-XX	XXX--X-XXX	XXXXXXXXXX	XX--
College of Saint Catherine	18	29	-XXXXXX	XXX--X-XXX	XXXXX--X-X	XXXXXXXXX-	----
College of Saint Elizabeth	17	12	--XXXXX	XXX-X-XXX-	----------	----------	----
College of Saint Mary	17	10	-----X-	XX---XXXXX	XX--------	----------	----
College of Saint Rose	17	3	-------	----------	----------	-------XXX	----
College of Saint Scholastica	18	8	-X--XX-	----------	-----XXX--	-X-----X--	----
College of Saint Teresa	17	10	-------	----------	--XXXXX-XX	XXX-------	----
College of Santa Fe	18	6	XXXXX--	-------X--	----------	----------	----
College of Staten Island	07	9	------X	----------	-X--X----X	X-X-X-XX--	----
College of William and Mary	09	6	-X--X-X	-----X----	-XX-------	----------	----
College of Wooster	13	18	-X--XXX	XXXX---XX-	--------X-	XXXXXXX---	----
College of the Atlantic	14	2	-------	--------X	--X-------	----------	----
College of the Holy Cross	18	17	XXXXXXX	XXXXXXXXXX	----------	----------	----
College of the Southwest	11	1	---X---	----------	----------	----------	----
Colorado Christian University	12	7	-----XX	XXXXX-----	----------	----------	----
Colorado College	14	14	-------	---X-XXXXX	XXXX-XX-X-	-------X--	----
Colorado State University	02	2	X------	----------	----------	----------	---X
Colorado State University-Pueblo	07	2	-------	----------	----------	----------	--XX
Colorado Women's College	11	3	-------	----------	----------	---XXX----	----
Columbia College	21	7	-X-----	X-----X-X-	X---------	X-------X-	----
Columbia University	06	17	X----XX	XXXXXX--X-	XX-X-X----	----------	-XXX
Columbus College of Art and Design	11	1	-X-----	----------	----------	----------	----
Concordia College (MN)	23	4	--X----	----X-----	----------	----------	--XX
Concordia College	21	23	X-XXXXX	X-XXXXXXXX	XXXXXXX--	----------	----
Concordia University (CA)	21	13	XX-XXXX	XXXXXXX---	----------	----------	----
Concordia University (OR)	21	13	X------	----------	----XXXXX	XXXXXXX---	----
Concordia University (TX)	20	5	-------	-------X--	XXXX------	----------	----
Concordia University Wisconsin	12	2	-------	----------	----------	XX--------	----
Connecticut College	14	39	XXXXXXX	XXXXXXXXX-	XXXXXXXXXX	XXXXXXXXX-	XXXX
Converse College	12	19	XXX-XX-	---------X	XXXXXXXXXX	XXX-------	----
Coppin State College	34	6	---X-X-	X--XXX----	----------	----------	----
Corban College	21	7	X-X-X--	---X-X-XX-	----------	----------	----
Cornell College	23	22	X--X-X-	--XXX-XXX-	X--XXXXXXX	XXX-XXX---	----
Cornell Univ-School of Human Ecol	06	1	-------	----------	----------	----------	-X--
Cornell University	06	9	XXXXXXX	----------	---------X	----X-----	----
Cornerstone University	21	12	X---X--	-XXXXXXXXX	----X-----	----------	----
Covenant College	23	9	-----X-	-X-X--X---	-X-X------	XXX-------	----
Creighton University	05	17	XXXXX-X	XXXXXXXXX-	XX--------	----------	----
Crown College	22	1	---X---	----------	----------	----------	----
Culver-Stockton College	22	1	X------	----------	----------	----------	----
Cumberland University	11	1	-------	X---------	----------	----------	----
D'Youville College	17	5	-------	----------	X----X----	---XX-X---	----
Daemen College	11	2	XX-----	----------	----------	----------	----
Dakota Wesleyan University	21	2	-------	----------	------X---	----------	-X--
Dallas Baptist University	21	1	-------	----------	----------	----------	--X-
Dana College	22	3	--X-XX-	----------	----------	----197----	----
Daniel Webster College	12	6	------X	XX------XX	X---------	----------	----

230

Institution	Strat Cell	# of Years	-200x-- 6543210	---199x--- 9876543210	---198x--- 9876543210	---197x--- 9876543210	196x 9876
Dartmouth College	14	39	-XXXX-X	XXXXXXXXXX	XXXXXXXXXX	XXXXXXXXXX	XXXX
Davidson College	23	25	XXXXXXX	XXXXXXXXXX	XX-------	---XXXXXX-	----
Davis and Elkins College	20	18	-------	----------	-----XXXXX	XXX-XXXXXX	XXXX
DePaul University	04	7	---XX--	---X-X-X--	--X-X-----	----------	----
DePauw University	23	29	------X	XXX-XXXXX-	XXXX-XXXX	XX-XXXXXXX	XX--
DeSales University	17	22	-X-X-X-	--X-X-X-X-	X-XXXXXXXX	X-XXXXX---	----
DeVry University-Columbus	15	14	-------	--XX------	-------XXX	XXX-X-XX-X	XX--
Defiance College	12	14	X------	----------	XXXX---XXX	---X-X-XXX	-X--
Delaware State University	34	9	-------	----------	---X-X-X--	-------XX	XXXX
Delaware Valley College	11	15	-------	---XX-----	--------X-	XX-XX-XXXX	XXXX
Denison University	13	6	---X---	--X-----XX	X---------	--------X-	----
Dickinson College	13	33	--XX--X	XXXXXX-X--	XXXXXXXXXX	-XXXXXXXXX	XXXX
Dillard University	35	31	-X-XXXX	-XX-XXXXXX	XXX--XXXXX	XXXXXXX--X	XX--
Doane College	22	4	-X-----	----------	----------	------XXX-	----
Dominican College of Blauvelt	16	33	XX-X-XX	XXXXXXXXXX	---XXXXXXX	XXXXXXX-XX	--XX
Dominican University	17	30	XXXXXXX	XX-XXXXXXX	XXXXXXXXX-	-XX-X-XX--	----
Dominican University of California	17	30	--XXX--	X---XXXXXX	X-XXXXXXXX	-XXX--XXXX	XXXX
Dordt College	23	1	---X---	----------	----------	----------	----
Drake University	04	32	---XXXX	XXXXX-XXXX	XXXXXXXXXX	X-XX-XXXXX	-X--
Drew University	23	10	XX--X--	--X--X-XXX	-----XX---	----------	----
Drexel University	13	4	--XX--X	-X--------	----------	----------	----
Drury University	13	7	-XX----	X--X-X-X--	X---------	----------	----
Duke University	06	19	XXXXXX-	XXX-X--X-X	--------X	XXXXX----	----
Duquesne University	04	1	--X----	----------	----------	----------	----
Earlham College	23	38	XXXXXX	-XXXXXXXXX	XXXXXXXXXX	XXXXXXXXXX	XX--
East Carolina University	01	8	----X--	-X-----X--	--X---XXXX	----------	----
East Central University	08	2	--X----	----------	----------	--------X	----
East Stroudsburg U of Pennsylvania	07	4	--X----	-X--------	----------	X-X------	----
East Texas Baptist University	21	6	XXXXXX-	----------	----------	----------	----
Eastern Connecticut State U	07	1	X------	----------	----------	----------	----
Eastern Illinois University	08	1	-------	-X--------	----------	----------	----
Eastern Kentucky University	07	1	--X----	----------	----------	----------	----
Eastern Mennonite University	22	22	X---X--	-X---XX---	XXX-XX----	-X-XXXXXXX	XXXX
Eastern Michigan University	08	2	-XX----	----------	----------	----------	----
Eastern Nazarene College	20	9	--XX--X	XXXXXX----	----------	----------	----
Eastern New Mexico University	07	10	-X-----	-X-XX-XXXX	XX--------	----------	----
Eastern University	22	4	X------	----------	---X------	-----XX---	----
Eckerd College	23	25	XXX--XX	XXXXXXXXXX	XX-------	-X-XXXXXXX	----
Edgewood College	17	12	-X-X--X	XXXXX-XX--	-------XX	----------	----
Edinboro U of Pennsylvania	08	1	---X---	----------	----------	----------	----
Eisenhower College	13	8	-------	----------	----------	-XXXXX-XXX	----
Elizabeth City State University	34	15	XXX-X--	--XX----X-	------XX--	X-X--XXXX-	----
Elizabethtown College	23	33	XXXXXXX	XXXXXXXXXX	XXX-XXXXX-	X--XXXX-XX	X---
Elmhurst College	22	9	XX----X	XXXXXX----	----------	----------	----
Elmira College	13	15	XXXXXXX	XXXXXX----	-------XX	----------	----
Elon University	23	26	XXXXXXX	XXXXXXXXXX	XXXXX-----	XX-----X--	----
Embry-Riddle Aeronautical U	12	5	-X-----	-------XX	XX-------	----------	----
Emerson College	13	18	X-X-X-X	-X-X-X-XXX	XXXXXXXX--	----------	----
Emmanuel College (MA)	17	5	XXX-X--	------X---	----------	----------	----
Emory University	06	36	XXXXXXX	XXXXXXXXXX	XXXXXXXXXX	-XXXXXXXX-	---X
Emory and Henry College	22	36	XX-XXXX	XXXXXXXXXX	X--XXXXXX-	XXXXX-XXXX	XXXX
Erskine College	23	22	X-XXXXX	X-X-XXXXXX	XXXXX-----	------XXX-	----
Eureka College	22	14	-------	XXXXXXXXXX	X-X-------	X-----X---	----
Evangel University	22	3	-------	--X--XX---	----------	----------	----
Fairfield University	18	23	XXXXXXX	XXXXXX-XX-	XX-------	XXXXX-----	----
Fairleigh Dickinson University	12	6	-------	--------X	X-X-------	---XX-X---	----
Fairmont State College	07	9	-------	----------	-----X-X-X	X-X--X-X--	----
Fayetteville State University	34	1	---X---	----------	----------	----------	-XXX
Ferris State University	07	1	-------	----------	-X--------	----------	----
Ferrum College	20	16	XXX----	XXXXXXXXXX	XX---X----	----------	----
Finlandia University	20	15	---X---	X--XX-----	------X-XX	--X-XXXXXX	X---
Fisk University	35	34	-XXX---	XX-XXXXXXX	XXXXX--XX	XXXXXXXXXX	XXXX
Fitchburg State College	07	1	-------	----------	--------X	----------	----
Florida A & M University	34	2	-------	----------	----------	---XX-----	----
Florida Atlantic University	08	1	-200x--	---199x---	-X---198x--	---------	196x
Florida Gulf Coast University	09	2	-------	X-X-------	---------	---------	----

231

Institution	Strat Cell	# of Years	−200x−− 6543210	−−−199x−−− 9876543210	−−−198x−−− 9876543210	−−−197x−−− 9876543210	196x 9876
Florida Institute of Technology	13	1	−−−−−−	−−−−−−−−−	−−−−−−−−X−	−−−−−−−−−	−−−−
Florida Southern College	22	7	X−X−−XX	X−X−X−−−−−	−−−−−−−−−−	−−−−−−−−−−	−−−−
Florida State University	03	21	X−−X−−−	−−XXXXXXX−	XXXXXXXXX−	−−−−−−−−−−	XX−X
Fontbonne University	17	1	−−−−−−−	−X−−−−−−−−	−−−−−−−−−−	−−−−−−−−−−	−−−−
Fordham University	04	20	XXXXXXX	XXXXXXXXXX	XXX−−−−−−−	−−−−−−−−−−	−−−−
Fort Hays State University	08	7	−−−−−−−	−−−−−−−−−−	−−−−X−XXX−	−−−−−X−X−−	−−−X
Fort Lewis College	07	3	−−−−−−−	−−XXX−−−−−	−−−−−−−−−−	−−−−−−−−−−	−−−−
Fort Valley State University	34	6	−−−−−−−	−−−XXXX−X−	−−−−−−−−−−	−X−−−−−−−	−−−−
Framingham State College	08	17	XX−−−−−	XXX−−−−−X−	X−X−−−−−−−	−−XX−XXXX−	XX−−
Franklin College of Indiana	12	8	−−−−−−−	X−−−−−−−−X	−−−−−−−−XX	XXXX−−−−−−	−−−−
Franklin Pierce College	11	4	−−−X−X−	−−−−−X−−−−	−X−−−−−−−−	−−−−−−−−−−	−−−−
Franklin and Marshall College	14	33	−−−−−−X	XXXXXXXXXX	X−X−XXXXXX	XXXXXXXXXX	XXXX
Free Will Baptist Bible College	20	2	−−−−−−−	−−−−−−XX−−	−−−−−−−−−−	−−−−−−−−−−	−−−−
Freed-Hardeman University	22	38	XXXXXXX	XXXXX−−XXX	XXX−XXXXXX	XXXXXXXXXX	XXX−
Fresno Pacific University	21	8	−−−−X−X	−X−X−X−X−X	−X−−−−−−−−	−−−−−−−−−−	−−−−
Friends University	22	5	−−−−−−−	−XXXX−−−−−	−−−−−−−−−−	−−X−−−−−−	−−−−
Frostburg State University	07	2	−−−−−−−	−−−−−−−−−−	−−−−−−−−−−	−−−−−−XX−−	−−−−
Furman University	14	32	XXXXXXX	XXXXXXXXXX	XXXXX−−XX	XXXX−XXX−−	−−−−
Gallaudet University	11	4	−−−−−−−	−−−−−−−−−−	−−−−−−−−−−	−−−−−−−−−−	XXXX
Gannon University	17	17	XXXX−X−	XXXXX−X−−−	−−−−XXX−−−	−XXX−−−−−−	−−−−
Gardner-Webb University	21	14	−−XXXXX	X−−XXXX−X	XX−−−−−−−−	−−−−−−−−−−	−−−−
Geneva College	22	12	X−X−−−X	−X−X−−X−X	−−−−−−−−X	X−−−−XXX−	−−−−
George Fox University	23	6	−X−−X−X	−X−XX−−−−−	−−−−−−−−−−	−−−−−−−−−−	−−−−
George Mason University	01	7	−X−−−XX	−−−−X−−−−−	−−−−−−−−−−	−−−−−X−X−X	−−−−
George Peabody Coll for Teachers	11	3	−−−−−−−	−−−−−−−−−−	−−−−−−−−−−	−−−−−−−−−−	X−XX
George Washington University	05	3	−−−−−−−	X−−−−−−−−−	XX−−−−−−−−	−−−−−−−−−−	−−−−
George Williams College	12	12	−−−−−−−	−−−−−−−−−−	−−−−X−−−−−	−−XXXX−XXX	XXXX
Georgetown College	22	8	−−−−−XX	XXXXX−X−−−	−−−−−−−−−−	−−−−−−−−−−	−−−−
Georgetown University	06	15	−X−X−X−	XX−XXXXXX	−XX−−−−−−−	−−−−−X−−−−	−−−−
Georgia College & State University	08	1	−X−−−−−	−−−−−−−−−−	−−−−−−−−−−	−−−−−−−−−−	−−−−
Georgia Institute of Technology	03	21	−−XX−X−	−X−−−XXXXX	X−−−XXXX−X	−−−X−X−−−X	−XXX
Georgia Southern University	09	1	−−X−−−−	−−−−−−−−−−	−−−−−−−−−−	−−−−−−−−−−	−−−−
Georgia Southwestern State U	09	14	−−XX−−X	−−−−−−−−−X	−X−X−−−−−−	XXXX−XXXX−	−−−−
Georgia State University	08	1	−−X−−−−	−−−−−−−−−−	−−−−−−−−−−	−−−−−−−−−−	−−−−
Georgian Court College	16	11	XXX−−−−	XXXXX−−−−	−−−−X−−−X−	−−−−−−−−−−	−−−−
Gettysburg College	14	36	XXXXXXX	XXXX−XXXX	XXXXXXX−−−	−XXXXXXXXX	XXXX
Glenville State College	08	1	−−X−−−−	−−−−−−−−−−	−−−−−−−−−−	−−−−−−−−−−	−−−−
Gonzaga University	18	20	XXXX−XX	−−−−X−−XX	−−XX−XXXXX	−−−X−−X−X−	−−XX
Gordon College	13	10	−X−XXX−	−X−−−X−−XX	X−X−−−−−−−	−−−−−−−−−−	−−−−
Goshen College	22	8	X−X−X−X	−X−X−−−−−−	−−−−−X−−−−	−−−−−−X−−−	−−−−
Goucher College	13	17	X−XX−XX	XXXX−−−X−	−XX−−−−−X−	XXX−−−−−−−	−−−−
Grace College	21	13	XXXXXXX	XXXXX−−−−	−−−−−−−−−−	−−−−−−−−−−	−−−−
Grand Canyon University	21	4	−−−−−−−	−−−X−−−X−	−−−−−−−−−−	−−−−−−−−XX	−−−−
Grand Valley State University	09	15	XXXXXXX	XXXXX−XXX	−−−−−−−−−−	−−−−−−−−−−	−−−−
Grand View College	11	9	−X−−−−−	X−−−−−−−−−	−−−−−−−X−X	−−XX−X−X−−	−X−−
Green Mountain College	11	2	XX−−−−−	−−−−−−−−−−	−−−−−−−−−−	−−−−−−−−−−	−−−−
Greensboro College	20	3	−−−−−−−	−−−−−−−−XX	X−−−−−−−−−	−−−−−−−−−−	−−−−
Greenville College	22	8	−−X−X−X	XXXXX−−−−−	−−−−−−−−−−	−−−−−−−−−−	−−−−
Grinnell College	14	24	−−XXXXX	−−X−−−−XX	XXXXXXXXXX	XX−−−−−−−	XXXX
Grove City College	13	1	−−−−−−−	−−−−−−−−−−	−−−−−−−−X−	−−−−−−−−−−	−−−−
Guilford College	23	25	XXXXXXX	XXX−X−−−XX	−XX−−−X−−−	−X−X−−XXX−	XXXX
Gustavus Adolphus College	23	34	XXX−XXX	XXXXXXXXXX	XXXXXXXXXX	XXXXXX−X−X	−−−−
Gwynedd-Mercy College	16	5	XXX−X−−	−−−−−−−−−−	−−−−−−−−−−	−−−−X−−−−	−−−−
Hamilton College	14	34	XXXXXXX	XXXXXXXXXX	XX−−XX−XXX	XXXXXXX−−X	XX−−
Hamline University	23	36	−−XXXXX	XXXXXXXXXX	XXX−−XXXXX	−XXXXXXXXX	XXXX
Hampden-Sydney College	23	24	−−−−−−X	X−−−−−−XX	XXXXXXXXXX	XXXXXXXXXX	−−−−
Hampshire College	13	2	−−−−−−−	−−−XX−−−−−	−−−−−−−−−−	−−−−−−−−−−	−−−−
Hampton University	35	3	−−−−−−−	−−−−X−−−−−	−−−−−−−−−−	−−X−−−−X−	−−−−
Hannibal-LaGrange College	22	28	X−XXXXX	XXXXXXXXX−	−XXX−−−−−−	−X−−XXXXXX	XXX−
Hanover College	23	9	−−−XXXX	XXXX−X−−−−	−−−−−−−−−−	−−−−−−−−−−	−−−−
Harding University	21	14	−−−−−−−	−−−−−−−−−−	−−−−−−−XX−	XXXXXXXXXX	XX−−
Hartwick College	13	12	X−X−XX−	XXXXXXXX−−	−−−−−−−−−−	−−−−−−−−−−	−−−−
Harvard University	06	1	X−−−−−−	−−−−−−−−−−	−−−−−−−−−−	−−−−−−−−−−	−−−−
Harvey Mudd College	14	34	−−X−−XX	XXXXX−XXX	XXXXXXXXXX	XXXXXXX−−	XXXX
Haverford College	14	32	XXXXXXX	−XXXXXXXXX	XXXXX−−−X	−−XX−−XXXX	X−XX
Hawthorne College	15	1	−−−−−−−	−−−−−−−−−−	−−−−−−−−−−	−−−−−−−−X−	−−−−

232

Institution	Strat Cell	# of Years	-200x-- 6543210	---199x--- 9876543210	---198x--- 9876543210	---197x--- 9876543210	196x 9876
Heidelberg College	21	9	------X	XXXX------	---------X	-X-X----X-	----
Hendrix College	23	19	-----XX	XXXXXX----	XX-XXXXXXX	XX--------	----
High Point University	21	15	XX--XXX	XXXXXXXXXX	---------	---------	----
Hilbert College	11	6	-X-----	----XXXXX-	---------	---------	----
Hillsdale College	13	1	-------	----------	--------X-	---------	----
Hiram College	13	32	XXXXXXX	XXXXXXXXXX	XXXX-XXXXX	---X-XXXXX	----
Hobart and William Smith Colleges	13	22	XXXXXXX	XXXXXXXXXX	X---------	---X-XXX--	----
Hofstra University	04	17	--X-X-X	-X-X-X----	-X-----X-X	-XXXXXXXX-	----
Hollins University	13	27	-X-XXXX	XXXXXXXXXX	XXXX--X---	----X----X	XXXX
Holy Family College	16	11	--XX--X	XXXXXXXX--	---------	---------	----
Holy Names College	16	1	X------	----------	---------	---------	----
Holy Redeemer College	19	2	-------	----------	-----X-X--	---------	----
Hood College	13	24	X-X----	-XXXXXXXXX	XXXXXXXXXX	XXXX------	----
Hope College	13	5	--X---X	----------	---------	------XXX-	----
Hope International University	20	3	-----XX	X---------	---------	---------	----
Houghton College	23	5	X------	-----X---X	------XX--	---------	----
Houston Baptist University	22	4	--X-X--	----------	---X------	---------	X---
Howard Payne University	21	2	-------	------XX--	---------	---------	----
Howard University	35	8	X------	---X------	-----X-X--	-XXX------	X---
Humphreys College	15	8	-------	------X-X-	-----XX---	---XX--XX-	----
Hunter College	08	1	-------	----------	---------	---------	-X--
Huntingdon College	23	6	XXXXXX-	----------	---------	---------	----
Huntington University	22	29	XXXXX-X	XXXXXXXXXX	XXXXX---X-	-X-X-XX-X	XX--
Huron University	20	6	-------	----------	---------	--XXX-X---	XX--
Husson College	11	2	-XX----	----------	---------	---------	----
Huston-Tillotson College	35	2	-------	-------X-	---------	---------	-X--
Idaho State University	08	3	-------	----------	---------	---------	XX-X
Illinois College	12	11	XXXXX-X	XX-XXX----	---------	---------	----
Illinois Institute of Art	15	1	--X----	----------	---------	---------	----
Illinois Institute of Technology	14	12	------X	XXX-X---X-	--X------	---------X	XXXX
Illinois State University	08	4	------X	-XXX------	---------	---------	----
Illinois Wesleyan University	14	13	X-XXXXX	XXXXXXX---	---------	---------	----
Immaculata College	11	2	-------	----------	---------	---------	--XX
Immaculata University	16	15	-XX-XXX	XXXXXXXXXX	---------	---------	----
Immaculate Heart College	17	3	-------	----------	---------	--------X-	-X-X
Indiana Institute of Technology	12	2	-------	----X-----	---------	----X-----	----
Indiana U of Pennsylvania	09	2	--X----	-X--------	---------	---------	----
Indiana U-Purdue U-Indianapolis	01	1	-------	-------X--	---------	---------	----
Indiana Wesleyan University	22	7	------X	----------	XX--X---XX	X--------	----
Iona College	16	2	-------	---X------	---------	-----X----	----
Iowa State University	03	34	XX--XXX	XXXXXXXXXX	X-XXXXXXX	XXXXXXXXX-	-X--
Iowa Wesleyan College	21	35	--XXXXX	XXXXXX---X	XXXXXXXXXX	-XXXXXXXXX	XXXX
Ithaca College	13	3	X-X----	----------	---------	--------X-	----
Jackson State University	34	2	-------	----X-----	---------	-X-------	----
Jacksonville State University	07	1	-------	--------X	---------	---------	----
Jacksonville University	12	3	-------	-XXX------	---------	---------	----
James Madison University	09	1	-------	----------	---------	-------X-	----
Jewish Theological Sem of America	24	1	-------	--X-------	---------	---------	----
John Brown University	13	16	-XXXXXX	XXXX------	X-X-X---X-	-X-----X-	----
John Carroll University	18	10	-X-XXXX	XXX-----XX	---------	---------	----
John Jay Coll of Criminal Justice	07	10	-------	----------	-------X-X	XXXXX-XXX-	----
Johns Hopkins University	06	40	-XXXXXX	XXXXXXXXXX	XXXXXXXXXX	XXXXXXXXXX	XXXX
Johnson C Smith University	35	34	------X	XXXXXXXXXX	XXXXXXXXXX	XX-XXXXXXX	XXXX
Johnston College	23	1	-------	----------	---------	-----X----	----
Judson College	12	8	-X--X-X	-XX-X-----	---X-----X	-X--------	----
Juniata College	13	25	XXXXXXX	XXXXXXXXXX	XXX--XXXXX	---------	----
Kalamazoo College	14	17	XXXXX-X	XXXX-X----	--------X	XXXX-X----	----
Kansas City Art Institute	12	14	---XX--	-----X---X	-XXX--XX-X	XXX-X-----	----
Kansas Wesleyan University	20	6	-------	----------	---X------	--------XX	-XXX
Kean University	08	5	-------	----------	-------XX	XXX-------	----
Keene State College	07	12	---X---	------X---	--XXXXXXXX	XX-------	----
Kent State University	01	8	---X---	-X--XXXXXX	---------	---------	----
Kentucky Christian College	21	6	-------	---XXXXXX-	---------	---------	----
Kentucky State University	08	4	-------	----------	---------	-----X-X--	-X-X
Kentucky Wesleyan College	21	20	XXXXXXX	XXX--X----	------XXXX	X--X-----X	-XX-

Institution	Strat Cell	# of Years	-200x-- 6543210	---199x--- 9876543210	---198x--- 9876543210	---197x--- 9876543210	196x 9876
Kenyon College	14	21	X---X-X	XXXXXXX--	XXXXXXXX-	X--------	----
Kettering University	13	34	XXXXXX	XXXX----XX	XXXXXX-X-X	XXXX-XXXX	XXXX
Keystone College	11	23	--X-X--	----------	XXXXXXXXXX	X---XXXXXX	XXXX
King College	23	18	XXXXXX	XXXXXXX--	-X-X------	-X--------	----
King's College (NY)	12	3	-------	----------	XXX-------	----------	----
King's College (PA)	17	13	-------	X-----XXXX	XXXXX-XXX-	----------	----
Kirkland College	14	9	-------	----------	----------	--XXXXXX-X	XX--
Knox College	13	21	--XXXXX	XXXXXX-XX-	--XXXX----	XXXX------	-X--
Knoxville College	35	3	-------	----------	----------	X-X-------	-X--
Kutztown U of Pennsylvania	08	8	XXXXXX	X---------	----------	----------	----
La Roche College	16	4	-------	-------XX	----------	-------X--	X---
La Salle University	18	9	-------	--------X-	X-X-XXXXX-	-----X----	----
La Sierra University	04	1	------X	----------	----------	----------	----
Lafayette College	14	39	XXXXXX	XXXXXXXXXX	XXXXXXXXXX	XXXXXXXXXX	XX--
Laguna College of Art & Design	15	2	XX-----	----------	----------	----------	----
Lake Erie College	12	4	-------	----------	----------	--XXXX---	----
Lake Forest College	13	39	XXXXX-	XXXXXXXXXX	XXXXXXXXXX	XXXXXXX-XX	XXXX
Lakeland College	21	15	----XXX	X---------	---------X	-X-X-X-XXX	XXXX
Lamar University	07	4	-------	---------X	-XXX------	----------	----
Lambuth University	22	5	------X	XXX-------	-----X----	----------	----
Lander University	08	14	-------	--------XX	XXXXXXXXX-	X---X-----	----
Lasell College	11	2	--XX---	----------	----------	----------	----
Lawrence Technological University	12	2	XX-----	----------	----------	----------	----
Lawrence University	14	17	XX-XXXX	XX-X-X--X-	XXX-X-XX--	----------	----
Le Moyne College	18	33	XXXXXX	XX--XX--XX	XXX--XXXXX	-XXXXXXXXX	XX-X
LeTourneau University	13	4	----X-X	--XX------	----------	----------	----
Lebanon Valley College	23	40	XXXXXX	XX-XXXXXXX	XXXXXXXXXX	XXXXXXXXXX	XXXX
Lee University	22	3	------X	-X-X------	----------	----------	----
Lehigh University	05	13	-X-----	-XXX------	-----XXXX	XXXX------	----
Lenoir-Rhyne College	21	20	X------	XXX-XXXXX	-XX--X----	--XXXXXXX-	----
Lesley University	11	19	---XXX-	XXXXXXX---	--XXXXXXXX	X---------	----
Lewis University	17	22	XXXXXX	XXXXX--XXX	XXX-XXXX--	----------	----
Lewis and Clark College	13	27	XXXXXX	XX----XXX-	--XXXXXX--	XXXXXXX-XX	----
Lincoln Christian College	20	1	-X-----	----------	----------	----------	----
Lincoln Memorial University	12	2	-------	--X----X--	----------	----------	----
Lincoln University (MO)	07	1	------X	----------	----------	----------	----
Lincoln University (PA)	35	20	--XX---	----X-XXXX	XXXXXX-XX-	-------XXX	XX--
Lindenwood University	22	12	-------	----------	----------	-XXXXXXXXX	XXX-
Linfield College	23	13	-----X-	---X------	-X-X-XXXXX	XXX---X---	----
Lipscomb University	22	3	----X--	X---------	----------	----------	-X--
Livingstone College	35	2	-------	----------	----------	----X-X--	----
Lock Haven U of Pennsylvania	09	14	-------	----------	X--X----XX	XX-X-XXXXX	-XX-
Long Island U-Southampton	12	4	-------	----------	--------X-	X-XX------	----
Longwood University	09	31	X-XXXXX	XXX-XXXXXX	XXX-----X-	XXXXXXXXXX	XX--
Loras College	17	1	---X---	----------	----------	----------	----
Louisiana College	22	6	-------	----------	--XXXX----	XX--------	----
Louisiana State U and A&M Coll	02	4	----X--	--X-------	----------	----------	-X-X
Louisiana State U-Shreveport	07	2	-------	----------	--------X-	----------	-X--
Louisiana Tech University	08	4	-------	----------	----------	-------X--	-XXX
Loyola College in Maryland	18	29	XXXXXX	XXXXXXXXXX	-XXXXXXXXX	XX-X------	----
Loyola Marymount University	04	18	--XXXXX	XXX-XXXXXX	X-----XXX-	----------	----
Loyola University	18	3	-------	----------	----------	----------	-XXX
Loyola University of Chicago	04	34	X-XXXXX	XXXXXXXXXX	----XXXXXX	XXXXXXXXXX	XX--
Loyola University-New Orleans	05	15	-------	----------	-XXXXXXXXX	XXX--X---X	X---
Lubbock Christian University	22	4	-XX---X	--X-------	----------	----------	----
Luther College	23	23	XXXXX-	XXXXXXX--	-------X-X	XX---XXXXX	----
Lycoming College	22	17	XXXXXX	XXXXXXXXXX	----------	----------	----
Lynchburg College	11	17	--XX-X-	X-X-X-XXXX	XXX-X----X	XX--------	----
Lyndon State College	07	1	-X-----	----------	----------	----------	----
Lynn University	11	8	XXX----	-------XXX	XX--------	----------	----
Lyon College	23	28	XXXXXX	XXXXXXXXXX	-XXXXXXXXX	--X-X-X---	----
MacMurray College	20	22	X-X----	--XXX-XXX-	-----X-X-X	X---XXXXXX	XXXX
Macalester College	14	27	XXXXXX	XXXXXXXXXX	XXXXXXXXX-	------X---	----
Macon State College	10	2	-----X-	X---------	----------	----------	----
Madonna University	16	8	-------	----------	----------	------XXXX	XXXX
Maharishi University of Management	12	3	-------	----------	-X---X----	---X------	----

234

Institution	Strat Cell	# of Years	-200x-- 6543210	---199x--- 9876543210	---198x--- 9876543210	---197x--- 9876543210	196x 9876
Maine Maritime Academy	09	9	XXXXX--	---XX---XX	----------	----------	----
Malone College	22	5	--X-X-X	X---X-----	----------	----------	----
Manchester College	21	23	XXXXXXX	XXX-------	-XXXX-XX--	X-X-X-XXXX	----
Manhattan College	18	30	XXXXXXX	XXX-XXXXXX	XXX-XXXXX	XXXX----X-	----
Manhattanville College	12	16	-------	-----X---X	XXXX-XXX-X	XXXXX-----	-X--
Mansfield U of Pennsylvania	08	7	X-----X	-X---X----	----------	-----XXX--	----
Marian College of Fond du Lac	17	20	X------	---X--X-X-	-------XX-	XXXXXXXXXX	XXXX
Marietta College	12	36	----XXX	XXX-XXXXXX	XXXXXXXXXX	XXXXXXXXXX	XXXX
Marist College	13	8	------X	X--X-----X	X------X--	--X---X---	----
Marlboro College	13	17	----X--	-XX--XX---	--XX------	----XXXXXX	XXXX
Marquette University	04	21	--X----	---X-XXXXX	XXXXXXXXXX	X-XXX-----	----
Mars Hill College	21	19	----XX-	-X--XX-XXX	X--X----XX	XXXXX--XX-	----
Martin Methodist College	24	3	-------	-XXX------	----------	----------	----
Mary Baldwin College	20	20	---X---	-X-X--XXXX	XXXX-X-XXX	-XX-------	-XXX
Mary Washington College	09	2	-------	----------	----------	-----XX---	----
Marygrove College	16	2	-------	----------	----------	---XX-----	----
Maryknoll Seminary	18	3	-------	----------	----------	----------	XXX-
Maryland Institute College of Art	12	13	-X-----	-----XX---	-XX--XXXXX	XX---X----	----
Marymount College (NY)	16	12	-------	-----X--XX	XXXXXXXXX-	----------	----
Marymount College of Kansas	16	15	-------	----------	-XXXXXXXX-	-X------XX	XXXX
Marymount Manhattan College	12	11	XXX---X	XX-----X--	--XX-X----	----X-----	----
Marymount University	16	17	----XXX	XXXX-XXXXX	XX-X-XX---	----------	----
Maryville College	23	13	-X-X-X-	X-XXXX----	--XX----X-	X----X----	----
Maryville Univ. of Saint Louis	13	4	XXXX---	----------	----------	----------	----
Marywood University	17	24	XXX-XX-	XXXX-XX---	-X---XXXXX	----XXXXXX	X---
Mass Col of Pharmacy & Hlth Sci	11	1	-------	-X--------	----------	----------	----
Massachusetts Coll of Liberal Arts	09	5	--X----	------X---	--XX--X---	----------	----
Massachusetts College of Art	09	7	-----X-	--XXXX--XX	----------	----------	----
Massachusetts Inst of Technology	06	2	X-X----	----------	----------	----------	----
Massachusetts Maritime Academy	08	1	-------	--X-------	----------	----------	----
Master's College	23	30	---XXXX	X--X-XX-XX	XXX-XX-XXX	XXXXXXXX-X	-XXX
Mayville State University	07	16	------X	X--XXXXXXX	--X-XXXXXX	----------	----
McKendree College	23	7	X------	--X-------	----------	XXXXX-----	----
McMurry University	22	3	-------	X---XX----	----------	----------	----
McPherson College	20	36	XXX-XXX	XXXXXXXXXX	XXXX-XXXXX	X--XX-XXXX	XXXX
Medaille College	11	14	X-X---X	X-X-------	------XX--	-X---XXXXX	-X--
Medgar Evers College	34	2	-------	----------	----------	--XX------	----
Mercer University	23	13	-XXXXX-	XXXXXXXX--	----------	----------	----
Mercy College	12	1	-------	----------	----------	-X--------	----
Mercyhurst College	18	29	XXXXXXX	--XXXXXXXX	XXXXX---X	--XX--XX--	-XXX
Meredith College	12	13	XXXXXXX	XXXXX-----	----------	-----X----	----
Merrimack College	17	13	-------	---X------	---X-XXXXX	X-----XXX-	XX--
Mesa State College	07	2	-------	----------	----------	----------	-X-X
Messiah College	23	15	-XXX-XX	XXXXXXXXX-	-X--------	----------	----
Miami University	03	40	XXXXXXX	XXXXXXXXXX	XXXXXXXXXX	XXXXX-XXXX	XXXX
Michigan State University	02	4	-------	----------	----------	----------	XXXX
Michigan Technological University	09	7	X-X-X-X	-XX---X---	----------	----------	----
MidAmerica Nazarene University	21	16	-------	--X-XXXX--	---XX---XX	XXXXXXX---	----
Middlebury College	14	24	XXXXXX-	XX-XXXXXXX	XX--------	------XX-X	XXXX
Midway College	22	22	--X----	---X-XXXXX	XXX-X-XXX-	X--X--XXXX	XX--
Millersville U of Pennsylvania	09	5	--X-X-X	-X-----X--	-X--------	----------	----
Milligan College	13	27	-------	----XXXXXX	XXXXXXXXX-	XXXXX-XXXX	XX--
Millikin University	23	5	-X---XX	XX--------	----------	----------	----
Mills College	13	19	------X	XXXXXXX-X-	---XXX----	X-XX-----X	-XXX
Millsaps College	23	3	-------	----------	----------	-------X--	XX--
Milton College	11	2	-------	----------	----------	-------X--	X---
Milwaukee Inst of Art and Design	15	3	---XXX-	----------	----------	----------	----
Milwaukee School of Engineering	13	6	-X-X-X-	X-XX------	----------	----------	----
Minneapolis Coll of Art and Design	12	2	-------	----------	--XX------	----------	----
Minnesota State University-Mankato	08	2	------X	----X-----	----------	----------	----
Minot State University	08	2	-------	---XX-----	----------	----------	----
Mississippi College	23	3	------X	X---------	----------	--X-------	----
Mississippi University for Women	09	3	-------	----XXX---	----------	----------	----
Missouri Southern State College	08	8	--XXXXX	XXX-------	----------	----------	----
Missouri Valley College	20	15	-----XX	XX-XXXXXX-	----------	XXX-XX----	----
Molloy College	16	12	XXXXXX-	XXXXX-----	-------X-	----------	----
Monmouth College	22	17	--XX--X	----------	-----XXXX	X---X-XXXX	XXXX
Monmouth University	12	23	XXXXXXX	XXXXXXXXXX	XXXXX-----	----------	----

Institution	Strat Cell	# of Years	-200x-- 6543210	---199x--- 9876543210	---198x--- 9876543210	---197x--- 9876543210	196x 9876
Montana State U-Billings	07	2	-------	----------	--------X-	X---------	----
Montana State U-Northern	07	1	-------	----------	X---------	----------	----
Montana State University	02	18	-------	-----X-X-X	X--XXX----	---XXXXXX	XXXX
Montana Tech of the U of Montana	09	2	-------	----------	------XX--	----------	----
Montclair State University	08	5	XX---X-	----------	----------	----------	--XX
Monticello College	11	3	-------	----------	----------	----------	XXX-
Montreat College	21	6	----XXX	---XXX----	----------	----------	----
Montserrat College of Art	12	1	---X---	----------	----------	----------	----
Moore College of Art and Design	11	10	XX-XX--	-X-XXXX---	--X-------	----------	----
Moravian College	23	11	XXX-XXX	X--XX-XX--	----------	----------	----
Morehead State University	07	3	-X-----	---X------	-X--------	----------	----
Morehouse College	35	27	XX--XXX	X-XXXXXX--	-XXXXXXXX	X--X------	-XXX
Morgan State University	34	11	X------	----------	------XXX	XXXX--X---	--XX
Morningside College	22	35	XXXXXXX	XXXXXXXXXX	XXXXXXX-X	XXXX-X-XXX	X---
Morris Brown College	35	4	-------	----------	----------	------XXX-	-X--
Mount Aloysius College	16	2	-------	XX--------	----------	----------	----
Mount Holyoke College	14	22	XX-----	---------X	----XX-XXX	XXXXXXXXXX	XXXX
Mount Ida College	12	1	---X---	----------	----------	----------	----
Mount Mary College	17	4	--XX---	X--X------	----------	----------	----
Mount Mercy College	17	2	-------	------X---	----------	---X------	----
Mount Olive College	20	30	---XXXX	XXXXXX-XX	-XXXXXX--	-XXXXXXXXX	X---
Mount Saint Mary College	12	29	XXXXXXX	XX-XXXXX-	X-XX-X--XX	XX-XXXXXX-	----
Mount Saint Mary's College (CA)	17	18	XXX-XXX	XX-XXXX---	--XXXX-X-	-X--------	----
Mount Saint Mary's College (MD)	18	38	XXXXXXX	XXXXXXXXXX	XXXXXXXXXX	XXX-XXXXXX	XX--
Mount Saint Scholastica College	16	4	-------	----------	----------	-------XX	XX--
Mount Senario College	16	1	-------	-X--------	----------	----------	----
Mount Union College	23	5	-------	----------	--------X	---XXXX---	----
Mount Vernon College	11	10	-------	----------	-X--XXXXX	XXX-------	----
Mount Vernon Nazarene University	22	23	XX-XXXX	XXXXXX----	XXXX-XXXX	XX--------	----
Muhlenberg College	23	17	X--XXX-	XXXXXXXXXX	X-X----X-	----------	----
Mundelein College	12	9	-------	--------X	-XXXX-X---	-X--XX----	----
Muskingum College	22	6	-------	----------	X---X-----	--XXXX----	----
Myers University	15	1	-------	----------	----------	----X-----	----
Naropa University	15	1	X------	----------	----------	----------	----
Nasson College	12	1	-------	----------	----------	--X-------	----
National-Louis University	11	9	-------	----------	----------	XX-X--X-X-	XXXX
Nazareth College	11	6	-------	----------	----------	----X--X--	XXXX
Nazareth College of Rochester	13	28	----X-X	XX-XXXXXX-	XX--XXXXXX	-X---XXXXX	XXXX
Nebraska Methodist College	24	1	--X----	----------	----------	----------	----
Nebraska Wesleyan University	23	6	----X--	---------X	-----XXXX	----------	----
Neumann College	16	13	XXXX-X-	XX--XXX-XX	X---------	----------	----
New College of Florida	09	9	X-X-X--	------X---	--XXX-----	-------XX-	----
New England College	11	3	-----X-	--------X	-X--------	----------	----
New Jersey City University	07	3	-------	XXX-------	----------	----------	----
New Jersey Institute of Technology	09	23	-------	--XXXXXXXX	X-X--X----	XXX-XX-XXX	XXXX
New Mexico Highlands University	07	2	-------	-----XX---	----------	----------	----
New Mexico State University	01	3	-------	----------	----------	----------	X-XX
New York University	05	2	X----X-	----------	----------	----------	----
Newberry College	20	1	-------	---X------	----------	----------	----
Niagara University	17	7	--X----	-X-XX-X--X	X---------	----------	----
Nicholls State University	09	1	-------	-------X-	----------	----------	----
North Carolina A & T State U	34	15	-------	------XXX-	--X----X-X	XXXXXXXXX-	----
North Carolina Central University	34	1	-------	X---------	----------	----------	----
North Carolina School of the Arts	09	1	-------	--X-------	----------	----------	----
North Carolina Wesleyan College	20	15	------X	---XX---XX	--------X	XX---XXXXX	XX--
North Central College	23	13	---XXXX	XX-XXXX-XX	X---------	----------	----
North Central University	22	5	-------	XXX-XX----	----------	----------	----
North Dakota State University	02	17	-XXX--X	X-XXX--X--	X---X----X	---X-X--X-	--XX
North Georgia College & State U	09	7	---X-XX	XXXX------	----------	----------	----
North Greenville College	21	16	--X----	XXX-------	--------X-	XXXXX---X	XXXX
North Park University	22	2	-------	-------XX	----------	----------	----
Northeastern Illinois University	07	3	-------	----------	-------X--	X-X-------	----
Northeastern State University	07	15	-------	--XXXXXXXX	----XXXXX	---X--X---	----
Northeastern U-Burlington	04	2	-------	----------	----------	----------	-XX-
Northeastern University	04	27	XXXXX-X	XXXXX-----	-X-X-XX-X-	X-XX--XXXX	XXXX
Northern Arizona University	01	2	X-X----	----------	----------	----------	----
Northern Illinois University	01	30	XX--XXX	XXXXXXXXXX	XXXXXXXXXX	XXXXX-----	----

236

Institution	Strat Cell	# of Years	−200x−− 6543210	−−−199x−−− 9876543210	−−−198x−−− 9876543210	−−−197x−−− 9876543210	196x 9876
Northern Kentucky University	07	1	X------	----------	----------	----------	----
Northern Michigan University	08	1	-------	----------	----------	--------X-	----
Northland College	13	12	X------	----------	----------	XX-X-X-XXX	XXXX
Northwest Christian College	21	7	-XXX--X	X-XX------	----------	----------	----
Northwest Missouri State U	08	33	XXXXXXX	XXXXXXX-XX	XXXXXXXXXX	XXX--X----	XX-X
Northwest Nazarene University	22	7	---X--X	XXXXX-----	----------	----------	----
Northwest University	21	7	XXX--X-	---XX-----	----------	-----X----	----
Northwestern College (IA)	23	18	X-X-X--	-------XXX	XXX-XX--XX	XX-XXX----	----
Northwestern College (MN)	12	6	X---X-X	-X-X-X----	----------	----------	----
Northwestern University	06	36	X-XX-XX	XXXX-XXXXX	XXXXXXXXXX	XXXXXXXX-X	-XXX
Notre Dame College (NH)	16	14	-------	XXXXXXX-X-	XX--XXXX--	----------	----
Notre Dame College (OH)	17	14	-XX-X--	XXXXX-X---	---------X	XXX-------	----
Notre Dame de Namur University	16	14	X-X--X-	---XXX-XXX	X--X------	----------	-XXX
Nova Southeastern University	12	3	XXX----	----------	----------	----------	----
Nyack College	21	6	----X--	X---X-----	-X-X-X----	----------	----
Oakland City University	20	3	-------	----------	-X--------	----------	--XX
Oakland University	08	35	X-XXXXX	XXXXXXXXXX	XXXXXXXXXX	-X-XXX-X--	XXXX
Oberlin College	14	28	X-XXXXX	X--XXXXXXX	-XXXXXXX-X	-----XX---	XXXX
Occidental College	13	27	X-----X	-XX-XXXXXX	X-XXX--X--	-XXXXXXXX-	-XXX
Ohio Dominican University	16	37	--XXXXX	-XXXXXXXXX	XXXX-XXXX-	XXXXXXXXXX	XXXX
Ohio Northern University	23	4	--XX---	----------	----------	-------X-X	----
Ohio State University	02	34	----XXX	XXXXXXXXXX	XXXXXXXXXX	XXXXXX-X--	XXXX
Ohio State University-Lima	08	3	-------	---X-X----	----------	----------	----
Ohio State University-Mansfield	08	1	-------	----------	---------X	----------	----
Ohio State University-Marion	07	7	-------	---------X	X---XXX-XX	----------	----
Ohio State University-Newark	08	1	-------	----------	---------X	----------	----
Ohio University	02	3	X-----X	----------	----------	----------	-X--
Ohio Wesleyan University	23	17	-------	----------	-XXXXXXXXX	XXX-XXXXX-	----
Oklahoma Baptist University	23	2	-------	----------	----X-----	--X-------	----
Oklahoma Christian University	23	8	----XXX	----------	----------	---X---XXX	X---
Oklahoma City University	22	3	XX-----	----------	----X-----	----------	----
Oklahoma State U	03	15	X-X-X-X	X--XX-----	--XX------	------XXX-	-XXX
Oklahoma Wesleyan University	22	3	X-XX---	----------	----------	----------	----
Old Dominion University	08	3	-------	----------	----------	------XXX-	----
Olivet College	11	1	-------	------X---	----------	----------	----
Oral Roberts University	12	7	-------	----------	---------X	XXXXXX----	----
Oregon Institute of Technology	08	4	---X-X-	X--X------	----------	----------	----
Oregon State University	02	2	XX-----	----------	----------	----------	----
Otis College of Art and Design	12	4	XX-XX--	----------	----------	----------	----
Ottawa University	21	11	-------	----------	----------	XXXX-XXXXX	XX--
Otterbein College	22	19	X------	-------XX-	XXXXXXXXXX	X-XXXXX---	----
Ouachita Baptist University	21	3	-------	---XXX----	----------	----------	----
Our Lady of the Lake University	16	15	X-X-X--	X--X--X--X	-X--X-----	-----X--XX	X-XX
Oxford College of Emory U	23	4	-XXXX--	----------	----------	----------	----
Pace University	12	11	---XXX-	-X--------	-X---X---X	-X-----XX-	X---
Pace University-White Plains	12	5	-------	---------X	XXX-------	---X------	----
Pacific Lutheran University	23	2	XX-----	----------	----------	----------	----
Pacific Northwest College of Art	15	3	---XXX-	----------	----------	----------	----
Pacific Union College	22	9	-X-----	XX-X-XXX--	X---------	----X-----	----
Pacific University	13	19	---XXX-	--X-X-XX--	----X-XXX-	XXXXXXXX--	----
Paine College	35	1	-------	----------	--X-------	----------	----
Palm Beach Atlantic University	22	7	X----XX	X--X-XX---	----------	----------	----
Park University	21	6	-------	----------	-X---X----	--XX------	-XX-
Parks College of St Louis U	15	3	-------	----------	--------X-	X---X-----	----
Parsons College	23	4	-------	----------	----------	-------X-X	XX--
Peace College	20	3	X--XX--	----------	----------	----------	----
Penn State Erie-The Behrend Colleg	09	11	X-X--XX	----------	-XX--XXX--	--XX------	----
Penn State U-McKeesport	10	6	-------	----------	----X--X--	XXXX------	----
Penn State U-Wilkes-Barre	10	18	-------	XX-----X--	XXXXXXXXXX	XXXX----X-	-X--
Penn State U-Worthington/Scranton	08	16	-------	----------	XXXXXXXXXX	XXXXX---X-	----
Pennsylvania College of Technology	10	10	-------	--X-X--X-X	X--XX-----	------XX--	X---
Pennsylvania State University	03	8	-------	----------	XXXX------	XX-X------	---X
Pepperdine University	23	21	---XXXX	XXXXXXXXXX	X---------	--X-XXX---	XX--
Peru State College	07	10	XXXXX--	----------	----------	-X--------	XXXX
Pfeiffer University	20	2	-------	----------	----------	----XX----	----
Philadelphia Biblical University	12	8	-------	-X--------	--XX------	--XX----XX	X---

237

Institution	Strat Cell	# of Years	-200x-- 6543210	---199x--- 9876543210	---198x--- 9876543210	---197x--- 9876543210	196x 9876
Philadelphia University	12	21	X-X-X-X	-X-X-XXXXX	X--XXXXXXX	XX-------	----
Philander Smith College	35	12	X------	X-XXX--X-X	----------	------X-XX	XX--
Phillips University	21	3	-------	-------X-	----------	-----XX---	----
Pikeville College	20	4	-------	----------	-XXXX-----	----------	----
Pine Manor College	11	20	---X-XX	--X-------	-X-XX-XXX-	X-XXXXXXX	-X--
Pittsburg State University	08	4	-------	----------	------XXXX	----------	----
Pitzer College	13	13	---XXXX	--X-------	-XXXX--X-	--X------	-X--
Point Loma Nazarene University	21	11	XX-XXXX	XXXXX-----	----------	----------	----
Point Park University	11	19	XXXXX-X	XXXXXXXXX-	XXX-------	----------	----
Polytechnic University	13	24	XX-XX-X	XX--X-XXXX	X---------	-X-XX-XXXX	XXXX
Pomona College	14	13	X---X--	XXXX-X-XX-	-X-X-----	---X-----	-X--
Post University	11	4	XXX----	X---------	----------	----------	----
Pratt Institute	04	5	----X--	X---------	----------	----------	-XXX
Presbyterian College	23	18	-XXXX-X	-XXX---XXX	XXXX--X--X	---X-----	----
Prescott College	13	2	-------	----------	----------	------XX--	----
Presentation College	19	5	-------	-XXX-XX---	----------	----------	----
Princeton University	06	33	-------	XXXXXXXX-	XXXXXXXXX	XXXXXXXXX	XXXX
Principia College	23	1	-X-----	----------	----------	----------	----
Providence College	18	12	XXXXXXX	XXX-------	----------	------X-X-	----
Purdue University	02	6	XXXXXX-	----------	----------	----------	----
Queens University of Charlotte	21	11	-------	------XXX	X------X-X	-XXXX----	----
Quincy University	18	11	-------	--X-----X-	--XX-XXXXX	XX-------	----
Quinnipiac University	12	12	--XXXXX	XXXXXXX---	----------	----------	----
Radcliffe College	14	1	-------	----------	----------	----------	-X--
Radford University	08	3	-----X-	XX-------	----------	----------	----
Ramapo College of New Jersey	09	17	XXXXXXX	XXX--XXXX-	XX--------	-------X--	----
Randolph-Macon College	22	11	-------	----------	--XXXX--XX	----XXXXX-	----
Randolph-Macon Woman's College	23	38	XXXXXXX	XXXXXXXXXX	XXXXXXXXXX	XXXXXXXXXX	-X--
Reed College	14	23	--XXXXX	XXXXXXXXXX	-X------X-	--X-X-XX--	XX--
Regis College	11	40	XXXXXXX	XXXXXXXXXX	XXXXXXXXXX	XXXXXXXXXX	XXX-
Regis University	18	17	-XXXXXX	XXX-XXXX-X	-----X-X-X	----------	----
Reinhardt College	15	20	X--X---	X-XXXXXXX	XX-X------	---XXXXX-X	----
Rensselaer Polytechnic Institute	05	16	XXXXXX-	X------XX-	X--------X	--XXX-XX--	----
Rhode Island College	07	37	XXXXXXX	-XXXX-XXXX	-XXXXXXXXX	XXXXXXX-XX	XXXX
Rhode Island School of Design	13	31	XXXXXXX	XXXXXXXXXX	XXXXXXXXXX	--XX------	-X-X
Rhodes College	23	21	XXXXXX-	XXXXXXXXXX	X-XXX-----	-----X----	----
Rice University	06	21	X-XXXXX	-XXXXXXXX-	----------	XX-X-XXXX-	----
Richard Stockton College of NJ	09	21	XXXXXXX	XXXXXXXXXX	X---------	--XXX-----	----
Rider University	12	38	-XXXXXX	-XXXXXXXXX	XXXXXXXXXX	XXXXXXXXXX	XX-X
Ringling School of Art and Design	15	3	--XX---	----------	X---------	----------	----
Ripon College	13	4	X-X-X-X	----------	----------	----------	----
Roanoke Bible College	24	2	XX-----	----------	----------	----------	----
Roanoke College	23	22	-XXXXXX	XXXXXXXXXX	XXX-X-----	--XX------	----
Robert Morris University	11	17	-XXXXXX	XX--XXXX--	XXX-XX----	----------	----
Roberts Wesleyan College	22	7	------X	----------	XXXXX-----	-----X----	----
Rochester Institute of Technology	13	13	--X-XX-	-XXXX-XXXX	XX--------	----------	----
Rockford College	12	21	----X--	X----XX-XX	XXXX--X---	--XXXXXXXX	--XX
Rockhurst University	18	21	-XXX-XX	X-XX-X----	------X---	XXXXXXX-X	XX--
Rocky Mountain College	21	4	--XX---	-XX-------	----------	----------	----
Roger Williams University	12	2	------X	----------	----------	----------	X---
Rollins College	13	24	-X-X-X-	X-X--XX-XX	XXXXXXXXXX	--------X	XXXX
Rose-Hulman Inst of Technology	14	7	----XX-	XXXXX-----	----------	----------	----
Rosemont College	17	17	XXXXX--	XXXXX-XXXX	X---------	---XX-----	----
Rowan University	09	7	-X--X--	--X-------	XXXX------	----------	----
Russell Sage College	12	27	-XX---X	--XXXX--XX	XX-XXXXXX	XXXXXXXXX-	----
Rutgers University-Camden	08	10	X------	------X-X-	---XXXX-X-	-XX------	----
Rutgers University-New Brunswick	03	8	XXXXX--	XXX-------	----------	----------	----
Rutgers University-Newark	01	8	X-X----	XX--X-----	----------	-XXX-----	----
Sacred Heart University	17	17	XXXXXXX	XXXXX-XXXX	----------	----X----	----
Saginaw Valley State University	08	2	-------	----X-----	----------	-X-------	----
Saint Alphonsus College	19	1	-------	----------	----------	X--------	----
Saint Ambrose University	17	3	-------	---XXX----	----------	----------	----
Saint Andrews Presbyterian College	21	28	XX--XXX	XXXXXX--XX	XXXXX-XXXX	X-XXXXX---	----
Saint Anselm College	18	8	-XXX-X-	XX-----X--	----------	-------XX-	----
Saint Benedict College	18	2	-------	----------	----------	----------	XX--

238

Institution	Strat Cell	# of Years	-200x-- 6543210	---199x--- 9876543210	---198x--- 9876543210	---197x--- 9876543210	196x 9876
Saint Bonaventure University	17	14	X-XXXXX	XXXXXXX--	----------	----------	----
Saint Edward's University	18	24	--XXXX-	------XXX-	XX--XXX---	XXXX-XX-XX	XXXX
Saint Francis College	16	7	XXXXXXX	----------	----------	----------	----
Saint Francis University	17	9	-------	XXXX---X--	-----X--X-	-XX-------	----
Saint John College	17	8	-------	----------	----------	-----XXXXX	XX-X
Saint John Fisher College	16	20	XXXXXXX	XX--X-XX--	-X--------	-------XXX	XXXX
Saint John's College (KS)	13	13	-------	----------	----XXXXXX	XXXXXXX---	----
Saint John's College (NM)	14	1	-------	----------	----------	--------X-	----
Saint John's University (MN)	18	31	-----XX	X-XXXXXXX	XXXXX--XXX	XXXXXXXXXX	XX--
Saint John's University (NY)	04	4	X--XX--	----X-----	----------	----------	----
Saint John's University-Queens	04	11	XXXXXXX	-X--------	----------	-----XXX--	----
Saint Joseph College	16	5	-X-----	--XXXX----	----------	----------	----
Saint Joseph's College	17	24	-------	----XXXXX-	X---XXXXXX	XXX-X-XXXX	XXXX
Saint Joseph's College of Maine	17	2	-XX----	----------	----------	----------	----
Saint Joseph's University	18	17	X---XXX	XXXX--XXX-	XX--------	-----XXXX-	----
Saint Lawrence University	13	23	XXXXXXX	XXXXXXXX-	XXX-X--X--	-X------X-	----
Saint Leo University	16	10	-XXXX--	--------XX	XXXX------	----------	----
Saint Louis College of Pharmacy	13	7	-------	---XXXX-XX	-X--------	----------	----
Saint Louis University	05	7	-------	----------	----------	----X--X-X	XXXX
Saint Martin's College	17	1	-------	----------	----------	-----X----	----
Saint Mary of the Plains College	16	11	-------	--------X-	---XX-XXX-	X-XXXX----	----
Saint Mary's College (IN)	18	28	XXXX-XX	XXXXXXXXX	XXXX----XX	X-XXXX----	----
Saint Mary's College of California	18	30	-XXXXX	XXXX-XXXX	XXXXXXX---	---XXXXXX	-X--
Saint Mary's College of Maryland	09	27	XX--X--	-XXXXXXX-	XX---X-XXX	XXXXX---X	-XXX
Saint Mary's Dominican College	17	12	-------	----------	----------	-XXXX-XXXX	XXXX
Saint Mary's U of Minnesota	17	25	-XXXXXX	X-XXXXXXX	XX-----XXX	----XX--X-	XX--
Saint Mary's University	17	15	X-X-XXX	XXXX-X-X--	---X------	X-X-X-----	----
Saint Mary-of-the-Woods College	16	2	-------	---X-X----	----------	----------	----
Saint Meinrad College	16	29	-------	---XXXXXX	XXXXXXXX-X	XXX-XXXXX	XXXX
Saint Michael's College	18	6	XX----X	X---------	XX--------	----------	----
Saint Norbert College	18	26	XXXXXXX	--XXXXXXX	----------	X-XXXX--XX	XXXX
Saint Olaf College	23	7	----X--	---X-X----	--XX----X-	X---------	----
Saint Peter's College	16	12	XXX---X	-XXXXX--X-	---------X	X---------	----
Saint Vincent College	17	20	X-XXX-X	XXXXXXXXX	XX-XX--X--	----------	----
Saint Xavier University	17	11	XXXX-XX	X---------	----------	---X---X-X	X---
Salem College	22	24	-------	--------X	XXXXXXXXX	XXXX-XXXXX	XXXX
Salem International University	12	2	-------	----------	----------	X--X------	----
Salem State College	07	3	--XX---	-------X--	----------	----------	----
Salisbury University	09	7	--X----	X---X--X--	X---------	-------XX-	----
Salve Regina University	16	5	-----XX	XX--------	----------	---X------	----
Sam Houston State University	07	2	-------	----------	----------	-----XX---	----
Samford University	23	4	-------	---X-XX-X-	----------	----------	----
San Diego Christian College	20	2	X-X----	----------	----------	----------	----
San Luis Rey College	18	3	-------	----------	----------	----------	-XXX
Santa Clara University	05	24	XXXXXXX	XXXXXXXXX	XXX-X-----	--X--X-X--	----
Sarah Lawrence College	13	19	-XXXXXX	XXXX-X-XXX	--X-------	----XXXX-	----
Savannah State University	34	6	XX-XX--	X---X---X-	----------	----------	----
School of Visual Arts	12	5	XX---XX	-------X--	----------	----------	----
School of the Art Inst of Chicago	12	4	-X-----	--X-----X-	-X-----X--	----------	----
School of the Museum of Fine Arts	15	1	----X--	----------	----------	----------	----
Schreiner University	21	17	X-X-XX-	--XX------	---XX-X--X	XX--X-XXXX	----
Scripps College	14	17	XXXXXX-	--XXX-XX-X	XX----X---	----X-----	-X--
Seattle Pacific University	23	8	XXXXX-X	----------	--------XX	----------	----
Seattle University	18	7	-------	-----X----	-------XXX	----------	X-XX
Seton Hall University	04	8	XXXX-X-	X---------	----------	-----X--X-	----
Seton Hill University	16	16	------X	-XXXXXXXXX	XXXX-X----	---X------	----
Shaw University	35	2	-------	------X---	----------	---X------	----
Sheldon Jackson College	11	2	------X	X---------	----------	----------	----
Shepherd College	09	1	-------	----------	----------	--------X	----
Shippensburg U of Pennsylvania	09	12	----X-X	-X-X---XX-	X---X-XXX-	-------X--	----
Shorter College	22	11	X-X--X-	-X--XXXXX	X---------	----------	----
Siena College	13	8	-----X-	-X-XXXX---	----------	--X---X--	----
Silver Lake College	18	3	-------	----------	--------X	XX-------	----
Simmons College	12	15	----X--	---X-X---X	-XXX----X	XXXXXXX---	----
Simon's Rock of Bard College	13	5	-------	----------	----------	-XX-XXX---	----
Simpson College	23	27	XXXXX-X	X--X-X-XXX	--XX-XXXXX	XXXX--XXXX	----
Simpson University	21	6	X---X-X	-X---X----	----------	-----X----	----
Skidmore College	13	20	---X---	X-X-X-X-XX	XX-XX-XXXX	XXXXX-----	----

Institution	Strat Cell	# of Years	-200x-- 6543210	---199x--- 9876543210	---198x--- 9876543210	---197x--- 9876543210	196x 9876
Slippery Rock U of Pennsylvania	07	12	-XXX---	XXX-XXXXX-	-------X-	----------	----
Smith College	14	24	-XXXX--	-X-XX-X-XX	XXXXXXXXXX	XXXX------	----
Sonoma State University	08	13	XXXXXXX	XXXX-XX---	----------	----------	----
South Carolina State University	34	5	-------	----------	----------	-XXX--X-X-	----
South Dakota Schl of Mines & Tech	09	1	-------	------X---	----------	----------	----
South Dakota State University	01	14	----XXX	XXXXXX-XX	XX--------	----------	----
Southeast Missouri State U	08	6	----X-X	-X---X-X-X	----------	----------	----
Southeastern State College	10	3	-------	----------	----------	-----XX-X-	----
Southeastern University (FL)	24	2	X---X--	----------	----------	----------	----
Southern Arkansas U	07	21	-------	--------XX	XXX-XXXXXX	XXXXXX-XXX	X---
Southern Illinois U-Carbondale	01	4	-------	----------	----------	---------X	XXX-
Southern Illinois U-Edwardsville	08	21	XXXXXXX	XX------XX	XXXXXXX---	-------XXX	----
Southern Methodist University	04	21	XXXXXXX	XXXXXXXXXX	X---------	----X-----	XX--
Southern Nazarene University	21	9	X-X-X-X	---X-X----	----------	--XXX-----	----
Southern New Hampshire University	11	3	XX-----	----------	----------	------X---	----
Southern U & A&M Coll-Baton Rouge	34	6	-------	-----XXXX-	----------	------XX--	----
Southern University-New Orleans	34	1	-------	----------	--------X	----------	----
Southern Utah University	08	3	---X-XX	----------	----------	----------	----
Southern Wesleyan University	21	7	--X-X-X	---XXXX---	----------	----------	----
Southwest Baptist University	21	2	X-X----	----------	----------	----------	----
Southwest Minnesota State U	08	4	-------	-----X----	----------	--------XX	-X--
Southwest Missouri State U	09	5	---XXXX	X---------	----------	----------	----
Southwestern Adventist College	21	1	-------	--------X-	----------	----------	----
Southwestern College	22	8	-------	----------	-X--X-----	XXXXXX----	----
Southwestern Oklahoma State U	08	2	-------	--XX------	----------	----------	----
Southwestern University	23	32	XXXXXXX	XXXXXXXXXX	XXXXXXXXXX	XXXXX-----	----
Spalding University	16	8	-------	-----X----	----XX----	-------XX-	-XXX
Spelman College	35	37	XXXXXXX	XXXXXXXXXX	XXXX-XXXX	XX-XXXXXXX	XX--
Spring Arbor University	21	23	-----X-	XXXXXXXXXX	XXX-XXXXX	XXX-------	----
Spring Hill College	18	33	---XXXX	XXXX---XXX	--XXXXXXXX	XXXXXXXXXX	XXXX
Springfield College	11	17	X-----X	-XX-XXXXXX	X---------	-------X-X	XXXX
Stanford University	06	28	---XXXX	XXXXXXXXXX	XXXXXXXXXX	XXX-------	---X
Stephens College	12	30	-X-XX--	---XXXXXXX	-XXXXXXXXX	---XXXXXXX	XXXX
Sterling College	22	6	------X	XX-XXX----	----------	----------	----
Stetson University	13	9	XXX----	-X--------	---X-XX--X	--------X-	----
Stevens Institute of Technology	14	28	-----XX	--X--XX-XX	-XXXXXXXXX	XXXXX--XXX	XXXX
Stillman College	35	2	-------	---------X	X---------	----------	----
Stonehill College	18	2	-X---X-	----------	----------	----------	----
Suffolk University	11	8	XXXXXX-	X---------	----X-----	----------	----
SUNY A & T College-Cobleskill	08	18	-------	----------	-XXXXXXXXX	XXXXXX-X--	--X-
SUNY College of Env Sci & Forestry	09	3	---X---	------X--X	----------	----------	----
SUNY College-Brockport	08	28	XXXXXXX	XXXXXXX-XX	--XXX-X-X-	X--XX--XXX	XX--
SUNY College-Buffalo	08	10	X--XXXX	XX--------	------XXX-	----------	----
SUNY College-Cortland	08	5	-------	----------	----------	------XX--	-XXX
SUNY College-Geneseo	09	35	XXXXXXX	XXXX-X-XX	XXXXXXX-XX	X-XXXXXXXX	XX--
SUNY College-New Paltz	09	7	-----X-	-X--X-X---	X------XX	X---------	----
SUNY College-Old Westbury	07	3	XX-----	----------	----------	----X-----	----
SUNY College-Oswego	09	7	-------	----------	----------	---X-XX---	XXXX
SUNY College-Plattsburgh	08	1	----X--	----------	----------	----------	----
SUNY College-Potsdam	08	22	-XXXXXX	X------XX	-----XXXX-	-XXXXX-X--	-XXX
SUNY College-Purchase	09	4	-------	----X-----	-----XXX--	----------	----
SUNY Institute of Technology	10	3	-XXX---	----------	----------	----------	----
SUNY-Albany	02	2	-------	------X---	----------	-X--------	----
SUNY-Binghamton	03	25	--X--XX	XXXXXXXXXX	XXXXXXXXXX	XX--------	----
SUNY-Stony Brook	03	23	--X--XX	XXXXXXXXXX	XXX--XXXX-	----------	-XXX
SUNY-University at Buffalo	03	23	-XXXXXX	--XXXXXXXX	XXXXXXX-X	----------	----
Susquehanna University	23	31	XXXXXXX	XXXXXXXXXX	XXXXXXXXXX	-----XXXX-	----
Swain School of Design	11	2	-------	----------	--------XX	----------	----
Swarthmore College	14	27	XX----X	--X---X-XX	XXXXXXXXX-	---XXXXXXX	XXXX
Sweet Briar College	13	34	XX-XXXX	XXXXXXXXXX	X----XXXXX	XXXXXXXXXX	XX--
Tabor College	22	9	--XXX-X	--XXXXX---	----------	----------	----
Talladega College	35	15	--X----	----XX----	--X---XX-X	X-X---XXXX	XX--
Tarkio College	21	2	-------	----------	----------	----------	XX--
Tarleton State University	08	1	X------	----------	----------	----------	----
Taylor University	13	15	-XXXXXX	XXX--XXXXX	-X--------	----------	----
Taylor University at Fort Wayne	11	5	--X---X	XX-X------	----------	----------	----
Teikyo Loretto Heights University	11	14	-------	----------	----X--XX-	-X--XXXXXX	XXXX

240

Institution	Strat Cell	# of Years	−200x−− 6543210	−−−199x−−− 9876543210	−−−198x−−− 9876543210	−−−197x−−− 9876543210	196x 9876
Tennessee State University	34	1	-------	----------	----------	--------X-	----
Tennessee Temple University	24	4	X-X-XX-	----------	----------	----------	----
Texas A&M U-Commerce	08	4	-----X-	X----X-X--	----------	----------	----
Texas A&M U-Corpus Christi	01	2	-----X-	-X--------	----------	----------	----
Texas A&M University-Kingsville	07	5	--X--XX	XX--------	----------	----------	----
Texas Christian University	04	39	XXXXXXX	XXXXXXXXXX	XXXXXXXXXX	-XX-XXXXXX	XXXX
Texas Lutheran University	22	3	-------	----------	-XXX------	----------	----
Texas Southern University	34	1	-------	----------	--------X-	----------	----
Texas State University-San Marcos	09	4	-X-X-XX	----------	----------	----------	----
Texas Tech University	02	5	-------	----------	-----X-XX-	----------	--XX
Texas Wesleyan University	21	4	-------	----------	----XXX---	------X---	----
Texas Woman's University	01	2	--X----	----------	----------	-X--------	----
The Evergreen State College	09	1	-------	----------	----X-----	----------	----
The University of Tampa	12	21	XXXXXXX	XXX----XXX	X--XXXXX--	----------	--XX
Thiel College	20	14	---XXXX	---XXXXXX-	-X-----XXX	----------	----
Thomas More College	16	6	-XXXXX-	----------	----X-----	----------	----
Tougaloo College	35	8	-------	---XX-X-XX	-XXX------	----------	----
Towson University	09	16	-X-X-XX	---XXX-XXX	-XXXX-XX--	----------	----
Transylvania University	13	14	------X	XXXXXXX---	----------	--X----XXX	XX--
Trevecca Nazarene University	22	2	-------	-------XX-	----------	----------	----
Trinity Christian College	12	8	X-X-X-X	-X-X-X----	----------	-----X----	----
Trinity College	14	24	XXXXXXX	XXXXX-X--X	XX-X-XXXX-	XXX-------	----
Trinity College of Vermont	16	5	-------	----X--XXX	X---------	----------	----
Trinity International University	22	1	-------	---X------	----------	----------	----
Trinity University (DC)	16	29	---XX--	---X-XXXX	XXXXX-XXX	XX--XXXXXX	XXXX
Trinity University (TX)	23	15	X-X-X-X	-X-X-X---	X-XXX--XX-	----X-X---	----
Truman State University	09	21	-XXXXXX	XXXXXXXXXX	XX-XX-----	----X-----	----
Tufts University	06	1	-------	----------	----------	----------	-X--
Tulane University	05	23	X-XXXXX	X-XX----XX	XXX---XXXX	X--X----X-	-XXX
Tusculum College	11	6	-------	XXXX------	----------	-XX-------	----
Tuskegee University	35	17	--X----	----XXXXXX	XX-XXXXXX-	XX-------	----
U of Akron	01	5	-------	---XX-----	----------	----------	-XXX
U of Alabama	02	6	-X--XXX	X------X--	----------	----------	----
U of Alabama-Birmingham	01	5	-X-X-X-	XX--------	----------	----------	----
U of Alabama-Huntsville	02	9	-------	----------	---XX-----	--XXX-XXXX	----
U of Alaska-Fairbanks	01	1	-------	----------	----------	----------	-X--
U of Arizona	02	5	-------	--------X	XXXX------	----------	----
U of Arkansas-Fayetteville	02	8	-XXXXXX	XX--------	----------	----------	----
U of Arkansas-Little Rock	07	2	-------	----------	X--X------	----------	----
U of Arkansas-Pine Bluff	34	10	X------	----------	-XXXX---X-	-----X-X--	-X-X
U of Bridgeport	11	3	----X--	-X--------	-------X--	----------	----
U of California-Berkeley	03	3	-------	----------	----------	--XXX-----	----
U of California-Davis	03	4	-------	--------X-	-X--------	---X-----	-X--
U of California-Irvine	03	6	-------	----------	--XX------	------X---	-XXX
U of California-Los Angeles	03	25	XXXX-XX	XXXXXX-XXX	XXXXX-X---	----XX---X	--X-
U of California-Riverside	01	15	XXXXXXX	XX--------	-X--------	--------X	XXXX
U of California-San Diego	03	9	XXXXX--	--------X-	-X-X------	----------	-X--
U of California-Santa Barbara	03	5	-------	----------	----------	-----X-XX-	-X-X
U of California-Santa Cruz	03	26	X---X--	-X-X-X-XXX	XXXXXXX--X	-X--XXXXXX	XXX-
U of Central Arkansas	09	1	-------	-X--------	----------	----------	----
U of Central Florida	09	3	----X-X	----------	----------	------X---	----
U of Charleston	11	4	-------	----------	----------	----------	XXXX
U of Chicago	06	3	X-X----	X---------	----------	----------	----
U of Cincinnati	02	1	-------	----------	----------	X---------	----
U of Colorado-Denver	01	2	-------	----------	----------	----X----X	----
U of Connecticut	02	10	-------	-X-X-----X	--X-X-X---	-XXX------	---X
U of Dallas	18	6	-----X-	X-X----X--	----------	----------	X--X
U of Dayton	18	1	-------	----------	----------	-------X-	----
U of Delaware	03	17	-------	----------	--XXXXX-XX	XX-XX-X-X-	XXXX
U of Denver	04	9	-------	--------X-	X---------	-X-X---X--	XXXX
U of Detroit	04	3	-------	----------	----------	----------	-XXX
U of Detroit Mercy	17	3	-------	----------	----------	--------XX	-X--
U of Evansville	23	6	-------	---XX-XXXX	----------	----------	----
U of Findlay	21	5	-------	----------	----XX----	------XXX-	----
U of Florida	03	1	X------	----------	----------	----------	----
U of Georgia	03	9	--------	-----X----	--XXX--X--	------X---	-XXX
U of Hartford	12	7	-------	----------	--XX---XXX	X---------	-X--

241

Institution	Strat Cell	# of Years	-200x-- 6543210	---199x--- 9876543210	---198x--- 9876543210	---197x--- 9876543210	196x 9876
U of Idaho	02	16	-XXXXX	XX-X-XXXX-	----------	-------X--	--XX
U of Illinois-Chicago	09	1	-------	-X--------	----------	----------	----
U of Illinois-Springfield	10	4	-XXXX--	----------	----------	----------	----
U of Illinois-Urbana-Champaign	03	12	----X--	-X---XX--	----------	--XX-XX-XX	XX--
U of Indianapolis	21	4	-------	---XXX----	----X-----	----------	----
U of Iowa	03	4	-------	--X-------	----------	---------X	XX--
U of Kansas	02	1	-------	----------	----------	----------	-X--
U of Kentucky	01	4	-------	----------	----------	-----X---X	-X-X
U of La Verne	11	13	----XXX	XXXXXXXXXX	----------	----------	----
U of Louisville	01	20	X------	-------XX-	-XXXXXXXX	XX-----XXX	XX-X
U of Maine-Augusta	07	3	-------	----------	----------	-------XXX	----
U of Maine-Farmington	08	4	-------	XX--------	----------	-------XX-	----
U of Maine-Fort Kent	07	3	-------	----------	----------	--X---XX-	----
U of Maine-Machias	08	10	-------	---------X	XX-X-XX---	-------XX-	XX--
U of Maine-Orono	01	6	-------	----------	X----XXXX-	-------X--	----
U of Maine-Presque Isle	07	16	---XXXX	XXXXXXX-XX	--X-------	X------X--	----
U of Mary Hardin-Baylor	21	4	--XXX--	----------	-X--------	----------	----
U of Maryland Baltimore County	09	5	-------	----------	----X-----	X--XX-X---	----
U of Maryland College Park	03	1	-------	---------X	----------	----------	----
U of Maryland Eastern Shore	34	1	-------	----------	----------	--X-------	----
U of Massachusetts-Amherst	03	36	X-XXXX-	XXXXXXXXXX	XXXXXXXXX	X-X--XXXXX	XXXX
U of Massachusetts-Boston	01	3	X-XX---	----------	----------	----------	----
U of Massachusetts-Dartmouth	08	5	-------	----------	----X-X---	------X-XX-	----
U of Memphis	08	2	-----X-	----------	X---------	----------	----
U of Miami	05	16	-X-----	----------	--XXXXXXX-	-XXXXXXX--	----
U of Michigan	03	16	-XX--XX	XXX-XXX---	----------	----X----X	XXXX
U of Michigan-Dearborn	09	14	-XXXX-X	XXXX-XXX--	----------	X-----X---	----
U of Michigan-Flint	09	30	XXXXXXX	XXXXXXXXXX	XX---X--XX	XXXXXXX---	----
U of Minnesota-Duluth	01	1	-------	----------	----------	---X------	----
U of Minnesota-Morris	09	4	-------	--X-X---X-	----------	---X------	----
U of Minnesota-Twin Cities	03	5	---X-X-	--X-X-X---	----------	----------	----
U of Mississippi	01	2	-------	----------	----------	----------	X--X
U of Missouri-Columbia	03	10	-------	----X-X---	-X--XXXXXX	X---------	----
U of Missouri-Kansas City	03	19	-------	XXXX----X	XXXXX-X---	--X--XXX-X	XX--
U of Missouri-Rolla	09	18	-------	---XXXXXXX	XXX-----X-	---XXX-X-X	XX--
U of Missouri-St Louis	02	8	-------	----------	---------X	----X-XXXX	XX--
U of Montevallo	08	16	XXXXXXX	XXXXXXXXX-	----------	----------	----
U of Nebraska-Lincoln	02	2	-------	-----X----	----------	----------	--X-
U of Nebraska-Omaha	08	3	--XXX--	----------	----------	----------	----
U of Nevada-Reno	01	6	----X--	----XX----	----------	---X---X--	---X
U of New Hampshire	02	15	-X-X-X-	XX-X---X--	-----X----	--X-XX----	XXXX
U of New Haven	11	1	-------	----------	----------	-X--------	----
U of New Mexico	01	3	-------	------XX--	----------	----------	-X--
U of New Orleans	07	1	-------	----------	----------	----------	-X--
U of North Carolina-Asheville	09	1	X------	----------	----------	----------	----
U of North Carolina-Chapel Hill	03	34	XXXXX--	XXXXXXXXXX	XXXXXXXXX	XX-X-XX-XX	--XX
U of North Carolina-Charlotte	01	2	-------	------X---	----------	----X-----	----
U of North Carolina-Greensboro	08	2	-------	--X--X----	----------	----------	----
U of North Carolina-Wilmington	09	4	X------	---X------	-----X----	--X-------	----
U of North Dakota	01	31	--XXXXX	XXXXXXXX-	-XXXXXXXX	-XXX-XX---	XXX-
U of North Florida	09	1	-----X-	----------	----------	----------	----
U of North Texas	01	1	-X-----	----------	----------	----------	----
U of Northern Colorado	08	1	-------	----------	----------	---------X	----
U of Northern Iowa	09	1	-------	----------	-------X--	----------	----
U of Notre Dame	06	32	XXXXXXX	XXXXXXXXXX	XXXXX-XXXX	X--XXXXX--	----
U of Pennsylvania	06	7	X------	----------	-X--------	---X---X--	-XXX
U of Pittsburgh	03	20	XXXXXXX	--XXXXXXXX	XX---XX---	----------	---X
U of Pittsburgh-Bradford	07	23	X-XXXXX	XXXXXXXXXX	XXXX-X----	-X--X-X---	----
U of Pittsburgh-Greensburg	08	15	-------	---X--XXXX	XXXXXXXXX	----------	----
U of Pittsburgh-Johnstown	08	26	XXXXXXX	XXXXXXXXXX	XXXXXX---	---X---X--	----
U of Portland	18	8	--X-X-X	-XXX--XX--	----------	----------	----
U of Puget Sound	13	6	XXXXXX-	----------	----------	----------	----
U of Redlands	13	33	XXXXXXX	--X--X---X	XXXXXXXXX	XXXXXXXXXX	-XXX
U of Rhode Island	01	6	-------	----X-----	X---------	-XXX-----	---X
U of Richmond	14	23	--XXXXX	XXXXXXXXXX	X-----XXXX	XX-X-----	----
U of Rochester	06	38	XXXXXXX	XXXXXXXXXX	XXX---XXXX	XXXXXXXXXX	XXXX
U of Saint Mary	17	22	------X	XXXX---XX	--XXXXX-X	X-XXXXXX--	----
U of Saint Thomas	18	27	-XXXXXX	XXXXXXXXXX	XXXXXXX-XX	X-X-------	----

Institution	Strat Cell	# of Years	-200x-- 6543210	---199x--- 9876543210	---198x--- 9876543210	---197x--- 9876543210	196x 9876
U of San Diego	05	31	X-XXXXX	XXX-XXXXXX	XX-XXXXXXX	X-XXX-----	-XXX
U of San Francisco	18	7	-X-----	-XX--XXX--	----------	-------X-	----
U of Science and Arts of Oklahoma	08	2	----X--	X---------	----------	----------	----
U of Scranton	18	18	-----X-	X-XXXXXXXX	X--------X	X-XXXXX---	----
U of Sioux Falls	22	7	--X-X-X	-X-X-X----	----------	----X-----	----
U of South Carolina-Aiken	08	16	XX-X---	----XXXXX	XX-------X	XX--XX-X--	----
U of South Carolina-Columbia	02	35	XX--X-X	XXXXXX-XX	XXXXXXXXXX	XXXXX-XX-X	XXXX
U of South Carolina-Upstate	07	2	-------	----------	X--------	-------X--	----
U of South Florida	09	3	-------	----------	--------X	XX--------	----
U of South Florida-St Petersburg	09	1	X------	----------	----------	----------	----
U of Southern California	06	18	-XXXXXX	-XXXXX-XXX	XXXX------	----------	----
U of Southern Indiana	01	1	----X--	----------	----------	----------	----
U of Tennessee-Chattanooga	08	7	-------	---XXXXX--	----------	-------XX-	----
U of Tennessee-Knoxville	02	20	-X-X---	X----XXXXX	X---X----X	XXXXX-X---	-XXX
U of Texas-Arlington	08	1	-------	----------	----------	-X-------	----
U of Texas-San Antonio	08	4	--XXXX-	----------	----------	----------	----
U of Toledo	01	2	-X-----	--------X	----------	----------	----
U of Tulsa	05	2	-------	----------	----------	----------	-X-X
U of Vermont	03	31	XXXXXXX	XX--XXXXXX	XXXXXXXXX-	--XX-----X	XXXX
U of Virginia	03	31	---XXX-	--XXX-XXXX	XXXXXXXXXX	XXXXXXXX--	XX-X
U of Virginia College at Wise	07	6	------X	XXXXX-----	----------	----------	----
U of Washington	03	2	-------	----------	----------	----------	--XX
U of Wisconsin-La Crosse	09	1	-------	----------	----------	----X-----	----
U of Wisconsin-Milwaukee	01	14	--X----	----------	-XXXXX---	--X-XXXXX-	---X
U of Wisconsin-Parkside	08	2	-------	-----X----	----------	----X-----	----
U of Wisconsin-River Falls	09	1	X------	----------	----------	----------	----
U of Wisconsin-Superior	08	2	------X	----------	----------	---X-----	----
U of Wisconsin-Whitewater	08	17	-------	--XXXXX--X	XXXX------	--XX----XX	XXX-
U of Wyoming	02	4	-------	----------	----------	----------	XXXX
U of the Arts	12	16	--XXXXX	XXX-X-----	--X-XXXX--	-------XX-	----
U of the District of Columbia	34	2	-------	----------	----------	-X---X----	----
U of the Pacific	04	28	XX-X-XX	XXXXXXXXXX	-XXXXXXXXX	XXX-------	-X--
U of the Sciences in Philadelphia	13	24	-XX-XX-	X-----X---	--XXXXXXXX	XXXXXXXXXX	----
U of the South	23	21	XXXXXXX	XXXXXXXXXX	X---XX----	-------X--	----
U of the Virgin Islands	34	4	--XXX--	----------	-------X--	----------	----
US Air Force Academy	09	36	-X-XXXX	X-XXXXXXXX	XXXXXXXXXX	XXXXXXXXXX	XX--
US Coast Guard Academy	09	40	-XXXXXX	XXXXXXXXXX	XXXXXXXXXX	XXXXXXXXXX	XXXX
US Merchant Marine Academy	09	17	--XXXXX	-XXXX-XXX-	----------	XX-XX-X---	----
US Military Academy	09	39	XXXXXX-	XXXXXXXXXX	XX-XXXXXXX	XXXXXXXXXX	XXXX
US Naval Academy	09	29	X-XXXXX	XXXX-X----	--XXXXXXXX	XXXXXXXXXX	----
Union College (KY)	20	1	-------	----------	----------	-----X----	----
Union College (NE)	22	12	-------	----------	-------X-X	-X-XX-XXXX	XXX-
Union College	13	24	XXXXX--	X--XXXXX-X	-X-X-XXXXX	XXX-XX----	----
Union University	23	9	X-X-X-X	XXXX----X-	----------	----------	----
Unity College	11	2	-------	----------	--------X	X--------	----
University of Saint Francis	17	22	X-XXXXX	XXXXXXXX-X	XXX------X	----XXX---	----
Upsala College	22	5	-------	----------	----------	------XXX-	XX--
Ursinus College	13	13	---XXXX	-XX-XX----	--XX---XXX	----------	----
Utah State University	02	5	--X--XX	XX--------	----------	----------	----
Utica College of Syracuse U	11	1	-------	X--------	----------	----------	----
Valley City State University	08	12	X-XXXXX	XXXXX-----	----------	----------	----
Valparaiso University	23	35	XX---XX	XX--XXXXXX	XXXXXXXXXX	X-XXXXXXXX	XXXX
Vanderbilt University	06	32	XXXXXX-	XXXXXXXXXX	XXXX-XXXX-	--XX----XX	XXXX
Vanguard U of Southern California	20	2	----XX-	----------	----------	----------	----
Vassar College	14	17	-------	----X--XXX	---XXX----	---XXXXX-X	XXXX
Vaughn Coll of Aeronautics & Tech	11	8	-------	--XXXX----	----------	----X-----	X-XX
Villa Julie College	12	5	XXXX---	----------	----------	X--------	----
Villa Maria College	16	1	-------	----------	----------	--X------	----
Villanova University	05	23	XX-X-X-	-XXXXXXXXX	XXXXX-X--	X-----XX--	----
Virginia Commonwealth University	01	5	-------	----------	-------XX	X-XX------	----
Virginia Intermont College	20	1	-------	----------	--X------	----------	----
Virginia Military Institute	09	26	-------	-------XX	XXXXXXXXX-	XXXXXXXXXX	XXXX
Virginia Polytechnic Inst and St U	03	27	--XXXXX	XXXXXXXXX-	--XXX----X	-XX-XXXXXX	-X--
Virginia State University	34	28	-------	-X--XXXXXX	XXXX-XXXX	XXXXXXXXXX	-XX-
Virginia Union University	35	13	-------	X-XX------	-X------X	--XXX--XX	XX--
Virginia Wesleyan College	23	25	XXXXXXX	XXXXXXXXXX	XXXXXXX--	----------	----

243

Institution	Strat Cell	# of Years	-200x-- 6543210	---199x--- 9876543210	---198x--- 9876543210	---197x--- 9876543210	196x 9876
Viterbo University	17	3	-------	----------	----------	----X-XX--	----
Voorhees College (SC)	35	5	X---X--	-X-X----X-	----------	----------	----
Wabash College	13	28	XXXXXXX	XXXXXXXXXX	------XXXX	XXXX-XXX--	----
Wagner College	22	12	----XXX	XXXX----X	------X-X-	--X-------	----
Wake Forest University	05	19	-XXXXX	XXXXX-X-X	X--X-X--XX	----------	----
Walla Walla College	22	2	-------	----------	----------	---X-X----	----
Walsh University	17	28	XXXXXXX	XXXXXXX--	----X-X--X	XX-XXXXXX	X---
Warner Pacific College	21	2	------X	----------	----------	-X-------	----
Warner Southern College	11	7	----X-X	XX--XXX---	----------	----------	----
Warren Wilson College	13	10	XX--X-X	-X---X-X-X	----------	------XX--	----
Wartburg College	22	3	X-X----	--X-------	----------	----------	----
Washburn University	08	1	-------	----------	----------	----------	---X
Washington & Jefferson College	12	24	--XXXXX	XXXXXXXXXX	XXXXX-XXXX	----------	----
Washington College	13	13	XX-XX--	--X-------	XXXXX----	----------	--XX
Washington State University	01	5	-------	---X-X----	----------	----------	-XXX
Washington University	06	6	---XXX-	----------	----------	----------	-XXX
Washington and Lee University	14	40	XXXXXXX	XXXXX-XXX	XXXXXXXXXX	XXXXXXXXXX	XXXX
Wayland Baptist University	20	3	-------	----------	----------	--------XX	--X-
Wayne State University	01	15	-X-XXXX	--XXXXX-XX	XX--------	--------X-	----
Waynesburg College	21	18	XXXXX--	X--XXXXX--	X---------	-X----XXX-	----
Webb Institute	14	32	XXXXXXX	XXXXXXXXXX	X----XXXXX	XXXXX-XX-	X---
Webster University	13	15	XXXXX-X	XXXXX---X-	----------	----X-X-X-	----
Wellesley College	14	27	X-XXXXX	XXXXXXX---	-XX-XXXXX-	-X-XX---X-	-XXX
Wells College	13	14	XXXX--X	XXXX----X-	XX-X---X--	--X-------	----
Wentworth Institute of Technology	11	21	-X---XX	XXX-XXX-X-	-XX------X	X--X--XXX-	-XXX
Wesleyan College	23	35	XX-XXXX	XXXXXXXXXX	XXXXXXXXXX	XXX--XXX--	-XXX
Wesleyan University	14	36	X-X--XX	XXXXXXXXXX	XXXXXXXXXX	XXXXXXXXXX	XX--
West Chester U of Pennsylvania	08	16	--X-X-X	-X-X-X-X-X	-X-X-X-X-X	XX------X-	----
West Virginia State College	07	6	-------	----------	----------	XXXX------	XX--
West Virginia University	01	3	-------	----------	-------X--	----XX----	----
West Virginia Wesleyan College	21	6	----XXX	XX--------	----------	----X-----	----
Westbrook College	11	3	-------	---XXX----	----------	----------	----
Western Carolina University	08	5	-------	----------	----------	----XXX--X	X---
Western Illinois University	08	10	-------	----------	----------	--X--XXXXX	XXXX
Western Michigan University	08	1	-------	---X------	----------	----------	----
Western New England College	12	26	XXXXXXX	XXXXX-XXXX	------XXXX	-XX----XX-	-X-X
Western New Mexico University	07	4	-------	-------XX-	----------	XX--------	----
Western Washington University	09	7	-------	------XXX-	X---X---X-	---X------	----
Westfield State College	08	4	-------	---------X	----------	-XXX------	----
Westmar University	20	12	-------	--------X-	XXXX---XXX	X---XXX---	----
Westminster College (MO)	23	31	--XXXXX	XXXXXXXXXX	XXXXXXXXXX	XXX-X---X	X---
Westminster College (PA)	22	31	-XXXXXX	XXXXXXXXXX	XXXXXXXXXX	XX---XXX--	----
Westmont College	13	12	--X---X	XXXXXXXXX-	-X--------	----------	----
Wheaton College (IL)	14	15	-X-X-X-	X-X-X-X-X-	X-X-X-X-X-	XX--------	----
Wheaton College (MA)	13	37	XXXXXX-	-X-XXXXXXX	XXXXXXXXXX	XXXXXXX-XX	XXXX
Wheeling Jesuit University	17	17	XX-X--X	---X-XXX--	--XXXX----	-X-XXXX---	----
Wheelock College	12	16	-XXXXXX	X-X--X----	-X----XX-X	XXX-------	----
Whitman College	14	28	XXXXXXX	XXXXX-----	-XX-X-X---	---XXXXXXX	XXXX
Whittier College	12	31	-XXXXXX	XXXXXXXXX-	XXXXXXXX-X	XXXXXXX---	----
Whitworth College	23	13	-X-XXX-	XXXXXX----	---XXX----	----------	----
Widener University	13	4	X-XX---	----------	----------	----X-----	----
Wilberforce University	35	7	-------	----------	XXX------X	XXX-------	----
Wiley College	35	1	-----X-	----------	----------	----------	----
Wilkes University	12	18	XXX-X--	---XXXXXXX	XXXXXXX---	----------	----
Willamette University	13	22	X-XX-X-	---XXXX-XX	XXXX-----X	X-XXXXXXX--	----
William Carey College	22	3	-------	----------	----------	----------	-XXX
William Jewell College	23	13	-----X-	--XXXX----	XXXXXXX---	X---------	----
William Paterson U of New Jersey	08	12	-X-----	----------	-XXXXXXXX-	--XX------	----
William Tyndale College	12	3	--X---X	-X--------	----------	----------	----
William Woods University	22	8	----XX-	XXXX-X---X	----------	----------	----
Williams Baptist College	21	23	--X-X-X	XXXX---XXX	XXX-XXXXXX	XXXX------	----
Williams College	14	41	XXXXXXX	XXXXXXXXXX	XXXXXXXXXX	XXXXXXXXXX	XXXX
Wilmington College	21	7	-----X-	---XXX----	XXX-------	----------	----
Wilson College	12	10	-X-X---	XXXX--X--	-------X--	-X--------	----
Wingate University	11	39	XXXXX-X	XXXXXXXXXX	XXXXXXXXXX	XXXXXXXXXX	XXX-
Winona State University	09	9	-------	X-XXXXXXX	----------	----------	----
Winston-Salem State University	34	25	XXXXXXX	XXXX------	-X-X-----X	XXXXXXX-X-	XXX-

244

Institution	Strat Cell	# of Years	-200x-- 6543210	---199x--- 9876543210	---198x--- 9876543210	---197x--- 9876543210	196x 9876
Winthrop University	08	2	-------	----------	----------	----XX----	----
Wisconsin Lutheran College	23	7	-----XX	XXXXX-----	----------	----------	----
Wittenberg University	23	37	XXXXX--	-XXXXXXXXX	XXXXXXXXXX	XXXXX-XXXX	XXXX
Wofford College	23	36	XXXXXXX	XXXXXXXXXX	X-----XXXX	XXXXXXXXXX	XXXX
Woodbury University	11	3	-------	----X-XX--	----------	----------	----
Worcester Polytechnic Institute	14	28	--XXXXX	XXXXXXXXXX	XX-XXXX-X-	XXXXXX----	----
Worcester State College	07	7	--XXXX-	-XX---X---	----------	----------	----
Xavier University	18	8	-------	----XXX--X	----X-----	------X-X-	X---
Xavier University of Louisiana	35	22	X-XXXXX	----XXXXX-	X-----XXX-	XXXXXX-X--	----
Yankton College	11	5	-------	----------	-----X----	--------X-	-XXX
York College	07	6	------X	----------	----------	--XX-XX--X	----
York College of Pennsylvania	12	2	XX-----	----------	----------	----------	----

Appendix D

Qualifications in
Assessing the HERI Trends

Appendix D
Qualifications in Assessing the HERI Trends

Some of the survey items used in the CIRP Freshman Survey can be very sensitive to changes in item text, presentation or order. While we at HERI make a considerable effort to present such items consistently over time, there have been occasions when items must be changed to keep relevance over time. On other occasions, errors in the presentation of an item for a particular year can render the results not comparable to results for other years.

This Appendix discusses results that were removed from this report due to non-comparability, as well as other results that may have been affected to a lesser degree by changes in questions but were left in place. Please note that in discussing these potential artifacts, the possibility still exists that they were actually due in whole or in part to a real change in response.

GENERAL

All results for the years 1971–2006 were prepared through direct analyses of the "raw data," that is, the individual survey responses, for baccalaureate-granting colleges included in the national norms sample. However, raw data were unavailable for the years 1966–1970. Results for baccalaureate-granting institutions were instead derived by performing an algorithm that algebraically removed the results for two-year colleges from those for all institutions, as reported in "The American Freshman" for each year. Individual percentages computed in this manner are subject to rounding error and may be different by as much as one-tenth of a percentage point from results that would have been obtained had the raw data been available.

CAREER

Between 1971 and 1972, the response option "housewife" was replaced by "homemaker (full-time)." The percentage of students marking this response dropped precipitously, with corresponding rises in the responses "business (clerical)," "unemployed" and "other."

The response options to the CAREER variables were changed so substantially in the period 1973–1975 that they deemed incomparable, and were not included in the Trends File. The original response set was restored in 1976.

MAJOR

Until 1971, students were asked to mark their first, second and last choices for major. Starting in 1972, students were directed to mark the major they were most likely to choose. The "undecided" response showed a large increase between these years.

Nine response categories, including specific business and education categories, were added in 1973, affecting many response percentages. "Pre-med, dental, veterinary" was removed from the response set in 1973 and restored in 1977, affecting the "biological sciences" and "health professional" categories.

RELIGION

Changes have been made in the number of responses in several years, primarily switching from a "short" list (5 responses) to a "long" list (17–19 responses). When the long list was used, the "Protestant" category reported in the aggregated version of the RELIGION variables was computed by adding together all Christian religions except Roman Catholic. In the short list, "Protestant" represents the only option for these religions. The short list was used in 1966–1969, 1971, 1972, 1979–83 and 1986. (NOTE: Results in the aggregated religious preference items for these years are *italicized*.)

The major result of these variations is a sharp drop in the "Protestant" category matched by an increase in "other religion" when the short categories were used. Presumably, many Christians do not consider themselves to be "Protestant."

In 1984, two long-list options (Episcopal & Presbyterian) were inadvertently left off the 1984 list, engendering. a rise in the "other Protestant" response. These options were restored in 1985.

In 1994, the response option "other Protestant" was replaced by "other Christian." This resulted in a large increase in the percentage of students responding to this item, with a smaller but substantial drop in the percentage responding to "other religion."

RACIAL BACKGROUND

The results for this item from 1966–1970 were removed because students in those years were allowed to mark only one racial background category, which yielded substantially lower percentages than seen in the years 1971–2006, in which students could mark as many racial background categories as were appropriate.

In 1997, the "Asian/Asian American" category was broken out into five more specific categories. This had the curious effect of substantially increasing the number of respondents that marked more than one category—regardless of what categories were marked. In 1998, the eight-category response set used in 1996 was restored.

In 2001, the category "American Indian" was changed to "American Indian/Alaska Native," and the category "Native Hawaiian/Pacific Islander" was added. For this report, the latter category was treated as "Asian American/Asian."

INCOME

The "parents' income" item has undergone more changes than any other item in the survey, mainly to keep up with inflation. Each change resulted in some artifactual effects on the results as compared with the previous year. In addition, until 1972, respondents were allowed to enter their own family income if they were not dependent on their parents. The elimination of this option undoubtedly resulted in a drop of respondents reporting low income observed in 1973.

In 1985, to accommodate a finer discrimination among income ranges at the high end of the spectrum, it was necessary to compress the low-end ranges. While these changes do not have a large effect on the overall results, they will cause medians computed from these data to be slightly higher, particularly among low-income groups.

FINANCIAL AID

While some version of the financial aid question has been asked since the beginning of the Freshman Survey in 1966, it was not until 1978 that the various items presented and the response set were sufficiently standardized to allow their inclusion in the Trends. In addition, the reordering of the Aid items in 1984 may have had some small effects on the results.

In 1992, the response set for these items was reduced from seven categories to five, covering the same overall range. In 2000, the long set of 20 sources of aid was reduced to five, which are shown separately in this report. In 2006, a longer set of 22 sources was used. Of these 22, 18 were compatible with the earlier long set of 20, and results for those 18 were included.

HIGH SCHOOL GRADES

The format of the response options was changed in 1973 and 1987. In both cases, the original order was restored the following year. The grades most affected by this change were B– and C+.

DISABILITIES

Although the disability item was included in the survey starting in 1979, a consistent format for the question was not developed until 1983.

In 1998, the item "hearing" was inadvertently omitted from the list of Disabilities. As a result, the item "other" was judged to be not comparable to earlier years (since students with a hearing disability may have marked it), and was not included in the Trends for 1998.

DEGREE ASPIRATIONS

The layout of this item was changed in 2000 in an attempt to make it more understandable to the respondents. The results were so at variance with those of earlier years that they were not included in the Trends database. The format used in 1999 and earlier was restored in 2001.

251

NUMBER OF OTHER COLLEGES APPLIED TO/ACCEPTED BY

Through 1996, the last response option was "6 or more." Starting in 1997, this response option was broken out into three: "6," "7–10," and "11 or more." For the Trends, these new categories were merged back into "6 or more."

MISCELLANEOUS

Questions which do not deal with established facts (such as self-ratings, opinions, projected future activities and life objectives) are more likely to be affected by changes in order of the items, their text, or the addition/deletion of items. In three instances (self-ratings in 1983 & 2004, and life objectives in 1988), the effects were so profound that HERI judged that the results should not be included in the Trends. Changes of a similar sort occurred in the "Reasons for Attending College" in 1998, and resulted in the exclusion of two items—"Become a more cultured person" and "Prepare for graduate/professional school."

In 2000, the "Time diary" item "Played video games" was changed to "Played video/computer games," yielding results not comparable to earlier years. The "future activity" items "Be elected to a student office" and "join a social fraternity, sorority or club" were changed to "Participate in student government" and "join a social fraternity or sorority" respectively, with similar results. All three of these newly worded items are included in this report.

Appendix E

The Precision of the Normative Data and Their Comparisons

Appendix E
The Precision of the
Normative Data and Their Comparisons

A common question asked about sample surveys relates to the precision of the data, which is typically reported as the accuracy of a percentage "plus or minus x percentage points." This figure, which is known as a confidence interval, can be estimated for items of interest if one knows the response percentage and its standard error.

Given the CIRP's large normative sample, the calculated standard error associated with any particular response percentage will be small (as will its confidence interval). It is important to note, however, that traditional methods of calculating standard error assume conditions which, (as is the case with most real sample survey data), do not apply here. Moreover, there are other possible sources of error which should be considered in comparing data across normative groups, across related item categories, and over time. In reference to the precision of the CIRP data, these concerns include:

1) Traditional methods of calculating standard error assume that the <u>individuals</u> were selected through simple random sampling. Given the complex, stratified design of the CIRP, where whole <u>institutions</u> participate, it is likely that the actual standard errors will be somewhat larger than the standard error estimates produced through traditional computational methods. In addition, while every effort has been made to maximize the comparability of the institutional sample from year to year (repeat participation runs about 90 percent), comparability is reduced by non-repeat participation and year-to-year variation in the quality of data collected by continuing institutional participants. While the CIRP stratification and weighting procedures are designed to minimize this institutional form of "response bias," an unknown amount of non-random variation is introduced into the results.

2) The wording of some questions in the survey instrument, the text and number of response options, and their order of presentation have changed over the years. We have found that even small changes can produce large order and context effects. Given this, the *exact* wording and order of items on the survey instrument (which is produced as Appendix B) should be examined carefully prior to making comparisons across survey years.

3) Substantial changes in the institutional stratification scheme were made in 1968, 1971, 1975 and 2000. These changes resulted in a revision of the weights applied to individual institutions between 1966 and 2006. Stratification cell assignments of a few institutions may also change from time to time, but the scale of these changes and their effect on the national normative results are likely to be small in comparison to other sources of bias.

Since it is impractical to report statistical indicators for every percentage in every CIRP norms group, it is important for those who are interested to be able to estimate the precision of the data. Toward this end, Table E1 provides estimates of standard errors for norms groups of various sizes and for different percentages[1] which can be used to derive confidence interval estimates.

For example, if the item we are interested in has a response percentage of 28.9 percent among freshman men in 1977 (a normative group containing 84,578 respondents—see Table A1 for unweighted respondent counts), we would first choose the column that most closely corresponds to that value, or "30%".[2] Next, select the row corresponding most closely to the unweighted sample size of the comparison group to find the appropriate standard error. With a sample size of about 80,000 and a percentage that is close to 30, the estimated standard error would be .162.

To calculate the confidence interval at the 95% probability level, multiply the estimated standard error by the critical value of t for the unweighted sample size (which, for all CIRP norms groups, will be equal to 1.96 at the .05 level of probability).[3] In this example, we would multiply the estimated standard error of .162 by 1.96, which yields .318. If we round this figure to a single decimal point we would then estimate our confidence interval to be 28.9 ± .2. In practical terms, this confidence interval means that if we were to replicate this survey using the same size sample, we would expect that the resulting percentage would fall between 28.7 percent and 29.1 percent 95 times out of 100.

Table E1. Estimated Standard Errors of Percentages for Norms Groups of Various Sizes

Unweighted size of norms groups	Percentage										
	1%	5%	10%	15%	20%	25%	30%	35%	40%	45%	50%
65,000	.039	.085	.118	.140	.157	.170	.180	.187	.192	.195	.196
80,000	.035	.077	.106	.126	.141	.153	.162	.169	.173	.176	.177
95,000	.032	.071	.097	.116	.130	.140	.149	.155	.159	.161	.162
110,000	.030	.066	.090	.108	.121	.131	.138	.144	.148	.150	.151
130,000	.028	.060	.083	.099	.111	.120	.127	.132	.136	.138	.139
150,000	.026	.056	.077	.092	.103	.112	.118	.123	.126	.128	.129
175,000	.024	.052	.072	.085	.096	.104	.110	.114	.117	.119	.120
200,000	.022	.049	.067	.080	.089	.097	.102	.107	.110	.111	.112
225,000	.021	.046	.063	.075	.084	.091	.097	.101	.103	.105	.105
250,000	.020	.044	.060	.071	.080	.087	.092	.095	.098	.099	.100
275,000	.019	.042	.057	.068	.076	.083	.087	.091	.093	.095	.095

NOTE: Assumes simple random sampling.

---

[1]Calculated by $\sqrt{\dfrac{x\%(100-x\%)}{N}}$, where x is the percentage of interest and N is the population count from Table A3, column 2.

[2]Since the distribution of the standard errors are symmetrical around the 50 percent mid–point, for percentages over 50 simply subtract the percentage from 100 and use the result to select the appropriate column. For example, if the percentage we were interested in was 59, 100 – 59 percent yields 41, so we would use the column labeled '40%.'

[3]To calculate the confidence interval at the 99% probability level the critical t value is 2.56.

Appendix F

Coding Scheme for Aggregated Items

STUDENT'S PROBABLE MAJOR

Aggregated Item	Disaggregated Item(s)
Agriculture	Agriculture, Forestry
Biological Sciences	Biology (general), Biochemistry or Biophysics, Botany, Environmental Science, Marine (life) Science, Microbiology or Bacteriology, Zoology, Other Biological Sciences
Business	Accounting, Business Administration (general), Finance, International Business, Marketing, Management, Secretarial Studies, Other Business
Education	Business Education, Elementary Education, Music or Art Education, Physical Education or Recreation, Secondary Education, Other Education
Engineering	Aeronautical or Astronautical Engineering, Civil Engineering, Chemical Engineering, Electrical or Electronic Engineering, Industrial Engineering, Mechanical Engineering, Other Engineering
English	English (language and literature)
Health Professional	Medical/Dental/Veterinary, Nursing, Pharmacy, Therapy (occupational, physical, speech)
History or Political Science	History, Political Science (gov't, international relations)
Humanities	Language and Literature (except English), Philosophy, Speech, Theology or Religion, Other Arts & Humanities
Fine Arts	Art (fine and applied), Music, Theater, Architecture or Urban Planning
Mathematics or Statistics	Mathematics, Statistics
Physical Sciences	Astronomy, Atmospheric Science (including Meteorology), Chemistry, Earth Science, Marine Science, Physics, Other Physical Science
Social Sciences	Anthropology, Economics, Ethnic Studies, Geography, Psychology, Social Work, Sociology, Women's Studies
Other Technical	Health Technology (medical, dental, laboratory), Data Processing or Computer Programming, Drafting or Design, Electronics, Mechanics, Other Technical, Computer Science
Other Non-technical	Journalism, Home Economics, Library Science, Other Professional, Building Trades, Communications, Law Enforcement, Military Science, Other Field
Undecided	Undecided

PROBABLE CAREER

Aggregated Item	Disaggregated Item(s)
Artist	Actor or entertainer, Artist, Interior decorator, Musician, Writer
Business	Accountant or actuary, Business executive (management, administrator), Business owner or proprietor, Business salesperson or buyer
Clerical	Business (clerical)
Clergy	Clergy (minister, priest), Clergy (other religious)
College Teacher	College teacher
Doctor (MD or DDS)	Dentist (including orthodontist), Physician
Education (secondary)	School counselor, School principal or superintendent, Teacher or administrator (secondary)
Education (primary)	Teacher (elementary)
Engineer	Engineer
Farmer or forester	Conservationist or forester, Farmer or rancher
Health Professional	Dietitian or home economist, Lab technician or hygienist, Optometrist, Pharmacist, Therapist (physical, occupational, speech), Veterinarian
Homemaker	Homemaker (full-time)
Lawyer	Lawyer (attorney) or judge
Military	Military service (career)
Nurse	Nurse
Research Scientist	Scientific researchers
Social Worker	Social, welfare or recreation worker
Skilled worker	Skilled trades
Semi-skilled worker*	Semi-skilled worker
Laborer*	Laborer (unskilled)
Unemployed*	Unemployed
Other career	Architect, Psychologist, College administrator/staff, computer programmer or analyst, Foreign service worker (including diplomat), Law enforcement, Policymaker/government, Other
Undecided**	Undecided

*Father's and mother's career only
**Student's probable career only

RELIGIOUS PREFERENCE

Aggregated Item	Disaggregated Item(s)
Christian (Protestant)	Baptist, Congregational (UCC), Eastern Orthodox, Episcopal, Latter Day Saints (Mormon), Lutheran, Methodist, Presbyterian, Quaker (Society of Friends), Seventh Day Adventist, Unitarian Universalist, Other Christian
Roman Catholic	Roman Catholic
Jewish	Jewish
Other	Buddhist, Muslim (Islamic), Other religion
None	None

NOTE: In 1966–69, 1971–72, 1979–83 and 1986 the religious preference item included only the five aggregated response options. In all other years, the disaggregated response options were presented. See Appendix D for the notes on the effect of the alternate response options sets.

Higher Education Research Institute
Publications List

The American Freshman

Provides national normative data on the characteristics of students attending American colleges and universities as first-time, full-time freshmen. In 2006, data from approximately 300,000 freshmen students are statistically adjusted to reflect the responses of 1.3 million students entering college. The annual report covers: demographic characteristics; expectations of college; degree goals and career plans; college finances; attitudes, values and life goals.

December, 2006/202 pages	$25.00	☐
December, 2005/188 pages	$25.00	☐
December, 2004/188 pages	$25.00	☐
December, 2003/186 pages	$25.00	☐
December, 2002/189 pages	$25.00	☐
December, 2001	(out of stock)	
December, 2000/187 pages	$25.00	☐
December, 1999/181 pages	$25.00	☐

Note: National norms for most years between 1966–1997 are available.

The American Freshman: Forty Year Trends

Summarizes trends in the CIRP survey data between 1966 and 2006. The report examines changes in the diversity of students entering college; parental income and students' financial concerns; issues of access and affordability in college. Trends in students' political and social attitudes are also covered.

April, 2007 $30.00   ☐

First in My Family: A Profile of First-Generation College Students at Four-Year Institutions Since 1971

First-generation college students are receiving increasing attention from researchers, practitioners, and policymakers with the aim of better understanding their college decision-making process and supporting their progress in higher education. First-generation college students are generally defined as those students whose parents have had no college or post-secondary experiences. This is a critical population of students to study because of the general perception that, relative to their peers, such students have poorer academic preparation, have different motivations for coming to college, have varying levels of parental support and involvement, have different expectations for their college experience, and have significant obstacles in their path to retention and academic success. As part of the 40th Anniversary of the CIRP, this report explores the changing dynamic between first-generation college students and their non first-generation peers by utilizing thirty-five years worth of longitudinal trends data collected through the Cooperative Institutional Research Program's (CIRP) Freshman Survey (1971–2005).

February, 2007 $15.00   ☐

Black Undergraduates From *Bakke* to *Grutter*

Summarizes the status, trends and prospects of Black college freshmen using data collected from 1971 to 2004 through the Cooperative Institutional Research Program (CIRP). Based on more than half a million Black freshman students, the report examines gender differences; socioeconomic status; academic preparation and aspirations; and civic engagement.

November, 2005/47 pages $15.00   ☐

Degree Attainment Rates at American Colleges and Universities

Provides latest information on four- and six-year degree attainment rates collected longitudinally from 262 baccalaureate-granting institutions. Differences by race, gender, and institutional type are examined. The study highlights main predictors of degree completion and provides several formulas for calculating expected institutional completion rates. The study also provides a section on trends in degree attainment in the last decade.

January, 2005/88 pages $15.00   ☐

The American College Teacher

Provides an informative profile of teaching faculty at American colleges and universities. Teaching, research activities and professional development issues are high-lighted along with issues related to job satisfaction and stress.

National Norms for 2004–05 HERI Faculty Survey report.
     September, 2005/156 pages $25.00   ☐
National Norms for 2001–02 HERI Faculty Survey report.
     September, 2002/146 pages $25.00   ☐
National Norms for 1998–99 HERI Faculty Survey report.
     September, 1999/128 pages $22.00   ☐
National Norms for 1995–96 HERI Faculty Survey report.
     September, 1996/127 pages $22.00   ☐
National Norms for 1992–93 HERI Faculty Survey report.
     September, 1993/107 pages $20.00   ☐

Race and Ethnicity in the American Professoriate, 1995–96

Highlights findings and draws comparisons between various racial and ethnic groups of faculty. Faculty's views and values about undergraduate education, professional goals and institutional climate are examined along with preferred teaching and evaluation methods, levels of work satisfaction and sources of stress.

April, 1997/141 pages $25.00   ☐

To Order: send this form with a check to:
The Higher Education Research Institute
UCLA Graduate School of Education and Information Studies
Mailbox 951521
Los Angeles, CA 90095-1521

(Add $5.00 for shipping, plus $1.00 for each additional book ordered)

HERI accepts Visa, MasterCard & Discover: Call (310) 825-1925 to order by credit card
Or visit the HERI webpage: www.gseis.ucla.edu/heri/heri.html